IDEOLOGICAL CONFLICTS IN MODERN CHINA

IDEOLOGICAL CONFLICTS IN MODERN CHINA
Democracy and Authoritarianism

WEN-SHUN CHI
Foreword by Chalmers Johnson

Transaction Books
New Brunswick (U.S.A.) and Oxford (U.K.)

Published with the assistance of the Center for Chinese Studies and the Institute
of East Asian Studies, University of California, Berkeley.

Library of Congress Catalog Number: 85-8580

ISBN: 0-88738-054-9 (cloth)

Printed in the United States of America

Library of Congress Cataloging in Publication Data

Chi, Wen-shun.
   Ideological conflicts in modern China.
   Includes index
   Bibliography: p.
   1. China—Politics and government—20th century.
2. Democracy. 3. Authoritarianism.   I. Title.
JQ1508.C4636 1985   320.5'0951   85-8580
ISBN 0-88738-054-9

This book is dedicated to the memory
of my parents and my sister,
all of whom died from the ravages of
the War of Resistance Against Japan

Contents

Foreword

Chalmers Johnson

One of the oddest things that happened in the modern history of East Asia is that many Chinese modernizers embraced Marxism. Given traditional China's long-standing and quite justified sense of cultural superiority toward all of its neighbors, and the enormous conservatism and hostility to novelty of imperial Confucianism, it was utterly unexpected that any group of twentieth-century Chinese would base its programs of national renovation on a foreign doctrine, least of all on one as foreign as Marxism. Far too many foreigners still believe that the victory of Marxism in China was inevitable and see it as a testimony to Marxism's relevance and power in conceptualizing the problems of social change in countries like China and in offering answers.

Writing as a true historian of ideas, Wen-shun Chi recalls the clash of ideological systems that occurred during China's century-long revolution and the numerous contingencies that propelled the country in a Marxist direction. His book, which can also be read as a text to introduce students to the main intellectual currents of twentieth-century China, describes nine major thinkers in detail and with the insight of a Chinese activist who lived through most of the period he is reviewing. Many of these, particularly K'ang Yu-wei, Liang Ch'i-ch'ao, Sun Yat-sen, Hu Shih, Liang Shu-ming, Ch'en Tu-hsiu, and Mao Tse-tung, have already received extensive biographical and monographic attention in both Chinese and English. However, they have never been treated together in a single volume, as they are here. Chi has also added to this list two other significant theorists of Chinese reform, Chang Chün-mai and Chang Tung-sun.

The result is a book that both reminds us of the humanistic and democratic alternatives to Marxism that existed in China and also helps to explain why, after the death of Mao Tse-tung in 1976, China began to turn away from the dead end of Marxism-Leninism. It has not yet happened, but the events of the decade after Mao have at least raised the possibility that China may one day become the first nation dominated by a Marxist party to free itself of that burden. If that should come to pass, one reason will be the lively heritage of democratic thought in China—a heritage that Chi details and that communism has been unable to suppress.

Why, then, in mid-century did Marxism nonetheless prevail? Chi cites many contributing factors. First, there was the tendency of many intellectual reformers to eschew politics altogether, an attitude that derived from traditional thought. Then there were those intellectuals who joined but subsequently deserted the latter-day Kuomintang, a desertion that Chi feels was justified but that also had its opportunistic side. Chi also notes the traditional Confucian aversion to capitalism and hence superficial compatibility between the Marxism of the Communist Manifesto and the prejudices of Chinese intellectuals. Finally, there was a tendency for democracy to be identified with Western imperialist nations and, as a result, to be discredited in Chinese eyes; and, above all, there was the social solvent of Japanese aggression against China and the disastrous conditions it created. Chi does not slight the insights of Marxism, particularly as modified and adapted to the Chinese scene by Mao Tse-tung. But he stresses those elements in Marxism that resonated with traditional utopian thought in China: the ideal of a classless society, Marxism's claim to be a universal truth, and the place of rebellion in Chinese theories of political change.

This is a book whose time has come. Even a decade ago it would have been impossible for an observer outside of China to imagine that democratic thought still survived, no matter how weakly, in the China of Mao and the Cultural Revolution. Wen-shun Chi had no doubt that it did survive and began to write this book to remind at least the elitist enthusiasts for the Cultural Revolution in foreign countries that Chinese were capable of democratic thought. As it turned out, Chi was prescient; the Cultural Revolution failed and the Chinese people themselves, in revulsion against it, began to study again the same thinkers whom Chi treats here.

Wen-shun Chi was a graduate of Tsinghua University and the University of Washington in economics (B.A. and M.A., 1932 and 1955). Between his two degrees he was the editor of the prominent Tientsin journal, *I Shih Pao,* which he also kept alive in Kunming during the World War II. After coming to the United States and studying in Seattle, Chi taught Chinese in several institutions, including the Army Language School at Monterey, California. From 1959 to 1977 he served as Senior Research Linguist in the Center for Chinese Studies, University of California, Berkeley. During his Berkeley years Wen-shun Chi educated a generation of China specialists (including this writer) in the language of Chinese communism. He also put together and annotated three widely used texts of readings in Chinese communist documents, and he headed the China Center's team that compiled and published the *Chinese-English Dictionary of Contemporary Usage* (University of California Press, 1977). These are all important accomplishments, but it is most fitting that Chi's major work, presented in *Ideological Conflicts in Modern China,* should return to the intellectual maelstrom in which he was engulfed virtually from the moment he received his baccalaureate degree. Differing from so many others who were destroyed by the Chinese Revolution, Chi mastered it intellectually and here offers us his analysis of its various ideological configurations.

Preface

Ideas are powerful forces in the shaping of the course of human events. When, in the early 1830s, Heinrich Heine, out of his concern for the future of Europe, wrote his *Concerning the History of Religion and Philosophy in Germany,* he was neither the first nor the last to recognize that ideas expounded by speculative philosophers can profoundly affect the future of nations. Ideas in the writings of several German philosophers have, as Heine feared, fueled continuing cultural and political anguish in Europe. Heine did not explicitly anticipate that some of those ideas and their consequent ideological compulsions toward ruthless social systems exalting a crude "nature philosophy" would spread rapidly around the globe, affecting the course of events in all nations, including China. Heine's concern was not solely with the dangers potential in the ideas of certain philosophers, among whom he included Kant, Fichte, and Hegel. Implicit in his book is his concern for the survival of other ideas, also current in Europe, more favorable for the future of nations.

In addressing his book especially to his friends in France, Heine's premise is that among these friends are those who value healthier ideas, including the spiritual insights supporting freedom of speculation and discussion. Heine's underlying assumption is that ideas healthier for the future of nations, so far as they are actively defended and propagated, can reduce the power of, as he says, the "pernicious" ideas he has perceived sprouting in Europe. Though beyond Heine's ken in the 1830s, corresponding ideological conflicts, including components of both the pernicious ideas and the healthier ideas coming in from the West, were also gathering force in China.

From the perspective of the early 1980s a pernicious utopianism and a ruthlessly pernicious materialism might indeed seem to have claimed all of China. But in China, as elsewhere, thinkers whose ideas have challenged and continue to challenge utopian illusions and the aggressions of that offshoot of nature philosophy which calls itself scientific materialism are also significant factors for the future of the Chinese people. A wider acquaintance, particularly among Western friends of the Chinese people, with not only the self-designated revolutionary ideologues but also with the ideas of other Chinese thinkers active in China during the past one hundred years can itself help to insure that their more generous and amiable hopes for the future can in time be actualized.

I have selected nine thinkers who, in my opinion, best represent the varying and competing ideological viewpoints that have influenced and will continue to influence the course of events in China. Except for Chang Chün-mei and Chang Tung-sun, books on the careers and viewpoints of all the others have long since appeared. My book, however, focuses on a single unifying theme: the persistence within the concerns of all these thinkers of the theme of social reconstruction.

The Communists habitually scorn all other programs for social reconstruction, label proponents of alternative programs as reformists, and claim for themselves preeminence as revolutionaries. Their insistence upon this distincton, however, is inadvertently useful. It underscores their goal of imposing social reconstruction through relentlessly alternating campaigns of covert violence and overt violence aimed at suppressing and eliminating all ideas of social reconstruction except their own. Though the noncommunist thinkers I am presenting also differ, and sometimes widely, all of them advocate social reconstruction achieved through nonviolent, genuinely and openly democratic procedures.

Democratic ideas and procedures and the rejection of dictatorship and of claims to absolute authority by any one person, party, or class, ideas and procedures brought over from the West and promulgated by Chinese intellectual leaders, have deeply influenced the minds of many Chinese. Recent daring and vigorous declarations for genuine democracy, though again denounced and suppressed in China, indicate that all of the preceding thirty years of violent suppression have not been able wholly to deflect or to extirpate the hope of actualizing a genuinely democratic system in China. In spite of past and current attacks on those who dare to speak of this hope, it will, I believe, eventually prevail. The idea of the equal dignity and value of every individual and the need for free and open discussion for the health of human society is a living idea in the hearts and minds of many Chinese. Its persistence, despite the calculating ruthlessness of its opponents, is itself impressive and will in time, I think, prove irresistible.

My descriptive report of nine thinkers whose ideas have been significant components of the ideological conflicts in modern China obviously proceeds within the context of the fact that I am a native Chinese, born in the early years of this century. Modern Chinese social problems and controversies through decades of desolating international wars and civil wars are vivid to me not solely from pages in print but from personal experience. This book may, I trust, provide some further illumination of the intellectual and emotional complexities within the ideological conflicts still going on in China.

Though recurrently denied open expression on wall space, in print, and by way of public broadcasts, ideas supporting a humane system of society and government of, by, and for all the people of China are still circulating among the people inside China. Those within China who scorn these ideas have attempted to stuff the ears of successive generations of children against ever hearing such ideas. Those attempts have not succeeded and, I believe, will never succeed in annihilating the hope for and the will to achieve a genuinely open and democratic society. These ideas are powerful and still shaping a course for the future of China.

W.S.C.

1984

Acknowledgments

My father, Wen-shun Chi, died on November 25, 1984, about six months after he had signed a contract with Transaction Books for the publication of *Ideological Conflicts in Modern China*. The manuscript at the time of signing was complete, and all that remained to be written was an acknowledgment note, plus an index. But during the last months of his life, my father's energy reserves were severely limited. He managed, nevertheless, to work an hour or two every day on other projects, thinking that the acknowledgments for this book could be done closer to publication time. His death, although not unexpected, came much too soon.

We found among my father's papers a list of friends and colleagues whom he wished to thank. Unfortunately, I am not in a position to acknowledge properly these individuals. I hope they will understand and forgive me if I simply list their names in alphabetical order, with the understanding that they have my family's deepest gratitude for their time, their support and their services. All of these people helped in various ways while my father was well, and they continued to help after his death. They are: Allison Campbell, Annie Chang, Po-yuan Chang, Chih-p'ing Chen, Lowell Ditmer, Irving Horowitz, Jeremy Ingalls, Chalmers Johnson, Sheila Johnson, Joyce Kallgren, Robert Scalapino, and John Service. A name that does not appear above, but one which undoubtedly would have been included, is that of my mother, Ellen Tso-fen Chi.

Had my father written his own acknowledgments, he would have accepted all responsibility for the intellectual content, as well as any omissions, in this book.

Alice Yun Chi
Princeton Junction, NJ
May 14, 1985

Introduction

China has undergone greater changes in the past hundred years than in the whole preceding historical period, and the greatest changes have been concentrated in the past thirty-odd years. Prior to 1800 China was a populous country which enjoyed a political stability and economic self-sufficiency that was admired by many European scholars. China was also a country which proudly regarded her civilization as the highest in world history and her position as being the center of the world surrounded by barbarians. It is possible that the Chinese viewed themselves as existing in a stage approaching a peaceful one-world kingdom, though such a view was based on an imperfect understanding of the scope of the globe. The Chinese devoted their energies more to civil and cultural activities than to military concerns. And because they were free from any serious external threat prior to 1800, they saw no necessity to provide for proper protection against external aggression.

China's relative stability was disrupted beginning with the Opium War of 1840–1842. The crisis began when the British forced the sale of opium on China under the pretext of trade. During the same period other foreign powers arrived and fought the Chinese in their own territory with superior weapons and gunboats that the militarily ill-prepared Chinese were unable to overcome. China then began to suffer humiliation after humiliation as she proved unable to defend herself against foreign aggression.

As one of the consequences of the Opium War and other wars which followed, China signed a number of treaties—generally known as the unequal treaties—with foreign powers. These treaties deprived China of the conditions necessary to retain her independence. Sun Yat-sen once described China's status at that time as that of a subcolony, for China was not subject to the oppression of a single country, as was Korea under Japan, or Indochina under France, but she suffered the oppression of most of the strong countries of East and West. The unequal treaties eroded China's prestige and abridged certain political and economic rights. The inequalities under the treaty terms, which the Chinese called national humiliations, are listed below:

1. Apology missions:
    a. Envoy sent to the British court to apologize for the Opium War;

    b. Envoys sent to Great Britian and France in 1860 as an outcome of the Arrow War of 1856;

    c. Envoys sent to Japan and Germany in 1901 to apologize for the Boxer Rebellion.

2. Annexations and leases of territories to foreign countries:

    a. Concession of Hong Kong to Great Britain (1842);

    b. Annexation of Annam by France (1885);

    c. Lease of Kowloon to Great Britain for 99 years (1898);

    d. Annexation of Burma by Great Britain (1886);

    e. Lease of Kwangchow Bay to France for 99 years (1899);

    f. Concession of the Ryukyu Islands to Japan (1879);

    g. Concession of Taiwan and Penghu to Japan (1895);

    h. Lease of Chiaochow Bay to Germany for 99 years (1898);

    i. Lease of Port Arthur and Dairen to Russia for 25 years (1898);

    j. Lease of Weihaiwai to Great Britain for 25 years (1898).

3. Indemnities:

    a. Twenty-one million dollars paid to Great Britain (Nanking Treaty of 1842);

    b. Eight million taels of silver paid to Great Britain and the same amount to France (Peking Treaty of 1860);

    c. Two hundred million taels of silver paid to Japan (Treaty of Shimonoseki of 1895);

    d. Four hundred fifty million taels of silver promised to the Allied Forces to be paid in 80 years, with a total, plus interest, of close to one billion taels of silver (Boxer Protocol of 1901).

4. Other privileges obtained by the Powers:

    a. Establishment of consular jurisdiction, or extraterritoriality;

    b. Direct control of Chinese customs by foreigners, including foreign control over tariff rates and tariff revenues;

    c. Foreign concessions established in different localities, such as Shanghai, Tientsin, and Hankow, where the foreign powers exercised extraterritoriality;

    d. Privilege of foreign warship navigation and anchorage along China's coast and at her inland ports;

    e. Right of coastal trade and the right of inland navigation;

    f. Right to garrison foreign troops on Chinese territory;

    g. Employment of foreign postal employees and foreign postal officers, plus foreign control of China's communications.

    h. Right of foreign powers to build factories in China;

    i. Opening of five ports to trade in 1892, with the condition that further ports were to be opened.[1]

The following quotation from R. R. Palmer may help to give an American reader a sense of the deep psychological shock the Chinese suffered from foreign intervention:

If the reader will imagine what the United States would be like if foreign warships patrolled the Mississippi as far as St. Louis, if foreigners came and went throughout the country without being under its laws, if New York, New Orleans, and other cities contained foreign settlements outside its jurisdiction, but in which all banking and management were concentrated, if foreigners determined the tariff policy, collected the proceeds and remitted much of the money to their own governments, if the western part of the city of Washington had been burned [the Summer Palace], Long Island and California annexed to distant empires [Hong Kong and Indochina] and all New England were coveted by two immediate neighbors [Manchuria], if the national authorities were half in collusion with these foreigners and half victimized by them, and if large areas of the country were prey to bandits, guerillas, and revolutionary secret societies conspiring against the helpless government and occasionally murdering some of the foreigners—then he can understand how observant Chinese felt at the end of the last century, and why the term 'imperialism' came to be held by so many of the world's people in abomination.[2]

Fighting imperialism has been a slogan of the Communist Party for years. Imperialism is considered to be one of the three great mountains on the backs of the Chinese people. In his Three Principles of the People, Sun Yat-sen warned them of the dangers of imperialist economic and political pressure which menaced the existence of China, and in his last will, he called for the abolition of unequal treaties. Antiimperialism was a major objective of the Kuomintang's Northern Expedition of 1926-28 against the warlords and their foreign backers. It is clearly true that foreign invasions did serious damage to China, and that they marked the decline of Chinese prestige and power. But solely to blame foreign pressures for China's own historical problems—the effect of her own internal inconsistencies which would emerge eventually—cannot be justified. An objective and dispassionate study China's problems would include careful consideration of both the impact of foreign powers and China's own internal shortcomings.

The Chinese had always regarded themselves as the most civilized people in the world but now, with repeated failures in the wars, the Chinese were suddenly labeled and treated as barbarians. Western thinkers who once showed deference to China were now contemptuous. The Chinese began to lose confidence in their own country and felt the loss of national pride. Chinese public opinion now exalted as advanced those countries it had once considered as barbaric and began to regard China as a backward country. The Chinese further realized that China was not, nor ever had been, the geographic center of the world. China, suddenly a prey of the colonial powers, was now confronted with the danger of partition—being cut up like a melon, as the Chinese referred to the situation—and her survival as a nation, as well as a culture, was in peril. The possibility that China faced a threat of extinction as a country and extermination as a race frightened and appalled the Chinese.

This situation was really an unprecedented challenge to the Chinese people as a whole. It could be viewed as an unfortunate situation, but it could also be viewed as fortunate. For, according to Toynbee, there are virtues in adversity. He holds that it is difficult rather than easy conditions that produce civilization; that man achieves civilization as a response to the challenge of a situation of special difficulty which rouses him to make a hitherto unprecedented effort;[3]

and that a sudden crushing defeat is apt to stimulate the defeated person to set his house in order and prepare to make a victorious response.[4]

Toynbee's concept of challenge and response finds a parallel in Mencius' famous aphorism: "Life springs from adversity and death from ease and comfort."[5] To many Chinese thinkers, the salvation of China politically and culturally became the cause to which they were anxious and willing to devote themselves. The responses of these thinkers to this challenge, i.e., their programs for China's rebirth, provide the subject matter of my study. The programs provided by these thinkers vary in approach, but their basic great goals are the same—to maintain China's national existence and cultural identity.

The latest serious threat to China's existence was the Japanese aggression, beginning with the Mukden Incident of 18 September 1931, and culminating with the War of Resistance against Japan between 1937 and 1945. This was the gravest disaster China had encountered since the Opium War. The Chinese realized that they had reached a critical stage, where they would either fight on to victory and survive or go down to defeat and extinction. Programs for national salvation took on a new immediacy and urgency. During the course of the war, the surviving thinkers mentioned in this study and intellectuals in general became ever more acutely aware of the conflict between the Kuomintang and the Communists in their struggle for political power and the ideological allegiance of the people. The United Front in fact prevented neither an intensification of this conflict nor the polarization of the supporters on either side.

The purpose of this book is to provide a narrative and analytical account of the programs for China's social reconstruction, programs that were only proposed and those that were actually undertaken by men concerned with saving China from extinction, both as a nation and as a culture. This study surveys the social programs of nine modern Chinese thinkers: K'ang Yu-wei, Liang Ch'i-ch'ao, Sun Yat-sen, Hu Shih, Chang Chün-mai, Chang Tung-sun, Liang Shu-ming, Ch'en Tu-hsiu, and Mao Tse-tung. The thoughts of these nine men represent the major trends in Chinese ideologies of social reform during the past one hundred years.

There are two methods of approach to the writing of intellectual history—the generic approach and the conceptual approach. The former treats the ideas of one thinker or a group stressing developmental chronology, while the latter stresses conceptual importance. I chose mainly the conceptual approach with a view to presenting the significant and representative ideas of each thinker. However, this study is not strictly a book of intellectual history. It concerns only that phase of the intellectual history predominating in the programs for social reconstruction that the representative thinkers had envisioned. Although it is only one phase in the intellectual history of China, the two methods can be selectively applied in its usage. In the case of momentous change in a thinker, such as Ch'en Tu-hsiu, who in his youth shifted from liberal to communist, and later shifted back to liberalism, I will also indicate their chronological development. Each of these nine thinkers had his own particular line of thought, and these are briefly outlined below.

K'ang Yu-wei was the first thinker in modern times who advocated a radical and complete change in China. His one-world ideal—variously translated as "great harmony" or "great unity"—consists of a much more radical vision than that of a communist society. Not only did he advocate the abolition of private property and of national governments, but also the complete dissolution of families and even the elimination of personal names, which were to be replaced by numbers. However, K'ang warned, this ideal was to be realized in the distant future. For his own time, he advocated a constitutional monarchy after the model of Great Britain.

Liang Ch'i-ch'ao, a disciple of K'ang Yu-wei, was more influential though less creative than his mentor. Politically, Liang first advocated constitutional monarchy and later supported constitutional republicanism when the Chinese Republic was founded in 1911. A prolific writer whose complete works have been estimated to run to at least 16 million characters, Liang achieved a tremendous and sweeping influence on the Chinese mind, an influence due perhaps as much to the magnetic attraction of his style as to the Western ideas and proposals for change which he introduced.

Sun Yat-sen advocated a revolution against the Manchu government and its replacement by a republic, whereas both K'ang and Liang had advocated peaceful change in China. Sun's activity in the early years before 1911 was primarily a nationalist movement, aimed at overthrowing the Manchu government by force, and was mainly motivated by nationalistic considerations that treated the Manchus as foreigners. By 1924, Sun had elaborated his revolutionary theory and had formulated his Three Principles of the People into a system. The three principles are nationalism, democracy, and people's livelihood. The principle of nationalism seeks equality among all peoples in China and China's equality with all foreign nations. His principle of democracy seeks to establish a democratic form of government, mainly after the U.S. model with certain modifications. His principle of the people's livelihood is a kind of socialism which provides programs for the regulation of capital and the equalization of land ownership.

Although the republican political system effected a great change in theory and form, China's difficulties nevertheless remained, and the problem of China's modernization still had to be solved. In the years subsequent to the establishment of the republic in China, three different ideals, represented by four scholars, emerged and became important.

Hu Shih was a protagonist of China's new cultural movement. To his mind, the new cultural movement meant the creation of a new Chinese culture. Actually, the new culture envisioned by Hu was virtually a replacement of Eastern civilization by Western civilization. Thus he emphatically maintained the position that the complete Westernization of China, particularly in the two outstanding features of Western civilization—science and democracy—was the way to save China.

5

Chang Chün-mai (known in the West as Carsun Chang) represented the line of thinking that advocated parliamentary democracy in China. The dream of his life was to draft and put into effect a national constitution and to organize a workable parliament, based principally on the British model with certain modifications to suit China's particular conditions. Chang Tung-sun, a close friend and colleague of Chang Chüng-mai, followed the same line of thinking; thus the two Changs may be grouped together. Hu and the Changs were strong opponents of any kind of dictatorship, of whatever variety, be it the Kuomintang's one-party dictatorship or the Communist party's democratic dictatorship.

Liang Shu-ming, who based his program on his own analysis and comparison of three patterns of world cultures, concluded that Chinese culture was supreme. He was convinced that the revival of true Confucianism would save China and even the world from decline and destruction. Interestingly enough, although Liang Shu-ming advocated Confucianism as a philosophical ideal, his proposed practical reform was what he called rural reconstruction, whereby intellectuals would work alongside farmers in the countryside. This was a program with obvious parallels to the communist program, yet it was based on a very different ideology.

Ch'en Tu-hsiu was another protagonist of China's new cultural movement, whose political thought had a checkered history. Prior to the May Fourth Movement, he was purely a bourgeois thinker who dreamed of making Western democracy and capitalism a perfect model for China. He was converted to Communism in 1920, and during this communist period, he believed in Marxism and favored the dictatorship of the proletariat. But his god of Soviet communism failed after some twenty years of bitter experiences with the Comintern, the Soviet Union, and Stalin. Shortly before his death in 1942, although he still believed in socialism, he reverted to his original belief, seeing democracy as having an intrinsic value which transcends time, classes, and social systems.

The last, but most influential of these thinkers is Mao Tse-tung. Unlike the others mentioned above, except Sun Yat-sen, Mao was both a thinker and a revolutionary. He envisioned a communist society to be effected by a revolution. At an early stage in his revolutionary career, he organized a peasant army to seize political power from the Kuomintang. After that had succeeded, he led a continuous revolution, divided into various stages, toward the building of socialism and communism. In theory and practice, Mao was different from all the other representative people in their various approaches to China's reconstruction.

The nine thinkers included in this study differ in their programs of social reconstruction, but there is one important dividing line that marks Mao Tse-tung off from the rest. Mao, representing the communist ideology, advocated violent revolution; the others favored a more gradual approach. Sun was a gradualist, in that once the Ch'ing dynasty was overthrown, he intended to proceed by peaceful and gradual means. Mao advocated a command or administered economy; the other thinkers advocated a free enterprise economy with varying degrees of socialism.

Communist power prevails over whatever other political parties exist in China today as well as over all other schools of thought. Mao stated: "Everything else has been tried and all failed."[6] What he meant by "everything else" included K'ang Yu-wei's ideal of the Great Harmony, Sun Yat-sen's Three Principles of the People, and the democratic and liberal ideals of other scholars. In a sense, Mao was right in saying that all avenues except the communist way have failed, because the Communist Party is the political party in power. However, it is not true to say that everything else had been tried, because many of the democratic and liberal programs had no chance to be carried out. For instance, the Kuomintang had neither the opportunity nor the ability to put Sun Yat-sen's principles into practice, partly because of internal strife among the warlords and the Kuomintang's fighting with the Communists and partly due to the circumstances of the Japanese aggression. The social programs of the other thinkers remained only theories on paper and were never put into effect for reasons we will discuss in the conclusion of the book. The reformers were never able to go beyond the stage of aspiration, inspiration, and persuasion in their programs of social reconstruction.

Since the introduction of communism into China at the turn of the twentieth century, communism has been an increasingly powerful and widespread current of thought. Although noncommunist thinkers with independent ideas for national salvation opposed communist theory, they were nevertheless forced to regard communist theory as a powerful force to be dealt with. For the choice was either to go along with communism or to oppose it; it was impossible to ignore it. Thus, we find that the intellectual history of modern China is a history of the struggle between those who support democracy and gradualism and those who support the Communist revolution. Communist writers are wont to categorize noncommunist thinkers of the past hundred years as reformists, while viewing themselves as revolutionaries. To use communist terminology, it is the struggle between two lines—the bourgeois against the proletariat line.

Representative communist intellectual historians hold that all thought struggles (including national struggle) are an inseparable part of class struggle, developing in accordance with the development of social, economic, and political struggles. Furthermore, all modern Chinese thought struggles focus on the solution to the problem of the Chinese revolution. Since the modern Chinese revolution is a revolution of the masses against imperialism and feudalism, it follows that the history of modern Chinese thought is the history of the genesis and development of antiimperialist and antifeudal thought among the masses for the past hundred years. At the same time, it is the history of the genesis, development, senility, and final decline of bourgeois and petty-bourgeois thought, and it is also the history of the growth to strength and the ultimate victory of proletarian thought. The modern revolutionary history of antiimperialism and antifeudalism in China can be divided into two stages: the old democratic revolutionary stage, and the new democratic revolutionary stage. Hence, the development of Chinese thought should also be divided into these two stages.[7] In a slightly different form, the development of modern thought is seen as a process by which reformist thought is replaced by revolutionary thought, and the revolutionary thought of other classes by that of the proletariat, ending in the proletariat victory over imperialism and feudalism in China.[8] What communist writers refer to as the bourgeois line or the reformist line is actually the democratic movement that began at the time of K'ang Yu-wei.

Whether called bourgeois line, reformist line, or democratic movement, it has been the liberal trend of Chinese political thought in the past century. The actions and beliefs of K'ang Yu-wei and Liang Ch'i-ch'ao, in their advocacy of a kind of constitutional monarchy aimed at the creation of a parliamentary form of government patterned after the British and at making the Manchu emperor a titular head, marked the beginning of the democratic movement in China. Politically, Sun Yat-sen's ideal government was also a form of democratic government. Other scholars, such as Hu Shih, Chang Chün-mai, and Chang Tung-sun, together with a large group of intellectuals, also strongly believed in democracy. Liang Shu-ming, although his central emphasis lay elsewhere, was definitely in favor of democracy. Ch'en Tu-hsiu began as an ardent advocate of democracy, was converted to communism for a time, and rejoined the democratic movement in his last years. But the communists claim that such people and their visions are gone.

I have attempted, in the following pages, to give a historical and analytical account of the chosen nine thinkers by presenting their ideas in regard to their social reconstruction programs as precisely, objectively, and comprehensively as possible, with a view of presenting a true ideological picture of each of them. A somewhat detailed account of the life of each thinker is given at the beginning of each chapter, based on the thesis that their activities provide good indicators of how extensive and deeply these people have swayed the minds of the Chinese politically and ideologically under their influences.

Since I am a native Chinese of the generation born in the early years of this century I grew up in an atmosphere of grave social upheavals, and I share —with both joy and sorrow—the concern for the destiny of China which resulted in the different programs for social reconstruction brought forth by the thinking of the men reviewed in this book. Thus, my understanding of their ideas is more intimate and direct than could be those of either a non-Chinese or a member of the younger generation. In general, I believe that my understanding of their ideas corresponds, to a considerable degree, to the great majority of the Chinese intellectuals' understanding of them and that, similarly, my aspirations for China agree with theirs.

It is my belief that ideas dominate human minds and that their influence is long-lasting. The present ideological conflicts in China are the outcome of conflicting ideas rooted in the past. The present political struggle in China is basically a reflection of past ideological differences. That is why thought reform or thought struggle has been tremendously emphasized in contemporary

China. To even begin to understand modern China's problems and their possible solutions, it is necessary to have a precise comprehension of the ideological conflicts between communist and noncommunist thinkers who competed for dominance.

In the concluding chapter an attempt is made first, to explain why only the communists have been successful in maintaining political power; and second, since accounts of the ideological conflicts between the communist and noncommunist thinkers are scattered throughout the earlier chapters, I try to bring them into focus with a summary of their predominant conflicting ideas in collective analyses by topic. The ideals of a political party are to be judged on performance. Over thirty years have passed since the inception of the communist regime, and it is now fitting and proper to use this yardstick to, third, measure the results of the communist ideals. This appraisal, both from the communist and noncommunist viewpoint, will consider both those hopes which have been realized and those which have not. I will also indicate certain other ideas which the Communist Party itself has modified or even abandoned in practice. Finally, I will venture to predict the future course of China's history during the next few decades.

Notes

[1] For a detailed account of the unequal treaties and their effect on modern China, see Chiang Kai-shek, "Chung-kuo chih ming-yün," in *Chiang tsung-t'ung szu-hsiang yen-lun chi* (Taipei: Chung-yang wen-wu kung-ying she, 1966), 4:11–23. Translated by Philip Jaffe, *China's Destiny and Chinese Economic Theory* (New York: Roy Publishers, 1947). Each item in category 4 involves treaties with more than one country. For simplicity, the names and dates of the treaties are not given.

[2] R.R. Palmer, *A History of the Modern World,* 5th ed. (New York: Knopf, 1978), pp. 637–38. We do not mean to suggest that this is a strict comparison, e.g. China had never integrated Indochina as the U.S. had California.

[3] Arnold J. Toynbee, *A Study of History,* abridgement of vol. 12 by D.C. Somervell (New York: Oxford University Press, 1957), p. 358.

[4] Ibid., p. 360.

[5] *The Works of Mencius,* bk. 6, pt. 2, ch. 15, sec. 5, in James Legge, trans., *The Chinese Classics,* vols. 1 and 2 (Reprint, Taipei: Wen-che ch'u-pan she, 1970). All translations of the Confucian classics are by James Legge, except where otherwise indicated.

[6] Mao Tse-tung, "Lun jen-min min-chu chuan-cheng," *Mao Tse-tung hsuan-chi,* 5 vols. (Peking: Jen-min ch'u-pan she, 1969–77), 4:1361. Hereafter referred to as *MTTHC*. Henceforth all translations of the quotations from *MTTHC* are based on the *Selected Works of Mao Tse-tung* (Peking: Foreign Languages, 1967).

[7] Shih Chün, Jen Chi-yü, Chu Po-k'un, *Chung-kuo chin-tai szu-hsiang shih chiang-shou t'i-kang* (Peking: Jen-min ch'u-pan-she, 1957), pp. 9–10. This is a collective work by the faculty of Peking University, supplying an outline for teaching the history of modern Chinese thought. It represents, in general, the official line of the Communist historians.

[8] Ibid., p. 17.

1
K'ang Yu-wei (1858–1927)

Biography

K'ang Yu-wei[1] was born on 19 March 1858 to a scholarly family. He began his education at a very young age under the guidance of his father, a district magistrate. As a child, K'ang was said to have had a photographic memory. By the time he was five he had memorized hundreds of T'ang poems; at six he studied the *Confucian Analects* and other classics, and at eight he began to compose essays. When K'ang was eleven and his father died, he continued his education under the tutelage of his grandfather, a scholar of the neo-Confucian school who taught in a country school.

In 1876 when K'ang was nineteen, he studied under the great neo-Confucian scholar, Chu Chiu-chiang (1807–1882). Chu, whose scholarship inclined toward an emphasis on the pragmatic utility of serving society rather than on fanciful abstract theory, specialized in the history of political institutions of former dynasties. This emphasis soon led to a breach between teacher and student. K'ang studied well and read widely under Chu's stern instruction, but they differed in their evaluations of ancient Chinese thinkers and writers. K'ang was contemptuous of certain of those whom his teacher respected, while Chu ridiculed and censured K'ang's independent and iconoclastic opinions as being wild.

K'ang finally left his teacher at the end of 1878 to study on his own and a year later retired to the Hsi-ch'iao mountains in Nan-hai (Kuang-tung) devoting himself to reading Taoist and Buddhist texts. During the same year K'ang made a brief excursion to Hong Kong where the magnificent buildings and clean streets as well as the careful efficiency of the British police impressed him. K'ang modified his attitude toward foreign people and foreign writings, feeling that foreigners should not necessarily be viewed as barbaric and that reading foreign books might be beneficial after all.

K'ang's new impressions of foreigners were reinforced when, after having failed the *chü-jen* examination in Peking in 1882, he was returning home by way of Shanghai and noted the orderliness of the foreign concessions. From his observations he inferred that these foreign governments must be even more superior in their native lands. The idea intrigued him and he decided to find out through careful study the secret of their order and efficiency. A reading of all the translations of foreign works put out by the Kiangnan Arsenal (Chiang-nan

11

chi-tsao chü) and Christian churches convinced K'ang that perhaps Western learning held the key to truth and prosperity.

But there was another side to K'ang's observant nature. He became increasingly vexed over the continuing humiliation China was suffering at the hands of foreign encroachment: France had annexed Annam in 1885, Japan had annexed the Ryukyu Islands in 1879, and Britain had annexed Burma in 1886. K'ang appealed to the authorities in Peking to end this humiliation, but being a commoner without an official appointment he had no status for submitting memorials to the throne. This however did not daunt him. He submitted some memorials to the most trusted aides of Emperor Kuang-hsu. His pleas to protect China from complete dismemberment through political reform and modernization were never passed on, but his efforts soon marked him as a political activist.

After his futile attempts to attract the attention of the emperor, K'ang Yu-wei returned to Canton in 1889 where he began to take on private students and where he later opened a formal school in 1891. One of those who enrolled was Liang Ch'i-ch'ao, a young scholar destined to become one of the chief supporters of K'ang's reform movement of 1898, and who was eventually lauded as one of the most influential thinkers in the intellectual and political history of republican China. K'ang did not teach orthodox Confucian studies in his school. In 1891 his famous work *Hsin-hsueh wei-ching k'ao*[2] (A study of the forged classics in the Hsin period) was published. A year later in 1892, with the assistance of his students, he wrote *K'ung-tzu kai-chih k'ao*[3] (A Study of Confucius as a reformer), which was published in 1897.

In these two works, K'ang broke away from the orthodox interpretation that Confucius stood for a static society. He tried to prove that Confucius favored institutional changes. Such a bold thesis naturally aroused intense controversies in academic circles. Actually, however, K'ang's works were more political than academic, for they provided the whole theoretical structure for his reform movement. Three years after his first book was published, government authorities in 1894 burned the wood blocks of *Hsin-hsueh wei-ching k'ao* on the pretext that its contents "deceived the world and misled the people, showed disrespect for the sages and disregard for the law." The effect of both works, referred to in more detail later, was aptly described in Liang Ch'i-ch'ao's metaphor: the *Hsin-hsueh wei-ching k'ao* had the force of a hurricane and the *K'ung-tzu kai-chih k'ao* had the effect of a volcanic eruption.[4]

K'ang's next activities stemmed from China's preparation to ratify the Shimonoseki Treaty with Japan, which ended the Sino-Japanese War and signed over to Japan the Liaotung Peninsula, annexed Taiwan and paid an indemnity of 200 million taels of silver to the Japanese. Chinese indignation turned to anger as unrest became widespread. K'ang had passed the *chü-jen* degree in 1893 and by April 1895 was in Peking to take the *chin-shih* examination. On 2 May 1895 he submitted a memorial, together with 1,300-plus signatures of *chü-jen* supporters, to Emperor Kuang-hsu. This "Ten Thousand Word Petition" urged the government to reject the peace treaty terms with Japan, to remove the capital to

Hsi-an (Sian), and to institute immediately certain fundamental political changes. This rather unusual event came to be known as *Kung-ch'e shang-shu* (Public Vehicles Presenting a Memorial). ("Public Vehicle" was the nickname given to *chü-jen* who were sent by public transportation to Peking to take the *chin-shih* examination.) Though little came of this, K'ang's image again rose in stature as a political figure. A few days after the submission of the memorial, K'ang was announced as a recipient of the *chin-shih* degree.

In the summer and autumn of 1895 K'ang founded and published a daily paper *Chung-wai chi-wen* and established an organization in Peking that he called Society for the Study of National Rejuvenation *(Ch'iang-hsueh hui).* In October of that same year a branch office opened in Shanghai. One of the society's activities was to translate and publish Western books and newspapers. Unfortunately, an Imperial Decree (initiated by the Empress Dowager) suppressed its operation after a short time.

K'ang Yu-wei continued to search for practical ways to popularize his reformist ideals. In 1897 he organized another society, the Society for Protecting the Nation *(Pao-kuo hui)* to attract aggressive intellectuals who favored reform.

But it was not just the intellectuals who worried over current events. The common man was also apprehensive that the German seizure of Chiao-chou in 1897 would further partition China. (To use a Chinese metaphor, it would have been similar to being sliced up like a watermelon.) When K'ang heard of the German action, he rushed to Peking to submit yet another memorial (his fifth) to the emperor; again, he pressed for immediate political changes to save China from complete dissection. His main point was the institution of a parliament and the adoption of a national constitution. He also proposed the study, and possible adaptation, of Russian and Japanese social, political and economic institutions. In the case of Russia, K'ang specifically mentioned Peter the Great as a model, and in Japan's case, he exemplified Emperor Meiji.[5] I am inclined to think that in his proposal to study these aspects of Russia and Japan, K'ang can be considered the forerunner of the advocates of industrialization (the Russian case) and Westernization (the Japanese case).

After many abortive attempts, K'ang Yu-wei's efforts at reform finally received the personal attention of Emperor Kuang-hsu. The emperor was deeply interested in reform, and he decided to put K'ang's recommendations into practice despite tremendous opposition from the Empress Dowager and her retinue of conservative supporters. On 11 June 1898 a decree was issued declaring a basic national policy of fundamental changes. Six months earlier, on 23 January, K'ang had been received by high officials rather than by the emperor, owing to K'ang's low official position. But on 16 June K'ang was granted an imperial audience by Emperor Kuang-hsu himself. The 11 June decree was followed by a number of more specific decrees actually influenced by K'ang and reflecting his proposals.[6]

Unfortunately, these reform measures, which came to be called the Hundred Days' Reform, lasted only 103 days.[7] The Empress Dowager had put an end to them when she assumed full power as regent and had placed Kuang-hsu in confinement on 21 September. Kuang-hsu's incarceration was to end only with his death the day before the Empress Dowager herself died on 15 November 1908. Naturally, all reform decrees were rescinded. Both K'ang and Liang Ch'i-ch'ao narrowly escaped arrest and death. Six others who were active in the reform movement were executed on 28 September 1898 and were martyred as the Six Gentlemen of Wu-hsu.

After the failure of the Hundred Days' Reform, K'ang's image changed from that of an ultraradical to an archconservative. This strange about-face was the result of K'ang's bitter enmity toward Sun Yat-sen; K'ang stood in opposition to Sun's revolutionary republican movement which, K'ang insisted, would bring to China only prolonged chaos and possible extinction.

K'ang's momentous work, as far as ideology is concerned, is his *Ta-t'ung shu* (The book of great unity).[8] It was initially formulated around 1884-1885, and finally completed in 1902 in India. He printed the first two portions in the periodical *Compassion (Pu-jen tsa-chih)* in 1913, and the whole book was not published until 1935, eight years after his death. This work was much more radical than the first two books mentioned above. K'ang warned his disciples that the blueprint of this book for a perfect society or utopia was designed for a distant future and that any attempt to apply it during the present time would create more harm than good. Liang Ch'i-ch'ao described the impact of the book as more powerful than an earthquake.[9]

For sixteen years, from 1898 until 1913, K'ang lived in exile. Shortly after his escape to Hong Kong, he sailed to Japan in October at the invitation of the prime minister of Japan, who had assured K'ang of assistance and protection. From Japan K'ang set forth in March 1899 on a trip which circumnavigated the globe three times and which took him to thirty-one countries where he studied their political, economic and social conditions. In 1911, "In the ninth month K'ang received news that at last the Ch'ing government had cancelled the order for his arrest. After twelve years abroad, he could finally go home to China. By this time the revolution in China was in full swing, and K'ang, deeply disturbed by the situation, wrote a long essay of ten sections entitled 'On Saving China from the Danger of Extinction' *(Chiu-wang lun)*. The essay warned the people against the dangers of protracted revolution. His solution for China was to establish what he termed a titular monarchical republic *(hsu-chün kung-ho)* as soon as possible to serve as an intermediate stage leading to a truly republican form of government."[10] This titular monarchical republic remained as his political faith until his death.

In 1913 K'ang published a magazine, *Compassion,* the contents of which consisted almost exclusively of his own writings. The publication ceased within a year after its inception but was revived in 1918. Little became of K'ang after this, although he grew more and more conservative, remaining faithful to the Ch'ing dynasty and to the cause of constitutional monarch; he even supported, in 1917, the restoration movement of Pu Yi, the young Manchu pretender to the Ch'ing throne.

K'ang Yu-wei died on 31 March 1927.

K'ang's Conception of Change

The Chinese philosophy of history is predominately one of stability or unchangeableness. The Confucian canons especially glorify the ancient sage emperors, their systems and institutions. In other words, the ideal society is one that emulates the golden age of the past. Because these ancient societies were set up as the supreme model, later generations were expected to follow and imitate the past rather than to look to the present or future. For two millennia, this attitude had contributed to the static conditions of Chinese society.

The influence of this philosophy of emulating the past was so strong and widespread that any bold reformer was doomed to failure. In the long history of China, only a handful of such progressive reformers attempted to bring about complete institutional change. At the end of the former Han dynasty, for example, Wang Mang (45 B.C.–23 A.D.) who is traditionally regarded as a usurper of the throne, tried to make certain far-reaching changes but failed. During the Northern Sung dynasty, Wang An-shih (1021-86) attempted reforms of an even wider and more ambitious scope. He, too, inevitably failed. But whether or not one agrees with his policies, it is to this courageous scholar and statesman that China probably owes the most rebellious idea of change. Wang boldly declared: "The changes of Heaven need not be feared. The [ways of] ancestors need not be followed. The words of others need not be concerned."[11]

As might be expected, Wang's iconoclastic remarks and attempts at reform were not only denounced by the majority of later Chinese thinkers but Wang's reforms also met with adamant opposition from most scholars and officials of his own day.

Eight centuries after Wang An-shih's failure to bring about reform, K'ang Yu-wei also tried to implement sweeping changes in China by arguing that change, not stability, is the natural way. K'ang asserted that, theoretically, change is the Heavenly law or the Heavenly course *(t'ien-tao)*. Throughout history dynasties have risen and declined. In general, a new dynasty of a certain ruling house instituted the necessary changes to replace the previous dynasty of another house that had failed to make the proper changes. Heaven showed no favor in the selection of any of these houses. Only those who acted in accordance with Heaven, and change, prospered; those who failed to follow the say of Heaven and did not change, perished.[12]

In practice, K'ang vigorously advocated institutional changes, from a philosophy of stability to a philosophy of continual change, a notion completely antithetical to orthodox Confucian teachings. Thus, "in the international realm of competition, those countries which change survive, those which do not change perish. A total change makes a country strong, while small changes still cannot avoid the fate of extinction."[13] (To illustrate his point more clearly, K'ang frequently used the metaphor of wearing fur in winter and light clothes in summer, and the use of vehicles on land and boats on water.) In applying a metapor to the actual international situation, K'ang asserted that "sticking to the old institutions without changing under the circumstances of international competition," referring to the arrival of the West in China, is like wearing a

15

heavy fur coat in the summer, and journeying on water in a land vehicle.[14] That is, when times (seasons) change, man must also change with a view to adapting to the new environment through new methods and new techniques and new institutions.

K'ang's ideas, despite their explosive force and shocking effects, still might not have been authoritative enough to convince the intellectuals and philosophers, steeped in the old dogmas, that change should be made. To lend credence to his ideas, K'ang worked out a theoretical foundation for his theory of change by reevaluating the Confucian classics.

In sum, K'ang was deeply convinced that the success of Western aggression was due mainly to China's own ignorance and weakness, and therefore China had no right to complain about it, for it was a natural consequence in the cruel world of fierce international rivalries. And, the only way China would be saved from complete colonization and from extinction was through institutional changes—immediate and complete.

Forged Classics

Let us begin with K'ang's academic works. Because K'ang was a voluminous writer, we must limit discussion to those writings relevant to his theory of institutional changes that led to his ideal of China's reconstruction and of her ultimate utopian development. Of particular importance are three of his books which his disciple Liang Ch'i-ch'ao described metaphorically as a hurricane, a volcanic eruption, and an earthquake.

After the burning of books in the Ch'in dynasty, the Six Classics (only five being extant, the *Book of Music* having been lost) were allegedly wholly destroyed. With the rise of the Han dynasty, scholars began to teach the classics, mostly from memory and by drawing on their own knowledge. (These five classics were: *The Book of Changes, The Book of Documents, The Book of Odes, The Spring and Autumn Annals,* and *The Book of Rites.*)

At the time of Emperor Wu (140-86 B.C.) and Emperor Hsuan (73-48 B.C.) of the Han dynasty, fourteen scholars were officially appointed to teach these five classics in government supported academies. The texts used and notes taken by their students and later used throughout the Han dynasty were written in "seal writing," the current written form of the time. It was this style that came to be known as the Modern Texts *(chin-wen),* as contrasted with the old text style of pre-Ch'in times.

Toward the end of the Western Han (206 B.C.-25 A.D.). a different version of the classics and their commentaries appeared. Among them, two were said to have been discovered sealed in the walls of the house of Confucius, having been put there to avoid discovery by Ch'in Shih-huang's officials. Other classics were said to have been transmitted from memory by certain scholars. These newly discovered classics were written in the ancient tadpole style and came to be called the Ancient Texts *(ku-wen).*

Liu Hsin (ca. 46 B.C.–23 A.D.), by taking advantage of his official position as Imperial Secretary, succeeded in establishing the Ancient Text school of

16

learning during the time of Wang Mang who, in 9 A.D., usurped the Han throne and established the Hsin dynasty. After he was deposed and the Eastern Han dynasty was restored, Emperor Kuang-wu (25-58 A.D.) abolished the Ancient Text learning. Nevertheless, the Ancient Text school continued to prosper and exerted a widespread influence, while the Modern Text school increasingly declined from the time of Cheng Hsuan (127-200 A.D.) to Tu Yü (222-85 A.D.) and Wang Su (195-256 A.D.). It was not until the Ch'ing dynasty (1644-1911) that the Modern Text learning revived.[15]

The most important work of the Modern Text school that is germane to K'ang Yu-wei's thought is the *Kung-yang Commentary* (Kung-yang chuan) of the *Spring and Autumn Annals*. The *Kung-yang Commentary,* according to Ho Hsiu (129-82 A.D.), a famous student of the classics, "abounds in unusually bizarre eccentric ideas." And it was mainly from these bizarre and eccentric ideas that K'ang extracted theoretical foundations for his institutional reforms—the great principles hidden in esoteric language, as K'ang put it. K'ang's first book, *Hsin-hsueh wei-ching k'ao,* not only aimed at reducing the authority, position, and prestige of the Ancient Text learning, but it also questioned the authenticity of the Ancient Text learning itself. In drawing his conclusion, K'ang brought out four essential points: (1)There had never been anything called the Ancient Text school in the Former Han dynasty, i.e., Western Han. All the Ancient Texts were forged by Liu Hsin. (2) The book burning during the Ch'in had not destroyed the Six Classics; all complete texts of the Confucian school were completely transmitted with nothing missing or omitted. (3) The written characters used at the time of Confucius were the same seal characters of the Ch'in and Han; there had never been the classification of "Ancient" and "Modern" texts. And (4) The motive of Liu Hsin's forgery was to aid Wang Mang to usurp the Han throne, Liu Hsin conspired to distort Confucius' "great principles" which were hidden in "esoteric language."[16]

In K'ang's search for the great principles hidden in esoteric language that aimed at effecting an institutional change involving a kind of political revolution and social change, he was fond of expounding two conceptions based on the *Kung-yang Commentary*—the unfolding of the three epochs *(chang san-shih)* and the passage of the "three legitimacies" *(t'ung san-t'ung).* The essence of both views is that history evolves progressively through changes. The three epochs consist of the epoch of disorder *chü-luan shih),* the epoch of gradual peace *(sheng-p'ing shih)* and the epoch of great peace *(t'ai-p'ing shih).* In political terms, K'ang conceived the world as evolving from autocracy to constitutional monarchy, and finally to republicanism. What K'ang meant by republicanism is, in modern terminology, perfect democracy. It should also be pointed out that although K'ang was opposed to Sun Yat-sen's republicanism, he did so only with reference to time and not in principle. That is, K'ang's belief in the evolutionary theory of step by step was so strong that he felt it premature and catastropic to build a democratic republic right after an autocracy.

K'ang also brought up the idea of the "minor peace" *(hsiao-k'ang)* in contrast to great unity *(ta-t'ung),* based on the chapter of the "Li Yun" in *Li Chi.* K'ang relegated the three dynasties upheld by historians for two thousand years as the golden age to the stage of minor peace, thus envisioning his utopia of great unity as a future accomplishment—quite a revolutionary view at the time.

The essence of the passage of the three legitimacies is that the three dynasties of Hsia, Shang, and Chou were different from each other, and therefore reforms should be made as time went on. According to the great Confucianist Tung Chung-shu's theory, each dynasty had a legitimacy that was conferred by the Mandate of Heaven: The Hsia dynasty received the "heavenly legitimacy" *(t'ien-t'ung),* the Shang dynasty received the "earth legitimacy" *(ti-t'ung)* and the Chou dynasty received the "man legitimacy" *(jen-t'ung).* Since each new dynasty begins by receiving the Mandate of Heaven, changing its calendars, establishing a national dress and choosing a national color, these three dynasties were also seen to have received the "black legitimacy" *(hei-t'ung)* the "white legitimacy" *(pai-t'ung)* and the "red legitimacy" *(ch'ih-t'ung)* respectively. The cycle of the three legitimacies goes through black, white, and red, and then begins again in subsequent dynasties.

Such concepts tend to look absurd by present day scientific standards, but K'ang's re-emphasis and reinterpretations added new life to these concepts, the consequences of which were profound. The concept of the unfolding of three epochs is based on a theory of evolution, asserting that human life is progressive, with each succeeding epoch better than the previous one. Such an evolutionary theory opposed the traditional theory that the millennium occurred only in the past. The concept of the three legitimacies adduces that no dynasty can hold power forever, and that any dynasty that has lost the support of the people would also have to lose the Mandate of Heaven, i.e., the legitimacy, and should yield to a new dynasty which would arise by receiving Heaven's Mandate or legitimacy.[17]

Although K'ang's opposition to the Ancient Text learning appeared, on the surface, to be only a question concerning different textual versions, he actually emphasized the fact that Ancient Text scholars ignored and omitted the greatest principles of Confucius—the highest truth in Chinese thought—namely, the concepts of the three epochs and the three legitimacies. However, the theory of the forged classics did not originate with K'ang; Liao P'ing (1852–1932) pioneered this theory and he understandably charged K'ang with plagiarism.[18] Actually, what K'ang did was to expand these ideas with greater boldness, ardor and intensity.

Confucius as a Reformer

K'ang Yu-wei's second book, *K'ung-tzu kai-chih k'ao,* was even more astounding and revolutionary than his first one. The first chapter begins with the theory that there was no reliable recorded history before the Six Classics. Near the end of the Chou dynasty, scholars attempted to create new theories and formulate new social systems according to their own originality. Since the people in China have had the propensity to "honor antiquity and despise the present, and to value the distant and hold lightly the near," the scholars appealed

18

to antiquity with a view to creating a sense of authority and sacredness in order to win the confidence and support of the people. Thus, Lao-tzu evoked the Yellow Emperor, Mo-tzu exemplified the Emperor Yü and Hsu Hsing glorified the Divine Husbandman (Shen-nung). Confucius honored Emperors Yao and Shun and King Wen, as well as their social and political institutions.

Traditionally, Confucius was considered to have transmitted the ancient principles without creating anything original. His contribution to the Six Classics was seen to have been only emendation and revision. But K'ang asserted that Confucius was the author of all six of the classics. This theory provided the seed for the concept he set forth as a blueprint for his ideal society and which was taken as a constitution of the world to come. Actually, K'ang contended, these accounts of the sage kings and their admirable virtues and institutions did not have to be factual. They were merely imagined by Confucius to be good models. What Confucius attempted to do, argued K'ang, was to bring about institutional changes by appealing to antiquity *(t'o-ku kai-chih)*.[19] And the implication of such a reevaluation of Confucius was to prepare the way for K'ang himself to play such a role in his own day.

Ta-t'ung shu 大同

The third important book which K'ang Yu-wei wrote is the *Ta-t'ung shu*. Liang Ch'i-ch'ao compared the far-reaching effects this work had on China to the effects of a major earthquake as we mentioned before. After the book had been written, K'ang kept it secret from others. Liang was one of the two disciples who were permitted to read the manuscript. They were bent on making parts of it public. Although K'ang did not approve this he could not stop them from doing so either. However, from that time on, K'ang's students all talked about the concept of *ta-t'ung*.

The somewhat detailed summary of *Ta-t'ung shu* which follows is motivated by two considerations. First, Marx said little about the form of organization that would replace capitalist society; nor did he describe the practical measures that would need to be taken to achieve the ultimate goal—the communist society. But K'ang had a detailed blueprint of his utopia, the summary of which can enable readers to know vividly K'ang's visions. Second, Marx and K'ang approached their problems and solutions differently. Marx's approach was more simplistic. He determined that in a capitalist society all social evils stem from the economic exploitation of the proletariat by the bourgeoisie. His solution simply was to destroy the bourgeoisie, such that "the expropriators are expropriated," and a happy society would emerge. Unlike Marx, K'ang took a pluralistic approach by juxtaposing a number of miseries of mankind, none of which is considered more basic or predominate. He determined, again in juxtaposition, various sources for these miseries, which he labelled as boundaries. Finally, he suggested, in juxtaposition, practical measures to remove these boundaries, the aim of which was to achieve a happy world in diversified fields.

K'ang's religious and humane compassion for all living beings is evident in the opening chapter of the *Ta-t'ung shu* where he lamented that all sentient beings suffered. Not only does every individual, rich and poor, noble and commoner, suffer, but birds and beasts have been unfortunate victims of humans who slaughter them, eat their flesh and use their skins and fur for personal comforts. Human history, he said, is a history of bloody wars that take millions of lives. The world is nothing more than a gigantic slaughterhouse and a huge prison filled with grief and misery.[20]

K'ang asserted that human nature, or the way of life, was characterized by the desire for pleasure and the avoidance of pain. Born in a chaotic world, full of suffering and pain, K'ang vowed to save human beings from suffering and lead them to the supreme happiness of a world of *ta-t'ung* as envisioned by Confucius.

K'ang organized this observation of human misery and suffering into six categories, as follows:

The sufferings from living:
- conception
- infant mortality
- disability and sickness
- aboriginal existence
- living in border areas
- slavery
- womanhood

The sufferings brought about by natural calamities:
- flood, drought, and famine
- plagues of locusts
- fire
- inundation
- volcanoes
- earthquakes and landslides
- collapse of buildings
- shipwrecks
- motor vehicular accidents
- epidemics

The sufferings from human relationships:
- bereavement of widows and widowers
- childlessness and orphanhood
- sickness without medical care
- poverty
- low social standing

The sufferings brought about by social and political institutions:
- punishment and imprisonment
- harsh taxation
- military service
- the state
- the family

The sufferings of human feelings:
- ignorance

- hatred and enmity
- love and affection
- emotional attachments
- toil
- desires
- bondage and tyranny
- class distinctions
  The sufferings of admired people:
- the rich
- the honorable and noble
- the elderly
- kings and emperors
- gods, sages, immortals, and the Buddha.[21]

This list reflects K'ang's feeling that the sufferings of mankind stemmed from all spheres of life and affected all human beings regardless of their status. Kings and emperors, the rich and the noble all had a share of misery. Man's suffering stirred within K'ang compassion *(pu-jen)*, or, to use the original Mencian phrase, the feeling of being unable to bear to see the suffering of others.[22] Compassion was one of the four principles of Mencius and from it sprang the cardinal virtue of benevolence which Confucius so highly valued. Moved by mankind's sufferings, K'ang sought to understand the reasons for them. He attributed the roots of suffering to nine barriers. His goal was to remove these barriers. At the time that these barriers are eliminated, the world would enter into the period of *ta-t'ung* and peace would reign eternally.[23]

National Barriers: Removal to Form One World. The state as an institution was a necessary evil for social coherence in primitive times, but thereafter no other institution had rendered greater harm to mankind. History, both in the East and in the West, has invariably demonstrated that the higher the civilization, the more disastrous the wars. In antiquity, one soldier was able to kill another soldier with a sword whereas in modern times the invention of firearms and poisonous gases permitted the slaughter of hundreds of thousands within a short time span. Since cruelty, murder and selfishness go hand in hand with the state, the state was evidently incompatible with the perfect virtue of man or with peace in the world. Thus, the state had to be abolished. The prerequisite for the abolition of the state was total disarmament of the state and the removal of state boundaries. Although a quick transformation to the goal of great unity was nearly impossible, historical development through time would guarantee the attainment of the goal. First, history showed that with the passage of time the number of states decreased as numerous small political entities were integrated into a few large ones. Second, the expansion of people's power which became increasingly evident after the American and French revolutions led to widespread constitutionalism and republicanism. Thus, it is easier for countries where people are in power to merge than for countries where selfish autocratic sovereigns are in power to merge.

Despite the inevitable trends of history, the goal could be achieved step-by-step. The first step would be to organize a "public deliberating government" *(kung-i cheng-fu)*, a world federation which resembled the Swiss political system but which differed widely from the American one. The public deliberating government would include at least one representative from each state and an elected speaker *(i-chang)* but it would not have a president. The chief responsibility of this international government would be to consider problems of international relations. Other political affairs would be left to member states. Some of its major tasks would be: to formulate international law; settle internal disputes among member states; equalize tariffs; standardize weights and measures; develop an international language; suppress any state which seriously damages civilization, public well-being or international law by an expeditionary force of the international government which would have the power to overthrow and replace the unyielding government, and gradually reduce the armed forces.

A few decades after the establishment of the public deliberating government, conditions would be ripe for the realization of a true world government that would be called the "public government" *(kung cheng-fu)*. The major problems of the public government would include: the complete reduction of armed forces, hence the abolition of the state; the abolition of the use of imperial and hereditary titles, a use that was synonomous with murder and slaughter; the expunging of the word "state" *(kuo)* from usage, which was the root of selfishness, wars and carnage, and was an obstacle to the attainment of good virtues of man; the division of the globe into ten continents, each one with a local government; the universal adoption of a new calendar commencing with the great unity, taking 1901 as Year One; the strict enforcement of the standardization of weights and measures; the use of the decimal system; and the replacement of all national languages with an international language (national languages would be obsolete and would be relegated to museums for linguists to study); the division of days and nights into ten hours each, with each hour divided into ten quarters, each quarter into ten minutes, and each minute into ten seconds.

The evolution from nation-state to world government had to be a gradual development that required three stages which corresponded to the three stages of the *Kung-yang* school of Confucianism, namely, the stage of disorder when the foundation of the great unity was laid, the stage of gradual peace when the great unity was coming into being, and the stage of great peace when the great unity was fully realized. K'ang detailed an outline of the political, economic, military and judicial conditions in the three stages.[24]

⊢ *Class Barriers: Removal to Achieve a Classless Society.* Class distinctions are a most unjustifiable man-made evil. The more obvious examples are the caste system of India, the class distinctions of Medieval Europe, and the feudalism of Tokugawa Japan. Prior to the Spring and Autumn period (772-484 B.C.) in China there existed feudal lords and noblemen. The principle of equality originated with Confucius.) He advocated the idea of a unified empire which meant feudalism would be replaced. He censured hereditary nobility with a view to eliminating hereditary office. He promoted the public land system in order to eradicate slavery. The *Spring and Autumn Annals (Ch'un-ch'iu)*, which Confucius wrote, was virtually a constitution that restricted the monarch's power and provided for social mobility.[25] Every individual was a "citizen" *(p'ing-min)*, and anyone could become a minister, a general, teacher, or scholar, regardless of social origin. It was due to the farsightedness and remarkable innovations of Confucius that China had a classless society two thousand years before Europe.)

A class society not only made the people ignorant and miserable, it also weakened their country. On the other hand, a classless society would find the people intelligent and content and their country prosperous and strong. America would be a good example. When classes vanish, a happy world would emerge.[26]

Racial Barriers: Removal to Achieve Racial Equality. Once the family and the state are abolished, the next goal toward achieving the world of *ta-t'ung* would be to abolish races. Distinguishing characteristics of race would be variations in skin color and certain other physical features. Four races were recognized to exist in the then-present world: white, yellow, black, and brown. Color difference is caused by a combination of ethnic, geographic, climatic, and dietary factors. As long as people differ in color no real equality can be attained. It would be impossible to force people by law to practice equality.

Among the four races, white was to be aspired to, and the ways to form a white race was by the following three methods: (1) migration—no maternity institutes or kindergartens would be located in tropical zones because these zones were reserved solely for children born elsewhere who, after coming of age, could migrate and reside there. Local natives would be encouraged to move away either voluntarily or by governmental assistance; (2) intermarriage—yellow and white people who take black or brown spouses would be awarded eugenic medals as an encouragement; and (3) change of diet—black and brown people would eat the same diet as yellow and white people. By applying these methods, it would take 700 to 1,000 years to transform all colored people into white people. By the time of *ta-t'ung*, then, all people on the globe would be of the same color, the same appearance, the same height and the same intelligence; all would be handsome, god-like figures.[27]

Morphological Barriers: Removal to Achieve Sexual Equality. Sexual differences were considered merely morphological differences—that is, a difference in structure and form with no relation to factors such as intelligence, personality and emotion. Men and women are created equal by Heaven and are born with equal human rights. Unfortunately, one-half of mankind has been ruthlessly suppressed, fooled, imprisoned, and tortured for thousands of years throughout the world by those close to them. The suppression of women by men was the suppression of one's own mother, daughter or sister. The infringement

23

upon women's rights was an infringement upon the fundamental human rights endowed by Heaven. The yielding of these rights by women was the abandonment of their heavenly duties.

The sad plight of inequalities inflicted on women by men has been shocking. Among the most notorious inequalities were the following examples where women were not permitted to serve as government officials, take imperial civil service examinations, serve as parliament members in Western countries, have a voice in local public affairs, be citizens, maintain independence (a woman could not establish a household, retain her maiden name after marriage, or take care of her own relatives; rather, she had to care for her husband's), and be free. A person, being free, was entitled to enjoy heavenly endowed freedoms, yet a woman's situation contradicted this principle. Women did not have the freedom of marriage; they lived like prisoners for they were confined to the house and banned from public social life, especially with men. Women suffered punishments as though they were criminals, such as the piercing of ears or noses, and the binding of the feet as well as the waist; women served as slaves at home, performing all the cooking chores and menial work for the whole family; women were regarded as the private property of men, rather than as a member of the country or society; women were treated as toys or pets that were painted with cosmetics and decorated with jewelry; women were deprived of an education; they could not be scholars because it was felt that ignorance in a woman was a virtue.

The above mentioned atrocities were more widespread in Asian countries than in Western countries. But inequality did still exist in the West. In order to save the 800 million women from their miseries and to bring about an independent and equal realm of the great unity for the many women in the endless years to come, the following were important measures: give women equal opportunity along with men to go to school and award them academic degrees such as the Chinese *chü-jen, chin-shih,* or the Western B.A. or Ph.D.; give equal opportunity to women to be teachers, parliament members, or to hold high political office, even the chief executive of a country; give the right to restore or retain one's maiden name; let women wear the same clothing as men; allow the practice of free marriage by making it a free contractual relationship of love with a maximum limit of one year and a minimum limit of one month, but renewable if both parties wish to remain together. During the period of *ta-t'ung,* when the above equalities were practiced, sex crimes and marital problems would vanish.[28]

Family Barriers: Removal to Become the People of Heaven. Confucius taught in the *Analects* that filial piety and brotherhood were supreme virtues because they were the source of benevolent actions and, furthermore, that the family was the institution where such virtues were generated and cultivated. In principle this was an idea to be valued but, in reality, the family was the root of all evil. While families did nurture love, protect their members and educate their young, families limited their responsibilities to members only. This exclusiveness encouraged selfishness and cunning, bred falsehood, theft, robbery and murder and intensified constant fighting. Such evils have plagued the family and have been handed down from generation to generation through intermarriage, multiplying the number of unsavory offspring. The selfish concern for one's family meant the negligence of public health and public education, which in turn helped produce more uneducated and unhealthy offspring. Under these circumstances, society would be unable to produce a humanity with good virtues and admirable social mores, nor could it enter into the period of great unity. The family system was a necessary and beneficial instrument for mutual protection of mankind in the period of disorder and of gradual peace, but it was a serious obstacle to attaining the period of great unity.

To achieve the great unity, states had to be abolished and families as well. The abolition of the family, of course, meant a drastic change and the process towards a final realization of the idea *ta-t'ung* involved agonizing separations between parents and children, and between husbands and wives. The process necessarily had to be gradual and comprehensive. Simply put, the responsibility of raising the young and for the burial of the old, that is, from cradle to the grave, should lie with the public government which would initiate and operate the proper institutions for the lifelong care of all individuals. In this way, the family system would automatically be dissolved, relieving individuals from the agony of leaving their families, yet permitting them to enjoy happiness without them.

The House of the Origin of People *(Jen-pen yuan)*—Public Obstetric Hospital. These houses would be located in areas with the most favorable natural environments and the most ideal climate. Pregnant women would receive the best prenatal care, physically and mentally, so they could breed eugenically perfect children who would all have the physical features of Caucasians.

Public Nurseries. After the children are weaned, they would be placed in public nurseries until the age of six.

Public Education. Children from the ages of six to ten would attend public elementary schools, ages eleven to fifteen to middle schools, and ages sixteen to twenty to public universities. In other words, the first twenty years of upbringing and education were completely free and at government accommodation.

Houses of Public Medicine and Care for the Sick and Dying. The infirm and disabled would go to public hospitals. Those who could not make a living because of sloth would go to the poor house. People over sixty would go to public old people's homes that were equipped with every comfort. This was their reward for past efforts and contributions to society. After death, one's body would be sent to a crematorium. A simple ceremony would be held with family members and friends attending. However, in the world of *ta-t'ung*, family names would be abolished and people would be known only by numbers assigned to them, and there practically would be no known family members. Moreover, since the children did not live with parents and barely knew them, and since parents would not bestow any special favor in raising and educating them, the parent-child relationship would be purely biological. Children would have no filial responsibility to return parental kindness, and therefore, there would be no point in observing the three years' mourning advocated by Confucianism. Generally, because in the ideal world of *ta-t'ung*, death would be a natural ending to an individual's happy life in this world, traditional mourning or even weeping would be no longer necessary.[29]

Property Barriers: Removal to Achieve Public Ownership. Whereas the modern world created spectacular economic advancements over medieval ages, miseries of people's livelihoods and the lack of public morality did not improve significantly. In agriculture, Chinese farmers, in general, possessed only small plots of land that could not be cultivated on a large scale by machines. Landlords usually did not cultivate their own land. They exacted high rents from tenants who actually tilled the land. As a rule, the lives of farmers in every country were miserable. Recognizing this difficulty, Confucius originated the spring-field system to free everyone from cold and hunger. In this connection Confucius laid down the lofty principle that where equality existed poverty did not. However, the failure to realize an equal distribution of land on a worldwide scale was due to the system of private ownership. Moreover, communism could not be effected as long as families and states existed *(kung-ch'an* is the Chinese equivalent for communism. K'ang's application of this term was in a very loose and superficial sense). The family and state were entirely selfish institutions. The family concentrated on exclusiveness among members and the state tended increasingly to impose high taxes to maintain military strength. Both family and state were contradictory to the communist ideal.

With the modern development of enormous industries and commerce there developed greater differences between the rich and the poor. In addition, the theory of evolution and its concept of competition (struggle) was considered an inexorable truth which, due to cut-throat competition and mutual deception, in turn brought about the financial bankruptcy of failed capitalists and the general moral degradation of mankind. The theory of competition was only suitable to chaotic times; it was detrimental to a world of great unity. In order to eliminate competition, the abolition of the selfish family system and the selfish system of private property were the prerequisites.

In the world of *ta-t'ung*, all land would become public, as would industries and commerce. Agriculture, industries, and commerce would be owned, controlled and operated by the government. That is, production and distribution of goods and services would be carried out by the government through comprehensive and centralized plans. During the time of *ta-t'ung*, goods would be plentiful and work would be a pleasure rather than the drudgery it had been. Working hours generally would range from one or two hours to three or four hours a day.

It was possible that people would fear that governmental control of all agriculture, industries and commerce would do more harm than good to the people because of corruption or embezzlement by government officials. These misgivings were reasonable in chaotic times, but would be superfluous in the period of great peace. Then governmental misconduct would not occur because of the nonexistence of a private ownership system for selfish motives, excellent individual virtues, education and social customs, all of which would exist alongside a guaranteed good material life and the social pressure to act for the public good.

The practical measure for the nationalization of land, industry and commerce would be a simple solution—the elimination of the family. When a husband-wife relationship became merely a contractual relationship of friendly cohabitation, sixty years after the initial contract, no family would exist and no children would inherit any property from the parents because there would be no known parents anyway. All property would go to the government. Once the family disappeared, it would be very easy to reach the realm of the world of *ta-t'ung*.[30]

Disorder Barriers: Removal to Achieve Peace and Good Order. In the world of *ta-t'ung*, national boundaries would be completely eliminated. The globe would be divided into one hundred degrees latitudinally and one hundred degrees longitudinally, thus forming 10,000 "degree units." The land mass of the globe covered 5,238 degree units, each one being 10,000 square miles. Each inhabitable unit was an administrative unit with its own local government. There would be about 3,000 local governments all subject to a higher, universal government.

All officials, local as well as global, would be elected by the people. However, the election campaigns as practiced in Western democratic countries should not be permitted. In such Western campaigns, candidates advertised themselves in ballyhoo, and savagely attacked opponents. The candidates gave sumptuous parties, organized colorful parades, secretly schemed and even resorted to assassinations. This was morally wrong and barbarous. In the world of *ta-t'ung*, virtuous individuals would be elected by the people with neither clamorous activities nor by conspiratorial or brutal means. Those who were elected would decline the post two or three times. They would not accept the post until they were repeatedly urged by the people to do so. This was a display of the virtue of modesty and yielding.

The world government would consist of twenty administrative departments. There would be no departments of war and punishment for they would be unnecessary. There would also be a Global Assembly, a lower house, an upper house, and a Bulletin Bureau. The degree or local governments would have similar and corresponding organizations. The basic political organizations were the local self-control bureaus. In the world of *ta-t'ung*, people essentially have no private residences but instead would concentrate in spacious public buildings either where they worked, mainly a farm or factory, or where they were accommodated by the public, such as schools, hospitals, nurseries, or rest-homes. Each farm, factory or other production branch constituted an administrative unit of self-government, the directors of which would also be the administrative chiefs. Each self-government unit would have all the necessary educational and welfare institutions (such as nurseries, schools) and tele-communication offices. These units would be run by elected people distinguished by virtue and talent. All public affairs were to be decided by the majority, with each individual enjoying an equal right of voice.

In sum, the political system in the *ta-t'ung* world was of three levels—global government, degree governments, and local self-control governments. However, there would be no difference between the officials and the people, i.e., between the ruling and the ruled, for every person in the world would manage the affairs of the entire world as though they were fathers, sons and brothers of one family. In carrying out the functions of the governments, people might have different jobs to perform for the sake of division of labor, but beyond that, everybody was equal.

There was always the possibility of course that some people would become lazy and unproductive as a consequence of the overly easy and egalitarian life in the *ta-t'ung* world due to a lack of incentive and competition. Although competition, incompatible with cooperation and harmony was bad, the lack of competition would lead to stagnation and retrogression, and ultimately a return to the chaotic stage. One way to alleviate such potential remisson in behavior would be to encourage a competitive spirit for beauty (*mei*), intelligence (*chih*), and benevolence (*jen*). People who had new ideas for improving the material environment, such as means of transportation, or ideas to nourish the arts, the writing of new books, inventing new theories, making new discoveries, or giving pecuniary contributions or services to their fellow men, would be rewarded.

There would be four prohibitions in the world of *ta-t'ung*: laziness, personality cult, competition (with the exception of competition for intelligence and benevolence), and abortion.

Among the four prohibitions, worship of individuals or personality cult was considered the worst. For in the world of *ta-t'ung*, all individuals were equal, with no difference in personal status. If veneration were given to a single person, inequality would creep in and this would involve the recurrence of tyranny, mass killings and finally the chaotic world. Any sign of this tendency should be checked and promptly prevented beforehand. Anyone who intended or tried to become an emperor or a sovereign or any important leader would be considered as having committed the most hideous crime.[31]

Species Barriers: Removal to Love All Creatures. Human beings limited their sympathies to their own species only at the expense of other species. Due to their selfishness toward their own species, humans killed millions of plants and animals without compunction. A saint who was selfish to his own species while excluding other species was not too much different from a tiger as far as cruelty was concerned. In fact, tigers killed on a limited basis while a saint killed millions. But tigers were considered as fierce, while human beings were reputed by themselves to be virtuous. If the world were ever to achieve great peace, it would be necessary for human beings to extend their love beyond their own species to include all other sentient beings.

In this connection, Confucius had a three-stage principle. Humans were affectionate towards parents in the chaotic period, they loved people generally in the gradual peace period, and they showed kindness to all creatures in the great unity period.[32] Slaughtering animals and eating their flesh was the practice in the chaotic period. Before a meat substitute is invented, animals would be slaughtered by using electric shock so as to alleviate their pain. This was a practice to be followed in the period of gradual peace. In the period of *ta-t'ung*, no slaughter would be permitted. The underlying basic principle was to avoid the evil of killing, and extend love to all creatures.

In the world of *ta-t'ung*, ferocious animals would be exterminated; at the most, a few could be kept for biological studies. Birds such as big eagles which could kill people should also be exterminated. All other tame animals and beautiful birds would be kept either for man's services or for his pleasure. While human beings should extend their love as much as possible to other species, they were not able to go to the extremes that Buddhism required. For example, they could not afford to tolerate those harmful worms which cause human diseases, nor could they avoid the unintentional killing of millions of microscopic organisms. After all, within the entire universe, human love or benevolence was extremely limited.[33]

Suffering Barrier: Removal to Attain Perfect Happiness. Primitive people with their simple desires and civilized people with their more complex and sophisticated wants were naturally satisfied when their desires and wants were fulfilled and were sorrowful when they were not. This search for pleasure and avoidance of suffering has made human society progressive. Within this society, the function of sages was nothing other than to create ways and means to seek happiness and to avoid suffering for all people.

In the world of *ta-t'ung*, people would have only pleasure; they would encounter no suffering because they would lack emotional anxieties and because material luxuries would be unlimited.

Shelter. In the period of great unity, people would reside in public houses. However, any period of residence would be unusually short, since the desire to travel widely to avoid the monotony of living in one spot for any length of time would prevail. Thus, there would be an abundance of traveling homes (similar to the idea of the modern recreation vehicles such as campers, motor homes, and house trailers). These travel homes would be hundreds of feet wide and over a thousand feet long, with lavish built-in comforts and equipped electrically to travel anywhere on huge expressways. In addition, luxurious and colossal flying houses and flying ships would enable one to traverse oceans and greater land masses. Finally, in the *ta-t'ung* era, residential districts would evolve from mountain tops to sea communities to societies in the sky.

Food. Food would be limited to extractions from fruits and vegetables. Meat would not be served because humans and animals were related, and the consuming of one's own kind would be held a sacrilege. Love was incomplete until it extended to all living sentient beings.

Clothing. People would wear the same general style of apparel regardless of sex, but the clothing would be comfortable and stylish, exquisite and extravagantly made. Novel and intriguing styles would be admired and although the fashion would not manifest any differences in social standing, the wise and benevolent would wear certain badges that would serve as an incentive for the advancement of wisdom and benevolence among humankind.

Furniture. All furniture, tools, and other implements would be machine made, although exquisitely produced. In addition, music would be played in every piece of furniture when it was in use, including music in bed to accompany intercourse because it would stimulate the reproduction of eugenically fine offspring.

What would the people in the world of ta-t'ung look like? They would have handsome features, as pure as jade, as fragrant as an orchid, as rosy as a peach, as delicate as flower blossoms, as brilliant as mirrors. Even an ugly person in the ideal world would be much more beautiful than a beauty of a previous age.

Life expectancy would be extended to several hundred or even more than a thousand years. Doctors would be widely available and medical science would be highly developed. During the first chaotic stage, military personnel were the most powerful group, since the main activity of that period was the killing of one's enemies; in the ideal world, doctors would be the most powerful group because they maintained life. Finally, after the attainment of ta-t'ung, mortals and the secular world would become religious. This was all implicit in the so-called celestial peregrination (t'ien-yu) which would result in the highest attainment and social realization.[34]

Ta-t'ung shu and the People's Communes

I have argued elsewhere that it seems reasonable to suppose that the ideological roots of Chinese communes did not come from the West; there are reasons to believe that Mao Tse-tung was heavily or almost exclusively influenced by K'ang in establishing the communes.[35]

The chief characteristics of the people's communes, as given by Mao in two Chinese characters, are ta (large) and kung (public). An official translation of these two characters renders the meaning as "bigger size" and "more socialist nature."[36] The famous chapter of "Li yun" in the Li Chi has the statement that "when the great course is pursued, the world will be for all."[37] The two key words in the sentence are ta, meaning great, in ta-tao, great course; and kung in wei-kung, meaning for all. The selection of ta and kung to characterize the people's communes is not coincidental and its philosophical source is evidently borrowed from this famous treatise.

Largeness. The first characteristic of the people's communes emphasizes expansion of organization and a wider scope of activities than the agricultural cooperatives. The largeness in size is obvious because communes are formed by merging of several cooperatives. The main activity of the agricultural cooperatives is, as the name suggests, limited to agriculture, while the people's communes cover a wide range of activities, including agriculture, forestry, animal husbandry, fishing, and other occupations. Furthermore, small-scale industry, agriculture, trade, education, local government and military affairs are channeled into a single entity. In other words, a commune is an organizational form characterized by the integration of town government and commune administration and the integration of government authority and the organization in charge of production.

There is a remarkable resemblance between the people's communes and the huge farms and factories outlined in the *Ta-t'ung shu*. A farm would be like a village, with a farm holder acting at the same time as the administrative chief, carrying out agriculture, forestry, husbandry, fishery and even mining, with shops, telecommunication offices, airport and railway stations attached. A factory would be like a town, whose size was beyond the present imagination, with thousands and thousands of workers, where the factory head acted at the same time as the administrative chief—like an ancient king—with shops, telecommunication offices, airport and railway stations attached.[38] Evidently the farm was suggestive of Mao's agricultural communes, and the factory of the abortive urban communes. On the whole, similar to the people's communes, the farms and factories envisioned by K'ang covered a wide range of activities and integrated government authority with the organization in charge of production.

Publicness. The second characteristic of the people's communes is that they are of a socialist nature. The Chinese character used, *kung*, basically means public and is the antonym of *szu* meaning selfish or private. The significance of "more socialist nature" has two aspects: the ownership system and the distribution system. As far as the ownership system is concerned, the people's commune enhances the collective ownership system *(chi-t'i so-yu chih)* of the old agricultural cooperatives and elevates, to a certain degree, the system of ownership by the entire people *(ch'üan-min so-yu chih)*. The people's communes are eliminating, step-by-step, the last remnants of private ownership of the means of production. Thus, it is claimed by Communist authorities that the people's communes are the best organizational form for effecting the transformation from collective ownership to ownership by the whole people.

The ownership system of K'ang's *Ta-t'ung shu* was simple and clearcut and similar to Mao's commune system. Everything belonged to the public; private property was nonexistent. The distribution system retained the wage system according to the principle "to each according to his work" (the same distribution system is found in the people's communes), with basic requirements well provided for by the public.

It seems clear, then, that all evidence suggests that *Ta-t'ung shu* supplied a detailed blueprint for an ideal society for Mao that was not available in Marxist writings. This means that the ideals of a perfect society embodied in the people's communes were borrowed by Mao from the *Ta-t'ung shu* and were not entirely of his own creation. Thus, on the one hand, the *Ta-t'ung shu* served as a strong ideological plan for the establishment of the people's communes, while, on the other hand, Marxism has been used as a tool to carry on the Chinese revolution, of which the communes are only one phase.

Is K'ang Still a Confucianist?

In view of the radical ideas of K'ang, can we still recognize him as a Confucianist? Kung-chüan Hsiao, for one, deems that K'ang is basically a Confucianist. Hsiao says that "In his thinking Confucian doctrines remained the frame of reference and Western ideas served to extend, modify, or replace traditional notions. His moral values remained predominately Confucian, although his institutional ideas often betrayed Western influence."[39]

My observations lead me to a somewhat different conclusion. Although K'ang continued to eulogize Confucius, his basic beliefs departed widely from and often were diametrically opposed to Confucianism. First, K'ang challenged an important central principle of Confucianism which teaches that the best life is one in which a person derives happiness from within, from his inner self rather than from the external world and material things. The highly affluent society depicted in *Ta-t'ung shu*, with a view to abolishing suffering while increasing happiness basically through material splendors was, in the main, a contradiction to the Confucian ideal of seeking inner satisfaction and self-contentment. The following Confucian remarks illustrate this ideal:

> He who aims to be a man of complete virtue in his food does not seek to gratify his appetite, nor in his dwelling place does he seek the appliances of ease.[40]
>
> A scholar, whose mind is set on truth, and who is ashamed of bad clothes and bad food, is not fit to be discoursed with.[41]
>
> The superior man is anxious lest he should not get truth; he is not anxious lest poverty come upon him.[42]
>
> With coarse rice to eat, with water to drink, and my bended arm for a pillow—I have still joy in the midst of these things.[43]

Moreover, in his *National Salvation Through Material Construction (Wu-chih chiu-kuo lun),* in which Hsiao claims K'ang was "putting forth his impassioned plea for China's industrialization,"[44] K'ang reflected his unqualified praise of material civilization. Bertrand Russell once remarked that "if the West can claim superiority in anything, it is not in moral values, but in science and scientific technology."[45] K'ang certainly shared Russell's view, stressing his own belief that China was superior to the West in morals but inferior in material construction, China's greatest area of deficiency. The difference between the strong West and the weak East lay in one sole factor: having or not having material construction.[46] K'ang was deeply impressed that in America a poor family living in a mountainous area could have carpets on the floor, wall paper on the walls, spotless rooms, elegant furniture and beautiful kitchen utensils, that roads and lavatories were clean, that workers, whether male of female, had gentlemanly manners and that even the attire of countryfolk resembled clothes worn by nobles. Such a civilization could not be attained in China without the

32

development of materials even if Emperors Yao and Shun were alive again or if Yi Yin and the Duke of Chou were in power, or even the era of the Great Unity of Confucius.[47] K'ang concluded that the lives and comforts of common workers in the West equalled that of oriental emperors, ministers and nobles.[48] These attitudes of K'ang reflect how much importance, worship and admiration he gave to the place of material development in a good life for mankind.

From the above, we can see that the society K'ang was passionately preaching was more akin to a Western, materially oriented society than a spiritually oriented Confucian society. What K'ang referred to as materials was actually what was generally meant at that time by science and scientific technology, with more emphasis on the latter. Specifically, however, K'ang was speaking in terms of industrial techniques, steam, electricity, gunboats and troops, that is to say, industrial technology, electric or steam powered machines, efficient armaments and armed forces.[49]

K'ang exalted scientific technology to a fanatical degree. For instance, he said that without technology and military strength, even with the powers of Emperors Yao and Shun, it would be impossible to establish one's country and repel invading enemies; that it would be impossible to save one's country from extinction even if there were great religious saviors. For example, the Jews perished decades after the birth of Christ, and India was repeatedly conquered even with the existence of Buddha;[50] and America was immensely strong even though she had not a single philosopher.[51]

K'ang's emphasis on military strength to maintain a country's independence deviated somewhat from Confucius' emphasis on morality to rule. In a practical sense, K'ang identified civilization with military strength because he thought that it was military force which protected the independence of a country, and which commanded respect from other peoples. The example he gave was the Japanese defeat of Russia whereby Japan won great respect from Europeans. K'ang related this event as a matter of course without feeling the need to censure the imperialists as many other writers did in their accounts of the Russo-Japanese War and its impact on China.[52]

The political philosophy of Confucius that the rule of people in a government depends on virtue reflects the moral primacy of Confucius.[53] Answering a question from a disciple about the essentials in the government of a country, Confucius mentioned three factors: sufficiency of food, sufficiency of military equipment and confidence of the people in their ruler. When pressed to indicate which one should go first if one were to be dispensed with, Confucius answered that it would be military equipment.[54] Thus, in the mind of Confucius, military equipment was the least important in ruling a country. K'ang's preference for military force was obviously a response to foreign invasions, but nevertheless it was definitely ideologically opposed to Confucianism.

Certain other viewpoints of K'ang's diametrically opposed Confucian tenets. The chapter on Royal Regulations (Wang-chih) in the Li Chi states: "Using licentious music; strange garments; wonderful contrivances and extraordinary implements . . . all who used or formed such things were put to death."

If we study in detail the provisions for dwellings, transportation, clothing and instruments so cleverly and wonderously designed in K'ang's dream world, [55] we can see that those designers or users would be put to death according to this Confucian classic. And certainly the music K'ang would have liked to be played during sexual intercourse would be considered licentious by Confucian standards.

It has been generally maintained that Confucius preferred substance (chih) to ornament (wen), parsimony or thrift (chien) to extravagance or luxury (she). K'ang, however, argued that Confucius preferred ornament to substance, extravagance to parsimony, justifying his belief by saying that a simple life was the norm in the chaotic world, and extravagance in a civilized world. The degree of extravagance was in direct proportion to the degree of civilization. Thus, what would be luxurious in a primitive society would be considered extremely simple in a civilized society. If Confucius were a sage who believed in progress and in the advancement of material well-being, he could not possibly prefer parsimony to extravagance, such an attitude would be a sign of retrogression to primitive times. The misunderstanding of Confucius, K'ang continued, was all due to the misinterpretation of the Sung neo-Confucianists, which ultimately had the disastrous effect of keeping China in materially backward and barbarous conditions for so many years.[56]

Furthermore, a preference for substance or a preference for ornament marked the difference between a barbarous stage and a civilized stage and it also led to either emphasis on agriculture or on industry. A society which preferred substance naturally emphasized agriculture, in order to provide its people with sufficient food only. A society which preferred ornament naturally emphasized industry, with a view to supplying it with exquisitely manufactured articles, and ever new wonders to satisfy the desires of its people.[57] Evidently K'ang hoped for an industrial society to supplant the agricultural society and for an affluent society to replace the old, simple rustic society. From the above, we can see that K'ang deviated from this belief in the Confucian inner spiritual life to an external material life.

Now, let us see how K'ang deviated from the basic Confucian moral philosophy. K'ang not only firmly believed that morality in China was superior to that in the West, he also professed himself as an ardent Confucianist. As we all know, benevolence is the cardinal virtue of Confucian ethics. Confucius considered filial piety and fraternal submission as the basis of all benevolent actions.[58] But in K'ang's ideal world of ta-t'ung the family would be dissolved. All children would be raised by the government and they would not know their parents and elder brothers for the parent-child relationship in the ideal world would be biological only. Parents would bestow no favors upon their children and children would owe nothing to the parents. Logically, filial piety would not make sense. Actually, filial piety would not exist, nor would it be morally admirable. Then, what would be the basis for benevolence? By K'ang's argument, true love would prevail and extend to all mankind. It would not be limited to the confines of private families. Although this was an admirable argument, the abolition of family undermined the basic tenet of Confucian ethics to take filial piety as the root of benevolence.

Another basic tenet of Confucianism is the so-called three bonds which prescribe that the subject must be absolutely obedient to his sovereign, the woman to her husband and the son to his father. Ch'en Tu-hsiu vigorously attacked these bonds as being the cause of gross inequalities and the disappearance of even one independent individual in Chinese society.[59] In addition to these three bonds of Confucianism are the five relations of humanity taught by Mencius: affection between father and son, righteousness between sovereign and subject, distinction between husband and wife, proper order between old and young, and loyalty between friends.[60] Once the family and state were abolished, as advocated by K'ang, the three bonds and the five human cardinal relationships, with the exception of the relation between friends, would dissolve automatically. These bonds and relationships were human relationships upon which the Confucian ethical tenets were built. If they were taken away completely and the foundation for ethical tenets collapsed, how much Confucianism would be left? K'ang's shift from the inner cultivation as the highest ideal of moral training to the external material satisfaction of the West to make a good life, and his elimination of the Confucian ethics as a result of his attempt to abolish the state and family both reflect K'ang's fundamental departure from Confucianism. Thus, it is highly problematic if K'ang could still claim to be a Confucianist or even to be considered as one along with other Confucianists. But, in spite of K'ang Yu-wei's major deviations from Confucian tenets, his enthusiasm for realizing universal love and brotherhood, peace and harmony is in line with the high ideals of Confucius. Evidently, K'ang must have chosen to inherit Confucianism in the abstract rather than in the concrete to meet the hopes of a changing world.

Criticisms of K'ang Yu-wei: Communist and Noncommunist Writers

Since 1950 the Chinese communists have produced numerous works on the thought of K'ang Yu-wei. Certain of his ideas are praised as progressive and, often, revolutionary. There is, however, an overwhelming tendency to categorize the nineteenth century political thinkers as reformists, K'ang being the most prominent. For instance, Hu Pin sees K'ang as the protagonist of reformist thought in modern China whose writings and advocacy of reforms contributed to the general revolutionary trend that reached a peak fifty years after the Opium War.[61]

Another tendency is to label K'ang's ideals as utopian, following Marx's dichotomy of utopian versus scientific socialism. Li Tse-hou is a representative of this school of criticism. He argues that the class essence of K'ang's utopia of *ta-t'ung* is a vulgarized theory of evolution. That is, K'ang's belief in gradualism and his denial of leaping progress was based on the different views of the progress of history. On the one hand, society will incessantly progress toward *ta-t'ung*, which is the inevitable result of evolution, but, on the other hand, this utopian world cannot be reached in one swift stroke, rather it would require a long and often tedious process of gradual evolution. Li considered K'ang's single-minded emphasis on *ta-t'ung* as futuristic society, and his belief that any attempt to realize it at the present time would result in chaos and disaster, to have class implications rather than being merely a personal view. Thus, Li argues that K'ang's attitude represents the dual contradictory nature of a typical bourgeois liberal who demanded democracy and freedom while, at the same time, expressing a fear of the masses. This is why, Li contends, bourgeois liberals dare not mobilize the masses immediately to fight for their political rights as they should. This would be fundamentally incompatible with the interests of the liberals of the bourgeois landlord class. Hence, Li comments that the thought of *ta-t'ung* is tinged with two different and contradictory aspects: a far-reaching ideal of *ta-t'ung* and a serious lack of a realistic spirit of struggle. Because of this, K'ang's ideas reveal deception and hypocrisy. Li concludes that such reformists who simultaneously demand change and also defend the interests of the landlord class compromised with and joined the reactionaries in order to share the latter's political power and interests at the expense of their own original beliefs. They are much more afraid of the masses, whom they consider as unruly mobs, than they are of the reactionaries.[62]

Following a line similar to that of Li, two histories of Communist Chinese philosophy also give K'ang credit for his application of Darwin's theory of evolution to China and for formulating his own revisionist theory of a three-stage evolution, the last stage of which was the ideal world of *ta-t'ung*. But these histories of Chinese philosophy also label K'ang's concept of evolution as vulgar, because it omitted a very important factor—the revolutionary leap. K'ang's insistence that society must evolve from monarchy to constitutional monarchy and finally to democracy without the possibility of omitting any step is criticized as being virtually a drop-by-drop reform which serves only the political line of the reformists. K'ang is further criticized as having inherited the bourgeois theory of human nature which is totally erroneous. That is, when K'ang discussed man, human nature, the way of life, universal love, and even the desire for pleasure and avoidance of pain, he observed, on the whole, the class nature of man. By making the sufferings of mankind a common denominator of all human beings, K'ang failed to discern the interests of different classes as being contradictory. He saw only an abstract man, and failed to see a class man; he noticed the abstract pleasure and pain, but failed to put interests and demands in a historical class perspective. K'ang's abstract man, and abstract pleasure and pain actually do not exist. The happiness of the exploiting class is built upon the sufferings of the exploited class; the day when the former is happy is exactly the day when the latter is miserable, and vice versa. K'ang dreamt of a class cooperation and harmony where all classes entered into the realm of *ta-t'ung* hand in hand. His denial of the existence of antagonistic classes in China made him oppose class struggle and fear the revolution of the people. Since K'ang stopped at the stage of the revisionist program without abolishing feudalism, which was out of date long ago, he degenerated into a counterrevolutionary.[63]

In his preface to *Wu-hsu pien-fa,* Chien Po-tsan, despite his lament over K'ang's reformist ideology and its doomed failure, gives credit to the movement K'ang led as having patriotic and progressive significance. Chien points out that the movement's influence of enlightenment exerted on the society at that time cannot be underestimated and he further recognized that the reformers of the movement not only waged a violent thought struggle against feudalist forces, but also served as forerunners of the development of bourgeois revolutionary thought in China.[64]

The most recent history of modern Chinese philosophy was published in 1978 under the editorship of the prominent communist historian Hou Wai-lu. Although this history adds very little to what has already appeared in print before, it serves as a summary of the criticism within the Communist regime of K'ang's ideas. First, it views unfavorably K'ang's philosophical ideas, labelling him an idealist who falls short of being a materialist, and then calling his theory of evolution vulgar and his theory of human nature bourgeois. Hou's book continues to censure K'ang's programs for social reconstruction as envisioned in his *Ta-t'ung shu,* particularly his denial of the existence of classes and class struggle, his fear of and hostility to the masses, and hence fear of revolution and his insistence on constitutional monarchy as the necessary step toward reaching *ta-t'ung,* thereby slandering the democratic revolution. It concludes that the so-called *ta-t'ung,* a utopian fantasy, has only served the function of corroding the democratic consciousness of the masses and of opposing the democratic revolution.[65]

Finally, it is important to include here the very influential criticism by Mao of K'ang that although K'ang wrote *Ta-t'ung shu,* he did not and could not find a way leading to the world of *ta-t'ung.*[66] To my knowledge, this short remark has been universally quoted as the truth in every mainland China book or article dealing with the thought of K'ang Yu-wei. No one argues that K'ang knew how to reach *ta-t'ung;* nevertheless, as an ideal, it still had merit. The significance of a high ideal lies in his inspirational and visionary value. It would be the duty of those of posterity who believed in it to carry it out. On the whole, K'ang's ideas are seen by the communists as being reformist rather than revolutionary because he opposed staging a revolution and is seen as utopian rather than scientific because he did not know how to reach his ideal world.

It should be noted that these criticisms mentioned above reflect more than personal opinions; more importantly, they reflect the official Chinese Communist line of thought. In sum, the one important point which stands out from all criticisms of K'ang is that being a reformist, he did not apply the tactic used in revolution of mobilizing the masses, but instead he tried to effect political change by seeking the emperor. This practice is one which the communists have depicted as "from top to bottom" and which caused K'ang to degenerate into a counterrevolutionary.

In a sense, this criticism is undoubtedly true. But it is doing K'ang an injustice to criticize him unfavorably by present day standards. During his own lifetime, he was unaware of the revolutionary tactics of the Soviet and Chinese Communists and therefore could not have applied such tactics. But K'ang's hope for a modernization from top to bottom was not without successful historical precedents. The industrial innovation of Russia under Peter the Great and the Japanese modernization by the Meiji Emperor were his favorite historical models. Generally, the communist writers depict other reformers as reactionaries because of moral degradation and then charge them with being hostile to the people and conspiring with the ruling class in power. In K'ang's case, he is criticized, on the one hand as being extremely afraid of the people, and on the other hand as protecting his own class interest, thus fearing and thwarting the revolution. Basically, K'ang did not think it right to launch a revolution at the expense of sacrificing thousands of lives. In this, and in his own mind, K'ang remained a soft-hearted pacifist. It is true that K'ang followed a different approach and path from the communist ideology and tactics, but his sincerity and good intentions should not be doubted. In all likelihood, K'ang would have retained and enjoyed his own and even also his class interests without risking his own and other's lives in the coup had he not chosen to stage a political change. To charge him as being morally objectionable is a prejudice of the Communist Party, for the communists are wont to claim that only they, not anybody else, wholeheartedly support the people.

The evaluations of two noncommunist scholars deserve our mention here to complete the picture of the criticism of K'ang.

Ch'ien Mu, the famous anticommunist historian, does not hold K'ang as a person in high regard, labelling him as a megalomaniac. He also regards *Ta-t'ung shu* with contempt, saying it was a book of fantasies, irrelevant to the actual background and needs of his time. He was really just toying with illusions, Ch'ien says, and merely assembled a variety of novel and attractive ideas belonging to others and attributed them all to Confucius. Ch'ien does analyze in detail K'ang's works, providing references to contents and ideological sources, noting mistakes and self-contradictions K'ang made at times, and commenting on his intellectual honesty. But Ch'ien's most savage attack is directed at K'ang's basic motivation. Ch'ien believes that K'ang's reverence for Confucius was not really for Confucius, but rather it was a disguise for his infatuation with Western civilization. That is, it was Western civilization which K'ang revered, not Confucianism, when he claimed that Confucianism had all the advantages of Western civilization. The truth, says Ch'ien, is that K'ang was paying court to foreign countries at the same time he censured others for doing so.

Among the evidence Ch'ien gives to support his accusations that K'ang's veneration of Confucius was actually his reverence for Western civilization are the two cases cited below: (1) The reasons K'ang venerated Confucius as a religious founder is, according to his disciple Liang Ch'i-ch'ao, because when K'ang took Christianity to be the foundation leading to the military and political superiority of Europe, he erroneously labelled Confucius as the counterpart of

Jesus Christ in China, and to substantiate his claim, he quoted from apocryphal classics. (2) K'ang admired Western democracy, but claimed that the democratic doctrine originated with Confucius. The difference between barbarism and civilization was autocracy with emperors and democracy without them. Evidently China, with its tradition of having autocratic emperors, was barbarous, and Europe was civilized. In the past two thousand years China experienced only the so-called small peace *(hsiao-k'ang),* but not the *ta-t'ung* of Confucius. Fortunately, however, K'ang claimed, he himself rediscovered the concept of *ta-t'ung* which paralleled Western civilization as he saw it. Ch'ien concludes that this is the reason K'ang advocated the necessity for a change, quick and complete.[67] We can see that whereas the communist historians give certain qualified credit to K'ang, noncommunist historians such as Ch'ien judge him as absurd and his ideas devoid of content.

Hsiao Kung-ch'üan, an American-trained political scientist with high academic standing in Chinese studies, praises K'ang highly and clearly alludes in the last chapter of his book *A Modern China and a New World* that K'ang should probably have been "credited with having endeavored, in his own way and to his own ability, to make a goal for mankind and to give meaning to history."[68]

Summary

China from the time of Confucius to the time of K'ang Yu-wei had been relatively static. Granted, there had been those individuals such as Wang An-shih and Wang Mang who determined to effect radical changes in the course of history but who failed. The fundamental principle held by the Chinese people was that Heaven did not change, nor did *tao.* Permanence or stability, or simply no change, was the inexorable rule of history.

K'ang was the first major Chinese thinker to theorize that change was the fundamental rule of human history. Change led to life, nonchange to death. Change was a prerequisite to the vitality of a country, a people and a civilization. K'ang personally initiated a movement to bring about a political and cultural change. These actions, plus his attempt to substitute a dynamic view of history for a static view, awakened the Chinese from two thousand years of slumber.

K'ang planned two steps to change China and the world. The first step was to make China economically into a capitalist state, and politically a constitutional monarchy. The second step, i.e., his ultimate goal, was to transform the globe into one world to which China belonged only as a geographical unit, but this was a goal he recognized to be very remote, and any attempt at present to effect it would be catastrophic.

K'ang's view of a future world in some respects was more radical than that of Marx. For instance, as we discussed above, families and countries would be dissolved; personal names would be replaced by the use of numbers; the marriage system would be practically abolished; free intercourse between the sexes would be accepted; men and women would wear the same clothing; and male homosexuality would be permitted legally.[69] In a nutshell, K'ang's ideal world would be—if we paraphrase Marx—to each, very plentifully, and from each, very little. There would be only happiness, and no pain.

A comparison of the similarities and differences of doctrines of K'ang and Marx follows:

1. Both K'ang and Marx attempted a radical change of the course of history on a worldwide scale. Marx appealed to the workers of the world to unite while K'ang envisioned a one-world utopia without class discrimination.

2. Both K'ang and Marx condemned the world of their times from an ethical point of view. Marx pinpointed the moral degradation of the bourgeoisie in exploiting the proletariat as the main cause of unhappiness in the world, while K'ang saw selfishness as the main cause of the miseries of mankind.

3. K'ang's discernment of human plight and its salvation differed conspicuously from that of Marx. For K'ang, suffering was universal to mankind, and all human beings were victims of one big slaughterhouse. He vowed to save them all by peaceful evolution through institutional changes. Marx's view was based on his economic interpretation of history and his class analysis. He saw that the degradation of human society resulted from the exploitation by a minority of the bourgeois class over a majority of the proletarian class; with the elimination of the bourgeoisie, a classless society would emerge.

4. Marx believed that in the classless society man would work for the good of all, and coercion would no longer be necessary. But he did not explain how this would come about after the capitalists had been eliminated. K'ang had the same idea, that everybody in the world of ta-t'ung would be morally sound, but he did not say how this would actually happen either. For the both of them, that a harmonious world would come was only a faith.

5. Marx said little about the form of organization that would replace the capitalist society, nor did he describe the practical measures that would need to be taken to achieve the ultimate goal—the communist society. On the other hand, K'ang had a detailed plan on how to change his present world— to remove the nine barriers—and a detailed blueprint of his world of ta-t'ung.

We can address the question of whether K'ang's ideas for the Ta-t'ung shu came from his own independent thinking or was influenced by others. From my studies it is evident that his ideas can be traced to three sources: Confucianism, Buddhism and Western ideas.

The Buddhist belief that all beings were miserable moved K'ang to love all mankind indiscriminately and to love all other living beings. The Mencian concept of the heart of passion—literally, a heart which cannot bear to see the sufferings of others—was the basic force motivating K'ang to devote himself to save the world. Of course, this idea of Mencius originated from the Confucian concept of benevolence and universal love. Thus, K'ang's philosophy to change the world, based on the extension of one's sympathy to all mankind did not contain the slightest notions of hatred, force, or despotic power over a certain class of people as the communist theoreticians have argued.

In portraying Confucius as one who appealed to antiquity for institutional changes, K'ang made him into a reformer or a revolutionary in modern terms.[70] The ancient sages to whom Confucius appealed were Yao, Shun, King Wen, figures whose actual existence K'ang doubted. But if they had been real people, K'ang said, they must have been very ordinary people. Their great virtues and achievements as depicted in the classics were nothing more than speculations made by Confucius.[71] K'ang himself appealed to Confucius for his own institutional changes—the immediate change to a constitutional monarchy and the visionary change to *ta-t'ung*, and he traced all his theoretical foundations to Confucius. K'ang wanted to follow the steps of Confucius and to play the role of Confucius in the twentieth century. In this sense, the Confucian influence on him was great even though he removed many elements from Confucianism and substituted his own interpretations.

K'ang was vaguely exposed to certain Western ideas such as Darwin's theory of evolution, Western industrial and commercial institutions, democratic concepts, especially constitutional monarchism, and some superficial socialism. It seems unlikely that these Western influences played a crucial role in molding K'ang's ideals for the central thesis in the *Ta-t'ung shu*. He knew no foreign language and few great books on Western ideologies had been translated into Chinese during his lifetime. Commenting on K'ang's originality, Liang Ch'i-ch'ao remarked in 1921 that "When he wrote this book thirty years ago, he relied on nothing and he plagiarized nothing. Yet his ideas correspond in many ways to the internationalism and socialism of today, and in statement of high principle he even surpasses them."[72]

In his last years, K'ang's reputation had shifted from being a radical like "a great flood and a fierce beast" to an ultraconservative, a reputation stemming from his stubborn loyalty to the Ch'ing dynasty. Two explanations, in my mind, can be given to understand K'ang's loyalty. First, there was in Chinese tradition a moral obligation or virtue which scholars were expected to observe. It came from a relationship whereby when a superior discovered and recognized the extraordinary ability of an individual from obscurity and trusted him fully to carry out great responsibilities, that individual was expected to feel grateful and to repay the superior's kindness by being faithful to him all his entire life. K'ang, a man with no reputation, no official position and no high degrees from imperial examinations, had won the confidence of Emperor Kuang-hsu and had received from him unprecedented power to reform the country. Being an old scholar in the traditional sense, K'ang observed the moral rule to be grateful and faithful to the emperor. I believe that is one reason he never deserted the Ch'ing house.

Second, K'ang believed that history proceeded according to a certain law, that it progressed from one stage to another. Thus, politically, history should go from absolute monarchy to constitutional monarchy, and finally to democracy. Each stage had to be followed precisely; a jump over a stage would create chaos and disaster. The turmoil of the early years of the Republican period supported and strengthened his belief. If we defend K'ang in a hypothetical way, his insistence on the transient constitutional monarchy would not be devoid of reason. In Marxism, there is a transitional period of the dictatorship of the proletariat between the revolution which would destroy capitalism and the establishment of the communist classless society. K'ang's transitional structure of constitutional monarchy paralleled the Marxian transitional period. K'ang's transitional monarchy was a democratic one in that he would retain the emperor only in name, in the form of an idol made of wood or earth, while the Communist dictatorship of the proletariat is a bona fide dictatorship or despotism. In actual practice, the dictatorship of the proletariat is much farther from democratic rule than is a constitutional monarchy. Thus, for the communist critics to denounce K'ang just for this reason is an injustice to him. However, critics, communist as well as noncommunist alike, would have been less severe in criticizing him if he had held this view only theoretically and had not insisted on putting a Ch'ing family member such as Pu Yi on the throne.

K'ang's contributions to China's modern currents of thought are many sided. Politically, he valued democracy as the best form of government, one which would prevail in the period of *ta-t'ung*. His opposition to any personality cult was intense and strong; he resented political dictators as well as religious leaders who tried to control the masses. He vowed to halt the growth of this tendency from its incipience by anyone who had such an ambition. The Chinese people who have suffered from the tyranny of modern dictatorships would have greatly appreciated K'ang's farsightedness.

K'ang vowed in his world of *ta-t'ung* to bring to all mankind a level of happiness and well-bring as had never hitherto existed. His confidence in his ability to do this was based on his confidence in the omnipotence of science. Science could create wonders, therefore material lives would reach an unprecedented height; with material affluence came the absence of anxiety and poverty, so people could devote their energies to higher cultural and recreational activities which would in turn bring about supreme spiritual satisfaction and happiness. K'ang, in his admiration for and emphasis on democracy and science, can be considered as a forerunner of the May Fourth thinkers who vigorously publicized science and democracy. Yet, a hundred years later the people of China are still struggling for basic democratic rights, and for the development of further knowledge of science and technology as manifested in the recent people's democratic movement and the official movement of the Four Modernizations.

K'ang's ideas of *ta-t'ung* have influenced two great revolutionary leaders— Sun Yat-sen and Mao Tse-tung. Though politically an adversary of K'ang, Sun was at least implicitly influenced by his *ta-t'ung* theory. For Sun stated explicitly that *ta-t'ung* was the highest ideal and his own Three Principles of the People belonged to a lower and more immediate stage of development. Mao Tse-tung's ideas for the People's Communes were heavily influenced by *Ta-t'ung shu*. We will dwell more on K'ang's influence on Mao in the chapter on Mao. Carsun Chang, who devoted his whole life to China's democratic movement, which we also discuss in a later chapter, took K'ang as his mentor. In varying degrees, K'ang influenced certain prominent thinkers, such as Hu Shih, Ch'en Tu-hsui and thousands of other intellectuals.

In sum, K'ang can be viewed from two perspectives. As a scholar, he was quick and prolific in writing, but his attitude was subjective, dogmatic, stubborn, and in many cases, lacked intellectual honesty. K'ang probably would have regarded these shortcomings as truly insignificant in light of his implementation of academic writings as a tool to present certain high principles in his lofty ideal of saving China to mankind. As a reformer, K'ang was creative, confident and bold. Regardless of the extent to which people disagreed with K'ang's ideas, few will disagree that K'ang was modern China's first dynamic and primary moving force for change, and that he was the expounder of a great vision for a better world, serving as a pioneer forerunner of other thinkers.

Notes

[1] K'ang's biographical sketch is mainly based on his own "K'ang Nan-hai tzu-pien nien-p'u" in Chien Po-tsan et al., comp., *Wu-hsu pien-fa* (Shanghai: Sheng-chou kuo-kuang she, 1953), 4:107–69; translated and enlarged by Jung-pang Lo, *K'ang Yu-wei: A Biography and Symposium* (Tucson: The University of Arizona Press, 1967), pp. 17–144, 175–252. See also: Chao Feng-nien, "K'ang Ch'ang-su hsien-sheng nien-p'u," *Shih-hsueh nien-pao*, vol. 2, no. 1 (Peking 1934). The ages given in the Chinese text follow Chinese reckoning, in which a child is considered one year old when born.

[2] K'ang Yu-wei, *Hsin-hsueh wei-ching k'ao* (Peking: Ku-chi ch'u-pan she, 1967); *Wei-ching k'ao* (Shanghai: Commercial, 1936).

[3] K'ang Yu-wei, *K'ung-tzu kai-chih k'ao* (Peking: Chung-hua, 1969).

[4] Liang Ch'i-ch'ao, *Ch'ing-tai hsueh-shu kai-lun* (Shanghai: Commercial, 1921), p. 129. Translated by Immanuel C.Y. Hsü, *Intellectual Trends in the Ch'ing Period* (Cambridge: Harvard University Press, 1959).

[5] K'ang, in *Wu-hsu pien-fa* 2:188–97. (See especially 194–95.)

[6] For a concise tabulation of these decrees, see T'ang Chih-chün, *Wu-hsu pien-fa chien-shih* (Peking: Chung-hua, 1960), pp. 28–30.

[7] For a concise tabulation of the highlights of the reform movement on a daily basis, see Tuan Ch'ang-t'ung, "Wu-hsu pai-jih wei-hsin ta-shih piao," *Wu-hsu pien-fa* 4:557–72.

[8] K'ang Yu-wei, *Ta-t'ung shu* (Shanghai: Chung-hua, 1935). Hereafter referred to as *Ta-t'ung shu*. Translated by Laurence G. Thompson, *Ta T'ung Shu: The One World Philosophy of K'ang Yu-wei* (London: Allen & Unwin, 1958).

[9] Liang, p. 129.

[10] Lo, *K'ang Yu-wei*, p. 218.

[11] Teng Kuang-ming, *Wang An-shih* (Peking: Jen-min ch'u-pan she, 1975), pp. 29–31.

[12] K'ang, in *Wu-hsu pien-fa* 3:1.

[13] Ibid., 2:197.

[14] Ibid., p. 198.

[15] For more details on the dispute between the Ancient and Modern text schools, see Liang, pp. 118–21.

[16] Liang, pp. 127–28. In the original, there are five points, which are grouped into four by the present author.

[17] For an explanation of the Three Traditions and the Three Epochs, see Sung Yun-pin, *K'ang Yu-wei* (Shanghai: Commercial, 1951), pp. 27–30. "T'ung" is rendered as "sequence" by Lo and "period of unity" by Hsü. For examples see Lo, *K'ang Yu-wei*, p. 52; Hsü, *Intellectual Trends*, p. 94. I venture to translate it as "legitimacy." See also: Hsu Kwan-san, "K'ang Nan-hai te san-shih chin-hua kuan," *Hong Kong Chung-wen ta-hsueh hsueh-pao*, vol. 4, no. 1 (Hong Kong, 1977). The summary of this article by the editor says that "According to the author, Kang's progressive interpretation of history, compared to other theories of the same sort developed by European thinkers in the late 19th century, is supreme, either in terms of its grandeur and magnificence or in terms of its depth, complexity and sophistication."

[18] Sung, pp. 34–5; Liang, pp. 126–27.

[19] This account is based primarily on Liang, pp. 129–31; K'ang, *K'ung-tzu kai-chih k'ao*, pp. 1–3.

[20] K'ang, *Ta-t'ung shu*, p. 2.

[21] For details and elaboration see K'ang, *Ta-t'ung shu*, p. 11 *ff*.

[22] *Mencius*, bk. 2, pt. 1, ch. 4, sec. 1.

[23] K'ang, *Ta-t'ung shu*, pp. 78–79.

[24] Ibid., p. 81 *ff*. For details of the political, economic, military, and judicial conditions of the three stages, see K'ang, *Ta-t'ung shu*, pp. 136–165.

[25] K'ang maintained that the function of a constitution is to guard against the despotism of the sovereign and to protect the people from tyranny. The *Spring and Autumn Annals* is the constitution written by Confucius for that purpose. K'ang himself wrote one for the Republic of China, hoping that the Parliament then might consider it as a reference, and, if possible, as a model. For this argument, see K'ang Yu-wei, *Ni Chung-hua Min-kuo hsien-fa ts'ao-an* (Shanghai: Kuang-chih shu-chü, 1916).

[26] For details, see K'ang, *Ta-t'ung shu,* p. 167 *ff*.

[27] Ibid., p. 177 *ff*.

[28] Ibid., p. 193 *ff*.

[29] Ibid., p. 255 *ff*.

[30] Ibid., p. 353 *ff*.

[31] Ibid., p. 383 *ff*.

[32] *Mencius*, bk. 7, pt. 1, ch. 45. This is a quotation from Mencius, but K'ang attributes it to Confucius. The three-stage explanation is K'ang's.

[33] For details, see K'ang, *Ta-t'ung shu,* p. 431 *ff.*.

[34] Ibid., p. 441 *ff*.

[35] See Wen-shun Chi, "The Ideological Source of the People's Communes in Communist China," *Pacific Coast Philology* 2 (April 1967):62–78.

[36] *People's Communes in China* (Peking: Foreign Languages Press, 1958).

[37] There are a number of slightly different translations; this one is mine.

[38] K'ang, *Ta-t'ung shu,* pp. 365–68, 371–72, 401–2.

[39] Kung-chuan Hsiao, *A Modern China and a New World* (Seattle: University of Washington Press, 1957), p. 95.

[40] *Confucian Analects,* bk. 1, ch. 14.

[41] Ibid., bk. 4, ch. 9.

[42] Ibid., bk. 15, ch. 31.

[43] Ibid., bk. 7, ch. 15.

[44] Hsiao, p. 516.

[45] Bertrand Russell, *New Hopes for a Changing World* (New York: Simon and Schuster, 1951), p. 114.

[46] K'ang Yu-wei, *Wu-chih chiu-kuo lun* (Shanghai: Ch'ang-hsing shu-chü, 1919), pp. 8–9.

[47] Ibid., p. 54.

[48] Ibid., p. 58.

[49] Ibid., p. 18.

[50] Ibid., p. 49.

[51] Ibid., p. 44.

[52] Ibid., p. 26.

[53] *Confucian Analects*. bk. 2, ch. 1.

[54] Ibid., bk. 12, ch. 7.

[55] K'ang, *Ta-t'ung shu,* pp. 441–48.

[56] Concerning K'ang's commentaries on the related remarks of Confucius, see K'ang Yu-wei, "Lun-yü chu" in *Wan-mu ts'ao-t'ang ts'ung-shu* (Peking, 1917), 3:2; 7:16. Also see Ch'ien Mu, *Chung-kuo chin san-pai nien hsueh-shu shih* (Chungking: Commercial, 1945), 2:546.

[57] K'ang, *Ta-t'ung shu,* p. 373.

[58] *Confucian Analects,* bk. 1, ch. 2.

[59] Ch'en Tu-hsiu, "Wo-jen tsui-hou chih chueh-wu," *Hsin ch'ing-nien,* vol. 1, no. 6 (Shanghai, February 1916): 1–4.

[60] *Mencius,* bk. 3, pt. 1, ch. 4, sec. 8.

[61] Hu Pin, *Chung-kuo chin-tai kai-liang chu-i szu-hsiang* (Peking: Chung-hua, 1964), p. 96.

[62] Li Tse-hou, *K'ang Yu-wei T'an Szu-t'ung szu-hsiang yen-chiu* (Shanghai: Jen-min ch'u-pan she, 1958), pp. 121–23.

[63] Chung-kuo k'o-hsueh yuan che-hsueh yen-chiu so Chung-kuo che-hsueh shih tsu, and Pei-ching ta-hsueh che-hsueh hsi Chung-kuo che-hsueh shih chiao-yen shih, *Chung-kuo che-hsueh shih tzu-liao chien-pien* (Peking: Chung-hua, 1972), pp. 248, 253; Jen Chi-yü, ed., *Chung-kuo che-hsueh shih chien-pien* (Peking: Jen-min ch'u-pan she, 1973), pp. 545–51.

[64] K'ang, *Wu-hsu pien-fa,* Preface, pp. 1–2.

[65] Hou Wai-lu, ed., *Chung-kuo chin-tai che-hsueh shih* (Peking: Jen-min ch'u-pan she, 1978), pp. 181–204.

[66] "Lun jen-min min-chu chuan-cheng," *MTTHC* 4:1360.

[67] Ch'ien, pp. 491–549. (See especially 516, 545, and 549.)

[68] Hsiao, p. 600.

[69] K'ang, *Ta-t'ung shu,* p. 424.

[70] The idea of "appealing to antiquity for institutional changes" is accepted by Kuo Mo-jo as a true and correct appraisal of the historical conditions at the time of Confucius. Kuo Mo-jo, *Shih p'i-p'an shu* (Shanghai: Ch'ün-i ch'u-pan she, 1950), p. 90. Kuo also holds that both Confucius and his disciples supported the activities of the rebels of certain states and that Confucius was one who accorded with the currents of the time and was sympathetic to the emancipation of the people. Kuo, pp. 77–78.

[71] Liang, p. 130.

[72] Ibid., pp. 135–36.

2
Liang Ch'i-ch'ao (1873–1929)

Biography

Liang Ch'i-ch'ao,[1] whose best-known courtesy name is Jen-kung, was born on 23 February 1873 in Hsin-hui, Kuang-tung province to a family that had been farmers for ten generations before his grandfather. It was only beginning with his grandfather, who passed the first degree in the imperial examinations, that the Liang family became scholarly. Liang's father, however, failed several times in the examinations and, without a degree, the best he could do was to become a teacher in his home town.

Liang's early youth was spent studying the Chinese classics under his grandfather and his mother, and later under his father and an outside tutor. Liang's precocity was extraordinary. When only nine years of age, after unexpectedly being asked to compose a verse while enroute by boat to a local imperial examination, Liang extemporaneously and verbally proceeded to do so. His father's friends, traveling in the same group, all marvelled at his quickness and wit. Liang's immediate reputation as a prodigy proved to be well founded for he became a *sheng-yuan* at the early age of eleven.

Being born of a poor family, Liang possessed only two of the ancient classics, the *Shih-shi* (Historical annals) and the *Kang-chien i-chih-lu* (Mirrors of history made easy). Liang, of course, developed a unique familiarity with these works and even in middle age could still recite most of their texts by heart. His father's friends who appreciated his intelligence bought him a few other books from which his grandfather and father taught him daily.

In 1887 two occurrences marked a new phase in Liang's life: first, his mother, who was very close to him, died, and second, he enrolled in the *Hsueh-hai-t'ang*, a higher education school in Canton which subsidized the expenses of the students and which specialized in the teaching of philology and textual criticism *(hsun-ku tz'u-chang)*. Up to this time Liang had remained preocupied only with studying the "eight-legged essays" (i.e., the highly stylized examinations for entrance into the Imperial service), thinking that it encompassed the whole range of scholarship. But at this school he decided to pursue a new interest in its specialties. However, even at this point with the new interest, he still did not know there existed any other disciplines of study.

In 1889, when Liang was sixteen, he passed the provincial examination and received the *chü-jen* degree. So impressed was the chief examiner with Liang's writing that he sought a matchmaker to arrange an engagement between his sister and Liang. Ironically, the matchmaker, who was also the examiner's deputy, had similar designs for his own daughter to marry this young and promising candidate. But he helped arrange the engagement, following Chinese courtesy by deferring to the chief examiner because he first mentioned the idea. To pass the imperial examination and to marry are traditionally considered to be the two most important blessings in a man's life. For Liang, these blessings came within a short span of each other. Two years after passing the imperial examination, he married the chief examiner's sister in Peking in 1891.

In 1890 Liang had made his way to Peking to participate in the metropolitan examination but, unfortunately, he failed. He tried again in 1892, 1894, and 1895, but failed each time. The failure of the examination in 1890 did not, however, deter Liang's advancement in learning in any way. Returning home via Shanghai, he bought a book on world geography; for the first time in his life he learned that there are five continents in the world. It was during this time that he saw and enjoyed tremendously other books translated from foreign languages which had been published by the Kiangnan Arsenal.

Another great event in Liang's life occurred in 1890. Accompanied by Ch'en Ch'ien-ch'iu, a schoolmate from the *Hsueh-hai-t'ang*, Liang for the first time met K'ang Yu-Wei in Canton. On the first day of the interview with K'ang, the conversation, or rather K'ang's lecture, lasted from early morning until late that night. So excited was Liang by the theories of such a great scholar that he was unable to sleep. On the following day he and his friend again called on K'ang and once more K'ang gave them a lecture, this time on the theories of the neo-Confucianists Lu Chiu-yuan and Wang Yang-ming, on Chinese history, and on Western studies. Liang and his friend were deeply impressed by K'ang and accepted him as their master.

There was a slight problem in that Liang had already received the *chü-jen* degree which K'ang did not yet have. To enroll as a student under one who has a lower degree was unusual unless there was profound respect for and great confidence in one's master. From this time on, and only from this time as Liang put it, he began to realize the existence of true scholarship. Consequently, Liang discontinued his studies at the *Hsueh-hai-t'ang*.

Upon the urging of Liang and his friend, K'ang Yu-wei opened a school in Canton in 1891 where he lectured on the origin and evolution of Chinese learning and the history and politics of China's past as compared and contrasted with that of foreign countries. Under K'ang's tutelage, Liang's solid foundation in Chinese scholarship was laid chiefly in this year of study, though in addition he browsed through some translations of Western works.

One of the highlights of this phase of Liang's education was when K'ang explained to him the principle of the great unity *(ta-t'ung)*. Liang became almost ecstatic over the idea of a great unity, so he began to publicize the idea. Although K'ang believed that the time was not yet ripe for implementing the period of the great unity, he could not restrain the enthusiastic Liang from making it known to others.

The year 1895, when Liang went to Peking to participate for the last time in the metropolitan examination, was also the year in which K'ang presented to the emperor his famous memorial of c. 1,300 alleged *chü-jen* signatures, including Liang's. It was also in 1895 that Liang assisted K'ang in organizing the *Ch'iang-hsueh hui* (Society for the Study of National Strengthening) and in publishing a paper called *Chung-wai chi-wen* (Chinese and foreign chronicle) in Peking. Liang's style of writing is lucid and eloquent and the flow of his pen held a magic power over his readers. He began to build up a steady readership and his influence grew with the paper as well as with the public. Unfortunately, when the *Ch'iang-hsueh-hui* was closed down by the Ch'ing court, the paper was also terminated. The following year, however, in 1896, Liang published a magazine in Shanghai called the *Shih-wu-pao* (The Chinese Progress) which appeared every ten days. It was in this periodical that Liang wrote his famous *Pien-fa t'ung-i* (A general discussion of reform) wherein he urged reforms by criticizing corruption within the government and advocated the abolition of the old examination system and its replacement by the establishment of modern schools. He also occasionally touched upon the theory of popular sovereignty (*min-ch'üan lun*).

In 1897 Liang became the chief lecturer of the *Shih-wu hsueh-t'ang* (School of Current Affairs) in Ch'ang-sha, Hunan—the same province from which many prominent Communist revolutionaries have come, notably Mao Tse-tung and Liu Shao-ch'i. In his lectures and notes, Liang inculcated among his students theories on popular sovereignty and revolution. Such teachings stirred up a great commotion among the conservatives.

In 1898 Liang went to Peking to give his whole-hearted support to K'ang Yu-wei's reform movement. Liang's influence was known by the emperor and he was granted an audience on 3 July. Liang was also appointed to be in charge of the translation bureau. After the September coup d'etat and the abdication of Kuang-hsu, the Empress Dowager ordered Liang's arrest, but he escaped by taking refuge in the Japanese legation. Japanese officials further aided him by spiriting him to Japan where he remained for fourteen years.

Immediately after his arrival in Japan, Liang started another paper, the *Ch'ing-i pao* (The China Discussion) which savagely and unremittingly attacked the Ch'ing court. Except for three trips abroad—to Honolulu in 1899, to Australia in 1900, and to the United States in 1903—Liang remained in Japan until his return to China in 1912 after the establishment of the Republic. During his sojourn in Japan, Liang studied Japanese and came into greater contact with Western ideas and thoughts that were then in vogue in Japan. His knowledge of the West was obtained largely during these years.

The year 1899 was an eventful one for Liang. First, he joined K'ang Yu-wei's newly established *Pao-huang-hui* (Society for the Protection of the Emperor). Then Sun Yat-sen tried to win him over to his side in the revolutionary movement. Partly because of Liang's close ties to K'ang and partly because of his own opposition to Sun's theories, Liang and Sun were unable to come to terms. Consequently, there resulted a final break between Sun's revolutionary line and Liang's constitutional line.[2] Liang also, in the following year, supported the unsuccessful restoration uprising of Emperor Kuang-hsu against the Empress Dowager in Hankow led by T'ang Ts'ai-ch'ang.

In 1902 the offices of the *Ch'ing-i pao* were destroyed by fire. Liang immediately set about to start another newspaper which he named the *Hsin-min ts'ung-pao* (New people journal), a name taken from a phrase in *The Great Learning*. The aim of the paper was to change the minds of the people primarily through educational means and secondarily through political arguments. As matters developed, the *Hsin-min ts'ung-pao* turned out to be a radically political publication in response to the deteriorating political conditions in Peking. The paper was published from 1902 to 1907.

Liang's influence and contributions among a whole generation of intellectuals is through his writings. In addition to the publications already mentioned he also published the *Hsin hsiao-shuo* (New novels) from 1902 to 1905, the *Cheng-lun* (Political review) from 1907 to 1908, and the *Kuo-feng pao* (National trends) from 1910 to 1911. The total readership of these magazines is estimated to have been almost half a million.[3] Given the low literacy rate and the primitive postal system in China at that time, Liang's large circulation included nearly the entire intellectual world. Further, in the republican period, Liang edited two other magazines of short duration: *Yung-yen* (The Justice) from 1912 to 1914, and *Ta Chung-hua tsa-chi* (The Great Chung Hwa Magazine) from 1915 to 1916.

Since Liang's chief contribution lies in the ideological realm, his political activities, in subsequent years, which are only secondary, will be only briefly summarized. These activities included his formation of a political society by the name of *Cheng-wen she* (Political Information Society) in Japan in 1907; and his participation and involvement in political parties beginning in 1912 in the *Min-chu tang* (Democratic Party), in the *Kung-ho tang* (Republican Party), in the *Chin-pu tang* (Progressive Party), and in the *Yen-chiu hsi* (Research Faction). Liang also thrice held ministerial posts in the Republican government: Minister of Justice in 1913, Chief of the Currency Bureau in 1914, and Minister of Finance in 1917. He also played a supportive role in the Yunnan revolt against Yuan Shih-k'ai when Yuan declared himself emperor in 1915, and was in opposition to the military attempt by Chang Hsun and K'ang Yu-wei to restore the Ch'ing dynasty in 1917.

In 1918 Liang left for Europe as an unofficial delegate to the Paris Peace Conference and to investigate post-war Europe. From this time on, he withdrew from political life to devote himself to educational and cultural work, engaging in writing and lecturing. Upon his return from Europe in 1920, he organized the *Kung-hsueh She* (Association for Learning Together), the purpose of which was to translate and publish books of Western ideas, issue magazines, send students to study abroad, and operate reference libraries. Another cultural organization that Liang started was the *Chiang-hsueh She* (Association for Lectures), the main activity of which was to invite Western scholars to lecture in China. Due to financial limitations, however, this group sponsored only four world-renowned scholars, Bertrand Russell, Hans Driesch, John Dewey and Rabindranath Tagore, to travel to China between 1920 and 1924. His important academic works of lasting value were completed in this period and include his *Ch'ing-tai hsueh-shu kai-lun* (Intellectual trends in the Ch'ing period),[4] *Chung-kuo li-shih yen-chiu-fa* (The method of studying Chinese history), *Hsien-Ch'in cheng-chih szu-hsiang shih* (History of Chinese political thought in the pre-Ch'in period), and the *Mo-tzu hsueh-an* (Study of Motzu).

On 19 January 1929 Liang died in the hospital of the Peking Union Medical College where Sun Yat-sen had died four years before. Liang is often remembered and referred to as a reformer. In fact, Liang the student and K'ang the mentor are generally labelled together as K'ang-Liang, and linked as being the initial protagonist reformers of the late nineteenth and early twentieth century.[5]

Liang's Political Conceptions

Liang Ch'i-ch'ao's political thought underwent two distinct phases. The first phase was characterized by radical ideas. His advocacy of the overthrow of the Ch'ing dynasty and the establishment of a republic through utter destruction in a revolution first appeared in the *Shi-wu pao*. In this magazine Liang "wrote *Pien-fa t'ung-i* (A general discussion of reform), which criticized the worthless government and proposed to abolish the old examination system and establish modern schools as ways of remedying the crisis. From time to time he also wrote on popular sovereignty but he touched on this only very generally, not daring to espouse it too overtly."[6]

In 1897, while lecturing at the School of Current Affairs in Ch'ang-sha, "Liang remained in the lecture hall for four hours a day, and at night wrote comments on the students' notes, a single comment sometimes running to several thousand words. . . . His discussions were concerned, in the main, with the current version of the theory of popular sovereignty, and he also talked of historical events of the Ch'ing dynasty, listing [episodes of] misgovernment and strongly advocating revolution. . . . At that time, all the students lived in dormitories and had no contact with the outside world; the atmosphere within the school became more radical day by day, but the outside world had no way of knowing this. Then, when the new year vacation arrived and the students went home, they showed their notes to relatives and friends, causing a great stir throughout the entire Hunan province."[7]

After the failure of the Hundred Days' Reform, Liang fled to Japan in 1898 where he daily propagandized the cause of revolution against the Manchus and of republicanism in the *Ch'ing-i pao*. To these activities and views his teacher K'ang Yu-wei was strongly opposed. For two years they argued through a correspondence that amounted to tens of thousands of characters.[8] However, it was also at this time that Liang's views gradually changed, for he began to feel dissatisfied with what the revolutionaries (i.e., the Kuomintang members) were doing. Accordingly, he altered his stand.[9]

In 1903 Liang made a drastic about-face in his political advocacy from constitutional republicanism *(kung-ho li-hsien)* to constitutional monarchy *(chün-chu li-hsien)*. He had come under the influence of the theories of Johann Kaspar Bluntschli and Gustav Bornhak, both professors at Berlin University. Bluntschli was quoted by Liang as advocating that constitutional monarchy is the best form of government and which he regarded as a future utopia. Liang cited Bornhak as saying that a republic obtained through tradition will be secure but that a republic obtained through revolution will be unstable.[10]

Liang's previous confidence in republicanism was completely shaken. He came to believe that the factors necessary for realizing a republic were nonexistent among the Chinese people who, because of their heritage, possessed, on the contrary, characteristics antithetical to those factors essential to building a republic. A republican form of government could not have been sought in China at that time for, given such a people, an attempt to create a republic through revolution would result in a long period of chaos and destruction rather than any national well-being, and despotism rather than freedom, as was evident in the upheaval of the French Revolution and of the South American countries.[11]

In the field of Chinese history Liang's abhorrence of revolution was intensified by a comparison he made between the history of revolutions in China and the West, discovering that there had been seven major evils in the Chinese revolutions. In contrast, he cited as commendable models of revolution, the British revolution under Cromwell and the American revolution under Washington. This led Liang to believe firmly that any forthcoming revolution sought in China could bring about the ruin rather than the salvation of the country, because those evils would probably linger on and repeat themselves. Liang's greatest apprehension was that under the name of revolution, countless self-seeking and ambitious military groups, arising simultaneously, would ravage the entire country, perhaps for several decades, and be followed by feuds among their rivals leading to foreign invasions.[12]

Defending and explaining this dramatic change (all of which was very painful to Liang emotionally) from a revolutionary to a gradualist in theory and in practice, Liang made his famous and widely quoted remark that "I do not shrink from myself of today challenging myself of yesterday."

Liang's denial of revolution, a line deviating from that of the Kuomintang, is reflected in another of his important articles in which he differentiated political revolution from racial revolution. Political revolution he defined as a revolution from despotism to constitutionalism, resulting either in constitutional monarchy or republicanism. Racial revolution, on the other hand, he defined simply as the overthrow by military force of the central government controlled by a foreign race. In the case of China, this racial form of revolution referred to the driving out of the Manchus.[13]

Liang was thus opposed to racial revolution as a proper means of change on the ground that Chinese revenge on the Manchus would not achieve the political goal of constitutionalism. In order to save China, a political revolution was necessary. Since he opposed using the revolutionary method, Liang advocated the pursuit of constitutionalism by peaceful methods. It was in this context that Liang stipulated that "Those who want to carry out a racial revolution should advocate despotism rather than republicanism, and those who want to carry out a political revolution should advocate demands rather than insurrection."[14] What Liang drove at was that a racial revolution by force would invite despotism rather than constitutionalism.

Constitutional republicanism was Liang's ultimate goal, whereas constitutional monarchy was a transition to that goal. However, even the latter was considered infeasible during this time; thus enlightened despotism was proposed as the practical step to take. The reasons for this expediency were twofold: (1) The Chinese people were not yet qualified for constitutional monarchy; and (2) an adequate political infrastructure did not yet exist in China.[15] The two phases of Liang's political thought from his advocacy and support of an utter destructive revolution to that of gradualism represent an abrupt, fundamental, and penetrating change of mind, a change which not only marked an irreparable breach with the Kuomintang but which, in turn and most importantly, influenced and shaped the minds of many others after him who began to believe in gradualism rather than revolution.

Liang's attitude in regard to the form of government and the revolution is clearly and summarily expressed in his talk during an interview with a newspaper reporter in 1915 on the occasion of Yuan Shih-k'ai's attempt to proclaim himself emperor.

> I have maintained that the form of the state *(kuo-t'i)* and the form of the government *(cheng-t'i)* are two different things. If constitutionalism is practiced, a monarchy or a republic makes no difference. If constitutionalism is not practiced, neither a monarchy nor a republic will do. Since there is no preference to either one of these two forms I would rather prefer to stick to the present foundation on which we gradually attempt to construct an ideal form of government. This has been my principle of belief in the past few decades. A nation should not change too often; if it does, much damage will be done, of which I am greatly apprehensive. Thus, on the one hand, I always wish to promote the ideal form of government and, on the other hand, I always want to preserve the existing form of the state. For the change in the form of government is often evolutionary but the change in the form of the state is often revolutionary. I have never heard that a revolution can benefit the country and the people. I have never opposed a republic or a monarchy but I have always opposed a revolution, which is the greatest misfortune to the country.[16]

Finally, Liang envisioned a kind of Western style democracy—a multi-party system. He wrote an article on what he called "the political opposition force," which he considered to be the foundation of modern political parties and the basis for the superiority of constitutional politics. His argument may be summarized as follows.

Strong and righteous political force springs from a group of elites in a society who are solely faithful to what they believe to be truth, and refuse to obey subserviently the commands of those in power. Based on this principle, they gather supporters with the purpose of opposing anything contrary to their beliefs. If they do this, a political opposition force has been formed and organized. It was this force which made strong political parties possible.

In a country with no political opposition in existence, the government is bound to be despotic and revolutions would erupt frequently, because as soon as the absolute power corrupts and declines, the people would start to revolt. Historical facts revealed that a country where strong and righteous political forces had been cemented, as in France and England, revolutions had ceased to occur. While a country where no such forces had existed, such as China, or the Central and South American countries, its history had abounded with revolutions. (Liang used the Chinese phrase *ko-ming,* which can refer either to revolt or revolution. He called all dynastic changes revolutions.) Furthermore, in countries with opposition forces, governments would be able to run their normal courses without interruptions, and where a maladministration occurred, it would be corrected by peaceful methods without resorting to bloody revolutions.[17]

From the above condensation, it is clear that what Liang advocated was a kind of constitutional democratic form of government run by political parties, with due respect and legal protection for the rights of opposition parties by the party in power. Under this system, the transition of political power could be achieved through peaceful procedures without a revolution, and the country could enjoy permanent stability and peace.

The idea of Liang Ch'i-ch'ao has since been shared by many thinkers and intellectuals, but, even today, the two regimes in China are still plagued by one-party dictatorships, with each of the two major parties now controlling its side of the Taiwan Straits, sometimes in a cold war and sometimes in a shooting war.

In essence, Liang advocated a true democratic government in reality, irrespective of the form of the state. Subscribers to Liang's views would cite the British case where the government, though monarchical in form, is highly democratic, and the Soviet case, where the government is undemocratic, but is republican in name.

Renovation of the People

Liang Ch'i-ch'ao attempted to create an entirely new Chinese people with a view to rejuvenating China as a nation.[18] He analogized the people of the country to the limbs, internal organs, muscles, and blood of the human body. It is inconceivable that a body can remain functioning properly where it is atrophied. So it is with nations; a country whose people are sick and effete cannot expect to be strong. The inefficiency and corruption of the Chinese government was, of course, the fault of the government itself. But do not government officials, Liang asked rhetorically, come from among the people?

Liang's program for the salvation of China begins with the "renovation of the people." This term is taken from *The Great Learning* and states that "What the Great Learning teaches is...to renovate the people."[19] Liang's usage of the term *hsin-min* can also be construed to mean the renovated people and rendered as "new people," or new citizenry.

The practical measure by which Liang sought to effect the renovation of the Chinese people was to change the minds of the people by instilling in them a new ideology to replace the old one. He proposed two basic principles as guide lines: first, to create something new by screening out and retaining what is best from the old; second, to create something new from scratch.[20] Liang made it clear that what he meant by renovation of the people was different from the views of those who, enamored by Western culture, rejected the age-old Chinese morality, scholarship, and tradition, and sought to match the West. Liang was also in disagreement with those who, stubbornly loyal to the old Chinese culture, took it as adequate to enable survival in the modern world.[21] The aim of the renovation of the people is to create a new citizenry. Tradition had taught the Chinese people to carry out responsibilities as independent and individual members of society, family, clan, and even of the entire world *(t'ien-hsia)*. But, argued Liang, because the Chinese people patently lacked the features to be citizens of a country, China had only tribal members *(pu-min)* rather than citizens *(kuo-min)*. China, in Liang's opinion, consists of millions of people of the primitive type who are fit for tribes and other old-type political systems. China has no citizens who are fit for a modern state, so the Chinese are unable to survive independently in the modern, competitive world. In this respect, Liang viewed the situation through the lens of social Darwinism. The principles of the survival of the fittest, and the struggle for existence, rendered into Chinese, are colorful and concrete expressions: "The superior wins and the inferior fails;" and, "the weak is like a piece of meat and is to be carved and devoured by the strong." These two principles are the rules governing all actions of the competitive world. Liang seemed to reason that China, in order to survive, must not only learn the merits of the West, but also the vices. His dream was to transform the Chinese from a contented, moderate people to an aggressive and pugnacious people like the Westerners, and to turn China from a loosely organized and peace-loving country to a militaristic modern state such as the Western powers which China was compelled to resist.

In comparing the different races by this perspective, Liang admitted candidly that Anglo-Saxons are the most superior, and that their hegemony over most of the world in the nineteenth century was not sheer good luck but was definitely due to their racial superiority. Liang thus came to the conclusion that weak people have a weak country and strong people have a strong country. This is an inexorable law. If China wanted to be strong she first had to find out the basic reasons which enabled Anglo-Saxons to be strong and to flourish and then compare those reasons with the ones that made China weak and backward. After finding these causes and deficiencies the Chinese should correct their mistakes and improve their deficiencies with a view to creating a new citizenry. Liang was convinced that this was an effective way to combat imperialism. The way to achieve this goal was to combine the best of both Chinese and foreign cultures and thus to attain a synthesis. This process is perhaps what the communists refer to as "walking on two legs." Interestingly, Liang had his own similar metaphor, "to walk with one leg and to stand firmly with the other leg."[22]

We now turn to the broad principles and details which Liang believed the Chinese should follow to renovate themselves and to develop the required features for a new citizenry, so that China could compete in the struggle for existence in building a strong and viable nation.

Moral Revolution

Public Morality. Liang basically wanted to provide new moral values to guide the Chinese through difficult times.[23] First and foremost, he argued that traditional moral principles were not immutable and that morality was subject to change just as times change. Such a view proved to be shocking during a period when people firmly believed that the moral principles of the ancient sages were unequivocally true. Liang labelled his own efforts at searching for a new set of values as a moral revolution.

In creating a new Chinese citizenry, Liang staged what he called a moral revolution by shifting the centuries-old Confucian moral emphasis on personal and inner cultivation to the inculcation of public-oriented morality with respect to the good of one's fellow man and society.

Morality, in Liang's view, can be divided into two categories—private and public morality. Private morality is to make oneself perfect in solitude. Public morality is to do good for the whole community. Liang noticed that in the Confucian classics, moral teachings are predominantly private virtues, and that teachings on public morality are exceedingly few.

When he compared Chinese and Western ethics, Liang found that the Confucian ethics on personal virtues are embodied in the five cardinal relationships, three of which have to do with family relationships, namely, those between father and son, between older and younger brother, and between husband and wife. The relationship between friends is viewed as affection between nonrelated individuals, while the relationship between an emperor and his minister is viewed basically as a personal relationship. Confucius taught that "a prince [emperor] should employ his minister according to the rules of propriety; ministers should serve their prince with faithfulness,"[24] Among these relationships, the relation governing an individual and the society and country in which he lives is conspicuously lacking. Thus Liang felt that the five cardinal virtues were detrimental to China. Indeed, he said, the poverty and weakness of China were the consequences of everybody catering only to their own moral cultivation without proper attention to public welfare. People were not fulfilling their obligations and they owed a debt to the community.

The inculcation of the concept of public morality, he felt, would save China from decline and extinction. Liang defined morality as anything which is good for the community or the public. That is, anything which is beneficial to the public is good; anything which is not beneficial to the public is evil. Yet, to be evil does not necessarily imply doing actual harm to the public. A passive virtue which does not benefit society is also considered an evil. Liang even went so far as to say that if one is satisfied in being a virtuous person privately without actively contributing to society as a whole, he may be viewed as committing a heinous crime against society.

In short, the new moral values Liang wanted to establish were a public morality which aims at active participation for the public good. All other virtues which Liang advocated stem from this basic and central concept. (These concepts will be treated separately in the following pages.) It should be pointed out that in order to balance his overemphasis on public morality and some misunderstanding of his advocacy of allowing moral relaxation, Liang followed with another article entitled "On Private Morality,"[25] which dealt mainly with the relationship between private and public morality and the importance of private morality.

Concept of the State. Liang felt that the Chinese people conspicuously and tragically lacked a concept of the state.[26] He expounded upon four areas which he considered vague in Chinese minds and in need of clarification: (1) The individual and the state. The individual should be conscious of the state as being above himself and realize that he cannot survive without the state; (2) The court and the state. The court is only a political organization representing the state and should not be identified with the state although, if the court is not legitimate, it should be corrected for the good of the state; (3) Foreign nations and the state. A nation should fight at any cost if its sovereignty is threatened or infringed upon by a foreign nation; and (4) The world and the state. The state is the highest organizational form at the present time and the idea of one world, though desirable, is not practical.

Actual conditions in China, Liang pointed out, were contrary to these four principles. In general, the Chinese people could not rise above the individual level in their understanding of the state. The worst individuals were those self-seekers of personal and family interests, even at the expense of the state. The best were devoted to abstract philosophy without any practical use. Though the latter group was superior to the former, they were equally contemptible in inviting disaster to the country, because neither group was public-minded and neither had a sense of obligatory loyalty to the state.

Liang had ascertained that, of the 1,700 years since the end of the Han dynasty, China proper had been completely under foreign occupation for 358 years, and the territory north of the Yellow River had been occupied for 759 years. What is more, it was the greatest disgrace to China that these foreign regimes were aided by Chinese quislings. Scholars and philosophers were wont to rationalize a weak China by viewing the state as something insignificant. These were incorrect values, Liang believed, which stemmed from an absence of understanding of the state and which, if not corrected, could lead to the ruin of China.

The reason for a lack of a concept of the state has two sources: the consciousness of the individual, and the consciousness of the world, *t'ien-hsia,* rather than any consciousness of the state. The two factors giving rise to the concept of *t'ien-hsia* are geographical and theoretical. Geographically, Liang argued that China was, for the most part of her long history, unified on a vast plain and surrounded by a number of small barbarous states, a situation unlike that of Europe which is divided into many smaller and more independent states by numerous mountains and rivers. Theoretically, philosophers such as Confucius, Mencius, Mo-tzu, Lao-tzu, Hsun-tzu, and Kuan Yin, who flourished before and during the Warring States period and who were weary of continuous warfare, all advocated unity in preference to having a number of independent states in constant strife. But this theory of the "nationalism" of the separate warring states during the early period came to an end after the unification by Ch'in and Han. However, Liang argued, a new knowledge of world geography and the introduction of Western theories can easily dispel and change the traditional views on the state and the world. The most difficult idea to shake loose, however, was the focus on oneself—at its worst, the concern solely for oneself without regard for the interests of the public good. Liang's theory of the renovation of the Chinese people is his solution to this glaring evil.

Aggressive and Adventurous Spirit. Liang observed with apprehension that in the global perspective no country had degenerated so fast and was in such a precarious situation as was China.[27] Liang felt that of the many superior qualities of the European races, vis-a-vis the Chinese, their aggressive and adventurous spirit was probably the most important. This spirit is compared to what Mencius called the "vast, flowing, passion-nature" *(hao-jan chih-ch'i).*[28] With it, an individul lives; without it, he dies. In the same manner, with it, a country survives; without it, a country succumbs.

This spirit, in which Westerners abound, is exactly what the Chinese lacked. Figures in history whom Liang praised included the daring Columbus whose sea voyages led to the discovery of the New World, the spirited Luther who struggled against Catholicism in initiating freedom of religion, the rebellious Washington whose war against England resulted in the American nation, and the morally courageous Lincoln who emancipated the Negroes. Even explorers like Magellan and Livingstone, though their activities were contrary to the interests of the oppressed peoples, were praised by Liang for their courageous, aggressive, and adventurous spirit.

The lack of this spirit among the Chinese was attributed by Liang partly to the passive philosophy of Lao-tzu, and partly to the understanding and biased interpretation of Confucianism. That is, the followers of Confucianism often failed to comprehend in their totality the teachings of Confucius. They missed the main points when they followed the principles of reservation or timidity rather than boldness or aggression,[29] when they followed his don'ts but neglected his do's, when they followed his negative principles but neglected his positive principles, and when they followed his teaching of the Mandate of Heaven but disregarded his teaching of continually striving to do one's utmost. Consequently, there is not an iota of adventurous and aggressive spirit left

58

among the Chinese people. As a result, China finds herself with "feminine-virtue," without "man-virtue"; with sick people, not strong people; with "evening atmosphere" rather than "morning air"; and even with ghosts rather than with men. Under such circumstances, Liang wondered, how could a country survive?

Concept of Rights. For Liang, human beings differ from other animals in the sense that they emphasize a metaphysical life— what Liang termed the enjoyment of rights.[30] Anyone without regard for his rights will degenerate to the status of a beast. Rights always go to the strong, as in the case of the lion over the other animals, or the tribal chief over his people. Lions and chiefs as representatives of the animal and human worlds, Liang thought, should not be blamed for their brutality. It is human nature to want to expand one's rights. But no one can obtain more rights over another unless the latter relinquishes some. Thus, the protection of one's rights always involves struggle. The only way, then, to consolidate a community and maintain it in good order is for everyone to remain strong enough to guard his own rights.

According to Liang, the Teutons, the Anglo-Saxons, and the other white groups of Europe, as well as the Japanese, are all very serious about their rights and they would tolerate no incursions into those rights. They would, moreover, fight for them at any cost. But, on the contrary, the Chinese are much less sensitive about their rights. For instance, the responses of the Chinese people in general were conspicuously less intense than they should have been at the burning of the Yuan-ming Palace, the signing of the Nanking Treaty, the annexation of Hong Kong, Chiao-chou, Port Arthur, and Dairen, and the opening of the five treaty ports. The Chinese people's lack of the concept of rights, Liang explained, was influenced by such Confucian philosophical remarks as: "To show forbearance and gentleness in teaching others, and not to take revenge on unreasonable conduct";[31] "Offended against, yet never contesting";[32] and "To recompense injury with kindness; to recompense injury with justice."[33] The spirit behind these aphorisms, under specific circumstances, Liang believed, could be noble and respectful. But he regretted that they were used as an excuse for the evils of slothfulness and cowardice, thus bringing about damage to the psychology of the whole country. How can such a people, Liang asked, survive in a world of fierce struggle for existence?

Another philosophical source for this lack of rights is the emphasis on benevolent government. Keeping such an attitude in mind the Chinese, expecting a benevolent emperor to work for their benefit, became like children when such a benefactor appeared. In actual practice, there were more tyrants than benevolent rulers and the people succumbed as their victims without any resistance. The Chinese had conceived of the basic right of demanding good government but they saw oppression as part of fate as something natural and avoidable.

It was Liang's belief that rights could not be obtained without struggle, often bloody and devastating. People strongly imbued with the concept of rights, such as the British and American peoples, would always fight for their rights.

The Chinese outlook of looking for a benevolent government to confer upon them some token rights actually disqualified them to be citizens. (Liang acknowledged that the theme of this passage on rights was taken mainly from Rudoff von Jhering's *Der Kampfum Recht* [Battle Right]. This book was considered by Liang as a prescription to cure China's illnesses.)

Behind all these divergent arguments, Liang's intention is simple and clear. He urged the Chinese people to fight for their rights against their government first. Any people who have been cruelly oppressed without enjoying civil rights within the country could not be expected to resist foreign invasion. Because of their passiveness, the Chinese did not manifest any strong reaction to foreign incursions as they otherwise should have. Such a reaction also served as a warning to the Ch'ing court which, in spite of its reluctance to grant constitutional rights to the people, did inspire them with the courage to fight the foreigners. So Liang appealed to the statesman to regard as a supreme principle the protection and maintenance of the concept of rights; to the educator the cultivation of the concept of rights; and to individuals irrespective of their position as scholars, farmers, workers, merchants, men or women, the insistence on the concept of rights. If the government denies the people their rights, they should fight for them. Whenever the people fight for them, the government should yield and give them rights. Before China can enjoy equal status with the countries of the world it is imperative that the Chinese people enjoy the same civil rights as do peoples in other countries.

Liberty. The Chinese paraphrase Patrick Henry's famous saying, "Give me liberty or give me death," as "Without liberty it is better to be dead."[34] Liang regarded this saying as the founding principle and the motive force of Europe and America in the eighteenth and nineteenth centuries. Trying to differentiate between the true meaning of liberty and a popular misconception, Liang defined freedom as liberty to do as one pleases provided he does not encroach upon the freedom of others. Liang further held that freedom is the freedom of the whole community rather than that of separate individuals. Freedom and liberty should be used as a tool to create a national constitution within the state and to achieve international equality without personal abuses (indulgence) rather than as an excuse for them.

It may be noted here that freedom and liberty often have philosophical differences in their connotations in the English language. There is only one term in Chinese, *tzu-yu*, which is translated either as freedom or as liberty as the case may be. Moreover, the concept of liberty or freedom had been foreign to the Chinese traditional mind before the introduction of Western ideas. Thus, Liang's introduction and popularization of this concept was significant and influential. Naturally, Liang's understanding of it was by no means profound and thorough. This imperfect understanding, realized by Liang at the time and pointed out recently by several scholars,[35] does not affect the value of his pioneering contribution and should not overly concern us here.

Maintaining that freedom is opposed to slavery, especially slavery of the mind, Liang discussed four kinds of slavery of the mind and ways to remove them. First, do not be a slave to the ancients. Confucius is not to be held as the only sage. Had Confucius been a slave to Emperors Yao and Shun there would have been no Confucius at all. In the Western world, for instance, Luther, Bacon, Descartes, Kant, Darwin, and Huxley were great thinkers who added new thoughts and dimensions to the teachings of Christianity after the decline from its zenith in the Middle Ages. Any improvement in modern thought would have been impossible had they been slaves to the ancients. Second, do not be a slave to faddish thinking. That is, think independently and creatively rather than ape popular trends. Third, do not be a slave to the environment. Fight against and conquer the difficult conditions in which men live as, for example, the Americans did in their fight for independence. Do not feel that China is doomed to failure in the face of foreign invasions. Finally, do not be a slave to the lusts of the flesh. Retain high ideals for the salvation of China and do not become corrupted by material incentives.

Progress. Progress dominates Western minds; conservatism dominates Chinese minds.[36] The Chinese cherish memories of the ancient Golden Age, while Westerners look forward to a new era. Chinese civilization tends to be static, while Western civilizations tend to be progressive. This contrast between Chinese and Western thinking was keenly felt by Liang. He grouped the causes for this contrast into two kinds: natural causes and human causes. Natural causes have two perspectives: (1) The political unity of China as a large empire was achieved without competition within the country. Competition is the motive force of progress. During the few centuries of disunity in the periods of the Spring and Autumn and the Warring States, remarkable progress was made. After China's unification under the Ch'in dynasty, stagnation and even retrogression ensued for more than a thousand years due to a lack of competition. (2) China's being surrounded by barbarian tribes, invariably with lower levels of culture, caused her to have an attitude of arrogance which subsequently induced in her a passive and therefore static attitude.

Liang adumbrated three perspectives of the human causes: (1) The general development of language goes from the initial pictorial form, through syllabic writing, to an alphabet. In China the last step never evolved. Not being a phonetic language, written Chinese, which is divorced from spoken Chinese, became a hindrance to the enlargement of new vocabularies corresponding to new changing conditions of society, to the adoption and spread of a new and practical learning, and to the development of popular education. Hence, the nature of the writing system retarded intellectual progress in China. (2) A long period of despotism thwarted the growth and development of the people's initiative and abilities. Under a constitutional form of government, both the political party in power and the party out of power must compete for the votes of the people by promising better performance and thereby the hope of realizing social progress. In the case of China, where the people were passive due to long periods of despotism (and their bad rulers far outnumbered the good rulers,) the order-chaos cycle was repeated. Thus, little progress was made in the past several thousand years. (3) Conformity to Confucianism as an orthodoxy

61

narrowed down and suffocated the development of other thought and learning. However, the damage done to the progress of China was not the fault of Confucianism itself but rather of those who manipulated Confucianism for selfish purposes.

In his endeavor to save China from extinction and to make progress, Liang raised rather radical ideas. Destruction, he posited, is necessary to progress; no construction comes without destruction, as exemplified in the bloody histories of Europe before the Middle Ages, in America and in Japan. Thus, he not only advocated an immediate and utter destruction of what is old, he also called for immediate destruction. Liang urged people to sacrifice the present, short-run pains for peace, order, and progress in the long run; and he encouraged people not to hesitate in sacrificing lives lest natural disasters and political mis-administrations kill millions of people every year even without deliberate and planned destruction. By utter destruction Liang meant, in his own words, the crushing of the despotic and corrupt thousand-years-old political system in order that the evil, greedy, parasitic, and ferocious officials who resemble tigers, wolves, locusts, and maggots, would have no place to take refuge. Only when destruction is complete can China progress. Liang also advocated the refutation and liquidation of the corrupt and effeminate scholarship of the past several thousand years so that millions of scholars, who resemble worms, parrots, jellyfish, and dogs, cannot manipulate words to support despots. In simple terms, Liang advocated the complete destruction of the government and of the old scholarship and the scholars.

As to the means to this end, two alternatives were discussed: one, by shedding blood, as in the case of the French Revolution, and the other, a bloodless transformation, as in the case of Japanese modernization. Reluctant-ly, Liang believed that bloody destruction might be necessary if a peaceful change proved unfeasible. However, he cautioned that no one is entitled to unleash destruction unless he is of a compassionate nature and finds no other alternatives; nor should anyone be entitled to engage in destruction unless he has the ability to bring about construction afterwards. In short, Liang was as cautious as he was radical. Actually, he himself did not engage in any de-structive revolution, although it is interesting to speculate how many people in later years, under his influence, did follow his advice in destructive revolution-ary activities.

Production. One economic virtue which Liang promoted was production.[37] Quoting Confucius that "Possessing the people will give him [the ruler] the territory, and possessing the territory will give him its wealth,"[38] Liang at-tempted to explain the paradoxical phenomenon of China's poverty with a large population and a great land area. Liang maintained that the basic principle governing national economies lay in Confucius' words: "Let the producers be many and the consumers few.[39] For Liang, economic theories in subsequent ages (after Confucius) had revealed nothing more than this. That is, the total production of a country is the sum of the production of its individuals, and the national total production cannot realize any advance or progress unless the

62

producers outnumber the unproductive consumers. Liang dwelt on the factors of production and the simple principle of the increase of the wealth of a nation quoting Adam Smith to support his views. Liang was by no means an economist and there is little point in examining his arguments by the standards of modern economic theories. What does concern us here are the contents of and the aims behind his views.

Liang's diagnosis of the poverty of China was that, according to his own estimates, out of a population of four hundred million, over two hundred million were unproductive. These unproductive parasites include beggars, thieves, Buddhist and Taoist monks, charlatans (including witches, fortune tellers, quack doctors), playboys, soldiers, a majority of the government officials and their dependents, local gentry, certain women, invalids, criminals, servants, actors, prostitutes, education people (including teachers), speculators, cosmetic, wine and tobacco vendors, and opium planters.

What is surprising is Liang's appraisal of educated people as unproductive. This class of people is generally known as scholars in English translation and as *tu-shu-jen* (literally, "read-books-people") in Chinese. Liang pointedly condemned such persons who made a career of futile learning, especially the writing of "eight-legged essays." These "read-books-people" were depicted as intellectually, physically, or morally deficient and regarded as parasites, harmful to the people and the country. Teachers were also classified as unproductive and, therefore, as parasitic for they helped to produce unproductive people. Liang even went so far as to censure as useless and unproductive the scholarly fields of phonology, textual studies, modern classics, and history. Liang did, however, think highly of those scholars who could advance knowledge and morality and thus benefit the country; and he regretted that they only constituted a very small percentage of the entire population. Government officials were also severely censured; the great majority of them performed no useful functions for the people but often brought actual harm to the people. They were both unproductive and criminal.

These two classes of people—the educated and government officials—are traditionally considered by Chinese as mental workers whose role is to rule the manual laborers, whose function is to support them.[40] So it is obvious that Liang's exaltation of economic production as virtuous and his degradation of mental performers, especially scholars, as parasitic, aimed at encouraging everybody to engage in productive economic activity. In this manner, total production, and accordingly the total wealth of China, would increase. Liang, thus, realized vaguely and in a layman's way that in the modern world economic forces underlie the rise and fall of a country.

Political Ability. In the political realm, Liang deemed that China's difficult problems henceforth would not be so much in theory as in practice.[41] While political theory can be introduced in a comparatively short time, it takes a much longer time to train and develop political ability within the people. Actually, Liang's thinking in this respect coincided with Sun Yat-sen's theory of easy-to-know but difficult-to-do. The evidence cited by Liang for China's lack of political competency is manifest in her not having developed a sound and efficient government for thousands of years. A few thousand British subjects in Shanghai could form an efficient government while tens of thousands of overseas Chinese in San Francisco, as well as elsewhere, were unable to organize a strong political organization.

Liang believed that the practicalities of training and developing political ability in the people was the responsibility of the middle class in society, which had been imbued with political ideas. In other words, Liang believed in the influence and functions belonging to the middle class.

Since the minority composed of intellectuals has the great responsibility of educating and leading the whole country, it should cultivate political abilities and set a good example for others. Liang suggested two practical measures for those in politics to follow.

First, a specialized division of labor. Chinese enthusiasts for politics, as Liang noticed, were prone to have an ambition, which was actually a mistake, to seek an overall solution for all of China's problems. Those who were engaged in political, economic, educational, and social reforms were the same people. The consequence of this was not only that China's overall problems could not be solved but that even specific areas also remained unsolved. So Liang's suggestion was a division of labor according to one's special training or interest. Some people should devote themselves to politics, others to education, still others to society. This would prevent everyone from seeking a general and total solution of the national problem, a solution which was seldom if ever realized.

Second, a cooperation rather than hostility between different political parties. In this respect, Liang specifically referred to the early Kuomintang members and to the Constitutionalists. He pointed out that although their intentions for the good of China were the same, their differences lay only in their means. Their common foes were the Ch'ing government at home and foreign powers abroad. Liang appealed for fair play between the two parties and warned against any conspiracy, hostile acts, or personal attacks against the other. It is evident that Liang favored a kind of multipolitical party which would encompass expert politicians and fair competition. He was totally opposed to the tendencies of one-party dictatorships.

Other Aspects. There are a number of less-important values which Liang tried to inculcate in the minds of the "new people" in searching for a cure of some failings of the Chinese people.

Self Government. Liang deplored the incapacity of the Chinese to govern themselves.[42] He showed no sympathy for those under foreign control and felt it inevitable that those who cannot govern themselves will be governed by others. He lauded the British for their capacity for self-government and he grudgingly admired them for their control of numerous colonies. Thus, whether China can build up a modern state based on freedom, equality, a constitution and a parliamentary system will depend on her self-governing ability. Liang warned his fellow countrymen that if they did not learn and develop this ability, China would remain chaotic forever and could never become a free and independent state.

Self-respect. Liang condemned the lack of self-respect among the Chinese people.[43] He conceived self-respect to be the respect one has of himself in the capacity of a citizen who has an obligation and a responsibility to make his country prestigious, prosperous, and powerful. Though self-respect begins with the respect of individuals, the ultimate aim of Liang was to invoke the passion of a strong nationalism.

Group-oriented mind. Liang lamented that the Chinese are not group-oriented *(ho-ch'ün)*, that is, they are self-oriented and they lack the concept of the group or community.[44] Liang urged the Chinese, in the main, to keep the group in mind and to be ready to sacrifice their individual, partial, personal, and immediate interests for the total, long-run public interest.

Perseverance. Among the hundreds of shortcomings of the Chinese national characteristics, Liang regarded the lack of perseverance as the most tragic.[45] He cited as an example the Boxer Rebellion (of which he disapproved), condemning it for its lack of persistence and tragic and swift termination. Liang thus advised people to be persistent in the course of pursuing their ideals, especially in the salvation of China.

The Concept of Obligation. Liang felt a conspicuous weakness in the Chinese concept of obligation toward the nation.[46] For instance, in the West, to pay taxes and to perform military duties are two basic obligations of the people toward their government in obtaining financial resources and in defending their country against foreign aggression. In contrast, the Chinese praised emperors who levied light taxes, and able-bodied young men tried by every possible means to evade military service. The result was that people had almost no concern for the fate of their country. Since four hundred million Chinese were not conscious of their obligations to their country, it would be tantamount to saying that China was a country without people. Liang admitted that traditional moral values place the stress more on obligations such as loyalty, filial piety, brotherhood, and integrity than on rights. Unfortunately, the stress is confined to personal obligations and there is a neglect of obligations to the country.

Martial Prowess. Martial prowess is the vitality of a people by which a country and a civilization can stand alone and remain independent.[47] A civilization without a military force cannot survive in a time of struggle. Liang favored Bismarck's theory of iron and blood and cited as exemplars of martial prowess the Spartans, Germans, Russians, and Japanese. He condemned the Chinese people's "unmilitarism," which was taken as a great disgrace to the nation, for China had suffered foreign invasions in her long history since the Chou dynasty (c. eleventh century B.C.–221 B.C.) and was suffering especially under modern imperialist aggression. The lack of military prowess was, among other things, due to the distortion of Confucian pacifist philosophy resulting in a weak and effeminate people who prefer meekness to war, praising of humility but submitting to oppression, killing, and the loss of personal and national properties and rights. Liang urged the Chinese people to develop a strong mind and a powerful body in the face of the struggle for existence.

Marxism and Socialism

Socialism in general and Marxism in particular were introduced to China at the turn of the twentieth century. Marxism, usually synonymous with communism, represents a new concept and a radical program for social reconstruction. Thinkers and social reformers since Marx have had either to go along with or to oppose Marxism; few could afford to ignore it. However, Marxism did not attract much attention among the intellectuals in the period before 1911 when most attention was focused on the choice between constitutionalism and republicanism.

In 1905 Liang only incidentally touched upon the problem of Marxism, thus giving one of the earliest Chinese reactions to this theory. He opposed the simultaneous implementation of social revolution (i.e., land nationalization based on Marxism) and the political and racial views of revolution held by the early Kuomintang. Liang deemed the seizure of land by brutal force without compensation as a kind of theft by the government, just as Marx had accused the landlords and property owners of exploitation.

Furthermore, Liang censured the Kuomintang use of land nationalization as nothing other than a means to win the sympathy and support of gamblers, robbers, thieves, beggars, vagabonds, criminals, and undesirables in general. Land nationalization, Liang predicted would accomplish nothing more than disturbance and ruin to the areas concerned. If it were successful everything would happen as Borndalh had predicted: in the initial state the propertyless lower class would be in power after the overthrow of the central government but, after prolonged chaos, either a despot would appear to restore law and order (at the cost of the freedoms originally fought for), or, when no such despot appeared in time, foreign domination would ruin China forever.[48]

If Liang were alive now he would be opposed to the theories of peasant revolution and the dictatorship of the proletariat currently held by the Chinese communists. His view of socialism in China was expressed primarily in a letter, dated 19 January 1911,[49] in answer to an earlier letter from Chang Tung-sun. Chang was one of the six people whom Voitinsky first approached with the intention of forming a Communist Party in China. Those approached also included Ch'en Tu-hsiu and Li Ta-chao. Chang himself declined to participate in the conference and never did join the Party. He ultimately turned out to be a lifelong anticommunist, except for a short period in his later years. Chang's letter was to seek Liang's view on the socialist movement in China; Liang's answer is summarized below.

The main difference between the socialist movement in Europe and America and that in China lies in the fact that the most urgent problem in the West is how to improve the conditions of the majority of laborers, while China's main problem is how to turn the majority of the Chinese people into laborers. Thus the West is faced with the problem of struggle between the propertied and propertyless classes, while China's problem concerns mainly the creation of employment, relegating the problem of the propertied-propertyless struggle to secondary importance. Unemployed Chinese had to seek jobs rather than fight for increased wages and reduced working hours. The reason that China did not have enough jobs for her workers was because of the monopolization of most manufacturing industries by foreign capitalists in London, Paris, New York, and Osaka. If there should be a class struggle it would be a class struggle between all Chinese workers as the exploited class against all foreign exploiting classes. Liang further postulated that the socialist movement in China should be a movement toward equal distribution of goods within the context of promoting production; it would be entirely meaningless if attention were wholly devoted to distribution with no regard to production.

It was Liang's contention that the laboring class, by which he meant the strict sense of the term, i.e., wage earners in modern enterprises, did not exist in China. Naturally, there was no capitalist class in China either. Since the promotion of production envisaged by Liang was the only way to save China from poverty, industrial enterprises had to be developed. As such industrial enterprises developed, the twin brothers of laboring and capitalist classes would emerge. With the emergence of the capitalist class the evils of capitalism would inevitably appear. In order to check the growth of these capitalist evils and to channel the development of socialism into the best interests of society, Liang suggested a few points to be used as guidelines. (1) Capitalists should be warned that they must not exploit surplus capital and thereby bring about the enmity and opposition of the laborers since this would undermine their own capitalist base. They should take into serious consideration the worker's livelihood and welfare. The aim should be to achieve cooperation and compromise between the workers and the capitalists. (2) Further attempts must be made to gradually shift the control of production from the hands of the capitalists to the general public through cooperatives. (3) The organization and development of strong workers' unions is instrumental in achieving the final victory over the world's capitalists.

Liang's aversion to social change by drastic methods and his advocacy of gradualism can be clearly seen from these guidelines. He warned that any attempt to utilize the vagabonds (*[yu-min]*, i.e., somewhat similar to lumpenproletariat in Marxian terminology, whom Liang recognized as not belonging to the laboring class in society) to effect an insurrection in the name of socialism or communism would be detrimental to socialism and to China. His suggestion of a solution was to convert this vagabond class into a laboring class.

Material and Spiritual Civilization

In his account of his trip to Europe in 1918 to inspect the ruins of World War I, Liang made the shocking statement that there were cries in Europe of the bankruptcy of science. In his observations, Liang understood that Europeans had dreamed of the omnipotence of science which would bring a millenium to mankind. After a century of material progress, which surpassed the entire preceding three thousand years in scientific advancement but which had unfortunately culminated in world war, it was suggested that science not only didn't bring humankind well-being and happiness but, instead, misfortune and disaster. Thus came the cries of the backruptcy of science.

Liang saw this and hence began a dramatic change in his thinking. During that period the average Chinese intellectual, who regretted that China was so backward in science, was anxious to catch up with the West in this area. Anticipating that his remarks were sure to arouse opposition, Liang added a footnote to the effect: "I do not belittle science. I absolutely do not admit the bankruptcy of science. But I do not admit its omnipotence, either."[50]

Liang tended to associate science with the material civilization of the West, which he regarded chiefly as the product of science. Because material progress had not brought mankind unlimited happiness and well-being, a new civilization should be created. This was to be the grave responsibility of the Chinese. That is, the Chinese must help create a new civilization in which Western civilization and Chinese civilization would complement each other, thereby forming a new world through synthesis. What the Chinese had to offer was the spiritual wisdom of their ancient philosophers—Confucius, Lao-tzu and Mo-tzu among others.

Liang appealed to Chinese youth to undertake the following: (1) learn a sincere respect, love, and pride in Chinese culture; (2) apply the Western (scientific) method in studying Chinese culture in order to understand and make clear its true meaning; (3) synthesize Chinese and Western cultures to form a new culture; and (4) propagate this synthesized civilization abroad in order to benefit all mankind. Liang admonished the young people that millions upon millions of people on the other side of the ocean, stricken by the bankruptcy of a materialistic civilization, were desperately in need of Chinese help and salvation. Such aid could be effected through the spiritual teachings, blessings, and guidance of the Chinese sages in Heaven.[51]

Such an attitude reflects Liang's own belief and love of Chinese culture and outlines his cultural ideal of mankind as a whole and his unfavorable attitude to the West's material culture. In the West, Liang pointed out, the ideal and the actual were separate and distinct. The best way to merge these two dimensions was to achieve a balance between mind and matter. That is, Liang stressed the combination of Western material progress and Chinese philosophical wisdom—a view predominant during his time.

Summary

Liang Ch'i-ch'ao's influence on modern China is especially noteworthy and many-faceted. First, he was highly versed and prolific in prose writing. His complete writings, flowing and lucid in style, are estimated to run to at least sixteen million characters. Liang appraised himself in the following manner:

> Liang never liked the ancient-style writing of the T'ung-ch'eng school. . . . He liberated himself from it and made it a rule to be plain, easy, expressive, and fluent of communication. He interlarded his writings with colloquialisms, verses, and foreign expressions fairly frequently, letting his pen flow freely and without restraint. Scholars hastened to imitate his style and it became known as the New Style Writing. . . . Nevertheless, his style had a clear structure and the flow of his pen was often passionate, with a rare magical kind of power for the reader.[52]

Liang's style of writing was in vogue both during his own lifetime and for many years after his death. His style is exceptionally effective as an instrument for either introducing Western ideas or refuting iconoclastic persuasions, two purposes that would have been most difficult if not impossible, to achieve had he written in the style of someone such as Chang Ping-lin. Furthermore, Liang's style, labeled as semiliterary, was the intermediate link between classical writing and vernacular writing. His development of this new style may even have served as a catalyst for the literary revolution, which served to popularize education, introduce more easily Western ideas, and which culminated in an entirely new intellectual period.

Chang P'eng-yuan has this to say about the influence of Liang's political writings:

> Without Liang's essays the Manchus would not have split and fought chaotically among themselves; the Chinese people would not have known the importance of popular sovereignty; the Han people [i.e., Chinese] would not have realized the crimes of cruelty and suppression at the hands of the Manchus for more than two hundred years; and the storm of anti-Manchu feeling could not have arisen so soon. . . . In the study of history, although facts say that the Manchu throne was overthrown by the revolutionary armies, it is not an exaggeration to say that it was overthrown by the pen of Liang Ch'i-ch'ao.[53]

Liang's contribution to the mind of China lies in his introduction of Western thinkers, Western theories, and Western ideas, with the result that the thinking of a whole generation was drastically changed. He had introduced to the Chinese people such thinkers as Bacon, Descartes, Darwin, Montesquieu, Bentham, Benjamin Kidd, Aristotle, Adam Smith, Kant, Rousseau, and their theories. By influencing Chinese moral values, Liang attempted to change the traditional Chinese man into a new citizen—from a passive, peaceful, conservative, individual-oriented man into a strong, aggressive, militaristic, adventurous, political-minded, and group-oriented man. He believed firmly in Darwin's survival of the fittest theory and never tired of warning people that the weak will be devoured by the strong—a stark principle which cannot be escaped or evaded in any aspect of life. To defend this principle, especially the survival of the fittest in the struggle for existence, Liang seldom blamed imperialist aggression, but constantly urged the Chinese to change their ways and attitudes and to become strong in order to survive.

One theory in particular which seems to have had a profound influence in China was his theory of revolution, although he himself later retracted it. His pen was so influential that even when Liang himself changed his mind he could not shake the beliefs of those who were originally convinced by him. His theory and justification of a total revolution in China was so passionately formulated and so persuasive that it swayed and captured the young minds of his time and probably many young minds after him.[54] How many communist revolutionaries, devoted persistently to the Communist cause, were either directly or indirectly influenced by Liang's appeals we cannot say. Nor can we exclude the possibly equally profound influence on those who persistently followed the course of gradualism as their guide to political action.

Among the prominent men who were directly and profoundly influenced by Liang were Carsun Chang, who took Liang as his mentor, and Mao Tse-tung who at a young age memorized Liang's works and was impregnated with his ideas.

Certain major events under Mao's leadership bore a striking resemblance to Liang's passionately held ideas. While Liang advocated total revolution and the utter destruction of the existing traditional political system, the old scholarship of the past several thousand years, and the millions of corrupt scholars, Mao in fact carried out a violent and sweeping revolution against the existing social structure, which included the total destruction of the political system, feudalism, scholarship, and both the traditional as well as new bourgeois intellectual thought. In addition, Mao engaged in ruthless suppression and reformation of intellectuals, and was especially savage in his persecution of intellectuals during the Cultural Revolution. Again, while Liang advocated the creation of a new citizenry in China, with new moral values replacing old ones to be destroyed, Mao vowed to create the communist man in accordance with communist ethics, and in defiance of all traditional ethics.

Whether Mao's unprecedented, bold, and destructive deeds were completely based on Liang's ideas is a question which cannot be definitely answered due to inconclusive evidence.

Carson Chang, who was intimately acquainted with Liang and appreciated his true intentions, had taken on Liang's later beliefs in democracy and gradual socialism. Chang thus devoted his whole life to trying to bring about these ideals.

On the whole, Liang was a liberal and did not hold any belief dogmatically. He changed his opinions from time to time, sometimes quite dramatically, a tendency which many people considered a shortcoming and which often completely exasperated his followers and sympathizers. But his liberal attitude and scientific inclinations should neither be ignored nor belittled for he held his views at a time when conservatism prevailed. A short passage from Bertrand Russell may well illustrate Liang's position:

> The essence of the Liberal Outlook lies not in what opinions are held, but in how they are held: instead of being held dogmatically, they are held tentatively, and

with a consciousness that new evidence may at any moment lead to their abandonment. . . .Science is empirical, tentative, and undogmatic; all immutable dogma is unscientific. The scientific outlook, accordingly, is the intellectual counterpart of what is, in the practical sphere, the outlook of Liberalism.[55]

Liang modestly described himself as a person with too few fixed ideas while his master, K'ang Yu-wei, had too many fixed ideas. That is, Liang was never dogmatic in the way he managed his affairs or in his methods of study. Of himself, Liang has this to say:

The point of greatest contrast between Liang and K'ang is that the latter had too many fixed ideas and the former too few, and this was reflected in the way they managed their affairs as well as their methods of study. K'ang often said, "My knowledge was complete by the time I was thirty; from that point on I made no more progress, as indeed there was no need to advance." Liang was different, feeling always that his knowledge was still incomplete and worrying that it might never be complete. For several decades he wandered about seeking [knowledge] daily. Consequently, K'ang's knowledge now can be discussed definitely, whereas Liang's cannot.[56]

Liang, for instance, originally supported and subscribed to K'ang's theories on the forged classics and on institutional reforms. Finding these unsatisfactory in reasoning, Liang abandoned his beliefs and "after thirty. . .never again spoke of the 'forged classics' nor did he refer very often to 'institutional reforms.'"[57] Furthermore, Liang, in his later years, did not adhere closely to K'ang's theory of the Three Epochs. The most dramatic change in his political thought is, of course, his shift from the advocacy of destructive revolution to constitutional monarchy. Liang was liberal, undogmatic, and tolerant with men whose opinions differed from his own, and he had the scientific spirit of seeking continually for the truth rather than fixing his mind on any dogma without being willing to change. Moreover, Liang constantly tried to improve himself and to progress. Liang never stopped learning as his master had.

Concerning Liang's personality, the late Professor Joseph Levenson presented an impressive theory in *Liang Ch'i-ch'ao and the Mind of Modern China,* first published in 1953. Nineteen years later, Philip Huang, in *Liang Ch'i-ch'ao and Modern Chinese Liberalism,* made known his own observations. As a graduate student, Huang had been dazzled by the neatness of Levenson's ideas and by the sparkling brilliance of this book. Levenson's theory was that Liang was emotionally committed to the East and intellectually to the West. Liang was described as a man who continually struggled between his emotions and his intellect, or, in the words of Levenson, he was trying "to smother the conflict between history and values." Huang suspected that this hypothesis was too neat and simple. Indeed, when Huang read Liang's writings, he could detect no such conflict and, instead, a completely different picture emerged.[58] Seeing no struggle between Liang's emotion and his intellect, I find him a man incessantly seeking for truth and improvement.

On the whole, Liang's influence in shaping the minds of the Chinese of his time and afterwards has been paramount, and his selfless sincerity and devotion to the cultural and political renovation of China without thought for personal ambition or power is to be highly esteemed.

Notes

1 This biography is mainly based on Ting Wen-chiang, *Liang Jen-kung hsien-sheng nien-p'u ch'ang-pien ch'u-kao* (Taipei: Shih-chieh shu-chü, 1958).

2 For details of Sun's attempt to approach Liang and of their final break, see Chang P'eng-yuan, *Liang Ch'i-ch'ao yü Ch'ing-chi ko-ming* (Taipei: Academia Sinica, 1964), pp. 119–36.

3 For a statistical tabulation of the publication and circulation of several periodicals edited by Liang, see Chang P'eng-yuan, p. 320.

4 See note 4, chapter 1.

5 L.T. Chen, trans., *History of Chinese Political Thought in the Early Tsin Period* (London: Kegan Paul, 1930).

6 Liang Ch'i-ch'ao, *Ch'ing-tai hsueh-shu kai-lun* (Shanghai: Commercial, 1921), p. 140. Henceforth all translations from *Ch'ing-tai* are based on Hsü's *Intellectual Trends*.

7 Liang, *Ch'ing-tai*, p. 140.

8 For a detailed account of these radical views, see Chang P'eng-yuan, pp. 47–116.

9 Liang, *Ch'ing-tai*, pp. 142–43.

10 Liang Ch'i-ch'ao, "Cheng-chih hsueh ta-chia Po-lun-chih-li chih hsueh-shuo," in Lin Chih-chün, comp. *Yin-ping shih ho-chi* (Shanghai: Chung-hua, 1936), pt. 1, vol. 5, bk. 13, pp. 77–81; hereafter referred to as *YPSHC*.

11 Ibid., p. 85.

12 For details of this argument, see Liang, "Chung-kuo li-shih shang ko-ming chih yen-chiu," *YPSHC*, pt. 1, vol. 5, bk. 15, pp. 31–41.

13 Liang, "Shen-lun chung-tsu ko-ming yü cheng-chih ko-ming chih te-shih," *YPSHC*, pt. 1, vol. 7, bk. 19, p. 4.

14 Liang, "K'ai-ming chuan-chih lun," *YPSHC*, pt. 1, vol. 6, bk. 17, p. 75.

15 Ibid., pp. 77–83.

16 Ting, pp. 458–59. On the problem of the revolutionary line of the Kuomintang and the K'ang-Liang constitutional movement there was a heated polemic between the two sides from 1905 to 1907. The articles appeared in Liang's magazine *Hsin-min ts'ung-pao* and the Kuomintang-published *Min-pao*. For a tabulation of the articles with their issue numbers and central themes, see Chang P'eng-yuan, pp. 211–20.

17 Liang, "Cheng-chih shang chih tui-k'ang li," *YPSHC*, pt. 1, vol. 11, bk. 30, pp. 29–32.

18 Liang, "Hsin-min shuo," *YPSHC*, pt. 2, vol. 3, bk. 4, p. 1 ff.

19 "The Text of Confucius," *The Great Learning*, ch. 1.

20 Liang, "Shih hsin-min chih-i," *YPSHC*, pt. 2, vol. 3, bk. 4, p. 5.

21 Ibid., p. 7.

22 Ibid.

23 Liang, "Lun Kung-te," *YPSHC*, pt. 2, vol. 3, bk. 4, pp. 12–16.

24 *The Confucian Analects*, bk. 3, ch. 19.

25 Liang, "Lun Szu-te," *YPSHC*, pt. 2, vol. 3, bk. 4, pp. 118–42.

26 Liang, "Lun Kuo-chia szu-hsiang," *YPSHC*, pt. 2, vol. 3, bk. 4, pp. 16–22.

27 Liang, "Lun chin-ch'ü mao-hsien," *YPSHC*, pt. 2, vol. 3, bk. 4, pp. 23–29.

28 *The Works of Mencius*, in James Legge, trans., *The Chinese Classics*, vols. 1 and 2 (Reprint, Taipei: Wen-chi ch'u-pan she, 1970), bk. 2, pt. 1, ch. 2, secs. 11-16.

29 Confucius said of two kinds of people, the *k'uang* and the *chüan*, meaning the ardent and the cautious: the ardent are aggressive, the cautious are reserved. "The ardent will advance and lay hold of the truth; the cautiously-decided will keep themselves from what is wrong." *Confucian Analects*, bk. 13, ch. 21.

30 Liang, "Lun ch'üan-li szu-hsiang," *YPSHC*, pt. 2, vol. 3, bk. 4, pp. 31–40.

31 *The Doctrine of the Mean*, ch. 10, sec. 3.

[32] *The Confucian Analects,* trans. Arthur Waley (New York: Vintage Books, 1938), bk. 13, ch. 5.

[33] Liang's quotation is not complete. For the complete questions and answers regarding this point, see *Confucian Analects,* bk. 14, ch. 37, secs. 1–3.

[34] Liang, "Lun tzu-yu," *YPSHC,* pt. 2, vol. 3, bk. 4, pp. 40–50.

[35] For instance, Chang Hao comments: "It is interesting that in discussing liberal ideals he drew upon the writings of John Stuart Mill and Rousseau without being aware of the significant differences which separate the English and French concepts of Liberty." Chang Hao, *Liang Ch'i-ch'ao and Intellectual Transition in China 1890–1907* (Cambridge: Harvard University Press, 1971), pp. 190–91. For Philip Huang's discussion of Liang's concept of liberty, see his *Liang Ch'i-ch'ao and Modern Chinese Liberalism* (Seattle: University of Washington Press, 1972), ch. 4 (see especially pp. 69–70.)

[36] This section is based on "Lun chin-pu," *YPSHC,* pt. 2, vol. 3, bk. 4, pp. 55–68.

[37] Liang, "Lun sheng-li fen-li," *YPSHC,* pt. 2, vol. 3, bk. 4, pp. 80–96.

[38] Confucius, *The Great Learning,* ch. 10, sec. 6.

[39] Ibid., sec. 19.

[40] "Some labor with their minds and some labor with their strength. Those who labor with their minds, govern others; those who labor with their strength are governed by others. Those who are governed by others support them; those who govern others are supported by them. This is a principle universally recognized." *Mencius,* bk. 3, pt. 1, ch. 4, sec. 6.

[41] Liang, "Lun cheng-chih neng-li," *YPSHC,* pt. 2, vol. 3, bk. 4, pp. 149–62.

[42] Liang, "Lun tzu-chih," *YPSHC,* pt. 2, vol. 3, bk. 4, pp. 50–4.

[43] Liang, "Lun tzu-tsun," *YPSHC,* pt. 2, vol. 3, bk. 4, pp. 68–76.

[44] Liang, "Lun ho-ch'ün," *YPSHC,* pt. 2, vol. 3, bk. 4, pp. 76–80.

[45] Liang, "Lun i-li," *YPSHC,* pt. 2, vol. 3, bk. 4, pp.96–104.

[46] Liang, "Lun i-wu szu-hsiang," *YPSHC,* pt. 2, vol. 3, bk. 4, Ibid., pp. 104–8.

[47] Liang, "Lun shang-wu," *YPSHC,* pt.2, vol. 3, bk. 4, pp. 108–18.

[48] Liang, "K'ai-ming chuan-chih lun." *YPSHC,* pt. 1, vol. 6, bk. 17, pp. 73–4. See also "Po mou-pao chih t'u-ti kuo-yu lun," *YPSHC,* pt. 1, vol. 6, bk. 18, pp. 1–55. The "certain newspaper" Liang referred to is the *Min-pao.* Liang's article gives thirty-three reasons from financial and economic standpoints to show the "fallacies" of the land nationalization theory. Chang P'eng-yuan says this article gives thirty-nine reasons, but I have been able to detect only thirty-three in my copy. See Chang P'eng-yuan, p. 220.

[49] Liang, "Fu Chang Tung-sun shu lun she-hui chu-i yun-tung," *YPSHC,* pt. 1, vol. 13, bk. 36, pp. 1–12.

[50] Liang, "Ou-yu hsin-ying lu," *YPSHC,* pt. 2, vol. 5, bk. 23, pp. 10–12.

[51] Ibid., pp. 35–8.

[52] Liang, *Ch'ing-tai,* p. 142.

[53] Chang P'eng-yuan, p. 85.

[54] Hu Shih says that Liang's idea, at that time, was the most radical, his stand the clearest, his influence the most profound. Liang unequivocally raised the revolutionary slogan of utter destruction although he later desisted from promoting it. Nevertheless, many young men marched on and would not retreat. Hu Shih, *Szu-shih tzu-shu* (Shanghai: Ya-tung t'u-shu kuan, 1933), pp. 103–4.

[55] Bertrand Russell, *Unpopular Essays* (New York: Simon and Schuster, 1962), pp. 15–16.

[56] Liang, *Ch'ing-tai,* p. 149.

[57] Ibid., p. 143.

[58] Huang, pp. 203–4.

3
Sun Yat-sen (1866–1925)

Biography

Sun Yat-sen,[1] born in 1866 of a poor farmer family in Ts'ui-heng Village, Hsiang-shan *Hsien,* Canton Province, was raised during the time of China's repeated defeats and humiliations at the hands of foreign powers. At the age of seven (1872), Sun began his education in a private tutoring school and in the following years (1873–78) he studied the Four Books and Five Classics. At eleven (1876) he heard legendary stories about the leaders of the T'ai-p'ing Rebellion vividly related by an old T'ai-p'ing soldier, and began to form revolutionary ambitions in his young heart. In 1878 Sun aspired to study what was then known as New Learning, influenced greatly by Western ideals. A year later he accompanied his brother to Honolulu where he attended missionary schools operated by British and American churches. After a brief sojourn in Canton, he went to Hong Kong to study and, in 1885, was baptised a Christian in the Congregationalist Church there. In the following year, at the age of 21, he again returned to Canton and enrolled as a student in the Canton Hospital. In 1887, Sun went back to Hong Kong to pursue further his medical studies, this time at the College of Medicine for Chinese, where he was graduated at the age of 27 in 1892.

Earlier, in 1885, when China was defeated in the Sino-French War, Sun Yat-sen had resolved to devote himself to the revolutionary cause with the aim of overthrowing the Manchu regime and establishing a republic. Meanwhile, his medical practice became merely a camouflage for contacting people in order to carry on his revolutionary activities. In 1894, he founded the Hsing-Chung hui, and in 1905, the T'ung-men hui, the prototypes of the Kuomintang. The Kuomintang was officially founded in 1912. Sun's basic programs for China's reconstruction are embodied in his famous Three Principles of the People. Though the basic concepts were first promulgated in the *Min-pao* in 1905, his complete book on the Three Principles of the People was not completed and published until 1914. He eventually did overthrow the last Manchu ruler, and served as the provisional president of the new republic of 1912. He died of cancer in Peking on 11 March 1925. In the following year, the Northern Expedition was launched under the leadership of Chiang Kai-shek. In 1927, upon the initial success of the Northern Expedition, the Nationalist government was founded in Nanking, and in 1940, officially gloried Sun Yat-sen the Father of the Republic.

Sun's Three Principles

Like other programs for China's reconstruction in recent times, Sun Yat-sen's program was aimed at saving China from national extinction. He therefore defined his Three Principles of the People as an *ism* to save the country; a literal rendering of the *ism* is National Salvationism.[2] The Three Principles are literally, first, *people's racialism;* second, *people's powerism;* and third, *people's livelihoodism.* These terms are generally known in English respectively as *nationalism, democracy,* and *people's livelihood* or *socialism.* This order of priority is in accordance with the lectures on the Three Principles Sun delivered in 1924, but in his *Chien-kuo ta-kang* (Fundamentals of national reconstruction), the order is reversed: people's livelihood is placed first and nationalism last, indicating that livelihood is of the foremost importance in the work of national reconstruction.[3]

Nationalism

Sun Yat-sen's first principle is "nationalism," which expounds the idea that nation and state in China merge into a unity. However, he pointed out that in actuality the Chinese people have been united in a great sense of worship of and loyalty to the family and clan, but that their unity stopped short at the clan level and scarcely extended to the nation. Still, he felt the conditions of China were most suitable for fostering the identity of nationalism with state-nationalism *(kuo-tsu chu-i).* For in other countries, a state may consist of a number of nations or one nation scattered among various states. But in China the overwhelming majority of the 400,000,000 Chinese belonged to the Han race. There were also several million Mongolians, more than a million Manchus, two million Tibetans, and more than a million Mohammedan Turks, totalling in all no more than ten million in minorities. Thus, the Chinese state was essentially one nation comprised of the Han race that has a common blood, language, religion and customs. With such a tremendous population and a continuous culture of more than four thousand years, Sun Yat-sen saw no reason why China could not emerge as a first rank country. He lamented the fact that due to the absence of a sense of national spirit *(min-tsu ching-shen),* she was at that time the weakest and poorest country in the world and had sunk to the lowest international position imaginable. Sun was appalled at the state of affairs and feared that China might be in danger of obliteration as a state and as a nation. To avert a possible impending disaster Sun sought to promote nationalism by arousing in the Chinese people a sense of national spirit.[4]

Sun's first step was to determine what factors caused China to lose her sense of national spirit. He maintained that this deplorable situation had already persisted for centuries. The apathy was attributable to two causes, which were most detrimental. First, the Ch'ing Dynasty engaged in a deliberate policy of destroying China's national spirit through the corruption of scholars and ruthless repression of any attempt at Chinese restoration. People were convinced that the Manchu domination was no more than a change of dynasties, having no bearing on the question of nationality. Second, the concept of "one world"—*T'ien-hsia*—had hampered the Chinese in giving due attention to the question of national unity.[5] Sun was correct in asserting that the Chinese people had lost their vigilance against the Manchus as a foreign people; but, this should not be generalized to mean that they had lost their national spirit completely. The Boxer Rebellion during his lifetime, and the War of Resistance against the Japanese invasion after his death, have fully demonstrated the passionate nationalism with which the Chinese people will oppose foreign encroachment. Sun's famous metaphor to depict China and the Chinese people as "a sheet of loose sand" seems appropriate.[6]

However, despite Sun's analysis, most observers have believed that China's deficiency was not in nationalism but rather the necessary discipline and ability to organize the building of a modern state. And this, incidentally, is what the Chinese Communists of the present day have achieved with remarkable success, though under a different ideology.

Logically, then, Sun Yat-sen's next problem was to find means to revive the national spirit: "that possession which enables a state to aspire to progress and a nation to perpetuate its existence."[7] The first step in Sun's proposal was to awaken the four hundred million Chinese to the fact that China's existence was in such great peril that as a country and a people they were face-to-face with the tragic possibility of perishing. This grave situation was, according to Sun's analysis, brought about by three threatening forces: a decrease in the population, plus political and economic aggression by foreign powers.[8] The first threatening force, a problem of demography, has been proven groundless by the fact that the Chinese population has never decreased since his warning, but, on the contrary, there has been a population explosion in recent years. The remaining two forces did prove threatening. As a result of external economic and political pressures, China had sunk to the level of a subcolony—a position even worse than that of a colony under a single imperialist country, as was the case for example of Korea under Japan or Indochina under France. For China had become the colony of not just one, but a number of, imperialist countries. The second step of Sun's proposal was to organize the millions of small units, such as the family and clan, into one strong national unit. Once unity was secured and the national spirit thereby aroused, efforts were to be made to restore China's past national position, a position based on culture, strength, and prosperity.[9]

Sun Yat-sen envisioned four cardinal tasks as necessary for restoration of China's national status. The first task, he said, is the restoration of China's national virtues, commonly known as the eight virtues. They are loyalty and filial devotion *(chung-hsiao)*, kindness and love *(jen-ai)*, faithfulness and justice *(hsin-i)*, harmony and peace *(Ho-p'ing)*.[10]

The second task is to restore China's knowledge or learning through what Sun

Yat-sen referred to as an excellent political philosophy. The principles of this philosophy which were laid down in the Confucian classic *The Great Learning (Ta-hsueh)* are as follows: search into the nature of things, expand the boundaries of knowledge, make the purpose sincere, regulate the mind, cultivate personal virtue, rule the family, govern the state, and pacify the world.[11] I shall refer to these two tasks later for a fuller discussion.

The third task necessary for the restoration of China's national position concerns the revival of China's ability for invention. China had in the past invented the compass, wood-block printing, gun powder; she also made contributions to the development of tea cultivation, silk production, the arched doorway, and the suspension bridge, among other things.[12]

The fourth and last task, equally indispensable, was that of learning the strong points of the West with a view to keeping abreast of the Western powers in every important respect.[13]

Sun Yat-sen's program for nationalism consisted of different schemes of action to correspond to various stages of development so he could cope with a particular situation as it arose. In the initial stage, from the start of revolutionary activities to 1911, the emphasis was laid solely on the overthrow of the Manchu regime. After the fall of the Manchus and the establishment of the Republic, Sun promoted the idea of a republic made up of the five nationalities—Han, Manchu, Mongolian, Mohammedan, and Tibetan—on equal standing. Then, from the end of World War I until his death he advocated a policy of national autonomy free from foreign rule. He devoted himself to combating imperialism in an effort to cast off the yoke of foreign oppression, with a view to attaining for China liberty and equality. Indeed these two goals, liberty and equality, were explicitly stated in his last will and testament as the supreme cause to which his forty years of revolutionary activity had been dedicated.[14]

In this connection, Sun's highest ideal and ultimate goal was the *ta-t'ung* or one-world ideal. This was a Confucian utopia generally known as Great Harmony or Great Unity, of which nationalism was only a passing phase, to be replaced ultimately by universal brotherhood.[15] For a time, however, Sun opposed the deceptive cosmopolitanism *(shih-chieh chu-i)* advocated by the Western powers, rejecting it on the grounds that it was no more than a plot to obstruct China in her struggle for independence. At the same time he warned the so-called new youth, who opposed nationalism and who had been bewitched by the beautiful ideal of cosmopolitanism, that it was an impractical doctrine for an oppressed people to follow at that time.[16]

Democracy

Politics is known as *cheng-chih* in Chinese. For Sun Yat-sen *cheng* meant the affairs of the multitude, and *chih* meant management or control. Thus, politics is defined as the management or control of the affairs of the multitude. Political power or *cheng-ch'üan* is therefore the power which manages or controls the affairs of the multitude. Management or control by the people is called the people's power or *min-ch'üan*. The word *min* or *jen-min* corresponding to "people" was defined by Sun as a unified and organized body of men.[17] It is obvious this does not carry the class connotation characteristic of communist theory. In Chinese minds, people's power is generally construed to mean the exercise of democracy, because the Chinese conceive of democracy as a form of government in which the power of control rests in the hands of the people. Hereafter we will use the word democracy for Sun's *min-ch'üan* or people's power.

Politically, Sun Yat-sen divided history into three periods—theocracy, autocracy, and democracy—the last being the latest and best development in human history, where its progression is like the implacable torrents of the Yellow and Yangtze rivers.[18] There are two important concepts related to democracy which Sun borrowed from the West—liberty and equality. Sun noted that liberty was a foreign concept hitherto unknown to the Chinese. But he went on to argue that while China had no liberty in name, she possessed abundant liberty in fact. His theory was that because Europe had suffered a long period of cruel tyranny since the fall of the Roman Empire, Europeans keenly felt distress and, therefore, desperately fought for liberty. Whereas, in the case of China, for thousands of years the Chinese enjoyed an excess of individual liberty to the extent of becoming a sheet of loose sand, completely uncontrolled and unorganized. The end result was that the average Chinese, as opposed to the intellectuals who belonged to the New Thought movement, was not at all enthusiastic in the pursuit of liberty. But, all the same, the average Chinese welcomed the prospect of alleviating prolonged poverty and becoming individually prosperous as soon as the clarion call of *fa-t'sai* or "make a fortune" was sounded. Sun Yat-sen himself did not raise such a call, which is narrow in itself, because the Three Principles, providing for the well-being of the individual, cover the aim of making a fortune, while making a fortune does not cover the aims of the Three Principles.[19] Incidentally, one of the slogans during the early years of the Chinese Communist movement was *fa-chia chih-fu*, or, "make the family prosperous and attain prosperity."[20]

Sun Yat-sen urged the people to sacrifice their personal liberty in order to attain national liberty, by using revolutionary theory as a tool to cement the 400 million Chinese into a solid rock of unity so as to transform China's status of being a subcolony of imperialist powers into one of independence. In other words, liberty resides in the whole rather than in the constituent parts, a view which appears on the surface to have an authoritarian and even a totalitarian overtone. Sun Yat-sen compared, in principle, his nationalism to the concept of liberty of the French Revolution, but contrasted with it the fact that the former stands for national liberty while the latter stands for individual liberty.[21]

As for the concept of equality, Sun Yat-sen rejected Rousseau's theory, which was adopted by the American Declaration of Independence and the French Declaration of Human Rights, that men are created equal. For Sun, human beings were naturally endowed with unequal intellects that led to different levels of achievement. Equality is never heaven-born and any attempt to coerce equality upon society produces a false equality. In history, autocratic emperors are known to have imposed social inequality on societies to an unbearable extent; their actions are justified as having the sanction of divine right, but in reality are due to selfish interests. The theory of nature-bestowed equality, hailed by revolutionaries striving to overthrow despotism, differs from Sun's vision of true equality: a man-made political equality where every individual has an equal political standing at the outset. Then, one can build upon it and go as far as natural endowments of intelligence and ability permit. Sun Yat-sen considered as retrogressive the type of equality which exists only among the elite of a society and which represses those who wish to rise through intelligence and hard work. Ideally, the essence of equality lies in each individual doing his best to serve society and mankind.[22] The Chinese Communists stress a class concept when selecting, for instance, students for admission to colleges from proletarian families, or when appointing government officials by seriously considering their class origins. At the same time, they level down and check possible marked differences in social positions, as in the downgrading of the position of experts and university professors. These two tendencies are in an opposite direction to Sun's ideal. However, both Sun Yat-sen's and the Chinese Communists' appeal and insistence on serving society rather than striving for personal gain are consistent with the traditional Chinese emphasis on duties instead of rights as a high moral standard.

Believing that the democratic movement in Europe and America in the past two or three hundred years has culminated in a system of representative government with few achievements beyond universal suffrage and eligibility for office, and believing that the newly developed Soviet system of the "people's dictatorship," supposedly far more advanced than representative government, had as yet offered little information for conclusive judgment, Sun decided to seek a new and better form of democracy, one to suit the existing conditions of China.[23] Sun Yat-sen also detected a perennial contradiction between an all-powerful government and the lack of power on the people's part to check it. He claimed to have solved the problem by a unique contribution to political thought. This was his separation of the government's *ch'üan,* or sovereignty, and *neng,* or ability. He compared a government to an automobile, whose owner corresponds to the people, and whose hired chauffeur and mechanic are the governmental officials. The people have the right of ownership, but are not experts of know-how; the officials are able to perform certain functions such as driving and repair, but have no rights of ownership. The government is also likened to a machine of tremendous power where officials are merely experts or workmen hired by the people to operate the machine. As to the controversial problem of whether the government should be doing more or doing less, resulting in either being too powerful or too weak, Sun Yat-sen's answer was that the government should be omnipotent with a view to serving the myriad needs of the people, but should also be under the complete control of the people. The functions of government he called the administrative power *(chih-ch'üan),* and the people's control he called political power *(cheng-ch'üan)* or people's power *(min-ch'üan).*[24]

In the actual practice of democracy in China, Sun Yat-sen planned to allow the people four major political powers. They would enjoy the powers of suffrage, recall, initiative and referendum, giving them control of the five powers of the government, which are the judiciary, legislative, executive, examination and censorate. The whole organization, with two separate and independent branches, or *yuan,* specializing in examination and censorial activities but equal in standing to the judicial, legislative, and executive branches, is known as the Five Yuan system.[25] A *yuan* is equivalent to the office of one branch of power; for example the Legislative Yuan would be equivalent to the United States Congress.

A critic of Sun's Three Principles of the People, especially in regard to the distinction between sovereignty and power, was Carsun Chang. Chang has written:

> Dr. Sun's distinction between the sovereign power of people and the ruling power of the government is open to criticism. It is indeed difficult to follow him in his belief that the legislature should form part of the government in the same way as in the case of those Western constitutional systems in which the executive organ comes under the control of the legislative body. If the people's power is limited to suffrage, referendum, recall, and initiative, while the legislature has no power over the rise and fall of the cabinet and the selection of high officials, then the executive power of the government is out of reach of the influence of popular opinion and free from popular control. There are important tasks that legislatures must perform, such as declaring war and formulating the national budget, which can make or break a cabinet, so it is hard to justify Dr. Sun's dividing the sovereign power of the people from the ruling power of the government. Experience during the last twenty years has shown us that under such a division, the government has very often, through its executive organ and the dominant party (for example, the Central Executive Committee of the Kuomintang), dictated and imposed their policies upon an unwilling but powerless legislature, thereby making Dr. Sun's five-power theory of government meaningless, and militating against the creation of an actual working democracy.[26]

In the same vein, Carsun Chang comments that the five-power theory defies its own ends:

> Dr. Sun's five-power theory, placing the executive, the legislative, judicial, control, and examination powers and functions of the government on an equal basis, is a theory that is actually the heritage of absolute monarchy. . . . Dr. Sun succeeded in establishing a five-power government, but in the process he neglected the importance of popular, democratic control by the people over the government through their representatives in the legislature, and thus he managed to undermine the very democracy he wanted to see prevail.[27]

That China does not have democratic institutions as such, notably representative government through general election, does not mean that China lacks democratic ideals. Sun attributed the idea of the foundation of people's power to ancient Chinese sages. He enumerated the following as evidence: 1) Confucius said, "When the great course is pursued, the world will be for all."[28] Sun

Yat-sen interpreted this as an ideal of one world in which the people would rule. 2) "When speaking, he always made laudatory reference to Yao and Sun."[29] These two emperors were highly revered by Confucius and Mencius because they actually implemented and practiced people's power rather than sovereign's power. 3) Mencius said, "The people are the most important element in a nation; the spirits of the land and grain are the next; the sovereign is the lightest."[30] "Heaven sees according as my people see; heaven hears according as my people hear."[31] "I have heard of the cutting off of the fellow Chou, but I have not heard of the putting a sovereign to death, in this case."[32]

Such evidence demonstrates, Sun contended, that democratic ideals and aspirations have been operative in Chinese society, and are exemplified in the writings of China's ancient sages of two millennia ago respecting the people's welfare on the one hand and justifying a revolt by killing a tyrant on the other.

People's Livelihood

Sun Yat-sen's third principle is "people's livelihood." In his first lecture on this principle, he explicitly stated that the Principle of People's Livelihood is synonymous with socialism and communism.[33] This statement caused the Nationalist leaders, after their split with the Communists, and especially after the latter's victory on the mainland, to go to great lengths to explain the meaning of the remark. Actually, Sun Yat-sen used socialism and communism in an extremely loose fashion, categorizing them together as one ideal whose aim is a solution to social problems in the process of realizing a utopian society. Inasmuch as the Chinese Communists today have gone so far as to label the Soviet Communists as revisionists and at one time condemned Liu Shao-ch'i as a capitalist-roader, they can hardly claim Sun Yat-sen as a communist in any strict sense.

Socialism was viewed by Sun as the outcome of the industrial revolution which replaced human labor by machinery. This in turn resulted in mass unemployment as well as other intense miseries of the workers. These evils constituted serious social problems. In anticipating China's industrial revolution, Sun Yat-sen attempted to avoid these evils by preventive measures. His preference in using the old Chinese term—*people's livelihood*—rather than the term *socialism* is not without reason. First, Sun argued that the West had talked about socialism for decades but produced only conflicting theories without a consensus as to a solution of the problems involved. Second, among the socialists of different schools, Sun respected Marx above all others, dubbing him the sage of socialism though disagreeing with him on certain fundamental concepts. The materialistic interpretation of history is one of the essentials of Marxism. But for Sun Yat-sen it was the social problem, not the material forces as Marx maintained, which was the center of gravity of history. Subsistence is, in turn, the center of gravity of the social problem. The problem of subsistence is precisely the problem of people's livelihood. From this reasoning Sun finally concluded that the livelihood of the people is the center of gravity of social evolution and thus he again chose the term people's livelihood in preference to socialism or communism.[34] This interpretation of Sun Yat-sen is known by the nationalists as the "livelihood interpretation of history" *(min-sheng shih-kuan)* to contrast it to Marx's materialistic interpretation. Sun admitted parenthetically that this particular idea of his coincided with that of the American writer Maurice William.[35]

Having asserted that the struggle for subsistence was the cause for social progress, Sun further repudiated Marx's notion of class struggle as the driving force. His view is based on the four practices given credit for the economic progress of the West in modern times: social and industrial reforms, public ownership of transportation and communications, direct taxation, and socialized distribution. (William's words are: government activity in the distribution of consumable wealth.) Sun observed that none of these four improvements had been effected through class wars, but had been achieved by peaceful means. Their results, benefiting both the capitalist and the worker, demonstrate that social progress was effected by the harmony of the economic interests of the majority of the people. He concluded that class struggle was, therefore, a disease in the course of social development and that it erupted only when the people were unable to subsist. Hence, Sun Yat-sen called Marx a social pathologist rather than a social physiologist. In sum, Sun held that striving for existence was the law of social progress, and, therefore, it was the center of gravity of history; Marx's mistake of assuming class struggle to be the driving force of social progress lay in his mistaking the effect—class struggle—for the cause.[36]

In reference to the problem of livelihood, Sun proposed two measures: equalization of land ownership, and the regulation of capital.

Equalization of Land Ownership. Observing that the land problem was a great social evil in the West, especially after industrialization, and a problem as yet without satisfactory solution, Sun saw that preventive measures were essential for China. He was aware of the fact that, under the impact of the West, China's economy was in a state of cataclysm, resulting, among other social evils, in a serious land problem. One case in point was the sudden and tremendous increase of land value, as seen in the astronomical rise of land value in cities, especially in port cities like Canton and Shanghai. Sun did not favor the nationalization of land. Rather, his aim was to preserve private land ownership through a general declaration of land value, to be determined by the people, while at the same time removing the evil of unearned income. If an owner undervalued his property, the government reserved the right to buy it at the owner's declared price; if the land were overvalued, the government would accordingly exact a heavier tax on the property. The tax rate proposed by Sun amounted to one per cent of the land value, which of course was a tentative suggestion. Any income from increments of value beyond this general declaration was to go to the public, because it was the result of social progress and of industrial improvement.[37]

Regulation of Capital. Sun Yat-sen's view on the regulation of capital was to control capital that accumulated in the hands of a few individuals, thereby checking in advance the polarization of the rich and the poor. State capital was to be created by development of various industries, and by the national operation of communications, mines, and other large industries.[38] The chief goal of regulating capital, as Sun reinterpreted it in the Manifesto of the First Kuomintang Congress of 1924, was to render the private capitalist system incapable of totally controlling the livelihood of the people. His detailed plans for creating national capital are given in his *Industrial Plans,* or *Material Construction (Shih-yeh chi-hua),* or *(Wu-chi chien-she).* This outline for the physical construction of China may be considered the prototype of the first Five-Year Plan initiated in 1953 by the present Chinese Communist government.

Sun Yat-sen held that a new world of the Three Principles would be one in which it was the government's duty to provide adequately the four necessities of life—food, clothing, shelter, and means of transportation. If people were in want they had the right to demand these basic needs from the government.[39] The first and most important problem of the people's livelihood was the food problem. Its production depended on agriculture, which in turn was derived from the toil of peasants. Thus, the government should make laws to encourage peasants to strive for greater productivity, as well as to protect them from exploitation by landlords. However, the final and complete solution of the peasant problem lay in the realization of Sun's famous dictum, land to the tillers.[40] As for the ways of achieving this goal, Sun Yat-sen did not elaborate. But he did propose seven technical methods for increasing agricultural production: 1) machine cultivation, 2) use of fertilizers, 3) crop rotation, 4) eradication of pests, 5) food preservation, 6) improved means of transportation, and 7) protection against natural disasters.[41]

Sun Yat-sen in summarizing his Three Principles of the People compared them to Lincoln's famous motto: government of the people, by the people, and for the people. The ideal state under the Three Principles in Sun's phrasing is a state which belongs to all the people, a government that is controlled by all the people, and rights and benefits which can be enjoyed by all the people. In other words, it is not only a communization of properties, but also of all powers of the state. Here, Sun has said, at least implicitly, that the best that a communist regime could accomplish is the communization of properties, but the state power probably would be more centralized. When his ideal state is reached, Sun Yat-sen concluded, then the people will have reached the true realization of the Principle of People's Livelihood, which is also exactly the hope of the *Ta-t'ung* or One World of Confucius.[42]

The Sources of Sun's Thought

The sources of Sun's thought, as he himself acknowledged, are three: Chinese tradition, Western influence, and his own thinking.[43]

Chinese Tradition

In answer to the question of what his ideological foundation for the revolution was, raised by H. Maring, a representative of the Third International, on his first visit to Sun in 1921, Sun had this to say: "There is a continuous moral tradition in China beginning with the ancient sage-kings down to Confucius. . . . The foundation of my thought is simply a perpetuation of this tradition and an expansion upon it."[44] This revelation shows clearly that the basis of Sun's thought is to be found in orthodox Chinese tradition in Confucianism. It should be noted that one of the Confucian tenets is the rule of a state through virtue in preference to rule by law as advocated by the Legalists. Sun Yat-sen believed that the foundation and spring of life of a state and nation is morality. It was traditional ethics, Sun asserted, which enabled China to survive two foreign military conquests of the Mongols and Manchus, whose powerful military conquests only resulted in their own assimilation by the Chinese. Therefore, Sun Yat-sen believed that the only path to China's regeneration was through restoration of the time-honored virtues.[45]

The problem of the inheritance of traditional morality and of its desirability has been a controversial problem for the Chinese in modern times. Sun Yat-sen believed that the Chinese should preserve the old virtues in content while only changing the form as was necessary to meet the exigencies of the times. For instance, the traditional notion of personal loyalty to the Emperor should be reinterpreted to mean loyalty to the state and people, i.e., to China and her 400 million inhabitants.[46] Sun's appeal to restore China's traditional morality was diametrically opposed to the ideas of the radical intellectuals of the May Fourth movement who advocated the complete elimination of Confucian doctrines, calling them a syndrome of all evils in China.

This same problem once again emerged during the Cultural Revolution in communist China in 1966. It led to the liquidation of Wu Han, who was singled out and accused of being a representative of those who sought to revive the feudal and bourgeois morality in opposition to the revolutionary, proletarian morality of Mao Tse-tung. Actually, Wu Han's ideas were quite similar to those of Sun. The Maoists insist on the complete rejection of traditional morality and upon the substitution of a new proletarian morality.[47] The problem of China's moral legacy has been, and will remain for some time to come, a crucial problem in China's social reconstruction.

Sun ardently cherished the eight virtues which we have already mentioned. Among them he considered filial piety the most complete moral principle ever known. His praise of it also indicates an adherence to and a belief in the preservation of the Chinese family ideal without radical change. Yet another traditional virtue which Sun Yat-sen deemed splendid is the love of peace, a natural disposition of the Chinese. In individual relationships, it stresses "humility and deference" *(ch'ien-jang)* rather than the fighting and contention or aggressive self-assertion which he felt characterized Westerners. In the political field, the concept of peace has been regarded a basic principle by Confucianists and by nearly all other ancient Chinese thinkers. Mencius, in answering the question as to who can unite the divided China of the Warring States period, replied: "He who has no pleasure in killing men can so unite it."

This famous statement of Mencius has been regarded a fundamental goal and a guiding principle in governing the country.[48] Sun Yat-sen's passion for peace explains why he made no attempt at a catastrophic revolution in China of the Marxian type which inevitably ends in dictatorships. Such an attitude foreshadowed his foreign policy, but he was not long in power. We will leave off Sun's discussion of other virtues which he cherished equally well and move on to his fundamental beliefs in Chinese philosophy.

Though passionately desirous to learn from the West the better models for solutions to China's problems, Sun claimed that the West was superior to China only in its science-based material civilization. But in the wisdom of China, he emphasized, there is an excellent political philosophy of man's relationship to society, country, and world: a philosophy whose profundity and breadth have not been surpassed or equalled by the thinking of any Western statesman or political thinker. In this respect, therefore, even the West should learn from China. Such a political philosophy teaches the cultivation of the inner self and the ways to progress to the realization of a happy one-world. The contents of his philosophy consist of eight parts too involved to be discussed here.[49] However, in view of its importance, it is worthwhile to quote its original source from *The Great Learning:*

> The ancients who wished to illustrate illustrious virtue throughout the kingdom, first ordered well their own states. Wishing to order well their states, they first regulated their families. Wishing to regulate their families, they first cultivated their persons. Wishing to cultivate their persons, they first rectified their hearts. Wishing to rectify their hearts, they first sought to be sincere in their thoughts. Wishing to be sincere in their thoughts, they first extended to the utmost their knowledge. Such extension of knowledge lay in the investigation of things. Things being investigated, knowledge became complete. Their knowledge being complete, their thoughts were sincere. Their thoughts being sincere, their hearts were then rectified. Their hearts being rectified, their persons were cultivated. Their persons being cultivated, their families were regulated. Their families being regulated, their states were rightly governed. Their states being rightly governed, the whole kingdom was made tranquil and happy.[50]

Historical events show that there exists a relationship between politics and philosophy. The measures of practical politics of government are bound up with a belief in theoretical philosophy, as reflected in the relationship between Marxism and communist governments. Sun Yat-sen's ardent admiration and veneration of what he called the political philosophy of Confucius stems from his basic acceptance of Confucianism as a guiding philosophy for national reconstruction. Thus, Confucianism inevitably influenced the practical policies of his ideals.

Sun's highest ideal and ultimate goal was the Confucian *Ta-t'ung* world as outlined in "Li-Yun," a chapter of *Li Chi* or *Book of Propriety*. This famous treatise depicts a beautiful ideal world of perfect social and moral order, in which everyone lives in harmony and happiness. Sun deeply cherished this ideal, which is further evidence that his thought is rooted in ancient Chinese philosophy. Further, this utopia, as described above in the original text, is to be attained through natural and peaceful evolution. Following the same line of thought, Sun himself had not the least desire to bring about such a millennium by conquest; nor had he anything to do with concepts of creating world communism through world revolution.[51]

In short, Sun Yat-sen cherished the "shining of old China with greater luster"[52] as opposed to a sweeping denial of tradition. Sun did not consider the salvation of China a choice between her existence on the one hand and her traditional culture on the other, but believed that a certain amount of Westernization plus the revival and restoration of China's excellent tradition and wisdom would, in the end, save China politically and culturally.

Western influence

Western influence on Sun's thought is quite conspicuous.[53] Just as he frequently compared his Three Principles to Lincoln's famous motto, government of, by, and for the people,[54] so he likened his principles to the slogans of the French Revolution with nationalism corresponding to liberty, democracy to equality, and livelihood to fraternity.[55] Furthermore, his five-power constitution was evidently derived from the Western separation of the three powers,[56] and his land reform program from Henry George.[57] Sun's studies of different schools of socialism and investigation of Western political conditions plus contact with prominent Westerners all took place after his release following an arrest in London, October 1896. He acknowledged that he had completed the Three Principles at this time by adding the People's Livelihood to the first two.[58] His later views on nationalism were influenced by Woodrow Wilson.[59] Finally, the success of the Russian Revolution also greatly influenced and encouraged him.[60]

Sun's own thinking: Theory of Revolution

Philosophically, as we have seen, Sun Yat-sen's theories were based mainly on Chinese traditional thought with rather extensive borrowings from the West. However, being a revolutionary, he needed a theory of revolution in order to carry out his program, so he formulated one for which he claimed originality. It is his famous theory of knowledge, the doctrine of "difficult to know and easy to do" *(chih-nan hsing-i)*, which concerns the relationship between knowledge and action. In China there had existed two theories before Sun's time in regard to knowing and doing. First, the traditional and widespread belief, beginning with the Shang Dynasty, was that it is "easy to know but difficult to do."[61] Second, the great Ming Neo-Confucianist Wang Yang-ming founded the well-known doctrine of the inseparability of knowledge and practice, that is, knowing is at the same time an act of doing. To know and yet not to do is, in fact, not to know. Sun's new theory was, according to his own account, an answer to the criticisms of his own Party members who complained shortly after the downfall of the Manchu Dynasty that his projected programs were too idealistic and impractical, that they hindered the task of national reconstruction.[62] Taking the traditional belief of "easy to know and difficult to do" as a stubborn enemy of his revolutionary task, and deeming Wang Yang-ming's theory as uninvigorating to the people, Sun offered instead his famous dictum as a stimulus to overcome the psychological block and to spur on his followers to face fearlessly the anticipated difficulties.

Sun cited ten examples in such matters as food, money, architecture, shipbuilding, the Great Wall, the Grand Canal, electricity, chemistry, and the theory of evolution, offering them as evidence of this easy-to-do concept. Many tasks are performed without much conscious knowledge of the mechanics of the act. For instance, everybody partakes of food, but few really know the principles of food value or the chemistry of metabolism. Or, again, everybody spends money and yet it takes an economist to know the function of money as a medium of exchange. Sun concluded that if one knows a thing, one must be able to do it, and thus by extension, once a revolutionary program is laid down by the leader or theoretician, to put it into practice by the multitude is almost a matter of course. Difficulties are unavoidable, but they can be overcome because the most difficult aspect of revolution—knowledge—would have been solved and elucidated. The leader's relationship to the masses is similar to that of an inventor and the technician. Naturally, Sun's idea is subject to criticism when viewed as purely philosophical, but when seen in the context of a guide for action, one must give some credence to his insight.[63]

The development of this idea is now contained in a book entitled *Sun Wen Doctrine (Sun-Wen hsueh-shuo)* or *Psychological Construction* (1918), to distinguish it from his sister treatises *Democratic Procedures (Min-ch'üan ch'u-pu)* or *Social Construction* (1917), and *Industrial Plans (Shih-yeh chi-hua)* or *Material Construction* (1921). These three together form the *Programs for National Reconstruction (Chien-kuo fang-lueh)*.

In practical procedures, Sun mapped out his whole revolutionary process in three stages. 1) Military stage: the unification of the country by military force and propagation of the Three Principles. 2) Tutelage stage: the training of the people to exercise their political rights and guidance toward local self-control. And 3) Constitutional stage: the establishment of the Five Yuan, drafting and adoption of the constitution, opening of the People's Assembly, and the holding of a general election for the governmental offices.[64]

Communist Criticism

Ch'en Po-ta, the Chinese Communist theoretician, published a book about Sun Yat-sen during the War of Resistance against Japan (1937–1945), when there existed a united front between the Nationalist and Communist Parties. His is a polite criticism of Sun's Three Principles, as well as a reply to Sun's criticism of Marxist theory and practice as it pertained to the Chinese revolution.[65] In essence, Ch'en argues that Sun's thought is dualistic and contains contradictions within itself. It contains elements of both radicalism and inadequacy *(pu-tsu)*. In this respect it is characteristic of the awakening of the

Chinese nation. Thus we see reflected the revolution and conservatism of the petty bourgeoisie; and the activism and compromise of bourgeoisie. All these aspects have been manifested in China's history and are now concentrated in Sun's thought.[66]

In consequence, the Three Principles is a complex product of revolutionary ideals interwoven with compromise. In the Principle of Nationalism, for instance, Sun supports both "revolutionalism" and "national reformism" at the same time. In the Principle of Democracy, he espouses both radical bourgeois democracy and bourgeois compromise. In the Principle of Livelihood, he holds both revolutionary and compromising views: he is revolutionary when he is passionately sympathetic with the oppressed laboring masses and hostile to the exploiting system; and he is compromising when he takes a passive view with respect to the liberation struggles of the oppressed classes.[67] In sum, the contradiction between the Three Principles and the tenets of communism, in spite of some similarities, is basically an ideological one. The realization of the Three Principles, as Ch'en Po-ta perhaps rightly asserts, is to create objective conditions favorable to the development of capitalism rather than socialism or communism.[68] He praised Sun, however, as a great bourgeois democratic revolutionary, but reserved the epithet of great proletarian revolutionary for men such as Marx, Lenin, Engels, and Stalin. Ch'en is certain that Sun Yat-sen's principles and doctrines represent only the democratic ideals of the progressive bourgeoisie, while Marxism-Leninism represents the scientific communism of the proletariat.[69]

Basically then, Ch'en Po-ta's criticism avers that Sun's principles have a duality of both revolution and compromise, but that it is mainly deficient in radicalism. Ch'en's remarks are undoubtedly justified, for, as we stated before, Sun cherished the Mencian philosophy of pacificism, and shunned bloody revolution, even though he felt some of its tactics could be tolerated as a necessary evil only in the absence of an alternative, as was the case in overthrowing the Manchus. Further, he felt the sacrifice of lives in bringing about change was not to be lightly regarded and should be reduced to a minimum. Another important idea of Mencius to which Sun subscribed is that people can only be subdued by virtue and not by force.[70] This involves Mencius' dichotomy of the kingly way and the despotic way (wang-tao and pa-tao). For Sun, the surest way to bring about the success of the revolution was to convince the people that the Three Principles of the People were superior to military force.[71]

Outside the political arena, in social and economic reform, he advocated mild and gradual change, because to him there was no insoluble barrier or irreconcilable antagonism between what the communists call conflicting classes. Therefore, a catastrophic revolution was by no means inevitable. In Sun Yat-sen's program of land reform, he proposed the voluntary declaration of land value, fearing that if land were taken away by force, the landlord would revolt when the chance arose in order to reclaim his property.[72] Obviously this contradicted communist methods that are characterized by a blood affair of land redistribution, followed by a policy of repression to prevent the resurgence of the landlord class. In such a case it would be necessary to maintain proletarian dictatorship for a long time to come. Revolution invariably entails violence, but in hoping for a minimum of sacrifice and cherishing the philosophy of the kingly way as opposed to the despotic way, Sun Yat-sen naturally came to believe that the less revolution the better. This is why he envisioned a total operation combining political and social reforms, completing, as it were, China's revolution once and for all.[73] As soon as the revolution is completed, however, he anticipated a democratic form of government that would be peaceful and lasting. Within this framework he never dreamed of, and could not have favored, either the theory of the dictatorship of the proletariat or of permanent revolution advocated by the Chinese Communists.

The theme of Ch'en Po-ta's criticism of Sun follows essentially that of Lenin, who commented that Sun is greatly similar to the Russian Narodniks and represents the revolutionary bourgeoisie of the eighteenth century with certain petty bourgeois utopian and reactionary views.[74]

A final word about the relationship between the so-called new Three Principles of the People and the old Principles may be pertinent as raised by Mao Tse-tung. The first united front of the Nationalists and Communists was formed in 1924. The First National Congress of the Kuomintang adopted the historic manifesto in January of that year. The Communists claim that they aided the Kuomintang in drafting and revising the manifesto, together with the internal and external programs.[75] Mao insists that this manifesto provides the true interpretation of the Three Principles of the People, and that all others are false; the Three Principles so interpreted are the new, as opposed to the old, ones. What Mao refers to as the true and new embodies the three significant policies of alliance with Russia, cooperation with the Communist Party, and assistance to peasants and workers.[76] This attitude of Mao persisted. In 1956, on Sun Yat-sen's ninetieth birthday, Mao praised Sun's grandiose achievement in the development of his old Three Principles of the People into the new Three Principles of the People. Mao further added that the Communists completed the democratic revolution which Sun failed to complete, and in addition, developed it into a socialist revolution.[77] Mao's only supporting evidence is based on certain passages of the Manifesto of the First National Congress of the Kuomintang. Communist writers have continued to glorify the new interpretation of the Three Principles of the People, and have claimed credit for their epoch-making influence on Sun Yat-sen's thought.[78] Nevertheless, the fact that the phrase "three principles" per se appears neither in the Manifesto nor in the Three Principles of the People, the bible of the Kuomintang, leads some people to assume that the Kuomintang merely took the three policies as a kind of policy which is subject to change, but not as anything basic or permanent. From the inception of the united front, important Kuomintang members suspected that it was a Soviet-supported Trojan horse of the Communist Party, aimed at usurping the leadership of the Chinese revolution.

After all, the three policies reflected only temporary and tactical conditions for Kuomintang and Communist cooperation, not a change in the basic principle. Sun was not interested in Marxian ideology; what he wanted to learn from the Soviet Union was its method, organization and discipline in carrying out the revolution to a success.[79] Sun Yat-sen never abandoned his anti-Marxist stand in his Three Principles of the People. As Wilbur points out, Sun "made it clear repeatedly that he did not favor bolshevism for China and that he admired the Soviet Union because it treated China as an equal."[80] Sun categorically stated in his will that he was convinced his goal of revolution could only be attained by a thorough awakening of the people, or the masses *(min-chung)*, but he did not specify peasants and workers.

At the present, almost sixty years after the introduction of the three policies, the controversy arising from the difference between the old Three Principles of the People and the new Three Principles of the People makes little sense. Kuomintang cooperation with the Communist Party was a failed event of the past, and under current circumstances seems highly improbable. Alliance with the Soviet Union is out of the question; for decades communist China and the Soviet Union have been hostile to each other. The problem of assistance to peasants and workers does not constitute a point of contention. Communist China professes to be a dictatorship of the people under the leadership of the workers, with the alliance of the workers and peasants. Theoretically, at least, they are in the leadership position of the state. But the Nationalists in Taiwan claim that under their rule peasants and workers are far better off in material lives than those under Communist rule.

Summary

In evaluating Sun's personal career, we find that although he succeeded in the overthrow of the Manchu despotism that led to the establishment of a republic, he accomplished practically nothing in the republic with his programs for social reconstruction. He did not live long enough to realize his basic principles in democracy and in people's livelihood. Even in his lifetime, he had more failures than successes. It is for this reason that Martin Wilbur calls him a "frustrated patriot because most of his career was marked by discouragement in his efforts to achieve patriotic goals."[81]

In evaluating the achievements of the three principles we find that only Nationalism manifested tremendous power and produced magnificent results. The first time it exerted historic influence was in the overthrow of the Ch'ing dynasty during the period prior to the Republic. The people were united and motivated by a nationalist spirit to drive out the Manchus. The second time it exerted historic influence was during the War of Resistance against Japan. Again, the people were of one mind against the Japanese invasion. At various times, the nationalist tide had been channeled against imperialist invasions with great success. Under ordinary circumstances in China, racial issues are small problems because the minorities, who are few in number, live in their own areas peacefully. The Nationalist government, before 1949, failed in its pursuit of the Principle of Democracy, thus disappointing the intellectuals, who clamored for civil and democratic rights. In China it is the intellectuals who are the determining factor in the success or failure of a regime. The Nationalists also failed utterly in pursuing the Principle of Livelihood, leaving the majority of the people, especially the peasants, to live a life of abject poverty and consequently losing the confidence and support of the common people. Furthermore, as far as I can see, few Chinese have the kind of feverish faith for the Three Principles of the People that some devoted communists have for communism. Nor has there been the kind of intense opposition to the Three Principles of the People that has been exhibited by anticommunists toward communism. Thus, the fall of the Nationalist government in 1949 has much less to do with ideology of the Three Principles than with the corruption and inefficiency of the then Nationalist government. The corruption and inefficiency of the government resulted, to a great extent, in people's disillusionment and apathy toward the ideological principles preached by Sun Yat-sen.

But, over thirty years after the debacle of the Kuomintang on the mainland, a new picture has emerged in Taiwan with regard to the achievements of the Three Principles of the People. In his Principle of Democracy, Sun Yat-sen had planned to allow the people four major political powers—the powers of suffrage, recall, initiative and referendum. At present time, people in Taiwan enjoy suffrage, but not the other three. They can elect magistrates, mayors, representatives of the provincial assembly *(sheng i-hui),* city assembly *(shih i-hui),* and county assembly *(hsien i-hui),* but the offices of the governor, two mayors of Taipei and Kaohsiung are excepted. The election of the president is a formality, for there is never another candidate. On the central government level, the representatives of the People's Congress, of the Legislative Yuan, and of the Supervisory Yuan elected in 1947 still serve as representatives. Thus, some citizens are not satisfied with the present representative situation, and have demanded more political participation and abolition of martial law. Nevertheless, the election of officials and representatives at the provincial level reflects an improvement which did not exist on the mainland before 1949. We also find that there is more freedom of speech and publication as well as other civil liberties on Taiwan than on the present-day mainland.

Taiwan's achievement in the field of the people's livelihood is so extraordinary, some people call it a miracle. Among the developing nations, Taiwan has a very high personal per capita income, $2,360 (U.S.) annually in 1981.[82] Its economic growth has been rapid and steady in recent years. A. James Gregor argues that this economic development is accountable to Sun's ideology, especially his theory of equalization of land ownership and his advocacy of international economic cooperation. In the former, Gregor argues that "By equalization of land rights Sun and his followers meant governmental appropriation of 'unearned increments' in value rather than the formal abrogation of private land holdings. . . . Governmental acquisition of the 'unearned increment' resulting from the rise of land values that accompanied modernization would provide the capital for self-sustaining growth to the national economy. Such a program would not only preclude the concentration of wealth characteristic of the West; it would free inert capital, otherwise locked into land speculation, for employment in the more dynamic sectors of the economy."[83] In the latter, Gregor points out that Sun's denial of the dependency theory of classical Marxism and neo-Marxism, which claims that "less developed communities once lodged in international money market (i.e., 'capitalist') relations are necessarily condemned to slow growth and pandemic poverty."[84] But, "Unlike contemporary dependency theorists, Sun saw no inevitability of 'underdevelopment' for China as a consequence of involvement in the international market economy."[85] According to Gregor, Taiwan's remarkable success in international trade and in cooperation with foreign firms is due to Sun's ideology.

Equalization of land ownership and regulation of capital are the two measures of Sun's principle of livelihood of the people. In regard to the first measure, Taiwan has completed a land reform in rural areas, but nothing has been done with regard to the urban land where the phenomenon of sudden and tremendous increase of land value has occurred. In regard to the regulation of capital, very little has been done to control capital accumulating in the hands of a few individuals. However, at present the polarization between the rich and the poor is not acute enough to constitute a menace to social stability.

Recently the Chinese Communists have published some articles and books friendly to Sun Yat-sen and the Revolution of 1911. The historians on mainland China even opened a dialogue with the historians from Taiwan. The April 1982 annual meeting of the Association of Asian Studies presented an unprecedented panel in which historians from both communist China and Nationalist Taiwan participated. Each group of historians was headed by a ranking party member. The major argument or controversy between the two sides was on the nature of the 1911 Chinese Revolution. The Communist group insisted that it was a bourgeois revolution that was necessary to prepare the way for the later Communist revolution. This view obviously coincides with Mao's point of view, as we mentioned, that the communists have completed Sun's unfinished democratic revolution, i.e., bourgeois revolution, and have developed it into a socialist revolution. The Nationalist group insisted that the 1911 Revolution was a popular or nationalist struggle of people of all classes. We can see here the reflection of the basic ideological conflicts of a class approach versus a nationalist approach. It should be noted that these hisorians are not independent private academicians: their views represent the official lines of the People's Republic of China and the Republic of China. Although the controversy on the surface concerns the nature of the 1911 Revolution, in reality it involves the claims of the two conflicting governments to political legitimacy.

Finally, recent communist gestures in showing respect for Sun and the 1911 Revolution could be motivated by the fact that there exists a sizable number of Chinese who ideologically prefer Sun's mild and pacifist programs to the Communists' radical and violent programs. The Communists are realistic and shrewd politicians who would not do anything without a political purpose.

Notes

[1] Sun's biography is brief in comparison with the biographies of other thinkers in this book because there has been published a tremendous amount of reference materials on Sun's life, both in Chinese and English, so only highlights of his life are presented here. For more details see Chung-kuo kuo-min tang chung-yang tang-shih shih-liao pien-tsuan wei-yuan hui, ed., *Kuo-fu nien-p'u* (Taipei: Chung-hua min-kuo ko-chieh chi-nien kuo-fu pai-nien tan-ch'en ch'ou-pei wei-yuan hui [hereafter referred to as Chung-hua], 1965); Fu Ch'i-hsueh, *Kuo-fu Sun Chung-shan hsien-sheng chuan* (Taipei: Chung-hua, 1965); Shang Ming-hsuan, *Sun Chung-shan chuan* (Peking: Pei-ching ch'u-pan she, 1979); Kuang-tung sheng che-hsueh she-hui k'o-hsueh yen-chiu so li-shih yen-chiu shih (et al.), *Sun Chung-shan nien-p'u* (Chung-hua 1980); Harold Z. Schiffrin, *Sun Yat-sen and the Origins of the Chinese Revolution* (Berkeley and Los Angeles: University of California Press, 1968); John C. H. Wu, *Sun Yat-sen: The Man and His Ideas* (Taipei: Commercial, 1971); Lyon Sharmon, *Sun Yat-sen: His Life and its Meaning: A Critical Biography* (John Day, 1934; Stanford: Stanford University Press, 1968).

[2] Chung-kuo kuo-min tang chung-yang tang-shih shih-liao pien-tsuan wei-yuan hui, ed., *San-min chu-i,* in *Kuo-fu ch'üan-chi* (Taipei: Chung-hua, 1965), vol. 1, pt. 1, p. 2. Hereafter referred to as *Ch'üan-chi. San-min chu-i* is translated by Frank W. Price, *San Min Chu I* (Taipei: China Pub., n.d.).

[3] Sun, *Ch'üan-chi,* vol. 1, pt. 3, p. 369.

[4] Ibid., vol. 1, pt. 1, pp. 2–5.

[5] Ibid., pp. 20–24.

[6] This metaphor, which Sun frequently used, first appeared in Sun, *Ch'üan-chi,* vol. 1, pt. 1, p. 2. Sun attributed it to a comment made by foreigners.

[7] Ibid., p. 20.

[8] For details of Sun's argument on population see Sun, *Ch'üan-chi,* vol. 1, pt. 1, pp. 8–10; on political and economic aggression, see pp. 11–19.

[9] Ibid., p. 42.

[10] Ibid., pp. 43–45.

[11] Ibid., pp. 45–47.

[12] Ibid., pp. 47–48.

[13] Ibid., pp. 48–49.

[14] For an account of the historical development of Sun's nationalism, see Ts'ui Shu-ch'in, *San-min chu-i hsin-lun,* 5th ed. (Taipei: Commercial, 1960), pp. 1–9.

[15] Sun, *Ch'üan-chi,* vol. 1, pt. 1, p. 50.

[16] Ibid., p. 30.

[17] Ibid., p. 51. "Min-ch'üan" is translated as people's sovereignty by Price, p. 51.

[18] Sun, *Ch'üan-chi,* vol. 1, pt. 1, p. 59.

[19] Ibid., pp. 63–67.

[20] Caption of a poster on land reform, *Hsin-hua yueh-pao* 1, no. 3 (15 January 1950):819. Ch'ien Mu, in his *Chung-kuo szu-hsiang shih* (Taipei: Chung-hua wen-hua ch'u-pan shih-yeh wei-yuan hui, 1957), p. 219, comments that this unused slogan—"to make a fortune"—is the plainest and also the most penetrating remark made by Sun Yat-sen, and Ch'ien Mu regrets that Sun's followers never sincerely endeavored to help the Chinese people "make a fortune" and, thus, he feels that the Three Principles of the People deserved to fail.

[21] Sun, *Ch'üan-chi,* vol. 1, pt. 1, pp. 70–71.

[22] Ibid., pp. 72–74.

[23] Ibid., pp. 92–93.

[24] Ibid., pp. 98–99, 103–6, and 114–15.

[25] Ibid., pp. 119–20.

[26] Carsun Chang, *The Third Force in China* (New York: Bookman, 1952) p. 61.

[27] Ibid., pp. 61–62.

[28] "Li-yun," *Li-chi*. "T'ien-hsia wei-kung" has been a political slogan of the Kuomintang.

[29] *Mencius,* bk. 3, pt. 1, ch. 1, sec. 2. This reference is to Mencius, but Sun erroneously attributed it to Confucius, though the latter also highly praises the two sage emperors.

[30] Ibid., bk. 7, pt. 2, ch. 14, sec. 1.

[31] Ibid., bk. 5, pt. 1, ch. 5, sec. 8; quoted by Mencius from the "Great Declaration" in *Shu-ching* and not the words of Mencius.

[32] Ibid., bk. 1, pt. 2, ch. 8, secs. 1–3. For the full import of this quotation I quote the entire passage: "King Hsuan of Ch'i asked Mencius, 'Is it true that T'ang banished Chieh, and King Wu overthrew Chou?' Mencius replied, 'It is said so in the historical records.' The king said, 'May a subject commit regicide?' Mencius answered, 'He who outrages benevolence is called a robber, and he who outrages righteousness is called a ruffian. Robbers and ruffians are called mere fellows. I have heard of the killing of a mere fellow [i.e., tyrannicide], but I have not heard of regicide.'" (Legge's translation with revisions.) For Sun's enumeration of the quotations referred to in footnotes 28–32, see Sun, *Ch'üan-chi,* vol. 1, pt. 1, p. 56.

[33] Sun, *Ch'üan-chi,* vol. 1, pt. 1, p. 122.

[34] Ibid., pp. 123–128.

[35] Maurice William, *The Social Interpretation of History: A Refutation of the Marxian Economic Interpretation of History* (New York: Sotery, 1921). A check of William's book reveals two definitions of his thesis: (1) "The Social Interpretation of History is based upon the theory that man's effort to solve his problem of existence is the propelling motive force in history." William, *Social Interpretation,* Preface, ix. (2) "We now know that the propelling motive power behind all social progress is the quest for a solution to the problem of existence and that throughout history all social change has been registered in response to the social interests of the majority. The majority is usually formed through a combination of the powerful and the useful as against the remnants of the past and useless of the present. This is the social interpretation of history." William, *Social Interpretation,* p. 231. The four practices attributed to the economic progress in the West mentioned by Sun are exactly identical with those of William. William, *Social Interpretation,* p. 115. In his *Sun Yat-sen Versus Communism* (Baltimore: Williams and Wilkins, 1932), William claims that Sun's Principle of Livelihood was greatly influenced by his (William's) book—*The Social Interpretation of History*—and thus Sun changed his views from his previous lectures on nationalism and democracy, which are completely Marxian in approach. For a detailed discussion and a denial of this influence, see Ts'ui Shu-ch'in, *Hsin-lun,* pp. 279–93.

[36] Sun, *Ch'üan-chi,* vol. 1, pt. 1, pp. 128–32.

[37] Ibid., pp.144–45.

[38] Ibid., pp.146–47.

[39] Ibid., p. 160.

[40] Ibid., p. 152. Ironically, the Nationalist government on Taiwan began to implement a land-to-the-tiller policy in 1953, three years after the Communist announcement of their basic completion of land reform on the mainland. For a complete account of the Nationalist land reform program, see Chen Cheng, *Land Reform in Taiwan* (Taipei: China Pub., 1961). In the preface Chen explains apologetically for the failure to carry out Sun's ideal while on the mainland.

[41] Sun, *Ch'üan-chi,* vol. 1, pt. 1, pp. 153–159. For the recent efforts in improving agricultural techniques on Taiwan, see T. H. Shen, *The Sino-American Joint Commission on Rural Reconstruction, Twenty Years of Cooperation for Agricultural Development* (Ithaca, N.Y.: Cornell University Press, 1970).

[42] Sun, *Ch'üan-chi,* vol. 1, pt. 1, p. 148.

43 "Chung-kuo ko-ming shih," dated 29 January 1923; Sun, *Ch'üan-chi*, vol. 2, pt. 7, p. 90.

44 Fu Ch'i-hsueh, *Kuo-fu Sun Chung-shan hsien-sheng chuan* (Taipei, Chung-hua, 1965), p. 514.

45 Sun, *Ch'üan-chi*, vol. 1, pt. 1, p. 43. For an elaboration of the orthodox tradition of the Chinese thought mentioned by Sun, see Jen Cho-hsuan, *Chung-kuo wen-hua ti chu-liu* (Taipei: Hsin Chung-kuo ch'u-pan she, 1968).

46 Sun, *Ch'üan-chi*, vol. 1, pt. 1, pp. 43–44.

47 Wen-shun Chi, "The Great Proletarian Cultural Revolution in Ideological Perspective," *Asian Survey* 9, no. 8 (August 1969):568–70.

48 Sun, *Ch'üan-chi*, vol. 1, pt. 1, p. 45. For the quotation by Mencius, see *Mencius*, bk. 1, pt. 1, ch. 6, sec. 4.

49 Sun, *Ch'üan-chi*, vol. 1, pt. 1, p. 46.

50 Confucius, *The Great Learning*, ch. 1, secs. 4–5.

51 For an elaboration of Sun's one-world vision, see Jen Cho-hsuan, *Kuo-fu te ta-t'ung szu-hsiang* (Taipei: Pa-mi-erh shu-tien, 1969).

52 Sun, *Ch'üan-chi*, vol. 1, pt. 1, pp. 44–45.

53 For a complete compilation of Westerners whom Sun mentions in his works, together with his respective comments, see Lin Tzu-hsun, *Kuo-fu hsueh-shuo yü hsi-fang wen-hua* (Taipei: Chung-hua wen-hua ch'u-pan shih-yeh wei-yuan hui, 1953).

54 Sun, *Ch'üan-chi*, vol. 1, pt. 1, pp. 148, 207, 215, 222, 223; vol. 1, pt. 2, p. 7; vol. 1, pt. 3, p. 175.

55 Ibid., vol. 1, pt. 1, pp. 63, 70.

56 Ibid., p. 85.

57 Ibid., pp. 197, 218; vol. 1, pt. 3, p. 127.

58 For Sun's own account, see "Tzu-chuan" in *Kuo-fu ch'üan-chi* (Taipei: Chung-yang wen-wu kung-ying she, 1957), 1:35.

59 Sun, *Ch'üan-chi*, , vol. 1, pt. 1, p. 28.

60 Ibid., p. 29.

61 King Wu-ting (1324–1265 B.C.) in need of counsel on the duty and conduct of government, dreamed that God described such a man to him and when he was found made him Prime Minister and said to him: "Excellent! Your words, O Yue, should indeed be carried out in the conduct. If you were not so good in counsel, I should not have heard these things for my practice." Yue said, "It is not the knowing that is difficult, but the doing." James Legge, "The Books of Shang," in *The Shoo King, The Chinese Classics,* vol. 3, bk. 8, pt. 2, sec. 13, p. 258.

62 Sun, *Ch'üan-chi*, vol. 1, pt. 1, pp. 113–114.

63 For the text of the theory, see "Sun-wen hsueh-shuo" in *Ch'üan-chi*, vol. 1, pt. 3, p. 113–173. For a critical comment on the fallacy and danger of Sun's doctrine, see Hu Shih, "Chih-nan hsing i pu-i" in *Hsin-yueh yueh-k'an* 2, no. 4 (Shanghai, 1929):1–15. Ch'en Po-ta commends Sun's theory, hailing it as a revolutionary idea in the history of Chinese thought; nevertheless, he politely points out that to act is arduously difficult at times during a revolution, while cleverly expounding the Marxian viewpoint that theory and action are one. See Ch'en po-ta, "Kuan-yü chih-hsing wen-t'i te yen-chiu" in *Tsai wen-hua chen-hsien shang* (Chungking: Wen-hua shu-tien, 1939), pp. 103–117. For a defense and elaboration on Sun's theory, see Ho Lin, *Tang-tai Chung-kuo che-hsueh* (Nanking: Sheng-li ch'u-pan kung-szu, 1947), pp. 84–142.

64 For details, see Sun, "Chien-kuo ta-kang," *Ch'üan-chi*, vol. 1, pt. 3, pp. 369–371.

65 Ch'en Po-ta, *Lun Sun Chung-shan chu-i* (n.p., Tso-che ch'u-pan she, 1946). For the analytical and critical account of the Three Principles, see pages 77–134; for the answer to Sun Yat-sen's criticisms of Marxism, see pp. 144–61.

66 Ibid., p. 32.

67 Ibid., p. 133.

68 Ch'en Po-ta, "Lun kung-ch'an chu-i-che tui-yü San-min Chu-i kuan-hsi te chi-ko wen-t'i," in Mao Tse-tung, Ch'en Po-ta, et al., *Lun San-min chu-i* (Tung-pei shu-tien, n.p., n.d.), p. 63.

69 Ibid., p. 70.

70 *Mencius*, bk. 2, pt. 1, ch. 3. sec. 2.

71 Sun, "Ta-p'o chiu szu-hsiang yao-yung San-min chu-i," *Ch'üan-chi*, vol. 1, pt. 1, p. 233. See also Sun's lecture before a banquet honoring the representatives of the First Congress of the Kuomintang on 20 January 1924, entitled "Chu-i sheng-kuo wu-li," *Ch'üan-chi*, vol. 2, pt. 8, p. 220.

72 Sun, "Keng-che yu ch'i-t'ien," a lecture on 23 August 1924, in *Ch'üan-chi*, vol. 1, pt. 1, p. 247.

73 Sun, "Min-pao fa-k'an tz'u," 26 November 1905, in *Ch'üan-chi*, vol. 1, pt. 1, p. 173.

74 V. Lenin, "Democracy and Narodism in China," in *Collected Works* (Moscow: Foreign Languages, 1963), 18:103–169.

75 Hu Hua, *Chung-kuo hsin min-chu chu-i ko-ming shih* (Peking: Jen-min ch'u-pan she, 1951), p. 50.

76 Mao Tse-tung, "Hsin min-chu chu-i lun," *MTTHC*, 2:650-653.

77 Mao Tse-tung, "Chi-nien Sun Chung-shan hsien-sheng," *MTTHC*, 5:311.

78 One instance can be cited; "In this period, Sun Yat-sen, under the influence of the October Revolution and the May Fourth Movement, had accepted the assistance of the Soviet Union and the Chinese Communist Party, and reinterpreted the Three Principles of the People. Though the period is short, nevertheless it is the most brilliant and important moment of Sun's whole life." Wang Hsueh-hua, *Sun Chung-shan te che-hsueh szu-hsiang* (Shanghai: Jen-min ch'u-pan she, 1960), p. 10. Another instance: "The lectures of Sun Yat-sen on the Three Principles of the People expound on his revolutionary theories and programs, and, at the same time, reflect his improvement under the help of the Chinese Communist Party." Shang Ming-hsuan, *Sun Chung-shan chuan* (Peking: Pei-ching ch'u-pan she, 1979), pp. 136–37.

79 Sun, *Ch'üan-chi*, vol. 2, pt. 8, p. 186.

80 Martin Wilbur, *Sun Yat-sen: Frustrated Patriot* (New York: Columbia University, 1976), p. 287.

81 Ibid., p. 288.

82 Directorate General of Budget, Accounting & Statistics, Executive Yuan of the Republic of China, *Statistical Yearbook of the Republic of China 1982* (Taipei, 1983), p. 453.

83 A. James Gregor, with Maria Hsia Chang and Andrew B. Zimmerman, *Ideology and Development, Sun Yat-sen and the Economic History of Taiwan* (China Research Monograph, Institute of East Asian Studies, University of California, Berkeley, 1981), p. 12.

84 Ibid., p. vii.

85 Ibid., p. 17.

4
Hu Shih (1891–1962)

Biography

Hu Shih[1] was born in Shanghai on 17 December 1891 to parents who were natives of Chi-hsi, Anhwei province. There is a story behind Hu Shih's name, having to do with Charles Darwin. Hu Shih was originally named Hu Hung-hsing. One day he asked his brother to give him a courtesy name, so his brother suggested the character *Shih*. Added to the character *chih* (the second character in one's given name is one which members of one generation in a family have in common), Hu Shih's courtesy name would be Hu Shih-chih. By that time sociological theories popularly attributed to Darwin's theory of evolution were well known in China. The Chinese phrase for "survival of the fittest" is *shih-che sheng-ts'un;* the character *shih* corresponds to "fittest" in English. From 1910 Hu Shih formally adopted this new name. Such is an example of Western influence on the Chinese mind.

Hu Shih was the son of his father's third marriage, to a woman thirty years younger than he. His father's first wife had died shortly after their marriage in 1863 as a result of the T'ai-p'ing Rebellion. His second wife, who bore him three sons and three daughters, had died in 1878, and, because of difficult economic conditions and his intention of traveling abroad, he did not remarry again until 1889. Immediately after his third marriage, Hu's father went back to his official post, leaving his bride at home. Being only seventeen years old, living with a group of stepchildren, some of whom were older than she, the position of Hu Shih's mother was painfully difficult. Her plight was relieved, however, after her husband brought her to Shanghai to live with him. But Hu's father very soon afterwards, in 1892, was transferred to Taiwan. There Hu Shih and his mother joined him in the following year. Again, the family's time together was short. Because the Sino-Japanese War broke out in 1894, Hu Shih was brought back to the mainland by his mother in February 1895. Unfortunately, Hu Shih's father died of an illness in August of the same year. His will provided that Hu Shih be sent to school for a formal education.

Hu Shih's study of Chinese began before he was three years old. His mother, of peasant stock, was illiterate at the time of her marriage. Her husband had taught her Chinese characters by the traditional method—learning characters by using red paper cards. The same cards were used by Hu Shih's father to teach his son; his mother served as a teaching assistant. Before leaving Taiwan, Hu Shih's mother had learned close to one thousand characters and he about seven hundred.

In his home town, Hu Shih was taught by his uncle and later by his cousin, at the family school. For the next nine years (1895–1904) he studied only ancient texts, such as the Four Books and four of the Five Classics. At the age of nine (in 1899) Hu found by accident the popular novel *The Water Margin*. This encounter led him to other novels. Some were eloquent; others vulgar; and many were in vernacular Chinese. These readings had an important influence on his writing style, and most probably on his later attempt at a literary revolution.

Like many great men in Chinese history, Hu Shih was deeply influenced by his mother. Despite financial difficulties, she paid six silver dollars a year, thrice the regular tuition, in order that the tutor might give him special training and attention. During his adolescent years, Hu Shih's scholarly studies were limited to reading books and writing characters. But he also received traditional moral training. To this end his mother served at the same time both as a stern father and a tender mother. Every morning she woke him up, telling him what he did or said wrong on the previous day and exhorting him to work hard. To her, her husband was perfect. When she related to Hu Shih the good points of his father, she enjoined him to follow in his footsteps, not to disgrace his good name, and, in the spirit of Chinese philosophy, to distinguish himself in order to glorify his parents.

Searching for new education, Hu Shih made his way to Shanghai, where he spent six years (1904–10) attending four schools, at high school and college levels, without graduating from any of them. He had gone to Shanghai with his mother's permission and encouragement, despite the realization that parting from her only son caused her much pain.

During his Shanghai days, Hu Shih was immensely influenced and inspired by the popular writings of Liang Ch'i-ch'ao. Subsequently Hu Shih often expressed deep gratitude to Liang. In 1910, Hu Shih took the examination for the Boxer Indemnity Scholarship for Chinese students to study in the U.S. He passed and sailed to the United States from Shanghai in August of that year.

In the United States he began university studies as a student in the College of Agriculture at Cornell University in the belief that technology in farming could save China. However, finding himself uninterested in farm practice and pomology, he transferred to the College of Arts and Sciences a year and a half later. He received his B.A. in 1914. The following year he went to Columbia University to study philosophy, being greatly influenced by John Dewey. He took his doctorate from Columbia in 1917. Subsequently he received thirty-five honorary doctorates from universities throughout the world. In January 1917, Hu had already published his momentous article on "Humble Suggestions for Literature Reforms" in *New Youth (Hsin ch'ing-nien)*, which touched off the literature revolution in China.

Returning to China in that same year, he married, in December, Chiang Tung-hsiu, whom his mother had chosen for him. Also in 1917, he became a professor at Peking University, a post which he continued to hold intermittently until 1937 when the War of Resistance broke out. Within this twenty-year period, Hu was for a short while president of the China National Institute *(Chung-kuo kung-hsueh)*. Appointed in Shanghai in April 1928, he resigned in May 1929 because of unpleasant relations with the Nationalist government.

The period between 1917 and 1937 marked Hu Shih's pinnacle of accomplishment, prestige and popularity. He was a leader in the May Fourth movement and one of the architects of the literary revolution which rejected the convention of continuing to write only in the classical language and encouraged writing in the living vernacular. By 1919 Hu's magnum opus, *The History of Chinese Philosophy*, Vol. I *(Chung-kuo che-hsueh shih ta-kang)* was published, the first book of its kind using Western methodology and written in vernacular style.

The value of this book lies not in any great novelty of its information but in its influence as a new model of approach to Chinese learning, the use of the new scientific method. It influenced not only the field of philosophy, but the approach in other fields as well. *A Collection of Experimental Poems (Ch'ang-shih chi)*, published in 1919, and his *History of the Vernacular Literature*, Vol. I *(Pai-hua wen-hsueh shih)*, published in 1928, had a corresponding pioneer influence. The former opened up a new road for free verse as an alternative to traditional regulated poetry; the latter brought to vernacular literature wider scope and literary prestige. Though it was unfinished, it was nevertheless the first book of its kind in China.

Besides publishing other books, Hu Shih was editing several magazines, which included most of his important published articles. He edited *Weekly Review (Mei-chou p'ing-lun)* 1919–20; *Endeavor (Nu-li chou-pao)* 1922–23; *Contemporary Review (Hsien-tai p'ing-lun)* 1924–28; *Crescent (Hsin-yueh)* 1928–33; and *Independent Critic (Tu-li p'ing-lun)* 1932–37. Each was, during its timespan, among the most authoritative and influential Chinese periodicals. The last magazine for which Hu Shih served as a nominal editor and publisher was *Free China (Tzu-yu Chung-kuo)*, published in Taiwan (1948–60). This same magazine had involved the noted case of Lei Chen who, in 1954 when he was managing editor, was sentenced to ten years of imprisonment on charges of subversive political activities.

Hu Shih was initially critical of the Nationalist government; his early political criticism chiefly apeared in the *Crescent* magazine. But following the invasion of Manchuria by Japan in 1931, his attitude toward the Nationalist government became less harsh. As the threat of Japanese militarism to China became more intense, Hu's support of the Nationalist government became increasingly evident. Though he regarded the Nationalist government as very unsatisfactory in many ways, it was nonetheless the target of deliberate destruction by the enemy and he saw that, to resist the ambitious Japanese neighbor, a unified and strong government was necessary. Hu urged that the Nationalist government be supported in order to strengthen a unified resistance to the invader.

In September 1938, during the War of Resistance against Japan, Hu was appointed Chinese ambassador to the United States, a post which he held until September 1942. His prestige as an international figure helped to win the friendship and aid of America against Japan. Ironically, Hu Shih's prestige among the young radical intellectuals, especially students, began at the same time to dwindle. In their eyes his image as a progressive intellectual reformer and leader was dulled. His compromise, cooperation, and partial apology for and involvement with the practical politics of the Kuomintang government offended intellectuals who were highly critical of the Kuomintang.

From September 1944 to June 1945, Hu Shih lectured at Harvard University. Upon his return to China, as the conflict between the Nationalists and Communists became more acute, Hu sent a cable to Mao Tse-tung, dated 4 August 1945, advising him to give up the use of armed force and establish instead a second political party not dependent upon military force. In September 1945 he was appointed president of Peking University, but did not assume his post until September of the following year. In 1948 with the termination of the tutelage of one-party dictatorship and the beginning of the Nationalist constitutional period, the newly ratified Constitution provided for the People's Congress to pass laws and to elect the president. Hu Shih served as the chairman of the first session of the first Congress. But when Communist troops encircled Peking and the city's fall was imminent, Hu Shih took the last available airplane on 15 December 1948 to Nanking. He made his way to Taiwan on 19 March 1949 for a brief visit, then returned to Shanghai, and from there he left for America in April, aboard the U.S. President Wilson. During the ship's stopover at Honolulu he gave a press interview expressing support for Chiang Kai-shek regardless of how difficult the situation might be.

In September 1950 published attacks on Hu Shih's ideology, attacks which continued for two years, began in mainland China. From December 1956 to January 1957 Hu lectured at the University of California in Berkeley. In December 1957 he was appointed president of the Academia Sinica and assumed the post in Taipei on 10 April 1958. On 24 June 1962 he died in Taiwan of a heart attack, at 6:30 p.m., during a reception for the new members of the Academia Sinica.

Philosophical Foundation of Hu's Thought

The Dialectics - Pragmatism Conflict

Hu Shih has said in his article "On Introducing My Own Thoughts," that the two people who had the greatest influence on his thoughts were Thomas Huxley and John Dewey. Huxley taught him to be skeptical and to refuse to accept anything without sufficient evidence. John Dewey taught him how to think and to consider at all times the existing problems and the effects of a thought, as well as to regard every theory as only a hypothesis to be verified. These two men taught him to understand the nature and function of the scientific method.[2]

As a disciple of Dewey, Hu believed in and preached the pragmatism of his mentor. For Hu, pragmatism and dialectical materialism, the two most important methods of thinking in modern times, were in direct conflict. At the beginning of "Introducing My Own Thoughts," Hu makes clear his position by declaring that Ch'en Tu-hsiu's hope for a reconciliation of dialectics and pragmatism was a mistake. Hu points out that dialectics originated in Hegel's philosophy as a metaphysical method prior to the emergence of Darwin's theory of evolution, while pragmatism was the scientific method that followed. Because in Hu's opinion, Darwinism set the two methods apart, he maintained, against Ch'en Tu-hsiu, that reconciliation of two incompatible methods— dialectics and pragmatism—was impossible.

Darwin's biological evolution, according to Hu, taught us that both natural evolution and man-made (artificial) selection, occurs through what Hu calls "drop-by-drop" changes. These changes reflect a very complicated process and no single goal can be reached in a single stroke or step. Further, Hu posits, if a goal were reached by a single step, it is improbable that the goal itself would then remain unchanged. Although dialectics itself posits continuous change through thesis and antithesis, Hu continues, the communists seem to have forgotten this principle of continuous change; they arbitrarily concoct an ideal communist world that supposedly can be reached in one stroke through the method of class struggle. That the ideal communist state, once obtained, could be maintained forever by implementing class dictatorship, Hu deems a simplistic notion that, furthermore, basically denies the principles of evolution. The communists, he says, have adopted an arbitrary pre-Darwinian concept that is even more antiquated than Hegel's.[3] Hu's argument—"Civilization cannot be created in one fell swoop but must be done drop-by-drop. Evolution cannot be completed overnight, but is developed drop-by-drop."[4]—reflects his belief that gradual reform is a basic principle to be derived from Darwinism.

Being also a believer in the pragmatism of Dewey, Hu does not recognize the possibility of a wholly objective truth. In expounding a genetic theory of truth, Hu says that "truth is created by and for the use of man. . . . truth is nothing but the instrument of man. . . . An idea which had fruitful consequences was called truth by the people in the past. If it has been useful, it is still called truth by the people of the present time. In case new facts have been found which render it no longer useful, it will be truth no more and we have to seek for new truth to replace it."[5] In addition, Hu does not recognize the existence of a panacea for all social evils, or of an eternal and universal truth.[6] Pragmatists, Hu contends, recognize all truths to be useful hypotheses and whether the hypotheses are true or not depends entirely upon whether they can produce the consequences that are expected. This is the viewpoint of the "laboratory attitude of mind."[7]

Hu's views are diametrically opposed to the tenets of Marx in that Marxism claims to expound a universal truth and to reflect objective truth. Mao, for example, says in his "On the People's Democratic Dictatorship" that Marxism-Leninism is the universal truth. Another of the Communist writers asserts: "The Marxist-Leninist deems that the objective physical world and its laws are knowable. Thus, man's knowledge, if it can correctly reflect the objective physical world and its laws, can correctly provide us with the real ideas of objective matters. This kind of correct knowledge, the conformity of man's ideas with objective reality, is what the Marxists call truth. For instance, fire is hot and ice is cold. The hotness and coldness are the qualities of fire and ice which exist independent of human will. Therefore, this kind of knowledge is objective truth. For instance, the idea that the proletariat would inevitably step on the historical stage to replace the bourgeoisie is an objective truth, because this idea reflects the law of social and historical development, which [law] is independent of human will."[8]

This argument, only one of the representative examples of the communist writers in China, expresses the type of outlook that Hu Shih opposes. Hu's introduction of pragmatism into China during the May Fourth period was expectedly criticized, being regarded by the communists as an attempt to kill the new buds of Marxism in China.[9]

Denying both the existence of a universal truth and of a single remedy for all social evils, Hu warned the Chinese in 1919 to carry out more studies of problems and to talk less of *isms*.[10] Though he did not mention communism in particular, it is very clear that his target was communism; it was the *ism* that, in 1919, had particularly begun to attract the attention of the intellectuals.

Hu holds that "all valuable thoughts began with the study of practical problems." However, he points out that this does not imply that he is advising people against studying theories or *isms;* rather, he means that a great danger lies in poorly informed enthusiasm for *isms*. Chatter about *isms* gives people a false satisfaction; they suppose they have found a panacea, a "fundamental solution" of all problems, and therefore feel they need not exert further efforts in dealing with practical issues.[11]

In response to Hu's article on the discussion of problems and *isms,* Lan Chih-hsien and Li Ta-chao separately published articles criticizing Hu's arguments.[12] Li's article, representing the Communist viewpoint, is more incisive than Lan's. Li argues that *isms* and problems have an inseparable relationship.[13] As regards the problem of fundamental solution, Li argues that according to Marx's economic interpretation of history, the solution to the economic problem is basic. When economic problems are solved, other problems, such as political and legal problems, the problems of the family system, of emancipation of women and workers, will be, Li believes, automatically solvable. But if people, although adhering to the economic interpretation of history, and believing that economic change is inevitable, neither pay attention to the theory of class struggle nor use the latter theory as an instrument to effect actual movement in uniting the workers, then the economic revolution, Li says, can probably never be realized. Even if they were able to undertake it, its completion would be considerably delayed.[14] Nonetheless Li believes that solving the economic problem is a basic solution for all social evils.

Thirty-six years later (1955), Li's attitude was hailed in the following way: "The forerunner of Marxism in China, on the eve of the birth of the Proletarian

Revolutionary Party, had already resolutely stood on the revolutionary stand of new democracy against imperialism and against feudalism, by using Marxism as an ideological weapon, and maintaining that only class struggle can solve various problems of China, waged an irreconcilable struggle against the bourgeois reformism."[15]

In answering the criticisms of Lan and Li by persisting in advice to people to study more concrete problems and talk less of abstract *isms,* Hu had this to say: "All *isms* and theories should be studied, but they should be taken as hypothetical opinions to be verified rather than immutable dogma; materials for reference rather than infallible religion; instruments to stimulate man's mind rather than an absolute truth obscuring man's wisdom and stopping man's thinking. This is the only possible way gradually to develop the creative thinking of mankind, to give man the faculty to solve practical problems, and to liberate him from the superstition of abstract terms."[16]

As to the practical process of achieving social change and progress, Hu reiterated that only continuous "drop-by-drop" reforms could achieve true and dependable progress. Hu saw the aim of the new cultural movement beginning from around 1917 as the reconstruction of China's culture. He also saw that the road to achieving that goal was entirely dependent upon the study of individual problems:

> At present, people are fond of talking of "emancipation" and "reconstruction." It must, however, be noted that emancipation and reconstruction cannot be achieved in one fell swoop. Emancipation is the emancipation of this or that system, the emancipation of this or that thought, the emancipation of this or that man—they are all "drop-by-drop" emancipation. Reconstruction is the reconstruction of this or that system, this thought or that thought, this man or that man—they all are "drop-by-drop" reconstruction.
>
> The way to begin reconstructing the new civilization is to study this and that problem; the carrying out of this reconstruction of the new civilization lies in the solution of this and that problem.[17]

Hu did not believe in absolute truth; he, along with all pragmatists, has been criticized as unprincipled.[18] His "drop-by-drop" theory was criticized as rejecting the idea that revolution can effect a fundamental solution to Chinese problems. According to Hu, it was sarcastically commented, the exploitation of the workers and peasants by capitalists and landlords would be in conformity with the law of struggle for existence, and the struggle for emancipation of workers and peasants would mean a violation of the "drop-by-drop" principle.[19]

Ideologically, Hu was a strong anticommunist scholar. In the conclusion of his article "On Introducing My Own Thoughts," Hu explicitly affirms that the aim of his voluminous writings is to inculcate in the minds of young people an ability to protect themselves from being misled by others. "It is unwise to be led by the nose like a cow, whether by Confucius or Chu Hsi, and to be led by the nose by Marx, Lenin and Stalin is no great wisdom either.[20] From Hu's basic philosophy, all his other conflicts with the Communists stem. Hu's outlook on Chinese tradition, political thought, culture, and scholarship, as well as his vision for an ideal China in the future, is consistent with his basic philosophy.

Revolution versus Evolution: Which Road?

After the Nationalist government was established in 1927 at Nanking, the Chinese watched with great attention and interest the direction of China's reconstruction. In 1930 Hu Shih published his famous article, "Which Road Do We Take?" He wrote this article on the basis of an outline report he had prepared for a discussion at an informal editorial meeting with his *Crescent* friends. It reflects Hu's basic stand with regard to the problem of whether China should stage a drastic revolution or pursue gradualism. Hu's general program for the reconstruction of China consisted of two stages: first, negatively, what China should destroy; and second, positively, what China should construct.

What China should destroy, Hu proposes, are five archenemies: poverty, disease, ignorance, corruption, and disturbances. Hu realized that his analysis ran counter to the prevailing sentiment of that time, so he makes a special point of saying that capitalism is not to be regarded as an enemy. He does not elaborate on this point, but merely mentions in passing four reasons for not considering capitalism, the bourgeoisie, feudalism, and imperialism to be archenemies. First, China was not qualified to talk about capitalism. Second, the bourgeoisie were not enemies because, at most, China's wealthy class was a minority; there was no large bourgeois class. Third, feudalism had already broken down as early as two thousand years ago. Fourth, imperialism need not be categorized as an enemy since imperialism was observably harmless in those countries that were already free from the five archenemies. He added that so far as China must be able to fight against the imperialists, China must first eradicate the five archenemies.[21]

After their destruction, the new state to be established, in stage two of Hu's program, was to be a unified state, orderly, generally prosperous, civilized and modern. An orderly state Hu defines as one which effects good law and government, lasting peace, and a minimum public health program. A generally prosperous state he sees as one which provides for a stable livelihood, develops industry and commerce, builds a convenient and safe transportation system, maintains a fair economic system, and supports public welfare. A civilized state he regards as one which has universal popular education, a sound high school education, advanced university education, and advancement and populariza-tion of the humanities. A modern state in his view, requires an efficient political, judicial, economic and educational system, as well as public health, academic research and cultural facilities adapted to the needs of contemporary life.[22] Hu's vision is manifestly an image of a well-developed Western state, one which conspicuously resembles the United States.

Once the goal of the new state was formulated, the next problem Hu wanted to solve was the method of achieving that goal. Hu mentions three possible methods: revolution, evolution, and a third, which he proposes as a theoretical possibility, not an actuality, and does not elaborate. Hu made known his unequivocal opposition to revolution created by violence and despotism, and to revolution motivated by propaganda directed to fabricated targets such as feudalism or the bourgeoisie. Such revolutions, he says, in their violence only waste the energies of the country, stimulate the evils of blind action and cruelty, disturb the social order, and provoke mutual slaughter among the people. In such revolutions, he continues, the real enemies are still at large and the people drift further and further from the unified state that is desirable.

Hu believes that the five enemies—the true targets of a Chinese revolution—cannot be destroyed by violent forces. The only way to combat them, he insists, is through a conscious evolutionary process: that is, after having recognized the five enemies as enemies, China should unite the manpower and intelligence of the whole country and, utilizing scientific methods and technological know-how, carry out, step-by-step, conscious reforms. The harvests of continuous reforms are to be reaped "drop-by-drop" until the goal is reached. Hu's basic attitude and method support neither blind and violent revolution, nor the revolution of fancy slogans and catchwords. Nor does he support what he calls the "lazy-evolution," evolution of merely waiting and hoping for changes; he advocates a road of uninterrupted reforms through conscious efforts. Hu used the term "conscious reform" in opposition to "blind revolution." By "blind," Hu means several things: not understanding clearly the goals; disregarding the effects of the means applied; failing to consider priorities in carrying out revolutionary targets; and placing the blame for Chinese faults all on the shoulders of foreign devils.[23]

Hu's "Which Road Do We Take?" attracted wide attention. And, it aroused vehement opposition, especially from the leftists. Even a number of the so-called conservatives were disturbed about some of Hu's ideas. Liang Shu-ming's response is representative of this minority conservative reaction. Liang expressed complete agreement with Hu's stand against blind revolution, but expressed only partial agreement with Hu's theory of the five enemies and the adoption of conscious evolutionary reforms. Liang challenges Hu's lack of attention to international capitalistic imperialism, feudalism and warlordism. These three evils had been considered, Liang points out, and are seen by the revolutionaries as the great enemies of China. By "revolutionaries," Liang loosely refers to the communists and the leftists. Liang concurs with those who regard imperialism and warlordism as the archenemies. He suggests that Hu elaborate more on his assertion about the nonexistence of feudalism and deal more fully with the nature of Chinese society, Hu's treatment of which Liang considered insufficient and unconvincing. Liang also challenges Hu's statement on conscious evolutionary reforms, remarking that Hu has proffered an empty principle, failing to provide practical and concrete programs for reaching the goal.[24]

In answer to Liang's challenge, Hu concentrated on the crucial point that he had wanted to make the Chinese aware that they must blame themselves rather than others (namely, the imperialists) for their difficulties. He added that he was an advocate of conscious reform rather than blind revolution because, under the conditions of a violent revolution, no relief work or reform can be accomplished.[25] Although Hu vaguely promised to give Liang a more thorough answer at a later date, he never did.

Liang accused Hu of being shockingly rash and frivolous in his attitude toward the important problem of revolution. He called Hu's article simplistic and his thinking processes shallow. Although Liang was, at this time, not actually in favor of revolution, he did favor revolutionaries who seemed to have a sound theory of their own on the problems of imperialism, feudalism, and warlordism, problems which, in his opinion, Hu had failed to take sufficiently into account.[26]

Hu's Political Thinking

Hu Shih's political image among the Chinese people has been that of an ardent advocate of Western liberty and democracy and a strong opponent of dictatorship and communism. But in the decades between 1927 and his death in 1962, his political thinking, as reflected in his writings and in his attitude towards the Kuomintang, passed through markedly different stages.

Immediately after the establishment of the Nationalist government in Nanking in 1927, Hu Shih was sharply critical of the Kuomintang. His first provocative article was an attack against the Nationalist government for its lack of protection of human rights, especially the lack of a constitutional law to restrain the government, central as well as local, from illegal activities. This article was largely devoted to criticism of a decree issued by the Nationalist government on 20 April 1929 on the protection of human rights.[27] The most important statement in Hu's article reads: "At the present time, if the Nationalist government truly wants to protect human rights, and to establish their legal foundation, the first thing to be done is to formulate a Constitution for the Republic of China, or at least a provisional Constitutional Convention for the so-called period of political tutelage."[28] In other words, there must be established first a law to regulate and to control the activities of the government itself.

In the same vein of criticizing the undemocratic and unconstitutional practices of the Kuomintang, Hu wrote: "We do not believe that tutelage can be practiced without a Constitution; a tutelage without a Constitution is merely despotism. We firmly believe that only a constitutional government is qualified to practice tutelage."[29] Moreover, against the powerful and overwhelming pressure of the official line, Hu bluntly refuted Sun Yat-sen's theory of "difficult to know and easy to do."[30] At that time the Kuomintang practically deified Sun and held his theory as infallible. Hu's attack on Sun's theoretical foundation for political activities was tantamount to a slap in the Kuomintang's face; it was regarded as an intent to discredit the newly established Nationalist government.

In criticizing the relation of the Kuomintang and the New Culture Movement, Hu condemned the Kuomintang, which represented the Nationalist government, as being reactionary on three accounts, one of which was the complete suppression of freedom of thought and speech. To support the charge, Hu offered as evidence the fact that while it was forbidden to criticize Sun Yat-sen's theory, the existence of God could be denied; that while religious service was not mandatory, Sun's weekly memorial service was compulsory in schools and government offices; that newspapers were devoid of true news and responsible public opinion; and finally, that a certain scholar's responsible remarks about a citizen's lawful rights caused a number of Kuomintang local and provincial headquarters to petition the government to arrest him, to remove him from his presidency, to punish him, and to deprive him of his civil rights. (This last example deducibly refers to an unhappy personal experience as the president of the China National Institute in 1928–29, after his outspoken remarks against the Kuomintang.)[31]

The following statement made by Hu Shih represents his harshest criticism of the Kuomintang and is a significantly dire prediction: "The Kuomintang's present drastic loss of popular confidence is, of course, partly because its political measures are unable to satisfy the people's hopes but also, and more importantly, because its ideological fossilization is unable to attract the sympathy of the progressive thinking groups. On the day when the sympathy of the progressive thinking groups is completely lost, that will be the time of the burning up of both the oil and wick of the Kuomintang."[32]

By the early 1930s China had already lost to Japanese aggression the Northeastern provinces and a considerable part of North China. Hu's attention increasingly shifted from political dissatisfaction with China's central government to concern for national salvation. He became less critical of the dictatorial aspects of the Nationalist government though he still insisted on democracy as his ideal. In these years, when a number of people were dazzled by the successes of Hitler and Mussolini, fascist ideas became a vogue in some Chinese circles. There were people favoring the opinion that a dictatorial form of government might better help China in tiding over the national crisis. Certain Kuomintang members inclined to introduce such a system into the framework of the Kuomintang and to support Chiang Kai-shek as a Chinese counterpart of Hitler and Mussolini. Debates were carried out in various newspapers and magazines between those favoring democracy and those favoring dictatorship. The polemic of democracy versus dictatorship was as heated a war of words as the earlier famous polemics on science and the philosophy of life.

These polemical debates were reflected in the articles published in the *Independent Critic,* of which Hu Shih was then the editor. An article by T. F. Tsiang, then Chairman and Professor of the Department of History of Tsing Hua University, advocated dictatorship as the step necessary for national salvation. He did not say this explicitly but in ways that led readers to understand, beyond any doubt, exactly what he meant. Being a historian, Tsiang cited three historical instances to support his theme that absolutism was a necessary prologue to the success of a revolution: the hundred years of the absolutism of the Tudor dynasty preceded the revolution of the seventeenth century in Great

Britain; two hundred years of the absolutism of the Bourbons preceded the great revolution of the eighteenth century in France; three hundred years of the absolutism of the Romanovs preceded the great achievement of Lenin and Trotsky in Russia. Tsiang instances further that each of these absolutistic periods was preceded, respectively, by a long period of internal turmoil and disturbances: the Wars of the Roses in fifteenth-century England, the frequent wars between the Guise and Bourbons in sixteenth-century France, and the civil wars at the end of the sixteenth century and the early seventeenth century in Russia. He cites the absolutism of a dynastic state as the necessary condition from which a national state emerges, its material and spiritual circumstances playing a decisive role in the success of the subsequent revolutions.

Tsiang likens the case of China to England without the Tudor absolutism, to France without the Bourbon absolutism, and to Russia without the Romanov absolutism. He concludes that though China could still have internal disturbances, she could not have a true revolution. To support his view that China had neither the ability nor the qualifications to engage in a true revolution, he proffers three reasons. He categorizes China as still a dynastic state rather than a nation-state; the loyalty of the majority of the people is still a personal, familial, or local loyalty rather than a loyalty to the state. He points out that China's absolutism of thousands of years has failed to create and bequeath a class which can serve as the center of a new regime; the historical mission of absolutist governments has been to destroy any other class or system that could be developed as a center of a new regime. Consequently, after the royal family fell, the whole country disintegrated like a pile of loose sand. Finally, he emphasizes, Chinese absolutism retarded material developments and, as a result, whenever a revolution began, foreigners took advantage of the situation to exploit China and China was unable to resist.[33]

Tsiang's use of the term "true revolution" overlapped and, in his usage, became practically synonymous with the term "national reconstruction." In sum, Tsiang advocated the establishment of a dictatorship in China to achieve national unification for national salvation; he regarded a unifying dictatorship as the necessary prologue to a "true" revolution of national reconstruction.

Hu Shih's rebuttal to Tsiang's article appeared in the immediately following issue of the *Independent Critic,* the rebuttal entitled "National Reconstruction and Absolutism." Hu comments that, though Tsiang doubtless genuinely believes that a united government is a necessary condition for national reconstruction, the word "absolutism," as used by Tsiang, suggests a conception of a united government that can be misconstrued since many people will equate it with unlimited dictatorship. (Many liberal readers did, in fact, understand Tsiang's article to mean the advocacy of unlimited dictatorship, and became highly indignant.) Hu urged Tsiang to make clear that a united government need not necessarily be a dictatorship.[34] Tsiang clarified his stand later, stating that in his view China must have a leader able to crush the second-rate warlords by greater military force and to achieve unification in this transitional period. He explicitly affirms his belief that the emergence of a great dictator is advantageous to the people.[35] Deducibly, the great dictator he had in mind was Chiang Kai-shek.

In a subsequent article, "More on National Reconstruction and Absolutism," Hu remarks that modern absolutism appears in three different forms, namely, personal dictatorship, one-party dictatorship, and one-class dictatorship. The Kuomintang slogan of democratic centralism—*min-chu chi-ch'üan*—identifies one-party dictatorship; the Blue Shirts' leader system is a combination of personal and party dictatorship; the Communist Party is a combination of one-class and one-party dictatorships. Moreover, Hu states his opposition to all three forms, averring his conviction that there is no person, party or class in China qualified to carry out such a dictatorship. Hu adds that though people realize that citizens in a republic must possess high intellectual capacities, they do not realize that a dictatorship requires special genius and even greater intelligence to operate.[36]

Because of the danger of a personal or party tyranny, Hu is vehement in his opposition to any form of dictatorship, to the concentration of power in the hands of one or a few people. Referring to his own opinion as "wild prejudice," he argues in a rather diplomatic and circuitous manner. Democratic constitutionalism, he says, is a simple system of politics, comparable to the kindergarten level, while a dictatorship is comparable to graduate school. Democratic constitutionalism, he insists, is best suited to train a people with little political experience or competence in order to learn how to practice politics. According to his own observation, those who ran the government in Britain and America were not the first-rate people, nor those who went into business and science; the common citizens, given the opportunity of political participation, learn to love and protect their own rights. Dictatorship, as he sees it, requires special genius, such as Stalin and Lenin and their cohorts possessed, and in his opinion China does not have such men of political genius. On this basis, Hu argues that it is wrong to assume that democracy is too advanced and difficult a political system for China to adopt, and wrong to assume that the Chinese people in general are not qualified. What China has to do, he proposes, is to enter the kindergarten first and learn the basics; she is not ready for graduate school yet.[37] Hu stresses his conclusion that democracy is the best form of government to train those people with little political experience to participate in politics and that the concentration of power in the hands of a few can never allow the people a chance to obtain modern political training. The most effective political training method is gradually to open political rights to the people, giving them political training through political participation, just as one learns to swim by plunging into the water.[38]

Among contributors to the *Independent Critic,* T. F. Tsiang, favoring a kind of dictatorship, dismissed Hu's argument about democracy being a kindergarten training in government as merely a joke, not worth discussing.[39] V. K. Ting, the famous geologist, characterized Hu's argument as absurd, and held that "in present day China, both democracy and dictatorship are impossible, but the degree of impossibility of democracy is greater than that of dictatorship."

Ting appealed to the Chinese people to strive to make a dictatorship possible in the shortest amount of time. The first step, he said, would be to abandon advocacy of democracy.[40] Ch'ien Tuan-sheng, Tsing Hua professor of political science, argued that what China urgently needed was a high degree of industrialization of the coast provinces within one or two decades, but this could be achieved only through a powerful and popular dictatorship. Ch'ien urged the Chinese not to waste their energy in advocating a democracy, a democracy which would not only be difficult to realize, but which would be basically weak anyway. Yet, at the same time, he warned the people to guard against the emergence of tyrannical dictatorship.[41] Wu Ching-ch'ao, a professor of sociology at Tsing Hua University, and also one of Hu's close friends, pointed out that he could see no alternative for unifying China except by military force. He based this opinion on his own studies of the patterns of the history of Chinese civil wars.[42]

These scholars, T. F. Tsiang, V. K. Ting, Ch'ien Tuan-sheng and Wu Ching-ch'ao, all in one way or another favored some form of dictatorship in preference to democracy. Implicitly they all considered—or at least did not exclude—the possibility of Chiang Kai-shek as the dictator and the Kuomintang as the dictatorial party. T. F. Tsiang, as we have seen above, explicitly stated that it would be to the advantage of the people for one single strong dictator to crush the second-rate warlords. At that time, Chiang Kai-shek appeared to be the only person powerful enough to do so.

Though comparatively pro-Kuomintang, Hu did not at that time favor armed unification of China; he continued to insist on democratic constitutionalism. He appealed to both Kuomintang and non-Kuomintang leaders to seek, formulate, and agree upon a minimum common belief for the good of China and her people. Hu argued that such a belief be one which would solve China's problems by political means rather than by force. To avoid the use of force, he said, everyone should, regardless of political affiliation, strive for and promote the success of democratic constitutionalism in order to unite and advance China as a people and as a country.[43]

In assessing and criticizing the various debates on the problem of democracy versus dictatorship in the year 1934, Hu held firmly that the formation of a democratic parliament consisting of elected representatives from all provinces and controlling the central government was the most effective way to unify China.[44] Meanwhile, Mao Tse-tung, we may pertinently recall, was already practicing his theory that China's revolution was destined to be an armed rebellion and that a political regime would emerge from the barrel of a gun. In other words, Mao had already sided with those who were in favor of military unification first in preference to democratic means.[45]

In the heated debate over democracy versus dictatorship, most intellectuals were in favor of a democratic form of government over a dictatorial or fascist form of government. Scholars like T. F. Tsiang and V. K. Ting were not popular, and especially not among the young generation. Probably responding to the pressure of public opinion, Chiang Kai-shek and Wang Ching-wei jointly issued a circular telegram to the entire country on 9 November 1934. The most important point of this joint communique was that "Given the conditions and times of China today, there is neither any necessity or possibility for China to produce the Italian or Russian political system." The terms *fascism* or *dictatorship* were not used but the meaning was quite clear. In the years just prior to the War of Resistance against Japan, Japan allied with Germany and Italy to form the Axis. Dictatorship was taken to imply some connection with Japanese aggression against China. Public opinion showed opposition and aversion to dictatorship even though the heat of debate between democracy and dictatorship gradually cooled. During the late 1930s and 1940s, the intellectuals characteristically shared a common belief in democracy; and a democratic form of government was in general sought and supported. Even the Communist Party, the largest and most powerful party in opposition to the Kuomintang, appealed, as did the minor parties, for a democratic coalition government.

Immediately before and after the Communist take-over of mainland China, Hu became more adamant in his advocacy of democracy and freedom and in his opposition to dictatorship, totalitarianism and communism. On 1 August 1948 Hu Shih made a radio speech in Peking in which he stressed three ideal common goals of modern world culture: the use of science for the diminution of human suffering and for the increase of human happiness; the use of a socialized economic system to raise the standard of living of mankind; the implementation of a democratic political system to emancipate the thoughts of man, to develop the talents of man, to create free and independent individuals.[46]

Aware that Communist sympathizers would laugh at him for insisting on democracy as one of the common goals of modern world culture, Hu anticipated their arguments. He knew they would claim that democracy had been out of vogue for the past thirty years and that the most popular form of government was the dictatorship of a minority party that represented the interests of worker and peasant classes. He knew they would still advocate liquidating opposition parties and ruling the majority of people by force and still assert that personal freedom was a useless legacy of capitalism and that individuals should sacrifice their personal freedom in favor of class freedom. In retort Hu declared that to look at social development in a historical perspective is to perceive that democracy and freedom have been the ultimate goal and the clearest orientation of the past three or four centuries and that the antiliberal and antidemocratic tendency of the past three decades is nothing but a minor reverse current. People, Hu warned, should not ignore the great trends and orientations of the past three or four hundred years solely on the basis of reverse currents in a mere thirty-year period.

At the time this radio speech was made, many people favored the success of the Soviet Union in preference to the Western democratic system. In attacking such an attitude, Hu argued that while the Chinese can sympathize with the Russian revolution that fought for the interests of workers and peasants, the use of the method of class struggle which has created an intolerant and antiliberal political system is the most unfortunate event in history. Hu said that the undemocratic Soviet system was upheld by brutal force and led to cruel oppression and destruction of opposition parties that had led to a one-party dictatorship developing into a one-person dictatorship. Hu added that, regrettably, the economic advantages obtained by the people in the Soviet Union in thirty years of bitter struggle were also less than those achieved through free enterprise and social legislation in democratic countries.[47]

At the time this speech was made, Peking's fall to the Communists was imminent. Evidently Hu was trying to reverse the antidemocratic and pro-communist trends. In answering letters from the listeners to his broadcast who criticized him as "partial" to democracy and as oversimplifying the problem of the existence of the opposing democratic and communist camps, Hu elaborated his reasons for resisting the despotism of communism and being partial to democracy. He reasserted his view that freedom of thought, of speech, and of the press are the basic conditions for social reforms and cultural advancement. He reaffirmed his belief that a democratic system is the most comprehensive and can best represent the interests of all the people. He reviewed for his correspondents the history of the development of the right of consent to the control of government by the people, beginning in Europe with a limited few such as nobles and church leaders, and later extended to tax-paying merchants and finally extended to the universal vote of all adult citizens. Only this system, he insisted, could attain the goal of representing the interests of the whole population by peaceful means, could attain the goal without resorting to cruel struggle or slaughter. He urged the recognition that the democratic system evolved especially in the past one hundred years was, though still imperfect, the system which has nourished a cultural society cherishing freedom and tolerating opposing ideas.[48]

Hu appealed passionately to his fellow countrymen to take clear account of the great trend of world culture in choosing their own road. He declared that only freedom could liberate China's national spirit, that only the democratic form of government could unite the whole population in solving their national difficulties, and that only freedom and democracy could produce a humanist cultural society.[49]

In 1952, three years after the Nationalist government had moved to Taiwan, Hu made the same appeal in Taiwan in a public speech, urging the audience to keep up their confidence and to believe firmly in the road of democracy, which has been the common goal of humankind for the last three hundred years. He declared his belief that the road against democracy, being a reverse current, would soon be destroyed.[50]

Hu very frequently mentioned liberty and democracy together. To mention liberty and democracy together has been the general practice among Chinese writers. However, Hu's particular treatment of liberty within the concept of liberalism is worth particular attention. Liberalism, in the simplest terms according to Hu, emphasizes respect for freedom; it is the great movement in history that promotes freedom, worships freedom, fights for freedom, and substantiates and extends freedom. Hu's exposition of liberalism is largely a personal interpretation, a personal selection of a few of its political aspects.

A liberal, Hu says, is one who loves freedom, who recognizes it as the basic condition for individual development and social progress, and who, realizing that freedom is easy to lose but difficult to gain, always carefully guards, protects and nourishes it.[51] Characterizing liberalism as the support of democracy, of the control of political power in the hands of the majority, Hu associates liberalism with a parliamentary system, a written but revisable national constitution, and the secret ballot. Hu also argues that the unique and unprecedented political characteristic in the evolution of liberalism in the past two hundred years has been its toleration of an opposition political party and its protection of the basic rights of the minority. He especially stresses the function of a freely operating opposition party of a kind which did not exist in China. The function of such an opposition party, which might begin as a minority group, is, Hu contends, to serve as an instrument through which people exercise strict criticism and supervision of the administration in power, enlarge their choice of leaders, and enable power to be transferred by legal and peaceful means. Liberalism as he defined it was, Hu felt, the main road through which peaceful reforms were accomplished in modern democratic countries.[52] This liberalism that Hu personally espoused is the context of his still remembered and often quoted criticism of the Communist government, including his trenchant comment that in such a government not only was there no freedom of speech but no freedom of silence.[53]

Appraisal of Ancient Political Philosophy

A survey of Hu Shih's political thinking appropriately includes his views on ancient political thought. Although Hu Shih has generally been grouped among iconoclastic scholars, his attitude toward Chinese history, especially in his later years, differed greatly from that of scholars who wanted to destroy everything traditional and who dismissed almost everything traditional as valueless. Hu's views on the history of ancient Chinese political thought, expressed in a succinct article called "One Way to Look at Chinese Ancient Political Thought,"[54] serve as an example of his attitude, more moderate than that of the iconoclasts. He appraised the Chinese past in terms of what he designated as the four great events in the political thought of ancient China.

He designated, as the first of these events, the "no-actionism" of Lao-tzu, interpreted both to imply that a government could be run efficiently by doing nothing and to suggest that such a government is the preferred form of government. Hu viewed this as a form of protest against the government, against its excessive restrictions and its control over the people politically and socially; he saw it as a laissez faire political philosophy propounded 2500 years ago. He speculated that the Western idea of laissez faire and of noninterference, which did not emerge in the West until the eighteenth century, reflected influence from China and concluded that this political philosophy of nonaction and of noninterference emerged in China earlier than in any other country in the world.[55]

Hu designated as the second great event, the free thought and individualism of Confucius and of subsequent thinkers. Although Confucius could not be claimed to have created anything original in the field of political thought, Hu credited Confucius with creating an educational philosophy characterized by democracy and freedom wherein all men were viewed as being equal. He cited, as underlying principle of this educational philosophy, Confucius' remark, "In teaching there should be no distinction of classes."[56] Hu attributes the origin of the examination system of later ages to this philosophy of education. With regard to Confucius' primary goal to inculcate in his disciples and others the concept of benevolence, *jen,* Hu interpreted *jen* to mean the character of man, or the nature of man, or the dignity of man. Believing that the concept of *jen* was totally original with Confucius, Hu cites the following passage to support his interpretation: "Tzu Lu asked what constituted the superior man. The Master said, 'The cultivation of himself in reverential carefulness.' 'And this is all?' said Tzu Lu. 'He cultivates himself so as to give rest to others,' was the reply. 'And is this all?' again asked Tzu Lu. The Master said, 'He cultivates himself so as to give rest to all the people.'"[57]

Hu viewed the phrase "to give rest to all the people" as signifying the provision of peace and happiness to all mankind. Because the aim of Confucius' concept of education was to link individual education with society, an education not for one's selfish profit or prosperity but for other individuals, for the regulation of families, of states, and of the whole kingdom, Confucius also believed that educated men, especially educated official-scholars, would feel the dignity and responsibility of bettering the world. And indeed, it has been the tradition among scholars in China for the past 2500 years to assume this responsibility, even to the extent of sacrificing their lives for this principle. After Confucius, men such as Tseng Tzu, Mencius, Fan Chung-yen and Ku T'ing-lin have been cited as models for such behavior. A sound individualism in China, Hu argues, has been created as a result of this Confucian philosophy of education. Individualism, according to Hu, means viewing oneself as a person who has a social mission and social responsibility, as a person who respects himself and who has the responsibility of "cultivating himself so as to give rest to all the people."[58] Deducibly, Hu's exaltation of this definition of individualism aims at combatting the prevailing totalitarian idea that an individual simply serves as a cog in a state machine.

The third great event, according to Hu's designation, was the rise of totalitarianism *(chi-ch'üan chu-i).* In the fourth century B.C. Duke Hsiao of Ch'in, in cooperation with a shrewd statesman, Lord Shang, instituted a totalitarian state. Influenced, Hu says, by the political thought of Mo-tzu, who advocated a theory of "conforming to the superior" *(shang-t'ung),* Lord Shang advocated the principle that whatever the sovereign or the ruler says must be accepted as right, and, further, that everybody else in the country should conform to him. Practically, the standard of right and wrong was equated with the sovereign and in theory that of the sovereign conformed to the standard of Heaven. Hu's illustration of the practical measures used in this system of government employs the modern term "spy system" to indicate that the whole

116

population was so highly organized that whatever anyone did, good or evil, regardless of where the act took place, would be reported to the sovereign directly even though it might not even be known to one's family and neighbors. Hu Shih categorizes this system as the highest form of democratic centralism, calling it a form of theocracy posited in a totalitarian philosophy.

Lord Shang was noted for his promotion of agricultural production and his glorification of war. Although he was liquidated and killed in a political struggle, his totalitarian politics survived him and within a hundred years, the totalitarian state of Ch'in had unified all China by force. Hu Shih reviews these matters, including the reports that the first Emperor of the Ch'in state, in order to effect uniformity of thought and to eliminate freedom of thought, carried through the proposal presented by his Prime Minister, Li Szu, to burn undesirable books and to bury alive scholars.[59]

Hu's attention to Ch'in totalitarianism and its philosophy, Legalism, as a third significant event in the Chinese past curiously foreshadows the movement in mainland China to degrade the Confucianists and to upgrade the Legalists that emerged in 1974, with the aim of showing the existence of a continuing struggle between Legalism and Confucianism. The movement has demonstrably tried to reevaluate and justify, as a necessity for social progress, the Ch'in bookburning and the burying alive of scholars, actions traditionally regarded as a product of the tyranny of Ch'in.[60]

The fourth great event in China's history, according to Hu's appraisal, was the downfall of a totalitarian state—the Ch'in autocracy—and the establishment of a government of "no action." This is Hu's categorization of government under the Han dynasty, which lasted for 420 years. Hu attributes to the Great Han Empire the absence of war, the establishment of a regular reserve army, and the training of policemen. Hu also mentions that the Han levied light taxes, a practice inviting the approval and love of the people. Hu believed that the political thought and institutions of the ensuing two thousand years of Chinese history benefited by the Han model of government, what he calls rule by no-action.[61]

Hu's treatment of Chinese history attaches to it the general image of freedom, democracy and no-action, despite the short but successful period of Ch'in totalitarianism. Hu's historical view opposes the school of thought that maintains China has a strong despotic and totalitarian tradition. In Hu's view, democracy in China is to be regarded as a kind of natural growth, albeit retarded, rather than a transplant from the West.

Hu's political image is clear. He stood for democracy, which he defined as political power controlled by the majority of the people. He stood for the freedom of the individual; in particular he held the freedom of thought most important. He stood for political toleration, especially the toleration of opposition political parties and opposition opinions against the government in power. He stood for a parliament to settle political disputes and differences by argument rather than by civil wars. He stood for peaceful transformation—social changes and progress by peaceful means rather than by bloody revolution. Hu was opposed to dictatorship, either from the Right or from the Left; that is, he opposed both fascism and communism. In a word, he was opposed to any form of dictatorship or totalitarian government. Hu's political visions may be criticized as unpractical and have been so criticized by both friend and foe. But adverse criticism never led him to waver in his conviction that he was acting responsibly in expounding and defending his view of civilized society.

Appraisal of Eastern and Western Civilization

A stereotype held not infrequently by both Western and Chinese scholars is that Eastern civilization is spiritual and Western civilization is materialistic. The concern over the superiority of one over the other produced heated controversy during Hu Shih's time. Before World War I, there seemed to be a predominant tendency in China toward imitating Western civilization as a means of bringing about China's national salvation. Hu observed in 1926, in his "Our Attitude toward Modern Western Civilization," that there were signs of a revival of the old idea of glorifying the Eastern civilization as spiritual and belittling the Western civilization as material. He pointed out that this idea should be recognized as a Chinese defensive reaction to the oppression of the Oriental nations by the West; that Easterners suffering from Western oppression identified themselves as a spiritual civilization to give themselves consolation and comfort. This idea was available, he suggested, because a number of Western scholars, despondent and horrified by the cruelties of World War I, had begun to laud the East as a spiritual civilization.[62] Being an ardent advocate and promoter of Westernization for China, he feared, as he said in his "The Civilizations of the East and the West," that "In recent years the despondent mood of a number of European writers has led to the revival of such old myths as the bankruptcy of the material civilization of the West and the superiority of the spiritual civilization of the Oriental nations. . . . Although these expressions represent nothing more than the pathological mentality of war-stricken Europe, they have already had the unfortunate effects of gratifying the vanity of Oriental apologists and thereby strengthening the hand of reaction in the East."[63]

Hu denied emphatically that there was a fixed dichotomy between West and East, a materialistic versus a spiritual civilization. Every civilization, he said, necessarily contained both elements, the material and the spiritual; moreover, every civilization has reflected the command of human intelligence and wisdom over material matter and natural forces and there could be no civilization that was exclusively spiritual or exclusively material. He cited an earthenware basin and an iron steam boiler, a sampan and a big steamboat, a single-wheeled cart and an electric trolley car as all equal examples of products of human intelligence applied to material matter and natural forces; each pair involved a material basis plus human intelligence and wisdom. He pointed out that the owner of a steam boiler should not denigrate the primitive nature of the earthenware basin, and, by the same token, the passenger in a wheelbarrow should not arrogantly imply that he belongs to a spiritual civilization and despise trolley car riders as representing a materialistic civilization. The only difference in civilizations then, concludes Hu, is in degree and not in kind.[64]

What then is the difference in degree between Eastern and Western civilizations? Hu answers: "The civilization of a race is simply the sum total of its achievements in adjusting itself to its environment. Success or failure in that adjustment depends upon the ability of the race to use intelligence for the invention of necessary and effective tools. Advancement in civilization depends upon the improvement of tools. . . . The difference between the Eastern and Western civilizations is primarily a difference in the tools used. The West has. . . moved far ahead. . . . The East. . . is left behind in the stage of manual labor while the Western world has long entered the age of steam and electricity."[65]

Hu not only rejects the idea of a dichotomy between the Eastern spiritual and Western materialistic civilizations but boldly asserts that Western civilization can satisfy spiritual demands of man much more than the traditional Eastern civilization could ever succeed in doing. He states outright that modern Western civilization is not exclusively materialistic, but includes values that are highly idealistic and spiritual.

The two spiritual phases of Western civilization, as Hu perceives them, he sees reflected in science and democracy. With respect to science, Hu argues that the aim of science is to seek truth, which is the greatest spiritual demand of man. The happiness and satisfaction derived from the discovery of a scientific law, he said, was never sought after by unmotivated Oriental sages such as Chuang-tzu, who would have turned away from the pursuit of scientific knowledge. Hu speaks of the spiritual joy of scientists such as Newton, Pasteur, and Edison, and especially of the ecstasy of Archimedes when he ran naked from his bath into the streets and shouted "Eureka! Eureka!" to passers-by. For Hu, science constitutes one of the most spiritual phases of modern civilization.[66] And the greatest spiritual element for scientists, he feels, is the element of skepticism, the courage to doubt everything and to believe nothing without sufficient evidence, the skepticism which liberates the human mind from slavish subjection to superstition and authority. He sees the scientific method of inquiry as the only legitimate road to belief, a method aimed at conquering doubt itself and at establishing belief on a firmer basis.[67]

Another strong spiritual phase of Western civilization, Hu asserts, is the rise of the religion of democracy. In this use of the term religion Hu may be stretching the meaning of the word, but he does limit his comments on "the religion of democracy" to human or social matters. In the scope of the religion of democracy he includes the eighteenth-century ideals of individualism and the socialistic ideals of the nineteenth century. The new creeds of the eighteenth century were liberty, equality and fraternity that, Hu says, underlay the French Revolution, the American Revolution, the revolutions of 1848, and all subsequent revolutions. These ideals, he goes on, motivated the creation of constitutional republics, brought about the downfall of monarchies, gave man equality before the law, provided freedom of thought, speech, publication and faith, realized the emancipation of women, and led to the establishment of universal education. He regards the ideals of socialism as merely supplementary to the earlier and more individualistic ideas of democracy, furthering numerous improvements for the majority of people, especially the workers.[68] Hu concluded "that civilization which makes the fullest possible use of human ingenuity and intelligence in search of truth in order to control nature and transform matter for the service of mankind, to liberate the human spirit from ignorance, superstition, and slavery to the forces of nature, and to reform social and political institutions for the benefit of the greatest number—such a civilization is highly idealistic and spiritual."[69] It is to be pointed out that the spiritual civilization spoken of by Chinese scholars only refers to the predominate emphasis on one's inner moral cultivation of life to the extent of neglecting and even belittling the pursuit of material happiness. What Hu describes as the spiritual satisfaction derived from scientific inquiry or the idealist pursuit of social reforms has never been excluded from the value of spiritual civilization, though has not been emphasized.

Hu's redefinition and clarification of the terms spiritual civilization and material civilization, terms which he considered much misused and very confusing, along with his zealous praise of modern science and technology as being highly idealistic and spiritual, were reiterated in his speeches and writings in Chinese throughout 1925 and 1926. From 1926 to 1928 he expressed these same ideas in English. It was Hu's strong belief that the adoption of Western civilization would liberate China from ignorance, poverty and evil social institutions, and he had constantly defended his ideas. Some thirty-five years after his first appeal in 1925, he repeated with the same vigor, in a speech delivered before the four-nation Science Education Conference held at Taipei on 6 November 1961, his opinions on Eastern and Western civilizations. He again appealed to the Chinese people to develop an appropriate attitude toward science and technology: an intellectual and emotional openness toward and a receptivity to the growth of science and the adoption of Western civilization. He repeats his old argument, albeit with new emphasis: "Without some such heart-searching reappraisals and reevaluations, without some such intellectual convictions, there may be only half-hearted acceptance of science and technology as an unavoidable nuisance, as a necessary evil, at best as something of utilitarian value but not of intrinsic worth. Without acquiring some such philosophy of the scientific and technological civilization, I am afraid, science will not take deep root in our midst, and we of the Orient will never feel quite at home in this new world."[70]

Hu denied the dichotomy of a demarcation between the material and spiritual civilizations, and he further asserted the superiority and spirituality of the Western scientific and technological civilization. Logically, then, he advocated "wholesale Westernization" of Chinese civilization (literally, ch'üan-p'an hsi-hua—the complete, or en bloc, transformation of the Chinese civilization into a Western civilization). This concept, as well as the term itself, provoked much opposition and severe criticism. Hu had first introduced the term wholesale Westernization in the *Christian Year Book* in the United States in 1929, in an article entitled "The Cultural Conflict in China." P'an Kuang-tan, the famous sociologist then living in Shanghai, took issue with Hu's terms—wholesale Westernization and "wholehearted modernization" *(ch'ung-fen hsien-tai-hua)*—in a book review article that appeared in the English language *China Critic Weekly* in Shanghai. P'an favored the term wholehearted modernization but objected to the term wholesale Westernization. The semantic difficulty of the terms gave rise to some unnecessary and involved debates.[71] Hu ultimately yielded to P'an's objections. Hu formally announced in an article that he preferred the term "wholehearted world civilization" to the term "wholesale Westernization."[72] (Literally, "wholehearted world civilization" is "wholehearted worldization" *[ch'ung-fen shih-chieh-hua]*.) His new choice of words indicates that he considered the civilization of science and technology to be a world civilization.

Although Hu discarded the term wholesale Westernization and created the term wholehearted world civilization, the popular image of Hu as an advocate of complete Westernization has remained unchanged; the term "complete Westernization" has continued in use among scholars, and Hu's term wholehearted world civilization has been neglected and almost forgotten. The fact that Hu dropped the term complete Westernization did not alter his advocacy of Westernization. Moreover, this advocacy of Westernization, whatever adjective he attached to it, did not alter the fact that Hu's concept of Westernization was selective. The West is predominately a Christian civilization, but Hu was an atheist. He professed social immortality as his own religious faith—a belief that individuals are mortal and society is immortal, and that the individuals are significant in being responsible for the achievement of the immortality of society.[73] His religious theory did not exert much influence on the Chinese mind. Suffice it to say that what Hu meant by wholesale Westernization, or wholehearted world civilization, signified for him a complete acceptance of Western science and democracy, with particular emphasis on science and technology.

Being firm and unequivocal in his belief, Hu was adamantly opposed to two theories with respect to the future path Chinese civilization was to take. First, he opposed the theory of the traditionalists. He alerted young people against those who, trying to incite a kind of megalomania among them, insisted that China's traditional culture and virtues were supreme in the world, and also those who had never been out of China but had the audacity to scream "Go East! The Western juggleries can no longer work!"[74] Here Hu discernibly had in mind people like Liang Shu-ming. The second type of theory that Hu opposed was the so-called theory of China-centric culture *(Chung-kuo pen-wei wen-hua)*. This view was expressed most fully in the *Manifesto of the Construction of China-centric Culture,* written in 1935 by ten university professors, including Sa Meng-wu and Ho Ping-sung. The central theme of the *Manifesto* lies in a few key principles: (1) China's culture, for the situation at that time, should be

China-centric, yet China should still maintain a world perspective; (2) the new culture should neither be one of conservatism nor a blind imitation of the West—that is, from the West should be absorbed whatever meets China's needs but without accepting all of Western culture; and (3) China, assuming the principle of China-centrism but maintaining a critical attitude, should use the scientific method, should examine her past, grasp her present, and create her future.[75]

Hu was particularly opposed to this theory of China-centric culture on the grounds that it was only a modified form of Chang Chih-tung's idea that Chinese learning is basic and Western learning is for occasional application. For Hu, the staying power of Chinese culture was so great that there was no need to worry about its ever being entirely lost. Therefore, he argued, the Chinese could wholeheartedly accept the world culture of science and technology and the spirit behind it, since after a process of selection, the best parts of Chinese culture would still survive and Chinese culture itself would emerge more fully developed and more lustrous than before.[76]

On the whole, Hu did not examine the problem of culture as a problem *per se*. He considered culture in terms of how best to insure China's survival; he identified the new culture he envisioned with national salvation. This was the immediate problem that concerned him—to save a senile and sick nation, to save a half-dead culture. He felt that any pattern of culture which could bring life to China, that could rejuvenate China, should be fully utilized, irrespective of its origins.[77]

Promotion of a Scientific Spirit in China

In the period of the New Culture movement, science and democracy were generally taken by Chinese as the two outstanding characteristics of Western civilization. They were also seen as the two goals China should adopt in the process of modernization. In later developments, while there were those who opposed democracy and chose other forms of government as being better suited for China, no one proposed to deny the significance of science or to reject it.

Hu Shih was without doubt one of the most ardent promoters and supporters of the introduction of science into China. There are various theories on the problem of why science failed to develop in China, but such theories need not detain us here.[78] Hu Shih often lamented the backward state of science in China; however, he did believe that the Ch'ing scholars had successfully applied the scientific method to the study of philology, semantics, textual criticism, and investigation into the authenticity of old books—all of which he considered marked a great turning point in the history of Chinese scholarship.[79]

Hu also claimed a remarkable scientific spirit and method for Chinese philosophy, saying there was a "Socratic tradition" in the traditional school of Confucius that comprised free questions and answers, free discussion, independent thinking, skepticism, and an eager and dispassionate search for knowledge.[80] In his opinion, Confucius and Socrates had many points in common; for example, Hu said, Confucius, like Socrates, did not consider himself a wise man, but only a man who loved knowledge.

One of the outstanding features of the Confucian tradition, according to Hu, was its encouragement of independent thought. This feature, Hu remarked, was particularly encouraged by Mencius, who declared: "To accept the whole *Book of History* as trustworthy is worse than to have no *Book of History* at all."[81] Hu also held that Mencius encouraged a free and independent attitude of mind as essential to the understanding of the *Book of Poetry*.[82] Another feature of the Confucian tradition was intellectual honesty; Hu quoted two passages to support this claim. One was Confucius' definition of knowledge: "To hold that you know a thing when you know it, and to hold that you do not know when you really do not know: that is knowledge." Hu chose, as another instance of Confucius' intellectual integrity, his answer to the question about how to serve the spirits and gods: "We have not yet learned to serve men, how can we serve the spirits?" And when asked about the matter of death, Confucius responded "We do not yet know life, how do we know death?"[83] Hu saw Confucius' answers not as evasions of the questions, but as moral injunctions to be intellectually honest about things one does not really know. That Confucius' agnostic position on death, gods and spirits has had a lasting influence on Chinese thought in subsequent ages, Hu regarded as representative of China's "Socratic tradition."

Hu regarded Lao-tzu as the representative of the concept of naturalism.[84] Regarding the naturalistic concept as having been germinated in the *Book of Lao-tzu,* Hu considered it one of the most influential philosophical inheritances from the classical age. Naturalism itself, said Hu, exemplified the spirit of courageous doubt and constructive postulation. He attributed to the humanist heritage of Confucius and the naturalism of Lao-tzu equal status and importance in Chinese history. He was of the opinion that, whenever China succumbed to periods of irrationality, superstition, and otherworldliness, it was always through either the naturalism of Lao-tzu or the humanism of Confucius, or both, that China rose and tried to rescue herself.

The further major movement in Chinese thought, according to Hu, was the movement beginning from the Sung dynasty (11th century) that "started out with the ambitious slogan of 'investigation of the reason of all things and extension of human knowledge to the utmost' but which ended in improving and perfecting a critical method of historical research and thereby opening up a new age or revival of classical learning."[85] This great movement, generally known as the Neo-Confucian movement, aimed at reviving the thought and culture of pre-Buddhist China and at returning directly to the humanist teachings of Confucius and his school, in order to overthrow and replace the much Indianized, and therefore non-Chinese, thought and culture of medieval China. This movement was essentially Confucian, but the Neo-Confucianists also adopted the naturalist cosmology which was at least partially of Taoist origin, so that Neo-Confucianism was a combination of Taoist naturalism and

Confucian humanism in protest against the alien, non-Chinese otherworldly religion of Buddhism. The Neo-Confucian movement spanned about eight hundred years, beginning with philosophy and later extending to other humanistic and historical studies, such as textual criticism, semantics, history, historical geography, and archeology. For the general trend of the period, Hu had this to say: "In the last 800 years, there has grown up a scientific tradition, first as an intellectual ideal taught in the most influential school of philosophical thought, then as a scientific technique, even though it was applied not to the objects of nature but to humanistic and historical studies. The ideal is to investigate the nature of all things and to understand them. The technique is to build up every theory or hypothesis on the firm ground of sufficient evidence."[86]

It was the scientific spirit and method of this period, Hu says, that was of tremendous importance to Chinese minds and Chinese history. He points out that, in spite of the striking similarity in the scientific spirit and method of both the great European and Chinese scientists, there was an important difference in their respective achievement. In the West, great seventeenth-century scientists such as Galileo, Kepler, Boyle, Harvey and Newton, worked with the objects of nature, with stars, spheres, inclined planes, telescopes, microscopes, prisms, chemicals, numbers and astronomical tables. But their Chinese contemporaries, likewise as great—Ku Yen-wu and Yen Jo-chü, for instance, two masters noted for scientific works in the fields of classics and humanistic studies—worked with books, words, and documentary evidence. In pointing out the difference between East and West, Hu is implicitly somewhat apologetic, concluding that while Chinese scholars did create three centuries of scientific book learning, Western scientists created a new science and a new world.[87]

This evaluation was made in 1933. However, by 1959 Hu thought this opinion was neither fair nor sufficient. He renounced the apologetic tone. He declared that, although the great Chinese scholars of the seventeenth century were confined to books, words, and documents, "the books they worked on were books of tremendous importance to the moral, religious and philosophical life of the entire nation. Those great men considered it their sacred duty to find out what each and every one of these books actually meant." And, "those great men working with only books, words, and documents have actually succeeded in leaving to posterity a scientific tradition of dispassionate and disciplined inquiry, of rigorous evidential thinking and investigation, of boldness in doubt and hypotheses coupled with meticulous care in seeking verification—a great heritage of scientific spirit and method which makes us . . . feel not entirely at sea, but rather at home, in the new age of modern science."[88]

Communist Criticism of Hu Shih

The Chinese Communist stance regarding Hu Shih is that his ideas were harmful and poisonous to the minds of Chinese intellectuals. Since Hu was felt to have had a deleterious effect in the realm of ideology, the Communists waged a campaign to discredit his ideas. The scope and vehemence of this campaign were unprecedented. It began in 1950 with an initial attack by Hu Shih's son, Hu Szu-tu, who wrote an article denouncing his father as a tool of the imperialists.[89] Hu Shih conjectured, as many others did, that this article had been ghost-written by somebody other than Hu Szu-tu, because of its style and terminology of accusation.[90]

In December 1954 there began, with the strong support of the Academy of Science, a formal and large-scale campaign against Hu Shih, a campaign which lasted into 1955. Hu's thought was repudiated from nearly every angle; his philosophy, political thought, theory of history, theory of literature and of literary history, and other related fields were all targets. During the campaign more than 180 articles—about 5 million words in total—were written against Hu. The articles have been collected into a set of eight volumes under the title, *The Criticisms and Repudiation of the Thought of Hu Shih.*[91]

The aim of the campaign against Hu Shih's thought was political and ideological. Kuo Mo-jo, president of the Academy of Science, who played a leading and influential role had this to say in a speech to a meeting of people in art and literature representing the whole country: "In the past thirty years, it is generally recognized that Hu Shih is the representative of bourgeois idealism. Before the liberation, Hu was dubbed as the 'sage' and 'the present Confucius.' Hu is suported by American imperialism and becomes the number-one spokesman for the comprador bourgeoisie. . . . Hu Shih's influence, the influence of the bourgeois idealism represented by him, has even now a substantial potential force."[92] Kuo Mo-jo declared in this speech that the two principles of scientific method which Hu had advocated and propagated throughout his life—the principles of making hypotheses boldly and finding evidence carefully—comprised an idealistic method and were, moreover, within a reactionary philosophy of pragmatism, a fundamental distortion of the scientific method. (Dewey's philosophy of pragmatism has also been strongly condemned in mainland China.) Kuo further criticized another basic tenet of Hu's pragmatism, asserting that "effectiveness is truth" was tantamount to saying that "might is right."[93] Kuo ended by stating his concurrence with a statement made by Wang Jo-shui, who, in an article appearing in *Jen-min jih-pao,* had said that "The fire power of the struggle must aim at the chief of the bourgeois idealism; it is the task of cultural and intellectual leaders at present to see clearly the reactionary nature of Hu Shih's thought and to liquidate its influence."[94]

Another important article, typical of the general anti-Hu Shih attitude, was written by Hu's friend of the *Independent Critic* period, the sociologist Wu Ching-ch'ao. He claims that Hu's role on the ideological front, "since the time of Chiang Kai-shek's conspiracy with American imperialists," has been to support the interests of the American imperialists and of the ruling class, and to oppose the revolutionary movement of the people, that this is Hu's basic road and basic stand.[95] Hu's practical method of upholding the interests of the reactionary ruling class, Wu goes on to say, is first to advocate reformism against revolution, and second, to advocate bourgeois individualism against organization of the people. Wu adds that, although the success of the revolution completely shattered Hu's reformism, the poisonous effects of his ideals of individualism had not yet been completely cleansed.[96] Wu concluded that, although Hu was in the past his friend, he is now his enemy.[97]

The details of other articles criticizing Hu do not concern us here; what is important and striking is the high frequency of the world *reactionary* in the criticism, whether it ostensibly concerned his philosophy or simply his remarks on fiction. The focus of the criticism of Hu Shih was steadily political and ideological, denouncing his advocacy of gradualism and his opposition to revolution, his advocacy of liberalism and his opposition to the communist ideology.

Summary

Hu Shih's influence on modern Chinese minds has been profound. Among Chinese intellectuals he is probably the most influential after the time of Liang Ch'i-ch'ao; in the scope and depth of his influence, he even surpassed Liang in certain respects. Hu's contributions to Chinese intellectual thought may be divided into the following areas:

Pai-hua Movement. Hu's most conspicuous achievement, with epoch-making influence, was his contribution to the literary revolution; he was a leading force behind the movement to use vernacular Chinese in reading and writing. The impacts of such a change were multiple. It facilitated the introduction of Western social and natural sciences into China through a less restricted and more direct expression, making the ideas more accessible to a general reading public. It also made written communication in all its forms far more widely understood. At the same time, the change from the use of literary to vernacular Chinese lessened the time traditionally required to explain, teach, and learn the Chinese language. In essence, it served as an effective and efficient instrument for the popularization of modern education.

Introduction of Science into China. Hu's unceasing efforts to introduce science into China had wide ramifications. His support for the development of science in China, plus his use of scientific and Western methods in what he called the clarification and systematization of the old Chinese learning *(cheng-li kuo-ku)*, served to create a new era of Chinese intellectual activity and helped to broaden the horizon for Chinese studies.

Individualism. Hu Shih strongly advocated individualism as a philosophy of life worth adopting. He believed individuals should enjoy freedom from social restrictions and have the right to personal dignity. In old China, family was all important; individuals were insignificant. Hu fought to liberate the individual from the family bondage that enforced the importance of family as a unit. He felt that individuals should be allowed their own independent personalities and not be compelled to act solely as a servant, or even a slave, of the family. A man, he said, should have and follow whatever career he himself preferred rather than have a career chosen for him because it was considered advantageous to the family. And Hu said that a woman should not be regarded as the property of her husband. Hu's fight for individualism was most particularly concerned with the liberation of individuals from the tyranny of family authority and the liberation of women from male authority.

As for the importance of the individual versus the state, Hu firmly believed in the supremacy of individuals over the state. This was a belief contrary to the communist theory that the individual is of no importance because the state, being exalted as supreme and almost divine, is important above all else. Hu advised people not to heed the admonition, "sacrifice your personal freedoms for national freedom"; he insisted that "a state of true freedom and equality could not be built up by a group of slaves."[98] Hu's firm stance on individualism has, I believe, profoundly influenced a large number of intellectuals who continue to fight to defend this freedom against the pressures of totalitarianism.

The Way to Solve Chinese Problems. The chief controversies about Hu's contributions concern his approach to solving China's problems. The judgments range from excessive praise to total condemnation. Along with these two extremes of judgment, a rather frequent adverse criticism is that Hu's political ideas had no relevancy to China's practical conditions. Jerome Grieder, for example says:

> Dewey speaks pointedly of the need for "insight into both social desires and actual conditions" as the necessary foundation for a liberal approach to social change. It is on this point that his Chinese disciples, Hu Shih more than others, seem most conspicuously to have misunderstood him. Hu's values and aspirations reflected little real understanding of the "social desires" of his people or the "actual conditions" of their lives. He could never reconcile himself fully to the knowledge that for them "freedom" meant not the eventual freedom to hold their own opinions but immediate freedom from the scourge of hunger, conscription and pillage—neither more nor less. The "problems" that engaged Hu's attention, meanwhile, were for the most part the kind of intellectul riddles likely to provoke the leisurely curiosity of the professional scholar.[99]

Like many other critics, Grieder depicts Hu's ideal of freedom as abstract and irrelevant to actual Chinese circumstances. It is true that Hu was not practical in that he was not a man of action; but it is too much to say that his ideal of freedom had little to do with the welfare or the fate of his country. In a country like China that was plagued by poverty, it is true that the people did care more deeply about their immediate needs than about freedom. But Hu was not so naive as to overlook this basic human fact. His political approach, however, posited that the responsibility for effecting social change lay in the hands of a few intellectuals and scholars. He believed great social changes were possible, and indeed have come about, as the result of an intellectual movement. This aspect of Hu's political approach was substantiated even by the Chinese Communist movement, which, in its initial stage was an intellectual movement, laying the foundation for its own kind of subsequent practical measures.

Feeling that the best solution for China's problems had to be supplied by intellectuals and scholars, Hu argued that the necessary foundation for subsequent practical measures was the achievement of an atmosphere of freedom under a democratic form of government, so that they could express their opinions. He believed that public opinion would not only serve as a guide but also exert pressure on government personnel to do what they should do. He believed that without such freedom, the fate of a country would be left to the mercy of ignorant and brutal military men (warlords) or to ambitious politicians whose fight for power would embroil the country in endless chaos and turmoil. Hu strongly opposed revolution by violence because he was convinced that this would only increase the sufferings of the people. The best way to serve his country, he thought, was to provide a democratic method—rather than a revolution—that could establish and guarantee the political freedom he advocated; once political stability was achieved, and human rights protected, he believed that the problem of the people's livelihood, along with many other problems, would be effectively solved also. Though he was unable to put his vision into effect, it is just to recognize that he himself considered his recommendations practicable, and he committed himself to the cause of his country and was not merely amusing himself with abstract theories.

Wholesale Westernization. Hu was adamant in his belief in China's need to be cordial to Westernization. But though, as indicated above, he later dropped the term wholesale Westernization and in fact advocated selective Westernization, the impression left with the people that he wished China to become uncritically and indiscriminately Westernized became deeply etched and hard to remove. Obviously, Hu's primary aim was to awaken China from slumber. In order to get his points across he risked an exaggerated rhetoric. He said, for instance, that the Chinese must admit their inferiority (to Westerners) in every respect, not only in material things and machines, not only in the political system, but also in morality, knowledge, literature, music, art and even the physical build of the body. [100] He urged the Chinese people to admit all this and proceed to learn wholeheartedly from the West. To do Hu justice, he did not mean that they should learn uncritically and indiscriminately. What he meant by Westernization was really very straightforward: take the United States as a political and scientific model. But his way of advocating Westernization came to be regarded by many as responsible, to a considerable degree, for Chinese loss of national confidence and pride. His attitude is denounced by the Chinese Communists as the worship-America mentality. Although Hu does not deserve to be denounced, it may be conceded that the kinds of overstatement which he employed in an effort to rouse the Chinese into action to save themselves inadvertently led some Chinese to lose self-confidence and others to resent his views since they felt such views to be a threat to national pride.

After all, Hu Shih is a great liberal in modern China. Although in the 1950s he had been singled out in communist China as the most notorious reactionary and the worst enemy of the people, his contributions to China cannot be overshadowed by these accusations. His influences have been sweeping and many sided. Hu's contribution to the literary revolution of abandoning the classical style of thousands of years in favor of the vernacular style in writing is monumental, benefitting every literate Chinese, irrespective of whether one is a bourgeois or a proletariat. His glorification of and efforts to introduce science into China is definitely an endeavor of classless nature. His fight for freedom and human rights aimed at the greatest happiness for the greatest number, rather than at the interests of a specific class of people. Thus, the communist accusations are only a groundless political prejudice.

Notes

[1] This biographical sketch is heavily based on Hu Shih, *Szu-shih tzu-shu* (Shanghai, Ya-tung t'u-shu kuan, 1933); Hu Sung-p'ing, *Hu Shih hsien-sheng nien-p'u chien-pien* (Taipei: Ta-lu tsa-chih she, 1971).

[2] Hu Shih, "Chieh-shao wo tzu-chi te szu-hsiang," *Hu Shih wen-ts'un* (Taipei: Yuan-tung tu-shu kung-szu, 1953), 4:608. Hereafter referred to as *Wen-ts'un.*

[3] Ibid., 609.

[4] Hu Shih, "Hsin szu-ch'ao te i-i," *Wen-ts'un* 1:736.

[5] Hu Shih, "Shih-yen chu-i," *Wen-ts'un* 1:309–10.

[6] Hu Shih, "I-pu-sheng chu-i," *Wen-ts'un* 1:646.

[7] Hu Shih, "Shih-yen chu-i," *Wen-ts'un* 1:294.

[8] Yao P'eng-tzu, *P'i-p'an Hu Shih shih-yung chu-i te fan-tung hsing ho fan k'o-hsueh hsing* (Shanghai: Shanghai ch'u-pan kung-szu, 1955), pp. 16–17.

[9] Ibid., p. 13.

[10] Hu Shih, "Tuo yen-chiu hsieh wen-t'i, shao t'an hsieh chu-i," *Wen-ts'un* 1:344.

[11] Ibid., 1:345–346.

[12] Lan's article originally appeared in *Kuo-min kung-pao* and was reprinted in abridged form, Hu Shih, *Wen-ts'un* 1:346–57; Li Ta-chao's article in Hu Shih, *Wen-ts'un* 1:357–63.

[13] For details of Li's argument, see Hu Shih, *Wen-ts'un,* especially 1:357–60.

[14] Ibid., p. 363.

[15] Yao P'eng-tzu, *P'i-p'an Hu Shih,* p. 70.

[16] Hu Shih, "San-lun wen-t'i yü chu-i," *Wen-ts'un* 1:373.

[17] Hu Shih, "Hsin szu-ch'ao te i-i," *Wen-ts'un* 1:736.

[18] Yao P'eng-tzu, *P'i-p'an Hu Shih,* p. 20.

[19] Ibid., p. 67.

[20] Hu Shih, "Chieh-shao wo tzu-chi te szu-hsiang," *Wen-ts'un* 4:624.

[21] Hu Shih, et al., "Wo-men tsou nei-t'iao-lu?" *Hu Shih yü Chung-hsi wen-hua* (Taipei: Buffalo, 1967), pp. 83–84 (hereafter referred to as *Chung-hsi wen-hua*).

[22] Ibid., p. 87.

[23] Ibid., pp. 92–94.

[24] Liang Shu-ming, "Ching i ch'ing-chiao Hu Shih-chih hsien-sheng," originally published in *Ts'un-chih,* 1930, no. 2. Reprinted in *Hu Shih lun-hsueh chin-chu* (Shanghai, Commercial, 1935), 1:454–59.

[25] Hu Shih, "Ta Liang Shu-ming hsien-sheng," ibid., p. 466.

[26] Liang Shu-ming, "Ching i ch'ing-chiao," *Hu Shih lun-hsueh chin-chu,* 1:457, 462–63.

[27] A decree issued by the Nationalist government on 20 April 1929 to protect human rights. It reads as follows: "The human rights of all the countries of the world are protected by law. At the time of the beginning of the tutelage, legal foundation is to be immediately established. Any individual or group within the jurisdiction of the Republic of China shall not by illegal behavior infringe the person, freedoms, and property of others. Those who violate this shall be punished by law." Hu Shih, "Jen-ch'üan yü yueh-fa," originally appeared in *Hsin-yueh yueh-k'an,* vol. 2, no. 2. Reprinted in Liang Shih-ch'iu et al., *Jen-ch'üan lun-chi* (Shanghai, Hsin-yueh shu-tien, 1941), p. 1.

[28] *Jen-ch'üan lun-chi,* p. 8.

[29] Hu Shih, "Wo-men shen-ma shih-hou ts'ai-k'o yu hsien-fa?" originally appeared in *Hsin-yueh,* 1928. Reprinted, *Jen-ch'üan lun-chi,* p. 32.

[30] For Hu's arguments against Sun's theory, see the section on the chapter on Sun Yat-sen of this book. Hu's articles criticizing the Kuomintang, supplemented by the rebuttals of his opponents are collected in a book by Chang Chen-chih et al., *P'ing Hu Shih fan*

tang-i chin-chu (Shanghai: Kuang-ming shu-chü, 1929).

[31] Hu Shih, "Hsin wen-hua yun-tung yü Kuomintang," *Jen-ch'üan lun-chi,* pp. 123–5. The other two accounts are (1) the Nationalist government was using classical Chinese as the official language; (2) the Nationalist government was in favor of the old classical Chinese culture in opposition to adoption of the New World Culture.

[32] Ibid., p. 142.

[33] T.F. Tsiang (Chiang T'ing-fu), "Ko-ming yü chuan-chih," *Tu-li p'ing-lun,* no. 80 (20 December 1933), pp. 4–5.

[34] Hu Shih, "Chien-kuo yü chuan-chih," *Tu-li p'ing-lun,* no. 81 (27 December 1933), p. 3.

[35] T.F. Tsiang, "Lun chuan-chih ping ta Hu Shih-chih hsien-sheng," *Tu-li p'ing-lun,* no. 83 (31 December 1933), p. 5.

[36] Hu Shih, "Tsai-lun chien-kuo yü chuan-chih," *Tu-li p'ing-lun,* no. 82 (24 December 1933), pp. 3–4. In this article, Hu used the word "chuan-chih" (absolutism), "chuan-cheng" (dictatorship) and even "hsun-cheng" (tutelage) synonymously to mean dictatorship. For the sake of simplicity and smoothness in English translation, the word dictatorship is generally used.

[37] Ibid., pp. 4–5.

[38] Hu Shih, "Ts'ung i-tang tao wu-tang cheng-chih," *Tu-li p'ing-lun,* no. 171 (6 October 1935), p. 11.

[39] Hu Shih, "Tsai-t'an hsien-cheng," *Tu-li p'ing-lun,* no. 236 (30 May 1937), p. 5

[40] Ting Wen-chiang (V. K. Ting), "Min-chu cheng-chih yü tu-ts'ai cheng-chih," *Tu-li p'ing-lun* no. 133 (30 December 1934), pp. 5-7.

[41] Ch'ien Tuan-sheng, "Min-chu cheng-chih hu, chi-ch'üan kuo-chia hu?" *Tung-fang tsa-chih* 31, no. 1 (1 January 1934):24.

[42] Wu Ching-ch'ao, "Ko-ming yü chien-kuo," *Tu-li p'ing-lun,* no. 84 (7 January 1934), p. 4. Wu's studies of the history of civil wars or internal disturbances *(nei-luan)* reveal three stages: (1) bad government or tyrannical government results in a revolution to overthrow the government; (2) different leaders fight for power until the new unification is achieved; (3) good government begins—which brings peace or national construction. At that time China was in the second stage of the fight for power by autonomous leaders. Hence, Wu saw no possibility of unification except by initial use of military force. For the three stages, ibid., p. 2.

[43] Hu Shih, "Ts'ung min-chu tu-ts'ai te t'ao-lun li ch'iu-te i-ko kung-t'ung te cheng-chih hsin-yang," *Tu-li p'ing-lun,* no. 141 (17 February 1935), pp. 18–19.

[44] For the summary and the evaluation of the debate by Hu, see Hu Shih, "I-nien lai kuan-yü min-chu yü tu-ts'ai te t'ao-lun," *Tung-fang tsa-chih* 32, no. 1 (1 January 1935):15–23. This particular reference, see p. 21.

[45] Mao Tse-tung, "Chan-cheng ho chan-lueh wen-t'i," *MTTHC,* p. 512.

[46] Hu Shih "Yen-ch'ien shih-chieh wen-hua te ch'ü-hsiang," *Wo-men pi-hsu hsuan-tse wo-men te fang-hsiang* (Hong Kong: Tzu-yu Chung-kuo ch'u-pan she, 1950), p. 8.

[47] Ibid., pp.10–11.

[48] Ibid., pp.14–15.

[49] Ibid., p.17.

[50] Hu Shih "San-pai nien-lai shih-chieh te ch'ü-shih yü Chung-kuo ying ts'ai te fang-hsiang," *Chung-hsi wen-hua,* p. 195.

[51] Hu Shih, "Tzu-yu chu-i shih shen-mo?" *Wo-men pi-hsu hsuan-tse wo-men te fang-hsiang,* p. 25.

[52] Ibid., pp. 26–27.

[53] Hu Shih, "Kung-ch'an tang chih-hsia chueh mei-yu tzu-yu," ibid., p. 61.

[54] Hu Shih, "Chung-kuo ku-tai cheng-chih szu-hsiang shih te i-ko k'an fa," *Chung-hsi wen-hua,* p. 197 ff.

[55] Ibid., pp. 203–4.

[56] *Confucian Analects*, bk. 15, ch. 38.

[57] Ibid., bk. 14, ch. 45.

[58] Hu Shih, *Chung-hsi wen-hua*, pp. 205–7.

[59] Ibid., pp. 207–211.

[60] For details of the movement see: Yang Jung-kuo, "Ch'un-ch'iu chan-kuo shih-ch'i szu-hsiang ling-yü nei liang-t'iao lu-hsien te tou-cheng," *Hung-ch'i*, no. 12 (1972), pp. 45–54; "K'ung-tzu—wan-ku te wei-hu nu-li chih-tu te szu-hsiang-chia," *Jen-min jih-pao*, 7 August 1973, translated under the title "Confucius—a Thinker Who Stubbornly Upheld the Slave System," *Peking Review*, no. 41 (12 October 1973):5–10; Shih Ts'ang, "Lun tsun-ju fan-fa," *Hung-ch'i*, no. 10 (1973), pp. 33–43.

[61] Hu Shih, *Chung-hsi wen-hua*, pp. 211–13.

[62] Although Hu used the word Eastern or Oriental, he employed the term to signify the Chinese. "Wo-men tui-yü hsi-yang chin-tai wen-ming te t'ai-tu," *Chung-hsi wen-hua*, p. 53.

[63] Hu Shih, "The Civilization of the East and the West," in Charles A. Beard, ed., *Whither Mankind* (New York: Longmans, Green, 1928), p. 25.

[64] Hu Shih, *Chung-hsi wen-hua*, p. 54.

[65] Hu Shih, "The Civilization of the East and the West," in Beard, op. cit., p. 27.

[66] For details, see Hu Shih, *Chung-hsi wen-hua*, pp. 56–8.

[67] Hu Shih, "The Civilization of the East and the West," in Beard, op. cit., p. 37.

[68] Ibid., pp.37–9; see also Hu Shih, "Tui-yü hsi-yang chin-tai wen-ming," *Chung-hsi wen-hua*, pp. 61–63.

[69] Hu Shih, "The Civilization of the East and the West," in Beard, op. cit., p. 41.

[70] Hu Shih, "The Social Changes and Science," in *The China News* (Taipei), March 1962, p. 41.

[71] For a historical account of Hu's terms used and the related debates, see Hsu Kao-juan, "Hu Shih-chih yü ch'üan-p'an hsi-hua," *Chung-hsi wen-hua*, pp.11–23.

[72] For Hu's account of the term see Hu Shih, "Ch'ung-fen shih-chieh-hua yü ch'üan-p'an hsi-hua," *Chung-hsi wen-hua*, pp. 139–140.

[73] For Hu's self-professed religious belief, see his "Pu-hsiu—Wo-te tsung-chiao," *Wen-ts'un* 1:693–702.

[74] Hu Shih, "Chieh-shao wo tzu-chi te szu-hsiang," *Wen-ts'un* 4:617.

[75] For the whole text, see Wang Hsin-ming et al., "Chung-kuo pen-wei te wen-hua chien-she hsuan-yen," *Chung-hsi wen-hua*, pp. 127–31. (For the three key principles see especially pp. 130–31.)

[76] Hu Shih, "Shih-p'ing so-wei Chung-kuo pen-wei te wen-hua chien-she," *Chung-hsi wen-hua*, p. 137.

[77] Hu Shih, "Chieh-shao wo tzu-chi te szu-hsiang," *Wen-ts'un* 4:618.

[78] Joseph Needham argues that Chinese science and technique were, generally speaking, very much more advanced than that of Europe between the third century B.C. and the fifth century A.D., but after the Renaissance Europe began to lead. As to why nothing corresponding to the Renaissance took place in China, he attributes this to the nature and development of Chinese society. For details of the argument, see Needham, *Within the Four Seas* (London: Allen & Unwin, 1969), pp. 83–7.

[79] Hu Shih, "Ch'ing-tai hsueh-che te chih-hsueh fang-fa," *Wen-ts'un* 1:391. For *k'ao-ting-hsueh*, Hu put "higher criticism" in parenthesis in his original Chinese text. For clarity, it is changed to "authenticity of old books" by the present writer.

[80] The following condensation is based on Hu Shih, "The Scientific Spirit and Method in Chinese Philosophy," in Charles A. Moore, ed., *The Chinese Mind: Essentials of Chinese Philosophy and Culture*, (Honolulu: East-West Center, 1967), pp. 108–10.

[81] *Mencius*, bk. 7, pt. 2, ch. 3. Translation mine. James Legge has this to say in his footnote to this section: "This is a difficult chapter of Chinese commentators. Chao K'e takes [the character] *shu* of the *Shoo-king [Book of History]* which is the only fair

interpretation. Others understand it of books in general." If we take the latter interpretation, it fits Hu's argument better and gives more weight to the attitude of doubt. In actual practice, many Chinese, in quoting this passage, do mean books in general.

82 In the original text, Hu did not give the reference for this statement. As shown in the editor's note of Moore's book, it is said that "Because of serious illness and death of Dr. Hu it has been impossible to provide complete references for some of his quotations from classical texts." Moore, *The Chinese Mind,* p. 108.

83 The sources for Confucius' quotations are not given in Hu's article. For Confucius' answer on knowledge, see *The Analects,* bk. 2, ch. 17; for his answers on spirits and gods and death, see ibid., bk. 2, ch. 11.

84 The following condensation of Lao-tzu's philosophy is based on Hu Shih, "Scientific Spirit and Method in Chinese Philosophy," Moore, *The Chinese Mind,* pp. 110–11. The definition of naturalism was not given by Hu; in Vincent Shih's interview with Hu Shih, Shih said that he regretted he had not pressed Hu for his definition of the term. Shih presumed Hu meant an attitude of resignation to the natural course of things, resulting in the paralysis of individual initiative. See Vincent Shih, "A Talk With Hu Shih," *China Quarterly,* no. 10 (1962):159.

85 Hu Shih, "Scientific Spirit and Method in Chinese Philosophy," Moore, *The Chinese Mind,* p. 115. For the subsequent points condensed, see ibid. pp. 127–128.

86 Hu Shih, *The Chinese Renaissance* (Chicago: The University of Chicago Press, 1934), p. 71.

87 Ibid., pp.70–71.

88 Hu Shih, "Scientific Spirit and Method," Moore, *The Chinese Mind,* pp. 129–31.

89 Hu Szu-tu, "Tui wo-te fu-ch'in Hu Shih te p'i-p'ing," *Jen-min jih-pao,* 22 September 1950. Hu's son was reported to have committed suicide.

90 Hu Shih personally told me this story in the mid-fifties in Monterey, California.

91 *Hu Shih szu-hsiang p'i-p'an* (Peking: San-lien shu-tien, 1955–1956).

92 Kuo Mo-jo, "San-tien chien-i," ibid., 1:9–10.

93 Ibid., pp.10–11.

94 Wang Jo-shui, "Ch'ing-ch'u Hu Shih che-hsueh te fan-tung i-tu," which originally appeared in *Jen-min jih-pao,* 5 November 1954. It is quoted in *Hu Shih szu-hsiang p'i-p'an,* p. 11.

95 Wu Ching-ch'ao, "Wo yü Hu Shih—ts'ung p'eng-yu tao ti-jen," *Hu-shih szu-hsiang p'i-p'an* 3:107–8.

96 Ibid., p.109.

97 Ibid., p.111.

98 Hu Shih, "Chieh-shao wo tzu-chi te szu-hsiang," *Wen-ts'un* 4:613.

99 Jerome B. Grieder, *Hu Shih and the Chinese Renaissance* (Cambridge: Harvard University Press, 1970), pp. 340–41.

100 Hu Shih, "Chieh-shao wo tzu-chi te szu-hsiang," *Wen-ts'un* 4:618.

5
Chang Chün-mai (1887–1969)

Biography

Chang Chün-mai[1] occupies a special position in modern Chinese intellectual history as a person who devoted his entire life more wholeheartedly than anybody else to a democratic movement that would bring about in China a government based on a national constitution and controlled by a parliament. His given name at birth, Chia-sen, was romanized in the Shanghai dialect as Car-sun, and thus he is generally known in the Western world as Carsun Chang. Among Chinese speakers, he is generally known by his courtesy name, Chün-mai. Chang came from a long line of scholars and professional men. Both his father and his greatgrandfather were medical doctors, and his grandfather passed the imperial examination with the *chü-jen* degree and was a magistrate in Szechwan province for more than ten years. Several of his eleven brothers and sisters became prominent in business and finance.

Carsun Chang was born in Chia-ting, Kiangsu, on 18 January 1887. At six he began his education in the family school run by his uncle, and at twelve he entered the Foreign Language School of the Kiangnan Arsenal *(Shang-hai Chiang-nan chih-tsao chü kuang-fang yen-kuan)* founded by Li Hung-chang. Here, in addition to Chinese, Chang studied English, physics, chemistry, and mathematics. During these early student days in Shanghai, the Hundred Days' Reform broke out in 1898. However, this early attempt at sweeping reform of China's military, political, and educational institutions was quickly and easily squelched by the Empress Dowager. At that time, large portraits of the two leading protagonists who were sought for high treason—K'ang Yu-wei and Liang Ch'i-ch'ao—were posted at the entrance to the school. The sight made such an impression on Chang that then and there he vowed to spend his life serving his country.

Carsun Chang passed the new imperial examination *(ts'e-lun)* at seventeen with the *hsiu-ts'ai*, or first, degree. A year later, he was inspired by an article by Liang Ch'i-ch'ao on the future of the Aurora Catholic University *(Chen-tan)*. He enrolled to study Latin but dropped out after half year due to financial difficulties and instead entered the Nanking Higher School *(Nan-ching kao-teng hsüeh hsiao)*.

Though he harbored vague thoughts of reform and service to his country during his early school days, it was not until he personally became acquainted

135

with Liang Ch'i-ch'ao that he articulated his ideals in concrete terms. Their first meeting, which took place in Japan, proved to be a turning point in Carsun Chang's life, both ideologically and politically. Chang had gone to Japan in 1906 to study at Waseda University on a government scholarship and received a B.A. degree in political science in 1910. Liang had taken refuge in Japan after the failure of the Hundred Days' Reform. After this first meeting (1906), Carsun Chang quickly committed himself in his political position by joining the *Cheng-wen She* (Political Information Society), a short-lived (1906–1908) political party under the leadership of Liang. In 1910, Chang returned to China and, by a new kind of imperial examination, received the so-called "foreign" *han-lin* degree.

Chang's ideological outlook was also influenced by contact with Western thinkers. From 1913 to 1915 he studied at the University Berlin. Further contacts with the West included travel in France and in England, where he visited the British Parliament. He returned to China in 1916 but was back in Europe on New Year's Eve of 1918, accompanying Liang Ch'i-ch'ao and a small group of friends to France in an unofficial capacity to the Paris Peace Conference, and later investigated postwar Europe. He personally studied philosophy under the famous German philosopher Rudolf Eucken in Jena before returning again to China in early 1922. These European experiences were responsible for a significant shift of interest from social science to philosophy.

On 14 February 1923, Carsun Chang launched the famous "Science and Philosophy Debate" with a speech before the students of Tsing Hua College on the topic of the Philosophy of Life *(jen-sheng kuan)*. Alarmed by the near idolatry of Western learning, especially of science, Chang argued that science is not omnipotent in solving man's problems. Instead, he believed that a philosophy of life must not rely on scientific laws but on the free will of man. This lecture aroused vehement opposition from those who believed in the cult of science. The first man to oppose Chang was his friend V. K. Ting (Ting Wen-chiang), the famous geologist, who ridiculed Chang as being possessed by the "metaphysical devil of Europe." A heated and lengthy polemic ensued, lasting almost the entire year, with the participation of almost all leading thinkers of the day.[2]

Chang's experience with educational work, either as a professor or as an administrator, was not a happy one. He taught for a year at Peking University (1917–18), at Yenching University (1932–33), and at the Sun Yat-sen University in Canton during 1933. He voluntarily resigned from the first post and was asked to leave the other two because of his political views. In addition, Carsun Chang's attempts at administration were all unsatisfactory—every one of his schools ended in failure. In 1923, for example, he was made president of the National Self-Government Institute *(Kuo-li tzu-chih hsueh-yuan)* in Shanghai, renamed the Political Science University *(Cheng-chih ta-hsueh)* in 1925. But in 1927, the university was closed down by the Nationalist government after its occupation of Shanghai. In 1934 he founded a graduate school in Canton, called the Hsueh-hai Academy *(Hsueh-hai shu-yuan)*, with the support of the governor of Canton, Ch'en Chi-t'ang. It was a post-graduate school of philosophy and political science named after the prestigious Hsueh-hai t'ang of the Ch'ing dynasty, noted for the studies and publications of classics. The academy came to an end with Ch'en's abortive rebellion against Chiang Kai-shek in 1936. Again, in 1940, Chang founded the Academy of National Culture *(Min-tsu wen-hua hsueh-yuan)* in Ta-li, Yunnan. It, too, was short-lived and closed by the Nationalists in 1942 on the allegation that Carsun Chang had stirred up the student riot against the government in Kunming, capital of Yunnan.

In the field of publications, Carsun Chang founded and edited, at various times, four different magazines. The first was *New Way (Hsin-lu)*, published in Shanghai in 1928 and suspended by the Nationalists the following year. A second publication was *National Renaissance (Tsai-sheng)*, founded in 1932, and still being published in Taiwan by his former students of the Political Science University. The third was *The Universe (Yü-chou)*, originally published in Hong Kong in 1934. It ceased publication in 1935 but was also resumed in Taiwan in 1960 by his students of the Political Science University. The last magazine he founded was *Liberty Bell (Tzu-yu chung)*, first published in March 1965 and ending with his death in February 1969. It was almost entirely his own personal work, consisting mainly of articles he wrote in his later years while residing in the San Francisco Bay area.

Carsun Chang's firm belief in, and persistent advocacy of, the democratic form of government, especially the parliamentary system, was unique in China. When the Nationalists triumphantly occupied Nanking in 1927, he was the first, contrary to the general enthusiasm expressed for the new government, to oppose the one-party rule of the Nationalists. He retained this stand throughout his lifetime, tirelessly inveighing against dictatorships of both the Right and the Left. Not content with mere verbiage, Chang, in order to effect a parliamentary system with an opposition party, organized, with the aid of some friends, a political party, the National Socialist Party *(Kuo-chia she-hui tang)*, in 1932. It was renamed the Democratic Socialist Party *(Min-chu she-hui tang)* in 1946, when it amalgamated with the Chinese Democratic Constitutional Party *(Min-chu hsien-cheng tang)*, formed by overseas Chinese living in North America, and originally founded by K'ang Yu-wei after his failure of the Hundred Days' Reform.

At the outbreak of the War of Resistance against Japan, Carsun Chang appealed passionately for national unity in order to preserve China's existence and independence. He accepted the invitation to become a member of the People's Political Council *(Kuo-min ts'an-cheng hui)*, an advisory and consultative organization sponsored by the government. In 1938, after an exchange of notes with Chiang Kai-shek and Wang Ching-wei (the Director-General and Vice Director-General of the Kuomintang), his underground party was given official recognition.

After the fall of Hankow, Chang wrote an open letter to Mao Tse-tung, dated

10 December 1938, urging the Communists to submit their troops to the control of the Nationalist government and to dissolve their autonomous government in order to achieve unity in the war against Japan. With a view to bringing together all minor political groups and parties together for national democratic reform, Chang was active in 1941 in the China Democratic League *(Min-chu t'ung-meng)*, which was previously called the Alliance of All Political Groups *(Ming-chu cheng-t'uan t'ung-meng)*. In 1945 Chang was appointed, as a representative of his party, by the Nationalist government as a member of the Chinese delegation to the United Nations Conference on International Organization in San Francisco. In this same year, when General George C. Marshall went to China in an attempt to mend the Nationalist-Communist rift, Carsun Chang, on behalf of his party, participated in the political Consultative Conference. His dream of adopting a constitution also came true when the Constitution of the Republic of China was adopted by the National Assembly on 25 December 1946. The draft constitution was drawn up by Carsun Chang. It was reviewed article by article in Chungking by the Constitutional Draft Reviewing Committee *(Hsien-ts'ao hsiao-tsu hui-i)*, a group made up of representatives of both the Nationalist and Communist parties, as well as other minor parties. The Communists also initially agreed to the Constitution, sending Chou En-lai as their delegate personally to attend many of the sessions. It is significant that ninety percent of the contents in the revised draft was retained in the final version.

In the latter part of 1946, the political parties and factions in China were split into two uncompromising camps, one siding with the Nationalist government and prepared to participate in the National Assembly seeking the adoption of the Constitution, the other siding with the Communists who were trying to boycott the National Assembly and defeat the constitutional proposals. Carsun Chang and his party chose the first alternative and withdrew from the Democratic League.[3] Eventually, the breach between the Nationalists and the Communists was beyond repair and led to the final break. When the situation of the Nationalists deteriorated to the point of their inability to maintain their position in the civil war against the Communists, Carsun Chang wrote a letter to Chiang Kai-shek, dated 8 November 1948, urging him to resign.

As soon as the People's Republic of China was established, Carsun Chang began to oppose it. Beginning in 1949, he joined the Democratic China Movement *(Min-chu Chung-kuo yun-tung)* in Hong Kong under the leadership of Ku Meng-yü and supported by such persons as Chang Fa-k'uei and Chang Kuo-t'ao. This is generally known as the third force, which died out around 1955.

Carsun Chang came to the United States in 1952, where he remained, except for some brief trips to India, Japan, Korea, Hong Kong, and Philippines, as well as Switzerland, England, and Germany, until the end of his life. He died on 23 February 1969, in Berkeley, California, at the age of 82. His collected works are published in Taiwan.

Carsun Chang's Political Conceptions

National Consciousness versus Class Concept

Unlike the communists, who put the blame on imperialist aggression from without and the bureaucracy and feudalism from within, for the weakness and poverty of China, Carsun Chang held that the misery modern China was essentially due to the moral bankruptcy of the scholar-official class *(shih ta-fu)*. This class, he conceded, was not the ruling class, but although subsidiary, it was of great influence in running the government. All the periods of good order in the dynastic history were probably due to their efforts. Under the impact of the West, China had no choice but to adapt to world trends. The old method mastered by the scholar-official class of running the government was obsolete and had to come to an end, but the scholar-officials were unable to accept this. Even worse, the scholar-officials, having lost traditional morality, became purely self-seeking. As an increasingly parasitic political group, they could no longer be given the responsibility of building a new China. Unlike the class struggle solution of the communists, Carsun Chang sought to awaken national consciousness to bring about a national regeneration by all classes of people and not just one special class.

The concept of nation, Chang claims, is most potent in the development of man and society—far more powerful than the concept of class. All history has proved that when national interest is aroused, it overcomes class barriers. In China the War of Resistance against Japan (1937–1945) is a case in point where labor and management, two factions usually in mutual conflict, united and cooperated during the crisis. And farmers and soldiers, often mutually hostile, joined ranks in opposition to Japanese invasion. In Japan, the proletariat, according to Marxist theory, should have been sympathetic to China, especially to the Chinese proletariat; in fact it was subservient to the national interests of the Japanese militarists. The Soviet Union is cited by Chang as a further example: the relative success of the Soviet Union does not lie in the pursuit of the policy of proletarian internationalism, but is due to the intensive development of socialism in one country, The Soviet Union is further viewed as a country practicing collective production within and imperialism without, which is in no way different from any other imperialist power. Carsun Chang made this accusation long before the phrase "social imperialism" was applied by the Chinese Communists to the Soviet Union.

Again, unlike the communists, who emphasize the conflict of class interest, Carsun Chang sees no advantage in one class fighting another. Anyone who takes the class stand aims at struggling against his fellow countrymen: struggle is generated by a "philosophy of hatred." Carsun Chang sought to replace it with a "natural benevolence"; for hatred begets hatred, and no harmony and peace can result from class struggle. It is Carsun Chang's profound belief that, regardless of how diverse the interests of different people, a common interest can be generated by taking the nation as a whole as a starting point to cancel out individual differences. It is this common interest which is the foundation upon which diverse personal interests are dependent. When one segment of the population suffers, the whole national body suffers. His view was thus an organic view. For instance, when one area of China is invaded by a foreign power, everybody suffers irrespective of whether he is worker, peasant, official, or soldier; it is not merely those immediately afflicted. Thus, Carsun Chang, borrowing a Marxist term, refers to all individual interests as the "superstructure" and all common interests as the "substructure." And the common interest of the people as a whole constitutes a tremendous and indestructible force.[4]

Carsun Chang's vision for China's reconstruction is to build up a regenerated nation-state. This is to be done through a national organization for all people. It will maintain national independence, particularly cultural independence, and aim at the development of individual freedom and equality. To elaborate upon his ideas, Carson Chang raises six important points:

1. A sovereign state differs from other organizations in its culture; the considerations of the interests of labor and management should *not* be the supreme goal.
2. The characteristic of a state lies in culture, which is a spiritual achievement, wholly different from the material interests of food, clothing, and shelter.
3. The essence of spiritual organization requires individual sacrifice for the good of the whole.
4. Taking the interest of the community as the goal, it is necessary to put obligation before rights; during a crisis involving a foreign state, such as in war, if one's life belongs to the state, how much less important are one's rights?
5. For the sake of protecting the whole community, there must be moral restraint; for example, one cannot force people to plant opium for financial purposes or be in collusion with a foreign state for the seizure of political power.
6. Since there is an innate difference in the intelligence and difference in professions of people, class distinction is unavoidable; the ultimate goal, however, should be equality and freedom, which is the justification behind the advocacy of socialism.[5]

Rejecting the desirability of material things, which he considers crass and destructible, Carsun Chang maintains that the basic foundation of building a country lies in spirit, which he calls mental power or spiritual power *(hsin-li)*. This mental power consists of three factors: true love, true reason, and true will. But in whom is the new spiritual power going to be nourished and cultivated? Since he dismisses the morally depraved class of scholar-officials as incorrigible, he turns to the masses, the common people of China. Chang argues that it is better to put one's hopes for the reconstruction of the country in the illiterate masses rather than in the intellectuals, in the villages rather than in the cities, in the toiling masses who earn their own living rather than the monied class which is supported by them.[6]

The above is Carsun Chang's general view of the way to rebuild China, obviously at odds with both Nationalists and Communists. Let us turn to a more detailed look at his specific views of political, economic, educational, and cultural institutions.

Democracy versus Dictatorship

One-party Dictatorship. Carsun Chang was a strong opponent of any kind of dictatorship. As early as 1928, when the national government was first founded, he voiced opposition to one-party rule.

In the introductory article to *New Way (Hsin-lu)*, a periodical founded and edited by Chang himself, he enumerated twelve basic political beliefs. These include a democratic government, opposition to both one-class and one-party dictatorships, freedom of speech and association, opposition to the denial of these basic human rights under the pretext of party or military rule, the opposition to party control of education, of judicial affairs, of civil servants, and the use of the army for personal or party purposes.[7]

Following the establishment of the dictatorship of the proletariat in the Soviet Union in 1917, Carsun Chang noticed that there emerged in China the argument for party rule over the state, and for one-party dictatorship. Here the party in question was the Nationalist Party. Chang came to the conclusion that the dictatorship of the Kuomintang was an utter failure and warned that any dictatorship would meet the same fate. To substantiate his theory that all dictatorships would fail, Carsun Chang urged four arguments against dictatorship, with particular reference to the Nationalists: (1) Because a dictatorship allows no opposition, its policy is unpredictable and liable to shift. (2) Dictatorship is not based on constitutional law. Usurpation of power by force is a frequent phenomenon. In a dictatorial state, the power of the party is greater than that of the national constitution. In China there is only a Party constitution and no national constitution. (3) Under a dictatorship it is never known to whom the government is responsible. This often gives rise to corrupt leaders. At various times there was alignment with and opposition to the Communists under the same leader and government, but this equivocation took the lives of thousands of young men, and neither the government nor the leaders were ever blamed. (4) Under a dictatorship, public opinion is manipulated by the government; thus, the people have no opportunities to develop their political capacity.

Thus, Carsun Chang concluded that the only road leading to the salvation of China is democracy. Negatively, he proposed the termination of the monopoly of political activities by the Kuomintang party organization and the end of its tutelage. On the constructive side, he recommended four measures: the protection of freedom of speech; the protection of freedom of association and assembly; the speedy preparation for the draft of a national constitution; and the practice of multi-party politics.[8]

Carsun Chang points to several shortcomings of dictatorship. The achievements of the dictatorships of Italy, Germany, and Russia have been attained at a high price: the sacrifice of liberty gained during the last hundred years. Once the freedom of speech and association is banned and parliamentary politics are smothered, liberty is lost and an environment is created that nurtures a kind of hidden hatred and anger in the minds of the entire country, sowing the seeds of further disaster.

First, a dictatorship requires extraordinary individuals, such as Alexander and Napoleon of earlier times, and Stalin, Hitler, and Mussolini in the modern world. But when a dictator dies, the problem of succession is open to power politics. Second, human opinions can never be unified: a dictator may try to coerce a country into unanimous agreement, but this causes strife and bloody struggle, especially during times of crisis and transition. In a democracy, on the other hand, conflicting opinions do exist, but the various parties are able to solve their differences by peaceful means. Third, since dictators glory in public adulation, they are thus forced to achieve impressive feats. In Russia, for example, the Five-Year Plan was carried out despite the hardship of the people. Italy and Germany, owing to their limited internal development, resorted to foreign aggression. But, requiring showy accomplishments, dictators cannot withstand defeat. Dictatorships that can dazzle for a moment are far inferior to a democracy that can last for centuries.[9]

Program of Revised Democracy. Carsun Chang believes that the democratic movement in China began immediately prior to 1911; before World War I, there seemed to be a consensus among Chinese leaders that China must adopt democracy. There was only one model to follow: the parliamentary form of government. But, after repeated failures in creating such a system, opinion differed in the 1930s. Those who did not favor democracy raised two main objections to the development of a democratic form of government in China: first, democracy is, by definition, dependent upon the equal participation of every citizen, but the educational level of the Chinese people was considered elementary; second, the currents of international political thought had turned away from democracy and leaned toward dictatorship.

Carsun Chang refutes both of these objections vigorously. He opposes the first objection by saying that democracy is basically a matter of principle, and, that while a perfect democracy is ideal, a democracy of 90 percent or even 50 or 40 percent is better than none at all. In other words, the government he wished to see is one based on democratic principles instead of dictatorial ones. The system, however, must fit the educational level of the people as far as the degree of democracy is concerned.

Next, he directed his criticism against the theory of tutelage of the Kuomintang. If the Chinese people were all unable to practice democracy because of their educational level, then how could the Kuomintang, a part of this same educational milieu and therefore inexperienced, claim to be qualified to train the rest of their countrymen in democracy?

Carsun Chang observed that people in the 1930s who believed strongly in the Anglo-American form of government naturally tended to favor democracy, while those who were dazzled by the quick and surprising achievements of dictatorships tended to favor either Soviet totalitarianism on the Left or German or Italian dictatorships on the Right. China found herself in the middle of the political spectrum, and Carsun Chang tried to find a solution for her wavering politics.

Though an ardent believer in democracy, Carsun Chang concedes that in times of crisis, a democratic government may not function as efficiently as a dictatorial one. However, he argues, the centralization of power in the hands of a democratic government, such as the coalition in Great Britain during World War I, should be equally efficient. Therefore, a concentration of power is not incompatible with democracy. The principle of democracy is unshakable, and flexible measures should be sought to cope with the problems only under particular circumstances and times.[10] Dictatorship emphasizes authority, while democracy emphasizes freedom. Carsun Chang offers a synthesis to strike a congenial balance between these two opposite emphases, that he calls a program of revised democracy.

Chang's basic belief is that the administrative work of the state requires efficiency so that the government can function smoothly and effectively, while society and culture, in order to be progressive, should be left free and diversified. Efficiency should not be achieved at the expense of freedom. It is this which Carsun Chang holds to be the guideline between centralization and freedom, and he lays down an eleven-point program of revised democracy. This is stated as follows:

1. A state must have a unified government which should be organized on a national basis, and the fragmentary conditions caused by warlordism must first be eliminated as a requisite for such a government.
2. A national People's Assembly is to be set up with delegates selected by all citizens, each delegate representing a proportion of the electorate. All political parties, with an open consitution and open activities, except those under the command of a foreign country, are free to participate in the election.
3. The Central Executive Council *(Chung-yang hsing-cheng yuan)* is to be organized by administrators elected by People's Assembly. The leaders of all parties are to be included in order to form a national coalition government.
4. The first convention of the People's Assembly should adopt a five-year administrative plan which has the same binding force as the national constitution and should not be changed by the executive council.
5. The chief function of the People's Assembly is to be the supervision of the budget and the enactment of laws. But it is not to exercise the right of a vote of confidence in changing the cabinet. A budget is to be merely a method for showing the financial policy in figures, the adoption or rejection of which is not to affect the stability of the government.
6. The People's Assembly may give the government the power of expedience in the execution of the administrative plan.

7. Ministers of the Executive Council are not to be lightly dismissed or relieved without reason, except when financial embezzlement or other illegal acts are proved.
8. The administrative plan is to be reviewed annually or at other appropriate times by the People's Assembly or by groups elected by separate professional associations. If any minister is remiss in achieving the goals of the administrative plan, he should be removed by a resolution of the People's Assembly.
9. Civil service employees are to be detached from political parties. Officials from administrative vice-ministers down cannot be dismissed upon the removal of the ministers in charge of them.
10. A certain number of delegates in the People's Assembly are to be elected from among people possessing agricultural, industrial, commercial, technical, or scientific knowledge.
11. An Administrative and Economic Outline Plan adopted by the People's Assembly is to be supplemented by detailed plans mapped out by experts in their field.[11]

Carsun Chang's proposed program is based on two goals. The first and most important is, of course, democracy. He defended this thesis and bitterly opposed either personal or party dictatorship. However, he clearly understood that the two-party system in England or the United States was not feasible in China. Thus, he was in favor of a coalition government, with a People's Assembly as the highest authority to be elected by the people on the widest democratic basis—equal representation for an equal number of population including a certain proportion of workers, industrialists, merchants, and scientists—and an executive council (i.e., a cabinet) with all the leaders of the various political parties participating. Carsun Chang appealed to the leaders of these parties to sacrifice their partisan interests for national interests in order to make a coalition government possible.

The second goal in Carsun Chang's proposed program is the stability of the government. Up to the time of his writing, China had suffered great political upheaval since the founding of the Republic in 1911. Naturally, the same instability affected all government workers. Obviously, they could not accomplish anything substantial toward national construction owing to the lack of job security, a situation which would have been otherwise under a stable government. The suggestion of a five-year administrative plan to be adopted by the People's Assembly with the same binding force as the national constitution, and the suggestion that the Assembly should not exercise the right of or vote of confidence in changing the cabinet, are to ensure the stability of the government. And these two suggestions, along with the proposal that the civil service employees should not be removed with the removal of their superiors, are all aimed at government security. This coalition government, as conceived by Carsun Chang, was not to be of a short-term nature but was designed to last a projected twenty years.[12]

Democratic Seeds. There is the question of the feasibility of democracy in

China. The problem came to the fore in the 1950s as the Communists came to power. The Communist government is obviously dictatorial, and there were discussions as to whether China is best suited to have a democratic or an autocratic government. There is a theory, especially among communist apologists in the West, that, since China has a totalitarian tradition, a Western-type democracy does not and cannot work in China. But for Carsun Chang, the democratic development in China is a natural tendency and a logical result of her traditional thought and institutions. That is, there have been democratic seeds in ancient China and what is needed today is to help democracy grow and flourish; the seeds of democracy themselves have already been planted.

Chang argues that although Chinese political systems in the past were monarchical they were basically different from those of the West. The main difference lay in the fact that since very ancient times Chinese political philosophy had identified the people's will with the providence of Heaven: that a sovereign should respect and represent the will of the people. Both Confucianist and Taoist philosophies hold that emperors should not enjoy unlimited political power. The Taoists assert the "no-action" of government, while the Confucianists uphold "rule by virtue." Moreover, the Confucianists praised the yielding of thrones to the virtuous by Emperors Yao and Shun, who established a precedent by passing the throne on to the most virtuous and worthy man in the kingdom rather than to the eldest son or closest relative; they also endorsed the revolutions of T'ang and Wu. All of these views clearly underscore the conceptions that: the kingdom (t'ien-hsia) belongs not to one man but to the whole people; dynasties and thrones can be overthrown; and, a government aims at the realization of what the people desire.

This line of Confucian political thought has been a tradition held from Confucius and Mencius down at least to the eminent Ch'ing scholar and political theorist, Huang Tsung-hsi. The above conceptions can be subsumed under two principles: the world or kingdom is for the public; all people are equal. These two principles are held to be the seeds, by Carsun Chang, of democracy in Chinese political thought. The development of these principles would unavoidably conflict with the monarchical system. For, under a monarchy, the t'ien-hsia belongs to a family instead, and the people do not enjoy the same political equality as the ruler. To realize these two ideals, it is necessary to change the monarchical system to a democratic system.

However, all these moral ideals with their related institutions, such as the admonitions of the ministers to the emperor, the petitions of his subjects, titled or vulgar, the impartial chronicles of the court historiographers, and his posthumous titling by his ministers which limited the emperor's powers and supplemented his scruples, are not enough to effect a democracy. There must be a law—the national constitution—to stipulate clearly the rights of the people and the legal procedure of effective transfer of power to persons of high moral integrity and ability. In other words, the highest executive position must be made accessible to all persons qualified for it. In this way the political equality for all citizens will be affirmed. This constitution should represent the general will of the people and be followed as a common course for exercising political rights of all people. This task of democratic reconstruction, i.e., the legalization or the institutionalization of democratic ideas, which is a natural development of Chinese history, remains to be carried out.[13]

Economic Programs

Carsun Chang's vision of China's future economic policy for national reconstruction is neither the British laissez faire pattern, which places the national economy mainly on the foundation of private enterprise, nor the Soviet Communist pattern, which exploits class struggle as a means of completely destroying private enterprise and replacing it with national enterprise. Rather, it is a kind of mixed economy that combines capitalism and socialism, which Chang calls state socialism *(kuo-chia she-hui chu-i)*. Carsun Chang's state socialism should not, of course, be confused with the state socialism of other governments.

Carsun Chang's programs for economic construction under his proposed state socialism consist of two goals: self-sufficiency of the state, and social justice.

Economic Self-Sufficiency. It is Chang's premise that China's primary economic problem is not so much one of better distribution as it is the increase of production, since China's basic economic evil is poverty. (In asserting this he is reversing a saying of Confucius: "It is not scarcity but the inequal distribution which is to be worried about.") Instead, the proper way to increase production is to rely on the efforts of the Chinese people. Other means, such as the utilization of foreign investments or unity with the international proletariat are brushed aside as useless.[14] It may be noted here that the idea of self-reliance through one's own efforts *(tzu-li keng-sheng)* of the communists is not a unique communist idea, but has been held by many individuals, including Carsun Chang.

Chang was struck by the Customs Report of 1930 that a tremendous amount of foreign articles of clothing, food, and shelter had been imported, among which were 200 million silver taels worth of rice, wheat flour, sea food, and cigarettes. Intensely deploring this situation, he passionately appealed to the Chinese people to make strenuous efforts to consume what they produce and to produce what they consume. This is what is meant by self-subsistence.

In order to achieve this goal within ten to fifteen years, Chang considered the following three aims as necessary:

1. To achieve self-sufficiency of foodstuffs and ban completely the importation of rice, wheat flour, and sea food
2. To strive for self-sufficiency in cotton and woolen goods
3. To engage in basic industries, such as iron and steel, and electrical and chemical industries

The 200 million silver taels that would be saved annually from an embargo on foodstuffs and cigarettes, according to Chang's proposal, should be used to buy machines to produce cotton and woolen goods. This would free China from dependence upon imports of foreign materials for clothing. In addition, China could export hundreds of millions of taels worth of tea, silk, bean curd, tung oil, etc., the proceeds of which could be used to develop electrical and chemical industries. This practice, Carsun Chang believes, could solve the problem of creating capital for construction of more enterprises in China.[15]

Social Justice. Ideologically, Carsun Chang is opposed to the tactic of class struggle for bringing about an economic change in China, on the premise that internally it would impede the consolidation of the nation as a whole, and externally it would not receive the support of the international proletariat. Instead, it would arouse the fears and suspicions of other peoples. He considered this to be too great a sacrifice to be worth the effort.

Carsun Chang's economic plan is based on a national scheme. He envisions a balanced proportion between public property and private property, and between public and private enterprise. These ideals should be carried out according to a national plan so that the evils of the monopoly of economic affairs by a minority of entrepreneurs, as happened in the West, could be prevented and social justice could be realized.

In discussing the highly controversial and most basic problem of private property, Carsun Chang advocates its preservation on the grounds that the iniquities of capitalism are not due to private property but to laissez faire. It is the maintenance of private property plus the practice of laissez faire that has produced capitalism. Thus, at most, it can be said that capitalism has grown out of the acquisition of private property, although it would be a mistake to believe that capitalism is an inevitable result of private property. Reasoning from these grounds, Carsun Chang concludes that drastic changes in capitalism may not necessarily affect the existence of a system of private property. Moreover, he believes that an economy is always made up of many elements and, therefore, it is possible that private property could be maintained under socialism. He believes, along with many other individuals, that private property could serve as a material incentive for stimulating production and encouraging savings, this being an advantage rather than a detriment. Realizing the evils of the concentration of wealth among a few individuals, he advocates more equal and more general distribution of property among the people.

In Carsun Chang's view, the ownership of private property consists of the rights of use, transference, enjoyment, and protection from infringement by others of what one has earned by his own labor. But it does not include the rights of control and management by the owner alone with no regard for the general welfare of society. For example, an acre of land may be owned by a farmer who can cultivate it and be protected from claims on it by others; but should he leave it to lie fallow, the government would have the right to interfere or simply to confiscate it. According to this view, the right of ownership is conditional rather than absolute. Thus, a private property system could coexist with socialism.[16]

Agriculture. In applying this theory to agriculture, Carsun Chang prefers the private ownership of land hand-in-hand with complete state planning and control, including requisition, rather than the nationalization of land, with the simultaneous right of the farmers to work it. Specifically, Carsun Chang's land program consists of: the ownership of land belonging to the tiller of the land; and the amount of land owned not exceeding the owner's ability to till it.

On one hand, this means a change from tenants to self-cultivating farmers. On the other hand, it eliminates the landlord class by doing away with hired peasants or farm laborers. But Carsun Chang does not favor either the seizure of land by the peasants without compensation to the owners, nor seizure through violence.

Finally, agricultural cooperatives are considered to be the best method of solving the financial problems of the villages. Collective farms of the Soviet type he also considered as a possibilty.[17] In considering such ideas by Carsun Chang, it can be seen that the practice of cooperatives or collectivization is supported by both communist and noncommunist thinkers. (Readers are recommended to refer to the chapter on Liang Shu-ming in this regard.)

Industry and Commerce. In Carsun Chang's view, the nationalization of the means of production would inevitably lead to state operation of all economic affairs, similar to the case in the Soviet Union. This would, in turn, create a large bureaucracy.

China's bureaucracy was already considered rather excessive by Carsun Chang, and he was apprehensive of putting China's entire economic affairs in the hands of the greedy bureaucrats. Honest officials are essential to the success of the system, but Chang seriously doubted the integrity of China's future officialdom. The Soviet system is praised by Chang as having created a new world in the field of economics since the Soviet Union was the first country which planned its economy on a nationwide basis. But he criticizes it as having contributed to nothing new in the balance between authority and freedom. Bertrand Russell's criticism of the Soviet system as being adverse to freedom was praised by Carsun Chang. Thus, Chang wishes to adopt state socialism while at the same time preventing bureaucratism.

In this sense, Chang's proposal is to make the state an overall planning organization which would entrust individuals, possibly the guildsmen, with the power of carrying out the operations of economic enterprise, but definitely to avoid a large army of bureaucrats.[18]

With respect to industry, basically, Carsun Chang does not idealize the highly industrialized society found in the West. Rather, he envisions a coordination between industrial development and agriculture so that marked differences between cities and villages would not emerge. This idea could have come out of the traditional Chinese view which romanticized the pastoral life of the farmer.

Based on his concept of social justice, Carsun Chang maintains that industry and commerce should be carried out through the division of labor between public organizations and private individuals. By public organizations he means to include the state apparatus, local authorities, and cooperatives. The state would play the role of a general staff in economic affairs, carrying out the planning and deployment of the industry as a whole. However, reluctant to see a state monopoly of economic affairs, he holds that certain enterprises should be operated by private individuals with a view to developing their potential. His line of demarcation is that those enterprises that, if privately operated, are not detrimental to the public welfare of the state should allow private individuals to have a free hand. Those enterprises that, if privately operated, are detrimental should be operated by the state.

Chang supports his ideas with various concrete examples. Trades ranging from the production of fine art objects to sundry stores and tailor shops are to be operated privately. Daily necessity stores, grocery stores, and furniture stores are to be operated either by individuals or by cooperatives. Public utilities are to be operated by local authorities. Large industries, such as cotton mills, will be operated under state supervision, though their ownership can still be retained by private individuals. Public communications, such as railroads and telegraph offices, natural resources, such as coal mines, hydraulic power, and electric power, and large industries, such as steel mills, should be state operated.[19]

In sum, Carsun Chang's economic program consists of two opposing aspects: a state-planned economy and private ownership. He did not wish to see the emergence of powerful monopoly-capitalists in China as had appeared in Europe and America, nor did he wish to see the monopoly of economic affairs by the state as in the Soviet Union. Chang asked rhetorically: "Since you want to carry out socialism, but you don't want to nationalize private property, how can you manage to get the tremendous amount of capital needed for building up the new China?"[20]

His answer is to retain the right of ownership for the factory owners, with all factories to be run under state supervision. For practical measures, Chang proposes a six-point program:

1. The right of ownership of factories to remain unchanged.
2. Operations and equipment of factories to conform with state plans under state supervision.
3. Proceeds in the current year to go to the state for the following year's national industrial expansion, except for a certain amount to be earmarked as an accumulation fund for the particular enterprises concerned and interests to be paid to the enterprise owners according to the market rate.
4. Newly established industrial and commercial enterprises to be exempted, for a certain period of time, from the previous regulations on profit disposal in order to provide an incentive.
5. In case of loss, the state to supply a loan to insure continuing operation.
6. Commerce of daily necessities to be run by cooperatives, and all other kinds of business to be run by private individuals; the profits to be taxed according to the law governing business gains.[21]

Culture

Culture, according to Carsun Chang, is the expression of the spiritual and material life of a society in its totality.[22] A new culture would emerge as a result

149

of the change in attitude towards life. With the emergence of a new culture, a new political system and a new economic construction would necessarily follow. These new political systems and economic constructions, without the support of a new philosophy of life, would be like trees without roots or rivers without sources. Thus, Carsun Chang argues that the first step to be taken is to change the philosophy of life of the Chinese people in order to effect a new politics and economics for China.[23]

His view is contrary to the material interpretation of history, which holds that existence determines consciousness and that the mode of production, which is independent of human will, is the dynamic force in historical development. The philosophy of life is only a part of the superstructure that is determined by the mode of production. Carsun Chang's belief is that it is the philosophy of life which determines and shapes the course of history and which creates a new culture which is the forerunner of political and social reforms.

His argument is based on his study of modern European history. Modern Europe realized great achievements in science and democracy, but these achievements are rooted in four important historical occurrences: religious reform, the Renaissance, the reawakening of science, and the democratic movement. But there is one basic spirit which underlies all of these, and that is the new outlook on life since the Renaissance, or, in other words, the development of reason and the concomitant emphasis on man. Basing his analysis on these observations, Carsun Chang came to believe that the only guiding principle for China for her academic and political reconstruction is the development of reason, or rationalism, as it occurred in Europe, and this is what he referred to as the foundation for a new life and a new philosophy of life in China.[24]

But, what prospects of a new culture does Carsun Chang envision? In a small pamphlet entitled *A Declaration to the World for Chinese Culture*, to which we referred previously for some of the points in regard to the seeds of democracy in China, he and his three coauthors proclaimed their views. The arguments set forth are complicated and highly philosophical. In the simplest terms, they establish that Chinese culture is ethic-centric, and that moral realization is the nucleus of Chinese history and thought. In addition, the authors urged the absorption of science and democracy for the advancement and perfection of Chinese culture. Their own words sum up Chang's ideas on this subject:

> According to our understanding, the direction of progress to be taken should extend the attainment of moral self-realization to the fields of politics, of knowledge, and of technology. In other words, China needs a genuine democratic reconstruction, and scientific and technological skills. For this reason, China must embrace the civilization of the world; for this will enable her national character to reach higher planes of perfection and her spiritual life to achieve a more comprehensive development.[25]

Education

Carsun Chang finds the educational system of his time objectionable for three reasons: (1) Students have been produced with no definite objective or goal, and this is little different from the anarchic situation in laissez faire economics; (2) only those who are wealthy and influential can buy an education, regardless of knowledge or innate intelligence; and (3) the teaching materials in schools do not meet well the needs of China. Thus, a new educational policy should be designed to attain national unity and to ensure a developed national economy.

In practice, it is necessary to have universal education without regard to one's wealth; only through educational equality will every person be able to realize his full potential and be a useful member of society. One should be taught to cooperate with others for the common good of the nation. In general, the three educational goals to be stressed are universal military training, universal productive ability, and the inculcation of a new ethic for living a communal life.

Carsun Chang calls his educational policy a planned education, just as he favors a planned political system and a planned economy. However, he attaches far more importance to education because of his belief that it is education that can best bring about the success of political and economic reforms.

The educational measures stressed by Carsun Chang in the 1930s are to a striking degree similar to the present Communist program. However, as far as the closely related problem of thought is concerned, there is a diametrical difference. Carsun Chang's primary belief is academic independence and freedom of speech, both closely related to freedom of thought. Academic independence requires the noninterference of outside force or influence. He vigorously opposes the charge that too much free speech and free thought would entail conflicting opinions, and thus lower administrative efficiency of the government. He argues that efficiency is an inherent factor in governmental operations and that government efficiency and social freedoms are not incompatible, but are often complementary. Actually, the development of free speech, argues Chang, enables a government to run more smoothly.

"We ardently love political efficiency," Carsun Chang declares, "but we love even more the freedom of thought." An inefficient government loses its ability to function as a government; a country devoid of freedom of thought becomes a country without a soul. Even if a conflict between freedom and efficiency exists, under no circumstances should the former be sacrificed.

In elaborating these ideas, two concrete examples are cited. One is the Soviet Union, in which a class dictatorship is exercised and all freedoms of the people are temporarily suppressed in the hope that a millenium of complete freedom will appear later. With respect to this, Carsun Chang points out that a country belongs to the whole people, and no one class has the right to monopolize it by force and at the sacrifice of the freedom of others. Naturally Chang's criticism of the Soviet Union equally applies to Communist China. Moreover, political efficiency does require centralized government control, but this control should not extend to society as a whole, infringing on public freedom.

The practice of the Kuomintang is cited as the second example. The Nationalists never sought efficient central control, but always suppressed the freedom of the people. An ideal government is exactly the opposite: the unification and centralization of the political and administrative power should be carried out to the greatest extent, and society and thought should remain as free as possible.[26]

Philosophical Background

In order to better understand Carsun Chang's social, political, and economic ideas and ideal, it will help to look at his philosophic background. In philosophic terms, Chang is an idealist rather than a materialist, a position which he explains at the end of his book *Li-kuo chih tao* in the last chapter on "Our Philosophic Background."

In applying the concept of mind and matter to human society, Carsun Chang contends that free will belongs to mind, and all economic, political, and social institutions belong to matter. The former is the dynamic force behind human achievement; the latter is a tool to facilitate the goals of man. Human will permeates every social phenomenon, and every human community. Thus, the institutions of economics, politics, and law, reflecting human will in the various phases of social relationships, are the three factors necessary for integrating the organization and development of society. Of these three institutions, each is equally indispensable, but none is primary. Furthermore, the relationships among the three factors are interdependent and the total social life or social system is a function of all of them. This is the functional theory of society which Carsun Chang believes is opposed to dialectical materialism. Believing that a man's total social life is a function of politics, economics, and law, he objects to the basic concepts of dialectical materialism which hold economics supreme, and to the concept that economics exists objectively and independently of the will and action of men, and, finally, to the theory of ideological superstructure and the economic base.[27]

Philosophically, both Carsun Chang and his close friend, Chang Tung-sun, are in strong opposition to dialectical materialism. As early as 1934, the former edited a book entitled *The Polemic on Dialectical Materialism.*[28] And in his *Refutation of Dialectical Materialism,* Carsun Chang points out that there are five ideas in this theory which have proved adverse to mankind: (1) the theory considers only matter, but ignores mind or spirit; (2) it considers only the change in matter, but ignores its permanence; (3) it considers only struggle and opposition, but ignores harmony and tolerance; (4) it considers only social classes, but ignores the individual; and (5) it considers only revolution, but ignores the value of order.[29]

Both Carsun Chang and Chang Tung-sun are undoubtedly anticommunist, although it may be more appropriate to say that they are opposed to communism in theory and dictatorship in practice. As we have seen, Carsun Chang was active for a time in bringing together the Nationalists and the Communists; and Chang Tung-sun was one of the chief mediators in effecting a peaceful settlement between the troops of Fu Tso-i defending Peking and the Communist forces attacking them. In fact, Carsun Chang broke with the Communists

152

because of their refusal to participate in the promulgation of the Constitution in 1946. Chang Tung-sun's trouble with the communists after 1949 in Peking was due to his outspoken criticisms of the Communist government.

Summary

It is amusing to note that during the Cultural Revolution, Liu Shao-ch'i was dubbed the "parliament addict" *(i-hui-mi)* for his advocacy of gaining state power by parliamentary process rather than by armed force.[30] Actually, this phrase does not fit him at all; the epithet is better suited to Carsun Chang, whose life was devoted to the untiring pursuit of a parliamentary form of government in China.[31] The following anecdote illustrates very well his stubborn nature and nonconformity. Under the Kuomintang regime on mainland China, and now on Taiwan, Sun Yat-sen's memorial service has been performed weekly in schools and government offices, as well as at the beginning of every formal meeting. This requires everyone to rise and bow three times to the flag of the Kuomintang and of the Republic of China, and to Sun's picture. Protesting that a citizen of a republic should not be required to bow to the flag and the leader of the party to which one does not belong, Carsun Chang, on such occasions, either remained seated or arrived at a meeting after the ritual. This was symbolic of his strong opposition to any practice he felt was undemocratic.

However, Chang's political influence in China was never very great. In the short introductory note to his chronological biography he alludes—as if to console himself—to the founders of the short-lived Ch'in and Sui dynasties, Ch'in Shih Huang-ti and Sui Yang-ti; they founded great empires which crumbled after a decade or two and they exerted little enduring influence on China. Although the great philosophers, from Confucius down to Chu Hsi, were political failures in their own lifetimes and even victims of persecution, their outspoken opinions have remained behind to affect all posterity. Like a true disciple of Confucius, Chang concludes that he would prefer to emulate the great men of failures of the past. So he disdained to try for cheap success by compromising his own views and toadying up to the powerful; he likewise refused to melt back into the crowd and remain silent.[31]

Notes

[1] The biographical sketch is heavily based on Ch'eng Wen-hsi "Chang Chün-mai hsien-sheng chih yen-hsing" in Wang Yun-mu et al., *Chang Chün-mai hsien-sheng ch'i-shih shou-ch'ing chi-nien lun-wen chi* (Taipei: Chang Chün-mai hsien-sheng ch'i-shih shou-ch'ing chi-nien lun-wen chi pien-chi wei-yuan hui, 1956), pp. 1–53.

[2] For the collection of the articles of the polemic, see *K'o-hsueh yü jen-sheng-kuan* (Shanghai: Ya-tung t'u-shu kuan, 1923). For Chang's recollections after ten years of the polemic, see his "Jen-sheng-kuan lun-chan chih hui-ku," *Tung-fang tsa-chih* 31, no. 13 (July 1934): 5–13. After forty years, see his "Jen-sheng kuan lun-chan chih hui-ku—Szu-shih nien lai hsi-fang che-hsueh chieh chih szu-hsiang-chia" (Hong Kong), *Jen-sheng* 313 (November 1963): 2–6, 18; 314 (December 1963): 7–14.

[3] For an account of Carsun Chang's part in the draft of the Constitution and the conflicting points between the Kuomintang and the Communists, see his *The Third Force in China* (New York: Bookman, 1952), pp. 188–222.

[4] For the discussion on national consciousness, see Chi-che (pseud.) "Wo-men so yao-shuo te hua," *Tsai-sheng* 1, no. 1 (20 May 1932): 3–7; hereafter "So yao-shuo te." This is the first article in the first issue of the magazine. It is the most important article expounding the basic thought and the blueprint of Carsun Chang, as well as his friends' ideal China. It was drafted by Carsun Chang and revised by his closest friend Chang Tung-sun, a philosopher.

[5] Chang Chün-mai, "Chung-hua min-tsu chih li-kuo neng-li," *Tsai-sheng* 1, no. 4 (20 August 1932): 25–26.

[6] Ibid., pp. 26–28.

[7] Chang Chün-mai, "Fa-k'an ts'u," *Hsin-lu* 1, no. 1 (1 February 1928):3–4.

[8] This account is mainly based on Chang Chün-mai's "I-tang chuan-cheng yü wu-kuo," *Hsin-lu* 1, no. 2 (15 February 1928): 31. For Chang Chün-mai's detailed arguments against Kuomintang tutelage, see his "P'i hsun-cheng shuo," *Hsin-lu* 1, no. 7 (1 May 1928): 23–24; also see his "Kuo-min-tang tang-cheng chih hsin ch'i-lu," *Tsai-sheng* 1, No. 2 (20 June 1932): 1–5.

[9] Chang Chün-mai, *Li-kuo chih-tao,* also called *Kuo-chia she-hui chu-i* (Kweilin, 1938), pp. 139–41. Hereafter referred to as *Li-kuo*. This book was first privately published by Chang Chün-mai with the permission of the Kuomintang. Reprinted in Taipei by the Democratic Socialist Party in 1969, and by Commercial Press in 1971.

[10] Chang Chün-mai and Chang Tung-sun, "So yao-shuo te," pp. 8–12.

[11] Chang Chün-mai, *Li-kuo*, pp. 157–159. For the expounding of this political idea of Carsun Chang, also see his "Kuo-chia min-chu cheng-chih yü kuo-chia she-hui chu-i," *Tsai-sheng* 1, No. 2 (20 June 1932): 1–38. The eleven points appear on pp. 30–31.

[12] Chang Chün-mai, *Li-kuo*, pp. 159–64.

[13] Chang Chün-mai et al., *Chung-kuo wen-hua yü shih-chieh* (Hong Kong: Min-chu p'ing-lun, 1958), pp. 36–40.

[14] Chang Chün-mai and Chang Tung-sun, "So yao-shuo te," p. 22.

[15] Chang Chün-mai, *Li-kuo*, pp. 238–42. In the second line, on page 241 of *Li-kuo chih-tao,* the figure 300 million is evidently a misprint. It should read 200 million.

[16] Chang Chün-mai and Chang Tung-sun, "So yao-shuo te," pp. 26, 29–33.

[17] Ibid., pp. 33–35.

[18] Ibid., pp. 26–28.

[19] Chang Chün-mai, *Li-kuo*, pp. 241–44.

[20] Ibid., p. 245.

[21] Ibid., p. 246.

[22] Ibid., p. 273. Readers are recommended by Carsun Chang to refer to his *Ming-jih chih Chung-kuo wen-hua* (Shanghai: Commercial, 1934).

[23] Ibid., p. 278.

[24] Ibid., pp. 280–84.

[25] Chang Chün-mai et al., *Chung-kuo wen-hua,* pp. 32–33. English translation is taken from Carsun Chang, *Development of Neo-Confucian Thought* (New York: Bookman, 1962), 2:469.

[26] Chang Chün-mai and Chang Tung-sun, "So yao-shuo te," pp. 39–45.

[27] For the discussion on the functional theory of society, see Chang Chün-mai, *Li-kuo,* pp. 375–87.

[28] Chang Tung-sun, *Wei-wu pien-cheng fa lun-chan* (Peking: Min-yu shu-tien, 1934).

[29] Chang Chün-mai, *Pien-cheng wei-wu chu-i po-lun* (Hong Kong: Union Research, 1958), pp. 187–88.

[30] "Chung-kuo i-hui-mi te p'o-ch'an," *Jen-min jih-pao,* 12 August 1967.

[31] Ch'eng Wen-hsi, "Chang Chün-mai"," pp. 1–2.

6
Chang Tung-sun (1886–ca.1976)

Biography

Chang Tung-sun and Chang Chün-mai were exceptionally close friends. Both loved philosophy and both were devoted to the democratic movement. Their close political and philosophical relationship can be seen in Chang Tung-sun's will, which he composed during imprisonment in the Sino-Japanese War. Anticipating death by execution, torture or suicide, he stipulated that after his death both his and Carsun Chang's writings be published in one book, called *The Works of two Changs,* with no indication of individual authorship.

Chang Tung-sun[1] was born in 1886 in Wuhsien (Soochow) county of Kiangsu province to parents who were natives of Ch'ien-t'ang, Chekiang province. During his youth, he received a traditional education in Chinese classics under the supervision of his elder brother, Chang Erh-t'ien. His interest in philosophy developed at the age of sixteen, when he first read Buddhist sutras with great excitement. In 1905, at the age of nineteen, he travelled to Japan to pursue a modern education in Buddhism and philosophy. Later, however, after much reading in psychology, Chang became skeptical about Buddhism and centered his interest on philosophy, though he never completely forgot about politics.

Upon his return to China, Chang became active in journalism. Between 1912 and 1915, he served as editor of the *Ta-kung-ho jih-pao* in Shanghai, and two Liang Ch'i-ch'ao sponsored publications in Tientsin, *Yung-yen* and *Ta Chung-hua* magazines. In addition, he wrote numerous articles on constitutional problems for *Cheng-i* (Righteousness), an anti-Yuan Shih-k'ai magazine in Shanghai. These reflected his political stand in support of the Republic. He also contributed many articles on political theory to *Chia-yin tsa-chih,* published in Tokyo by Chang Shih-chao, a scholar who had studied in England and used his journal to advocate the British parliamentary system. (Years later in 1949, Chang Shih-chao, a native of the same province as Mao Tse-tung, joined the Communist government and denounced the British political system as useless and futile.)

In 1917 Chang Tung-sun succeeded Carsun Chang as editor-in-chief of the independent daily, the *Shih-shih hsin-pao* (The China Times) of Shanghai. In *Hsueh-teng* (Academic lamp), the literary supplement of the newspaper, Chang Tung-sun played an important role commenting on the ideology of intellectuals and the social currents of the day. From this time, he also edited a magazine,

Kai-tsao yü chieh-fang (Reconstruction and Emancipation), later renamed *Kai-tsao* (La Rekonstruo) for the sake of simplicity. *Kai-tsao*'s goal was to promote political democracy and gradual socialism.

Chang later abandoned the journalistic world; he deplored that the true freedom of speech he personally experienced in the first five to six years of the Republic was dead, and that since 1927 people had been unable to speak their thoughts. Chang also attempted to introduce Western ideas to China by translating two philosophical works of Henri Bergson, *Creative Evolution* in 1918, and *Matter and Memory* in 1922. He published, among other things, *Hsin che-hsueh lun-ts'ung* (Essays on contemporary philosophy) in 1929 and *Tao-te che-hsueh* (Moral philosophy) in 1931, an introduction to and interpretation of the history of Western moral philosophy, with strong condemnation of Marxist ethics. In 1924 he joined the science and philosophy debate on the side of Carsun Chang. His highest ambition in philosophy was to expound a new theory of knowledge, an epistemological synthesis which he called epistemological pluralism. Although Chang Tung-sun was confident that he had discovered such a synthesis, Carsun Chang, his best friend in philosophy and politics, doubted the success of a philosophical breakthrough. Nevertheless, Chang Tung-sun's philosophical works are responsible for his image as a neoidealist among academicians such as H. H. Dubs. It is an image which Chang denied but of course he was not a materialist either, for he regarded the dispute between materialism and idealism to be actually meaningless.

Politically, Chang Tung-sun had a close relationship with leaders of the Progressive Party, notably Liang Ch'i-ch'ao, but he never joined it. He did, however, join an association that Liang organized, called the Research Faction, which had the appearance of an academic organization. In 1911, Chang joined Sun Yat-sen's Nanking government. After this government was dissolved, many of its supporters left to join Yuan Shih-k'ai's government in Peking. Chang stayed and Sun appointed him a member of his Kuomintang, a membership he declined to accept. In 1920 when Voitinsky met with Ch'en Tu-hsiu in Shanghai, Chang attended some of the secret discussions which led to the creation of a small communist organization, but he withdrew from the group before the communist nucleus was formed in the summer of 1920. According to Chang, Ch'en and his associates did not ask him to join the Communist Party because they knew that though Chang was in favor of socialism, he opposed class struggle in a China without industrial development.

He called himself a man of no party affiliations. The reason that he cooperated with Carsun Chang to form the National Socialist Party in 1932 was purely as a protest against the Kuomintang's misguided assertion that no other political party could be permitted. This action was based on his belief in democracy, his opposition to one-party dictatorship, and his basic belief in freedom of thought. Chang was one of the principal drafters of the National Socialist party platform *(Wo-men yao-shuo te hua)* and a major contributor of articles on theoretical and political problems to the Party magazine, *Tsai-sheng*. However, he did not make this his career. At the outset of organizing their party, he made a pact with

Carsun Chang that as soon as the Kuomintang abandoned one-party dictatorship, they would automatically dissolve their party. The reason was very simple; he had realized long ago that he was not a man for political life.

Chang's university teaching career began in 1925. When Carsun Chang became the president of the Political Science University *(Cheng-chih ta-hsueh)*, Chang Tung-sun became a professor. For the next five years, he also served as professor of philosophy and dean of the college of arts at Kuang-hua University, and as president of the China National Institute *(Chung-kuo hung-hsueh)* at Woosung. In the autumn of 1930, Chang joined the faculty of Yenching University in Peking as professor of philosophy—a post which he held until his forced resignation in 1952 (?) because of ideological differences with the Communist regime. During an academic leave in 1934, he also served for six months as the chancellor of the Hsueh-hai Academy in Canton, founded by Carsun Chang.

On Pearl Harbor Day, 1941, Japan seized Yenching University. With many others, Chang was detained in one of the university buildings for a night and then arrested. He was sent to the Japanese Gendarme Headquarters and charged with anti-Japanese activities. After being imprisoned and tortured for six months and ten days, he was sentenced to imprisonment for eighteen months but released on parole for three years.

Before the age of sixty, Chang had completed three books on his philosophical and political ideas: (1) *Li-hsing yü min-chu* (Rationality and democracy), 1946; (2) *Chih-shih yü wen-hua* (Knowledge and culture), 1947; and (3) *Szu-hsiang yü she-hui* (Thought and society), 1947. He once remarked that these were his last books and that he would stop writing, but he did publish another small volume in 1948 entitled *Min-chu-chu-i yü she-hui-chu-i* (Democracy and socialism) which marks the culmination of his political ideas.

At the end of 1945, Chang left Peking for Chungking to attend the Political Consultative Conference as a representative of the Democratic Socialist Party. He and other conference members sought to mediate between the Nationalist government and the Communist Party. Evidently his sympathy lay with the Communists. At this time, he joined and became an important member of the Democratic League, fighting for the democratic rights of the minor parties. In the latter part of 1946, negotiation and mediation between the Nationalist government and the Communist Party completely failed. The Kuomintang decided to call the National Assembly and to proclaim the new Constitution, which the Communists opposed. Chang Tung-sun was sympathetic to the Communist cause, while Carsun Chang sympathized with the Kuomintang. (As mentioned before, Carsun Chang had drafted the new Constitution which the Communist representatives had examined and initially approved.) This event marked the breakup of the friendship of the two Changs.

When the Communist government was inaugurated in Peking, Chang Tung-sun was reappointed a member of the renamed People's Political Consultative Conference. As he became increasingly critical of the Communist dictatorship, he was charged in 1950 with the crime of high treason and cooperation with an

159

enemy country, obviously the United States. After repeated confessions, he was excused from punishment, but was forced to resign from his professorship. An unconfirmed report states that it was Mao, saving Chang from serious trouble, who personally suggested that Chang resign and who guaranteed Chang's livelihood and safety on the condition that he would "read books behind closed doors." Chang probably died in 1976 at the age of ninety. One of his sons, Chang Tsung-sui, a physicist, was officially reported to have been persecuted to death by the Gang of Four.

General Outlook on Democracy

Chang lauded democracy as mankind's greatest achievement. He regarded democracy as the normal form of government and all other forms as abnormal or ailing. Even though he was a devout Confucianist, he placed a higher value on the Western great tradition *(tao-t'ung)* characterized by democracy, than he did on Confucianism. There are many elements in Western learning from which China can benefit, he said, but democracy as a civilization is the most precious treasure of the West and of mankind as a whole, and China must learn it if she wants to absorb Western civilization. To learn democracy is sufficient; it is the essential element.[2] Chang's view obviously contradicts the Marxist idea that democracy belongs to one class and hence is called bourgeois democracy.

Chang's central theme is that democracy is not merely a political system, but is a civilization characterized by constant progress, i.e., the ability to improve itself by its own mechanism. For this reason, scholars describe Western civilization as dynamic, and Chinese civilization as static. How can a civilization leap from its static condition into the realm of progress? The answer lies in rationality, which plays a vital role in the progress of civilization from primitive to modern societies. Democracy is a system of civilization which can best promote the rationality of man, and conversely, only those people who are rational can successfully operate such a system. The two elements, democracy and rationality, are both complementary and supplementary. As a system, democracy is the initial path to be followed: as an ideal, it is the ultimate goal to be pursued. This goal has not yet been realized. (Chang quotes Rousseau, "So perfect a government is not for man.") In the continuing process of development of the democratic civilization, the more democratic the system is, the better the lives of the people become, and eventually the system can perpetuate itself to achieve a society close to that ultimate goal. Thus, it is not feasible to expect China to reach a high degree of democracy in a short time.

In a democratic society, proper social conduct emphasizes the healthy attitude among its members of pursuing the common good of the community. Although each individual is an agent of his will, no collective goal can be accomplished if everyone insists on his own will. Therefore, in regard to public affairs, all must compromise to reach a consensus on which a society or community can be built. In a despotic government, the free will of the people is subjugated to a ruler. No single person's will is absolutely free in a democracy, but the freedom of the whole, through compromise and reconciliations, comprises true freedom. This democratic unity of a society resulting from the recognition for and respect of others as one's equals, and the willingness to compromise, is the best form of unity.

To achieve such unity, certain virtues and social mores are absolutely essential. Individuals must be accustomed to free discussion, tolerant of compromise, generously yield their opinions to truth, and show equanimity and courtesy in heated arguments based on reason. Thus, in a narrow sense, democracy is a political system; and in a larger sense, it is a civilization that embodies the principles of society, thought, morality, outlook on life, and the moral standards of good character in the relationship between man and man.[3]

Rationality

It is Chang's belief that democracy is based on the assumption that human beings are rational in nature, and that the rationality of man is the prerequisite for democracy. Rationality plays a vital part in civilization, for it has enabled civilization to progress steadily. The rise of the theory at the end of the nineteenth and the beginning of the twentieth century of the irrationalism of man as a potent force in countering rationalism did not escape Chang's notice; he simply believed that the foundation of rationalism was not affected. Rationalism, Chang said, assumes that man is rational, while irrationalism assumes that man is irrational. Irrationalism further assumes that there are only irrational elements in human nature. This is exactly like the classical Chinese philosophical argument of whether human nature is good or evil. In fact, not everyone is good, nor is everyone evil, but some are good and some are evil. To say that everyone is irrational cannot be proven. There are people who in fact are irrational, but this particular proposition cannot negate the universal proposition. Rationality, like liberty and freedom, is a postulate, a faith, and an assumption. Thus, irrationalism has not been able to overthrow rationalism, and rationalism has not been shaken by irrationalism, the reason being that rationalism is based on faith rather than wholly on facts.

It is the common physical structure and mentality of man, which to a certain degree is influenced by one's social and educational environment, that make man rational and give each individual the same sense of right and wrong, good and evil. Since people have the same rational nature, everyone can understand and accept an ideal for a better world through reasoning. As Mencius remarked on the uniformity of human nature: "All palates have the same preference in tastes; all ears in sounds; all eyes in beauty. Should hearts prove to be an exception by possessing nothing in common? What is common to all hearts? Reason and righteousness."[4] The rationality of man predominates in a democratic society, and democracy can be established only in a community where man appeals to reason.

A basic assumption in democracy is that it is human nature to seek one's own happiness. However, individual interests are generally common interests and therefore can be pursued collectively. The concepts of general will, common

161

good, and general happiness all point to the same line of thought. Although democracy cannot make everybody fully satisfied, it aims at realizing the greatest good for the great majority. If this is so, then certain ideas of the Left and of the Right are questionable: on the Right, the Nazi claim that people in general do not clearly know what their true interests are but must be told by the superman, i.e., the leader; on the Left, the Marxian dichotomy of the so-called bourgeois truth and proletarian truth. Self-interested parties advocate their own prejudiced political theories, and their fallacies should be exposed. These theories cannot support a conclusion that truth is confined only to one party or class, and therefore has a class nature.[5]

Freedom of Speech

To speak of democracy, Chang maintained, is to speak of freedom, for without freedom there will be no democracy. Freedom provides a kind of immunity to protect society from corruption and decadence, and helps to make society progressive and healthy. Freedom falls into various categories, the basic one being freedom of speech. Through free expression and exchange of ideas, unreasonable ideas are negated and reasonable ideas affirmed and respected. It is a practice that leads to the advancement of civilization in that it produces the maximum and the best result under a democracy. In a despotic or dictatorial regime, any free discussion is narrowly limited within a party or faction.

It may be said that free expression and democracy are one and the same. A government in which the people enjoy freedom of speech is entitled to be called truly democratic. Conversely, if a government limits freedom of speech, it cannot be considered democratic, even if it has a constitution and a parliament. In this particular situation, Chang evidently had in mind the then Chinese Nationalist government.[6] The reason that democratic politics is responsible politics, Chang said, is simply because the reality of free speech holds the government responsible to the people, who are able to censure or impeach it for wrong doing. Without freedom of speech, there is no way to judge whether a government is right or wrong, and naturally there is no possibility of raising the question of government responsibility, let alone of censure or impeachment. A government of this kind is responsible to no one but itself. Irresponsible government is always a usurpation of power, regardless of the terminology used; autocracy in olden times and dictatorship in modern times belong to the same category. Without freedom of speech civilization cannot progress and the public cannot be mobilized by appeal to reason. Thus, freedom of speech is the life and soul of a nation; without it, a country becomes a corpse.[7]

Freedom of Thought

What is central to all freedoms, Chang wrote, is the freedom of thought, without which no other freedoms can exist. It is essentially freedom of thought that makes modern European and American cultures stand out in human history. Thus, freedom of thought, or academic freedom, is the necessary condition to the advancement of civilization.[8]

Freedom of thought or the lack of it brings about two entirely different worlds. In a society with freedom of thought, an individual is an agent who exercises free will and makes free judgments. Under a dictatorship, only the dictator exercises free will, while the common people can only take orders and parrot what the authorities desire. The people are used as tools, cheated, and goaded as children and animals. Thus, a dictatorial state is not a community of independent individuals with free will, as in a democracy, but one of slaves. Two entirely different views of the state are reflected here. In one case, the state belongs to all, and is what the Chinese have called a "public vehicle" *(kung-ch'i)*. The government in power, like a board of directors elected by the shareholders, is only temporary. In the other case, all dictators identify themselves with the state and have lifelong tenure. In a democratic state, education is aimed at producing independent individuals; in a dictatorial state, it produces followers.

In essence, freedom of thought is the basic condition for peace and order. Without freedom in discussion and reasoning, people will resort to force in settling problems; consequently, disorder and turmoil will ensue. Freedom of thought is also the basic condition necessary for the development of culture. In its absence, there is no creative thought, and even if there were, criticisms and improvements would be lacking: the exchange and interaction of diversified ideas and theories are conducive to the advancement of culture. A culture will stagnate if an orthodoxy in any one particular theory is established. Freedom is also the basic condition for the cultivation of good morality among citizens. A community of ignorant slaves, blindly obedient, and afraid to criticize, will ultimately lead to moral degradation and the decline of a people.[9]

Chang repeatedly emphasized that freedom is a moral principle, and should not in any way be construed to mean indulgence, moral relaxation, or doing as one pleases. In this respect, Chang's warnings are not purely theoretical, but are of practical significance. Usually those in power who are against freedom and democracy believe that freedom without restriction breeds anarchy and disorder. The Nationalist government used this line of reasoning to combat the Communists and other democratic minor parties, and it is used today by the Communist government on mainland China against those who demand democratic rights. Chang categorically maintained that the fight for freedom is a moral struggle against unfree and unequal situations. A most notable illustration was the Puritan founders of America who fled to America because they suffered unequal treatment and were not free in England. They led a rigorous life and were highly religious. It was purely moral principles that motivated them to become members of a political party of democracy.

Those Chinese who mistakenly believe that democracy creates disorder, that freedom means indulgence, and that equality means the leveling of the higher to the lower simply have completely missed the point. Liberty, equality and democracy are moral issues whose basic spirit is to regulate and discipline oneself rather than to demand from others. A democratic society can only be achieved when everyone, in his word and deed, is conscious of establishing himself morally and able to be tolerant of others. In the West, democracy is considered as a way of life. However, this way of life must be based on rationality, in harmony with morality. Freedom is a positive concept that enables an individual to develop moral excellence; equality is a negative concept that restrains one from discriminating against others.[10]

How to Introduce Democracy in China

It was Chang's belief that in order to create a new culture from two different cultures, it is best to study those areas common to both cultures. With regard to the introduction of democracy in China, he applied this principle to liberty and equality. Chang's argument is condensed as follows. Ancient China lacked the Western concept of liberty and equality. The closest thing China had is what is called in the West spiritual freedom, a prerequisite to political freedom. In China, Confucianism stresses inner moral discipline, but neglects institutionalized political liberty, a fact that probably accounts for the failure of Confucianism in regard to political problems. (There is a linguistic problem here. Liberty is *tzu-yu* in Chinese, while spiritual freedom is a free translation for *tzu-te*. Both *tzu-yu* and *tzu-te* have the same first character.) Chang's analogous interpretation of these two terms gets deeply involved in philosophy, which does not concern us here. It will suffice here to mention his attempt to link these two concepts.

The Confucian golden rule, "Whatever you do not wish others to do unto you, do not do unto them," serves very well to explain Western liberty in Confucian terms. The essence of liberty is not indulgence or relaxation as some people believe, but acceptance that one's own liberty is limited to the extent that it does not infringe upon the rights of others. To paraphrase the Confucian dictum: since you do not wish your liberty to be violated by others, you should not infringe upon another's liberty. This implies the concept of equality, for everyone has the same privileges and limitations of liberty. Confucius says that "all men within the four seas are brothers," a strong theoretical parallel to the Western concept of equality. The Confucian tenet can be explained to mean that everyone is the equal of everyone else. Among equals, no one should enjoy special privileges and no one should suffer discrimination. How much more equal would it be among brothers? Equality in the Western democratic sense means the social equality of opportunities; it has nothing to do with natural inequalities, e.g. the difference in individual intelligence. What is to be opposed is the artificial inequality created by man, for example, poor but intelligent children cannot receive a good education, while rich but stupid children can, as a result of unreasonable distribution of wealth and other man-made privileges. Most important, if there are people in China who really understand democracy, they would be Confucianists. This should not be misunderstood to mean that Confucianism coincides with democratic theory. It is only that the self-regulatory and self-disciplined tenet of Confucianism agrees with the basic view of an ideal personality in democracy.[11]

164

Democracy and Socialism Are One

For Chang, freedom and equality are the basic concepts underlying democracy. These concepts, together with their related and derived concepts, such as rationality, justice, human rights, tolerance, individualism, can be labelled as a group of ideas or network of ideas. Every culture has its basic group of ideas, serving as the determinates and bearing the characteristics of that culture. In the case of Western culture, it is rationality, freedom, and equality that form a conceptual system, which can be generally called democracy.

However, the basic concept of democracy is also the basic concept of socialism. Democracy and socialism are not to be separated. The great contributions of thought in the eighteenth century are the theories aimed at the elimination of social inequalities. These theories diverged in two directions, democracy and socialism. The former aims at eliminating inequality caused by political power, i.e., autocracy or despotism; the latter aims at eliminating economic inequality caused by exploitation. Political despotism and economic exploitation are closely related and are the two sides of the same thing. There is no political despotism which is not virtually economic exploitation. But, unfortunately, these two sides have developed into separate and even conflicting movements, with no satisfactory solution. The reason is the preference of the theorists for one side or the other. Democrats stress personal liberty, and therefore advocate the policy of lassez faire and the resulting free competition. Seeing that an economic revolution must depend on force, socialists advocate the suppression of antirevolutionaries during the revolution and thus seek political despotism. Obviously, democrats have sacrificed equality in upholding individual liberty, and socialists have sacrificed democracy in fulfilling their ideal. Historical facts now show that without democracy there is no true socialism; and without socialism, there is no true democracy, Actually, democracy should not be taken as a stage prior to socialism, and socialism should not be taken as something different from democracy. These two sides, which have unfortunately developed into seemingly conflicting movements, should unite.

Chang's advocacy of the unity of democracy and socialism contradicts the theory of dividing democracy into bourgeois democracy and proletariat or socialist democracy, and also undermines the basis for withholding people's democratic rights during a socialist revolution.[12]

Democracy to Be the Norm of Politics

Based on his analysis, Chang concluded that democracy should not be considered merely one of the forms of political institution, as Plato and Aristotle maintained, but it should be the norm or normality of a healthy form of political institution. All other forms, such as autocracy or dictatorship, are abnormal or ailing. His arguments are recapitulated as follows.

Freedom of speech is the soul of a state and the life of a society. This is exactly what autocracy and dictatorship lack and why they are both lifeless.

Moreover, in a democracy, free discussion can develop to its fullest extent, while it is restricted in an autocracy or in a dictatorship. In a democracy, consent of the ruled is achieved by freedom of speech. In an autocracy, on the other hand, consent is achieved through force or oppression, and in a dictatorship through propaganda at the expense of a liberal education, i.e. by deception. Consent is genuine only in a democracy because it is achieved on the basis of free will and, therefore, of equality. Thus, the people have a dual qualification, being both the ruler and the ruled. They are not subject to the ruler, but are self-governing. Accordingly, the interests of the ruler and the ruled can be harmonized. These are the reasons that democracy is considered as normal and all other forms are abnormal.[13]

Sometime in the 1930s the Yenching students asked Chang to write an inscription for the school paper, a common practice in China. Chang wrote, "If I were given a choice between communism and the guillotine, I would choose the latter." His anticommunist attitude, although strong, was mainly intellectual. However, Chang's writings in later years were more circumspect and, thus, less harsh on Marxism or communism and indirectly more cooperative towards the communists. His change of attitude was because, like many other intellectuals, he was dazzled by the Soviet success, especially its planned economy. Chang hoped that the Communists could reconstruct China after the Soviet pattern. In his last book, *Democracy and Socialism,* Chang dismissed as meaningless all the crucial controversial issues regarding Marxism or communism. He portrayed as issues of fact controversial questions such as: "Is revolution necessary?," "Is revolution to be catastrophic?," "Is terrorism to be practiced?" These issues, he now said, are the result of fortuitous and accidental events, or the collision between revolutionary activities and the targets of the revolutionaries. Events are dictated by the particular conditions of the time concerned and are neither questions of theories nor have anything to do with theories. The fears and horror commonly believed to be inherent to Marxist or communist revolution should be disassociated from theoretical considerations because these unpleasant events can be avoided by practical wisdom. They are not the logical consequences of revolutionary theory. Chang praised the Soviet achievements, particularly the planned economy, collective farms, and cooperatives. He concluded in *Democracy and Socialism* that politically, economically, and socially, the Soviet Union offered mankind valuable lessons, for it had discovered, while groping through the dark, a bright road for others to follow.[14] Nevertheless, he remained critical of Marxism and communism.

Dictatorship of the Proletariat

To many great communists, the dictatorship of the proletariat is a necessary and unavoidable stage in the socialist revolution, and it must be carried out to the end before its ultimate goal of communism is reached. Chang challenged this view as a deviation, even a misreading of Marxism. First, he quoted a passage from Marx's 1872 Amsterdam speech to substantiate his argument:

"Some day the workers must conquer political supremacy, in order to establish the new organization of labour; they must overthrow the old political system whereby the old institutions are sustained. . . . Of course, I must not be supposed to imply that the means to this end will be everywhere the same. We know that special regard must be paid to the institutions, customs and traditions of various lands; and we do not deny that there are certain countries, such as the United States and England, in which the workers may hope to secure their ends by peaceful means." Chang took this to mean that, first, for Marx, the revolution of the proletariat is the last resort, but not the only resort, and that it would be much better if social reforms are achieved by peaceful means, and with fewer sacrifices. Second, Marx did not regard the dictatorship of the proletariat to be a political system but rather a transitional means. Even in this transitional period, it would not mean that the government was an irresponsible one, but that it must be responsible to the whole proletariat. This is not, in theory, contradictory to the spirit of democracy. Third, Marx never supported the idea of the dictatorship of one party; rather, he advocated the dictatorship of only one class. To assert that one party can represent the interests of the class is contrary to Marxism. In capitalist countries, such as England and France, there have been more than one political party representing the interests of the bourgeoisie. Chang wondered how the interests of the proletariat could be represented by one and only one political party. He concluded that no scholar ever existed who was bold enough to declare that a state should be monopolized by a minority of the people. Marx had never been for dictatorship and against democracy; on the contrary, he regarded the then prevailing democracy as insufficient and wanted to widen it by including both economic equality and political freedom in order to achieve greater democracy.[15]

Aside from theory, Chang challenged the dictatorship of the proletariat from the practical side by evoking the principle that truth must be proven by practice. He did not, however, claim credit for this idea and admitted it was Marx's idea. In practice, Chang said, communist governments that exercised proletarian dictatorship are irresponsible, and the proletariat are powerless to control them. Thus, communist governments inevitably degenerate into the dictatorship of a minority. Furthermore, when intellectuals are condemned because they are related to the propertied class, there is no healthy expression of public opinion, and the whole culture will be degraded. In such a dictatorship, when the bourgeoisie is persecuted, the damage they suffer is less severe than the damage done to the majority of the proletariat. The indulgence on the part of the proletariat of the evil sentiments of revenge, sadism, and animosity will result in irrational emotions for the whole country. In actual practice, the dictatorship of the proletariat is certainly detrimental but it has nothing to do with Marx's theories. Marx's dictatorship of the proletariat simply consists in the denial of the right of the bourgeoisie to be elected but does not consist of their persecution, arrest, and death. Whether or not violence is to be used depends on the time and particular situation of the place concerned. There is no universal law to follow. To insist that there is such a law without giving due consideration to the particular time and place is a distortion of Marxism. On the whole, Marxism cannot be used as a theoretical foundation for violence and bloodshed.[16]

Principle of Struggle

In Communist usage the word "struggle" is usually linked to class struggle. Chang gives struggle a much wider scope. He interprets the historical conflict between individual freedom and centralized state authority with what he calls the principle of struggle. According to Chang, this principle applies to political behavior beginning from primitive tribes to modern dictators. Naturally, class struggle can be included in this category, but he seems to play it down purposely. The following is his argument of the theory of struggle.

There are two opposite and natural forces in a society: social solidarity and social antagonism. The former may be regarded as the centripetal force, the latter the centrifugal force. These two forces manifest themselves in a society in different situations. Both politicians and revolutionaries tend to exploit these two forces for their respective purposes. Politicians, after obtaining political power, tend to do their utmost to strengthen the centripetal force to consolidate their power at the expense of individual freedom; the revolutionaries, on the other hand, tend to utilize and enhance the centrifugal force, the existing conflicts of interests in society, to promote revolutionary zeal in order to overthrow the government they oppose.

But politicians, exploiting the natural centripetal force of solidarity, have employed the so-called principle of struggle. As far as human nature is concerned, to fight is not a human instinct; it is only some animals who start to fight as soon as they see each other. However, struggles among men can be instigated and manipulated by politicians to such a degree that men may become addicted and relish it. Ancient tribal leaders, attempting to expand their influence, grasped this principle unintentionally by first establishing an assumed enemy to fight against, and next controlling the minds and cultivating certain virtues of the masses, e.g., obedience, to a specific designed pattern. With obedience, orderly organization can be achieved, that is, disciplined actions and centralized power. The leader is then able to command the herd according to his will. For the benefit of the leaders, there must always be a target to fight. When one target has been conquered, another will be chosen. Accordingly, struggle becomes a constant task so that the strict organization does not disintegrate. In modern times, politicians, following the same line as the tribal leaders, are prone to emphasize the importance of national interest at the expense of personal liberties and they always like to change a peaceful state into a war or semi-war situation so that they can exploit it for their own purposes. Thus, they promote totalitarian theories and advocate state supremacy. By these pretexts, the leader or dictator succeeds by political trickery in identifying himself with the state.[17]

The principle of struggle conflicts with democracy in two ways. First, it contradicts the view that the state is simply an instrument for the welfare of its citizens; instead, it takes it as something to be worshipped. Second, struggle and freedom are incompatible. In a country where a group of people are singled out as the target to be struggled against, they will obviously be deprived of some of their freedom. Those who persecute these victims will also suffer a diminution of freedom because their organization must maintain a high degree of discipline and obedience at the expense of their personal spiritual freedom. Furthermore, constant struggle degenerates good human characteristics and deprives a society of an atmosphere of serenity. Under these conditions of struggle, there is neither freedom nor peace.

Chang remarked that modern socialists, for the sake of revolution, prefer the practice of struggle at the expense of freedom. As we mentioned before, Chang was soft and circumspect towards the communists in his later writings. Although he strongly censured struggle, he never touched class struggle, nor the name of communists, even though class struggle is the most typical characteristic of communist movements. As to the struggle against a portion of the people in one's own country, the concrete example Chang referred to was, by innuendo, the Kuomintang repression of the Communists. When he spoke of this burning issue of his time, he only used the word "modern socialists." Since his censure of struggle as a principle was strong, he naturally would not have approved of class struggle, but on this question he was neither explicit nor direct. His attitude on the problem of struggle may be summarized in the following points.

He did not totally oppose struggle, nor curse revolutions; he maintained that struggle can only be viewed as a tactic, an expediency, a temporary means, but not as a theory to be adhered to forever. What he truly opposed was the theory of permanent struggle. Advocates of such a theory maintain that struggle will continue even after the great success of communism, being transformed into the struggle against nature. His rebuttal was that struggle between man and man is different from that of man against nature. To take them as the same thing is a wrong analogy, for man's struggle against nature actually started at the dawn of history, and it need not wait until the success of communism. Chang felt that taking the principle of struggle as a universal truth and everlasting law, and failing to see it as wrong, is due to a misunderstanding of Marxism. Actually, the theories of ceaseless struggle and permanent revolution are fallacies promoted by the ambitious thirst for power of politicians, aimed at the destruction of people's freedom. In essence, Chang urged that all people in a country are to be treated as brothers, and under no circumstances should they struggle against each other. With struggle, there can be no peace; without peace, there can be no social construction; without construction, neither freedom nor democracy can be established.[18]

Class and Class Struggle

Chang also addressed the question of class and class struggle apart from what he called the principle of struggle. Since democracy requires the full participation of all the people, it must first solve the problem of class struggle. Marx in his *Communist Manifesto* stated that all human history, past and present, is the history of class struggle and that the emergence of classes is due to the mode of production. However, sociological studies show that in primitive societies there was only communal production and no private production, so that no antagonistic classes existed. Thus, neither class distinction nor class struggle began with human history. (After the publication of the *Manifesto,* Marx noticed the existence of primitive communist society from Morgan's crowning discovery, and realized that only after the dissolution of these primeval communities does society begin to be differentiated into separate and finally antagonistic classes. But Chang did not mention this point specifically.) Since Marx envisioned a classless society in the communist stage, there would naturally be no more class struggle at that time. Thus Marx could not believe that class struggle coexisted with human history from beginning to end.

Marx's definition of class differed from a sociologist's definition. For Marx, class is determined by ownership relations. People are divided into wage earners who own nothing but can sell their labor, and capitalists who own the means of production and who do not work but live on interest. Sociologists define class by profession. According to Marx's definition, as noted above, class did not exist at the beginning of history, and would be abolished in the future communist society. According to the sociologist's definition, classes would still exist in a highly socialist society, but there would be no class struggle. Moreover, when a high degree of democracy materializes, class and class struggle would not occur at all.[19]

As stated previously, Chang's strong censure of the principle of struggle in general would lead people to surmise his logical opposition to class struggle, for class struggle is one form of struggle. Since struggle is viewed as nothing but trickery and manipulation by politicians to enhance their power in order to command the people at the expense of their freedom, one must use this standard to evaluate class struggle. The following questions at least may be raised: Is the theory of class struggle true? Is its practical policy likely to bring about more social harmony and human happiness? Is class struggle, as other forms of struggle, stimulated, exploited, and manipulated by power-seeking socialists? Chang did not explicitly explore these questions. The reasons, I believe, are twofold. First, he was not sure about the answers because socialists are after all different from nonprincipled politicians. Second, he did not want to offend the Communists so he was circumspect in his language. One thing we can say for sure is that he was at least theoretically not in favor of class struggle, and tactically he tried to comment on it as vaguely and innocuously as possible.

Gradual Socialism versus Radical Revolution

Revolution and Permanent Revolution

Chang basically opposed the practice of revolution. His attitude toward revolution and permanent revolution was dictated by his philosophical beliefs, as follows. Democracy requires all members of a society to be treated as brothers. No section should be singled out as enemies. The Confucian tenet that all men within the four seas are brothers should be observed. The Western ideal of fraternity as seen in the French Revolution is an important addition to liberty and equality. Thus, the philosophy of hatred is to be rejected. If democracy is to prevail, the prevailing theory of revolution should be rectified. Revolution can only be a last and unavoidable resort. It should be carried out in as short a period as possible, and under no circumstances should it be permitted to last long. Revolution, after its short duration, should be immediately followed by construction. It is absurd to maintain a second, third, or even a continuous revolution. The advocacy of continuous revolution along with ceaseless struggle are pretexts of politicians to monopolize power indefinitely. If such a practice is followed, the country would be constantly in a state of chaos, belligerency, and evil, and destitute of harmony and cooperation.

Those socialists who believe in democracy should remember that in the literature of Marx and Engels there is an indication that communist transition can be achieved by peaceful means. This shows that both these great communist theorists regarded revolution only as a means and not an end. People who either fail to understand or ignore this point do not take revolution as a means but as a necessary passage. This mistake entails all sorts of evils. It is called formalism. Actually, revolution should be limited to effecting the change of government during a short time span, after which revolution will not be in existence and nothing violent under the name of revolution can be justified. Accordingly, "reactionaries" and the "suppression of reactionaries" make no sense at all.[20]

Chang did not favor revolution, but could tolerate it if absolutely necessary. He definitely opposed continuous or permanent revolution, his belief being that only democracy is an everlasting ideal to be pursued, while revolution is a temporary and transitory event. He also asserted that those who consider democratic revolution as a preliminary stage to socialist revolution obviously misunderstood the true meaning of democracy.[21]

Class Distinctions in China

According to Chang's classification, there are three classes in China: bureaucrats, civilians (mostly peasants), and military men and bandits. The bureaucratic class is subdivided into scholars, who are potential bureaucrats; business men, who do business and make money primarily through official influence and privilege (the small shop clerks or employees are excluded from this class); landlords, who are often the offspring of bureaucrats; and gentry *(shen)*, who are retired bureaucrats.

Among these classes, the peasants are the most painfully and cruelly exploited. In China, the only significant source of wealth comes from agriculture. Although artisans and merchants pay taxes, they can pass on the tax burden; ultimately, the poor peasants shoulder the heaviest taxes. Burdened with a crushing weight, the only outlet for them in avoiding the intolerably heavy levies is to join the army or become bandits. Superficially, peasants and

171

warlords appear to belong in two entirely antagonistic classes. Actually, all troops are recruited from peasants and the warlords come from the peasants. The peasants do not form a class with class consciousness, and cannot cement themselves into a solid entity so as to relieve their sufferings as a whole class. Of course, in history there are innumerable instances of peasant leaders who started revolts, and vowed to save the people from "the deep water and hot fire," that is, to lessen or do away with taxes and misery. As soon as they were in power, however, they exploited the peasants in exactly the same way as their predecessors. In China, class distinction is not clearly defined in economic terms, but rather set by lines of political influence. In other words, exploitation is mainly political, and economic exploitation is only effected through political exploitation. What the rebels have attempted to do is to change their status from being ruled to that of ruler, from being exploited to being exploiters.[22]

The Role of Intellectuals in China's Reconstruction

Who are the people qualified and capable of carrying out the great task of revolution and reconstruction? For Mao, it is the proletariat, mainly the workers and peasants. For Chang, it is what he called the scholar class *(shih chieh-chi)*, those generally referred to as intellectuals. Chinese scholars have always had a long tradition in helping the ruler run the government. Chang rejected people outside of the scholar class as unqualified. They are the peasants, he said, who are intellectually unable to shoulder the task of modernization. Moreover, they cannot leave their land to participate in political activities. Workers and artisans are too few in number. The military are even less qualified for the task. Confucius believed that there is bound to be a minority with high intelligence and more knowledge to lead the masses from going astray. It is the mission of the intellectuals to lead the people first to moral advancement and subsequently to intellectual enlightenment. However, scholars have degenerated in the recent decades into a hypocritical, irresponsible, self- and profit-seeking, sycophantic class as a result of the alien oppression of the Ch'ing dynasty. Their failure to carry out the Confucian mission, due to their corruption, constituted the main cause of all the chaos and turmoil of the decades since 1911. Thus, a morally reformed scholar class is the only class suitable for carrying out social reconstruction in China.[23] Clearly in Chang's mind the Chinese revolution should be an intellectuals' revolution.

Chang believed that every culture has its own tradition, which cannot be transplanted from a foreign land. However, men living on the same planet Earth must have a cultural exchange. China, though having her own tradition and culture, cannot but assimilate some Western culture. For this reason, Chang suggested a two-sided program to revitalize the Chinese scholars' mission in assimilating the Western system. First, the failed mission of the scholar class should be revived. The scholars should perform the function of an organ to create new blood, to perform the process of social metabolism to generate an atmosphere of serenity in society, and to provide the criteria of right and wrong in politics. This means the creation of public opinion to lead the country on the correct path with guiding influences.

It is important that such public opinion be protected by law and by an established system. Thus, second, the practical course to follow is British guild socialism. Among its programs, the one which China can best adopt in its education is the guild system, the spirit of which is the "automony of education" (*chiao-yü tzu-chih*). This British plan has some similarities to a Chinese system. The academy system (*shu-yuan*) of the Sung dynasty, mainly private or locally operated, has a spirit of educational automony similar to that of the British system. Here, again, is Chang's belief that it is easier to adopt a foreign system that has elements common to one's own culture rather than one entirely foreign. However, for modern China, Chang continued, the curriculum in the academy should be entirely different from the past. For instance, Chinese classics should be taught selectively rather than exclusively, and science and social philosophy should be introduced and added. In the past, the scholar class devoted themselves solely to moral cultivation with a view to assisting the emperor to run the government. In modern time, they should still remain in the assisting position, but not to the emperor, nor even to the government, but to the whole culture. In other words, they should persistently make an effort to contribute to the whole culture by preventing it from being fossilized. They should also serve as a ventilator, constantly expelling stale air and letting in fresh air, thus preventing the nation from becoming corrupt and stagnant. They are also to provide guidance so that justice and truth always prevail. The government should provide the expense for education. It can only ask the scholar guild to be responsible for training a certain kind and number of experts and fulfilling certain educational policies laid down by the government, but it should not interfere in any way with educational autonomy.

Chang did not specify the practical measures enabling scholars to succeed in gaining the position of guiding and influencing the government. He simply set out the principle that scholars should guide society and culture to the correct course. However, Chang did anticipate an international aid for China's social, economic, and political reconstruction. The practical measure he envisioned was the creation of an international cultural organization, consisting of top scholars from various countries who are devoted to the welfare of mankind as a whole. The aim of the organization is to help all countries through moral pressure and rational persuasion to achieve economic and political renovation. Economically, the aim is to eliminate the exploiting class without bloodshed, and politically, it is to promote democracy. Cooperation between this international organization and the scholars in various countries would be necessary to ensure the success of the goal.

Chang admitted that his suggestion did not originate with himself, but that it was based on the idea of Plato's philosopher king. However, Chang criticized Plato's mistake of allowing philosophers to become administrators. Once they become administrators, they would give in to practical conditions at the expense of their ideals. Further, philosophers in the modern world are no longer sufficient and should be supplemented by scientists.

In summary, Chang believed that the adoption of the educational autonomy policy of the British guild socialism would elevate the level of Chinese culture. This policy would correlate with international moral influences on the one hand, and agree with the traditional mission of Chinese scholars on the other hand. It would lead China on her way to democracy and economic justice without going through a social revolution.[24]

It was Chang's belief that to create a new culture as the new situation called for, the scholar class is indispensable. Most important, in Chinese history scholars have symbolized morality. Ideal scholars are those who hold the moral law firmly until death, are ready to sacrifice their lives for moral principles, set themselves as models of good conduct, and engage in educational work to inculcate moral teachings to others. This spirit has a great deal to do with the fact that Chinese culture has persisted for thousands of years while many other cultures perished. For Chang, therefore, morality has an absolute nature in value. This view obviously contradicts Marx's materialistic interpretation of history that morality is a reflection of economic and social conditions, and that moral values change as the relations of production change. Chang commented that this was a great weak point in Marxism. Admitting that there are certain virtues that change as the times change, he insisted that in the abstract sense of morality, there remain unchanging fundamental principles. His argument is based on Kant's theory of morality, which Chang said was Kant's most immortal contribution to human thought, rather than on his theory of knowledge as people have generally considered. Kant, as Chang interpreted him, maintained that morality consists of laws that an individual sets up through his free will for the purpose of restricting and disciplining oneself. At the same time, these are laws that any reasonable person can follow and practice. Morality is created for one's own inconvenience, not for one's own selfish convenience.

This self-restraining principle is indispensable to the coherence of society, and without it harmony and agreement between man and man would be impossible. This fundamental principle of morality remains immutable no matter how social and economic conditions have changed. Thus, morality, in this abstract sense, has an absolute nature. The emphasis on the abstract principle, rather than the concrete contents, is what is generally called formalism or formal ethics. Chang, in his *Moral Philosophy,* discusses in detail Kant's theory of morality and Marxian ethics.

Chang further argued that although some people view Kant's abstract moral theory as vague and empty, it truly has binding power, and that economic factors cannot be considered as the only factors determining a good society. Those who believe this do so because of their failure to distinguish between the necessary and sufficient conditions. Economic betterment can, of course, serve as a necessary condition in eliminating certain crimes, such as theft, but cannot serve as a sufficient condition to eliminate all other crimes. This fact necessitates the uplifting work of scholars to educate peasants and workers to bring

174

about their moral advancement. In addition, the idea, held by some, that people of common origins naturally possess noble virtues is questionable. Finally, history has proven that the theory of the dictatorship of workers and peasants is harmful rather than beneficial.[25]

Chang envisioned two paths for the future of the scholars. One is to devote themselves to a lifetime job in educational work by organizing themselves into autonomous guilds after the pattern of British guild socialism, as discussed above. Another is to go to the rural villages to integrate with the peasants. This idea is evidently in line with the advocacy of the communists, and shows that intellectuals' going to the village has been an idea of many thinkers and is not unique to the communists. For instance, Liang Shu-ming, discussed in this book, is one. The integration, Chang believed, will free the peasants from the oppression of the bureaucrats. For bureaucrats, big businessmen, and gentry belong to the same oppressive class, which must be eliminated. However, the elimination is not to be effected by brutal revolutionary means, but by legislative measures and a new land system.

Chang said very little about the land system. He simply echoed Sun Yat-sen's principle that the tillers should own the land. He also shared the popular belief that the permanent solution to the problem of land reform lies in the promotion of scientific methods of cultivation. Collective farming is considered to be the most suitable means for scientific cultivation. However, collective farming can go hand in hand with private ownership of land to accord with the peasants' love for the land. In addition, Chang advocated self-government in villages, on the model of the traditional village convention *(hsiang-yueh)* formulated by Lü Ta-fang of the Sung dynasty. The attempt must be to integrate education and politics. In short, Chang believed that the hope of China in the land problem lies in the integration of intellectuals and peasants, and the severance of the peasants from the bureaucrats.

Summary

Chang's ultimate faith in the future of China is a gradual socialistic democracy. By gradual, he meant the achievement of social reconstruction by peaceful means. His studies of Chinese history, and perhaps of Western history as well, led him to reach an instructive conclusion that a radical change is always followed by a reaction, which is able to cancel the reform and cause a retreat, in a considerable measure, to the original situation. Thus he was convinced that the more radical the reform, the faster the retreat; and that only the effects of peaceful reform can be stable and long lasting. This does not mean that radical reforms are entirely fruitless, but rather that they generally involve a process of going forward one hundred steps and going back sixty or seventy steps. Chang declared that he does not oppose revolution, but does not believe that real progress of mankind is dependent on revolution.

Since revolutions, whether political or social, do not signify true progress, the periodization of history, in Chang's opinion, should not be based on revolutions as landmarks. He cites the example of the 1911 Revolution: on the surface it marked the beginning of a new epoch, but in reality the true social conditions remained almost unchanged in the early years of the Republic. The idea that a democratic revolution of today must precede a socialist revolution of the future is inappropriate. True progress does not occur at the time of radical change, but rather after the radical changes have taken place. Radical changes in and of themselves have no beneficial value; hence, nothing good results directly from radical changes. In order to achieve progress, the Chinese people are urged to move forward toward social progress at any time and at any place without waiting for a revolution as the starting point.[27]

Chang passionately hoped that China would transform herself from a society of natural evolution to one created and guided by reason. He saw it as the duty of scholars to reconstruct and plan this new society based on reason.[28]

Notes

1. See also Howard L. Boorman "Chang Tung-sun," *Biographical Dictionary of Republican China* (New York: Columbia University Press, 1967) 1:129–33.

2. Chang Tung-sun, *Szu-hsiang yü she-hui* (Shanghai: Commercial 1947), pp. 167, 179–80. Hereafter referred to as *Szu-hsiang*.

3. Chang Tung-sun, *Li-hsing yü min-chu* (Chungking: Commercial, 1946), pp. 1–7, 145. Hereafter referred to as *Li-hsing*.

4. *Mencius*, trans. D. C. Lau (England: Penguin, 1970), p. 164. In Chang's book, he did not include the last three sentences. The present author has added them to make it clearer. It is presumed that Chang thought this a very famous quotation in China, so no complete quote was necessary.

5. Chang, *Szu-hsiang*, pp. 166–69; Chang Tung-sun, *Chih-shih yü wen-hua* (Shanghai: Commercial, 1947), pp. 87–98. Hereafter referred to as *Chih-shih*. Chang Tung-sun, *Min-chu chu-i yü She-hui chu-i* (Shanghai: Kuan ch'a-she, 1948), pp. 4–5. Hereafter referred to as *Min-chu*.

6. Chang, *Li-hsing*, p. 126.

7. Chang, *Szu-hsiang*, pp. 171–72.

8. Chang, *Li-hsing*, pp. 134-35; *Chih-shih*, p. 225.

9. Chang, *Chih-shih*, pp. 230–33.

10. Chang, *Li-hsing*, pp. 152–53.

11. Chang, *Szu-hsiang*, p. 164; *Li-hsing*, pp. 49, 125–26, 128, 152.

12. Chang, *Li-hsing*, p. 130; *Szu-hsiang*, p. 178; *Min-chu*, pp. 5, 10, 26.

13. Chang, *Szu-hsiang*, pp. 165–67, 171–72; *Li-hsing*, p. 175.

14. For the changed attitude of Chang, see his *Min-chu*, especially the latter part, pp. 39–74.

15. Chang, *Szu-hsiang*, pp. 172–73.

16. Ibid., p. 177; Chang, *Min-chu*, pp. 70–72.

17. Chang, *Li-hsing*, pp. 138–39.

18. Ibid., pp. 142–43.

19. Ibid., pp. 149–50.

20. Ibid., p. 146.

21. Ibid., p. 151.

22. Ibid., pp. 166–68.

23. Chang, *Szu-hsiang*, pp. 185–88.

24. Ibid., pp. 192–95.

25. Chang, *Li-hsing*, pp. 176–77. For Chang's own treatment on the problem of morality, readers are recommended to refer to his book *Tao-te che-hsueh* (Shanghai: Chung-hua, 1931), 1:322–36, 2:617–47.

26. Chang, *Li-hsing*, pp. 178, 182–83.

27. Ibid., pp. 184–85.

28. Chang, *Szu-hsiang*, p. 199.

7
Liang Shu-ming (1893–   )

Biography

From 1924 until at least 1956, Liang Shu-ming actively defended traditional Confucian values and upheld their relevance to the welfare of China's predominantly rural society. Whether agreeing or disagreeing with the details of his particular perspective, Chinese intellectuals who have not conceded to the prescriptive categories of praise and blame current in the People's Republic of China retain an image of Liang Shu-ming as an independent thinker who devoted his energies to direct application of his ideas in education and in the practicalities of rural life.

Liang Shu-ming[1] was born in Peking of a bureaucratic family from Kweilin, Kwangsi, on 9 September 1893. His father was a *chin-shih,* an official of the fourth rank in Peking, and seems to have been part of the intellectual movement for modernization, since he enjoyed reading the works of Liang Ch'i-ch'ao and sympathized with his constitutional monarchical movement. Liang Shu-ming attended a modern primary school, where English was taught, and a middle school in Peking. After his fifth year in middle school, with the coming of the 1911 Revolution, he ceased his formal schooling. He joined the *T'ung-meng hui* and, for a while in Tientsin, engaged in "playing the game of guns and bombs." He then essayed a few weeks of newspaper and propaganda work for the Republican cause. This he found also uncongenial as well as, it seems, best relinquished because it provoked an unwelcome disagreement with his father. Liang Shu-ming, during his school days, which ended before he was twenty, had been drawn to practical affairs and had leaned toward utilitarianism and socialism. Now he turned to Buddhism and spent the ensuing four years (1912–1915) in self-study and contemplation.

An article on Buddhism which he contributed to the prestigious *Tung-fang tsa-chih* (The Eastern Miscellany)[2] attracted the notice of Ts'ai Yuan-p'ei, President of Peking University, and earned him an invitation, which he accepted, to teach Indian philosophy at Peking University in 1917 at the age of twenty-five. However, his father's suicide in 1918, a suicide protesting the abandonment of the values of China's traditional culture, marked, for Liang Shu-ming, the onset of his own further personal intellectual crisis. He began to occupy himself intently, from this point on, in a reconsideration of Confucianism, interpreting it in terms applicable to twentieth-century China.

By 1921, his thinking reached the stage formulated in his first major work, *Eastern and Western Cultures and Their Philosophies.*[3] The views embodied here deal with cultural patterns and their evolution, and basically reject the iconoclasm of the May Fourth Movement; he affirms the view that Confucianism is superior to the philosophies of the West. This work established Liang Shu-ming's fame and was influential in academic and political circles throughout China.

However, in self-appraisal Liang Shu-ming rejected the title of scholar. He declares that purely academic work does not appeal to him and that he is neither scholar nor philosopher in the usual sense.[4] He claims for himself only that he lives in strict adherence to his own ideas. This description, he says, is sufficient and that, should anyone describe him as both a thinker and a social reformer, he would be flattered.[5] The events of his life seem to substantiate his self-appraisal. He had always been serious, even as a child. His commitment to the practice of whatever views were persuasive to him was already evident during the period of his early twenties when he was, for a few years, much absorbed in Buddhism. Obeying the commandments of celibacy and vegetarianism, he remained a bachelor and ate no meat. Subsequently he became convinced that Buddhism contradicted human nature and was incapable of leading him to the good life. Gradually shifting his devotion from Buddhism, an otherworldly philosophy, to Confucianism, a worldly outlook on life, he married in 1921 and also gave up his vegetarian diet.

Liang continued his search for a philosophy which would provide a personally satisfying way of life, an adequate explanation of society and social problems, and a basis for a positive program of practical reform. By 1923 he began to believe that this search could best be furthered through what he regarded as the basic elements in Chinese society: the countryside and the life of the peasantry. He resigned from his professorship at Peking University in 1924 in order to found a senior middle school at Ts'ao-chou, Shantung. His hope was that this would lead eventually to the creation of a new type of university at Ch'ü-fu, the birthplace of the sage Confucius. His plans, however, soon ran into difficulties and in 1925 he had already returned to Peking. Here, he spent the next several years (1925–1928) independently in self-study and contemplation, living with a small group of students who were attracted to him, and seeking for practical plans through which to carry out a program of rural reconstruction that, he was now convinced, offered the best hope for China's salvation.

By 1930 his rural reconstruction movement had attracted the favorable attention of Han Fu-chü, then governor of Honan. Liang was invited to become one of the founders of the Honan Village Self-Government Institute. His theories began to be tested in the curriculum. He also expounded them in his post as editor of the *Village Self-Government Monthly (Ts'un-chih yueh-k'an).* Han Fu-chü's loss of power in Honan forced the termination of these enterprises in Honan in 1931. But, within the same year, Han reestablished himself in Shantung and again invited Liang and his group to resume their activities.

Accordingly, the Shantung Rural Reconstruction Research Institute was set up before the end of 1931. The provincial government facilitated practical application of the Institute's policies by designating Tsou-p'ing *hsien* (and later Ho-tse *hsien*) as an experimental area. As the guiding spirit, Liang directed teaching and research, served concurrently as magistrate of Tsou-p'ing *hsien,* and was able to experiment with a number of economic, political, educational, and social reforms. The measures adopted had some influence in the rest of Shantung province, and Liang had some basis for his hope that this was the modest beginning of a national movement.

The thinking that underlay the rural reconstruction movement he set forth in several books that were widely read, books which we will consider in more detail below. In brief, he posited that the unique character of China's culture and social system made it wrong and impractical for China to attempt to adopt Western political systems. In his view, Marxist class analysis had no validity for China. Social relations, he believed, could be improved peacefully, on the basis of the tenets upon which Chinese culture is founded, through an educational process which creates an enlightened leadership of intellectuals and the peasant masses. Through such leadership there would emerge institutions combining the functions of local self-government with economic cooperation and eliminating any need for violent revolution.

There was little opportunity to test these theories on a large scale or for any length of time.[6] Shantung was overrun by the Japanese in the autumn of 1937, forcing the institute to close. Liang followed the Nationalist government to Hankow and Chungking. He came to hold an increasingly prominent role in China as an independent intellectual who maintained his reputation for selflessness and integrity, supporting China in the war against Japanese agression, and seeking to ameliorate the growing conflict between the Kuomintang and the Communists.

During the Sino-Japanese war, Liang served as a non-Kuomintang member on the People's Political Council *(Kuo-min ts'an-cheng hui).* Having visited the communist areas in 1938 and frontline areas in 1939, he saw the deterioration of the political situation. Hoping to create a third force in China to bolster the United Front, he became a leader in bringing the minor political parties and groups in China into a union that eventually gained national importance as the China Democratic League. As the political climate in Chungking was uncongenial, he went to Hong Kong to establish there, in September 1941, the *Kuang-ming jih-pao* as the League's newspaper and organ of public expression. Liang served as chief editor, and the staff included a number of other prominent intellectuals. This effort was, however, soon aborted by the Japanese capture of Hong Kong in December 1941.

Successful in escaping from Hong Kong in January 1942, Liang took refuge in Kweilin. The Japanese offensive in the summer of 1944 forced him to flee once more. By late 1945 he was in Chungking. There he served as secretary-general of the Democratic League till October 1946. He now became active in attempts to avoid civil war in China through creation of a coalition government.

This included membership, as a representative of his Rural Reconstruction Group *(hsiang-ts'un chien-she p'ai),* in the Political Consultative Conference set up as a result of General Marshall's mediation efforts in early 1946.

Liang remained in China after the Communist take-over, but declined participation in the Chinese People's Political Consultative Conference held in September 1949 to establish the new government of the People's Republic. He did, however, accept membership in 1950. In October 1951, the *Kuang-ming jih-pao* (originally founded by him in Hong Kong in 1941 and by now revived in Peking as the organ of the United Front elements working with the Communists) published a lengthy statement by him: "What changes in my thinking have taken place in the past two years?"[7] This gave recognition to the success of the Chinese Communists, but was in essence a restatement of earlier views.

A storm finally broke over Liang's head in the summer of 1953 during an enlarged meeting of the National Committee of the People's Political Consultative Conference. Liang, attending as a member, bluntly criticized the severe inequality of living standards between city workers and peasants. Mao Tse-tung himself was reported to have taken part in driving him from the rostrum, while Ch'en Ming-shu, another United Front leader, intervened on his behalf.[8] Liang became from that time on, a marked man. Along with Hu Shih, he was the chief target of a major campaign in 1955. This led to the official publication of two volumes of articles attacking him;[9] epithets were hurled at him, such as "spokesman of the landlord class," "comprador scholar," "helper of the imperialists in oppressing the Chinese people," "extreme idealist," "extreme reactionary," "defender of feudalism" "anti-Communist," "anti-people," and so on. Liang made no reply until February 1956. Then, in a talk before the Consultative Conference, he gave what can only be regarded as a limited self-criticism.[10] He welcomed criticism of himself, he said, adding that his understanding of Marxism had improved and that he was continuing to study. Since then Liang has dropped completely out of the news from mainland China for a long period of over twenty years.

Liang's Philosophy

The Basic Role of Culture

The importance of culture is the core of Liang's thinking. This was the subject of his first book, the widely read and controversial *Eastern and Western Cultures and Their Philosophies,* first published in 1921 and reprinted many times.

Culture, to Liang, is the creation of genius and the product of human will.[11] The different patterns of culture are due to the divergence of human wills. In his view culture, understood as the philosophy of life shared by a people, shapes the development of history.[12] He divides world cultures into three patterns: Western, Chinese, and Indian. Regarding Western culture as the product of a spirit that drives the will forward to obtain satisfaction, Liang associates it with science and democracy;[13] he sees Chinese culture as the product of the will's pursuit of self-adjustment and moderation; while Indian culture, he believes, expresses a spirit that retreats rather than explores or adjusts, trying to cause problems of life to disappear by conquering desire.[14]

These three cultures thus have produced three ways of life. People of the Western mode strive for material things and try to change their environment to satisfy their wants. People of the Chinese pattern seek contentment by adjusting to the environment rather than combating it. People of the Indian pattern try to eliminate problems by conquering desire.

It is not surprising that the Chinese Communists find this view of culture intolerable. To the Marxists, the mode of production, independent of human will, is the dynamic force in historical development. In this view, culture—including politics, law, literature, philosophy, and religion—is no more than a part of the superstructure which is determined by the mode of production. Accordingly, Liang is attacked as holding an idealistic conception of history and, on two principal counts, as an anti-Marxist. First, he is denounced for putting Eastern and Western cultures on the same plane, as the manifestation of different philosophies, instead of treating them as stages—namely, feudalism and capitalism respectively—in the development of history.[15] Second, he is rebuked for asserting that differing philosophies give rise to different cultures. Since his viewpoint makes thought a cause and the mode of production an effect, his position runs counter to the Marxian axiom that successive stages in social organization determine consciousness.[16]

The communist philosophy asserts that history must develop according to a law that communists have discovered and that victory of communist social organization is therefore certain. Should Liang's theory of the inner will determining the pattern of culture or the course of history be tolerated, the communists would lose the basis of their certainty of victory and even the justification of their revolution. The result inevitably would be to shake the confidence of many of their followers. Further familiar tenets of communist belief are that the laboring people create history, and that the communists themselves are the vanguard of the proletariat bringing about the communist millennium. Liang's assertion that a few geniuses can determine the main course of history does not accommodate itself to communist doctrine with regard to the roles of the proletariat and the communist vanguards.

Advocacy of Confucianism

As the result of their way of life, which emphasizes self-contentment, the Chinese people, Liang admits, have made little material progress compared with the modern West, and conspicuously remained backward in science and democracy.[17] This does not, in Liang's opinion, mean that China's culture is backward. He sees China's culture as one of the three patterns of culture which he posits as stages in the evolution of mankind. The natural progress of man, he says, is to follow, first, the Western path, then the Chinese, and eventually the

183

Indian. The first, the Western, seeks primarily to solve the problems between man and his environment. The second, the Chinese, concentrates on solving the problems between man and man. The third, the Indian, seeks to deal with the problems of man's soul. Chinese culture, in his perspective, is thus at a higher, not a lower, stage than the Western. China's difficulties have arisen from moving into the second stage of cultural evolution before having made sufficient progress along the first. He explains the paradox of a superior culture appearing inferior by calling the development of Chinese culture premature, comparing it to a precocious child who excels in some areas but remains childish in others.[18]

Liang associates the essence of this Chinese culture, or the Chinese way of life, with Confucianism.[19] Its true spirit lies in the seeking of self-adjustment and the pursuit of moderation. Liang has persistently, and with great courage in a hostile environment, urged the cultural superiority of Confucianism. He has argued not only that it will revive but that it will become a world culture. He deals with trends pointing in this direction under the headings of economics, psychology, and philosophy. The arguments are as follows.

Economics. The highly developed modern system of capitalism is unreasonable. Its many economic contradictions include such evils as large-scale production for profit rather than for consumption; mass unemployment; poverty in the midst of plenty; impersonal relationship between employers and employees. The cause of these evils is the misuse of science devoted to the invention of machines and the ensuing mechanization of production. Liang sees these as the logical consequences of the Western outlook: striving for material happiness, and attempting to utilize nature to conquer nature.

The life of the workers is miserable because of work tedium and economic insecurity. But the condition of persons enjoying better economic status is equally lamentable. In Liang's view, everybody in a capitalist society, rich as well as poor, lives a life that is mechanical, empty and devoid of humane feeling. Everyone is forced to exhaust himself in unrelenting competition to amass wealth, or to avoid failure and degradation, if not poverty. The cold calculation of profit suppresses the finer sentiments and emotions in the individual.

This unendurable kind of life must be changed. He sees socialism as the only alternative to this capitalism. He describes this change as a change from unreason to reason; from an individualistic to a socialistic society; from a society stressing production for profit to one stressing production for distribution. It will be a change from the first to the second pattern of culture, from the Western to the Chinese attitude toward life. The West has, in his opinion, reached the end of the first road; the new road will be the Chinese road.[20]

Psychology. From Socrates to the end of the nineteenth century, according to Liang's interpretation, the West based its culture on assumptions that considered only the conscious aspects of human psychology but neglected the unconscious. From this emphasis stem all kinds of fallacies such as hedonism, the doctrine that all activities are motivated by desire for pleasure and aversion to pain—a doctrine which became the foundation of utilitarianism. He sees the psychology of William McDougall as pointing correctly in a different direction: The intellectual processes are but the servants, instruments, or means of mental forces; men are moved by a variety of impulses; mankind is reasonable only to a limited extent, and largely moves in unreasonable ways; psychologists must cease to be content with the narrow conception of their science as the science of consciousness, and must assert its claim to be the positive science of the mind in all aspects.

From this basis, Liang argues that the springs of life come from the emotions (ch'ing-chih) rather than the intellect. Life is not based on reasoning, nor on a search for pleasure and the avoidance of pain. Neither hedonism nor utilitarianism, then, are valid. The recognition that neither is valid will, Liang believes, turn Western thought in a direction closer to Confucianism, which also opposes utilitarianism while cherishing the emotions.[21]

Liang acclaims Kropotkin's theory of mutual aid as a refutation of Darwin's theory of survival of the fittest. While Darwin, according to Liang's interpretation, stressed struggle and self-interest, Kropotkin argued that society is formed on the basis of mutual aid, that ethics and morality stem from the social instinct, and that harmony and cooperation in society ensue from concern for the welfare of all human beings. Hoping that Kropotkin is the trend of the future, Liang sees this shift as another indication of the turning of the West to the Chinese road.[22]

Philosophy. The general trend in the West, Liang contends, has changed from emphasis on looking outward to looking inward. As examples, he cites philosophies as diverse as those of Eucken, Russell, Bergson, and Tagore. This change he sees as another indication of a move from the Western to the Chinese way.[23] Prior to Chinese culture becoming world culture, what is the solution to the problem of China? Liang postulates the following guidelines for China: (1) China should reject the Indian attitude completely; (2) China should completely accept Western culture but with a basic qualification that there be a change in emphasis; and (3) China should critically revive the Chinese attitude.[24]

To paraphrase his three postulates, it may be said that Liang rejects Indian culture, but accepts Westernization plus Confucian philosophy, and also Confucianism plus science and democracy. From 1921 to the beginning of the 1930s, Liang assumed the necessity of accepting complete Westernization.

The Uniqueness of Chinese Society

Liang's most extensive analysis of Chinese society is set forth in *The Essence of Chinese Culture.* This was first published in 1949 in Chungking, but is introduced here to provide perspective on his matured proposals for the solution of China's problems.

Ethic-Centricism. [25] A principle characteristic of Chinese society, according to Liang, is that it is centered on one cultural code of ethics. Western society, by contrast, is individualistic with various individuals following different cultural codes, as in England and America, or prescriptively socialist, as in the Soviet Union. The influence of Christianty on the development of Western society has been, in Liang's view, chiefly that churches have led the people into the experience of an organized life. He sees religious intolerance and religious wars as having kept Western organizations strong. Westerners have lived in organizations, be they guilds, city states, modern cities, or nation states—all larger than the family unit. Thus, family does not play an important role in the West. Chinese culture on the other hand is Confucianist, where family life plays a basic role.

The ethical relationship of the Chinese family is applied in the organization of society: the whole society is regarded as a single extended family. In a sense, property is considered communal among relatives and even among friends, for people have a moral obligation to support relatives and to help fellow townsmen and friends in need. It is no coincidence that Chinese law has historically neglected property rights and debt obligations, and treated human relationships as more important than wealth.

The political philosophy of China is profoundly affected by this principle. An emperor is both son of Heaven and an ancestor. A magistrate is likened to the parent of the people under his jurisdiction. To serve an emperor is to serve one's father; and to govern the people wisely is to rule with fatherly love. Where progress and wealth are goals of Western government, the highest goal in China is peace in the kingdom. This depends on the attaining of proper ethical relationships, where a father acts as a father, a son as a son, and so on.

In such an ethic-centered society as a Confucian society, mutual affection and harmony prevail. The individual's life is expected to be devoted to the good of others. Thus, society achieves balance and harmony, with no overemphasis upon either individuals or organizations. Though China has no religion, in Liang's view of Confucianism, family-centered morality takes its place. Morality belongs to the sphere of reason *(li-hsing),* which, in Liang's terminology, is to be differentiated from intellect *(li-chih).* Liang relates reason to feeling, behavior, and morality; he associates intellect with knowledge, science, and logic. For instance, the manufacture of deadly weapons is a product of intellect; but whether mankind can be saved from destruction by these weapons is a function of reason. Liang's definitions of reason, ethics, and morality are often synonymous and overlapping. But what he regards as reason he sees as a basic characteristic of Chinese culture. It gives meaning to Chinese concepts of the value of life, knowledge, education, politics, state, and law.[26]

Professional Differentiation. This Confucian society does not contain opposing classes. Classes, in Liang's view, are a characteristic of Western societies. They are exemplified by opposition between lords and serfs in feudal times, and between capitalists and workers in modern times. China lacks such antagonistic divisions; it is, rather, a society of professional differentiation.

Because China is an agricultural country, the situation in land distribution determines the existence or absence of opposing classes. According to Liang, an examination of land-holding patterns in North and South China indicates that (1) land can be freely bought and sold by everyone, and (2) the majority of

186

people own land, and there is no noticeable phenomenon of land concentration and monopoly. Industry and commerce are subordinate to agriculture and have not been highly developed. Since China has not had an industrial revolution, there is no great concentration of capital. The absence of primogeniture, resulting in the custom of equal distribution among heirs, checks the concentration of capital just as it does the concentration of land. Thus, there have been only small industrialists and merchants, but no bourgeoisie or proletariat in the Western sense. The development of agriculture and industry in China has not, in Liang's view, produced antagonistic classes. Instead, he sees validity in the customary division of the Chinese people into four groups: scholars, farmers, artisans, and merchants. He regards the relationship between them as one of interdependence and coordination, rather than class opposition.

Liang argues that there is also no ruling class in China because there has been no hereditary, feudal nobility since the Chou Dynasty. Scholars filled posts from prime ministers to petty officials, but they neither passed on privileges and titles, nor were their positions hereditary. For thousands of years, political power from central government down to local administration was in the hands of these salaried scholars, but their periods of rule were always limited. Moreover, official status was always open to those who studied the classics and were able to pass the imperial examinations.

It is true, Liang admits, that classes are a general phenomenon in human society, but China, where class formation is not conspicuous, is an exception to this rule. Similarly, economic exploitation and political control are universal facts. But, whereas these two conditions are centralized and fixed in Western countries, they are decentralized and flexible in China. And, whereas there are antagonistic classes in Europe, there is, he believes, only professional differentiation in China.[27]

Finally, Liang contends that these two basic characteristics of Chinese society—ethic-centrism and professional differentiation—mean that China is not a state in the full sense of the term. Instead, China is only a big society, loosely organized, with some features of a state. Strictly speaking, in Liang's definition, a state is formed on the basis of class rule. But China has no class rule because she has not formed clearly antagonistic classes. State and society are merged into one, and state power is reduced to a minimum. This, he says, is exemplified in the influential governing policy of inaction *(wu-wei)*. Nor were China's rulers energetic about her defenses, being accustomed to think in terms of one world *(t'ien-hsia)* rather than one state *(kuo-chia)*.[28]

Liang's Political Thinking

Conflict with the Communists

In arguing for ethic-centricism and professional differentiation rather than class struggle, Liang is in conflict with the Chinese communists on at least three principal points:

- Denial of the universality of Marxism. For the Chinese Communists, Marxism-Leninism is a universal truth which is applicable to all societies, wherever existing. Although Liang never directly challenges Marxism, he insists that China is an exception to the rule because of the unique qualities of her culture and the resulting social structure.
- Denial of classes in Chinese society. Class struggle is basic to Marxist theory, which regards all history as the history of class struggle. Liang, on the other hand, denies the existence of distinctive, antagonistic classes in Chinese society. His characterization of that society as ethic-centered, and as preferring reason over force, dismisses the whole theory of class struggle.
- Denial of dialectical change. The communists see the antagonism between classes as creating contradictions; they declare that it is through the resolution of the contradictions that human progress is achieved. Confident in this theory of dialectical process, they see class struggle as the dynamic force which moves the world forward. Liang sees Chinese society as being without classes; positing that it is inherently static, he virtually denies that it can develop dialectically.

That class conflict is inherent to the process of development is insisted on by the communists. In 1949, Mao wrote in *On the People's Democratic Dictatorship:* "The problem of the Communists is . . . one of working hard to create the conditions for classes, state power, and political powers to wither away . . . and for mankind to enter the era of one world."[29] But if Liang is right in regarding China as having no classes and no massive state and political power to wither away, then the conditions to be created by Mao are irrelevant, because, from Liang's viewpoint, China has already approached closer to "one world" than she can approach through the conditions Mao wished to create.

Dismissal of Western Solutions

Liang argues that no nation can survive by abandoning its traditions and adopting a foreign culture wholesale as its own. Essentially he emphasizes two themes. First, China is grievously wrong in discarding her tradition and seeking a solution from outside.[30] Second, beyond the question of their own existence, the Chinese people have the historic mission of contributing to a better future world.[31] China must reject all Western tricks and deceptions (literally, juggleries) and build a new country in her own way.[32] The fullest exposition of this view is found in his *The Final Awakening of the Chinese Nation's Self-Salvation Movement*. This book was first published in 1933; but Liang's views have remained, since 1933, substantially unchanged. This book marked his momentous change with respect to his attitude toward Western culture and his approach to his final summation of his program for China's reconstruction. We have noticed earlier that one of the requisites he had set forth for the Chinese people to adopt, prior to an emergence of a new world culture, was a total acceptance of Westernization, i.e., the assimilation of science and democracy.

By 1933 he resolutely rejected all of what he termed "Western juggleries"—both European democracy and Russian communism—which he condemned as "dead ends" for China. This rejection, and the newly gained confidence in China's solutions, constitute what he calls the final awakening of China's national salvation.

First Dead End. Democracy, by Liang's definition, is rule by a majority which creates a system—a constitution and set of laws—to be maintained by this majority. But, in China, the majority is apathetic to politics. The sector of society concerned with political processes and political reform is only a limited number of intellectuals, perhaps one-hundredth of one percent of the population. Since only a handful desire to imitate this foreign system, it would, Liang argues, be futile to try to adopt the democratic form of government.

Moreover, the physical conditions of China are, in his opinion, not suitable to democracy. The standard of living of the Chinese people is generally very low; most people exist on a subsistence level and have no energy to be concerned with politics. The vast size and poor communications in China make it difficult to carry out elections, which are an essential feature of the democratic system. Because of underdeveloped commerce and industry, China does not have a middle class comparable to that in Europe, a class which is the main strength of democracy.

He also enumerates certain mental obstacles which he regards as preventing the possibility of China's adopting democracy. His view of these obstacles may be summarized as follows.

First, the philosophy of life of a nation determines the pattern of its culture, including its political system. European democracy was won through struggles and revolutions, especially in France. It was the spirit of fighting for one's rights that created and sustained democracy. But the Chinese have entirely different goals; they seek self-contentment and the exercise of self-restraint *(an-fen shou-chi)*. Liang sees the West as pugnacious and China as pacifist. In the words of the Chinese proverb: "It is easy to move mountains and rivers, but it is difficult to alter one's disposition." He believes it is equally difficult to change the national spirit of China.

Second, one of the most important features of a democratic system is the election campaign. In a campaign, the candidates, while attacking their opponents, engage in self-glorification. This practice is diametrically opposed to the traditional virtue of a Chinese gentleman. Chinese ethics require that a gentleman be modest about his own merits and refrain from speaking ill of others; when he is offered a position because of his prestige, he should decline one or more times before accepting. To copy Western campaign techniques, Liang points out, would mean degrading the traditional Chinese virtues.

Third, because Westerners invest their energies in the desire for individual achievement, Westerners have developed, Liang deduces, their mutual checking, mutual opposition, and mutual supervision which, in the political system, becomes the principle of checks and balances; the Western system implicitly assumes that no one is to be trusted. The Chinese ethic-centered society, Liang asserts, operates through mutual trust and respect and dispenses with checking among the individuals or between the government and its people. This spirit stems from the belief that human nature is basically good. In practice, government in China rules by *li* (propriety) rather than by law as in the West. Chinese are encouraged to follow the ritual rules in their daily life. China cannot imitate the West because the Western and Chinese spirits are incompatible.

Fourth, European systems have realized material well-being for the people. But there are three inherent defects. Europeans follow a policy of aggression, sacrificing the interests of other countries to their own. Domestically the interests of one part of their people are often sacrificed to the advantage of another. Finally, though there may be superficial appearances to the contrary, there is no true happiness in life. These are the results of their belief in individualism and the importance placed on worldly well-being.

This type of government, which only caters to external standards, according to Liang's appraisals, without concern for the meaning of life, is incompatible with the traditional Chinese ethic because it cannot satisfy the spiritual demands of the Chinese people. Chinese tradition has emphasized the unity of government with education and morality. But Western democracy rests on the separation of the state and the Christian church. A state should be an education force for the fulfillment of the higher goals of mankind rather than for the attainment of material satisfaction only. China, therefore, cannot and should not try to emulate Western government.[33]

Second Dead End. The second unsuitable system is the one "invented by the Russian Communists" and is primarily economic. Liang admits some advantages but points out four principal objections.

1. The revolution envisaged by Marx is made by industrial workers, or the proletariat. China lacks such a class. Other groups—even if they can be classified as peasants, petite bourgeoisie, and bourgeoisie—are unable to play this role.
2. The targets of the revolution in China are difficult to determine. China has no military strength to fight the foreign imperialists. Even economic boycott is ineffective, because China is economically weak and dependent in many ways on foreign economic agression. Warlords cannot be a target because warlordism is not a unified system.
3. China has no generally accepted revolutionary theory. Even the Three Principles of the People (*San-min chu-i*) as expounded by Sun Yat-sen are a "hodgepodge."
4. The Russian method of tight organization and intensive indoctrination is directly counter to the Chinese tradition which, in these respects, is characterized by looseness in organization and the reluctance of the people, especially the intellectuals, to be regimented and disciplined under party control.[34]

Rural Reconstruction versus Revolution

The traditional society of China, though admirable and unique, has been endangered by the impact of the West. It is in the process of disintegration; it can be saved only by building a new social order. Rejecting the dominant trend of Westernization, Liang Shu-ming became convinced that the source of the new life of China must be sought in the rural villages; that it is impossible to have a new life for China unless there is a new life in the villages. Firmly confident of his own observation, he goes so far as to say if a sage were born today, he would not change an iota of what he says.[35] His full exposition for his new social order appears in his book *Theory of Rural Reconstruction*.[36]

Liang is not uncritical of China's weaknesses. He observes that the two greatest impediments to the reconstruction of China are, first, lack of organization and, second, lack of scientific knowledge and skill.[37] These are precisely the strong points of the West. Liang, nonetheless, rejects direct copying from the West. Instead, he contends that these problems can be solved by organizing the villagers to participate vigorously in community affairs, and by maintaining communications between village society and the outside world so that knowledge and skills can be brought to the countryside.[38] Liang calls the program to carry out these objectives the Rural Reconstruction movement.

Two important features of his plan are the "village contract" and the "village school." Under the village contract, villagers are to pledge mutual aid for the collective achievement of social reconstruction. In Liang's words: "The organization to which we aspire is based on ethics and affection, and also takes the advancement of life as its goal."[39] As each village binds itself under the village contract, linkages will be set up among villages, then among larger units such as *hsien,* and finally among provinces.[40]

Rural schools are to be established for the study of rural problems and for training in carrying out rural reconstruction work. These schools are to be guided by the principles of the movement: (1) agriculture has precedence over industry; (2) the villages are primary and cities secondary; (3) man is the "main body" *(chu-t'i)* of society—that is, man should control material things, not vice versa; (4) the new society is to be ethic-centered, shunning both the individualistic and socialistic extremes; (5) education, politics, and economics are to be combined into one entity, rather than separated into different compartments; and (6) order is to be maintained by reason rather than by armed force.[41]

The crucial need for achieving this reconstruction is to be met by the intellectuals going into the villages and serving as the brains for the society as a whole. Stated slightly differently, there must be a fusion of intellectuals and common people: "The solution of China's problem, from the initiation of active participation to its completion, lies in the strength achieved by welding the intellectuals and rural inhabitants into one."[42] Liang purposely uses the term rural inhabitants rather than peasant or proletariat because he does not recognize the existence of clearly differentiated classes, but only admits a geographical distribution of population which, he says, has created political and economic differences between urban and rural inhabitants.

Finally, this reconstruction of the village society is, according to Liang, to be carried on as a strictly nongovernment movement. Participants should not seek nor hold political power. Liang concludes: "We should firmly maintain our social flexibility, and should absolutely not assume political power.... Only by doing it this way can we represent society and form a strong force. Only by not holding political power can we avoid splits among ourselves and achieve a united alliance for the movement. This is the most important."[43]

Mao and Liang

Earlier we alluded briefly to a virulent attack on Liang by Mao Tse-tung at a meeting of the National Committee of the People's Political Consultative Conference. According to an eyewitness, Liang had remarked that "the peasant life in the country is very hard," and "comparing the remuneration of factory workers with what peasants receive, it was as if one was in the ninth level of heaven, while the other was in the ninth level of hell." At this point Mao is said to have lost his temper, seized the microphone on the rostrum from Liang, and shouted: "You stink! You have stinking bones!"[44]

There was no official version or confirmation of this incident until the publication in April 1977 of the fifth volume of the *Selected Works of Mao Tse-tung*. Mao's repudiation of Liang is summarized in the following passage:

> There are two ways to kill people, one by guns, and the other by pens. The most sophisticated way to kill people is by using a pen without shedding blood. Liang Shu-ming is such a murderer. He is reactionary to the core. He thought he was the most beautiful person in the world, surpassing all the famous beauties in history, such as Yang Kuei-fei or Hsi Shih. I have never failed to criticize his erroneous ideas whenever I saw him. I have never believed his advocacies, such as: "China has no classes," "China's problem is one of cultural maladjustment," "a colorless and transparent government" [i.e., a government that transcends political parties], "China's revolution has no internal but only extraneous cause," and the recent ones consisting of the excellent ideas of "the ninth level of heaven and of hell," "the Communists have lost the peasants," "the Communist Party is less reliable than the Federation of Industry and Commerce," etc. [All these points, Mao brushed aside as unbelievable.] The problems of China are semi-feudalism and semi-colonialism. To deny this is virtually to have helped imperialism and feudalism. No one would listen to Liang except a reactionary or a muddle-minded person. What Liang should do is to confess clearly his reactionary anti-people and anti-Communist record of serving the interests of the landlord class. On the whole, Liang is a careerist, a hypocrite; his program for rural construction is for "landlord construction" and for "national destruction." The significance of repudiating Liang is not to repudiate a single person, but the whole reactionary thought represented by Liang.[45]

Mao's repudiation of Liang's thought clearly reflects the important ideological conflicts between them; and Mao's severe criticisms of Liang indicate that Liang's ideas were still powerful in the minds of a large number of people in China.

After Mao's public abuse of Liang, nothing was heard about him for the next twenty-five years. Then a news item surprisingly appeared in the Hong Kong

192

Ta-kung Pao in 1977, reporting Liang's recent participation in a symposium discussing the newly published fifth volume of the *Selected Works of Mao Tse-tung*. The main points of Liang's remarks are as follows:

> In the fifth volume of the *Selected Works of Mao Tse-tung,* there are quite a few criticisms of me, including a speech article. Generally speaking, my thought lacks the class concept and opposes violent revolution. In 1953 Chairman Mao reproached me as killing people by pen instead of by gun, precisely because I had opposed violent revolution. I had even urged the Communist Party to stop fighting when the powerful Communist armies were preparing to cross the Yangtze River. This was directly contrary to Chairman Mao's views and represented a position against the revolution. Had the civil war not been fought through there would have been no national unity, no completion of the new democracy, no achievements of socialist revolution and construction, and no national flourishing and international prestige. I am grateful for Chairman Mao's instruction and affection in trying to remould my thought; whenever I think of Chairman's affection and reproach, I always want to improve. This will be true until my death.[46]

Liang is a person most proud and adamant in his beliefs. If this report is true, and represents Liang's true sentiments, it marks a great success of Mao's thought. However, this is only an official news item and is not Liang's own writing. Hence, many observers are unsure of its significance as showing a change in Liang's thought. As of this writing, there has not been any conclusive evidence to indicate whether this is government propaganda or Liang's retraction.

Finally, in 1982 Liang broke his silence after so many years since the 1953 incident, by publishing an article in the Hong Kong semimonthly, *Pai-hsing (Common people)* entitled "The Origins of the Many Mistakes Made by Mao in His Later Years." This was probably the first time since 1949 that an officially unpopular scholar published his views outside of mainland China. The forty year old disagreement between Liang and Mao lay in their conflicting opinions toward class and class struggle. Back in January 1938, Liang and Mao had two long talks for two whole nights in Yenan. Liang insisted that in traditional China, for instance, during the Ming and Ch'ing dynasties, rich and poor, or people of different social ranks, could easily change their social status; class distinction was neither conspicuous nor prominent. The medieval, European class antagonism between feudal lords and peasant serfs, or the modern class distinction between capitalists and laborers did not exist in China. Mao criticized Liang for overemphasizing the particularity of Chinese society and neglecting the universality of societies. Liang retorted that Mao committed the mistake just the other way around, lacking an understanding of one's own national characteristic.

Liang was unable to express his independent opinion in the long period since 1949. At present, in 1982, he claimed that he had regained his confidence as things had changed. He concluded that many of Mao's mistakes are rooted in his overemphasis on class struggle, which he carried out vigorously by using his unchallengeable power, causing a great deal of disaster and crime, and that in his later years, Mao's manifestation of class prejudice, in its intensified absurdity and blundering, reached a ridiculous height.

Liang's argument is simple: first, Mao taught people, "Never forget class struggle," "Class struggle should be talked about yearly, monthly, and daily," "Class struggle works miraculously as soon as you grasp it." Liang asks rhetorically, "If class antagonism does exist and class struggle naturally follows and cannot be avoided, why should you remind people not to forget about it?" In Liang's eyes, this was evidence that class struggle is a kind of artificial creation.

An entry in Liang's diary for 18 December 1970 relates an incident in which Mao told his American friend Edgar Snow that China is a huge ocean of petit bourgeois whose history is short and where industrial workers are few. Liang thought this expressed a valuable truth. He reasoned that since China is a huge ocean of petit bourgeois, which means the nonexistence of two great antagonistic classes, then, why should Mao forcibly create troubles and turmoil, and create class struggle? The slogans "to destroy the four olds," or "the great cultural revolution of the proletariat," were absolutely senseless. How painful and sorrowful it was that the turmoil lasted for ten years throughout the whole country. All this insanity and aberration came from the disease of a great man in his old age; it could not happen to a common person. Such an extraordinary person would not apear again. Henceforth, what China needs is collective leadership, compliance with a legal system, and democratic consultations.[47]

Conclusion

It is easy to understand why Liang has not been popular with the Chinese Communists. His ideas in many obvious respects are antithetical to Marxist doctrine. Indeed, it may be assumed that they were more or less consciously formulated to provide a noncommunist alternative. At the same time, though accorded great respect, no serious attempt to implement Liang's ideas has ever been made by the Kuomintang, either while on the mainland or in Taiwan.

Still, the fact that the Communists accepted and honored Liang for several years, and then devoted a major campaign to his condemnation, is some indication that his ideas were influential and feared. Among the Chinese, wherever they may be, the image of Liang is still clear and distinct. He is an ardent advocate of China's traditional culture who believes that the revival of Confucian virtues will make the world a more humane place. He stands for Confucian morality, for the social responsibilty of the intellectuals, and the need for their personal involvement in solving China's basic problems in the rural villages. And all this, he resolutely insists, can accomplish a sweeping but nonviolent revolution. His career can be said to exemplify the "superior man" extolled by his Confucian sage. He might be dismissed as idealistic, visionary and impractical. But his views and efforts have been a tangible force in the intellectual currents of twentieth-century China.

Notes

[1] This biographical sketch is extensively based on Hu Ying-han, "Liang Shu-ming hsien-sheng nien-p'u ch'u-kao," *Jen-sheng* (Hong Kong) 295–301 (10 February 1963–16 March 1963). Readers may wish to refer to: Wen-shun Chi, "Liang Shu-ming and Chinese Communism," *China Quarterly* (London) 41 (January–March 1970):64–82.

[2] Liang Shu-ming, "Chiu-yuan chueh-i lun," *Tung-fang tsa-chih* (Shanghai), May 1916, sec. 3, pp. 6–10; June 1916, sec. 3, pp. 5–9; July 1916, sec. 3, pp. 8–12.

[3] Liang Shu-ming, *Tung-hsi wen-hua chi-ch'i che-hsueh,* 4th ed. (Shanghai: Commercial, 1923). Hereafter referred to as *Tung-hsi.* An anecdote as to how this book came to be written, revealing just how serious a person Liang is, tells that it was inspired by a farewell party for the president and a group of Peking University professors on their departure for Europe in the summer of 1920. The speakers hoped that these gentlemen would take Chinese culture to Europe and bring Western culture back to China, whereupon Liang embarrassed them by demanding a definition of precisely what Eastern and Western cultures are. Evidently no immediate answer could be given. After the meeting Professors T'ao Meng-ho and Hu Shih said to him smilingly that the question he raised was indeed good, but that the weather was too hot for people to give it serious thought. Taking this as intellectual dishonesty, Liang Shu-ming made up his mind to provide the answer, and his book is the result. Liang Shu-ming, *Tung-hsi,* pp. 1–2.

[4] Liang Shu-ming, *Tung-hsi,* pp. 1–2 of Preface to 1st ed. appended; and his *Chung-kuo min-tsu tzu-chiu yun-tung chih tsui-hou chueh-wu,* 3d ed. (Shanghai: Chung-hua, 1936), pp. 1–2. Hereafter referred to as *Chueh-wu.*

[5] Liang Shu-ming, *Chung-kuo wen-hua yao-i* (Hong Kong: Chi-ch'eng t'u-shu kung-szu, 1963), p. 4. Hereafter referred to as *Wen-hua.*

[6] Several attempts to implement Liang's Rural Reconstruction Movement seem to have been made in different parts of the country, but have been poorly reported. This is presumably because neither Kuomintang nor Communists supported them. One was in Honan (where Liang had planted the seed in 1930). This was led by a "local scholar" named Liu T'ing-fang, and seems to have lasted through the Sino-Japanese war, eventually extending to thirteen *hsien.* Some similar trials of Liang's ideas were also made in his native province of Kwangsi. Ch'ü Hao-jan, "Hui-ku 'Wu-szu' yü chan-wang pao-wei Tiao-yü t'ai yun-tung," *Min-pao yueh-k'an* (Hong Kong) 65 (May 1971): 10. Although this article gives the name of the "local scholar" as Liu T'ing-fang, it is generally believed to be Pieh T'ing-fang. See also Sheng Liang-jui, "Wan-hsi kuai-chieh Pieh T'ing-fang (shang)," *Chung-wai tsa-chih* (Taipei) 84 (February 1974):37–41.

[7] Liang Shu-ming, "Liang-nien lai wo-te szu-hsiang yu shen-ma chuan-pien?" *Kuang-ming jih-pao,* 5 October 1951.

[8] Chou Ch'ing-wen, *Feng-pao shih-nien* (Hong Kong: Shih-tai p'i-p'ing she, 1959) pp. 434–36. Translated by Lai Ming, *Ten Years of Storm* (New York: Holt, Reinhart and Winston, 1960), pp. 254–56.

[9] *Liang Shu-ming szu-hsiang p'i-p'an* (Peking: San-lien shu-tien, 1955). Hereafter referred to as *P'i-p'an.*

[10] "Liang Shu-ming te fa-yen," *Kuang-ming jih-pao,* 7 February 1956.

[11] Liang Shu-ming, *Tung-hsi,* pp. 24, 44.

[12] Ibid., p. 24.

[13] Ibid.

[14] Ibid., p. 55.

[15] Fung Yu-lan, "P'i-p'an Liang Shu-ming hsien-sheng te wen-hua kuan ho 'ts'un-chih' li-lun," *P'i-p'an,* 1:3.

16 For a detailed critique on this point, see Wu T'ing-ch'iu, "P'i-p'an Liang Shu-ming fan-tung li-shih kuan-tien," *P'i-p'an,* 2:35–43; also Wu Ching-ch'ao, "P'i-p'an Liang Shu-ming te Chung-kuo wen-hua lun," *P'i-p'an,* 2:86–90.

17 With respect to the backwardness of science in China, Joseph Needham has put forth a theory recently which Liang had not seen. For Needham's argument, see note no. 78 of chapter 4.

18 Liang Shu-ming, *Tung-hsi,* pp. 199–200; *Wen-hua,* pp. 265-77.

19 Liang Shu-ming claims that he found the true spirit of Confucianism. His interpretation, unique and original in certain respects, is too involved for consideration here. His most complete work on Confucianism is *K'ung-hsueh i-chih* which was never published in book form; rather, it appeared in stencil form as records of lectures he delivered at Peking University in 1923–24. Although Liang felt this stencil copy was unsatisfactory because he did not have a chance to check it, it nevertheless was in circulation. Later, he decided to write his own version by expanding the *K'ung-hsueh i-chih* under the new title *Jen-hsin yü jen-sheng.* Again, he first lectured on the topic at Peking University in 1927, and made public the preface he wrote to this forthcoming book, but the completion of the book was delayed for a long time. In an interview with Liang in October 1982, by *Ching-pao* (Hong Kong) no. 11, 1982, it is reported that Liang began to write *Jen-hsin yü jen-sheng* in 1955 and finished it in 1957. But the book remains unpublished.

20 Liang Shu-ming, *Tung-hsi,* pp. 161–68.

21 Ibid., pp. 168–71 for the change in psychology. McDougall's quotations are supplied here in order to make Liang's ideas more clear. See William McDougall, *Introduction to Social Psychology* (Boston: John W. Luce, 1918), pp. 3, 10, 11, 15. This may be cited as an instance of how a Chinese scholar took a Western idea through translation, to support his evaluation of the West.

22 Liang Shu-ming, *Tung-hsi,* pp. 171–75.

23 Ibid., pp. 175–87.

24 Ibid., p. 202.

25 Ethic-centered or ethic-centricism is my translation for Liang's *lun-lin pen-wei.*

26 For the discussion of the first characteristic (ethic-centricism) of the Chinese society, see Liang Shu-ming, *Wen-hua,* pp. 45–142.

27 For the discussion of the second characteristic (professional differentiation) of the Chinese society, see ibid., pp. 143–62.

28 Ibid., pp. 163–74.

29 Mao Tse-tung, "Lun jen-min min-chu chuan-cheng," *MTTHC,* 4:1358.

30 Liang Shu-ming, *Chueh-wu,* pp. 101–2.

31 Ibid., pp. 110.

32 Ibid., p. 12.

33 Ibid., pp. 117–62 for the first dead end.

34 Ibid., pp. 163–201 for the second dead end.

35 Ibid., p. 338.

36 Liang Shu-ming, *Hsiang-ts'un chien-she li-lun* (also called *Chung-kuo min-tsu chih ch'ien-t'u*) (Ts'o-p'ing: Ts'ou-p'ing hsiang-ts'un shu-tien, 1937). Hereafter referred to as *Hsiang-ts'un.*

37 Liang Shu-ming, *Hsiang-ts'un chien-she ta-i* (Ts'ou-p'ing hsiang-ts'un shu-tien, 1936), p. 47.

38 Ibid., p. 89.

39 Liang Shu-ming, *Hsiang-ts'un,* p. 190.

40 Ibid., p. 199.

41 Ibid., 441.

42 Liang Shu-ming, *Chueh-wu,* p. 208.

43 Liang Shu-ming, "Wo-men liang-ta k'un-nan," *Hsiang-ts'un,* Appendix p. 3.

[44] See note no. 8 of this chapter.

[45] Mao, "P'i-p'an Liang Shu-ming te fan-tung szu-hsiang," *MTTHC,* 5:107–15.

[46] *Ta Kung Pao* (Hong Kong), 21 June 1977. I wrote to Liang Shu-ming in January 1982, asking him, among other things, whether or not the news item was true. Although he promptly answered my letter, he neither affirmed nor denied the news item. He simply said that in a meeting with Mao he was at fault in offending Mao with words which caused Mao to reproach him. Liang's answer to my letter would appear to be an example of his Confucian virtue whereby he would not resort to censure.

[47] Liang Shu-ming, "Shih shuo-ming Mao Tse-tung wan-nien hsu-to kuo-ts'o te ken-yuan," *Pai-hsing pan-yueh k'an* (Hong Kong), no. 1 (1 January 1982):4–5.

8
Ch'en Tu-hsiu (1879–1942)

Biography

Ch'en Tu-hsiu,[1] born in Huai-ning, Anhwei province, on 8 October 1879, a few short months before the death of his father, was raised by his mother and older brother and sister and educated by his grandfather, a stern scholar nicknamed "Grandfather White Beard." Ch'en's formal studies began at the age of six with the *Four Books* and *Five Classics* in the traditional manner of learning by rote. Whenever he failed to recite a passage properly, Grandfather White Beard would beat him, but Ch'en never shed a single tear over a beating, no matter how severe it was. Ch'en's stubborn determination not to cry angered his grandfather and more than once while his grandfather angrily cursed Ch'en, he also sadly reflected, "When this little tyke grows into manhood, he will become a ruthless bandit who will be able to murder without batting an eyelash. What a true misfortune for the whole family."

Ch'en Tu-hsiu was to prove his grandfather's fears as unfounded, for Ch'en neither became a bandit nor took pleasure in killing. In later years he was to show, for example, in his opposition to insurrection under Ch'ü Ch'iu-pai or Li Li-san, his attitude that killing, even in a revolutionary war, was both cruel and barbarous.

Ch'en Tu-hsiu relates in his autobiography that while he feared neither beatings nor killings, he found weeping unbearable, especially the tears of women. He had refused to succumb to the brutal force of his grandfather, yet was moved by his mother's tears when she admonished him, "You should study hard, so that you might become a *chü-jen*, a rank which your father never reached. It was the sorrow of his whole life." Ch'en further states in his autobiography that although his mother was an able and generous woman who adhered to high moral values and was ready to fight against unfair treatment inflicted on others, she was, nevertheless, often a kindly but weak person, tolerant of evils, and lacking in resoluteness. Ch'en saw himself as having inherited his mother's weakness of irresolution even to toleration of evils. This character, Ch'en insinuated, made him compromise politically with the Comintern, and the Kuomintang.

In other matters, Ch'en remained independent of his mother's desires; for example, he remained uninfluenced by her ambition to see him climb the official ladder by taking the imperial examinations, even though in 1896 at the

199

age of seventeen, he passed the local imperial examination and thus received the first degree, the *hsiu-ts'ai*. Then, to please her, he grudgingly participated in the next year in the provincial examination at Nanking, but he failed. The testing experience gave him an insight that helped shape the next ten years of his life. He perceived the degree candidates as ignorant, lawless, corrupt, dirty and evil, and the examination hall as filthy, ludicrous, grotesque and depraving. Ch'en was absolutely convinced that the examination candidates would, should they some day rule China, bring near disaster to the people. This newly formed perception of the candidates and the examinations turned him against further participation and instead brought him to join the ranks of the two reformers, K'ang Yu-wei and Liang Ch'i-ch'ao. Under the influence of K'ang and Liang, Ch'en sought a modern education by attending the Ch'iu-shih Academy at Hangchow in 1898, where he studied French, English, and naval architecture.

Ch'en married in 1897 under his mother's order to do so. His wife bore him three sons and one daughter. The first two sons studied in France and became Communists, but were executed in 1927 and 1928 on Communist charges by the then Chinese authorities. Without formal divorce, Ch'en cohabitated with a woman by the name of Kao Chün-man, who left him after some years because she was unable to adapt to a revolutionary's dangerous and unsettled life. She died from poverty and sickness in the 1930s in Nanking after Ch'en's arrest.

In 1902 Ch'en made his way to Japan to pursue his studies. Between 1902 and 1915 he made altogether four trips to Japan: 1902–3; 1906; 1907–9; and 1914–15. In addition to his studies during these trips, he also became politically active. It has been reported that at some time between 1907 and 1910 Ch'en studied in France, where he grew to admire French culture, but this information has proven groundless.[2] Various sources have suggested that Ch'en attended six schools in Japan, including Kobun Institute, Tokyo Higher Normal School, English Language School, and Waseda University. However, exact dates of his enrollment are missing, and attendance at some of the schools he supposedly studied at, is dubious, due to lack of conclusive evidence. But the significant fact is that Ch'en clearly absorbed his knowledge of the theories of democracy and of Communist revolution during his years of study in Japan.

Between trips to Japan and after his return to China in 1909, Ch'en taught at various schools, participated in different political activities, and propagandized his revolutionary ideas through journalism. In 1917, Ts'ai Yuan-p'ei appointed Ch'en as Dean of the College of Letters at Peking University.

Two years earlier in 1915, he had begun to publish, in Shanghai, his own periodical, *Ch'ing-nien tsa-chih* (Youth Magazine), later renamed *Hsin ch'ing-nien* (New Youth). This magazine became the most powerful and prestigious organ in promoting the New Culture movement. The editorial policy of the periodical supported three cultural movements. First was the literary revolution, which basically fought for the substitution of the classical language by the vernacular. The second was the repudiation of Confucianism as unsuitable for modern China. Third was the promotion of science and democracy. Ch'en stood out among the many supporters of these three movements as one of the protagonists of the New Culture movement. But as *New Youth* had an editorial policy of not talking practical politics, Ch'en and Li Ta-chao founded in Peking a new periodical, *Mei-chou p'ing-lun* (Weekly Critic), in December 1918, that could deal more directly with political topics.

Ch'en moved to Shanghai toward the end of 1919 following the May Fourth Movement and his arrest by the Peking police on charges of antigovernment activities. The next year, 1920, George Voitinsky, Secretary of the Far East Department of the Comintern, went to China. He first met with Li Ta-chao in Peking, and then went to Shanghai to approach Ch'en Tu-hsiu and a select number of other scholars. Ch'en, after the meeting with Voitinsky, adopted communism and founded a forerunner of the Communist Party, called the Provincial Party Center. From that time on, *New Youth* changed its stand from the advocacy of democracy and liberalism to that of Marxism. It commemorated International Labor Day, the first such celebration in the history of China, by publishing a special issue on 1 May 1920.

The Communist headquarters was located in the French Concession of Shanghai and in July 1921, the new Chinese Communists held their first Congress there, marking the formal establishment of the Party. A politburo of three members was elected, with Ch'en elected as Party Secretary in absentia. He had not attended the meeting because six months earlier, in December 1920, he had accepted an offer to head the Education Department of the Canton Provincial Government and hence had been busy with duties in Canton. But, at the urging of Representative Maring of the Comintern, Ch'en returned to Shanghai, in August 1921, to devote more time to Party work.

Ch'en headed the Chinese Communist Party from 1921 to 1927. One important event of this period concerned the problem of collaboration with the Kuomintang. Ch'en had originally opposed collaboration but finally, at Maring's insistence, agreed. In September 1922, Ch'en founded in Shanghai another new, party publishing organ, the *Hsiang-tao chou-pao* (Guide Weekly), in which he promoted the official policy of Communist-Kuomintang collaboration as a means of propagating a national antiimperialist revolution in China. Still later, he went along, reluctantly, with the Comintern view that the Communist Party in China was still too weak to be effective independently and that it should thus seek to extend its influence among the working class within the Kuomintang. But the consequence of his support of the Comintern position was to be accused, in the August Seventh Meeting of 1927, of practicing the line of rightist opportunism toward the Kuomintang. And, as a further consequence, he was replaced as Secretary by Ch'ü Ch'iu-pai. As it turned out, however, the Communist Party under the leadership of Ch'ü Ch'iu-pai adopted the so-called insurrection line.

Another important event was the Chinese Eastern Railway incident that broke out in 1929 after the attempted seizure of the railway by Chang Hsueh-liang, the Young Marshal. The Soviet Union sent a large number of troops to Manchuria. The Chinese Communist Party sided with the Soviet Union, espousing slogans such as "Oppose the Chinese Imperialist Invasion of the Soviet

Union," and "Support the Soviet Union in Arms," referring to China in the term Imperialist. Ch'en opposed the supporters of the Soviet Union and denounced their slogans and actions as treasonous to China. This stand led to his expulsion from the Party by the Central Committee of 15 November 1929 (the resolution itself was not formally adopted until 11 June 1930).

Disillusioned with Stalin and the Comintern and expelled from the Party, Ch'en began to favor Trotsky's theory of revolution. He thus established contacts with the followers of Trotsky in Shanghai. The most important document published as a result of Ch'en's switch of political position is "A Statement of Our Political Opinions" *(Wo-men te cheng-chih i-chien shu)*, of 15 December 1929. The document bitterly attacked the Stalin leadership and the Comintern for their early disastrous policy of alliance with the Kuomintang and it further criticized the current line of the Chinese party leaders which, in spite of repeated failures, still called for armed uprisings and the immediate establishment of a workers' and peasants' dictatorship. In addition, Ch'en also published a magazine, *Wu-ch'an che* (Le Proletaire), in Shanghai in 1930, expounding Trotsky's revolutionary theories, and propagandizing Ch'en's own revolutionary ideas. Because of this, the Communist Party always afterward labeled Ch'en a Trotskyite, even though, in his later years, Ch'en announced that he was independent and belonged to no party.

Ch'en Tu-hsiu was arrested by the Nationalist government on 15 October 1932. According to a Nationalist source, the Nationalist government had acted on information of Ch'en's whereabouts that was supplied by his Communist opponents.[3] In April of the next year he was sentenced to thirteen years in prison on the charge of treason for engaging in antigovernment propaganda writing.

After the outbreak of the War of Resistance against Japan, the Nationalist government declared a general amnesty, and on 19 August 1937, Ch'en was released on parole. He then moved from Nanking to Wuhan and finally to Chungking, but when his health deteriorated, he went to Chiang-chin, a small village near Chungking, for recuperation. There he died on 27 March 1942, at the age of 63.

Ideological Change: The Road to China's Salvation

Ch'en Tu-hsiu believed that China's humiliating confrontation with the West could be made less traumatic if the Chinese could somehow be aroused from their conservative and out-dated mentality. Ch'en first analyzed the reason why China was so conservative and static, then he traced China's responses to the Western impact at different historical stages in the past few hundred years, and he finally came to the conclusion that the only way to save China was to replace the old ideology by a new ideology. This is what he meant by the "final awakening" of the Chinese people.[4]

Ch'en viewed China as an ancient East Asian country that had achieved an advanced state of civilization several thousand years ago. Situated amidst what

China regarded as barely civilized tribes, China herself had developed a unique philosophy, political structure, and social tradition without having recognized that such institutions existed in foreign lands as well. Ch'en believed that foreign influence had no part in bringing about any major change in China. The one exception he admitted as being influential to Chinese civilization occurred during the Wei and Chin dynasties (220–420) when Indian Buddhist ideas enlightened scholars and laymen alike. Nevertheless, Ch'en still felt that Buddhist doctrines as a kind of other-worldly philosophy never really dramatically or comprehensively affected Chinese life. It was, he believed, only the introduction of Western ideas in recent years that had increasingly changed the daily lives of the Chinese people.

Like other scholars, Ch'en acknowledged basic differences in the nature of Eastern and Western cultures and attributed the social and political upheavals of past centuries to the confrontations between these two cultures. In looking at China's responses and adaptation to the contact with the West, Ch'en outlined seven stages of development.

1. The introduction of Christianity and Western articles into China during the middle of the Ming dynasty (1368–1644) was given little attention. The only person worthy of mention was Hsu Kuang-ch'i.[5]
2. During the early Ch'ing dynasty (1644–1911), when Ch'ing emperors adopted Western cannons and the Western calendar, conservative scholars reacted by strong opposition. A conflict between the old and the new factions was emerging.
3. The artillery power of the Westerners in the Opium War (1840–1842) shocked the Chinese people, officials and commoners alike. Tseng Kuo-fan (1811–1872) and Li Hung-chang (1823–1901) advocated the introduction of Western weapons and the Western way of military training. There was again strong opposition from conservative scholars and officials.
4. China's defeat in the Sino-Japanese War (1894–1895) shocked the entire country out of complacency and into the realization of the absolute necessity of seeking a means to make China rich and strong. Two scholars, K'ang Yu-wei and Liang Ch'i-ch'ao tried to make some changes by staging a coup d'etat in 1898 against the Ch'ing ruler. The coup was unsuccessful. The conservative forces, by supporting the Boxer Rebellion that sought the complete expulsion of Western influences, invited the invasion of 1900 by the Eight Powers, the disastrous outcome of which nearly ruined the country. The conservatives then lost support, and people began to turn their attention from administrative problems to fundamental political problems.
5. Seeking a political solution, a number of progressive Chinese pondered the question of republicanism versus autocracy. The revolution in 1911 overthrew the thousand-year-long autocratic monarchy and founded a constitutional republic.
6. The Republic proved to be a republic in name only. The people, having suffered greatly from misrule in the first years of the republican government, were by now clearly aware of the importance of bringing about an effective republic.

7. The final stage was to be the ultimate awakening of the people into a realization of a true constitutional republic.

Political awakening

What Ch'en meant by the ultimate awakening of the people was the awakening of the political consciousness of the people. The process is divided into three steps.

First was the realization of the importance of politics as the people's own business and concern. The Chinese people, through long-term mistreatment under autocratic oppression, had become both ignorant about and apathetic to political issues. The common man's experience with politics was confined to paying taxes and obeying the whims of rulers; it was beyond his, the common man's, comprehension that a nation was the common property of the people or that human beings were political animals.

The second step of political awakening was to abandon the thousand-year-old bureaucratic and autocratic governmental structure headed by one person and to replace it by a free and self-governing political forum of the people in order to survive in the new world. For constitutionalism is the irresistible trend.

The third step was the direct participation in political movement by a majority of the people.

Whether the changes could be effected depended solely on one crucial condition: whether or not the people realized that they were the masters of their own nation. If so, they should then organize their own government and make their own laws and obey them. They were to carry out these actions by themselves instead of depending on others, specifically a benevolent emperor or a benevolent minister. In order for a constitutional republic to be achieved, it had to be done by the conscious as well as the spontaneous efforts of the majority of the people, for otherwise it would be a pseudorepublic and serve only as political window dressing.

Ethical Awakening

Ch'en believed that ethical principles, that is, values of political philosophy, affected politics in every country, but that it had been more the case in China than in other nations. The basic political and ethical principles of Confucianism, which essentially advocated a class system, were manifest in the concept of the Three Bonds: the relationship between prince and minister, between father and son and between husband and wife. The principles of freedom, equality and independence, which are diametrically opposed to a class system, serve as the foundations of Western civilization—hence are the fundamental difference between East and West. Since ethical doctrines determine political thought, it is impossible to have in existence at the same time ethical principles contradictory to political principles. Ethical and political principles have to be consistent in order for a nation to function properly. It is impossible to have a constitutional republic and at the same time preserve the class system of the

Three Bonds because constitutional republicanism and the Three Bonds are contradictory principles. In other words, a republic based on the principle of freedom and equality is incompatible with the class system based on the Three Bonds.

Ch'en points out that the Chinese people first realized their backwardness in learning, and later in their political institutions. But these two aspects were only secondary: the most fundamental problem was ethical. Without true awakening to the ethical problem the other two awakenings would be futile. For Ch'en, the ethical awakening was the final and ultimate awakening after all other awakenings.

In essence, what Ch'en meant by ultimate awakening was the rejection of Eastern civilization based on Confucianism and the adoption of Western civilization based on freedom, equality, and independence.

Eastern and Western Culture

The problem of Eastern culture versus Western culture has always been controversial among Chinese thinkers. The most unique analysis of this problem was Liang Shu-ming's idea of the three directions of human will: Western culture is the product of a spirit that drives the will forward to obtain satisfaction; Chinese culture is the result of the will's pursuit of self-adjustment and moderation; Indian culture arises from a spirit that goes backward in seeking a solution to life's problems. Equally attractive but most likely more far-reaching in influence are Hu Shih's ideas on what he called the material civilization of the West in material achievements and in physical sciences.[6]

Ch'en Tu-hsiu's treatment of Eastern and Western civilization is perhaps the most radical.[7] A fundamental antagonism, he said, as polar as north and south and as incompatible as fire and water, existed between Eastern and Western thoughts. Chinese survival in the modern world would depend on discarding Eastern thought and adopting Western thought. According to Ch'en, the salient differences between the two systems of thought can be explained in three areas.

Belligerent versus pacific: The three great Eastern schools of thought are Confucianism, Taoism and Buddhism. Confucianists do not favor feats of strength and daring, and in particular are not inclined favorably toward war. Taoists teach people to cease from rivalry and contention and also preach that weapons augur evil. Killing is taboo among the Buddhists. In general, the teachings of Eastern philosophy generate passivity, femininity, and weakness.

Westerners on the other hand are belligerent, as manifest in their nature and their social tradition. They have waged political wars, religious wars, and commercial wars; and in fact European history has been written in blood. The Western spirit to prefer death over humiliation is superior to the Eastern willingness to suffer humiliation rather than death.

Individualistic versus familial: Western peoples design their ethical, moral, social, political, and legal principles to protect individual freedoms, rights, and happiness. Hence, the basic social unit in a Western society is the individual. But in the East, the basic social unit is the family. An individual, whose social position is determined by his status as a family member and not as an independent entity, must subordinate himself to the head of the family. On a wider scale, the emperor is the head of a great family, the nation, and everyone takes orders from him. The familial system, which is the basic moral as well as institutional principle underlying a patriarchal or feudal society, still prevails in the East and has given rise to four evil consequences: a deleterious effect on the independent and self-respecting moral character of an individual; the stifling of individual free will; the denial of equal treatment before the law, depending on age, rank, and position; and the breeding of dependence by certain family members on other members that is harmful to individual productive power. All the tragedies of the East can be traced to these four evils; the remedy is the adoption of a system where individuals are more important than families.

Legal, utilitarian versus sentimental or formalistic: Western governments, as well as Western families and societies, respect rule by law. Confucianism views every institution as an ethical relationship. Westerners, whether they are strangers, friends, or relatives, use legal procedures in their business transactions. Their legal relationships are clearly differentiated from any social relationships. In addition, Western marriages are also legal relationships and not purely a relationship of love. The practice of separate property held by husband and wife, unlike the Chinese practice of joint property, is the most impressive of Western legal relationships. Also worthy of admiration is the Western act of suing one's husband without the slightest embarrassment.

Since every member of a family is governed by the same law, individual rights and obligations are not permitted to be impaired by sentiments. For instance, Western parents are not socially obligated to bear children, so they can practice birth control if they do not have the financial means to raise children. In China, childlessness is considered the ultimate unfilial act and even promotes the institution of concubinage. The attachment to the family system has created a vicious circle where a father has to raise and support many children. In turn, they have the duty of supporting their parents in their old age.

The small conjugal family system of the West is to be preferred to the extended family system in China. When familial love becomes an obligation, as is often the case in families where several generations live together, superficial affection is generated and genuine feelings are lacking. The cant of family obligation is economically harmful to both family and to society because it encourages excessive dependence by some family members on the other members of the family. When extended to friends, it results in loans without a definite date for repayment or any collateral; or, in friends installing themselves as permanent house guests. Thus, it happens that some rich people flee from their homes, for they fear their relatives and friends as they fear bandits.

In comparing Chinese and Western society, Ch'en saw a paradox. The West, by encouraging individual acquisitiveness and self-interest, has created independent individuals, an ordered society, and sound economy; while the

Chinese, with their emphasis on lofty sentiment and moral ideals in personal relationships, have produced a weak society and poor economy. The Western system is worth the sacrifice of the lofty sentiment venerated by Chinese tradition.

Ch'en's preference for the West reflects an economic analysis similar to Adam Smith's, although not clearly and explicitly expressed. Smith argued that in a capitalist society, where individuals see only their own profit or self-interest and hence collide with each other, an invisible hand promotes the common good of that society. That is, the philosophy underlying a Western economy is based on the idea of individual selfishness producing social well-being. People who oppose Smith's thinking contend that a capitalist society can at best be a rich society but not a just society. If Ch'en knew of this criticism, I assume from his general argument that he would find an identity in common good and justice. In this regard, Ch'en separates economics from morality or ethics. In his mind, economics takes precedence over ethics. This attitude was manifested most sharply in his evaluation of the Chinese society. To some superficial observers, he contended, the emphasis on sentiment is a sign of the genuine and generous spirit of the Chinese tradition,[8] but usually it is a kind of false sentiment. Instead, an ordered society and economy are a sign of genuine and generous spirit. As long as we have achieved such a goal, there is no harm in dispensing with the so-called genuine and generous spirit.

Ch'en's preference for Western culture over Eastern culture, as described above, was formulated in the first decade of the 1900s when he was not yet converted to communism and when he still cherished the democratic West as a model for China to follow.

Opposition to Confucianism

Since Ch'en believed that a change in the old Chinese ideology was an absolute necessity for the salvation of China, it is not surprising that he opposed Confucianism, the most influential and representative element of traditional Chinese thought. Indeed, during the New Culture movement in the early decades of twentieth-century China, Confucius was the common target of attack by reformers.

Ch'en, one of the most vigorous opponents of Confucianism, felt that in order for China to create a Western-type society so as to survive in the modern world, the Western principles of equality and human rights must be adopted by the Chinese. But, these fundamental principles of equality and human rights were incompatible with certain basic tenets of Confucianism. This meant, then, that Confucian ideals must be destroyed before any new belief could be introduced and established.[9]

Ch'en saw the core of Confucianism in the Three Bonds. This ethical principle, while preaching loyalty, filial piety, and obedience, justifies a class society that clearly distinguishes noble and high birth from base and low birth. Ch'en further contended that a well-defined class structure as such is common to any patriarchal society in a feudal system; but the Three Bond principle, the unique characteristic of Confucianism and Chinese culture, had been developed, from the Han through the Sung dynasties, into a complete ethical system as well.[10]

Ch'en discredits the existence of any universal and everlasting truth. The image of Confucius, accorded the distinction of being a teacher of ten thousand generations (that is, everlasting), was an image Ch'en was determined to destroy. In Ch'en's mind, if no everlasting truth existed, then Confucianism was no longer valid as an ethical guide for modern life.

To stress the incompatibility of Confucianism and modern life, Ch'en pointed out that Confucian teachings, having flourished in feudal times, were feudal and had become unsuitable to the conditions of the modern world in the following areas.[11]

Economy: In the modern world, economics is the base from which modern societies are built. Individualism, being the dominant factor in economics, affects ethics. The idea of an independent "personality" in ethics and in property, both firmly established in modern times, gives rise to great progress in social morality and material civilization. But Confucianism, which preaches dependence of sons and wives on their fathers and husbands, denies an individual an independent "personality" and personal independent property. Still further contradictory to the idea of individual independence was the attitude that fathers and older brothers should support sons and younger brothers, and vice versa.

Politics: As a rule, every constitutional country has political parties where a party member can maintain his own belief and act according to his own judgment: fathers and sons, husbands and wives do not necessarily need to agree on any political issue. But in China, the Confucian teaching that sons should obey fathers, and wives should obey husbands and even their sons after the death of their husbands, is incompatible with Western political freedom. Female participation in politics is a phenomenon of the modern world. But in Confucianism women are not only subordinate to men but should not even leave the inner chambers of the house. Under these circumstances, they cannot readily participate in politics.

Social life: Social interaction among men and women is common in the West, but Confucian teaching restricts almost all contact between the sexes, even to the degree of discouraging the touching of hands between men and women when something is given or received. Other admirable Western practices, such as allowing women to work at jobs ranging from clerical to professional positions in order to make an independent living, or else the custom where married children establish households separate from their parents, are not allowed by Confucian ethics. Under the Confucian extended family system, a woman's freedoms are limited because she lacks financial and personal independence, though both men and women are frequently victims of such a system. A further example is the Western practice of a simple funeral which is more sensible and more economical than the elaborate funeral for parents that is emphasized by Confucianism.

In sum, the underlying theme of Ch'en's opposition to Confucianism is that the teachings of Confucius were feudal principles that were current in his time and benefited an aristocratic minority, but that these feudal teachings have nothing to do with the great majority of the common people in modern times. The unsuitability of Confucianism to modern life led Ch'en to conclude that Confucianism should be completely abandoned.

It may be interesting to compare Ch'en's arguments with Communist China's theme in repudiating Confucius. The recent Criticize Confucius movement was based on the class approach in which Confucius was attacked primarily because he represented the interests of the landlord and aristocratic classes, preached the virtues of a feudal society, and even as a thinker stubbornly supported the slave system. [12] Thus, he is condemned as an enemy of the masses, especially of the laboring class.

New Youths

Thus far the account and analysis of Ch'en's thought has centered on his destructive attitude toward Chinese tradition. Now we turn to a more constructive attitude, his vision of the ideal man and the ideal society. Ch'en's ideal man was the image of the new youth which he envisioned. [13] In his theory of social organism, individuals within a society can be compared to the cells of an organism. During human metabolism, the old cells are continuously destroyed and replaced by new living cells. The new cells of a society are the new youths who replace the wornout older members of society. The new youths use their freshness and vitality in the fight for a national rebirth. Ideally, Ch'en says, the new youth possesses six qualities of character which qualify him to be the fittest for survival.

Independent rather than servile: Every man has the right to be independent; but he does not have the right to enslave others, nor should he allow himself to be enslaved. An individual, rather than be enslaved by others, should exercise his free will in thought and action to achieve individual freedom, independence, and equality.

Progressive rather than conservative: History shows that nations which cling to their old ways without change will decline and eventually perish, but those which constantly undergo change will advance rapidly. This is a basic law of human affairs and of the universe.

China cannot afford to remain static while the rest of the world advances. Her case is critical because she has lagged behind not only in education and politics but even in the production of daily necessities. Further, the great number of her people are extremely conservative. Chinese ethics, laws, learning, and social traditions are only remnants of feudal practices and thousands of years behind China's contemporaries. If the Chinese try to preserve their culture without change, they will without a doubt fail to survive the struggle for existence in the twentieth century. It would be preferable, Ch'en felt, to witness the complete elimination of a culture of five thousand years of accomplishment rather than see the extinction of the Chinese race.

Aggressive rather than retiring. To be aloof from an evil society is considered a virtue. However, an individual should not separate himself entirely from society, for it is an individual's duty to fight and conquer difficulties and to make progress in life. Thus, under no circumstances should one withdraw from society and live in solitude. Retirement, put positively, is an otherworldly behavior of the superior man; expressed negatively, retirement is a sign of weakness and impotence, unsuitable for the struggle of existence. In Europe, to struggle ahead dauntlessly is valued as a superior virtue; in Asia, resignation and peacefulness have been considered a noble tradition. This is the reason for the prowess of the West and the weakness of the East.

Those who believe in a philosophy of maintaining a distance from evil forces instead of fighting them are lazy and indolent, for they do not benefit a society in any way. People should fight the evil society rather than be conquered by it, and people should wage war against evil rather than seek one's own escape and evasion.

Cosmopolitan rather than isolationist: As the world becomes smaller, political and economic changes in any one country affect the rest of the world. At present a nation's rise and fall are determined by both internal and external political factors. To survive, it is impossible for China to adopt a policy of isolation on the claim that China has her own peculiar conditions and therefore can resist rather than conform to the international trends. Youths are urged to acquire a knowledge of the world and adopt an attitude conforming to the inevitable trend of global participation.

Utilitarian rather than formalistic: Old Chinese tradition emphasized the principle of "honoring the utilization of material things and the betterment of life" (li-yung hou-sheng). Unfortunately, since Chou and Han times this tradition and spirit has been increasingly less influential; it has become common in China to belittle material life and material improvement and to value greatly abstract learning and formalism. Since abstract learning is not always compatible with the practical life within a society, China has become backward in material development and is in extreme poverty. The Chinese people should change their attitude, putting a high value on fighting poverty and improving the material life of individuals and society rather than abstract learning.

Scientific rather than imaginative: Science is synonymous with objectivity and systematic reasoning, while imagination is synonymous with subjectivity and even ignorance and superstition. The development of science is the dominant factor in the superiority of Europeans to other peoples in modern times. Its contribution is as important as the theory of human rights—democracy. Science and democracy are like the two wheels of a vehicle. Science is essential to the development of Chinese agriculture, commerce, industry, and medicine.

Youths must study science. (Today this is common knowledge, but in Ch'en's day it had to be emphasized to the young people.)

In discussing educational policy, Ch'en raised a point that was extremely radical and revolutionary in the context of Chinese thought. The idea is literally "beastism" or, freely translated, "barbarism." His theory, which he borrowed from a Japanese educator, was that both human nature and "beast nature" should be developed in education. Beast nature includes, among other things, a dauntless and stubborn will power, the ability to fight without yielding, a strong and robust body, and the ability to resist nature. The colonization of the world by the white people can be attributed to this beast nature, just as Japanese hegemony over Asia is also due to this nature. A strong nation should simultaneously possess both human nature and beast nature, for a nation would degenerate and weaken if it only had beast nature or if it only respected human nature and completely lost the beast nature.[14]

In Confucian philosophy, human beings and beasts are contrasted as the two extremes of good and evil. Ch'en wanted to develop what the traditional philosophy tried to avoid. He lamented that the educated Chinese were generally weak in mind and in body. How could they, he asked rhetorically, shoulder the heavy and arduous burden of becoming successful politicians, military men, religious missionaries, or industrialists? So it is the beast nature that youths must cultivate. Naturally, Ch'en did not approve of the colonial aggression of Westerners and the Japanese but he argued that the typical traditional Chinese youth would be pushed aside in the struggle and competition among violent beasts of the world. To save China from being vanquished. Ch'en appealed to educators to consider seriously his point.

Actually, the idea of cultivating a beast nature can be seen as a seventh quality Ch'en hoped Chinese youths would possess. It was an extremely daring point of view. Though extreme, it was intended to combat traditional Chinese weak points.

Science and Democracy

In answering charges against *New Youth* by readers (conservatives as well as young students), Ch'en clarified the position of the magazine. In doing so, he presented a good picture of what he and the magazine stood for and opposed. The charges against *New Youth* were that it sought to destroy Confucianism, the national cultural essence, chastity of women, traditional ethics, propriety, art, religion, literature, and politics. Ch'en accepted all these charges as true, but he contended that the magazine justified its perspective on the basis of its support of two gentlemen—"Mr. Science" and "Mr. Democracy." Support of these two gentlemen meant that *New Youth* had no choice but to oppose the basic elements of Chinese society. Westerners, having shed tremendous blood and having undergone great trouble and difficulties, had gradually emerged from darkness to a bright world led by these gentlemen. Thus, Ch'en believed, "Mr. Science" and "Mr. Democracy" could lead China away from darkness in politics, in ethics, in learning, and in thought. Therefore, he and *New Youth* were determined to carry on regardless of the cost to themselves.[15]

Science and democracy were the two catchwords and the two cardinal goals of the New Culture movement. Except for a small handful of conservatives, there was no significant opposition to the introduction and development of science in China. Although Ch'en was among the strong promoters of science, his arguments do not now seem to need any detailed account. Thus, we can be brief with Ch'en on this point. With respect to democracy, the second cardinal goal of the New Culture movement, democracy has been a main trend in China's political development during modern times. Ch'en's views on democracy, not only important but also unique in certain points, had quite a checkered history.

Political Thinking

Ch'en's political thinking can be divided into three phases. Phase One covers the period before the May Fourth Movement; it reflects his belief in Western democracy and his hope of creating a new China patterned after Western democracy. Phase Two covers the years of his conversion to communism; he believed a worker and peasant revolution could bring about a society after the ideal of Marx. The Soviet Union would serve as a model. Phase Three covers the last years of his life after his release from imprisonment by the Nationalist authorities. This phase reflects disillusionment with the Soviet leadership and a return to the belief, stronger than before, in Western democracy.

Phase I: Democratic Period.

Ch'en's political ideas on democracy were in particular influenced by a series of lectures by John Dewey in China from 1919 to 1920. Ch'en simply quoted and accepted with a minimum of qualification Dewey's definition of democracy which is divided into four categories.

- Political democracy: the constitutional protection of people's rights and the expression of the people's will through a parliamentary system.
- Democracy of rights: the freedom of speech, publication, religion, and domicile.
- Social democracy: i.e., egalitarianism, such as the breaking down of the system of classes, the elimination of inegalitarian thinking, in order to obtain equality of social status for all individuals.
- Economic democracy: the elimination of economic inequalities and the leveling of the rich and poor classes to one equal status.[16]

Ch'en looked upon democracy only as the means for improving society. So, while politics was important, it nevertheless, he stressed, remained only a means toward a goal. In similar fashion, he looked upon Dewey's classification of democracy in political, social, and economic realms as the tools with which to work toward a better society. Of these three realms of democracy, he felt social and economic problems should receive greater emphasis, for socio-economic problems are the foundation of politics, and no major political problem can be solved without first solving socio-economic problems.[17]

Ch'en criticized Dewey's political democracy as not being thorough enough. Accordingly, he modified it by stressing that true democracy must guarantee that civil rights be under the direct control of the people. The people should directly formulate the constitution, which should prescribe the rights of the government and of the people; and the will of the people should be executed in accordance with the Constitution, through representation. In this way distinctions between ruling and ruled classes would be eliminated. In other words, bureaucratic control would be abolished and the people's self-control would be realized. These are the prerequisites for a true democracy.[18]

Ch'en suggested the two practical measures of local self-rule government and trade associations to lay the foundation for democracy. Organization should begin from the bottom and work toward the top, and from the small unit to the large unit. Thus, the self-rule government should be organized first at the village or town level and then extend to the national government. The trade association should start from the association of carpenters or bricklayers, journalist or lawyers of a city. The advantage of small organizations would be to involve the direct participation of all individuals rather than to have a delegate system.[19]

During this phase, Ch'en was not yet convinced of the efficacy of a communist revolution. Rather, what he wanted was a cooperative social structure in which pure capital, that is, capital divorced from labor, would gradually disappear, thus forestalling the emergence of class struggle.[20]

Phase II: Communist Period

As we mentioned above, Ch'en was arrested by the Nationalist government in 1932 and was charged with treason and endangering the Republic. Ch'en's rebuttal to these charges, dated 20 February 1933, reflects precisely his political thinking during his communist period.[21] He stated that since his twenties he had devoted himself to the movement of China's reconstruction, but that while his pre-May Fourth Movement activities had centered solely on the intellectuals, he later shifted his emphasis to the worker-peasant laboring masses.

Ch'en's analysis of the nature of Chinese society, shown in the *Rebuttal*, was in line with communist principles and represented the communist ideology. He saw China as a semicolonial and economically backward country, beset by warlords and bureaucrats within and international capitalist imperialism without. The liberation of the Chinese people from foreign aggression, and the achieving of democracy, unity, and economic prosperity within the country, depended, certainly not on the exploitative upper classes, but on the most oppressed and revolutionary worker-peasant laboring masses and on the forces of the world's proletariat. Ch'en explicitly stated this belief was the reason why he organized the Communist Party after the May Fourth Movement. The ultimate aim of the Communist Party, he said was to realize a classless free society without exploitation, and one in which the principle "from each according to his ability and to each according to his need" governed. Ch'en's attitude, typically communist, also had similarities to Sun Yat-sen's appeal to awaken the masses and to ally with all the nations in the world that treated China on an equal basis.

During this period some people argued that communism was not suitable to China. Ch'en dismissed this argument as absurd, though he did concede that communism could neither be achieved in one day nor by peaceful means. The implication was that there would be a violent revolution.

Ch'en's plan to achieve communism, the ultimate goal, required the communists to undertake the following: (1) to fight against imperialism so as to secure China's independence; (2) to fight against warlords and bureaucrats in order to bring about national unity; (3) to improve worker and peasant life by confiscating land held by landlords and giving it to the poor peasants, thus enhancing their purchasing power and subsequently benefiting urban commerce and industry; and (4) to set up a thoroughly democratic people's congress to write a constitution. On this last point he was vague. I gather that what Ch'en referred to was a people's congress that would, through universal suffrage, draft a constitution first and then later organize a parliament. In this connection he emphasized that the realization of the complete freedoms of assembly, speech, and publication, and of the people's congress were the prerequisites to national salvation.

In his *Rebuttal* Ch'en also included sharp criticism of the Kuomintang. He charged the Kuomintang with substituting its own party headquarters for a parliament, tutelage for people's civil rights, replacing the ordinary criminal law by special laws (such as Emergency Regulations against Activities Endangering the Republic, and Law on Publications), arresting, trying, and slaughtering people under the guise of martial law, depriving the people of freedom by bayonets. Ch'en further charged the Kuomintang with usurpation by having created a "party state" *(tang-kuo)* instead of a "people's state" *(min-kuo,* or republic).

A few words on how Ch'en perceived the nature of the Kuomintang may be appropriate here. In 1929 Ch'en was expelled from the Communist Party on charges of opportunism. After the expulsion, he issued two important public statements.[22] In both statements he attacked the Comintern leadership led by Stalin for its policy of opportunism toward the Kuomintang and for the disastrous failure of the Chinese Revolution of 1925–1927. Ch'en claimed that it was not his own opportunism that led to the failure of the Chinese Revolution; but rather that failure resulted from the wrong policy of opportunism pursued by the Comintern leadership.[23] Indeed, he continued, he had repeatedly opposed the Comintern's opportunistic policy to ally with the Kuomintang, and he had repeatedly suggested withdrawal from the alliance. The alliance was kept and the policy of opportunism was followed on the Comintern's insistence, and he was only obedient to that order.[24]

Theorizing about the reasons for the debacle, Ch'en maintained that the main cause was the fundamentally erroneous failure to understand the bourgeois nature of the Kuomintang. His attitude toward the Kuomintang also reflects his perception of the nature of Chinese society. In Chinese society, Ch'en maintained, capitalistic economic relations held an absolute dominant position, even though there still existed remnants of certain feudal forces.[25]

Ch'en further felt that the Kuomintang was definitely a bourgeois political party, as shown by the history of its activities, its programs of the Three Principles of the People, its industrial plans for reconstruction, and the component elements in its higher leadership. It was, in addition, reactionary in its hope for imperialist aid, in its refusal to confiscate land, and in its theory of "large-poor" and "small-poor" in China without essential class distinction.[26] It was a serious mistake, he believed, to overlook the class nature of the Kuomintang. The strategy that the Communist Party had adopted actually helped and supported the bourgeoisie, and made it impossible for the Chinese proletariat to have its own genuinely independent political party with which to lead the revolution. Due to the illusions of the Comintern leadership and the Communist Party, the Chinese proletariat were led into being unconscious tools of the bourgeois Kuomintang in overthrowing the rule of the Northern government, which represented bureaucrats, compradores, and capitalists. This (Communist-aided) victory paved the way for the Kuomintang compromise with the imperialists. And as soon as the Kuomintang had power, it immediately began, by an unprecedented white terror, to destroy the proletariat which had supported it.[27] Ch'en's analysis, from a class approach, of the antagonism between the two parties suggests, as we can see today, one of the basic reasons for the impracticality—if not impossibility—of any true cooperation between the Kuomintang and the Communist Party.

No summary of Ch'en's political thinking during the Communist period is complete without mention of his important article on labor. During the first year of Ch'en's organizing efforts, *New Youth* magazine served as the propaganda organ of the Party. On 1 May 1920, a special issue was published to commemorate International Labor Day. It was devoted exclusively to the labor movement in Western countries and in Japan, and to labor conditions in the metropolitan areas of China.

Ch'en's article, "The Awakening of the Workers," threw new and revolutionary light on the traditional view of labor in China and on the relationship between the ruling and the ruled classes.[28] Ch'en's argument ran as follows:

In the present world in which we live, only the workers can be said to be the pillars of society, for without them there would be no food to eat, no clothes to wear, no vehicles to drive. In a word, society would not be able to function. Evidently then, workers are the most useful and important of all members of society. But in actual practice, workers are lightly viewed as the most useless group. And, those who do not perform physical work are seen as the most useful and most important group. In order to rectify the situation, nonworkers should quickly recognize their uselessness while workers should realize their own usefulness and importance. Two steps will awaken the workers' awareness of their own usefulness. The first step is to demand better treatment; the second step is to place in worker control the power to rule over politics, military affairs, and industry. To demand better treatment from the capitalists is still a kind of begging, and the workers' power and rights cannot be secure unless they possess the power to rule. There is a famous passage in which Mencius expressed his attitude on manual and mental labor: "Some labor with their minds, and some labor with their strength. Those who labor with their minds govern others; those who labor with their strength are governed by others. Those who are governed by others support them; those who govern others are supported by them."[29] Ch'en maintained that the Mencian description should be reversed: those who labor with their strength should govern others and those who labor with their minds should be governed by others. Ch'en's advocacy of the rule of laborers over intellectuals in politics, military affairs, and industry is, of course, similar to the Marxist dictatorship of the proletariat.

Ch'en's acceptance of Marxism in this period is evident in an article, "Talk About Politics."[30] He observed that nothing in the world is more inequitable and painful that the oppression of the hard working proletariat in a capitalist system where the machinations of politics and law make the proletariat's life worse than being a machine or animal. The only exit from this unequal and painful situation is the seizure of political power by the proletariat. Such a capture of political control would completely subdue the bourgeoisie thus abolishing the system of private property, the wage system and unequal economic conditions. This is possible, however, only through violent force, class war, and seizure of the state and political apparatus.

Phase III: Last Views

Ch'en's political thinking in the third phase represents the crystallization of six to seven long years of deep thinking and thorough study of the two decades of the Soviet Russian experience. This phase is reflected in a collection of letters and articles written in 1940–1942, shortly before his death, entitled *The Last Views of Ch'en Tu-hsiu*.[31] These views were characterized, on one hand, by a strong condemnation of dictatorship in general and the Soviet dictatorship in particular, and, on the other hand, by a high esteem for the values of democracy.

For Ch'en, the god of Soviet communism had failed. He concluded that Soviet Russia was the first country to practice dictatorship, which he labeled as G.P.U. (i.e., secret police) politics, and he further felt that there was no evil the Soviet Russian government would not perpetrate. The governments of Germany and Italy had only followed Russia's example. Ch'en felt that these three reactionary governments, the Soviet Russian, the German, and the Italian, all attempted to turn thinking human beings into mindless machines and animals by forcing the general populace to follow the dictators' whips. If these three reactionary fortresses—in Ch'en's opinion even more reactionary and cruel than the ecclesiastical court of the middle ages—were not overthrown, human beings would be fated to become machines and animals.[32] Ch'en admonished people "to comprehend, without the slightest prejudice, the twenty-odd years of lessons from Soviet Russia and to re-evaluate scientifically instead of religiously the Bolshevik leaders and their doctrines. Complete responsibility for actions in Soviet Russia should not be attributed to Stalin alone, e.g., in such matters as the problem of democracy under the rule of the dictatorship of the proletariat."[33]

Ch'en claimed that the Soviet Union since the October Revolution had used the empty and abstract term "democracy of the proletariat" as a weapon to destroy the "concrete democracy" of the bourgeoisie. The Soviet government under Stalin was an outcome of this practice,[34] and all the crimes of Stalin were the logical outcome of this dictatorial system, for none of his crimes could have been perpetrated without reliance on dictatorial and undemocratic measures such as the secret police, single party system, suppression of the freedoms of thought, press, strike, and election. Clearly, it was the dictatorial system which produced a leader like Stalin, and not Stalin who produced the dictatorial system.[35] It should be noted that Ch'en made these comments at the time when Stalin was revered by leftists and liberals and the Soviet Union was considered a paradise for workers. This was thirty years before Krushchev made known, before the Twentieth Soviet Congress, Stalin's atrocities.

How did a dictatorship such as this which produced a leader like Stalin originate? Ch'en traced the theoretical foundation from Marx's advocacy of the dictatorship of the proletariat that follows the overthrow of the bourgeoisie. But it was Lenin who first put it into practice. On this point, Ch'en only commented that "though Lenin was then keenly aware that 'democracy is the antidote to bureaucracy,' nevertheless, he did not seriously adopt democratic measures, such as the abolition of the secret police, the permission of the opposition party to exist legally, the realization of the freedoms of thought, press, strike and election, etc."[36]

As for the ideological base of dictatorship, Ch'en, in one of his last letters to a friend, wrote that "the root of your mistakes lies, first, in your failure to understand the true value of bourgeois democracy, including Lenin and Trotsky and their followers who take democracy as being the forms of bourgeois control, hypocrisy and deception."[37] Now let us see what Ch'en viewed as the true value of democracy.

Ch'en made several very important points in regard to the value of democracy, especially as it relates to communism.

Democracy transcends time: "Since the advent of political organization among mankind until the period when politics wither away, throughout various eras, whether Greek, Roman, modern times or the future, democracy remains the banner of the classes of the majority in the opposition to the privileges of the minority."[38]

Democracy transcends class: "Modern democracy, richer in content and wider in scope than during the Greek and Roman periods, is called bourgeois democracy because it is practiced, in modern times, when the bourgeoisie is in power. Actually, bourgeois democracy is not limited to or welcomed by the bourgeoisie only; it was developed by the blood shed by hundreds of thousands of people and through five to six hundred years of struggle. Science, democracy, and socialism are the three marvelous inventions of modern mankind and are extremely precious. Unfortunately, since the October Revolution, the democratic system was inappropriately overthrown along with the bourgeois control, and consequently dictatorship replaced democracy."[39] Moreover, "the so-called 'proletarian democracy' should have been the same as bourgeois democracy as far as contents are concerned, but there could not be a different kind of democracy for the proletariat."[40]

Democracy transcends social systems: "Political democracy and economic socialism are mutually complementary rather than contradictory; democracy is not inseparable from capitalism and the bourgeoisie. If one were to oppose at the same time bourgeois capitalism and democracy, there might emerge a proletarian revolution. But without democracy as an antidote to bureaucracy, it could only be a Stalin-type of government with cruelty, corruption, hypocrisy, deception, and deprivation: it could never be real socialism. No such thing as the dictatorship of the proletariat exists. All that can develop is the dictatorship of the party, which becomes the dictatorship of one person—the leader."[41]

Contents of democracy: Democracy is more than an abstract idea; it has concrete contents which consist of the following points:

1. No government agencies, except the courts should have the right to arrest individuals.
2. No taxation without representation.
3. The government cannot levy taxes without parliamentary approval.
4. Opposition parties should have the freedom to organize, and the freedom of speech and press.
5. Workers should have the right to strike.
6. Peasants should have the right to cultivate land.
7. There should be freedom of thought, of religion, and so forth.[42]

Among these freedoms, Ch'en singled out the right of existence for opposition parties as especially important, for he felt a parliamentary or soviet system would be utterly worthless when this freedom is lacking.[43] His strong feelings about this are reflected in his appeal to restore not only Trotsky's party membership but also that of the members of Trotsky's opposition party. In addition, Ch'en appealed to restore Trotsky's leadership work in the Soviet Union.[44]

To illustrate the obvious differences between a democracy and a dictatorship, Ch'en drew up a comparison list:

Democracy of England, U.S., and France before its defeat in World War II.

1. The election of the parliament is participated in by many parties (including the opposition parties) which "monopolize" the precincts, but still have to issue

Fascist system of the Soviet Union, Germany, and Italy (since the Soviet political system served as Germany's and Italy's teacher, these three are categorized together).

1. All the members of the soviet or

campaign platforms and make public speeches to meet the demands of the people, for after all the power of the ballot rests with the electorate. When the parliament is in session, there is considerable discussion and debate.

parliament (legislature) are chosen by the ruling party. When in session, one can only have the right to express approval, not to debate.

2. Without an order by the court, no one shall be arrested or executed.

2. Secret political police can arrest or execute people arbitrarily.

3. Opposition parties, including the Communist Party, have the right to exist openly.

3. The single party system is the rule; other parties are not permitted.

4. There is considerable freedom of thought, speech, and press.

4. There is no freedom of thought, speech, and press.

5. The act of striking is not criminal.

5. There is no right to strike; strikes are considered criminal.[45]

Ch'en maintained that the democracy of England, U.S., and France, though imperfect, was worth preserving.[46] What remained to be done was to widen the scope of bourgeois democracy to what he called the "mass democracy" *(ta-chung min-chu)*. Although he did not elaborate on this idea, I gather from the context that what he meant was that democratic rights as he listed them should be enjoyed by the masses rather than be limited to one class or to a minority. He valued democracy above all other forms of government. Without mass democracy, he said, the dictatorship of the proletariat would inevitably degenerate into the Stalin type of G.P.U. government; this would be an inevitable consequence, not because Stalin's heart is especially wicked but because of the nature of the system itself.[47]

On the whole, Ch'en's final viewpoints on democracy coincided with the general trends of the democratic movement in the decades since the May Fourth Movement in China. Those men such as Carsun Chang and Hu Shih who fought for the realization of a democratic form of government desired nothing more than civil liberties for the people, a parliament, and the legal status of opposition parties. In other words, the hope was that the people could be free, and that government could be changed through peaceful means by the choice of the people. And, it was hoped, an opposition party could exist alongside the government party in power and enjoy full legal protection. Obviously, some of Ch'en's later views disagreed with Marx and communist practices. First, the theory of the dictatorship of the proletariat is one of the essential tenets of Marxism, but Ch'en opposed it as being nonexistent, or as a root of political crimes perpetrated in its name. Second, his hope of giving to all people democratic rights, especially the freedoms of thought and press, denied the theory of antagonism between the bourgeois and the proletariat, for those freedoms are generally denied to the bourgeoisie or people labeled as reactionaries. Third, his advocacy of the legal position of opposition parties contradicted the practice of the single party system in communist countries. Fourth, Ch'en rejected the orthodoxy of Marxism. He contended that his reevaluation of Bolshevik doctrines and leaders, including Lenin and Trotsky, was not based on the criterion of Marxism, but on the twenty-odd years of lessons learned from the Soviet Union; that if the principles of the Soviet Union were right in building up a new nation, irrespective of success or failure, no one could object even if they had deviated from Marxism. The *orthodoxy* of Marxism was the same as the orthodoxy of Confucianism. Thus, he would oppose the new orthodoxy as he did that of Confucianism.[48]

Conclusion

Ch'en's thought was greatly influenced by three elements from the West, namely, Social Darwinism, democracy, and Marxism. Social Darwinism was most noticeable in his early thought, and the references to that theory were copious in his early writings. His programs for China's reconstruction stem from his basic thesis that reform was necessary, even though it meant the destruction of the old tradition and ideology, in order for China to survive in a world where the struggle for existence was brutal. Since survival was possible only for the fittest, China faced the choice of adapting to new conditions or perishing in the new world. China of course had to survive. In one part of the survival program, Ch'en even went so far as to advocate the inclusion of "beast nature" or barbarism in the educational system to make the Chinese strong. This, he deemed, was the best cure for the overly civilized and effete Chinese. With the popularization of Social Darwinism came the urge to be strong or even ferocious. This line of thought, to which Ch'en's contribution has been influential, has shaped, I believe, the outlook and behavior of the young generation of Chinese to a considerable degree.

During the period before the May Fourth Movement, Ch'en was entirely a believer in Western democracy. For the period of his communist activity, he naturally followed the Communist theory of the state, the dictatorship of the proletariat, and so on. However, the theory of democracy is closely related to individualism. It is possible that Ch'en felt the importance and dignity of individuals so deeply that in his later years he grew to abhor the Moloch-like power of the state, the Party, the dictator, especially the atrocities of Stalin, and the individual's dwindling into insignificance in the Soviet Union. But he continued to sustain a strong faith in a socialism which aims at the advancement of life for all people in society. So he envisioned a society in which the traditions of democracy and socialism were combined. In other words, he dreamed of a society of socialism minus dictatorship, or socialism plus democracy, but he did not propose any practical measures for achieving such a goal.

Ch'en's life in thought and in action underwent two dramatic changes. Before 1920 he was a strong believer in democracy and liberalism; from 1920 he became a communist revolutionary in theory and in practice; from 1937 after his release from the Kuomintang prison when his god of communism failed, he turned back to democracy and liberalism again. There have been a number of anticommunist scholars in China who study and oppose communism intellectually, but who never had practical experiences with the communist movement. However, Ch'en was a founder, participant and leader of the Communist Party for some time. His opposition to communist practice in China was based upon his practical experience through participation, direct observation of the inner conditions, and his awareness of the darkness, injustice and atrocities of Soviet Communist practices, under whose supervision and direction the Chinese Communist Party operated. Ch'en's dramatic change reflecting the failure of and his disillusionment with the Soviet system is far more real, direct, and significant than that of the other thinkers discussed in this book. Moreover, Ch'en's turnover from liberal democracy to dictatorial communism and again back to liberal democracy brought nothing but misery and hardship to his personal life. The first change invited his arrest by the Nationalist government and resulted in a seven-year prison term, and the second change caused all the defamation, slanders as a Trotskyist bandit, a renegade, a traitor serving Japan from his former fellow communist comrades. I believe Ch'en struggled devotedly and unselfishly all his life for a faith, rather than for personal gain, power or fame; his reaffirmation of democracy and liberalism is thus particularly worth noting.

Notes

[1] The biographical sketch, especially for the early years, is heavily based on Ch'en Tu-hsiu, *Shih-an tzu-chuan* (Taipei: Chuan-chi wen-hsueh tsa-chih she, 1967). This autobiography was written by Ch'en in prison in Nanking, 1937. It is not always possible to determine whether the figures given for Ch'en's age in his autobiography are based on Chinese or Western reckoning. In these cases, we have simply given the figures as they appear in the original. For other details of Ch'en's life, see Howard L. Boorman, *Biographical Dictionary of Republican China* (New York: Columbia University Press, 1967), vol. 1, pp. 240–248.

[2] Chih Yü-ju, *Ch'en Tu-hsiu nien-p'u* (Hong Kong: Lung-men shu-tien, 1974), pp. 1–24.

[3] Ch'en Tu-hsiu, *Shih-an tzu-chan*, p. 6.

[4] The account below is based on Ch'en Tu-hsiu, "Wu-jen tsui-hou chih chueh-wu," *Hsin ch'ing-nien* 1, no. 6 (February 1916):1–4.

[5] Hsu Kuang-ch'i (1562–1633), minister of the Board of Rites, accepted both Christianity and Western sciences. He studied astronomy and mathematics with Matteo Ricci and was converted to Catholicism.

[6] The details of Liang Shu-ming and Hu Shih's arguments are treated in chapters 7 and 4, respectively.

[7] The discussion below is based on Ch'en Tu-hsiu, "Tung-hsi min-tsu ken-pen szu-hsiang chih ch'a-i," *Hsin ch'ing-nien* 1, no. 4 (December 1915): 1–4.

[8] The term Ch'en used is *ch'un-hou*—translated in the text as "genuine and generous"—has been used to describe the noble virtue of the ancient people or ancient China. It suggests the characteristics of being simple, pure, sincere, of generous and deep sentiment, etc. It is difficult to translate into one English term.

[9] Ch'en Tu-hsiu, "Hsien-fa yü K'ung-chiao," *Hsin ch'ing-nien* 2, no. 3 (November 1916): 5.

[10] Ibid., pp. 3–4.

[11] The account below is based on Ch'en Tu-hsiu, "K'ung-tzu chih tao yü hsien-tai sheng-huo," *Hsin ch'ing-nien* 2, no. 4 (December 1916): 2–5.

[12] Yang Jung-kuo, "K'ung-tzu—wan-ku te wei-hu nu-li chih-tu te szu-hsiang-chia," *Jen-min jih-pao,* 7 August 1973.

[13] The account below is based on Ch'en Tu-hsiu, "Ching-kao ch'ing-nien," *Hsin ch'ing-nien* 1, no. 1 (September 1915): 1–6.

[14] Ch'en Tu-hsiu, "Chin-jih chih chiao-yü fang-chen," *Hsin ch'ing-nien* 1, no. 2 (October 1915):5–6.

[15] Ch'en Tu-hsiu, "Pen-chih tsui-an chih ta-pien shu," *Hsin ch'ing-nien* 6, no. 1 (January 1919): 10–11.

[16] Ch'en Tu-hsiu, "Shih-hsing min-chih te chi-ch'u," *Hsin ch'ing-nien* 7, no. 1 (December 1919): 13.

[17] Ibid., p. 14.

[18] Ibid.

[19] Ibid., pp. 17–18.

[20] Ibid., p. 21.

[21] This account is based on Ch'en Tu-hsiu, "Ch'en Tu'hsiu hsien-sheng pien-su chuang," pamphlet dated 20 February 1933, n.p. This written statement, made in his own defense, was a plea of not guilty against the charges of endangering the Republic and of treason.

[22] Ch'en Tu-hsiu et al., *Kao ch'üan-tang t'ung-chih shu,* pamphlet dated 10 December, 1929, n.p. Ch'en Tu-hsiu et al., *Wo-men te cheng-chih i-chien shu,* signed by Ch'en and eighty others, pamphlet dated 15 December 1929, n.p.

[23] Ch'en, *Kao ch'üan-tang t'ung-chih shu,* pp. 1, 14. Ch'en, et al., *Wo-men te cheng-chih i-chien shu,* pp. 1, 26.

[24] Ch'en, *Kao ch'üan-tang t'ung-chih shu,* pp. 3–5.

[25] Ch'en et al., *Wo-men te cheng-chih i-chien shu,* pp. 16–7.

[26] Sun Yat-sen says that China has no specially rich class, but there is only a general poverty. See Sun Yat-sen, *San-Min Chu-I* in *Ch'üan-chi,* vol. 1, pt. 1, p. 140.

[27] Ch'en et al., *Wo-men te cheng-chih i-chien shu,* pp. 1–3.

[28] The account below is based on Ch'en Tu-hsiu, "Lao-tung che te chueh-wu," *Hsin ch'ing-nien* 7, no. 6 (May 1920): 1–2.

[29] See *Mencius,* bk. 3, pt. 1, ch. 4, sec. 7.

[30] The account below is based on Ch'en Tu-hsiu, "T'an cheng-chih," *Hsin ch'ing-nien* 8, no. 1 (September 1920): 4.

[31] Ch'en Tu-hsiu, "Kei Hsi-liu te hsin," *Ch'en Tu-hsiu tsui-hou tui-yü min-chu cheng-chih te chien-chieh* (Hong Kong: Chung-kuo tzu-yu ch'u-pan she, 1950), p. 19. Hereafter referred to as *Tsui-hou chien-chieh.* Hsi-liu is the pen name of P'u Te-chih, a follower of Ch'en, who spent four long years in the same prison in Nanking with Ch'en. In Ch'en's remarks he chose often to use the term Soviet Russia rather than Soviet Union.

[32] Ch'en Tu-hsiu, "Kei Hsi-liu teng te hsin," *Tsui-hou chien-chieh,* p. 14; Ch'en, "Kei Hsi-liu te hsin," *Tsui-hou chien-chieh,* p. 22.

[33] Ch'en Tu-hsiu, "Wo-te ken-pen i-chien," *Tsui-hou chien-chieh,* p. 26.

[34] Ch'en Tu-hsiu, "Kei Lien-ken te hsin," *Tsui-hou chien-chieh,* p. 15.

[35] Ch'en Tu-hsiu, "Kei Hsi-liu te hsin," *Tsui-hou chien-chieh,* pp. 20–21.

[36] Ibid., p. 22.

[37] Ch'en Tu-hsiu, "Kei Lien-ken te hsin," *"Tsui-hou chien-chieh,* p. 15.

[38] Ch'en Tu-hsiu, "Wo-te ken-pen i-chien," *Tsui-hou chien-chieh,* p. 26.

[39] Ch'en Tu-hsiu, "Kei Hsi-liu te hsin," *Tsui-hou chien-chieh,* p. 21.

[40] Ch'en Tu-hsiu, "Kei Lien-ken te hsin," *Tsui-hou chien-chieh,* p. 15.

[41] Ch'en Tu-hsiu, "Wo-te ken-pen i-chien," *Tsui-hou chien-chieh,* pp. 26–27.

[42] Ch'en Tu-hsiu, "Kei Lien-ken te hsin," *Tsui-hou chien-chieh,* p. 15.

[43] Ch'en Tu-hsiu, "Wo-te ken-pen i-chien," *Tsui-hou chien-chieh,* p. 26.

[44] Ch'en et al., *Wo-men te cheng-chih i-chien shu,* p. 44.

[45] Ch'en Tu-hsiu, "Kei Hsi-liu te hsin," *Tsui-hou chien-chieh,* pp. 23–24.

[46] Ibid., p. 22.

[47] Ibid., p. 19.

[48] Ibid., p. 30.

9
Mao Tse-tung (1893–1976)

Biography

Mao Tse-tung[1] was born on 26 December 1893, in Shao-shan village in Hsiang-t'an *hsien,* Hunan province. At the time of Mao's birth his family was poor, but Mao's father had managed to rise from a poor peasant to a middle peasant and finally become a wealthy peasant by doing a profitable grain and pig business and investing savings in land. Mao's birthplace was a quiet and unproductive village, but the city of Hsiang-t'an was a bustling business center that served not only Hunan but also Kwangtung province to the south. Mao thus was able to get news of both the latest currents of thought from Canton and of the activities of progressive elements in his native Hunan.

By the time he was six Mao was helping his family in various farm activities at home. When he was eight, Mao enrolled in an old style private school, staying there until the age of thirteen. The traditional custom of learning the classics by rote bored Mao. He turned instead to popular literature, becoming fascinated by Chinese novels such as *Travels to the West, Water Margin* and *The Romance of the Three Kingdoms.* Mao admitted in later years that he benefited ideologically from these novels more than from the formal classics.

From the ages of thirteen to sixteen, Mao worked as an adult farm laborer on his father's farm. During these years he continued his habit of self-study. The first book of a political nature to which he was introduced was *Sheng-shih wei-yen* (Words of warning) by Cheng Kuan-ying, a book dealing with the salvation of China by making her rich and strong. When he was sixteen, Mao's rebellious nature was fully revealed in a fierce fight with his father. After this confrontation between father and son, Mao was given permission to leave for Hsiang-hsiang, a town fifty *li* from his home village, to attend the senior class in an elementary school. There he studied some basic principles of the natural sciences and a smattering of new Western doctrines in addition to the Chinese classics. Mao was now free of his home environment; at the age of sixteen, the impressions made upon him through access to new knowledge of the outside world must have been profound and lasting.

Mao's intellectual vision was vastly widened by the study of Western knowledge. He was further greatly influenced by the newspaper edited by Liang Ch'i-ch'ao, written in an emotional and passionate style, which advocated democracy and an aggressive spirit in individuals and nations. By that time,

K'ang Yu-wei and Liang Ch'i-ch'ao had already won Mao's great admiration. Mao read and reread certain writings of K'ang and Liang to the point where he could remember them by heart. After one year in the elementary school, Mao was admitted in 1911 to the Hsiang-hsiang High School at Ch'ang-sha. He immediately became an avid reader of the newspaper published by the T'ung-meng hui under the leadership of Sun Yat-sen. After the outbreak of the 1911 Revolution, Mao voluntarily enlisted in the new army. But, disillusioned with the revolution, he quit the army six months later. Thereafter, he attended several schools, but also found them unsatisfying. Finally, he decided to continue self-study by going to the library at Ch'ang-sha every day. Included among the books Mao had read by now were the translations of Charles Darwin, *The Origin of the Species;* Adam Smith, *Wealth of Nations;* Thomas Huxley, *Evolution and Ethics;* James C. Miller, *Logic;* Herbert Spencer, *Study of Sociology;* John S. Mill, *Ethics;* Charles Montesquieu, *The Spirit of Law;* and Jean-Jacques Rousseau, *Theory of Social Contract.* The chief translator of these works was Yen Fu, whose translation of Darwin's theory of evolution influenced Mao the most, for the theory expounded the law of the struggle for existence and it contradicted the traditional Chinese ideal of the superiority of ancient times over the present. These Western works exercised tremendous influence on the thought of Chinese intellectuals in general and naturally exercised at least an equal influence on Mao. Later in life, as he came to accept communist ideology, Mao rejected these Western democratic ideals.

In 1913, at the age of twenty, Mao was admitted through competitive examination to the Hunan Fourth Normal School, which later combined with the First Normal School, where he studied for the five years between 1913 and 1918. At this school Mao acquired a solid foundation in the Chinese classics, history and literature. The Confucian *Analects* and *Mencius* were among the classics he read, and in his book notes, some of which are still extant, Mao expressed an appreciation for certain Confucian passages and, indeed, showed no signs of disagreement. Of the later Chinese scholars whom Mao read, Mao preferred, and was influenced by, the pragmatic theories of Ku Yen-wu (1613–1682), Yen Hsi-chai (1635–1704), and Wang Ch'uan-shan (1619–1692). It appears, then, that Mao was at one time influenced by Confucianism and Neo-Confucianism.

Mao distinguished himself at school in Chinese composition, and he occasionally wrote poems, which won warm praise from his schoolmates. In addition to academic work, Mao emphasized physical fitness; he especially enjoyed swimming. The ideal scholar possessed, in his words, a "civilized spirit and a barbarian body."

Mao's stay at the five-year normal school can be considered the only formal education he ever received, yet it was sufficient not only to lay the foundation of his learning, but also to give some shape to his political ideas. In addition, these five years provided opportunities for social activities. Mao made many friends and he studied with good teachers. When he organized the New People's Study Association *(Hsin-min hsueh hui)* in 1917, the majority of the members were his

226

schoolmates and many of the backbone members of the early Chinese Communist Party were recruited from the teachers and students of the normal school.

Among the teachers, the most respected and for Mao the most influential in his life and thought was Yang Ch'ang-chi, a returned student who had studied abroad in Japan and England for nine years. Yang, a specialist in Neo-Confucianism, had developed his own school of thought by adapting and combining the theories of Wang Ch'uan-shan, T'an Szu-t'ung and the German philosopher Kant on the one hand, with ideas of Western democracy and institutions on the other hand. Yang Ch'ang-chi taught courses in education and on moral cultivation and ethics, a required course in all schools at that time. Yang was an esteemed teacher and a man of profound learning and high moral character. Mao frequently sought him out for consultation in the Chinese tradition of after-class, student-mentor discourse. The student-teacher relationship was a close one and, in 1921, Yang gave his daughter in marriage to Mao at Ch'ang-sha. But, in 1930, Mao's wife was executed in the same city by the government then in power on charges of communist activities.

When *New Youth* began publication in 1915, it was Yang who introduced this new magazine to Mao; Mao slowly established a preference for the writings of Hu Shih, Ch'en Tu-hsiu and Li Ta-chao over that of K'ang and Liang, the two men whom Mao had earlier worshipped. It was also Yang who introduced Mao personally to Li Ta-chao. When Mao first visited Peking in 1918 Li Ta-chao gave Mao a job in the library of Peking University. In Peking, the center of China's revolution, Mao made new friends and widened his horizons. He also absorbed new ideas and began to dabble in Marxism-Leninism.

Even as late as 1918 and a year after the October Revolution had begun, Mao's thought remained a mixture of liberalism, democratic reformism and utopian socialism. In 1919, Mao returned via Shanghai to Hunan where he reported on his Peking trip and also introduced Marxism and other schools of socialism, which he had learned in Peking, to the New People's Study Association. In order to propagandize his revolutionary ideas and especially to eugolize the victory of the October Revolution and to promote Marxism, Mao published a weekly called *Hsiang-chiang p'ing-lun (Hsiang-chiang Review)*. But this weekly was suspended by the authorities after only five issues had been published.

In 1920, Mao made his second trip to Peking. At this time, he read extensively in Chinese publications on the Russian Revolution and communism. It was not until this particular point in his life that Mao established a complete faith in Marxism and accepted the Marxist theory of historical materialism. Beginning in 1920, Mao claimed himself as a Marxist in theory and in action and his faith afterward never wavered. In this year, upon instructions from Li Ta-chao and others, Mao began to organize the Socialist Youth League in Hunan, a prototype Communist party organization. He also organized Communist small groups, or cells, in Peking and then one such cell in Ch'ang-sha.

The history of the Chinese Communist movement following the founding of the Party is generally divided into four periods; this periodization is followed in Mao's *Selected Works* as well as in other communist history books. Thus, it is convenient to use this time scheme as a guideline in discussing Mao's biography after 1920.

The Founding of the Party and the First Revolutionary Civil War (1921–1927)

The First Communist Congress was held in Shanghai beginning on 1 July 1921. This is regarded as the birth of the Chinese Communist Party. Mao was one of the twelve delegates attending the Congress, who represented a total of fifty-nine Communist Party members in the whole country. After the conference, Mao returned as the Party secretary of the Hunan area. In subsequent years, he was active in the labor movement in Hunan, organizing and leading numerous strikes, the most notable being the general strike of the Anyuan miners in 1922. Mao also headed a peasant movement. In response to those who censured the peasant movement in Hunan as "terrible," Mao investigated five *hsien* in Hunan and in 1927 wrote his famous "Report on an Investigation of the Peasant Movement in Hunan" in defense and praise of the peasant movement, which he called "excellent."

The Third Party Congress convened in Canton in 1923 and Mao was elected a member of the Central Committee. A year later, in 1924, the Communist Party and the Kuomintang formed its first united front. In 1926, Mao headed the National Institute of the Peasant Movement in Canton, training cadres to lead the peasant struggle, and in the same year Mao formulated his observations, based on a Marxist-Leninist perspective, on the peasantry and other classes in China in an essay called "Analysis of the Classes in Chinese Society."

The Second Revolutionary Civil War (1927–1936)

In July 1927, the Kuomintang in Hankow decided formally to break with the Communist Party. This split between the two parties caused the killing of many Communists and left a wound which was never to be healed. Mao said of the Kuomintang/Communist split, "But the Chinese Communist Party and the Chinese people were neither cowed nor conquered nor exterminated. They picked themselves up, wiped off the blood, buried their fallen comrades and went into battle again."[2] To meet the critical situation, the Communist Party called an emergency conference on 7 August 1927, which rectified Ch'en Tu-hsiu's so-called opportunist line and removed him from leadership, though Ch'en did not admit the charge. The conference also called upon the peasants to save the revolution by launching an Autumn Harvest uprising. Mao was sent to western Kiangsi and eastern Hunan to lead the uprising. It was in this capacity that Mao succeeded, in September 1927, in organizing the first division of the Red Army. By October, after numerous battles, Mao marched his troops to Ching-kang Mountain where he established the first revolutionary base and established the Hunan-Kiangsi Border Region Workers' and Peasants' Government. After converging with the troops led by Chu Te, Mao and Chu established the Central Revolutionary Base using as its center Jui-chin, Kiangsi. Several years later, in 1931, a Soviet Republic was set up at Jui-chin. In his 1930 article, "A Single Spark Can Start a Prairie Fire," Mao confidently pointed out that the correct policy was to establish and develop the Red Army and its revolutionary bases, to build up a revolutionary regime, and to develop agrarian revolution *(t'u-ti ko-ming)*. This was a policy designed to encircle and ultimately to seize, through armed revolutionary rural villages, the Kuomintang-occupied cities.

By 1930, the Red Army had grown to about 60,000-strong throughout the country. From 1930 to 1934 Chiang Kai-shek launched five encircling-annihilation campaigns against the Red Army. The Communist position in Kiangsi held firm against the first four campaigns. But it weakened with the fifth campaign in 1934 when Chiang, on the advice of a German general named Hans von Seekt, successfully blocked the Communist movement by building lines of encircling blockhouses, and placing an embargo on salt importation to Communist areas. In October 1934, the Central Red Army decided to break through the Kuomintang encirclement. The Red Army thus withdrew from Kiangsi and started on its famous Long March.

In January 1935, the Communist Party called a meeting at Tsun-i, and corrected the wrong military strategy which earlier had resulted in the failure to hold out against the fifth Kuomintang encirclement campaign. At this meeting, Mao's leadership in the Party was firmly established. During the Long March, there was a disagreement as to which route to take. Mao advocated marching to Shensi. Chang Kuo-t'ao favored going to Hsi-k'ang or Tibet. In a meeting held at Mao-erh-kai to decide which direction to take, Mao triumphed over Chang. A full year after starting out in the Long March, the Red Army reached northern Shensi in October 1935 and joined forces with the Red Army units there.

The War of Resistance Against Japan (1937–1945)

After the War of Resistance broke out, Mao's proposal, the Ten-Point Program for National Salvation and Resistance to Japan, was adopted by the Communist Party Conference held at Lo-ch'uan in August 1937. A second united front against the Japanese invasion was formed between the Kuomintang and the Communist Party. Mao's two important treatises dated 1937, "On Practice" and "On Contradiction," were reputed to having been written to expound Marxist dialectical materialism and to serve as a theoretical framework for China's Communist revolution. Mao's 1938 article "On Protracted War" was one of the major contributions to the War of Resistance. The article analyzed the political and military situations in China and Japan. It further stated that China could be sure of ultimate victory, but that victory would not be quick; rather, victory over Japan could only come after a protracted war fought according to the principles of a people's war. In 1940, Mao published his "On New Democracy," an article which greatly furthered the ideological unity of the Party and the so-called democratic people outside of the Party throughout the country.

In 1942 the Communist Party carried out a rectification movement of the Party work style. Incorrect tendencies, such as subjectivism, sectarianism, and the Party "eight-legged essay," were censured as being contrary to true Marxism-Leninism. The chief architect of the movement was Mao himself. He charged that many party members, especially those comrades returned from Russia such as Wang Ming, were guilty of these mistakes and incorrect tendencies. To combat the wrongdoings, Mao gave a series of lectures under the titles, "Reform Our Study" "Rectify the Party's Work Style," and "Oppose Party Eight-Legs." Also in the same year, Mao gave a talk entitled "Talks at the Yenan Forum on Art and Literature," the central theme being that the aim of art and literature is to serve the workers, peasants and soldiers. This speech prescribed the basic policy for art and literature and has been followed as the official line since 1941. In 1945, the Seventh Party Congress was held in Yenan at which the Congress unanimously approved Mao's political report "On Coalition Government." A new Central Committee with Mao as the head was elected.

The Third Revolutionary Civil War and the Founding of the People's Republic of China (1945–1949)

On 25 August 1945, Mao Tse-tung personally flew to Chungking to negotiate with Chiang Kai-shek on the peaceful cooperation between the two parties. The result of the talks, made public on 10 October contained an agreement on measures to safeguard internal peace. However, the measures were never carried out and civil war never actually ceased. Neither side assumed responsibility and both sides accused the other as the violator of the agreement. The civil war lasted four years, culminating in the complete victory for the Communist Party. On 1 October 1949, the Central People's Government of the People's Republic of China was proclaimed with Mao elected as its first chairman. Mao had earlier discussed the nature of the new government and defined the People's Republic of China in his "On the People's Democratic Dictatorship," published on 1 July 1949, as a people's democratic dictatorship led by the working class through the Communist Party and with the alliance of workers and peasants as its foundation; he defined democratic dictatorship as the combination of democracy for the people and dictatorship over the reactionaries. Mao further emphatically stressed that China must learn from the Soviet Union and, he diplomatically added, that China must lean to one side of the Soviet Union. This foreign policy was followed until the split between China and the Soviet Union in 1958. Mao's first visit to the Soviet Union was from December 1949 to March 1950. But his second visit, in November 1957 to celebrate the fortieth anniversary of the October Revolution, lasted less than three weeks.

After 1949, the first and most important measure carried out in China was land reform. Land was confiscated from landowners and redistributed to peasants who had little or no land. Mutual aid teams and agricultural producers' cooperatives were set up with a view to establishing agricultural collectivism and socialism. The cooperatives took two forms: the primitive type of cooperative that was introduced in 1951, and the advanced type of 1956. Finally, the highest communist form of the people's communes was adopted in 1958. At each stage which led to the next stage of higher degree of collectivism, blood was shed and there was opposition from conservative peasants. It was Mao who directed the reforms and it was he who served as the chief motive force and architect of these changes. Without his direction, these changes might not have been realized.

In 1958, the Great Leap Forward Movement began. The slogan "Go All Out, Aim High" is reputed to have been coined by Mao. The People's Communes, the Great Leap Forward Movement, together with the General Line to Build Up Socialism, introduced in 1956—that is, "More, Faster, Better and More Economical—are known as the Three Red Banners. All are credited to Mao's creation. Unfortunately, these movements proved to be too ambitious and hasty for they led to economic disorders and poor harvests. Even though the three trying years after the great leap were officially labeled as temporary difficulties caused by natural calamities, Mao was, nevertheless, deprived of the chairmanship of the government in 1959. However, he did retain the Party chairmanship. Liu Shao-ch'i saved the economy by instituting more compromising and practical measures which brought about economic revival. But, years later, under Mao's personal initiative and leadership, a great cultural revolution was launched in 1966, in which Liu Shao-ch'i and his cohorts were charged with being revisionists and capitalist roaders. After three years of tumultuous and bloody struggles throughout the whole country, Mao triumphantly liquidated Liu and his cohorts in 1969.

Mao always paid special attention to ideology; he personally initiated and directed numerous ideological campaigns: in 1951 against the depiction of Wu Hsun as a proletarian hero, for his lack of class consciousness; in 1954 for the reevaluation from a Marxian viewpoint of the novel *Dream of the Red Chamber;* in 1955 against Hu Feng, a long-time communist writer, for his alleged anti-Party and antisocialist crimes; in the early 1970s against Confucius and Lin Piao; and in 1975 against the novel *Shui-hu chuan* (Water Margin). In 1975 a campaign was launched, in Mao's name, to study the Marxist theory of dictatorship with a new emphasis on establishing a total proletarian dictatorship and the elimination of bourgeois rights.

The T'ien-an Men incident occurred on 4 April 1975. Mao personally removed Teng Hsiao-p'ing, then the Vice-Premier of the State Council, and appointed Hua Kuo-feng as his successor. On 9 September 1976, Mao died in Peking at the age of 83.

Philosophical Foundation

On Practice

Mao needed a philosophical framework for his revolutionary theories. Being a revolutionary, he believed that a thorough preparation in ideology was requisite for anyone participating in a revolution.[3] His two famous treatises of

1937, "On Practice" and "On Contradiction," serve as the philosophical foundation for the Chinese revolution. They also serve to criticize the dogmatism which prevailed in the Party at that time. A consideration of the historical background in which the two essays were written is essential to understanding their contents. An important footnote to the article "On Practice" provides a partial explanation of how the article came to be written:

> There used to be a number of comrades in our Party who were dogmatists and who for a long period rejected the experience of the Chinese Revolution, denying the truth that "Marxism is not a dogma but a guide to action" and overawing people with words and phrases from Marxist works, torn out of context. There were also a number of comrades who were empiricists and who for a long period restricted themselves to their own fragmentary experience and did not understand the importance of theory for revolutionary practice or see the revolution as a whole, but worked blindly though industriously. The erroneous ideas of these two types of comrades, and particularly of the dogmatists, caused enormous losses to the Chinese revolution during 1931–34, and yet the dogmatists, cloaking themselves as Marxists, confused a great many comrades. "On Practice" was written in order to expose the subjectivist errors of dogmatism, from the standpoint of the Marxist theory of knowledge. It was entitled "On Practice" because its stress was on exposing the dogmatist kind of subjectivism, which belittles practice.[4]

Further background is provided in a *Jen-min jih-pao* editorial which describes how Mao repeatedly made the point that the reason why the opportunism of Ch'en Tu-hsiu had prevailed in the latter part of the first revolution (1924–1927) was because of the lack of ideological preparation among the majority of the Party members. The consequence was that the revolution failed to crush Chiang Kai-shek and Wang Ching-wei's counterrevolutionary attacks. In the latter part of the second revolution (1927–1936), again because of cadre inability to distinguish true Marxism from false Marxism, "left" opportunism was able to exert a wide influence that resulted in a serious setback to the revolution. Because of these two debacles, the editorial continues, Mao put greater effort and time into ideological work during the post-1935 period after he had led the Red Army to North Shensi and also in the initial period of the War of Resistance against Japan.[5] Mao's ideology was not just a purely philosophical approach independent of actual struggles; his goal was to bring the communist revolution to victory, and the way to reach that goal was to teach ideology and to practice ideology.

Mao's theory of practice is his version of Marx's dialectical theory of knowledge. We are not concerned here with the "correctness" of Mao's interpretation of Marx; rather, our only concern is in discussing the contents of Mao's interpretation and adaptation of Marxian theory, and Mao's application of it to the Chinese revolution. Mao's theory of practice is briefly summarized in the following five points based on his article "On Practice."

First, exponents of materialism prior to Marx failed to understand the relationship of the dependence of knowledge upon social production, that is, upon production and class struggle. This is because these early materialists

examined the problem of knowledge apart from man's social nature and his historical development. Marx wrote that man's productive activity is the most fundamental practical activity and is the determinant of all other activities. This is basically correct; human knowledge derives from material, productive activities. It is through productive activities that man gradually gains an understanding of nature's phenomena, nature's characteristics, nature's laws, and the relationships between man and nature. It is also through productive activities that man gradually understands, in varying degrees, certain relationships between men. The problem of the material life in a classless society is solved when man as an individual of society enters into certain relationships of production with others, just as he enters into certain relationships of production with others as a member of a class in a class society. However, man's social practice is not limited to productive activities, for his social activities include activities in the political and cultural life as well. Through social activities he acquires further knowledge concerning the relationships between man and man. It is within these social activities that various forms of class struggle exert a particularly profound influence upon man's knowledge. Since every person belongs to a particular class, every kind of thought is invariably stamped with the mark of a class.

Second, social practice alone is the criterion of the truth of man's knowledge. It is the objective results of social practice, rather than one's subjective feelings, that determine the truth of any knowledge or theory.

Third, the development of knowledge occurs in two stages: the perceptual stage of knowledge and the rational stage of knowledge. Perceptual knowledge is the understanding of the separate aspects, the phenomena and the external relationships of things. Rational knowledge, a step following perceptual knowledge, is the recognition of the totality, the essence, and the internal relationships of things. Rational knowledge is the ability to draw logical conclusions concerning the internal contradictions of the surrounding world. That is, with rational knowledge one can grasp the development of the surrounding world in its totality and perceive the internal relations between all its aspects.

Fourth, although perceptual knowledge and rational knowledge are different in nature, they both belong to the same single process of knowledge. There are two stages: a lower stage and a higher stage. Knowledge emerges in the lower stage, where it appears in its perceptual form and it is in a constant movement to the higher stage, where it appears in its rational form. The two stages are united on the basis of practice. The movement of perceptual knowledge to rational knowledge is a process whereby knowledge deepens. This development of stages from lower to higher, or from perceptual to rational, is basically the dialectics of the theory of knowledge.

Fifth, the Marxist theory of knowledge does not end with an understanding of the laws of the objective world and the consequent ability to explain that world. A further, more crucial goal is to change the world by actively applying the knowledge of its objective laws. An active application of knowledge to change the world is not merely a leap from perceptual knowledge to rational knowledge; it is, more importantly, the leap from rational knowledge to revolutionary practice. Thus, the struggle of the proletariat and revolutionaries to change the world entails the goal of reforming both their objective world and their subjective world, that is, to reform their faculty of knowing as well as to reform the relationship between the subjective and objective world. Mao's own summary of his theory of practice concludes:

> Discover the truth through practice, and again through practice verify and develop the truth. Start from perceptual knowledge and actively develop it into rational knowledge; then start from rational knowledge and actively guide revolutionary practice to change both the subjective and objective world. Practice, knowledge, again practice, and again knowledge. This form repeats itself in endless cycles, and with each cycle the content of practice and knowledge rises to a higher level. Such is the whole of the dialectical-materialistic theory of knowledge, and such is the dialectical-materialistic theory of the unity of knowing and doing.[6]

In addition to the five points summarized above, Mao emphasized several other points. First, in his repeated emphasis on the dichotomy between idealism and materialism, he explains in simple and concise terms that a person is an idealist if he thinks that rational knowledge need not be derived from perceptual knowledge. And, one is a materialist if he believes that knowledge starts with experience. This is the materialist aspect of the theory of practice.

Second, in addition to opposing idealism, Mao opposes mechanistic materialism, opportunism and adventurism for they are all characterized by the separation of knowledge from practice.

Third, Mao opposes both empiricism and dogmatism. Those who believe in empiricism emphasize perceptual knowledge only, while dogmatists emphasize only rational knowledge. Both groups are in error.

The sub-title to "On Practice," reads, "On the relation between knowledge and practice—between knowing and doing." The problem of knowing and doing has been a controversial problem in the history of Chinese philosophy. A traditional widespread belief, reaching back to the Shang dynasty, is the idea that it is not difficult to know but difficult to do.[7] Originally, the statement was made in regard to the administration of government policies, but, since ancient times, it has been extended to other aspects of human affairs in general, and in particular to ideal moral behavior. Centuries later, Wang Yang-ming, the Ming dynasty Neo-Confucianist, explained in his theory of the unity of knowing and doing that knowledge and practice are inseparable, and that knowing is at the same time an act of doing. Wang's theory was directed at achieving ideal moral behavior and had little to do with practical affairs. In modern times, Sun Yat-sen argued that it is easy to do but difficult to know. Sun's aim, unlike Wang Yang-ming's moral injunctions, was to rouse revolutionary fervor and confidence. His approach, which he called psychological construction, was to persuade fellow countrymen that once they understood and accepted his theory of revolution, they could easily carry it out. The Chinese people had to overcome the traditional belief that even when an ideal is clearly known, that ideal is difficult to realize. Once this belief was destroyed, Sun felt, he could then lead his followers to face fearlessly anticipated difficulties and to work with confidence to make China strong again. Mao's advocacy of the unity of knowing and doing, that is, the association of theory and practice is, as he puts it, the unity of knowing and doing dialectical materialism.

Traditionally, the ancient Chinese idea of knowing and doing is applied to individuals, generally in reference to moral realizations, but Mao has given this idea a social basis. For Mao, knowing primarily refers to theories of social reform and reconstruction while practice basically refers to production and class struggle. Mao aimed towards a revolution in his goals for reconstruction. By his standards, any theory that could successfully be put into practice for the purpose of revolution for social reconstruction is called truth. The notable characteristic of Mao's theory is his emphasis on actual action over theoretical principles. He believed a theory sterile if the truth could not be confirmed by practice. Most of the thinkers acounted for in this book, whose theories are sound in many ways, had not attained enough political power to be able to put their ideals into practice. Mao elevated practice to the first priority and he regarded practice as the standard of truth. For him, the goal of practice was to change the world, not merely to explain it. In Mao's eyes, practice is the essence of all philosophies. However, in his treatment, little attention has been given to purely abstract learning such as mathematics or to personal virtue such as filial piety, both of which would be difficult to master through productive practice. Thus, I would say that Mao's theory of practice is limited to the theory of practice for social reconstruction or revolution.

On Contradiction

Another of Mao's important treatises on Marxian philosophy is "On Contradiction." It deals with the basic law in materialist dialectics. His exposition is based on Lenin's interpretation of dialectics, who, in turn, took over the philosophy from Marx. Marx borrowed his dialectical philosophy from Hegel, but transformed it into materialist dialectics. For Marx, the material world is the ultimate reality, whereas for Hegel, the real world is something immaterial. Thus, Marx claimed to have found Hegel standing on his head and to have " set him the right way up." In this respect, Mao's view does not reflect any originality. To criticize Mao it is necessary first to criticize the dialectical materialism of Marx, which is beyond the scope of our studies. What we attempt to do here is to summarize some of the highlights of the theory of contradiction as Mao saw them and to explore the way Mao utilized this theory as a philosophical foundation on which his revolutionary theory could be built.

Mao began his article "On Contradiction" by saying that "The law of contradiction in things, that is, the law of the unity of opposites, is the most basic law in materialist dialectics." Immediately after this statement, he quoted Lenin as saying that "in its proper meaning, dialectics is the study of the contradiction within a very essence of things."[8] This is the general theme upon which Mao attempted to elaborate.

Mao proceeded to argue that, in the West as well as in China, there are two opposite world outlooks, metaphysical and dialectic. Again, he quoted Lenin as an authoritative support of his argument that the two basic conceptions of development (evolution) are: (1) development as decrease and increase, as repetition; and (2) development as a unity of opposites (the division of the one into mutually exclusive opposites and their reciprocal relation).[9] Mao then elaborated the historical background of these two outlooks. He argued that the metaphysical viewpoint is idealistic and occupied a dominant position in Europe until the time of Marx. In the early days of the bourgeoisie in Europe, materialism was also metaphysical. After the emergence of the materialist dialectics of Marx, besides the extremely reactionary idealism, there emerged the vulgar evolutionism which stood in opposition to materialist dialectics. In ancient China, the famous maxim of Tung Chung-shu, as quoted by Mao, that "heaven changes not, likewise the Way changes not," reflects an idealistic world outlook. In modern times, Darwin's theory of evolution has become popular and maintained a dominant position in the Chinese mind. However, Mao deplored vulgar evolutionism for it does not accept a leap in social development and is in opposition to materialist dialectics.

Now, let us see the difference between these outlooks as envisioned by Mao. For Mao "the so-called metaphysical world outlook or the world outlook of vulgar evolutionism consists in looking at the world from an isolated, static and one-sided viewpoint. It regards all things in the world, their forms and their species, as forever isolated from one another and forever changeless. Whatever change there is, means merely an increase or decrease in quantity or a transplacement in space. Moreover, the cause of such an increase or decrease or transplacement does not lie inside things, but outside them, that is, propulsion by external forces."[10] From the above quotation, it can be seen that, according to Mao, the characteristics of the outlook of metaphysics and vulgar evolutionism are that they view the world as static, without changes; and, whenever there is a change, it is minor rather than a leap, and is due to external rather than internal causes.

Further on, Mao expounded the contents of the outlook of materialist dialectics:

> Contrary to the metaphysical world outlooks, the materialist dialectical world outlook advocates the study of the development of things from the inside, from the relationship of a thing to other things, namely, that the development of things should be regarded as their internal and necessary self-movement, that a thing in its movement and the things around it should be regarded as interconnected and interacting upon each other. The basic cause of development of things does not lie outside but inside them, in their internal contradictions. The movement and development of things arise because of the presence of such contradictions inside all of them. This contradiction within a thing is the basic cause of its development, while the relationship of a thing with other things—their interconnection

and interaction—is a secondary cause. Thus, materialist dialectics forcefully combats the theory of external causes, or of propulsion, advanced by metaphysical mechanistic materialism and vulgar evolutionism.[11]

But what has this to do with the Chinese revolution? For Mao, the connection is obvious and important. Following directly the teachings of Lenin, Mao sees in dialectics the general laws of change, not only in society and in human thought, but also in the external world which is mirrored by human thought. Dialectics is the principle which controls everything in the world and contradiction is the motive force behind all development. Mao's article emphasizes mainly social development, with a view to supplying a theoretical foundation for the Chinese revolution. However, there are formidable obstacles to the concept of revolution in China. First, traditional Chinese thought conceived of the world as static, without seeing that the world is in continual change, let alone revolutionary change. It could only see that history repeats itself in dynastic cycles, but failed to see that it can develop dialectically to a higher stage.

Another traditional and influential concept serving as an obstacle to revolution is the concept of harmony. Confucianism values harmony between nature and man and among men; Taoism values not contending. There are a great number of people in modern times who believe that class struggle is merely a communist invention and that the different classes can coexist peacefully and harmoniously.

Second, those who have accepted the theory of evolution naturally accept the concept of change, but the change they believe in is a gradual change, leading to gradual socialism. Mao not only believes in change, but also drastic and swift change—a leap. Thus, he labeled the theory of evolution which refuses to accept a leap as vulgar evolutionism. In modern China, the most influential protagonist of evolution—"drop by drop" change was his favorite phrase—was Hu Shih. Hu and his sympathizers are the targets Mao attacked. In short, Mao wants to inculcate the concept that a revolution is inevitable because it is based on dialectics which is the law that governs the operation of the universe. To arouse the enthusiasm and confidence of his readers, Mao proclaims: "The supersession of the old by the new is the universal, forever inexorable law of the world. A thing transforms itself into something else according to its nature and the conditions under which it finds itself and through different forms of leap; that is, the process of the supersession of the old by the new. Everything contains a contradiction between its new aspect and its old aspect, which constitutes a series of intricate struggles. As a result of these struggles, the new aspect grows and rises and becomes dominant while the old aspect dwindles and gradually approaches extinction."[12]

Evidently, what Mao means by the old and the new can be applied to the Kuomintang and the Communist Party or the bourgeoisie and the proletariat. The new, though small, is fated to grow, replace the old, and occupy the dominant position. Thus, Mao concludes: "It is very important to know this situation. It enables us to understand that in a class society revolutions and revolutionary wars are inevitable, that apart from them the leap in social development cannot be made, the reactionary ruling classes cannot be overthrown, and the people cannot win political power."[13]

Mao's emphasis on the inevitability of the revolution and its victory is of great psychological significance. Since it is fated that social development is inevitably moving in the direction of the desired revolution, people are encouraged to join the revolution and fight for it dauntlessly, in spite of formidable difficulties, and feel assured of victory, for the laws of the universe are on their side.

Not only has Mao used the theory of contradiction as a theoretical foundation for his projected revolution, he has also extended the application of this theory to political conflicts and economic imbalances in the post-revolutionary period. Following Marx, Mao holds that the law of contradiction—the unity of opposites—prevails everywhere and at all times. For the unity and struggle of the contradictory phases of things propel the movement of things and the progress of society; however, the unity of opposites is only conditional, temporary, and transient, and the struggle is absolute and, therefore, permanent. Mao deems it unrealistic and naive to imagine that there will not be contradiction or struggle in a socialist society. There are people who dream and expect that with a socialist society the millennium will come. Actually, this is impossible. To guard against possible disillusionment with socialism and to arouse enthusiasm and courage in building up socialism, Mao clearly utilizes the theory of contradiction. The word "contradiction" has been used in such an extensive way that at times it becomes almost synonymous with problem or difficulty. For instance, a shortage of manpower in a construction project may be described as a contradiction between the supply and demand for labor. This interpretation provides people with a psychological preparation and even a comfort when difficulties are encountered. It thus buttresses their confidence in socialism.

Mao anticipated that after the initial establishment of socialism, the basic contradiction would still be between productive forces and production relations, and between superstructure and economic base. Generally, after certain contradictions of these types have been solved, new contradictions will emerge and require solution in their turn. Thus, an economic contradiction, through struggle, reaches a balance or the so-called temporary unity of contradictions; this balance or unity, after a period of time, is broken by a new contradiction, which requires the same process to reach another new balance or unity. This process goes on and on. Since this is dictated by the law of the universe, there is nothing to be alarmed about in new problems or difficulties.

Mao did not foresee a smooth and tranquil political development in the years to come. Unlike the Soviet line of thinking, Mao did not expect that the advent of socialism would bring the class struggle to a close. Mao contended that classes and class contradictions continue to exist even after the socialist transformation of the system of ownership has basically been completed. Class struggle between the proletariat and bourgeoisie will continue to be long, tortuous, and at times very acute. However, Mao regarded the contradictions which arise in a socialist society as being fundamentally different from those arising in a capitalist society. The contradictions in capitalist societies are characterized by class struggle of an antagonistic nature and can only be resolved by a socialist revolution. In the socialist stage in China, contradictions are divided into two kinds: the contradictions between the economy and ourselves, and the contradictions among the people. The former is antagonistic and the latter is nonantagonistic. The ways of handling them are, accordingly, different.[14] Since contradictions will continue to exist in the socialist stage, so political struggles even of an acute nature at times are not unexpected. This theory of Mao's, that classes and class contradictions continue to exist in a socialist society, constitutes the foundation for his other theory: continual revolution under the dictatorship of the proletariat.[15]

Chinese Social Structure and Revolution

Communists and noncommunists have their own unique ways of looking at past history and contemporary events, both national and international. Communist Chinese analysis of modern China differs from noncommunist Chinese analysis. Communist Chinese regard modern Chinese history from a Marxian point of view, that is, through an economic interpretation of history and the class approach. The following is a discussion of Mao's analysis of Chinese history and how he views the impact of recent Western influences.[16]

According to Mao, China had been a feudal society since the beginning of the Chou and Ch'in dynasties about three thousand years ago. But, after the Opium War of 1840, China became a semifeudal and semicolonial society, and after the Incident of 18 September 1931, when Japan seized Manchuria, China became a colonial society. The greatest changes in Chinese history occured during the middle of the nineteenth century when the foreign economic system of capitalism reached China. The impact of capitalism on Chinese society accelerated the change from a feudalistic to a capitalistic social structure, and the penetration of capitalism into China's social economy undermined the foundations of her self-sufficient natural economy and crippled the handicraft industries both in the cities and in peasant homes. It further promoted the growth of the commodity economy in urban and rural areas.

During the transformation from a feudal to capitalist economy, two distinct and antagonistic classes, which had never before existed, emerged: the bourgeoisie and the proletariat. The emergence of the proletariat coincided with the emergence of the bourgeoisie at the same time that imperialists had begun to control directly Chinese enterprises. The imperialists did not want a complete transformation of China into a capitalist country; rather, they preferred to mold her into a semicolony or a colony under their control. In fact, Mao continued, the imperialists colluded with local feudal forces to suppress the development of capitalism in China. In their attempt to suppress capitalism, the imperialists applied every kind of military, political and economic pressure on China, as manifest in the aggressions against China in the Wars of 1840, 1857, 1894 and 1900, or in the claims made against China under the unequal treaties as a result of these wars. Cultural pressures were also exerted, in the guise of missionary work, the operation of hospitals, schools, newspapers, and in the enticement of students to study abroad. These were all aggressive measures, Mao believed, designed to enslave and to dupe the Chinese masses for selfish imperialist purposes. [17] He further believed that since it was imperialist and Chinese feudal forces which turned China from a feudal society into a semifeudal society, and from an independent China into a semicolonial and colonial China, then the primary contradictions within modern Chinese society were the contradiction between feudalism and the Chinese masses. Imperialism, thus, was a major and formidable enemy. Contemporary Chinese revolutions grew out of these contradictions, Mao concluded.

Thus, the targets and main enemies of the Chinese revolution were imperialism and feudalism, and more specifically, the imperialist bourgeoisie and the Chinese landlord class. It would seem then that the Chinese revolution had two goals: (1) to overthrow foreign imperialism through a national revolution, and (2) to strike down feudal landlord oppression through a democratic revolution. The Chinese revolution necessarily had to be an armed revolution so it could fight against powerful imperialist and feudal landlord armed counterrevolution. The initial stage was to wage a guerrilla peasant war in order first to establish a strong military, economic and cultural base in the countryside prior to achieving the final conquest of cities and the complete victory for the revolution. But Mao said that due to the fact that the conditions in China were special, the nature of the Chinese revolution was special too: "the character of the Chinese revolution at the present stage is not proletarian-socialist but bourgeois-democratic."[18] But the bourgeois-democratic revolution he referred to was no longer the former and obsolete type of bourgeois-democratic revolution; rather, it was a new-democratic revolution, the nature of which will be discussed in the next section.

New Democracy

Toward the end of the War of Resistance against Japan and for several years thereafter, Mao's "On New Democracy" (1940) was the most influential of all his writings. It was also the critical article that helped to bring the sweeping victory of the Communist Party in 1949. In "On New Democracy," Mao stated that the direction and character of the Chinese revolution were determined by the nature of the Chinese social structure. Thus, because Chinese society was colonial, semicolonial and semifeudal, the direction which the Chinese revolution therefore had to follow was divided into two stages: the first stage of revolution was to transform China into an independent democratic society; the second stage was to continue the revolution to build a socialist society. The first stage covered the period from the Opium War in 1840 to the War of Resistance against Japan. Among all the struggles within this first stage, the 1911 Revolution was the most significant in the revolutionary sense because it was an antiimperialist and antifeudal struggle which sought to build an independent and democratic society. In terms of social character, the 1911 Revolution was a bourgeois democratic revolution.

Mao wrote further to divide the idea of a bourgeois democracy into two distinct categories and periods, an old bourgeois democracy and a new bourgeois democracy. The period of the old bourgeois democracy and the old bourgeois democratic revolution covered the time prior to World War I and the Soviet Union's 1917 October Revolution. The new bourgeois democracy and the new bourgeois democratic revolution were the phenomena of the time after World War I and the October Revolution. Thus, Mao's breakdown of old and new types put China's revolution in the category of new bourgeois democratic revolution and, furthermore, now made China's revolution a part of the proletarian-socialist world revolution. Mao wrote: "It is no longer a revolution of the old type led by the bourgeoisie with the aim of establishing a capitalist society and a state under bourgeois dictatorship, but rather a new revolution led by the proletariat with the aim, in the first stage, of establishing a new democratic society and a state under the joint dictatorship of all revolutionary classes."[19] Since Mao's analysis was based on a class approach, and since he saw dictatorship as the only viable form of government, it follows that he would regard the joint dictatorship of all classes as a form of joint government. The new bourgeois democratic revolution had to be led by the proletariat. This is because, Mao said, of the dual character of the Chinese bourgeoisie which has, on the one hand, the potential to participate in the revolution against a formidable enemy by allying with the workers and peasants, yet which, on the other hand, is also prone to ally with the enemy when the conciousness of the workers and peasants is awakened. Thus, in their fight against imperialism and feudalism, the two mortal enemies of the Chinese people, the bourgeoisie wavers between revolution and compromise. History has proven that the bourgeoisie cannot overthrow imperialism and feudalism, so therefore, Mao concluded, the responsibility must inevitably fall on the shoulders of the proletariat.[20]

The Politics of New Democracy

Mao combined theory with practical strategy in his attempt to gain Kuomintang support. At the same time, he tried to win the cooperation of those liberals who had a strong faith in democracy. The ideal state Mao wanted to establish was a New Democratic Republic that would be under the dictatorship of all antiimperialist and antifeudal people; these same people would be led by the proletariat. Mao linked his vision of the New Democratic Republic with three genuinely revolutionary cardinal policies: allying with the Soviet Union; including Communists in the Kuomintang Party; and aiding workers and peasants. Mao's New Democratic Republic differed from the old, and now obsolete, capitalist republic that was under the dictatorship of the bourgeoisie. It also differed from the socialist republic under the dictatorship of the proletariat, a form of government then developing in the Soviet Union and which would also develop, he predicted, in other capitalist and industrially advanced countries.[21]

Mao especially favored a passage contained in the Kuomintang *Manifesto* of the First National Congress held in 1924 during the period of the Kuomintang and Communist cooperation. This passage appears in "On New Democracy" and also in his "On the People's Democratic Dictatorship," published in 1949, and a number of other articles. The passage reads:

> The so-called democratic system in modern nations is usually monopolized by the bourgeoisie and has simply become an instrument for oppressing the common people. As to the Principle of Democracy of the Kuomintang, it stands for something to be shared by all the common people and not to be monopolized by a few.[22]

Mao's intent in quoting this passage was to suggest that the bourgeoisie should not monopolize the political power of the state and that political power should be open to all other revolutionary classes. The passage also served to meet the demands of the slogan, "To open the political power" (Kung-k'ai cheng-ch'üan), which was espoused by the democratic people of the minor political parties. The intent here was to suggest an end to the one-party dictatorship of the Kuomintang. Thus, Mao outlined two distinct features concerning the politics of New Democracy: the state system, which was to be a dictatorship of all revolutionary classes, and the political system, which was to be democratic centralism.[23]

The Economy of New Democracy

In the economic aspects of the New Democracy, Mao did not make any new points; rather, he chose to follow the two basic principles of Sun Yat-sen's Principle of People's Livelihood: the regulation of capital and the equalization of land ownership.[24] However, Mao did add an extra element here by construing Sun's slogan of "land to the tillers" to mean the state confiscation and distribution of land to peasants who owned little or no land, whereas Sun had only proposed either land tax or government purchase of land as a measure of equalization. Mao felt that the economy of the New Democracy must not follow either the European-American pattern of capitalism or the old Chinese semi-feudal economic structure. Rather, the New Democracy had to establish an economy which incorporated basic socialist elements founded on the two economic principles of Sun Yat-sen.

The Culture of New Democracy

Echoing Marx and Lenin, Mao defined a given culture as the ideological reflection of the politics and economy of a given society; at the same time, that culture in turn exerts a tremendous influence upon the politics and economy of the given society.[25] Mao states that because traditional China was dominated by feudalism, naturally its politics, economy and culture were all essentially feudal. But, with the entry of capitalism into China and with the growth of capitalist elements in Chinese society, China gradually became a colonial, semicolonial, and semifeudal society. Thus, China's politics, economy and culture were all now of a colonial, semicolonial and semifeudal nature. The struggle in culture, Mao said, like the political struggle, had lasted approximately one hundred years beginning with the Opium War to the time when "On New Democracy" was written in 1940. The century-long struggle in culture is divided into two periods, marked off by the May Fourth Movement of 1919. Mao referred to these two periods as "the first eighty years" and "the last twenty years." In political terms, the first eighty years belonged to the old category of bourgeois-democratic revolution and the last twenty years to the category of the New Democracy. In cultural terms, the eighty-year period prior to the May Fourth Movement was the struggle between the new culture of the bourgeoisie and the old culture of the feudal class. During the twenty years after the May Fourth Movement, a new force emerged, namely the communist cultural ideology guided by the Communist Party, that is, the communist world view and the theory of world revolution. In other words, the new culture of China before the May Fourth Movement was led by the bourgeoisie, was characterized by the old democracy, and was part of the capitalist cultural revolution of the world bourgeoisie. After the May Fourth Movement, the new culture of China was led by the proletariat, was characterized by new democracy, and was part of the socialist cultural revolution of the world proletariat. Mao concluded that "New Democratic Culture is, in a word, the anti-imperialist, anti-feudal culture of the broad masses of the people under the leadership of the proletariat."[26]

Three Characteristics of the New Culture

The New Democratic Culture, according to Mao, had three characteristics: it was nationalistic, scientific, and of the masses. The New Democratic Culture was nationalistic in the sense that "it opposes imperialist suppression and upholds the dignity and independence of the Chinese nation."[27] Although it rejected the idea of accepting total Westernization, the New Democratic Culture would nevertheless assimilate beneficial elements of foreign cultures. In the case of Marxism, the New Democratic Culture advocated a unity of the universal truth of Marxism and the concrete practice of the Chinese revolution. I would presume this was the so-called sinification of Marxism, where Marxism was given a definite nationalistic form.

The New Democratic Culture was also scientific: "It is opposed to all feudal and superstitious ideas and it stands for the objective truth and for the unity between theory and practice."[28] It was obvious to Mao that superstitious beliefs were unscientific. He thought it was also unscientific to accept the ancient Chinese culture indiscriminately, to eulogize the ancient and disparage the present, or to extol feudal elements. But he did feel it was scientific to reject the feudal elements of the ancient Chinese culture and to absorb its democratic and revolutionary aspects.

The New Democratic Culture was also of the broad masses and thus was democratic; it opposed elitism. "It should serve the toiling masses of workers and peasants who account for more than 90 percent of the entire population, and gradually become their culture."[29]

Significance of New Democracy

The significance of Mao's "On New Democracy" was not so much as theoretical analysis as strategy of winning over the support and cooperation of the group of people known as the democrats or the democratic people, namely, liberal Kuomintang members, small political party activists, and the great majority of independent liberals and intellectuals. Mao's strategy was, first, to offer a new interpretation of Sun Yat-sen's Three Principles of the People by bringing into prominence its socialist and progressive features and identifying them with communist programs at a certain stage. Mao announced: "It is only such Three Principles of the People that the Chinese Communist Party describes as 'being what China needs today,' and declares itself 'pledged to fight for their complete realization.' It is only such Three Principles of the People that basically agree with the Communist Party's political program for the stage of democratic revolution, that is, its minimum program."[30] Mao's new interpretation and announcement altered the democrats' original image of the Communists. With a changed image in mind, the democrats now believed that no irreconcilable ideological conflicts existed between the two major parties, Kuomintang and Communist, at least for the immediate future.

Mao's second step in his strategy to win over the democrats was to trace the Chinese democratic movement from 1840 to 1940 as one continuous movement. He attached the Communist movement after 1921 to the general democratic movement of the past one hundred years as a stage which he called the New Democracy. This linkage created the general impression and belief that the Kuomintang and the Communist parties were practically like one single party that had worked together, at least in the initial period, toward the same goal. A further image was that the Communists and the general public in favor of democracy were all members of one political family. Of course, there were some who were apprehensive of the temporary nature of the Kuomintang and Communist cooperation and who foresaw a split at the time when the Communists would begin to enter the second stage, that is, socialism or communism. But Mao made it explicitly clear that "we Communists will from start to finish persist in long-term cooperation with all true followers of the Three Principles of the People."[31] There were also those who were apprehensive of the practice of the dictatorship of the proletariat once the Communists were in power. To this fear, Mao answered that throughout the entire new democratic period, there cannot be and should not be a political system of one-class dictatorship or one-party monopoly; and for a long time to come, there will exist in China a political system characterized by an alliance of several democratic classes.[32] With these assurances from Mao, a part of the Kuomintang members and the members of the minor parties felt it safe to cooperate with the Communists. Most of the democratic people held an optimistic hope that the New Democratic stage would last for a fairly long time. As it turned out, however, the period of New Democracy was short-lived and was terminated as soon as the People's Republic was inaugurated in 1949. The establishment of the People's Republic also officially marked the beginning of the socialist stage.

Mao's campaign was actually a psychological war to win over the popular conscience of the people. In the minds of the democrats, the Communists had become the most effective instrument in bringing about democracy because they had the military strength to bargain with the Kuomintang, whereas the Kuomintang, the democrats felt, had disillusioned the people by paying mere lip service to democracy. Once the liberal progressive elements, the democrats, sided overwhelmingly with the Communists, the fall of the Kuomintang government was inevitable. Hu Shih's prediction had come true that "on the day when the sympathy of the progressive thinking groups is completely lost, that will be the time of the burning up of both the oil and the wick of the Kuomintang."[33]

Mao's Political Thinking

Mao never dwelt exclusively on the subject of political thinking in one specific treatise to the extent that he did in "On New Democracy," "On Practice" or "On Contradiction." In order to furnish a more complete picture of his political thinking, it is necessary to pull together statements he made over time, either in theory or in practice.

If we were to identify one central principle in relation to a political system that runs through Mao's political thinking at different times, it would be democratic centralism. Of course, this idea is not original with Mao. The political system which the Chinese Communist Party and government adopted is Leninist democratic centralism. With respect to the party system, Mao said in 1937 that to lead a great revolution, it is necessary to have a great party and many excellent cadres; and that to make our Party powerful, we must rely on practicing democratic centralism in the Party to arouse the activism of the whole Party.[34] Mao also had suggested in 1940 in his "On New Democracy" that the form of government in the new democratic period should be democratic centralism. In actual operation, this system is closely related to the *mass line*. The mass line consists of two aspects: coming from and going back to the masses. Mao first expounded this in 1943 when discussing the method of Party leadership. In a resolution on methods of leadership written by Mao for the Central Committee of the Communist Party, Mao explained the mass line as follows:

> In all the practical work of our party, all correct leadership is necessarily "from the masses, to the masses." This means: take the ideas of the masses (scattered and unsystematic ideas) and concentrate them (through study turn them into

concentrated and systematic ideas), then go to the masses and propagate and explain these ideas until the masses embrace them as their own, hold fast to them and translate them into action, and test the correctness of these ideas in such action. Then, once again, concentrate ideas from the masses and once again go to the masses so that the ideas are persevered in and carried through. And so on, over and over again, in an endless spiral, with the ideas becoming more correct, more vital and richer each time. This is the Marxist theory of knowledge.[35]

The mass line seems to respect the opinions of the masses, but actually this line, as Liu Shao-ch'i put it, is the class line, or the mass line of the proletariat. Liu was still in power when he made this qualification, which has not been repudiated by the authorities and is, presumably, still accepted.

Liu stressed that the masses must have their vanguards—the Communist Party—that their thorough emancipation may be possible. Otherwise, the revolution would have no leadership and would fail. The Chinese people's thorough emancipation cannot be achieved unless they struggle under the firm and correct leadership of the Communist Party, and in the political direction pointed out by the Party.[36] Thus, the mass line is, in one important sense, a line mapped out and directed by the Communist Party. Evidently, Liu's view had Mao's endorsement, for there is no evidence that the two were in ideological conflict at that time.

In sum, the mass line is not only regarded as the basic political line of the Party, but is also the organizational line of the Party. Both the political line and the organizational line are based on the principle of democratic centralism. The principle of democratic centralism has been provided in the Constitutions of the Communist Party, e.g., the version which was adopted in 1973.

Democratic centralism is also the guiding political principle practiced in the government and among the people. The 1978 version of the Constitution of the People's Republic explicitly states that the National People's Congress, the local people's congresses at various levels, and all other organs of state practice democratic centralism. In his blueprint of China's political system, Mao proclaimed in 1949 that the People's Republic of China is a people's democratic dictatorship. "People" was then defined as consisting of the working class, the peasant class, the petite bourgeoisie, and the national bourgeoisie. These classes, under the leadership of the working class and the Communist Party, unite to organize their state and elect their own government and exercise dictatorship over the running dogs of the imperialists, i.e., the landlord class and bureaucratic capitalist class, and Kuomintang reactionaries and their accomplices representing these classes. Among the people, democratic rights are to be enjoyed, freedom of speech, assembly, association, etc., which are denied to the reactionaries. The combination of these two aspects—the practice of democracy among the people and the dictatorship over the reactionaries—is called the people's democratic dictatorship.[37]

In 1957, in his famous article "On the Problem of Correct Handling of Contradictions Among the People," Mao pointed out that, among the people, democratic centralism is practiced, indicating that democratic centralism and

246

democratic dictatorship are somewhat parallel or even analogous. For, one can discern a parallel in the discipline required of the reactionaries in their practice of dictatorship. In expounding on the Constitution of China, which provides that the organs of the state must practice democratic centralism and that the people enjoy civil rights, which Mao defined as the rights of freedom and democracy, he explained that this freedom is freedom with leadership and this democracy is democracy under centralized guidance, not anarchy, He further stated that both democracy and freedom are relative, not absolute; that among the people, democracy is relative to centralism and freedom to discipline; that they are two opposites of a single entity; that among the people we cannot do without freedom, nor can we do without discipline; we cannot do without democracy, nor can we do without centralism. This unity of democracy and centralism, of freedom and discipline, constitutes democratic centralism. Mao concluded that under this system, the people enjoy extensive democracy and freedom, but at the same time they have to keep within the bounds of socialist discipline.[38]

Democratic centralism theoretically means a system which combines democracy and centralism. But, in actual practice, the system depends on where the emphasis is laid, on democracy or on centralism. First, Mao's promise to give the people freedom of speech, assembly, association and so on seems to be cancelled by his other statements. Mao said that the people enforce dictatorship over the reactionaries, suppress them, allow them only to behave well, and not to be unruly in word or deed; if they speak or act in an unruly way, they will be promptly stopped and punished.[39] Also, he asserted that after the elimination of the landlord class and the bureaucratic class, the only exploiting class remaining is the national bourgeoisie. The national bourgeoisie cannot provide leadership but it can be used for national construction; because the people possess a powerful state apparatus, they are not afraid of rebellion by the national bourgeoisie.[40] The threat of using a powerful state apparatus to suppress the national bourgeoisie is a threat to all other people who may deviate from the official line in thought or act. Under these circumstances, the democratic rights of freedom of speech, etc., are nothing more than a piece of paper, tantamount to no democracy at all, while the all-powerful government exercises without restraint the authority of discipline.

Second, the words *people,* and, its opposite, *reactionary,* are flexible. The reactionaries against which the people's democratic dictatorship was to be exercised originally were interpreted as the running dogs of the imperialists, i.e., the landlord class and bureaucratic capitalist class, and Kuomintang reactionaries and their accomplices representing these classes. However, Mao later shifted the meaning of the term reactionary from reference to specific individuals to a vague political outlook, such that anyone could be called reactionary and be deprived of the right to be considered people if he deviated from the official line. Even Liu Shao-ch'i, a lifelong Communist, was suddenly called all these names. As a result of these accusations, he no longer was a member of the people, but had become an enemy of the people and was treated accordingly. He was tortured to death in 1969. From the above quotations, it is evident that Mao did not intend to tolerate anyone who would think, speak, or act differently from the official line. Obviously, dissent—a characteristic of the democratic form of government—is not allowed.

Third, Mao seems to stress centralism at the expense of democracy, though, on the surface, he puts democracy and centralism on the same footing. In criticizing the danger of extreme democracy, Mao condemned the proposals to carry out in the Red Army "democratic centralism from the bottom to the top" or "ask the lower levels to discuss first, then let the higher levels decide" as an incorrect or erroneous idea. Mao saw this kind of thinking as detrimental to the Party and the revolution, and as growing out of the petit bourgeois aversion to discipline which is incompatible with the fighting tasks of the proletariat.[41] I wonder if these ideas agree with the principle of coming from the masses, or with the principle of democratic centralism. His position here is at odds with his principle of democratic centralism and would make free discussion from the bottom impossible.

In defense of Mao, one might argue that generally democracy is not practiced in any army. However, the emphasis on centralism is not limited to the army sector. The line of demarcation between democracy and extreme democracy is hard to draw. Being against extreme democracy can frequently be used as an excuse, even as a weapon, to suppress democracy. This attitude of Mao reflects clearly his favoring centralism over democracy, with damaging consequences to the latter.

The value of democratic centralism is to be judged by the extent to which the masses enjoy democratic rights. On this question, I quote the reflections of a scientist who lived and studied in the West and returned to China, but left disillusioned. These observations reflect the eyewitness reactions and personal experiences of one staying in China, rather than an abstract judgment of an outsider.

> Democracy always involves a distrust of the Government, hence power is kept in the hands of the people to check or replace it; but in "democratic centralism," which the Communist government in China is called, trust in the Government is taken for granted and the public, though nominally the master of the nation, is actually left helpless under the political machine. "Centralism" refers to the right to joint predetermined elections and to pass upward "well-meant suggestions within the limits of socialist ideals and Marxist-Leninist methods."[42]

> "Democratic centralism" is described as a form of government "from the people and to the people." Theoretically, this means that the motive force of the Government comes from the people and the benefits of the policies go back to them, the idea being that only what the people want can ever be carried out and that is the "correct" line; but the catch is: all this happens under the leadership of the Communist Party in whose eyes the people are wards as well as potential enemies. Actually, "to the people" means the extension of the control apparatus to them and "from the people" means the measurement, through the control system, of their reaction in order to determine how far the Government can go in putting pressure on them.[43]

In the previous section, we have discussed Mao's idea of the politics of New Democracy. As we have explained before, the purpose of New Democracy is to contract alliances with other small political parties and those portions of the general public which favor democracy. The Chinese reconstruction movement since the time of K'ang and Liang has pursued the democratic line as the mainstream. Though during the heyday of the German and Italian dictatorships, a minority of Chinese were attracted to dictatorship, the inclination was ephemeral and subsided when the Axis was formed, one of whose member states was Japan, the aggressor against China. The German and Italian dictatorships evoked a sense of fear and hostility; British and American democracy evoked sentiments of hope and friendship. During the last years of the War of Resistance the small parties representing the Western democratic tradition were unprecedentedly vigorous in pressing for a democratization of political life, including the abolition of the one-party dictatorship, and came to rely on the Communists who, unlike themselves, had the military force to compel the Kuomintang to negotiate seriously. The minority parties were convinced that the Communist Party championed the cause of democracy for which they had fought unsuccessfully in the past. In his treatise on New Democracy, Mao simply mentioned, in passing, that the form of government of the parties would be democratic centralism without any elaboration. At that time, few people seriously studied or understood the exact connotations of the term, and very few people even bothered to determine its meaning. Mao proclaimed the New Democracy period as beginning from the year 1919 and he promised it would be practiced indefinitely. The minority parties took him at his word, believing it would be so. However, the so-called New Democracy period was officially terminated in 1949, when the People's Republic was established. With the advent and practice of the democratic dictatorship of Mao, the high hopes and dreams of the minor parties for the New Democracy were shattered.

On the negative side, the most conspicuous feature of Mao's political thinking was his apparent aversion to Western parliamentary democracy. Let us analyze this attitude of his under the following points:

Individual Freedom

Individual freedom, an essential element of democracy, has been a goal for which the Chinese democratic movement has fought for the last one hundred years. With respect to this point, Mao wrote an important article entitled "Combat Liberalism" in 1937. Liberalism has different connotations at different times. For instance, it has stood for less government in the eighteenth century, and for more government in recent times. Its essential feature to Chinese minds is individual political freedom tending in the direction of democracy. The Chinese would link democracy and freedom together almost as a single phrase, tending to identify democracy with liberalism. However, Mao has a different understanding of the term, condemning it from a different angle. In his article, he cited eleven types of concrete manifestations of liberalism to be rejected. For instance, one who disobeys orders of the Party and places his personal opinion above everything else, or one who makes no attempt to rectify his mistakes, but adopts a liberal attitude, etc.[44] All the features Mao attributed to liberalism are indeed bad ones, but it is unlikely that a self-styled liberal would cherish them more than Mao would. Mao's characterization of liberalism is valuable for what it tells us about Mao's views rather than what it tells us about liberalism.

Mao asserted that the Communist Party should pursue active thought struggle, which is a weapon for achieving solidarity within the Party and the revolutionary organizations; but liberalism negates thought struggle, and advocates unprincipled peace. Here the word *peace* evidently suggests the opposite of a struggle, though Mao did not define it. Here Mao obviously recognized only one correct line of thinking and denied any other line which might deviate from Marxism. So Mao held that Marxism and liberalism are fundamentally contradictory to each other. Starting from the demand for uniformity in thought, he further advocated uniformity in action. Thus, he insisted that at all times and under all circumstances one should maintain loyalty to correct principle, and wage a tireless struggle against incorrect thoughts and actions. Furthermore, Mao held that a Communist should view the interests of the revolution as his very life to which his personal interests should be subordinated.[45] Revolution is an abstract term. In actuality, what Mao demanded was the subordination of individuals to the Party, which amounted to their subordination to the people controlling the Party.

In the West, two very different conceptions of human life are struggling for the mastery of the world. In the democratic countries, individualism has been stressed. Individuals are not supposed to be all alike, and their individuality and independence are respected. The Marxian view, as exemplified in the Soviet Union or in China, stresses the greatness of the Communist Party and the state, to whose wishes the individuals are collectively subject to conform. Before the Moloch state power, individual dignity counts for nothing. This view is fundamentally opposed to individualism.

In the name of combatting what he deemed the unwholesome aspects of liberalism, Mao actually suppressed true liberalism in its sense of free thought, free expression, and individualistic action. Mao said before the second plenum of the Eighth Party Congress that certain high ranking intellectual cadres sought to practice "greater democracy," by which they meant the adoption of Western bourgeois parliamentary system, Western parliamentary democracy, freedom of the press, freedom of speech, etc.; but that all these advocacies, which lack the Marxist and class points of view, are erroneous.[46]

Freedom of speech or freedom of thought never entered Mao's mind as political virtues to be cherished. For instance, the movement to "let a hundred schools of thought contend and a hundred flowers bloom" in 1957 did not aim at the realization of freedom of speech or thinking for the people at all. The motive was to induce the people to divulge opinions hidden in their hearts which they had not dared to express openly. The Chinese people, especially intellectuals, were encouraged to contend and bloom freely and were promised that no punitive measures would be taken no matter what one might say. But, when they had expressed their criticisms openly, when the vast reservoir of discontent, anger, and hatred against the government which had been built up exploded, they were immediately labeled as rightist reactionaries and punished. To use Mao's words, this was "to establish the opposites," i.e., a target of attack. Mao said that "we" determined to carry out the great contending and blooming in order to set free the rightists to serve as opposites, and then to mobilize the laboring people to rise up and argue against them, oppose them, and finally bring them down. He also asserted that the establishment of opposites is very important in dealing with rightists and that giving them free rein and freedom of speech was planned so that their position as opposites might be brought into prominence.[47] According to Mao's explanation, the Hundred Flowers movement was nothing but a preconceived plan to trap the opposition.

In this connection, incidentally, Mao coined a phrase which has gained currency since the Cultural Revolution—*yang-mou*. Traditionally, *yin-mou* (conspiracy) means to plan together secretly evil or illegal activities. The new term, *yang-mou*, means to conspire openly, publicly, and even officially, i.e., "open conspiracy." The reference was originally made to the practice of getting people to voice their grievances and then "fixing" them. Clearly, this violates both the principle of human decency and human rights.

Burning of Books

In an informal talk, Mao applauded Ch'in Shih Huang-ti as an expert at respecting the present and belittling the ancient, because he held that one who uses the ancient to deny the present shall be punished not only by his own death but by the death of his parents, his wife, and children as well. Lin Piao interrupted, pointing to the fact that Ch'in Shih Huang-ti burned books and buried scholars alive, to which Mao responded as follows: "What did Ch'in Shih Huang-ti amount to? He only buried alive 460 scholars, while we buried alive 46,000 scholars. In suppressing counter-revolutionaries, did we not kill some counter-revolutionary intellectuals? I argued with the democratic people that it is a mistake for you to accuse us of being like Ch'in Shih Huang-ti; we have surpassed Ch'in Shih Huang-ti a hundred times. When you berate us for acting like Ch'in Shih Huang-ti, like a dictator, we admit it all. The pity is you don't say enough. We have often had to supplement (great laughter)."[48]

The conversation above indicates Mao's evaluation of the Ch'in emperor. Prior to the recent glorification of Ch'in Shih Huang-ti in mainland China, Chinese intellectuals through the centuries had invariably condemned the burning of the books and burying alive of the scholars as the worst atrocities in Chinese history.

Now let us see how the official Communist line appraised Ch'in Shih Huang-ti and his burning of books and burying alive of scholars. He was portrayed as a distinguished statesman who first unified China; during the great period of change in Chinese history when the slave system was replaced by feudalism, he supported reforms, resolutely attacked the forces seeking a restoration of the slave system, and established the first unified feudal dynasty, and thus played an important role in propelling Chinese history forward.[49]

The burning of books and burying alive of scholars are defended on the grounds that "the burning of books aimed not at the destruction of civilization, but at the unification of thought" (a quotation from Lu Hsun whom the Communist government esteems very highly), and that certain books, such as books on medicine, divination and forestry were not burned, proving that the books burned were not many. The burying of scholars alive aimed at attacking the opposition faction who advocated restoration of the ancient system, not at killing all scholars.[50] It is further argued that the burning of books and the burying alive of scholars were part of a political struggle being waged by the landlord class that had newly won political predominance against the slave-holding aristocrats, who had been swept from the political stage and were conspiring to effect a restoration of their class. The Ch'in emperor is seen as daring to take these steps to shatter this conspiracy of the restorationists, and to uphold the rule of the new feudalism, and hence these are seen as progressive measures which promoted the principle of respecting the present and belittling the ancient. These acts are considered to have been completely necessary at that time.[51] On the whole, they are considered as having a great deal to do with the consolidation and unity of the feudal state and the strengthening of the feudal and aristocratic centralization of power.[52]

It is to be noted that the word feudalism as used above is in accordance with the Marxian theory that feudalism follows the slavery system in human history. This is thus an attempt to force Chinese society into the Procrustean bed of the schema: primitive communism—slavery—feudalism—capitalism—communism. According to traditional history books, it is the Ch'in dynasty that abolished the feudal system and initiated the "Commandery system" (chün-hsien chih). Levenson and Schurmann have noted their disapproval of periodizing Chinese history in conformity with Marxist theory. They say: "The Marxist view is unacceptable to most Western scholars because it squeezes the particulars of history into a rigid developmental scheme. The rigidity of the scheme reflects the classic error of the doctrinaire: the bending of particulars to conform with one's own universals."[53]

The official line on periodization conforms to the view of Kuo Mo-jo, who said that, in its development, Chinese society had passed through primitive communism, a slave system, and feudalism in complete accord with the stages of social development as delineated by Marxism. He held that the displacement of the slave system by the feudal system occurred during the time of transition from the Spring and Autumn Period to the Warring States Period and that the Ch'in dynasty was most successful in completing this transformation and in establishing an extensive feudalism under centralized authority.[54] The term "chün-hsien" is also mentioned in the article laying out the official Marxist line, but the author in one way or another tries to obscure this point by describing the Ch'in dynasty as practicing feudalism. The problem of feudalism in Chinese history, its nature and its period of genesis and breakdown, is a very controversial one, which we cannot explore fully at this point. It suffices to point out that the feudalism of the Ch'in dynasty as seen by the official line is characterized by autocratic centralization of power in the hands of the emperor. Ch'in Shih Huang-ti was commended for his success in accomplishing this. In addition to his various reforms, his attack on the restoration forces, and his advocacy of the principle of respecting the present and slighting the ancient, all the characteristics mentioned above have the endorsement of the Communist government. Judged by the principle "make use of the ancient for the present," at least one thing is sure: the reevaluation and glorification of Ch'in Shih Huang-ti does not show any fondness for democracy.

The aim of the glorification of Ch'in Shih Huang-ti and its related campaign to elevate the Legalists and downgrade the Confucianists was to promote and to strengthen the concentration of power in the central government. It is common knowledge that a reference to Ch'in Shih Huang-ti of ancient times was an allusion to Mao of present times. This movement, like much else, has been attributed to the Gang of Four. One interesting statistic shows how intensive and extensive the efforts were to promote the idea of centralization of power. According to the publishing departments of the Communist government, in the years from 1973 to 1976, 9,070 books, each title running from the hundreds of thousands to one million copies, and over 5,000 articles were published, consuming an amount of paper totalling 40,000 tons.[55]

Elections

Another essential element of democracy is elections, in which Mao showed no trust at all. In a talk before the Albanian Military Delegation on 1 May 1967, Mao had this to say: "Some people say that elections are very good, and very democratic. But as I see it, elections are so much fine-sounding rhetoric and I don't recognize that there is any true election. I was elected as the people's representative of Peking, but how few in Peking truly understand me. I hold that Premier Chou was appointed by the Central Committee."[56]

Mao was not in favor of the American presidential election every four years, nor its freedom of the press, regarding them as drawbacks of democratic countries.[57]

In Mao's interview with France's President Pompidou, Mao praised Napoleon because he dissolved all parliaments and worked with the persons he appointed to manage state affairs. Mao went on to argue that China in the past had tried to have some kind of parliament; it was only afterward that she realized how much money the election of a parliament would cost. In the U.S. an election costs tens of millions of dollars. Moreover, Mao said that he was at a loss to say why de Gaulle wanted to have a universal vote just for some minor problems.[58] Bertrand Russell once remarked that "Stalin could neither understand nor respect the point of view which led Churchill to allow himself to be peaceably deposed as a result of a popular vote." I believe Mao would share the same feeling.[59] This is probably why Mao lamented and was puzzled that

Nixon, whom he regarded as a great president, could be toppled by forces that began with newspaper attacks.

Though Mao occasionally spoke of the importance of democracy, what he meant by democracy is not that the powers of the government are to be derived from the consent of the people as stated in the American Declaration of Independence. Nor did he respect the freedom of speech, of thought and of popular election of government representatives as practiced in the West. At most, the democracy allowed to the Chinese people is the discussion or suggestion of details as to how to carry out a policy which has been decided by Party organizations or government units. Mao's often quoted statement concerning his ideal democracy is: "It is necessary to create a political situation in which there are both centralism and democracy, both discipline and freedom, both unity of will and personal ease of mind and liveliness."[60] But when centralization is emphasized, as is usually the case, freedom and democracy tend to be stifled; and when thought control and struggle constantly prevail, the springs of life and happiness tend to dry up. We are convinced that Mao did not believe in Western or parliamentary democracy at all. As Edmund Wilson put it, "The government which Marx imagined for the welfare and elevation of mankind—though he sometimes speaks of democratic institutions inside the new dominant class—was an exclusive and relentless class despotism directed by highminded bigwigs who had been able to rise above the classes, such as Engels and himself."[61] I believe the same thing can be said of Mao, just by substituting Mao for the names of Marx and Engels.

Mao's Economic Thinking

Mao did not say much about pure economic thought, though he talked a great deal on economic policies. Rather, he emphasized political thought for he maintained that political work is the lifeline of all economic work.[62] Thus, economics serves politics; politics should take command. The political aim of China, then, was to carry out the socialist revolution and socialist construction within, and to support the world revolution without. Economic policy was to be coordinated with this political goal. The national economy was to be developed in a planned and proportionate way, through state planning and leadership. This practice is regarded as characteristic of socialism and as an important indication of the superiority of socialism over capitalism. In making plans, the highest goal is for the good of the proletariat.

Mao's idea may be clarified by contrasting it with an opposite idea, which became one of the main targets of the Cultural Revolution. Liu Shao-ch'i allegedly maintained that economic affairs should be managed by economic methods and that for the state and Party to lead economic development is to use "supra-economic methods."[63] The main target under fire in the economic realm was Sun Yeh-fang, a prominent economist and at one time the director of the Institute of Economics of the Academy of Sciences, who was supposedly the brains behind Liu's economic ideas.

Sun was accused of attempting to use his "black line" to replace Chairman Mao's "red line" with respect to the political economy. The "red line" consisted of the following contentions: a very great advancement in Marxism-Leninism was made by Mao in his assertion of the existence, within the stage of socialism, of class struggle between the bourgeoisie and the proletariat, of struggle between the two roads of capitalism and socialism, and of contradictions between both the enemy and ourselves, and among the people. Mao's theory of contradictions, classes and class struggle in a socialist society is the "red line" pervading the entire socialist revolution and construction. It is also the "red line" that is to be followed in the study of political economy. Sun asserted, on the other hand, that the most serious contradiction in a socialist economy is the contradiction between man and matter, between labor and product, and between value and use-value. Moreover, Sun's "black line" in the study of political economy, in a socialist economy, would be a policy of " using the least labor to obtain the greatest useful effects."[64]

Sun Yeh-fang maintained that the law of value is the basic economic law in a capitalist society as well as in a socialist society. According to his interpretation, in a socialist society this law consists of the relation between socially necessary labor and useful effects, in other words, the use of the least cost to create the greatest use-value. Thus, he advocated that all planning and statistical work of the national economy should be put on the basis of the law of value. The indicator for value to be used is profit. The state, therefore, should "grasp" one target only—profit, and leave the method of achieving that profit to the individual. Sun is said to have likened the relationship between profit and the entire economy to the relation between the ox's nose and the ox. When you pull a string attached to the nose, the ox (the entire economy) will follow; but the multitudinous planning targets set forth by the government are likened to the stupid method of moving the cow by lifting its legs. Sun advocated that profit be used as the key to determine how much of a product is being produced, which enterprises are to be developed and which sectors of the economy are to receive investment.[65] Sun's desire to dispense with state planning and to utilize profit as the adjustment mechanism was evidently contrary to Mao's theory that the characteristics of socialist economy constitute the planned and proportionate development of the national economy.

What would have happened if Sun's economics had prevailed? The Maoists argued that had the law of value been adopted as the foundation for planning, the unproductive national defense industry, heavy industries, inland industries and industries supporting agriculture, whose products were low priced and temporarily less profitable, would not have been developed. Further, they asserted that a locality or a province would not have been able to develop industries in accordance with its local conditions and with a view to preparing for war. (To prepare for war, for famine and for the people, are the three main aims of the national strategic policy set forth by Mao.) The state would have neither provided subsidies to develop production of the people's daily necessities, nor produced the necessary products for the support of the struggles of the revolutionary people of the world based on the international proletarian spirit. All this indicates not that the Maoists do not want efficiency or profit, but that they are determined that political necessity will reign supreme, even at the cost of economic loss. The Maoists thus stressed that if Sun's principles had prevailed, the great task of socialist construction would have had to have been discarded and the revolution would have deviated from the course mapped out by Mao.[66] These two views indicate clearly the antagonism between Mao's economic thinking and the so-called revisionist line on economics. Though the concept of profit in a socialist state as advocated by Sun was denounced during the Cultural Revolution, it was urged by a famous economist, Hsu Ti-hsin, after the fall of the Gang of Four. Hsu reaffirmed the necessity and reasonableness of this concept and maintained that the pursuit of profit in a socialist state is an important measure leading to the "great order" of the world and the modernization of China.[67]

That politics is basic and economics only serves politics are the general and fundamental principles of Mao's economic thinking. In practice, when politics takes command, it means that economic development is to be carried out under the leadership of the Party; what Sun asserted was that economic activities were to be dominated by an objective economic law. Besides this basic principle, there are a few more of Mao's economic concepts which are worth mentioning here: productive forces, production relations and superstructure; economic reconstruction; and "walking on two legs."

Productive Forces, Production Relations and Superstructure

A basic Marxist tenet is that the production forces are the decisive factor in social development. Marx said: "In the social production of their subsistence men enter into determined and necessary relations with each other which are independent of their wills—production relations which correspond to a definite stage of development of their material productive forces. The sum of these production-relations forms the economic structure of society, the real basis upon which a judicial and political superstructure arises, and to which definite social forms of consciousness correspond. The mode of production of the material subsistence, conditions the social, political and spiritual life-process in general. It is not the consciousness of men which determines their existence, but on the contrary it is their existence which determines their consciousness."[68]

But Mao had a modified interpretation of the relationship between productive forces, production relations and superstructure. He conceived this relationship as follows: an ideological struggle always precedes a political struggle; so ideology is the most fundamental driving force. He said, "We recognize that in the general development of history it is material things that determine mental things, i.e., social existence determines social consciousness, but at the same time, we also recognize, and must recognize, the reaction of mental things, the reaction of social consciousness on social existence, and the reaction of superstructure on the economic base."[69]

Mao observed that the world history of bourgeois and proletarian revolutions reveals the same general law of development: the first step is always to change the superstructure, the second to seize the power of the state machine which is used to greatly affect the production forces. Mao postulated a general law that public opinion is always created first, in order to seize political power, and that then the problem of the system of ownership is solved and the productive forces are greatly developed.[70] In the sequence of revolution, Mao considered the superstructure the primary element.

In China, the revolution began with Marxist propaganda, aiming at creating new public opinion in favor of the revolution. After the old superstructure was overthrown in the course of revolution, the old production relations were destroyed and the new ones established, which paved the way for the development of productive forces, and consequently it was possible to engage in technical revolution vigorously, and greatly develop the social productive forces.[71]

Mao once indicated that the new production relations established under the new government after 1949 permitted the productive forces of China to develop at an unprecedented speed.[72] Mao stressed this point by saying that the gigantic development of production forces always follows the development of production relations. Evidently, in these remarks Mao stressed the primacy of production relations, though he qualified his point by saying that the revolutions in production relations are due, to a certain degree, to the development of productive forces.[73] Thus, Mao postulated that it is a general rule that first the production relations have to be changed, and then, and only then, the productive forces can be greatly developed.[74] Based on this logic, he maintained that the main subjective matter of political economy is the study of production relations.[75]

But Mao at the same time observed a situation in which productive forces take the lead. He argued: "When productive forces advance so fast as to create a situation in which the production relations do not correspond to the productive forces, and the superstructure does not correspond to the production relations, it is necessary to change the production relations and the superstructure in order to meet the new situation."[76] In this argument, he stressed the primacy of the productive forces.

As for the mutual relationship among the three factors, Mao further argued that when the superstructure does correspond to the production relations, and the production relations correspond to the productive forces, the three factors will reach a balance. But the balance is only relative, because "the productive forces are increasingly progressing, therefore, it is always in a state of imbalance. Balance and imbalance are the two phases of contradiction in which imbalance is absolute and balance is relative; otherwise productive forces, production relations, and superstructure cannot continue to develop and will be inalterable."[77] What Mao says here is simply that the process of continual shifting from balance to imbalance and vice versa, between productive forces and productive relations, between production relations and superstructure con-

257

stitute the dynamic force of progress, otherwise they would remain static. Mao also asserted that in a socialist society the relationship between the production relations and productive forces and the relationship between the production relations and the superstructure are both contradictory and harmonious.[78]

Though he juxtaposed the three factors and gave primacy to one or the other at different times, Mao's emphasis was definitely on superstructure or ideology. The change in people's thinking is not only regarded as the motive force in starting a revolution but also as the basic instrumentality in effecting economic programs for socialist reconstruction. Thus, in practice, Mao insisted on political work to arouse the consciousness of the workers rather than the use of material incentives to arouse their enthusiasm, and he stressed the change in production relations first prior to the development of technology or machines.

Economic Reconstruction

China's revolution led by the Communist Party is, as recounted by Hua Kuo-feng, divided into two stages: the revolution of New Democracy and that of socialism. The first stage aims at overthrowing the imperialist, feudalist and bureaucratic capitalist rule in China and at changing the semicolonial and semifeudalist society into the New Democratic Society. This task was claimed to be completed right before the establishment of the People's Republic of China in 1949. The second task has been the attempt to establish a socialist society. The fundamental concept during this transition is seen as the upholding and development of the Marxist principle of continued revolution, which is characterized by the switch over from the democratic revolution upon the seizure of political power by the proletariat, to the socialist revolution and carrying it on under the dictatorship of the proletariat.[79]

Mao envisioned a transitional period from capitalism to socialism in China. In 1952, Mao formulated the general line to be executed by the Party in this period as follows: The transitional period begins with the establishment of the People's Republic and ends with the basic completion of socialist transformation. The general line and fundamental task for the Party in this transitional period, a fairly long time, are to realize the socialist industrialization of the state and also the socialist transformation to agriculture, handicrafts and capitalist industry and commerce conducted by the state.[80] As to the actual date of termination of this transitional period, no official announcement has been made yet.

The General Program of the Constitution of the Communist Party of China, adopted in 1956, provides that, "During the period of transition from the founding of the People's Republic of China to the attainment of a socialist society, the fundamental task of the Party is to complete, step by step, the socialist transformation of agriculture, handicrafts and capitalist industry and commerce and to bring about, step by step, the industrialization of the country."[81]

There is a difference between Mao's statement and the provision of the Constitution. The problem of periodization has not yet been resolved. For Mao the transitional period ends with "the basic completion of socialist transformation," while the Constitution provides that the transitional period ends with the "attainment of a socialist society." The road from "the basic completion of socialist transformation" and "the attainment of a socialist society" is a long one.

The policies pursued in carrying out the socialist construction in the transitional period were in two major divisions, agriculture and industry.

The Agricultural Sector. In the agricultural sector, land reform was initiated on a national scale in 1949 and was completed in 1952. This reform consisted of the confiscation of the land of landlords and its distribution to peasants with little or no land. After the distribution of land, the authorities established mutual aid teams (1950–1951) and primitive agricultural producers' cooperatives (1951–1953), which were characterized by putting in one's land as shares. These primitive cooperatives were later developed into advanced cooperatives (1956–1957), under which all peasants lost their lands. The mutual aid teams and cooperatives were considered to be the necessary steps in the transition from a small-scale individual economy to a large-scale collective economy. Finally, the advanced cooperatives developed into the people's communes, which were considered as the best form of organization not only for the transition from collective ownership to ownership by the entire people but also for the future transition from socialism to communism. The final stage of agricultural transformation would be effected by the change of the production relations from the collective ownership system into the ownership of the entire people. In other words, all agricultural means of production are to be nationalized, and all peasants are to be turned into workers paid in wages by the state.

The Industrial Sector. A series of important steps was taken in effecting the socialist transformation of handicrafts and capitalist industry and commerce. For small-scale handicraft and commercial enterprises, the form of cooperative was used. With respect to large-scale industry and commerce, the first step was confiscation of eighty percent of the bureaucratic capital of the entire capitalist economy. This was followed by the Three-Anti and Five-Anti movements. The joint operation of enterprises by the state and private parties was practiced for a brief period (1955–1956) and an overall economic reorganization took place in 1958, which practically nationalized all industries and commerce. These measures brought about the forced transformation of the national bourgeoisie.[82]

Certainly the most important problem is that of industrialization. As early as 1945 Mao warned that "Without industry there can be no national defense, no people's warfare, and no national prosperity and power."[83] We can assume that in Mao's mind, heavy industry was stressed as the foundation of national economic development. Parenthetically, China's first Five-Year Plan was notable for its almost exclusive reliance on heavy industry. Later, Mao realized the mistake of its lopsidedness and could only lament that China was then so inexperienced and ignorant that she had no choice but mechanical copying from the Soviets.[84]

In 1956, Mao explicitly expressed his preference for the development of

259

heavy industry, but emphasized not at the expense of light industry and agriculture. To make his policy more flexible, Mao further added that heavy industry still remains to be the central point of investment, but the investment in agriculture and light industry should be proportionally increased.[85] In 1957, following the same line, Mao said that the problem of China's industrialization was mainly the problem of the relationships of the development of heavy industry, light industry and agriculture. He stressed the point that heavy industry must be affirmed as central to China's economic reconstruction. However, he also said at the same time that attention must be given to the development of agriculture and light industry.[86]

China was, by 1957, considered to have completed, in the main, the socialist transformation of the ownership of the means of production. From then on, a new question confronted the Chinese revolution—whether contradictions, classes and class struggle still existed in socialist society, whether it remained necessary to continue the socialist revolution and how this revolution was to be carried on. According to Hua Kuo-feng this was a question for which no correct answer had been found in the international communist movement for a long time and no ready answers could be found in the Marxist-Leninist works of the past. It was Mao, Hua held, who answered this question and founded the great theory of continuing revolution under the dictatorship of the proletariat.[87] Mao's words to the solution of this problem, often quoted and deemed to be of immense importance, are as follows:

"The class struggle between the proletariat and the bourgeoisie, the class struggle between the various political forces, and the struggle between the proletariat and the bourgeoisie in the ideological field will be long and tortuous and at times very acute."[88]

In 1958, Mao formulated the general line for socialist construction: "Go all out, aim high and achieve greater, faster, better and more economical results in building socialism." The policy of walking on two legs was introduced the same year by Mao.

Walking on Two Legs

The central theme of this policy was not to emphasize one thing to the neglect of other things but, rather, to develop pairs of relations simultaneously, such as the balanced relations between industry and agriculture, heavy industry and light industry, large enterprises and medium-to-small enterprises, modern production methods and indigenous methods, and enterprises run by the central government and those run by local authorities.[89] "It enables China to mobilize all positive factors for the building of socialism, thus accelerating the country's economic development and guaranteeing that the General Line for Socialist Construction...is put into effect." The long-range significance of the policy was to reduce the differences between workers and peasants, city and countryside and mental and manual labor, because it brought an increasing number of modern industries to China's vast countryside, which trained many workers and engineers from among the peasants.[90]

The general line together with the people's communes and the Great Leap Forward of 1958 are generally known as the "Three Red Flags." To Mao's mind, heavy industry was to be emphasized with steel production as the core. During the Great Leap Forward he set the target of steel production in 1958 as high as 10,700,000 tons and also initiated the backyard furnace movement, which turned out to be a disaster. Mao admitted his mistakes in advocating this.[91]

Later, Mao presented a more balanced view of industry and agriculture in carrying out the general line of socialist construction. In 1960, he initiated the policy of "taking agriculture as the foundation and industry as the leading factor" in developing China's national economy. Under this new guideline, grain production was regarded as the core of agriculture; steel production was to be the core of industry. However, this policy stressed that the two sectors could not advance separately. Agriculture is basic to the production of food grains and raw materials for light industry, which in turn promotes the growth of heavy industry. Thus, agriculture plays the basic role on the way to achieving industrialization—the ultimate goal. As *China Reconstructs* puts it, "In China the development of industry is based on agriculture; the advance of agriculture and rise of its labor productivity cannot be separated from industry's leading role. The two are interdependent and promote each other.[92]

As mentioned above, Mao's program for economic construction stressed ideology more than economic forces. To his mind, economic development depends basically on man, rather than on material factors, exemplified by the productive forces; therefore, initially, chief attention is to be given to the revolutionization of man's thinking, i.e., ideology or superstructure. The essential features of the new communist man envisioned by Mao may be summarized as follows:

The ideal attitude of a worker in a communist society would be to devote himself voluntarily to the interests of the revolution and of the people. Thus, he should be selfless; his service is not for fame, nor for gain and, while working, he must not fear hardships, or even death. Those familiar with the *People's Daily* have read many of the stirring stories about workers who have been glorified and extolled for superhuman feats, for courageously suffering unbearable hardships, and for sacrificing their lives in the performance of dangerous tasks for the common good. That new attitude definitely represents a sharp break with the self-seeking attitude in a capitalist society. To promote this new ideal labor attitude, material incentives were discouraged and moral incentives were strongly advocated.

Moreover, Mao admonished the Chinese people to persist in the conviction that "Man's determination can conquer Heaven." Though this is an old saying, Mao instilled new blood and new vigor into it, making it a guiding principle for economic construction in the face of apparently overwhelming unfavorable material conditions. Mao believed in self-reliance rather than in foreign assistance, either in technology or in finance. This brought to the Chinese people a new national pride and self-confidence. Mao not only encouraged people to endure hardships during the revolution for socialist construction, he simply did not cherish material comforts for the people as a lofty ideal. He emphasized egalitarianism, the disappearance of classes and exploitation, rather than more enjoyment or amusement for the people, at least in the foreseeable future. As Edgar Snow observed: "Benefits commune life has brought to the peasant are not all to be measured by a full belly, bodily warmth, better dwellings, good bedding, thermos bottles, bicycles, or a bit of cash. If it means no more than that, the revolution will fail, in the eyes of Mao Tse-tung and his 'activists.'"[93]

Mao's preference for a society of egalitarianism rather than affluence was not without its traditional background. In the West, from roughly the fifteenth century to the eighteenth century, many thinkers extolled political liberty; up to the mid-nineteenth century there was great success in extending freedom to all citizens. The rise of industrial magnates, however, resulted in a remarkably unequal distribution of wealth, so the emphasis shifted from love of liberty to the love of equality. Economic equality, i.e., the elimination of the gap between rich and poor, has thus been the main target of socialism. However, the idea of equality was emphasized in ancient China two thousand years ago. Confucius said: "I have been taught to believe that rulers of states should not be worried about scarcity of possessions but should be worried about unequal distribution of possessions; they should not be worried about poverty, but should be worried about the people being discontented. For with equal distribution there will be no poverty; with harmony there will be no scarcity; and with contentment among the people, there can be no rebellious uprisings."[94] This early idea of equality has had a powerful influence on Chinese minds throughout history. Ironically, an age-old Confucian theory reappears under the cloak of modern Marxism.

As for more recent economic conditions, Mao held that after twenty-five years of Communist revolution and reform, there was only one thing basically changed—the system of ownership. Mao is quoted as saying the following: "China is a socialist country. Before liberation, she was more or less like capitalism. Even now she practices an eight-grade wage system, distribution to each according to his work, and exchange by means of money, which are scarcely different from the old society. What is different is that the system of ownership has changed."[95] There are people who object to Mao quotes filtered through the Gang of Four, asserting that they fabricated Mao's words. But I do not think they could do so while Mao was still alive. Moreover, this quotation coincides with Mao's ideas. As we have seen above, Mao put emphasis mainly on the change of the production relations in a revolution, of which the ownership system is one of the elements. However, this attitude led Mao to underestimate the time and work required in the task of modernization or industrialization. It is a familiar story that Mao thought, in 1958, that it was possible for China to equal or surpass the production of steel and other major industrial products of England in fifteen years or a little longer.[96] He again optimistically anticipated, in 1960, the realization of China's four modernizations in two more five-year plans after the second Five-Year Plan, and to beat the schedule, he even conceived it possible to complete the task by the year 1969.[97]

Lastly, there is one point to be clarified. Mao's emphasis on an egalitarian rather than an affluent society should not mislead one into supposing that he did not cherish an affluent society as an eventual goal. He regarded an affluent society as both possible and necessary in the future, though not in the present. In 1956 Mao made the remark that in the next fifty or sixty years it was not only possible but absolutely necessary for China to overtake the U.S. in economic development. If China should fail to do so, she should be wiped off the face of the earth.[98]

Mao's Cultural Views

As noted in the section on New Democracy, following Marx and Lenin, Mao defined a given culture as the ideological reflection of the politics and economy of a given society, and at the same time that culture in turn exerts tremendous influence upon the politics and economy of a given society. The New Democratic Culture, according to Mao, had three characteristics: It was nationalistic, scientific, and of the masses. However, even though Mao rarely described the new culture in these same exact words after 1949, the general concept nevertheless still held true for the socialist stage. This section will be limited to the discussion of three basic aspects of Mao's views on culture: his policy for art and literature, the educational system, and the problem of intellectuals.

Policy for Art and Literature

Mao's *Talks on Art and Literature at the Yenan Forum* (1942), has served as the guiding principle and the orthodox doctrine of the Chinese Communist position on art and literature since the Yenan period. Mao's position, considered to be the correct and official Marxist line of art and literature in theory and practice, was also the position which all communist artists and writers were to take. During the Cultural Revolution, writers and artists were criticized and repudiated for their alleged deviation from this Marxist line. The basic ideas of this line are presented in the form of four questions.

The first question asked, "For whom are art and literature intended?" Mao's unequivocal answer was that art and literature are intended for the broad masses of the people, which include the workers, peasants, and soldiers.

The second question asked, "How are the masses to be served?" The answer involved the two elements of elevation and popularization. Workers, peasants, and soldiers had been fighting in a ruthless and bloody war against Japan; in addition, they had also suffered under a long period of feudal and bourgeois rule. Consequently, the masses remained illiterate and uncultured. Hence, popularization for the masses was basic and urgent. Once popularization was realized, elevation was achieved on the basis of the popularization. Even though popularization had priority over elevation, art and literature in both elementary and advanced forms had to be created for the workers, peasants, and soldiers and enjoyed by them, rather than for and by a minority of privileged people.

The third question concerned the relation between the works of art and literature of the Party and the entire work of the Party. For Mao, all art and literature basically belonged to a definite class and followed a definite political line. In reality, he said, the idea of "art for art's sake," did not exist; nor was there any such reality as art which transcended classes, or art which paralleled or was independent of politics. The art and literature of the proletariat was only a part of the entire revolutionary cause of the proletariat. Although art and literature were subordinate to politics, they exerted, at the same time, a great influence on politics. For Mao, politics meant the politics of the proletariat, i.e., the masses, not the politics of a minority of so-called statesmen.

Mao saw literary criticism as one of the major methods in the struggle within art and literature. He created two standards, one political, the other artistic. Although these standards were juxtaposed, it is evident that the political standard enjoyed greater significance since, according to communist theory, politics is of supreme importance.

The fourth question concerned whether to expose or to praise, and whether to write the "bright" side or the "dark" side. Mao believed that the basic task of revolutionary artists and writers was to expose all dark forces harmful to the masses of the people and to praise all revolutionary struggles of the people.[99]

Mao's policy on art and literature can be condensed into two important postulates: (1) Art and literature should serve the broad masses of the people i.e., the workers, peasants, and the soldiers; and (2) Art and literature are subordinate to politics, that is, class politics.

Educational System

In 1966, Mao personally initiated the Cultural Revolution. He was its principal leader. Whether the Cultural Revolution was a struggle for power as some suggest, or whether it was a struggle in ideology as others believe, or, most likely, whether it was a combination of both motives, the point to remember in terms of ideology is that the main purpose of the Cultural Revolution was twofold: to fight the revisionism of Liu Shao-ch'i and to establish Mao's revolutionary cultural line of the proletariat. The most drastic change in education during the Cultural Revolution occurred in educational policy and in the school system. There were two directives concerning education issued by Mao, both of which served as basic guidelines for education. The first directive, dated 7 May 1966, and in the form of a letter addressed to Lin Piao, stated that while students should regard the learning of culture *(wen)* as a primary objective, they should also learn to be competent in industry *(kung)*, agriculture, military affairs *(chün)* and in the criticism of the bourgeoisie. Mao further stated in this directive that school terms were to be shortened, that education was to be revolutionized, and that bourgeois intellectuals would no longer control the schools.[100]

The second directive, dated 21 July 1968, was a report written by reporters of

Wen-hui Pao and the *Hsin-hua* News Agency in Shanghai, concerning an on-the-spot investigation of the training of engineering and technical personnel in a machine tools factory. The publication of the report was accompanied by an editorial note which lauded the report as a vivid illustration of how the Cultural Revolution brought changes to the training of engineering and technical personnel. The editorial, in addition, singled out another Mao "directive" (unidentified) which laid out the educational program for the proletariat in opposition to the revisionist and bourgeois educational line. In other words, this unidentified directive sets the orientation for education during and after the Cultural Revolution. The directive or the instruction of Mao reads as follows:

> Universities, mainly universities of sciences and engineering, have still to be operated, but school terms should be shortened, education should be revolutionized, proletarian politics should take command so as to follow the road of the Shanghai Machine Tool Plant in training the technical personnel from among the workers. Students should be selected from workers and peasants who have had practical experiences, and they, after entering school for a few years, will go back to practical production again.[101]

The report itself—the second directive—outlined a four-point program that reflected the educational thought of Mao Tse-tung and which allegedly represented the ideas of the workers and technical personnel of the factory. The following is a brief summary:

1. Since the aim is to train workers with social consciousness and socialist culture, rather than "intellectual aristocrats" produced by revisionist education, college graduates should begin their careers as manual workers.
2. Teachers should be selected from among experienced workers, rather than from the college graduate bookworms.
3. New engineering and technical personnel should be recruited from workers and high school graduates who have good political thought.
4. The reform of revisionist engineers should be carried out by refuting their idea that technique is primary and by sending them down to work as factory labor.

In addition to the principles of Mao outlined in the report, he discussed at length on different occasions the importance of practice. Mao valued practical experience far more than he valued theoretical learning gained from books. This attitude was clearly reflected in his discussions on military affairs, medical education, and even in science. He said that in military science, while it is fine to read a little, it is of little use to read a lot. In military affairs, Mao said he never consulted a book to fight a battle. His advice to foreign students studying military science in China was that their most valuable experience would be to return home to participate in actual fighting since a few months of study sufficed and since class lectures were of little use.[102]

Medical education was an area which Mao felt needed reform. The most basic improvement, he said, would be to cut down on the amount of required reading. Admission to medical school would not be limited to junior or senior high school graduates because three years of training beyond elementary school was sufficient. In essence, then, Mao basically believed an individual could elevate himself through practice in medicine and that the more books an individual read, the more stupid he became.[103] Mao extended his belief even to the so-called "apex science," which refers to any highly specialized, highly sophisticated science, such as solid-state physics in the 1950s. Three years, or slightly more time, he felt, would be required for such study.[104] Furthermore, Mao urged philosophers and historians to work on farms and in factories, students of the humanities to work in agriculture, industry and business, and students of engineering and science to work in factories and in their laboratories.[105]

In summary, the following principles were observed as guidelines in educational policy in the wake of the Cultural Revolution: (1) Education must serve proletarian politics; the aim of education is to train, for the cause of the revolution, the proletariat masses rather than the bourgeois elite; in other words, what is sought is an entirely new generation of intellectuals, drawn from the workers, peasants, and soldiers, and totally free of the traditional elitist ideology; (2) Education must be integrated with labor and production; (3) Domination of schools by intellectuals must cease; schools are to be controlled by the proletariat, i.e., the Party.

The Problem of Intellectuals

As early as 1939, Mao had already suggested that the Communist Party recruit a large number of intellectuals into the Party, army, government, and schools so that the intellectuals could aid in developing the cultural movement. Without the participation of the intellectuals, the victory of revolution would be impossible.[106] Mao repeated this idea in his essay, *On Coalition Government,* when he again stressed the importance of the people's government in bringing forth from among the broad masses various categories of intellectuals to serve as cadres and the importance of uniting and reeducating all the existing useful intellectuals.[107] It was Mao's intention to train intellectual cadres of all backgrounds and at the same time to remold the old ones. Mao had recognized the crucial role of the intellectuals in China's last fifty years, especially during the post-May Fourth Movement period and during the War of Resistance. He anticipated that intellectuals would play an even more important role in subsequent struggles. Thus, a thought reform movement was carried out immediately after the establishment of the People's Republic in 1949. In order to meet completely the needs of the new society, it was necessary for intellectuals to adopt new attitudes in their ideology. Intellectuals were urged to give up their bourgeois world outlook and establish a proletarian communist world outlook; thought reform, especially political thought, was of utmost importance. Mao declared that being "without a correct political viewpoint is just like being a man without a soul."[108] Intellectuals were urged to regard serving the people as the highest goal, to integrate with the worker-peasant masses, to accept the attitude that education was meant to serve proletarian politics and that education should integrate with labor and production.

266

Beginning in 1949, eminent scholars were set up as model cases in which they were urged to remold their thoughts by writing confessions that displayed a switchover from bourgeois to socialist or communist ideology. One intellectual after another, in nearly every field of scholarship, wrote confessions to denounce their old thoughts. A collection of their confessions was published under the title, *How Have My Thoughts Been Changed?*[109] This confession campaign completely altered the high social position enjoyed by the intellectuals. They invariably admitted that they had wrong ideology before and vowed to learn from workers and peasants and make a new start. Against the tradition of intellectual elitism the communists set new revolutionary criteria of manual labor, upgrading greatly the social position of workers and peasants, and downgrading that of intellectuals, branded as a useless and selfish group. During the Cultural Revolution, it became the practice to send intellectuals and cadres down to the countryside to be "re-educated by the poor and lower-middle peasants."

Mao, who had little faith in formal school education or learning from books, directed that "our educational policy must enable everyone who receives an education...to become a worker with both a socialist consciousness and culture."[110] He generalized that in history all creators of new thought and founders of new schools of learning were young and barely erudite. He cited as examples Confucius, who began his career at twenty-three and Shakyamuni, who founded Buddhism at nineteen. Mao asked rhetorically, "What knowledge did Christ have?" Sun Yat-sen, he continued, knew very little, having had only a high school-level education when he started a revolution in his early youth. Marx formulated his theory of dialectical materialism when young and wrote the *Communist Manifesto* at around the age of thirty. K'ang Yu-wei and Liang Ch'i-ch'ao both were active, aggressive and famous, making a sweeping impact throughout China at young ages. Mao cited other men, including Luther, Darwin, Franklin, and Gorki and the inventors of sleeping pills and penicillin, men whose names he probably did not know but who, he pointed out, were of low social status and unschooled. Mao further noticed that this was also true in the political and military fields. Among many examples he cited, the most striking one was Li Shih-min, the founder of the T'ang dynasty, who started the revolt as a teenager and became the emperor at the age of twenty four.[111] Mao concluded that the young would overcome the old, those with less learning would overcome those who were well-schooled and that what counted was the courage to think, to speak, and to act without being frightened into timidity by authorities, or famous or learned people.[112]

Formal education thus meant very little to Mao. With regard to his own peer group, Mao noted that few of the Central Committee members of the Chinese Communist Party were the products of college training.[113] Following in the same vein, Mao, in a talk with the responsible members of the Capital Red Guard Assembly, stressed that long years of schooling were not significant. Lenin, he said, studied law for just one year. Engels never completed high school. Stalin never attended college after graduation from a church high school. Gorki had two years of elementary school—even less formal education than Chiang Ch'ing's six years. Then, to fit himself into this category of great revolutionaries, Mao revealed that his marks in school had averaged only 70 points out of a possible 100. In geometry he submitted a "blank answer" and marked a zero grade on his own examination paper.[114] Could this be the theoretical foundation for the case of Chang T'ieh-sheng, a 1970 college applicant who turned in a blank physics exam and, upon receiving a zero mark, was given nationwide publicity? He was held up as an example for the youth of the country to emulate.

Mao even went so far as to praise totally uneducated, but successful people. Do not show any disrespect to clods *(lao-ts'u)*, Mao warned his audience in a speech. Extreme examples of prominent but illiterate personages were Genghis Khan, the founder of the Yuan dynasty; and Liu Pang, founder of the Han dynasty, who could barely recognize a few characters. The two most successful emperors of the Ming dynasty were Ming T'ai-tsu, the founder of the dynasty, who began as an illiterate cowherd, and Ming Ch'eng-tsu, who could hardly read. In contrast, Mao continued, during the Chia-ching period, when intellectuals were in power, the dynasty suffered from excessive internal turmoil. Ch'en Fa-chih was illiterate but he nevertheless became the prime minister during the reign of Liang Wu-ti. Conversely, Mao cited Liang Wu-ti and Li Hou-chu, who lost their thrones because they suffered from too much culture. Sui Yang-ti, and Ch'en Hou-chu, both of whom excelled in prose and verse, and Sung Hui-tsung, a poet and a painter, all failed tragically as emperors. Degree holders did not escape Mao's contempt for scholarship either. He noticed that seldom did *chuang-yuan* degree holders accomplish anything extraordinary. The two greatest T'ang poets, Li P'o and Tu Fu, did not have advanced imperial degrees. Nor did other prominent prose writers, novelists, and dramatists, such as Han Yü, Liu Tsung-yuan, Wang Shih-fu, Kuan Han-ch'ing, Lo Kuan-chung, P'u Sung-ling or Ts'ao Hsueh-ch'in. In fact, those who did earn *chin-shih* or *han-lin* degrees have invariably been unsuccessful. These degrees reflected, Mao implicitly hinted, merely a kind of social or academic ladder to be climbed rung by rung by ordinary people rather than by geniuses. Too much book learning, Mao asseverated, would be "deadly harmful."[115]

Since, according to Mao, intellectuals were supposed to be workers with socialist consciousness and culture, the function of schools should be to train them as such. Thus, intellectuals were to be trained and used by the government for the cause of the revolution. The pursuit of knowledge and participation in academic research for personal satisfaction were not primary concerns for Mao, and in fact came close to being completely denied. Theoretically, being both red and expert were equally emphasized; however, in actual practice, being red was given much more preference to being an expert. Because intellectuals were seen as tools, as the cogs and gears of the revolution, they were to be uniform in ideology and in action. It is for this reason that thought reform has been persistently carried on, and that the Hundred Flowers movement was only short-lived.

Mao's lack of faith in the ability of formal education to produce great men is very closely related to his advocacy of the principle of genius, or the "great man" theory of history, which parenthetically, has always been vigorously attacked officially. Great men were born to be great. They did not become great through formal schooling; rather, they trained themselves through private self-study. In a society where politics takes command, intellectuals should do as they are told, according to the course mapped out by a leading genius. In the case of China, Mao, by virtue of his position as the genius leader, was bound by no ordinary laws or custom, whether traditional, moral, or legal (for example, he was not filial to his father; in his poems, he wrote in purely classical style when virtually no one else was allowed to do so; and, he did not comply with the Constitution when he personally dismissed and appointed a premier). Some people may argue that Mao believed in Marxism, but it must be remembered that Marxism, to Mao, was only a guide to action, a tool. He believed that any action a leader decided upon depended upon his personal genius and insight, and not on anything he could learn from books or school.

Conclusion

Mao has been the most influential and powerful person in recent Chinese history. His influence is not limited to one aspect, but is comprehensive. He has greatly affected politics, economics, individual lives, and thought. A new world in China has emerged, and, as he himself put it, he was courageous enough to "replace a new sun and a new moon in effecting a new Heaven." Certainly Mao's thought plays a very important role in his achievements. Then what is the origin of his thought? Modern Chinese thinkers generally inherit two ideological resources, one Chinese and one foreign. Marxism is definitely a foreign ideology to the Chinese. This part of Mao's thought came from the West, though Mao has his own interpretation of it. We will return to this point later. Mao's debt to Chinese thought can be divided into two sources: old books, and modern people. Mao was supposed to have had a thorough study of Chinese history, with special emphasis on the causes and processes of the rise and fall of dynasties. He is reputed to have found the key principle of the development of Chinese history—the peasant revolution. This discovery helped him to use the tactics of peasant revolts, or speaking militarily, guerrilla warfare, in effecting his communist revolution that culminated in the overthrow of the Kuomintang government and the establishment of the People's Republic. Mao's guerrilla warfare is basically what in tradition is derogatorily called "roving"—a tactic practiced by the so-called roving bandits, but Mao had modernized it as a revolutionary means and renamed it guerrilla warfare. Mao's debt to contemporary thought originated with K'ang and Liang. The early life of Mao revealed that he was strongly influenced by the writings of K'ang Yu-wei and Liang Ch'i-ch'ao at an age when young minds are receptive to new ideas. Mao held these two men in great esteem, and he read and reread their political writings to such an extent that he could remember almost all of these works by heart.

K'ang is noted for his propaganda and promotion of the *ta-t'ung* ideal in his book *Ta-t'ung shu,* which had a powerful and startling impact on intellectuals then and afterwards. Undoubtedly Mao was tremendously fascinated by the book and its ideal. Many scholars have speculated that Mao borrowed heavily in his ideas for people's communes from *Ta-t'ung shu.* To my mind, both the principles and the institutional organizations of the people's commune are very close to those depicted in *Ta-t'ung shu,* as I have noted in the chapter on K'ang Yu-wei.[116] It is interesting to note that in one of the Soviet-produced pamphlets, *Mao's Pseudo Socialism,* attacking Mao, the charge is made that "Mao calls the 'ideal world' or 'world of great harmony' for which he is striving, 'socialism,' which in hundreds of thousands of years will develop into 'communism.'" It concludes that "One can only suppose that Mao's 'ideal world' and 'world of great harmony' are something different from the socialism and communism of Marxism-Leninism."[117]

A reliable personal source reports that Mao, upon his triumphant entry into Peking as the highest leader in 1949, made a personal call on K'ang T'ung-pi, the second daughter of K'ang Yu-wei, to express his appreciation for the beneficial influences her father's work, *Ta-t'ung shu,* had had on him.[118] When we recall that in his last years, he often said, in jest, that he was going to see Marx, it seems that these two sources, K'ang and Marx, were recognized by Mao himself. K'ang's and Liang's influence on Mao was not confined to traditional Chinese ideas. I suspect that Mao received certain Western liberal ideas from them, especially from Liang, who was known for his introduction of Western liberal ideas into China through his lucid and passionate style of writing. However, Mao's absorption of Western liberal ideas must have been, at most, minimal. Although Mao's official biography revealed that he was exposed to the classical writings of Western ideas, such as the works of Mill and Montesquieu, translated by Yen Fu, I seriously doubt the extent to which Mao could absorb and be influenced by these great works. I do not suggest that Mao had a natural inclination to reject Western liberal and democratic ideas. The fact is that Yen's translations are hard to comprehend. In his *Translation Guidelines* to *On Liberty* by J.S. Mill, Yen deplored the fact that many Chinese readers often complained his translations were abstruse.[119] This fact must be attributed to his use of classical Chinese in translating those books. His readers, then, were generally very learned and wholly familiar with the literary style. If even they found them esoteric, I wonder how the young Mao could have read them easily. This fact alone suggests that Mao received very little influence from the liberal thought of the West.

All of Mao's poems and prose poems are in the classical style. His success in treating contemporary themes in this medium has won the admiration of many professional writers, including some who opposed him politically. Furthermore, his example refuted the May Fourth position that the classical language was a dead language unsuited to the living scenes of the present. Mao used it to extoll the Communist revolution, a most modern and unclassical event. Paradoxically, he also, in a sense, refuted his own theory on literature as advanced in his Yenan talks which advocated the use of the common people's language as a literary medium. Mao's spontaneous use of a traditional Chinese literary form reinforces our sense that his thought was indeed imbued with tradition and it would be surprising if this element were not expressed in his interpretation and application of Marxism.

However, while Mao's poetic talents have been recognized and acclaimed, particularly in the West, he was a poet by avocation just as he was a philosopher by avocation. The roles of poet and philosopher of dialectical materialism were subordinated to his vocation—his calling—that of revolutionary. He claims that a few famous Chinese novels were of more benefit to him than the classics; and he quoted freely in his writings and conversation from *The Water Margin, The Romance of the Three Kingdoms,* and the *Dream of the Red Chamber.* He was particularly indebted to *The Water Margin* for his ideas on peasant revolution. This contrasts with his attitude toward the classics which he felt could only teach him dead knowledge. Of course, since the novel had popular roots and had been traditionally disparaged by the scholars, Mao, the rebel, could hardly side with the novel's critics. The point to note here is that he valued the novel primarily insofar as it contributed to carrying out the revolution.

Mao and Marxism

Mao was one of China's earliest converts to Marxism. His standing as a Marxist theoretician is a subject of dispute, some scholars regarding him as a genius, others regarding him as only mediocre. The correct appraisal of Mao's knowledge of Marxism does not mainly concern us; what we want to stress is that Mao was not interested in the purely abstract and academic study of Marxism but that his basic stand was to use Marxism as an instrument for revolution. To Mao, therefore, Marxism is a tool, a weapon, rather than a dogma.

"For a hundred years," Mao said, "the finest sons and daughters of the disaster-ridden Chinese nation fought and sacrificed their lives. . . in quest of the truth that would save the country and the people. . . . But it was only after World War I and the October Revolution in Russia that we found Marxism-Leninism the best of truths, the best of weapons for liberating our nation. And the Communist Party of China has been the initiator, propagandist and organizer in the wielding of this weapon."[120]

Mao stressed this point by saying that Marxism-Leninism is a science which will lead the proletarian revolution to victory; that Marx, Engels, Lenin, and Stalin have repeatedly said that their theory is not a dogma but a guide to action; and that those who look upon Marxism-Leninism as a religious dogma are simply foolish and ignorant.[121] Mao ridiculed those who treat Marxism as dogma: "Your dogma is useless and frankly is even less useful than dog's manure. We can see that dog's manure can fertilize fields and human excrement can feed dogs. Dogma can neither fertilize land nor feed dogs. What's the use of it?

(laughter)."[122]   Instead, Mao expounded the correct and true relationship between Marxism-Leninism and the Chinese revolution in the following analogy:

> This is the attitude of "shooting one's arrow at the target." The "target" is the Chinese revolution, and the "arrow" Marxism-Leninism. The reason that the Chinese Communists have sought the "arrow" is purely for the purpose of hitting the "target" of the Chinese revolution and the revolution of the East, otherwise the "arrow" is nothing but a curio to be played with, entirely useless.[123]

Since Mao did not regard Marxism as a dogma, he ridiculed those who study Marxism abstractly without putting it into application: "One cannot be considered as theoretician, even if he has read ten thousand books by Marx, Lenin, Engels, and Stalin a thousand times and can recite every sentence by heart."[124] Again he said: "If one person can only recite glibly Marxist economics or philosophy from chapter 1 to chapter 10, and is utterly unable to apply it, can one be considered a Marxist theoretician? No, he cannot."[125] Mao's suggestion on the proper way of studying Marxism is this: "Books on Marx should be studied, but not too many of them. Ten-odd books will do. To read more of them will lead one in the opposite direction, and turn one into a 'book-idiot,' dogmatist, and revisionist."[126]

From the above quotations, it is clear that Mao does not approve the study of Marxism only as a doctrine, but insists on using it as a tool. It is not how much one knows about Marxism that counts, but the extent that one can apply it to the Chinese revolution. To master the theory of Marxism is useless unless one can use it as a sharpened tool. In other words, for Mao it is a means rather than an end.

Obviously, the attraction of Marxism in China cannot be explained in the strict framework of the Marxist system, for the victory of communism had little to do with the breakdown of capitalism as Marx originally envisioned. So in practice, Mao attemped a sinification of Marxism for its application in China. What did Mao take from Marxism? I believe the most important concept is the class struggle. This was the Marxist concept that Mao saw, with some modifications, as most directly relevant to his revolutionary movement. By applying class struggle initially in the Chinese rural society, Mao mobilized millions of landless peasants to fight the landlords and then organized them into an enormous army that brought the Chinese Communists to power. Mao managed to arouse class consciousness among the peasants, permitting them to kill the landlords. Once that was done, the peasants who had a blood debt to the landlords could not leave the Communist-controlled areas for the Nationalist-controlled areas where they would be condemned to death also. Thus, the peasants not only had strong reasons for identifying with the Communist regime but really had no place else to go. Since 1948, the tactic of class struggle has been used almost continuously in a series of mass campaigns to carry out political and economic objectives. One of Mao's warnings to Party members at the Eighth Party Congress was never to forget class struggle.

Class struggle, which justifies brutal and often violent action in realizing political goals, runs counter to the mainstream of traditional Chinese political philosophy of a benevolent government based on peace and love. In answering the question raised by one of the kings of the Warring States, of how the turmoil of the whole empire could be settled, Mencius answered tersely, "Through unity." Pressed by the king, "Who can unite it?" Mencius answered, "He who has no pleasure in killing people can unite it."[127] Mencius also argued that "None of them [sages of antiquity] in order to obtain the empire, would have committed *one* act of unrighteousness, or put to death *one* innocent person."[128] The traditional philosophy's stand against brute force and against the committing of even one single improper act or the killing of a single innocent person was an obstacle to a revolution by force, for Mao conceived that a revolution is bloody and is not like a dinner party.[129] The concept of class struggle thus supplied Mao with a theoretical justification for using force in solving the problem of China's reconstruction.

For Mao the class struggle was a necessary means to realizing an ideal and he did not hesitate to break with Mencius' principles on this issue. It was from this standpoint that Mao launched, first, the peasant revolution, then the cooperative movement, then the people's commune movement, and, finally, the Cultural Revolution. His struggles against political enemies, such as Liu Shao-ch'i, Lin Piao and Teng Hsiao-p'ing also used the same tactic. Class struggle came to be considered an efficient weapon in any movement and against an enemy, and Mao consistently held that once the concept of class struggle was grasped, miracles would follow.

Another important concept Mao took from Marxism is that of the dictatorship of the proletariat. Democracy has been an ideal in China's political philosophy since very ancient times. However, the problem is that the idea has never been institutionalized. Democracy has also been the main trend of political thinking of the past hundred years; a form of democratic government has been the aspiration of most Chinese intellectuals. In contrast to democracy, in which power rests with the majority of the people, Mao attempted to reconstruct China by centralizing power in himself plus a few others around him. It is difficult to resist the general trend of a democratic movement by arguing undemocratic ideas. Under these circumstances, the dictatorship of the proletariat gave Mao a theoretical foundation for exercising dictatorial power, while at the same time it gave the people the impression of being somewhat democratic. We will explore this point more fully below.

Mao as a Person

Understanding Mao's character is essential to the study of his achievements and failures. Thousands of articles have been written inside and outside of China on this subject. Mao did not respond to any of them except to two terse evaluations made by Chang Hsi-jo and Ch'en Ming-shu. Chang was a professor of Political Science at Tsing Hua University, a leader of the Democratic League in the 1940s, and Minister of Higher Education in the People's Republic of China in the 1950s. He had a sharp tongue and a charismatic appeal among the radical intellectuals. Ch'en was a Kuomintang general, who joined the Fukien rebellion against Chiang Kai-shek and fled to Hong Kong after its failure. He joined the Political Consultative Conference under the Communist regime. These two people had one thing in common—strong opposition to Chiang Kai-shek. Each of them gave Mao a brief (consisting of 16 Chinese characters) appraisal.

Chang Hsi-jo	Ch'en Ming-shu
1. Ambitious for great achievements	1.[†] Ambitious for great achievements
2. Impatient for recognized success and immediate profit	2.[†] Listening to and believing only one side [prejudiced, biased]
3. Belittling the past	3.[†] Unstable in feeling of joy and anger [emotionally unpredictable]
4. Blind faith in the future	4.[†] Dislike of antiques[130]

In these two appraisals, point 1. of Chang and 1.[†] of Ch'en are identical. Chang's points 3. and 4. and Ch'en's point 4.[†] are almost the same. The difference lies in Chang's point 2. which Ch'en does not have, and in Ch'en's points 2.[†] and 3.[†] which Chang does not include. On the whole, all these are the standards commonly used in China to evaluate administrative leaders, including the emperor. We may summarize these criticisms into four points: (1) ambitious for great achievements; (2) intense fondness for the new and dislike of the old; (3) capricious; and (4) biased. Mao answered these two appraisals on three occasions, once at his talks at the Nanning Conference, the second time at his talks at the Supreme State Conference, both occurring in January 1958, and the third time at the Ch'eng-tu Conference in March 1958. Like his other informal talks, Mao made his responses in a somewhat sophistic and humorous way.

Mao appeared to concede Chang's comments, acclaiming them as being "Excellently said, right to the point,"and then proceeded to construe their meaning in his own way. For instance, point 1., literally meaning "love of greatness and successes," traditionally suggests an unfavorable criticism of one who is overly ambitious, and loves to do things in a big way for personal aggrandizement. The phrase is difficult to translate fully and accurately in a compact way. However, its meaning can be clarified by giving concrete examples. For instance, the Chinese have often used this epithet to characterize Ch'in Shih Huang-ti or Han Wu-ti, and would probably use it to criticize such Western historical figures as Alexander the Great and Napoleon. However, Mao argued that the "love of bigness and successes" does not mean anything by itself; it all depends on who is doing the pursuing of "bigness and successes"—

the revolutionaries or the reactionaries. Furthermore, revolutionaries can be divided into two kinds: Those whose pursuit of "bigness and successes" is subjective, and those whose pursuit is in accordance with reality. Mao then argued that the bigness he loved was the bigness of 600 million people; the successes he loved were the successes of socialism.

Chang's point 2. "impatient for recognized success and immediate profit," suggests seeking for a quick utilitarian result, possibly heedless of long-range implications. Mao said, however, that this depended on whether one aimed at personal prominence, which would be subjectivism, or at a progressive production norm, which would be both realistic and attainable. As for his contempt of the past, Mao simply responded that it wouldn't do *not* to belittle the past, or to dwell on the ancient sages every day. On blind faith in the future, Mao answered only that people have always vested their hopes in the future. Mao also said that in the past, the average acre production in the North was only 100 odd catties, and only two or three hundred catties in the South, and that after twenty years Generalissimo Chiang Kai-shek left China with a mere 40,000 tons of steel; what hope can Chinese have if they don't belittle the past and have blind faith in the future? To sum up, Mao concluded that the four points raised by Chang were "well taken."

Responding to Ch'en, Mao answered that it was impossible not to be partial to one side. The question is whether one is partial to the side of the bourgeoisie or to the side of the proletariat, partial to what the rightists say or to what socialism says. Some comrades were not partial enough and should be more partial. For example, Mao argued that one should not listen with a favorable bias to the words of Liang Shu-ming or Ch'en Ming-shu. As for his "unpredictable" emotions, Mao twisted the meaning of the Chinese original before responding to Ch'en. The Chinese means "to be inconstant in joy and anger." Mao has taken the positive form, "to be constant," to mean unchanging and concluded that it is not correct to be constantly loving toward the bourgeois rightists, for example. As Mao put it, we can only love good people, and when they become rightists, we will be unable to love them and begin to be angry with them. This comes close to being a play on words for the expression has always referred in Chinese to a capricious, unpredictable temperament and not to emotions which respond to understandable provocations. Concerning his dislike of antiques, by which Ch'en obviously meant ancient artifacts and culture, Mao asked rhetorically whether we should not have contempt for such antiques as the binding of feet, eunuchs, bedbugs, and so forth. In this connection, Mao argued that this was a question of whether things are advanced or backward, and "antiques" are always a little bit backward. The elimination of flies, mosquitoes, and sparrows was never attempted before and will never occur again (that is to say, it would be unprecedented and unique). In general, Mao argued that what happens later is superior to what precedes and that it is not true "the present is inferior to the ancient." Mao conceded that "antiques," of course, cannot be unloved, but should not be loved too much.

At the Ch'eng-tu Conference, Mao said that Chang's comments describe exactly what the proletariat is and should be. Not only that, Mao argued, every other class "loves bigness and success." If we don't "love bigness and success," do you mean to say that we should "love smallness and failure?" Moreover, in history, the Great Emperor Yü, Confucius, and Mo-tzu were all "impatient for recognized success and immediate profit." Mao raised the following evidence to support his point. The Great Emperor Yü loved preciously even an inch of time. "When Confucius was not being employed by some sovereign for three months, he became agitated" (a quotation from the *Analects*). While touring through the various countries to preach their beliefs, Confucius did not let his mat (on which he sat) warm and Mo-tzu did not let the front of his cooking range blacken before starting another trip. (It takes a longer time to blacken the front of the cooking-range. The idea is that Mo-tzu stayed only a short time in each place and then hurried on.) All these exemplify the attitude of "impatience for recognized success and immediate profit." These, Mao argued, are our guidelines. Are we not "loving bigness and recognized success" when we are engaged in water conservation projects, rectification of work style, the anti-Rightist movement, big campaigns involving 600 million people? Are we not "impatient for recognized success and immediate profit" when we are engaged in reaching progressive production norms? What else shall we do if we don't have contempt for the old system, and the reactionary productive relations? What else do we do if we do not have blind faith in socialism and communism?[131]

Mao's technique in responding to these evaluations is to give them a different interpretation than one would generally attribute to them and then largely explain them away. However, since Mao did not bluntly reject these criticisms as unwarranted, we may infer that he admitted them to some degree. Furthermore, the criticisms of Chang and Ch'en conform to the general impressions and opinions of overseas Chinese intellectuals regarding Mao's personality. There is a considerable measure of truth in them.

Mao's Position in History

One of the ways Chinese scholars used to evaluate an eminent political leader was to apply the two criteria of learning and statecraft. The practice is based on a quotation of a negative appraisal from the biography of Huo Kuang in the *Han-shu* (History of the Han Dynasty) evaluating a great general and statesman, Huo Kuang, as "lacking in learning and statecraft." In subsequent years, people often used these two criteria in evaluating leaders. Theoretically, eminent persons can be divided into four kinds: (1) those having both of these qualities, which is ideal; (2) those lacking both of them, which is the worst; (3) those having learning but no statecraft; and (4) those having statecraft but no learning. It is difficult to find examples extreme enough to fit the first two categories. Most scholarly statesmen belong to the third category. For instance, Liang Ch'i-ch'ao, a nice scholar and an influential writer, did not have the ability to handle state affairs, and thus failed in politics. Liang Wu-ti and Li

Hou-chu, as pointed out by Mao, were too cultured and thus lost their thrones. Type four includes the successful men of action. The first emperor of the Han is a good example. He was a good emperor, noted for his statecraft but had not learning at all. Some of China's notorious warlords may be cited as examples of those lacking both qualities. As for the first type, true examples are so rare that one may doubt if history can supply one. Plato's philosopher-king suggests the ideal of that type of ruler. In actual practice, these two qualifications generally do not go hand in hand in one person. Trotsky was incomparably more brilliant in scholarship than Stalin, whom he dismissed as as "gray, colorless mediocrity." But the mediocrity made history, and the Marxist genius was not only defeated politically but also murdered by him. I would guess that Mao would put Lenin in the first category, and he himself may be regarded as approaching this category—at least, so Mao claimed.

Perhaps a word of explanation concerning our translation of "statecraft" would be in order here. The Chinese word "shu" in its broadest sense corresponds in many respects to the English word "art." It may have a rather highbrow connotation as in "fine arts," it may suggest accomplished skill as does the English "artisan," and it may include some of the connotations of the English "artful"—all, of course, depending on context. In a political context, as here, it suggests the kind of political knowhow required for effective administration and for the forming of alliances leading to the attaining and maintaining of power. It may include such ruthless tactics as conspiracies, cruelties, and treacheries. Machiavelli's views are concerned with "shu" in this sense.

To judge Mao by these two standards, we find that his achievements in statecraft surpassed those in learning. In ancient Chinese political philosophy, two distinct roles were supposed to be created by Heaven to rule the people—a ruler and a teacher. In the *Book of History,* it is said:

> *Heaven populates the earth below,*
> *Made people a lord*
> *And made him their teacher*
> *That he might assist God in loving them.*[132]

Incidentally, one cannot be certain from the text whether this duty is to be performed by one person or by two different persons. In history, the emperor was definitely the ruler, while the role of teacher was played by Confucius. Mao clearly wanted to be both. Thus, he is labeled as the great leader and the great teacher. His position as the great leader, i.e., the ruler, is beyond the slightest shadow of doubt, but his position as the great teacher is incongruous, since Confucius has been regarded traditionally and universally as the most holy teacher. Evidently Mao aspired to play such a role on top of being the ruler. As Chou Yang put it when he was in charge of cultural affairs, "We will fundamentally overthrow the thought of Confucius and establish the thought of Mao Tse-tung as the absolute authority."[133] It is evident that the Maoists attempted to replace Confucianism with Maoism. Mao told Edgar Snow that he preferred, among all the epithets honoring him, to be called the teacher. As far as learning is concerned, it seems to me that Mao must base this self-evaluation on his creation of a number of excellent poems, and on his interpretation, development and application of Marxism-Leninism in connection with the Chinese revolution.

Mao was a genius in manipulating statecraft. He had begun to establish his leadership in the Communist Party at the Tsun-i Conference, and he remained the Communist Party leader until his death. Like other founding emperors, Mao knew how best to use people for his purposes and how to win their loyalty. Liu Shao-ch'i and Chou En-lai were his faithful supporters. Even Lin Piao had helped him stay on the top. Mao was also a genius in mobilizing the masses to overthrow a government. In the very beginning, Mao had to start from scratch since he had no political base. Utilizing tactics historically used to cause dynastic change, Mao manifested his military genius by modifying the traditional "roving bandits" tactic to topple dynasties, and developed his guerrilla warfare tactics. By mobilizing peasants to form the backbone of the army, and by using villages as the base to encircle cities, he finally conquered all of China.

Realizing the vital importance of the strength and influence of the intellectuals, Mao's handling of the intellectuals was the most clever. There is a story told by a former Chinese Ambassador to the United States, T.F. Tsiang, that during the civil war, when the Communist forces were closing in on Peking, Mao invited Wu Han, a popular anti-Kuomintang writer and historian to Shih-chia-chuang, where they talked all night long exclusively about Wu's writings. When Wu returned to the Tsing Hua campus, his praise of Mao was exceedingly high. The compliments he paid Mao were undoubtedly inflated and certainly enhanced Mao's popularity and the Communist cause among the large academic community of Peking. After the Communist occupation of Peking, Wu was made deputy mayor of the city, a post unprecedented for a university professor. However, as soon as Wu's writings came to be seen as thinly veiled criticisms of the actions and policies of Mao's leadership, his downfall ensued. He was persecuted to death, although the blame of this, according to a belated official report, has now been put on the Gang of Four. Wu's wife and daughter also suffered tragic deaths due to his disgrace.

Immediately after the founding of a new dynasty, emperors as a rule would slaughter many loyal supporters who helped put the emperor on the throne. In similar fashion, Mao liquidated P'eng Te-huai and Lin Piao, both of whom had helped him militarily in founding the Communist regime. He also liquidated Liu Shao-ch'i, who was the most important person in elevating Mao to the position as the leader and the teacher in the Party and in the country. It was Liu who first coined the term "the thought of Mao Tse-tung" and introduced it into the Party constitution in 1945 as the guiding principle of the Communist Party. Lin Piao was the person who, at a later date, also helped Mao to wipe out Liu during the Cultural Revolution. Chou En-lai, who helped Mao by organizing and running the government in good order so that Mao could carry out his reforms, narrowly escaped liquidation by his "timely death" from illness.

Those democrats who helped Mao tremendously by undermining the Kuomintang government were labeled Rightists and severely punished when they criticized the Communist government under the slogan of "let hundred schools contend and let hundred flowers bloom." As we mentioned earlier, these individuals were tricked into contending or blossoming, and they suffered the punitive actions that they had been assured beforehand would not occur. The punishment was so severe and widespread that a situation of complete silence prevailed in the whole country for a long time thereafter. Thanks to the fall of the Gang of Four, people have since been able to voice their grievances by attributing all evils to these four people.

As far as the clever and successful manipulation of statecraft is concerned, I would include Mao among those great emperors who founded a new dynasty. This observation is shared by most Chinese. Among Westerners, Dick Wilson for one, has a similar idea, as shown by the title of his book *Mao, the People's Emperor*.[134] More significantly, Chinese often compare Mao to the great founder of a great dynasty. In his heart of hearts he might well make such a comparison himself. In his famous prose-poem on snow, he criticized the founders of Ch'in, Han, T'ang, and Sung as lacking literary brilliance, and Genghis Khan as being too rude, for he knew nothing more than to shoot at vultures. The last sentence of the poem says that "The truly great man can only be found in the present age." Because Chinese grammar does not formally indicate singular or plural the meaning is ambiguous. The suggestion could be that only in the present age will the truly great men be found, with Mao among them, or that Mao is the great man. In reading the poem, most Chinese get the latter impression. It is safe to say that Mao's ideal great man is one who combined the two qualities of learning and statecraft, and that he himself possesses learning, in the form of his knowledge of Marxism-Leninism and his literary talents, and excelled in statecraft.

Mao's mind held two opposite ideologies—feudalism and communism. Although he was a communist, certain feudalist thoughts or tendencies nevertheless dominated his behavior. Like other great feudal emperors, Mao was, as has been pointed out, fond of bigness and recognition. He lusted for power and fame, and immortality. The personality cult of glorifying him had developed to an extreme during his lifetime. In the Party and in the government, he acted as a patriarch, which in modern terms is called a dictator. He enjoyed writing poems in the classical style—a heritage from the pundit aristocrats—the like of which I have not found in any other modern dictator. In his later years, Mao had become a god among the Chinese, who worshipped him morning and night. As we know, all past Chinese emperors were deified. While some may argue that Mao's deification was Lin Piao's doing, it would be inconceivable to believe that Mao did not know and approve. He was strong and shrewd enough to stop anything he did not like. The Sung founding emperor was made an emperor by his generals who put a yellow robe on him, we are told. Could we say that this ran against the will of Chao K'uang-yin and that he was reluctant to become an emperor? 'Feudal socialism,' a phrase coined on mainland China, aptly describes this phase of Mao's versatile career.

I am inclined to think that Mao, with the talents of an emperor in founding a new dynasty, could have succeeded in creating a new regime of any ideology, even if he had not been a Marxist. However, his chances of success were enhanced by his professing to be a Marxist, which entitled him to the support of international communists and of foreign and domestic progressive elements in addition to his own Party. In modern terms, Mao's ambition was to change the world as Marx envisioned. To express this idea in Mao's own poetic diction as we quoted in the beginning of this section, he vowed "to replace a new sun and a new moon in effecting a new Heaven." His achievements can be viewed from two sides, destructive and constructive. On the destructive side, in the political realm, he succeeded in destroying the Kuomintang government on the mainland. In the economic realm, he succeeded in destroying the multicentury-old system of private property ownership of the Chinese society. This led to the disappearance of the marked difference between the opulent rich and abject poor. The military seizure of state power, followed by certain destructive measures, was only the first step, but the most important task was the construction of a new society according to Marxism as Mao envisioned. Let us examine what Mao had accomplished in this respect.

On the constructive side, a wide spectrum is to be noted. Under Mao's leadership, the Communist government achieved unprecedented unity throughout the breadth and width of the whole country. With the socialist system, there was a sharp upgrading of the social status of poor workers and peasants. In the same vein, a woman's position was immensely elevated; soldiers too were now to be respected, contradicting the old conception that good people would never be soldiers. A certain amount of material construction had been achieved, but whether this should be labeled, within a period of thirty years, as great and significant, and whether this lives up the the needs of a modern state, is subject to evaluation. But on the whole, China remains a poor country, with a low per capita income, even in comparison with other developing countries.

On the spiritual side, Mao vowed to change human nature from selfishness to communist selflessness. From the voluminous reports published in Hong Kong, including the leftist magazines, and the eyewitness reports that I heard from overseas Chinese returning to China, there has been no evidence that the bloody and cataclysmic turmoils, such as the Cultural Revolution, brought improved changes in human nature. Nor does China's future hold in store a lofty selfless society.

On the cultural side, few books were published during the Mao period; what publications were available either echoed Mao's quotations or the official Party line. Schools were closed for almost ten years. One Communist educator lamented that universities were such in name only (actually, they use high school textbooks and have primary school standing).

280

The crucial and central point is: did Mao contribute a permanent model for building socialism? Marx and Engels both said little about the form of organization that would replace capitalist society, nor did they describe the practical measures necessary to achieve the ultimate goal—the communist society. Any blueprint of the new society was actually discouraged as being utopian. Nor was Lenin in favor of making such an attempt. After his military seizure of power, Mao had more visions than he had concrete plans for building socialism. The only model for Mao to follow was, as Mao himself proclaimed, the Soviet Union. Beyond this, he had to grope for specific solutions for China. After breaking relations with the Soviets in 1958, Mao, forced to rely on his own resources, intensified the policy of self-reliance. The Three Red Flags campaign—the general line for socialist construction, people's communes, and the Great Leap Forward—begun in 1958, are a credit to Mao's ingenuity. The general line for socialist construction was only an abstract principle; the Great Leap Forward was definitely a disaster; and the success of the people's communes is increasingly doubtful. If we judge present China by the following facts, that production is meager, that people's confidence in the government and in socialism is sagging, and that discontent among the people is widespread, we are tempted to say that Mao failed in his effort to build socialism.

The words of Stuart Schram in 1963 are still applicable to Mao today. Schram wrote, "Whatever his future contribution may be, there is little doubt that his theories and his example regarding the road to power in the undeveloped countries will continue to exercise an influence for many years to come. But for the moment, the question of whether he has anything to say to China and to the rest of Asia, Africa, and Latin America about the road to industrialization and modernization remains entirely open."[135] To summarize, Mao's contribution in China, as well as in the underdeveloped countries, is more remarkable for its destruction, which he carried out spectacularly, than for construction. With regard to the peaceful construction of Chinese society, it is almost as though Mao had turned in a blank examination paper, as he did in his student days for a geometry examination. This is unfortunate for Mao himself, and more importantly, for China's modernization. It meant a waste and delay of at least thirty years.

The image of Mao's infallibility has begun to shatter in the years following his death. People have begun to ask what his merits and demerits are. Such evaluations, including those of the Communists themselves, vary greatly among different people. There are those who grade Mao's merits over demerits in a ratio of 70:30; there are others who hold an entirely opposite view, putting the ratio at 30:70. There are also the in-between people who suggest a ratio of 60:40, or 40:60, or 50:50. Teng Hsiao-p'ing, evading the question, shrewdly suggested that history should decide this problem, for history can give a definite and just conclusion, and people of later years will be wiser than we. Top Communist leaders such as Yeh Chien-ying and Teng Hsiao-p'ing, while conceding that Mao did make some mistakes, including serious ones, still insist that Mao's contribution to new China is incomparable.

The appraisal of the achievements under the Communist regime, dominated by Mao's dictatorial design, both materially and spiritually, will be discussed in more detail in the next chapter. At present we wish to point out that Mao's most damaging harm to China lies in his squandering of human resources. What China needs most urgently is modernization to cure her poverty and backwardness, the success of which primarily depends on her human resources.

If we view China's problem from an historical perspective, we find that China's modernization movement has been a tardy and slow process. Modernization mainly consists of industrialization through Westernization. World history reveals that there have been two industrial revolutions. The first one began in the middle of the eighteenth century to the mid-nineteenth century, gradually spreading throughout Europe. Essentially, the first industrial revolution substituted human labor with machines. Obviously, China missed that one. Moreover, China started her modernization by adopting Westernization several decades even after Japan did. The second industrial revolution, as some call it, is the extensive use of computer machines. This revolution has replaced certain kinds of mental labor with machines in data processing.

The development of computer science, which began in the 1940s and 1950s, progressed rapidly in the 1960s. Unfortunately, China, in this period, was preoccupied with revolutionary struggles and movements. These struggles and movements generally resulted in the transfer of wealth from one social class to another class rather than in creating wealth for the nation. In construction work, emphasis was laid on primitive methods, using people's two hands to create miraculous wonders. 'To learn from Ta-chai' is a good example of one campaign of that period. The central aim of this movement was to apply primitive methods, notably human labor, to build bridges, dams, and other much-needed infrastructure. Although one can admire the spirit of the industrious and hardworking Chinese people, this is hardly an efficient and effective way to modernize in the twentieth century. During the revolutionary period, the best talents of the Chinese were not engaged in the study of science and technology with a view to saving labor and increasing efficiency. Rather, the people were encouraged by Mao's teachings to glorify improper labor-intensive working processes over labor-saving machines. The blame for the backward economic conditions of today which resulted from the retardation of modernization, must be placed on the ideas of Mao.

What is most tragic is that there existed an official policy to show contempt for educational, scientific, and cultural work, and to discriminate against, and even persecute, intellectuals. As a result of this policy, the educated adults of Mao's heyday could not perform their professional work; they wasted, in various ways, their prime years of life. There was also created a lost generation of youth who did not receive a proper education and who know nothing but fighting, struggle, and revolution. When the time comes for this generation to shoulder the responsibilities of social reconstruction, politically, economically, and culturally, there will be a vacuum of competent, responsible and educated citizens.

Mao was gifted in seizing political power through a revolution, and in establishing a new government of unprecedented centralized personal power. But while he not only failed to elevate the material and spiritual life of the masses to an appreciable level according to socialist visions, he also incurred through his mistakes an awesome and irreplaceable waste of human resources by actually ruining two whole generations of people. Judging from all these facts, I painfully come to the conclusion that Mao did more harm than good to China.

Notes

[1] The life of Mao in this biographical sketch is heavily based on Li Jui, *Mao Tse-tung t'ung-chih te ch'u-ch'i ko-ming huo-tung* (Peking: Chung-kuo ch'ing-nien ch'u pan-she, 1957). Other chief works include: Hu Hua, *Chung-kuo hsin min-chu chu-i ko-ming shih* (Peking: Jen-min ch'u-pan she, 1951); Hu Ch'iao-mu, *Chung-kuo kung-ch'an tang te san-shih nien* (Peking: Jen-min ch'u-pan she, 1951); Hsiao San, *Mao Tse-tung t'ung-chih te ch'ing shao-nien shih-ti* (Peking: Hsin-hua shu-tien, 1950).

[2] Mao Tse-tung, "Lun lien-ho cheng-fu," *Mao Tse-tung hsüan-chi* (1969) 3:937.

[3] Quoted in Chung-kuo kung-ch'an tang chung-yang wei-yuan hui, "Kuan-yü wu-ch'an chieh-chi wen-hua ta ko-ming te chueh-ting," *Jen-min jih-pao*, 11 August 1966.

[4] Mao, "Shih-chien lun," *MTTHC*, 1:259.

[5] *Jen-min jih-pao*, editorial, 29 January 1961.

[6] Mao, "Shih-chien lun," *MTTHC*, 1:273.

[7] Refer to note no. 61, Chapter 3.

[8] Mao, "Mao-tun lun," *MTTHC*, 1:274.

[9] Ibid., p. 275.

[10] Ibid.

[11] Ibid., pp. 276–77.

[12] Ibid., pp. 297–98.

[13] Ibid., pp. 308–9.

[14] For details of Mao's arguments on the two kinds of contradictions, see Mao, "Kuan-yü cheng-ch'ueh ch'u-li jen-min nei-pu mao-tun te wen-t'i," *MTTHC*, 5:363–66, 389.

[15] For an elaboration of Mao's theory and practice in continual revolution, see Hua Kuo-feng, "Pa wu-ch'an chieh-chi chuan-cheng hsia te chi-hsu ko-ming chin-hsing tao-ti," *Jen-min jih-pao*, 4 May 1977.

[16] This account is based on Mao, "Chung-kuo ko-ming ho Chung-kuo kung-ch'an tang," *MTTHC*, 2:584–617.

[17] For Mao's ten accusations against foreign invasion, see Mao, *MTTHC*, 2:591–3.

[18] Ibid., p. 610.

[19] Mao, "Hsin min-chu chu-i lun," *MTTHC*, 2:629.

[20] Ibid., p. 635.

[21] Ibid., pp. 635–36.

[22] Ibid., 2:637; Mao, "Lun jen-min min-chu chuan-cheng," *MTTHC* 4:1366.

[23] Ibid., 2:637–38. Mao did not elaborate on democratic centralism in this article.

[24] Refer to Chapter 3 on Sun Yat-sen for a discussion on these two principles.

[25] Mao, "Hsin min-chu chu-i lun," *MTTHC*, 2:624.

[26] Ibid., p. 659.

[27] Ibid., p. 666.

[28] Ibid., p. 667.

[29] Ibid., p. 668.

[30] Ibid., p. 653.

[31] Ibid., p. 655.

[32] Mao, "Lun lien-ho cheng-fu," *MTTHC*, 3:963.

[33] See note 32, Chapter 4, on Hu Shih.

[34] Mao, "Wei cheng-ch'ü ch'ien-pai-wan ch'ün-chung chin-ju k'ang-Jih min-tsu t'ung-i chan-hsien erh tou-cheng," *MTTHC*, 1:255–56.

[35] Mao, "Kuan-yü ling-tao fang-fa te jo-kan wen-t'i," *MTTHC*, 3:854.

[36] Liu Shao-ch'i, "Lun-tang," *She-hui chu-i chiao-yü k'o-ch'eng te yueh-tu wen-chien hui-pien* (Peking: Jen-min ch'u-pan she, 1958), 2:38.

[37] Mao, "Lun jen-min min-chu chuan-cheng," *MTTHC*, 4:1364.

[38] Mao, "Ch'u-li jen-min nei-pu mao-tun," *MTTHC*, 5:366–68.

[39] Mao, "Lun jen-min min-chu chuan-cheng," *MTTHC*, 4:1364.

[40] Ibid., p. 1366.

[41] Mao, "Kuan-yü chiu-cheng tang-nei te ts'o-wu szu-hsiang," *MTTHC*, 1:86.

[42] Mu Fu-sheng, *The Wilting of the Hundred Flowers* (New York: Praeger, 1962), p. 152.

[43] Ibid., p. 165.

[44] For details, see Mao, "Fan-tui tzu-yu chu-i," *MTTHC*, 2:330–31.

[45] Ibid., p. 332.

[46] Mao, "Tsai Chung-kuo kung-ch'an tang ti-pa-chieh chung-yang wei-yuan hui ti-erh tz'u ch'üan-t'i hui-i shang te chiang-hua," *MTTHC*, 5:323.

[47] Mao Tse-tung, "Pien-cheng fa chü-li," in *Mao Tse-tung szu-hsiang wan-sui* (n.p., 1967 and 1969), 1:130–31. Hereafter referred to as *Wan-sui*, the 1967 volume as book 1 and the 1969 volume as book 2. There is another 1967 volume, indicated as volume 3 by the original publisher, which began to circulate in this country at a later date than the first two volumes and contains some articles overlapping with those in the other two volumes.

[48] Mao, "Tsai pa-ta erh-tz'u hui-i shang te chiang-hua," *Wan-sui*, 2:195.

[49] Shen-hsi shih-fan ta-hsueh hsieh-tso tsu, "Ch'in Shih-huang shih chien-chueh ta-chi nu-li chu fu-p'i te cheng-chih-chia," *Jen-min jih-pao*, 31 October 1973. For more information, see *Ch'in Shih-huang tsai li-shih shang te chin-pu tso-yung*, enlarged edition (Hu-nan jen-min ch'u-pan she, 1973). This book is a collection of articles, including the above *Jen-min jih-pao* article.

[50] Shih Ting, "Fen-shu k'eng-ju pien," *Ch'in Shih-huang tsai li-shih*, p. 26.

[51] Ibid., p. 28.

[52] Ibid., p. 29.

[53] Joseph R. Levenson and Franz Shurmann, *China: An Interpretive History* (Berkeley: University of California Press, 1969), p. 37.

[54] For details, see Kuo Mo-jo, "Chung-kuo ku-tai shih te fen-ch'i wen-t'i," *Hung-ch'i* 7 (1972), especially pp. 61–62.

[55] "Szu-jen pang tsun-fa ch'ou-chü te mu-ch'ien mu-hou," *Li-shih yen-chiu* (Peking), no. 5 (May 1978):15.

[56] Mao, "Tui A-erh-pa-ni-ya chün-shih tai-piao t'uan te chiang-hua," *Wan-sui*, 2:678.

[57] Chou Yü-jui, *Hung-ch'ao jen-wu chih* (New York: Shih-chieh jih-pao she, 1976), p. 169.

[58] "Mao Tse-tung yü Peng-pi-tu te hui-t'an," *Ming-pao yueh-k'an* (Hong Kong), no. 131 (1976):29–30.

[59] Bertrand Russell, *Unpopular Essays* (New York: Simon and Schuster, 1962), p. 140.

[60] Mao, "I-chiu-wu-ch'i nien hsia-chi te hsing-shih," *MTTHC*, 5:456–457.

[61] Edmund Wilson, *To the Finland Station* (New York: Doubleday, 1953), p. 326.

[62] Mao Tse-tung, "Yen-chung te chiao-hsun," *Chung-kuo nung-ts'un te she-hui chu-i kao-ch'ao* (Peking: Jen-min ch'u-pan she, 1956), p. 123.

[63] "Tui Sun Yeh-fang te p'i-p'an ho ching-chi chan-hsien te tou-p'i-kai," *Jen-min jih-pao*, 24 February 1970.

[64] Kung Wen-sheng, "Po Sun Yeh-fang te hsiu-cheng chu-i 'ching-chi kang-ling,'" *Jen-min jih-pao*, 10 August 1966, p. 4.

[65] For details of Sun's arguments, readers may wish to refer to Wen-shun Chi, "Sun Yeh-fang and his Revisionist Economics," *Asian Survey* 22, no. 10 (October 1972): 887–900.

[66] Chi-lin sheng ko-ming wei-yuan hui hsieh-tso hsiao-tsu, "She-hui chu-i chien-she yü ching-chi hsueh liang-yü chung te chieh-chi tou-cheng," *Hung-ch'i*, no. 2 (1970):55.

[67] "Hsu Ti-hsin lun li-jun wen-t'i" *Ta Kung Pao* (Hong Kong), 24 November 1977.

[68] Karl Marx, "Introduction to 'Critique to Political Economy,'" *Capital and Other Writings of Karl Marx* (New York: Modern Library, 1932), pp. 10–11.

⁶⁹ Mao, "Mao-tun lun," *MTTHC*, 1:300–301.

⁷⁰ Mao, "Tu Cheng-chih ching-chi hsueh chiao-k'o-shu (she-hui chu-i pu-fen) te pi-chi," *Wan-sui*, 1:194-195.

⁷¹ Ibid., p. 182.

⁷² Mao, "Ch'u-li jen-min nei-pu mao-tun," *MTTHC*, 5:373.

⁷³ Mao, Tu Cheng-chih ching-chi hsueh," *Wan-sui*, 1:195.

⁷⁴ Ibid., p. 218.

⁷⁵ Ibid., p. 208.

⁷⁶ Mao, "Su-lien Cheng-chih ching-chi hsueh tu-shu pi-chi," *Wan-sui*, 2:359.

⁷⁷ Ibid., 2:359–60.

⁷⁸ Mao, "Ch'u-li jen-min nei-pu mao-tun," *MTTHC*, 5:374.

⁷⁹ Hua Kuo-feng, "Pa wu-ch'an chieh-chi chuan-cheng," *Jen-min jih-pao*, 4 May 1977.

⁸⁰ Liu, *She-hui chu-i chiao-yü*, 1:347.

⁸¹ "Chung-kuo kung-ch'an tang chang-ch'eng," *Chung-kuo kung-ch'an tang ti-pa chieh ch'üan-kuo tai-piao ta-hui wen-hsien* (Peking: Jen-min ch'u-pan she, 1956), pp. 821–22.

⁸² Mao, "Tu Cheng-chi ching-chi hsueh," *Wan-sui*, 1:192–193.

⁸³ Mao, "Lun lien-ho cheng-fu," *MTTHC*, 3:981.

⁸⁴ Mao, "Tsai Ch'eng-tu hui-i shang te chiang-hua," *Wan-sui*, 2:161.

⁸⁵ Mao, "Lun Shih ta kuan-hsi," *MTTHC*, 5:269.

⁸⁶ Mao, "Ch'u-li jen-min nei-pu mao-tun," *MTTHC*, 5:400.

⁸⁷ Hua Kuo-feng, "Pa wu-ch'an chieh-chi chuan-cheng," *Jen-min jih-pao*, 4 May 1977.

⁸⁸ Mao, "Ch'u-li jen-min nei-pu mao-tun," *MTTHC*, 5:389.

⁸⁹ *Some Basic Facts about China*, supplement to *China Reconstructs* (Peking: January 1974), p. 53.

⁹⁰ Ibid., pp. 56–57.

⁹¹ Mao, *Wan-sui*, 2:303.

⁹² *Some Basic Facts about China*, p. 53.

⁹³ Edgar Snow, "China's Communes, Success or Failure" *The New Republic*, (26 June 1971):21.

⁹⁴ *The Confucian Analects*, bk. 16, ch. 1, sec. 10, my translation. For details concerning this point and other traditional sources, readers may wish to see Wen-shun Chi, "New Economic Ideas and Their Traditional Sources in China," *Current Scene* 13, nos. 5 and 6 (May–June 1975):1–13.

⁹⁵ Yao Wen-yuan, "Lun Lin Piao fan-tang chi-t'uan te she-hui chi-ch'u," *Hung-ch'i*, no. 3 (March 1975):22.

⁹⁶ *Jen-min jih-pao*, editorial, 3 February 1958, supposedly written by Mao.

⁹⁷ Mao, "Tu Cheng-chih ching-chi hsueh," *Wan-sui*, 1:194.

⁹⁸ Mao, "Tseng-ch'iang tang te t'uan-chieh, chi-ch'eng tang te ch'uan t'ung," *MTTHC*, 5:296.

⁹⁹ For details of these four questions, see Mao, "Tsai Yenan wen-i tso-t'an hui shang te chiang-hua," *MTTHC*, 3:804–35.

¹⁰⁰ Mao, "Wu-ch'i chih-shih," *Wan-sui*, 2:642–43.

¹⁰¹ "Ts'ung Shang-hai chi-ch'uang ch'ang k'an p'ei-yang kung-ch'eng chi-shu jen-yuan te tao-lu," *Jen-min jih-pao*, 22 July 1968.

¹⁰² Mao, "Ni ta ni-te, wo ta wo-te," *Wan-sui*, 2:614–15.

¹⁰³ Mao, "Tui wei-sheng kung-tso te chih-shih," *Wan-sui*, 2:615–16.

¹⁰⁴ Mao, "Yüu Ch'en Po-ta, Ai Szu-ch'i t'ung-chih te t'an-hua." *Wan-sui*, 2:631.

¹⁰⁵ Mao, "Tsai Hang-chou hui-i shang te chiang-hua," *Wan-sui*, 2:625–26.

¹⁰⁶ Mao, "Ta liang hsi-shou chih-shih fen-tzu," *MTTHC*, 2:581.

¹⁰⁷ Mao, "Lun lien-ho cheng-fu," *MTTHC*, 3:983–84.

¹⁰⁸ "Ch'u-li jen-min nei-pu mao-tun," *MTTHC*, 5:385.

¹⁰⁹ Pei Wen-chung et al., *Wo-te szu-hsiang shih tsen-mo chuan-pien kuo-lai te?* (Peking: Wu-shih nien-tai ch'u-pan she, 1952).

[110] Mao, "Ch'u-li jen-min nei-pu mao-tun," *MTTHC*, 5:385.

[111] Mao, "Tsai Ch'eng-tu hui-i shang te chiang-hua," *Wan-sui*, 2:176–77.

[112] Mao, "Tsai pa-ta erh-tz'u hui-i shang te chiang-hua," *Wan-sui*, 2:192.

[113] Mao, "Tsai Hang-chou hui-i shang te chiang-hua," *Wan-sui*, 2:626–27.

[114] Mao, "Chao-chien shou-tu hung tai-hui fu-tse jen te chiang-hua," *Wan-sui*, 2:693–94.

[115] Mao, "Tsai Lu-shan hui-i shang te chiang-hua," *Wan-sui*, 2:298; Mao, "Ch'un-chieh t'an-hua chi-yao," *Wan-sui*, 2:460 (on this page, the reference to Han Wu-ti [the emperor Wu of Han] as the Chinese text reads is evidently a misprint. It should read Liang Wu-ti [the emperor Wu of Liang] as in the English text); Mao, "Tsai i-tz'u hui-pao shih te ch'a-hua," *Wan-sui*, 2:476–77.

[116] Wen-shun Chi, "The Ideological Source of the People's Commune in Communist China," *Pacific Coast Philology* 2 (April 1967):62–78.

[117] V. Gelbras, *Mao's Pseudo-Socialism* (Moscow: Novosti Agency, n.d.), pp. 6, 24.

[118] This story was told to me by Carsun Chang who was told it by a high official from mainland China in India. Another version, from a Chinese official visiting this country, is that Mao did make this remark when he met K'ang T'ung-pi at the National Congress but not at her house.

[119] Yen Fu, *Ch'ün-chi ch'üan-chieh lun* (Shanghai: Commercial, 1931), p. 3.

[120] Mao, "Kai-tsao wo-men te hsueh-hsi," *MTTHC*, 3:754.

[121] Mao, "Cheng-tun tang te tso-feng," *MTTHC*, 3:778.

[122] Mao, "Cheng-tun hsueh feng, tang-feng, wen-feng," *Cheng-feng wen-hsien* (Hong Kong: Hsin min-chu ch'u-pan she, 1949) p. 17. This passage has been deleted from Mao's *Hsüan-chi* of 1953 and subsequent editions.

[123] Mao, *Cheng-feng wen-hsien*, p. 50. The last clause of the quotation, from "otherwise" to "useless" has been deleted from *MTTHC*.

[124] Ibid., p. 10. This passage has been deleted from *MTTHC*.

[125] Mao, "Cheng-tun tang te tso-feng," *MTTHC*, 3:772.

[126] Mao, "Ch'un-chieh t'an-hua chi-yao," *Wan-sui*, 2:464.

[127] *Mencius*, bk 1, pt. 1, ch. 6, secs. 2–4.

[128] Ibid., bk. 2, pt. 1, ch. 2, sec. 24.

[129] Mao, "Hu-nan nung-min yun-tung k'ao-ch'a pao-kao," *MTTHC*, 1:17.

[130] Mao, "Tsai Nan-ning hui-i shang te chiang-hua," *Wan-sui*, 2:147.

[131] Ibid., pp. 155–56, 178 for Mao's answers to the criticisms.

[132] Trans. by D. C. Lau, *Mencius*, p. 63.

[133] Chou Yang, "Niu-kuei she-shen tsai K'ung-tzu t'ao-lun hui shang fang-le hsieh shen-ma tu?" *Jen-min jih-pao*, 10 January 1967.

[134] Dick Wilson, *Mao, The People's Emperor* (London: Hutchinson, 1979).

[135] Stuart R. Schram, *The Political Thought of Mao Tse-tung* (New York: Praeger, 1963), p. 84.

10
Conclusion

Why Mao Alone Triumphed

Of the nine people described in this book, only Sun and Mao—the revolutionaries—succeeded, to different degrees, in their political and revolutionary careers, while the rest, who esteemed learning, remained thinkers only. For convenience, at this point, we will label the six scholars—K'ang Yu-wei, Liang Ch'i-ch'ao, Hu Shih, Liang Shu-ming, Chang Chün-mai, and Chang Tung-sun—as the scholar group. Ch'en Tu-hsiu does not belong in either the revolutionary or the scholar category, though I would classify him more as a scholarly person than as a man of action. Now we turn to the question of why Mao alone finally triumphed.

Teacher to the King

The success or failure of the revolutionary and scholar groups may, in one important sense, be attributed to a primary reason—a difference in their tactics, the tactics of effecting social change from the bottom upward versus from the top downward. Obviously, Mao mobilized the masses to a far greater extent than did Sun. The scholar group attempted to carry out their programs for social reconstruction by trying to influence the rulers. The important concept that underlies and dominates their activities is the concept of being the teacher to the king *(wang-che shih)*. This position implies specific duties and the highest moral prestige. The most dramatic manifestation of a teacher to the king is illustrated by the following episode from *Mencius*.

Mencius was about to see the King of Ch'i, when a messenger came from the king with the message, "I was to have come to see you, but I am suffering from a cold and cannot be exposed to the wind. In the morning, I will be holding court. I wonder if you will give me the opportunity of seeing you." To this, Mencius replied, "Unfortunately, I am ill too and will be unable to come to the court." The next day Mencius went on a visit of condolence to the family of a high official. One of his distinguished disciples said to him, "Yesterday you excused yourself on the grounds of illness, yet today you go on a visit of condolence. May this not be regarded as improper?" Mencius replied, "Yesterday I was ill, and today I am recovered. Why should I not go on a visit of condolence?"

The king was very courteous and sent a messenger accompanied by a doctor to inquire about Mencius' illness. Mencius' cousin, who was clever, replied that "Mencius was ill yesterday and was unable to go to the court when the King's summons came. Today he is somewhat better and has hastened to court. But I am not sure if he has reached there by this time." Having said this, he sent several men to intercept Mencius with the message, "Don't, under any circumstance, come home but go straight to court." Mencius insistently refused to go to the court and was forced to go to another high official's house to spend the night. The high official politely observed that he had seen the king's respect for Mencius but not Mencius' respect for the king. After a few exchanges between the guest and the host, Mencius made his famous reply: "A prince who is to achieve great things must have subjects he does not summon. If he wants to consult them, he goes to them. If he does not honor virtue and delight in the Way in such a manner, he is not worthy of being helped towards the achievement of great things."[1]

This is a vivid description of the services which a teacher to the king would perform and of the prestige and dignity a king should accord him. He is not to teach the king ordinary academic subjects, as the tutors to the kings in Europe and in China generally did, but to advise and assist the king in ruling the empire and running the government properly. He is to be respected by the king as a teacher is respected by his student. Such is the dignity of the teacher to the king that he cannot be summoned but rather must be sought out by the king, who respectfully asks his advice.

In history, such modest rulers were exceedingly rare, but to be teacher to the king remained the dream and aspiration of scholars who were interested in creating a period of good government. This concept has dominated the thinking of scholars, or at least was exceedingly influential before the contemporary period.

In Chinese history, intellectuals have been in the position of advising and assisting in the governing of the country. They themselves were not the rulers. If a scholar could not become the teacher to the king, the next best thing was for him to become a prime minister (though this was less prestigious), a position which also permitted him to advise and help the ruler. In either case, the orthodox scholar was prevented by his ideology from attempting to assume the throne himself.

In contemporary times, scholars still cherish the concept of playing the role of teacher to the king or of prime minister, but in different form. Of course, there have been no imperial rulers since the last years of K'ang Yu-wei's time, but scholars have persisted in trying to play the role of mentor to whoever was in power. In other words, they would advise the ruler on how to achieve modernization and industrialization but would not themselves seek to establish an essentially new political order, as would Sun or Mao. Let us illustrate this psychology from a widely known episode found in the famous novel, *The Romance of the Three Kingdoms,* a book that Mao enjoyed immensely. (This episode was based on *Hou-Han shu.*)

Prior to the time of the Three Kingdoms, there was a scholar, Hsu Shao, renowned for his accurate appraisal of people. This scholar was visited by Ts'ao Ts'ao when he was an obscure government official before his virtual usurpation of the Han dynasty throne. The scholar at first declined to respond to Ts'ao Ts'ao's request for a personal appraisal, but due to Ts'ao Ts'ao's insistence, he later consented. He said of Ts'ao Ts'ao's character, "You would be an able minister in a good government but would be a capable scoundrel in a time of chaos." Ts'ao Ts'ao was extremely pleased. The Chinese for "capable scoundrel" is *"chien-hsiung,"* which has no exact equivalent in English. It refers to a man of undeniable ability who uses his ability for nefarious, and, above all, treacherous purposes. In private conversations, the famous geologist, V. K. Ting, was wont to say sentimentally that "We are people who would be able ministers in a period of good government, but are rice kegs in a period of chaos." "Rice keg" is a Chinese expression which refers to a person who is good for nothing except for consuming rice, i.e., food. By "we people" he meant himself and his good friends, notably Hu Shih and other scholars.

In the ancient connotation, the phrase "capable scoundrel" was, in a sense, synonymous with treason. In modern connotation, it may be construed to mean a rebel, someone who breaks away from traditional moral principles. By paraphrasing the original quotation and substituting rice keg for capable scoundrel, Ting was suggesting that he and people like him could only give counsel to achieve a good government in peaceful times, but could never be revolutionaries in chaotic times. These scholars were limited by the traditional view of a scholar's role in government and by the lack of intrepid courage and exceptional ability required to create a new dynasty.

Moreover, these thinkers of the scholar group were primarily scholars. Their basic interest was in learning, not in politics. Their interest in politics derived from the lofty tradition that scholars assume the responsibilty of the whole world. Again, their role was chiefly limited to advice and assistance. But Mao was entirely different. He was a practical man, a man of action. As we have indicated, although he studied Marxism and wrote poems, he did not stop at being a theoretical Marxist or a poet describing the beauty of nature. Rather he used Marxism and poems as instruments to effect a revolution according to his own visions. In other words, Mao vowed to create a new government on his own, the way emperors had established new dynasties, while the other scholars had no such ambitions.

The Importance of a Political Party

Another factor which determined the success or failure of the two groups was the existence or nonexistence of a political party as an instrument to further each one's programs. In summarizing the first twenty-eight years of the Chinese Communist Party, Mao attributed a crucial role to the Party as a weapon for achieving a Communist victory, a victory which had eluded other revolutionaries who had lacked this weapon.[2] Elsewhere, Mao pointed out that the Chinese and Russian experiences proved that a well-organized and experienced party was an important condition for the success of the revolution.[3] Mao's account of his experience shows the importance of a political party to a revolutionary's career.

Now let us review the history of the other political thinkers. Sun's initial success in overthrowing the Manchu government can be mainly attributed to the activities of his party. However, the scholar group either did not organize a party at all or did so only halfheartedly. K'ang Yu-wei's Monarchical Party was hardly a political party in the strict sense of the word. Liang Ch'i-ch'ao organized and joined the Progressive Party, but not in a serious way. Hu Shih refused to join any party, even though in his later years his admirers begged him to lead a democratic party. Carsun Chang did found a party, the Socialist Democratic Party, which was to serve as a symbol of an opposition party. However, he did not organize it as a modern political party whose main function was to gain political control. Rather, he and his cofounder, Chang Tung-sun, pledged to dissolve it when the Kuomintang abolished its one-party dictatorship and a multiparty system was realized. Their intention was to show that their primary aim was for principle, not for political power.[4] Liang Shu-ming vowed that he and his followers would under no circumstances seek or hold political power. Evidently, Liang had not the slightest intention of organizing a political party. Ch'en Tu-hsiu, after his disillusionment with Soviet communism, proclaimed his resumption of independence from any political affiliation.

Under such circumstances we find that, on the one hand, there was the Communist Party, well organized and well disciplined, assiduously striving for the realization of their ideals. On the other hand, there were the other reformers in the scholar group, who had no organization to carry out their programs and who limited their individual actions to propagandizing their ideas on paper. They refused to accept any political power, which is obviously indispensable for effecting any important social change. This unrealistic attitude of not wanting to hold power was rooted in the old Chinese ideological tradition of belittling practical politics. Thus, the reformers of the scholar group just talked and waited for competent government leaders to invite them to advise and to adopt their programs. The success of the one and the futility of the other was only the natural and clear consequence of the different courses they took.

The Causes of the Kuomintang's Failure

From the above analysis, we have seen the importance of a political party to the success of a reform movement and the futility of a reform movement carried out by unorganized individuals without the support of a party. However, since the Nationalists and the Communists were supported by their respective political parties, other elements must have been decisive in producing the Communist victory on the mainland. Sun Yat-sen did found a party with clearly stated principles and programs for social reconstruction. The party was organized after the pattern of the Soviet model and its first constitution was drafted by Borodin.

Marxism as a theory is far more attractive and much more systematic than Sun's principles. It appealed to the intellectuals as a beautiful utopia to seek and a meaningful goal for which to fight. The intellectuals were dazzled by the highly publicized successes of the Soviet Union's five-year plans and they hoped the same plan could be copied and realized for China. But to my mind, a consideration of greater weight than either the theoretical appeal of Marxism or the example of the Soviet Union's economic success, and which tipped the balance of success heavily to the side of the Communists, was the corruption of the Kuomintang and its Nationalist government. In the last years prior to its downfall on the mainland, the Kuomintang was plagued by corruption, notably manifest in favoritism, nepotism, and inefficiency. Ambitious and serious intellectuals were disillusioned; seeing little chance to devote themselves to meaningful careers, a great number of them "went Communist." This intellectual shift to communism actually was the deciding factor which brought about the downfall of the Nationalist government on the mainland. In the past one hundred years, it was the intellectuals who handled every great political change. Actually, the Communist movement in China is also an intellectual movement. In 1932, Hu Shih prophetically predicted that it would be the end of the Kuomintang if it should lose the support of the intellectuals.[5]

In a broader sense, the Communist Party had long been taken as a last resort for all kinds of dissatisfied or desperate people. There was a common saying during the War of Resistance that "If I can't get a decent job here, I can find it elsewhere. If no place can offer me a decent job, I'll join the Eighth Route [Army of the Communists] as a last resort."[6]

Immediately before the Communist conquest of mainland China, the dissatisfied political and military personnel, for one reason or another, pinned their hopes on the Communists, in the hope that their positions could be improved. There was also a common saying in Kuomintang circles that "When this road is blocked, go and look for Mao Tse-tung."[7] Naturally, it was easy for the Communists to pay lip service to the dissatisfied and the disillusioned to win their sympathy and support. Consequently, as people lost confidence in the Nationalist government and as its morale shattered, the whole edifice of the government disintegrated much faster than the Communists had anticipated.

The Aversion to Capitalism

Traditional Chinese philosophy has exerted great influence in bringing Chinese intellectuals close to the ideal of communism. Chinese intellectuals have a built-in aversion to capitalism. To them, capitalism is a system in which the capitalists, or businessmen, dominate the scene. It is a system which they find absolutely impossible to admire. In the *Communist Manifesto*, Marx has this to say: "The bourgeoisie, wherever it has got the upper hand, has put an end to all feudal, patriarchal, idyllic relations. It has pitilessly torn asunder the motley feudal ties that bound man to his 'natural superior,' and has left no other nexus between man and man than naked self-interest, than callous 'cash-payment.' It has drowned the most heavenly ecstasies of religious fervor, of chivalrous enthusiasm, of Philistine sentimentalism, in the icy water of egotistical calculation. It has resolved personal worth into exchange value."

The Chinese intellectuals were not much interested in Marx's definition of the kind of human relationships that existed in Western society and which perhaps did not apply to the Chinese. Rather, they were obsessed with the cherished human ties found in Chinese tradition and were especially concerned with the destruction of such ties by the introduction of capitalism. At the same time, they concurred with Marx's attack on the cash nexus and on cold calculation, since these two features of capitalist society were also traditionally detested.

The preeminent reason that brought the Chinese intellectuals close to communism was a deep-seated philosophical aversion to the pursuit of profit on the part of both individuals and the nation. In the *Confucian Analects,* one criterion on which the doctrine of the superior man is based is: "The superior man is conversant with righteousness; the mind of the small man is conversant with profit."[8] The *Book of Mencius* begins with Mencius giving advice to King Hui of Liang: "Why pursue profit? What matters is benevolence and righteousness."[9] Furthermore, in the social framework of Chinese traditional society, money-making merchants never enjoyed respect, and of the four classes of people, merchants were the lowliest, behind the scholars, farmers and artisans. Thus, a government by businessmen was detestable to the Chinese people. Socially, money was associated with odium. Such abhorrence is illustrated by a story of a fourteenth-century scholar who never used the word "money." The anecdote has it that his wife surrounded his bed with coins to force him to use the word, but he still refused and simply said, "Remove that thing!"

From this tradition against profit making and an aspiration for the *ta-t'ung* society of equality and brotherhood—which coincides with the ideal society of Marxism—the acceptance of the attractive aspects of the utopian elements of communism, although with reservations, is not hard to understand.

Change in the Communist Image

In the years of the May Fourth Movement, Western civilization was characterized in the Chinese mind by science and democracy. The Chinese admired and accepted both. However, Western political ideas and economic institutions were often associated with unpleasant memories of Western aggression, as was shown in the introductory chapter. For this, Mao had a very good explanation. From the 1840s to the beginning of the twentieth century, Mao observed, China was determined to learn from the progressive Western capitalist countries how to obtain salvation and achieve modernization. Mao said, "But the aggressions of the imperialists have shattered the dreams of the Chinese. How strange! Why do the teachers always carry out aggression against the students?... The October Revolution brought Marxism-Leninism to China. To take the road of the Russians—this is the final conclusion."[10]

On the other hand, the Soviet system was generally perceived as totalitarian, which was not acceptable to most Chinese intellectuals. But there were certain explanations of and justifications for the Soviet system, according to the leftist writers. First, Western democracy was criticized as being a kind of bourgeois democracy or false democracy. Second, the prevalent theory in China during the 1930s was that the capitalist countries had political democracy but not economic democracy, while the Soviets had economic democracy, but at the expense of certain political rights which were seen as being of little value if they failed to secure a livelihood for the masses.

Western democracy appeared to address no urgent reality and might therefore well be irrelevant. Furthermore, the theory of the New Democracy which Mao developed during the War of Resistance served to provide the appeal of political democracy to the Chinese Communist movement. Thus, the communist image conveyed to the intellectuals included both the economic democracy attributed to the Soviet model and a general political democracy, as distinct from the now discredited Western bourgeois democracy. In this way the ideological reservations that had earlier characterized the intellectual view toward communism were removed.

Tactically, after the Mukden Incident of 18 September 1931, the Communist Party manifested its sympathy for and support of the democratic movement in order to close ranks with all political forces against Japanese aggression. On 17 January 1933, Mao and Chu Te jointly issued a manifesto demanding, among other things, the guarantee of the people's democratic rights as the basis for cooperation between the Kuomintang and the Communist Party. In 1937, prior to the opening of the Third Plenum of the Kuomintang, the Communist Party sent a telegram to the Kuomintang, demanding the granting of freedom of speech, assembly, and association to all people; the release of political prisoners; and the promise of a meeting for national salvation, consisting of representatives from all parties and factions, all walks of life, and all military units. After the formation of the National United Front, the Communist Party appealed to the people of the whole country to join in the struggle for democracy and in resistance against Japan.[11] Thus, the Communist Party not only became an enthusiastic member of the democratic movement, but was also seen as perhaps its strongest promoter.

Japanese Aggression and Mao's Ability

The overwhelming loss of sympathy and confidence among the intellectuals for the Kuomintang, combined with a corresponding gain for the Communist Party, had a great deal to do with the failure of the former and the success of the latter, but this was not all. Other conditions favorable to the Communists must also be considered. We must remember the effect of the Japanese invasion on the balance of power between the Kuomintang and the Communists. In 1964, Mao said: "We have to show our appreciation to the Japanese Imperial Army. After the Japanese troops came, we fought against them and cooperated with Chiang Kai-shek. After eight years of war, the result was that our troops expanded from 25,000 strong to 1,200,000 strong, and the population of the territory under our control reached 100,000,000 people. Should we or should we not thank the Japanese?"[12] Chalmers Johnson regarded the Communists as the beneficiaries of the war,[13] and Tetsuya Kataoka said more explicitly that "in the sense that the revolution in China could not have succeeded without the war, one can conclude the revolution itself was a contingent event."[14]

Finally, and probably most important, Mao was an exceptionally able revolutionary. As we said, he was a man who combined both learning and statecraft, a rare event in history. Although communist historians hold that it is the people who create history and although they reject the great-man theory of history, it is beyond doubt that without Mao contemporary Chinese history would have run a different course. Even if we concede that the masses make history, the masses had to be mobilized to play this creative role, and it was Mao's ingenuity that recognized this necessity and developed the methods for achieving this mobilization.

Ideological Conflicts between Communist and Noncommunist Ideologies

Since its introduction into China in the beginning of the twentieth century, communism has become a powerful and widespread current of thought. Even noncommunist thinkers were forced to regard communist theory as a powerful force with which to contend. For the choice was either to go along with communism or to oppose it; communism was not to be ignored. Thus, we find that the intellectual history of modern China is in a sense a history of the conflict or struggle between communist and noncommunist thinkers. Generally speaking, communists are wont to categorize noncommunist thinkers of the past one hundred years as bourgeois reformists, in contrast to themselves as proletarian revolutionaries. To use communist terminology, it is the struggle between two lines—the bourgeois against the proletarian line. Mao capitalized on this conflict. Even at present, those who do not follow the official line are labeled capitalist roaders. Ideological conflicts existed in the past and still exist in contemporary China.

The so-called struggle between the two lines is very broad in scope. We find certain fundamental and sharp contrasts in ideas between the thinkers representing these two lines. Needless to say, these conflicting ideas originated in Europe and the Chinese thinkers adopted them. By and large, the main conflict may be seen as between communism and democracy and their related and supporting ideas. Except Chang Tung-sun among the thinkers, no one is a philosopher by profession. He is the only one who made an academic study of democracy and he politely conceded that this work was outside his specialty, but said he did it because no one else had done it.[15] Mao, the recognized great Marxist theoretician of China, told people that there was no need to read all the works of Marx, a portion of the basic ones would do.[16] The ideas of democracy or communism of the thinkers under consideration are all colored by their particular viewpoints or promulgation in China. Their common aim is China's social reconstruction, not academic validity. Hence, their version is unavoidably basic and general in nature. And I have made no attempt to provide a comparison of their explanations with the original thinkers as to fine academic details. Their conflicting ideas have been presented in various chapters of this book. Here we are summarizing the question of ideological conflict according to topic in an attempt to bring them into sharper focus.

The Class Concept

The aim of all Chinese social thinkers was directed toward the same great end—the salvation of China and the Chinese people. For the noncommunist thinkers, the term Chinese referred anthropologically to every Chinese, including minorities on the mainland. The communist approach is one of a strong class concept. Early pioneer thinkers such as K'ang Yu-wei and Liang Ch'i-ch'ao, both self-proclaimed Confucianists, did not have the slightest idea of class. It was a Confucian virtue to love everybody. Hu Shih, a strong defender of democracy, believed in the equality of all Chinese. Chang Chün-mai, another strong advocate of democracy, believed that national consciousness transcended all class distinctions. Chang Tung-sun, close friend and colleague of Carsun Chang, held that class distinction in China is not clearly defined in economic terms. Liang Shu-ming, on the other hand, denied the existence of distinctive and antagonistic classes in Chinese society; the traditional division of Chinese society into four groups—scholars, farmers, artisans, and merchants—was one of professional differentiation rather than of class distinctions. He purposely used the term "village inhabitant" in place of the communist term "peasant."

Sun Yat-sen advocated the equality of all Chinese people, and concerning his ideological principles, Stalin had this to say: "In the 'Three Principles' [nationalism, democracy, socialism], the concept 'people' obscured the concept 'classes'; socialism was presented, not as a specific mode of production to be carried on by a specific class, i.e., by the proletariat, but as a vague state of social well-being. . . . The epigones of Sun Yat-senism, by emphasizing and exaggerating the very features of this ideology that have become objectively reactionary, have made it the official ideology of the Kuomintang, which is now an openly counter-revolutionary force."[17] With respect to classes in China, here are Sun's own words: "There is no especially rich class, there is only a general poverty. The 'inequalities between rich and poor' which the Chinese speak of are only differences within the poor class, differences in degree of poverty. As a matter of fact, the great capitalists of China, in comparison with the great foreign capitalists, are really poor; the rest of the poor people are extremely poor."[18]

Noncommunist thinkers took all Chinese as a whole, and their programs for social reconstruction were based on nationwide cooperation, while the Communists confined their hopes and wishes to one class of people—the proletariat. Their affections and kindly feelings for this one class were paralleled by hostility toward another class—the bourgeoisie. Since the people were taken as two antagonistic classes, they were depicted as entirely different. The bourgeoisie was described as reactionary, decadent, selfish, and immoral; the proletariat was described as very courageous, revolutionary, unselfish, and highly moral. The upgrading of one and the downgrading of the other served as the driving force of the revolution and aimed toward achieving a classless society through the elimination of the bourgeoisie.

The acceptance or denial of Marx's theory of class and class struggle was the basic ideological conflict between the communist and noncommunist thinkers. Accordingly, the Chinese individual was treated either as a "class man" or a "national man."

In general, noncommunist thinkers rejected class struggle because it was based on a philosophy of hatred and because it was to be carried out by force and violence. It was diametrically opposed to the mainstream of traditional Chinese political philosophy of benevolent government based on peace and love. Those who cherished such a philosophy of kindness and who abhorred violence naturally would not subscribe to such a doctrine. The habit of hatred among those who achieved victory of the propertied class would continue as they searched for new targets of destruction. Such a condition was hardly an asset to the ideal society. The theory of class antagonism was further diametrically opposed to the Confucian tenet that all men are brothers; according to the Communist doctrine, all men are no longer brothers. Only the proletarians were brothers, and the propertied class were class enemies. When the class enemies were completely liquidated, then all men would be brothers again. But according to the theory propounded by Mao, this process would require a long, long time for it was to be achieved through an uninterrupted revolution under the dictatorship of the proletariat.

Marx, in fact, never defined what he meant by *class*. He simply raised the question in the last two pages of his third volume of *Capital*, and the manuscript then breaks off. It is noted that the terms used by the Chinese Communists are, for the most part, derived from Marx, but some of them have acquired new meanings. Class is one of them. Mao altered the meaning of the word "class" from *actual people* defined by *actual* (past or present) *ownership relations*, to a more vague moral attitude or outlook. By so doing, he greatly diluted the "materialistic theory of history," making class more of an ethical concept than an economic or sociological concept.

The extension of the connotation of the term *class* produced certain political consequences. Mao's interpretation prolonged the period of class struggle. It was Mao's contention that class and class contradictions continue to exist even after the "basic completion" of the socialist ownership system, and that the class struggle between proletariat and bourgeoisie will be long, tortuous, at times very acute. The Maoists contended that Liu Shao-ch'i held the contradictory theory of "class struggle extinguishment" which envisaged the disappearance of classes and the conclusion of class struggle. Liu's theory was linked to Soviet revisionism.

It is supposed that Mao's theory of prolonging class struggle had the effect of heightening the noncommunist opposition to the class concept. Since class has an ethical character or broader meaning, it can be used as a weapon in the political struggle against those with different viewpoints. For instance, Liu Shao-ch'i, a lifelong Communist, was labeled a capitalist roader. And, during the Cultural Revolution, the Gang of Four accused others of being capitalist roaders, only to suffer the same accusation themselves at a later time. Among the common people, the class concept has inflicted certain injustices. The bourgeois character, a synonym for bourgeois criminal, is supposed to be hereditary. Thus, the children of the propertied classes are denied college educations and even entrance to high schools. They are discriminated against socially in many other ways as well. As a consequence, the children of the bourgeoisie find it difficult to get married; no one will risk associating with the children of a capitalist or landlord because that will cause him great difficulty throughout his life, as well as for his children, whenever his family background or his children's is to be reviewed.

Communists as well as other thinkers regarded a classless society as a noble ideal. But in practice, a new bureaucratic class emerged in China consisting of Communist high officials and cadres. It is evident by now that this new class monopolizes political power and enjoys privileges and comforts which the common people cannot aspire to due to restrictions of law or of ideology. For instance, only high officials can ride in cars, travel by air or in pullman cars (called soft-bed in Chinese), live in spacious and beautiful houses, eat good food and have servants. The comrades in charge of a unit are supposed to have beautiful secretaries and young and pretty lovers to facilitate their revolutionary work. Even the lower cadres in the countryside lead better quality lives than the theoretical masters of the country—the people. The concentration of all political and economic power in the hands of the bureaucrats naturally produces a new privileged class and in a certain sense, an even more rigorous class society.

The Universal Truth

It is generally known that the Communists believe that Marxism-Leninism is the universal truth. In old China, a similar doctrine prevailed. Traditional Confucianists believed Confucianism to be such a truth. This belief was shaken at the time of the May Fourth Movement and was subsequently discarded. Among the modern thinkers, Hu Shih was the most conspicuous opponent of the existence of a universal and everlasting truth. He was a disciple of Dewey and a believer in the pragmatism of Dewey. Hu contended that the pragmatists did not recognized the existence of a universal or everlasting truth because truth was only an instrument created by and for man's use. Moreover, Hu did not believe in an objective law according to which a society could be developed by a single leap. Evidently his views countered the tenets of Marx, in that Marxism expounded a universal truth which reflected the objective reality. Mao believed that Marxism-Leninism was a universal truth and that a Communist revolution based on Marxism-Leninism could effect a fundamental solution to Chinese problems.

Ch'en Tu-hsiu also opposed the existence of a universal and everlasting truth. In his early writing against Confucianism, he especially emphasized this point, arguing that Confucianism was useful in the feudal period but was outdated in modern times. In Ch'en's last years, he reevaluated the Bolshevik doctrines and leaders, including Lenin, Trotsky, and Stalin, and, subsequently, rejected the orthodoxy of Marxism just as he did that of Confucianism.

Behind the acceptance or rejection of the existence of a universal truth, there lies the basic difference in one's attitude in looking at things of the world. This can be described as a difference between a scientific attitude and a dogmatic attitude. Since the introduction of Western science to China, the scientific attitude received respect from the scholars. This attitude was generally held in favor by liberal intellectuals. The Communist practice of taking Marxism-Leninism as a universal truth and regarding Mao as infallible is contrary to this spirit. In *Jen-min jih-pao* and other publications, we can find ample evidence attesting to this attitude.

The Chinese intellectuals acquired their liberalism from Western thinkers. The idea may be better illustrated by quoting Western sources. As Bertrand Russell, who was well known in China, has pointed out: "The philosopher Locke was never tired of emphasizing the uncertainty of most of our knowledge, not with a skeptical intention, such as Hume's, but with the intention of making men aware that they may be mistaken, and that they should take account of this possibility in all their dealings with men of opinion different from their own."[19] This suggested to the Chinese that knowledge and opinions are not infallible and therefore one should not be dogmatic.

This idea of the fallibility of knowledge is well reflected in a passage by David Spitz, written at a later time (1975), in connection with his appraisal of J.S. Mill, another well-known advocate of liberalism: "What is fundamental to Mill's whole approach, of course, is the altogether salutary reminder that we are not infallible creatures; that truth cannot be attained in any complete and final sense; that what we take to be truth we must always be prepared, as rational men, to subject...to the test of new data and new experiences."[20]

The Communists are generally very confident in their unshakable belief in the righteousness and certain victory of their cause. It is a belief that has contributed to their courageous struggle under extremely difficult conditions. But the drawback is that they tend to distort facts in the interests of theory, and to coerce the people to toil at arduous and often fanatical projects regardless of how great and harsh the sacrifice. To those devoted Communists, communism is almost a secular religion; many others take it as a dogma. So the conflict between the communist and noncommunist thinkers was whether or not they specifically accepted Marxism-Leninism as a universal and immutable truth or, in a broad sense, whether they were dogmatic or tentative in accepting a theory.

In general, people who believe in the existence of a universal immutable truth tend to be dogmatic, despotic, and intolerant of different ideas, and people who hold liberal ideas tend to be democratic, tentative, and tolerant of different ideas.

Revolution versus Gradualism

Since the very beginning of China's salvation movement, there was an ideological conflict between revolution and gradualism. Among the early thinkers, K'ang Yu-wei and Liang Ch'i-ch'ao were gradualists. Although K'ang Yu-wei envisioned extremely radical changes, he never advocated force or revolution. His disciple, Liang Ch'i-ch'ao was averse to a brutal and violent catastrophic revolution to achieve his society. Compared with K'ang and Liang, who were gradualists because they merely wanted to reform the Ch'ing court by constitutional means, Sun Yat-sen was a revolutionary who advocated the overthrow of the Manchu dynasty by military force. Compared with Mao, however, Sun was a gradualist who wanted to achieve his reforms through peaceful methods after his revolution. Other thinkers such as Carsun Chang, Chang Tung-sun, and Hu Shih shared the belief in gradualism. Liang Shu-ming must be put in this category, for he completely denied the necessity, practicability or advisability of a revolution in China. Hu Shih especially emphasized the theory that "drop-by-drop" evolution was the only way to achieve true and dependable progress and he abhorred violent or blind revolution. For, he believed, revolutions, by their very violence, would only waste the country's energies, stimulate the evils of blind action, disturb the social order and sow the seeds of mutual slaughter among the people. Mao and his followers held that the existing order must be completely swept away and that this could not be done without violence. He thus brushed aside gradualism as either reactionary or revisionist and called Hu's evolutionary theory vulgar evolutionism. Mao believed in a leap, or a revolution, to achieve a new and better society and he asserted that the nature of China's revolution was definitely to be one characterized by the use of armed force. On the whole, what the noncommunist thinkers seriously sought in social reconstruction was to minimize the human cost and to avoid violence and bloodshed as much as possible.

As to the human cost of the Chinese revolution, figures differ in the number of lives lost, varying from hundreds of thousands to millions, and even to tens of millions. *China Quarterly* quotes dispatches to the effect that over 400,000 people have been killed in the Cultural Revolution and 100 million have been directly or indirectly victimized by political measures.[21] A Japanese newspaper, the *Yomiuri Shimbun,* claims that 20 million were killed during the Cultural Revolution according to the statistics compiled by the Central Committee.[22] Professor Richard Walker estimated casualties to communism from the time of the first Civil War (1927–1936) to 1971, from 34 million lives to as high as 63 million lives.[23] Of course, all these figures are subject to controversy in one way or another, but their magnitude, even discounted many times indicates a staggering sacrifice on the part of the Chinese people. The gradualists sought to avoid revolution or to restrict it if possible, feeling that the less revolution the better. We thus find that Sun Yat-sen advocated the completion of both political and social revolution at the same time.[24] The theory of uninterrupted revolution had not been introduced in Sun's time; he would have been shocked at such an idea.

With respect to the Chinese revolution, there are two more important Maoist theories which have profoundly affected the lives of the people. First, Mao trusted and depended on the lumpen-proletariat. In the West, Bakunin championed the revolutionary potential of the lumpen-proletariat (of whom Marx and Engels spoke with contempt). Mao believed that the lumpen-proletariat provided a vital basis for the revolution. In his *Report on Investigation into the Peasant Movement in Hunan,* Mao said that the poor peasants were the most revolutionary, and that without the poor peasants, there could be no revolution. Among the poor peasants, a significant portion belonged to what can be called the lumpen-proletariat.[25] Mao's faith in the lowest stratum of society came from his belief that the poorer the people, the more revolutionary they were.[26]

In 1964, Mao raised the point once more before the Central Work Sit-and-Talk Conference. He said that "When we began to fight, we depended on those vagabonds *(liu-mang),* for they do not fear death. At one moment, the army wanted to eliminate them, which I objected to."[27] These vagabonds can be technically called the lumpen-proletariat, though the Chinese translation for the term is "vagabond proletariat."

Mao's dependence on the lumpen-proletariat created a serious consequence for the people. While Mao took advantage of the desperate straits of the poor peasants by using them as tools of the revolution, society generally treated them with deep contempt. Mao defined as abject poor peasants those who had neither land nor money, and who, without any means of livelihood, were forced to leave home and become mercenary soldiers, hired laborers or itinerant beggars.[28] This quotation is taken from the *Selected Works* of Mao of 1951. The first version of the report had a more vivid description of the revolutionary peasants with special reference to the lumpen-proletariat, but those passages were deleted from this version of the *Selected Works.* "Those who previously resided in the countryside wore badly worn out leather shoes and long ragged coats, carried foreign tattered umbrellas, gambled and played mahjongg. In a word, they previously had neither social position nor voice; now, not only have they raised their heads, but they have taken power into their hands."[29]

After the victorious revolution, many of these communists became more powerful, holding different posts in the government, including high ranking positions. It is believed by communist theorists that these were basically good people. If they had committed sins or crimes it was because they were victims of a vile social system. But, once the social system was improved, they would behave with virtue. Judging from impressions offered by the common man under the Communist rule, it appears that once in power these people did not change much. They are incompetent administrators, corrupt handlers of public funds, and oppressors of the common people.

The second Maoist theory that severely affected the people's lives is the uninterrupted revolution. Mao once remarked, "We advocate the theory of uninterrupted revolution. For instance, the mutual aid team came after the land reform, which was followed by cooperatives, the state-private joint operation, the handicraft cooperatives, and then the 1957 readjustment movement which was immediately followed by the technical revolution of 1958. One revolution should immediately follow another, with no interval left in between."[30] Actually, the people were exhausted and tormented by these revolutions. Mao nevertheless realized his aim of uninterrupted revolution, culminating in the Cultural Revolution. People were horrified by the excesses and the havoc that was wrought throughout the country, but Mao insisted that the Cultural Revolution should be repeated every few years. Historical sites, precious cultural and artistic objects, including rare books, were destroyed. Ts'ao Yü, the Chinese playwright who visited the United States in 1980 at the age of seventy after long years of hardship and torture, said that the reason he could live today was because of his faith that the Cultural Revolution would not recur. Pressed to respond to the question of what would happen should it recur, he said that it would signal the end of China as a culture and a nation.[31]

Democracy versus Dictatorship

The democratic movement developed in China over the past hundred years. Pioneer reformers such as K'ang-Liang advocated a constitutional monarchy patterned after the British model. What they dreamed of was a titular monarchy system, which was to be democratic. Theoretically, Sun Yat-sen favored democracy, but in actual political practice, followers deviated from his principles of democracy. The later thinkers, such as Hu Shih, Carsun Chang, and Chang Tung-sun, were ardent supporters of democracy. They opposed both the one-party dictatorship of the Kuomintang and the people's democratic dictatorship of the Chinese Communist Party.

Mao Tse-tung had a different approach to the problem of democracy. He saw the objective character of Chinese society as being colonial, semicolonial, and semifeudal—a character which determined that China's revolution must be taken in two stages: first, to change it into an independent democratic society, and second, to carry the revolution forward to build a socialist society.

According to Mao, the first stage began at the time of the Opium War in 1840 and continued up to the May Fourth Movement. The line of demarcation was World War I, beginning in 1914, and the October Revolution in Russia in 1917. These two events had changed the course of history and divided human history into two different epochs. Before these events, China's revolution belonged to the old category of the bourgeois democratic revolution; after these events, it changed to the *new* category of bourgeois democratic revolution. The period beginning with the May Fourth Movement up to 1949, which marked the beginning of socialist revolution under the dictatorship of the proletariat, was called the new democratic period. The new democratic revolution was led by the proletariat with the aim of creating a new democratic society and state under the joint dictatorship of all revolutionary classes. Mao seemed to believe that there was only one form of government—dictatorship. The problem lay in determining whether it would be a dictatorship of the bourgeoisie, of the proletariat, or of all the revolutionary classes.

Western democracy, labeled as bourgeois democracy, was condemned by the Communists as false, hypocritical and deceptive. Actually, Western democracy or bourgeois democracy in principle was what the democratic Chinese thinkers and intellectuals seriously sought. It was not that these people failed to recognize the imperfections of Western democracy, but rather that they preferred it to a dictatorship. For dictatorship is characterized by the concentration of power in the hands of one or a few people, thus constituting the danger of personal or party tyranny.

Furthermore, the democratic thinkers believed in individualism and cherished a society that would produce creative and independent individuals. The emphasis of communist theory on the principle that excellence resides in the whole has been used to justify in practice the supremacy of the state and the complete subordination of the individual. The actual measures Hu and the two Changs hoped to realize were nothing more than a parliament to be elected by the people, the peaceful transfer of political power, the protection of civil liberties, and the legal status of opposition parties. China is still lacking in all these practices.

The last to join, or rejoin, the democratic movement was Ch'en Tu-hsiu. After his disillusionment with communism in his last years, he became firmly convinced of the intrinsic value of democracy. He saw Western democracy as being welcomed, not only by the bourgeoisie, but by everybody; timeless in being the banner of the majority of the people against the privileged minority at various times in history, from the time of the Greeks and Romans until the distant future when politics withers away; precious in any social system, capitalistic as well as socialist. Aside from theoretical appeals, Ch'en sorrowfully pointed out that Stalin's atrocities would not have happened had there been a democratic system to control him.

In a word, the advocacy of democracy or dictatorship constitutes the basic ideological conflict between the communist and noncommunist thinkers. So the problem in China has been and still is whether democracy is implemented.

Hopes Realized and Disappointed

The cause to which all the thinkers we have discussed devoted themselves was the political and cultural salvation of China. Although their approaches varied, their basic goals remained the same—to maintain China's independent existence and her cultural identity. The response of the Chinese people to the Western impact was not that of a few isolated intellectuals—it was the response of the whole Chinese people. The ideas of the scholars were the reflections and crystallizations of the hopes and aspirations of millions of Chinese yearning for China's salvation. After one hundred years of humiliation and struggle that ultimately culminated in the communist revolution and the institution of a Communist government, it is appropriate to ask which of the Chinese people's hopes have been fulfilled and which have been disappointed.

Since the Communist regime controls the vast majority of the Chinese people, the following analysis will tend to focus on conditions on the mainland. I view these problems from the standpoint of the Chinese people as a whole and not from the ideology of either the Communist Party or the Kuomintang. I believe that most of these hopes have little to do with party ideology, and that they reflect the hopes and aspirations of all Chinese.

Abolition of the Unequal Treaties

With respect to China's foreign relations, the most encouraging development has been the abolition of the "unequal treaties." This was the initial goal of the Chinese salvation movement and represented the concerted will of the entire Chinese people. It was also prominently stressed in Sun Yat-sen's "Last Will." Chiang Kai-shek has this to say on the topic:

> On October 10, 1942, the American and British Governments simultaneously informed the Nationalist Government of the abolition of extraterritorial rights and related special privileges in China, and announced their readiness to begin the negotiation of new treaties based upon the principle of equality and mutual benefit. On January 11, 1943, the new equal treaties between China and the United States, and China and Great Britain were signed. . . . Therefore, it may be said that, beginning today, the letter and the spirit of the unequal treaties of the past hundred years have been permanently abolished.[32]

In addition to the recovery of treaty rights, before the establishment of a communist regime on the mainland, virtually all territories lost by the Chinese government in the preceding hundred years had been returned to Chinese sovereignty. Port Arthur and Dalien were returned to China through the negotiations of the Communist government in 1955. A notable exception to this list of recovered territories was the loss of sovereignty over Outer Mongolia. It had already slipped into the Soviet orbit, and this de facto condition was confirmed by the Yalta Conference in 1945. It is ironic that China, one of the Big Four in World War II, was forced to cede considerable territory after the victory. Hong Kong-Kowloon and Macao remained in foreign hands until the 1980s, when negotiations with Britain and Portugal established firm dates for their return to Chinese sovereignty.

Material and Spiritual Achievements

Material Achievements. The material construction movement began at the end of the Ch'ing dynasty during which time evidently little had been accomplished. Nor was much accomplished in the first years of the Republic. It was not until the 1930s that the national government engaged in a planned and comparatively large scale economic development leading to modernization. But, just as some signs of accomplishment became apparent, Japan embarked on a military invasion of China beginning in 1937 that obviously had a twofold purpose: to obstruct China's attempt to industrialize, and to colonize agrarian China in order to force her to supply raw materials for Japan's expansion as an emerging industrial power. Since the Communists took power in 1949 there have been ambitious plans, but again, no significant progress was apparent in modernizing China.

On the mainland the most epoch-making economic change has been the abolition of private property—a reform advocated at least as early as K'ang Yu-wei. The fundamental change was the land reform program which, through the nationalization and redistribution of land ownership, was also one of Sun Yat-sen's economic policies. This drastic change was achieved both on the mainland and on Taiwan (on the mainland rather brutally and on Taiwan by peaceful methods). In addition to land reform, the commerce and industry, including urban real estate, of the whole country was nationalized. Egalitarian practices on the mainland have eliminated the marked differences between rich and poor. The lives of the very poor workers and peasants have improved while the lives of the formerly well-to-do (and even the middle classes) have been leveled. Of course, the ideal would be to make all people equally well-to-do. What was actually accomplished was only to have socialized poverty, making everybody almost equally poor. The personal income per capita, even in comparison with developing countries, is still very low in China: 344 *yuan* in 1979; 372 *yuan* in 1980; and 390 *yuan* in 1981.[33]

Some people might argue that with China's tremendous population it is a great achievement to feed so many millions of mouths. But the actual picture is not as rosy as it is generally painted to be. Sun Yeh-fang, a prominent Communist economist, reported that the mortality rate in 1957 was 10.8 percent and was increased to 25.4 percent in 1960.[34] If we correlate these figures with the population census of the *People's Handbook* of 1957, which gives total population as 660 million, the total number of deaths would be 7.09 million. If we use the same population figures for 1960 (1960 figures are not available), the number of deaths would total 16.68 million. Sun Yeh-fang's point, strongly hinted at, was that the increase of about 10 million deaths in three years was due to starvation. Judith Banisters, Chief of the China Branch at the U.S. Bureau of the Census, concluded, on the basis of the population figures published in 1984, that the Great Leap Forward cost in lives was near 30 million, largely due to famine.[35]

In the industrial sector, coal is the key raw material in the development of industry. The *People's Daily* reported that in 1979 the average production of a Japanese steel worker is 300 tons per year, while that of a Chinese worker is only 10 tons per year.[36]

Economic growth in China is distinctively slow, lagging far behind its ambitious plans. The causes are accountable to both government policies and people's productivity. China, under the Communist regime, has a centralized planned economy. To centralize the economic power at the top may not necessarily be harmful, but it is fatal to centralize power at the bureaucratic level where bureaucrats are both ignorant and fanatical. Such a policy has given rise to complaints of "confused guidance" and "blind guidance" of the government. In other words, the economy is directed under policies contrary to correct economic principles. The result is a terrible waste. For example, according to the *People's Daily*, Mao, through no one's fault but his own, wasted 100 billion *yuan* during the Great Leap Forward.[37] Throughout the thirty-odd years of

Communist administration, the total amount wasted has been approximately 1,200 billion U.S. dollars, according to Cheng Chu-yuan, a professor of economics in this country.[38] Naturally these figures are staggering. But the first one is official, which we should have no argument with. The second figure is, of course, subject to further verification and careful computation.

As for the people themselves, most of the Chinese are not enthusiastic workers. For Marx, only the capitalists are nonworking parasites. Let us see how the Chinese peasants work under the socialist state. Seymour Topping, in his article, "China's Long March into the Future," says, "The government [i.e., Xinjiang Government] has found that in many communes private plots that take up only 7 percent of the land are producing as much as 25 percent of the total output."[39]

Based on Topping's findings, the efficiency of a peasant working on his private plot is 4.43 times higher than if he worked on communal land. Although this is a local instance, it reflects the general tendency expressed in a common saying: "When one works on his own private lot, he goes all out, or works like mad; when he works on the communal land, he goes so slow, as if he were convalescing in a hospital."

Among industrial workers, the same phenomenon is apparent. Although no accurate figures are available, there is an apt saying: "Work or not work, three meals a day." Industrial workers have what is called "iron rice bowls"— absolute job security. Thus, when they go to work, they work halfheartedly and take a long daily siesta. This is why the government has tried in recent years to change these habits by offering more work incentives. Communism may be too lofty an ideal which cannot operate under the present educational level of the masses. Even so, it was the wrong policies, including impractical policies of the government, which led to the slow economic growth, poor economic conditions, low gross national product, and low personal income per capita.

The foregoing account is very sketchy and highlighted, and further elaboration is beyond the scope of this work. For a better understanding of the economy of China for the past three decades, the publications of the U.S. Congress Joint Economic Committee, of the World Bank, and of the Chinese government are valuable reference sources.[40]

Spiritual Achievements. As stated earlier, Liang Ch'i-ch'ao wanted to rejuvenate China by trying to create an entirely new Chinese citizen through the implementation of a new ideology to replace the old one. Ch'en Tu-hsiu passionately envisioned the new youths of freshness and vitality to fight for a national rebirth. Whether or not the new Chinese of the present generation live up to the standards set forth by Liang and Ch'en is too complicated to evaluate in simple and precise terms. The Chinese at present are, in general, more developed intellectually and physically than those of Liang and Ch'en's time. The physically unattractive and mentally backward Chinese of the old China, whom Liang and Ch'en deplored, is a phenomenon of the past. Steps toward the establishment of equality between men and women have gone in the main as all thinkers would have wished. Mao, being more ambitious, vowed to change human nature, and to create a communist man in a communist society. Before assessing the most recent Chinese society, I wish to single out one strikingly encouraging phenomenon in China: the resumption of the national confidence that had disappeared with the humiliations suffered at the beginning of the Opium War. It is to the Communist regime's credit that China has regained, and now enjoys, high prestige in the family of nations.

But we have found certain discouraging aspects in present communist China, especially as a result of the Cultural Revolution. Chinese people all over the world are noted for their industriousness, but ironically, an adverse condition has emerged among the common people. The leader of a Singapore Trade Commission reported in 1980 that life under communism has done what he never would have thought possible: the Communists took a naturally industrious people and made them lazy.[41] This phenomenon has been confirmed by many people who have access to Chinese workers. Under Marx's ideal, compulsory work would be abolished in the promised land. In China the threat of starvation no longer forces anyone to work. As the earlier quoted saying goes, "Work or not work, three meals a day." Such an attitude has, in practice, atrophied the vigor and diligence of the traditionally industrious Chinese and accounts for China's economic sluggishness. Many thinkers of the past, including J. S. Mill, were of the opinion that due to the indolence of human nature, socialism would make people lazy and society stagnant. Marx disregarded this kind of argument as nonsense. Unfortunately, China has verified these misgivings. This lack of work incentive in particular, together with other shortcomings in China's great experiment in socialism, can serve as a useful lesson for those countries trying to build socialism.

The communist ideal is to create a classless society in which cooperation rather than competition prevails, and altruistic and selfless people work voluntarily for the good of the whole society without seeking personal gain or fame. But in fact, it seems that people in general are more selfish and more pragmatic. The explanation is that the political struggle and persecutions against individual citizens were so overwhelming and acute that the importance of self-protection and the realization of the unreliability of others, whether friends, relatives, or government promises, were indelibly imprinted on people's minds.

The situation among the young generation is more discouraging. It is reported that at present the majority of youth is interested in nothing but the cash nexus. In China, there is an edifying maxim that, "in everything, look forward to the future."[42] Ironically, this maxim has been twisted, without changing one word in pronunciation, to mean, "In everything, look forward to money." In Chinese, "future" and "money" are homonyms; the interchange of the two words makes a pun. Thus, youths in general are not idealistic but pragmatic. Their interests lie not with Marxism or social reconstruction but with immediate personal gains. Hu Yao-pang confirmed this tendency in one of his speeches when he admonished youths not to look forward to money.

Two further discouraging tendencies in connection with youths exist. The first is the rise of juvenile crime stemming from the Cultural Revolution. The

Chinese Ministry of Public Security disclosed, in 1979, that China had ten times more juvenile delinquency in that year than in the early 1960s.[43] The cause for this is quite simple. During the Cultural Revolution, youngsters were taught that rebellion was justified; they were allowed and even instructed to engage in "beating, smashing, and looting," actions considered revolutionary and virtuous. As a consequence, young Red Guards ransacked millions of homes, destroyed or robbed personal properties, ruined historical remains, humiliated, tortured and even killed individuals, All these atrocities, which we see now as frightening, were considered normal and righteous during the Cultural Revolution. These bad influences instilled into young, receptive minds have lingered on even as the youths grew older.

A second discouraging habit of youngsters, even young adults, is the use of obscenities and rude language. It has become a social custom that plagues every part of the country such that there is a movement aimed at cleansing and beautifying the language *(yü-yen mei)* in daily conversation. Peking has been noted for the urbanity and sophistication of its natives. In the past, they were even ridiculed as being too extreme in their politeness. But, a special book published in Peking not long ago instructs people on how to speak politely, for many genteel expressions have been forgotten due to disuse when political struggles were rampant.

Another unfortunate social custom is that both the government and the people are wont to tell lies. Governmental lies are deliberate while the people's are involuntary. The government is dishonest in not reporting "true" facts through its official organ the *People's Daily.*[44] It has admitted that in the past, it has often printed lies and distortions, as well as boastful and untruthful reports. The public has known that the papers everywhere have been filled with unfactual stories for years. The most notorious instances are the fabrication, often greatly inflated, of production figures. Examples include the production figures of the Great Leap period, and the incredible stories of Ta-chai's miraculous achievements.

A Shanghai-born businessman, whom I met in Hong Kong in 1977, boasted to me, when he realized I was doing studies on communist China, that in order to know the real conditions of the grass roots of China, he was the one to talk to, not the China watchers, for he had long years of firsthand experience with the Chinese conditions before 1970, plus his frequent travels from Hong Kong to the mainland afterwards. He reasoned that every Chinese suffers from a split personality, saying one thing but thinking another entirely different thing in his heart. No Chinese will tell the truth because longtime political persecutions have taught him how to protect himself by telling lies. This gentleman also said that if he were to meet me on the mainland, he would say something entirely different from what he was saying to me then.

The most serious and damaging spiritual setback is what is called the faith crisis. This can be seen from three aspects. First, the common Chinese are disillusioned with what they once believed to be the noble and saintly spirit possessed by all Communists: the Communists were supposed to be, and indeed were believed to be, selfless individuals who devoted themselves to the welfare of the people. But the common Chinese person discovered from personal experience that this is not true. The internal struggle for personal power, especially among the top leaders, is horrible in its cruelty and severity. The people detect none of the comradeship and love which the Communists often boasted of possessing. The people also suffered bitterly from the corruption and lawlessness of the lower cadres, of whom they are the direct victims.

Second, the common Chinese people are bewildered as to how to determine who is a revolutionary, and who is a counterrevolutionary. Liu Shao-ch'i was at various times considered Mao's successor and was acclaimed as a great Marxist and a great revolutionary. Then, suddenly he was labeled a revisionist, a traitor, a scab, a spy of the Kuomintang, and a counterrevolutionary. Several years after he was persecuted to death, Liu Shao-ch'i was rehabilitated posthumously as the great Marxist, a great revolutionary, and was honored with all other good names. Lin Piao, Mao's comrade-in-arms and legal successor, as provided in the Constitution, astonishingly was reported to have made an attempt on Mao's life and then been killed mysteriously in an airplane crash. Naturally, he was called all sorts of vile names, and was depicted as the perpetrator of all sorts of evil doings. There are numerous cases, too many to mention, of minor cadres who follow the same pattern of changing from a revolutionary to a counterrevolutionary and from angel to devil. It is no wonder the people find it difficult to determine who is a true Marxist and a true revolutionary.

Third, people are confused as to the nature of true Marxism. Interpretations of Marxism vary with the ups and downs of the top leaders. When Mao was alive, his interpretation of Marxism was official and the truth. After his death, many of his interpretations were actually refuted, though his name was not explicitly mentioned. Liu Shao-ch'i's interpretation of Marxism was also official when he was in power, but it was denounced as absurd when he was disgraced. Lin Piao and the Gang of Four all had their interpretations of Marxism, but were all later denounced. Naturally, these events have caused confusion in the minds of the people. A visiting scholar from China told me that at present no one has any confidence in the Communists or in Marxism. Even though this is an exaggerated statement, a faith crisis undoubtedly exists among the majority of people.

Education and Science. It may be appropriate to mention briefly these two fields under the topic of spiritual achievements. China started Western-style schools with Western learning at the end of the Ch'ing dynasty. Through the Republican years up to 1949, many schools from the primary to university level, were established; to a large extent, Western learning replaced classical learning. Outstanding Western-style universities of high academic caliber, such as Peking University and Tsing Hua University, emerged. After 1949, the Communist regime renovated the educational system by introducing ideological indoctrination and by involving students and faculty in political movements at every level of schooling. Although the number of schools increased tremendously, the quality of education suffered, as we mentioned previously, especially during the Cultural Revolution, due to the unbalanced emphasis of political activities over academic pursuits. Certain changes begun in the last few years are still ongoing.

Western science was introduced into China as early as the Ming dynasty, but it did not receive significant respect and popularity until the May Fourth Movement period. What happened in China during the first half of the twentieth century as a response to science is what D. W. Y. Kwok terms scientism, which, as he put it, can be considered the tendency to use the respectability of science in areas having little bearing on science itself.[45] The acceptance and adoption of science by the Ch'ing government was motivated by the goal of national salvation. It has been used as an instrument by successive governments to increase material wealth and military strength. Among the people, there has developed the apotheosis of science, worshipping science as omniscient and omnipotent. In schools, science has been taught with special emphasis and prestige; and departments of natural sciences have been established and developed in universities. In the past, a number of prominent scientists, including three recent Nobel prize winners in physics, with basic training in China and advanced studies in America or Europe, have attained international recognition in their fields. Two of the Nobel laureates had undergraduate training in China before 1949, and one even attended high school in Taiwan. But in the past thirty-odd years, due to a lack of academic surroundings and facilities conducive to research, brought on by political turmoil, few scientists on the mainland, as far as we know, have been able to excell to the point of international standing. At present, the Chinese government is sending a great number of students abroad for training. On the other hand, thousands upon thousands of young scientists who received their undergraduate training in Taiwan and pursued advanced studies in this country have been amazingly successful in academia and industry. It is to be noted that the two Chinese governments, irrespective of their political stance, invariably accept, respect and worship science. But what they actually worship is not science, but scientific technology. The basic spirit of science is to seek for truth, supported by objective evidence. It is precisely this spirit that neither Chinese government encourages nor even tolerates to develop and prevail. If under the Kuomintang regime one doubts the truth of the Three Principles of the People, that individual would find himself in trouble. The situation is worse under the Communist regime, where if a person questions the tenets of Marxism, he would be considered a criminal, for in doubting Marxism, he automatically becomes a counterrevolutionary.

Suppression of Individualism

The problem of whether value inheres in the individual or in the whole has been a perennial subject of debate since Plato's time. The noncommunist thinkers in China that we have discussed believed, either explicitly or implicitly, in individualism. Individual progress was valued as necessary to social progress. The communists believed in collectivism, arguing that individuals were less important than the collective and that excellence resided in the whole, not in the parts. China has developed into a collectivist society. This sharp contrast between individuals and collectives forcibly struck Jan S. Prybyla, an American professor of economics at Pennsylvania State University, during his visit to China when he was treated to a performance by a group of small children. The skit portrayed a goose, which chose to leave the gaggle and strike out on its own, in what most Americans would approvingly regard as the spirit of entrepreneurial initiative. But the goose was thoroughly criticized for its manifestation of individualism. Terrible things happened to the deviant goose as it wandered blindly through the world, away from the stern but warm group. It finally rejoined the group and thenceforth worked unstintingly for the common good with no thought of self. Professor Prybyla considered that the message of this morality play was that the self is not legitimate. The ego must be torn out and dissolved in the mass. Any thought of personal advancement is by definition at odds with the interests of the collective and is, therefore, wrong and harmful.[46] Since this show was especially performed for the foreign guests, it can be supposed to be representative of official ideology.

Collectivism is applied to every field. For instance, students from elementary school to college study collectively. The aim of study is not personal satisfaction or distinction—least of all personal profit—but service to the whole people. College students are not permitted to choose their own majors. College graduates have no right to choose their own jobs, but must accept obediently any government assignments. The guidelines are based on what and where one is particularly needed. After schooling, the same principle applies to academic work. Articles and books are usually the product of a collective, the author's name being either wholly fictitious or the name of a study group. The traditional scholarly ambition to become a famous authority is discouraged. As with the scholars, workers in every field, whether factory hand, peasant, office cadre, shop clerk, or even a soldier, are not supposed to labor for personal gain or fame. The common good, not individual interests, is the supreme goal to which everyone should devote himself. The individual gradually disappears. Again what remains is the collective.

To explore this question further, we must involve ourselves with a question of the means and ends. Bertrand Russell made a telling point in this context. He said, "People do not always remember that politics, economics, and social organization generally, belong in the realm of means, not ends. . . . But a society does not, or at least should not, exist to satisfy an external survey, but to bring about a good life to the individuals who compose it. It is in the individuals, not in the whole, that ultimate value is to be sought. A good society is a means to a good life for those who compose it, not something having a separate kind of excellence on its own account." [47]

Russell's premise is certainly subject to controversy. But if we go along with him, we will find that the Maoist collectivist society that China has erected now seems to be making the very mistake that Russell inveighed against. First, Marxism-Leninism is, as I see it, what Russell called an external survey; and this foreign ideology had been made a holy and orthodox doctrine in China. Second, the Communists have mistakenly placed the general well-being of the abstract state of the masses above the happiness of the individual. They have taken the means of mobilizing the populace by collectivization to attack their common problems and turn it into an end. Thus the collective has come to be thought of as an entity and not as the aggregate of the individuals that compose it. They have gone so far as to maintain that ideas and emotions, ideals and hopes, in a word, the minds of the populace, must conform to the orthodox norm of the collective. An example of the regimentation of emotions will show the excesses of this practice. People must either hate or love the Soviet Union depending on instructions. One would find himself in serious trouble if he loved the Soviet Union when he should hate it, or if he hated the Soviet Union when he should show love.

No sacrifice is thought too great or too harsh for the attainment of the highest good of the whole. This condition is obviously contradictory to Riesman's insistence that no ideology, however noble, can justify the sacrifice of an individual to the needs of the group.[48] The Chinese people who actually live under this system privately complain that the slogan whereby the party is to serve the people has actually turned out to be one where the people serve the party; further, that the exercise of the people's dictatorship has actually turned out to be the exercise of dictatorship over the people by the governing minority.

The basic question remains: do the Chinese people have a good life? China's goal is to provide a good life for her people, but life in a society in which an individual has no identity but simply serves as an instrument to the whole can hardly be called a good life. It was in this sacrifice of the individual to the mass that many of the dreams of our thinkers were disappointed.

Destruction of Intellectuals as a Class

Mao not only destroyed individualism but he also crushed intellectuals as a dominant class in Chinese society. He belittled the usefulness of formal education and even went so far as to say that certain of China's great emperors were actually illiterate. To this he juxtaposed his belief that many of the more highly educated emperors were failures. In a sense, he regarded intellectuals as the most ignorant people.[49]

Lo Lung-chi (a hero and ultimately a victim of the Hundred Flowers Movement) once complained that by no means could the "small intellectuals" of the proletariat lead the "big intellectuals" of the bourgeoisie. To this Mao answered that not only the "small intellectuals" but even those among the proletariat who could barely read a few characters were superior to Lo. Mao ranked the less educated peasants higher than the better educated peasants. He said that as far as culture (i.e., education) and ability were concerned, poor peasants were inferior to well-to-do middle peasants. But as far as revolution was concerned, they were superior.[50] Based on this principle, Mao asserted that it was a general law that only laymen (*wai-hang*) could lead the experts (*nei-hang*).[51] Mao's meaning was clear: experts are mere technicians who perform specialized functions for the revolutionary leadership, the proletariat. Thus the president of a hospital often was an Eighth Route Army officer, and the vice-president a trained physician. Similarly, the president of a university would be a party functionary (presumably from the lower classes) and the vice-president an academician. Mao's belittling of formal education and specialized learning and his placing of revolutionary zeal ahead of technical competence and expertise tended to create a new obscurantism. I suspect that Mao's downgrading of intellectuals was motivated, in part at least, by selfish considerations rather than ideology. First, Mao was snubbed by the intellectuals in Peking when he was only a low library clerk. As he recalled ruefully, he was attracted to those prominent new cultural movement intellectuals who used the library, and he was intensely interested in discussing with them political and cultural problems, but they were too busy to listen to a library assistant who spoke in a heavily accented Hunan dialect.[52] Second, and most important, Mao's deep distrust of intellectuals stems from an extreme fear of their potential to influence public opinion to the point of starting a new revolution. He believed, as we noted earlier, that it was necessary to form public opinion prior to starting a revolution. Undoubtedly this kind of work could only be done by intellectuals. Mao is widely quoted on mainland China as saying, "Let the intellectuals behave with their tails between their legs."[53] That is, intellectuals should live obediently and tamely, acting as an instrument of the Party; as soon as they raise their tails, i.e., try to assert themselves, they should be immediately suppressed. To safeguard and to consolidate his Communist regime, Mao subjugated intellectuals to strict regimentation and control even at the expense of culture and education.

In actual practice, China has become a country in which the uneducated proudly control the educated. For example, in J. H. Ch'en's *Returning,* when a prominent military officer noticed during a high school inspection that a track field lay unused, he promptly ordered faculty members to plant cabbage on this large tract of land.[54] A United Nations employee, who has toured China several times, related to me the following anecdote: When a new Communist party secretary of an orchestra assumed his post, in accordance with established practice, a command performance was given in his honor. At the end of the performance, after making routine comments about his pleasure in hearing the music, he declared: "The violinists in the front were excellent in their spirit, and this showed in the performance. However, the drummers in the back row were lackadaisical and did not show much enthusiasm for their work. It is my hope that the drummers will learn from their colleagues, the violinists, and I am sure your performance will improve tremendously." Numerous instances such as this can be cited.

Statistically, only 15.8 percent of the 40 million Communist Party members have as much as a high school education.[55] Uneducated party members thus rule the country, and to protect their own interests, they prohibit intellectuals from sharing any political power. They also claim that intellectuals cannot be trusted to hold power, but can only be used. This belief is the basis for

314

intellectuals being labeled as the ninth class, filthy citizens. What is most serious about this is that such an attitude has been translated into national policy and is very difficult to change. The Central Committee in 1981 proclaimed that those gross fallacies which have long existed and escalated to the extreme during the Cultural Revolution, of showing contempt for education, science, and culture and of discriminating against intellectuals, should be resolutely swept away.[56] The Central Committee's use of the phrase "long-existed" signifies that these fallacies existed quite some time prior to the Cultural Revolution. In spite of such official denunciation, a *Jen-min jih-pao* editorial notes this attitude still lingered on, as late as the end of 1982, among the Communists.[57]

The most tragic consequence of this tendency has been the destruction of intellectuals as a class; they were humiliated, tortured, and persecuted. Anyone who was educated fell victim to the Cultural Revolution simply because he was educated. Those who survived the Cultural Revolution are either too old to advance themselves in academic, cultural or other highly specialized work, or they simply refuse to return to former posts because the wounds were too deep to heal. An entire generation of youth lost its chances and incentives for education. No society can progress where it is ruled by ignorant bureaucrats and where ignorance prevails. Between the old heart-broken intellectuals and the ignorant lost young generation, there hardly exist enough capable people in the prime of life who can assume the work of social reconstruction. This problem is further intensified in the current lack of freedom of thought.

Lack of Freedom of Thought

Freedom of thought has been a major goal of all Chinese intellectuals for the past one hundred years. During the May Fourth Movement period, it received particular attention. However, the thought of Mao Tse-tung, or Marxism-Leninism interpreted by Mao, has become the only acceptable orthodoxy on the mainland. No competing *ism* or ideology is allowed to develop.

Theoretically, of course, along with the other intellectuals we have studied, Mao was in favor of intellectual freedom. His slogan "Let a Hundred Schools Contend" was derived from an expression depicting the flourishing and exuberant conditions of the *Ch'un-ch'iu* (Spring and Autumn) period when scholars of diverse philosophies vied with one another to produce a spectacularly vivid and rich culture. We find not a few statements by Mao praising the value and significance of the few intellectual rebels who were courageous enough to create new ideas and challenge the prevailing orthodoxy. For instance: "Truth is usually in the hands of one person. Truth is usually in the hands of a few people. For instance Marxism is in the hands of one person only— Marx."[58] "Truth—all truths—in the beginning is always in the hands of a minority, who suffered oppressions from the majority.... such as Copernicus....[and] Galileo."[59]

However, in practice Mao did not tolerate the "intellectual rebels" he praised; nor did he tolerate thought at variance with his own. Would Mao have conceived that it was still possible to produce a Chinese Copernicus or Galileo under such conditions where non-Mao thought was equated with counterrevolutionary thought? If thought control had been practiced in Marx's Germany or in England to the extent it is in China today, would Marx have been able to survive?

The Communists shared with other intellectuals the demand for intellectual freedom during their fight for existence. Since coming to power, however, they have practiced thought control more efficiently and rigorously than their predecessors. During Mao's time, nearly all books and magazine articles began by quoting Mao. In this period, we find hardly any book with independent thinking.

The lack of freedom of thought was compounded by the fact that the people were not permitted to do their thinking. Students, intellectuals, and scholars were not supposed to think creatively. They had to parrot the official line. The role of established scholars was to prove and give academic credence to what the government professed to be truths, and to support governmental proposals. For instance, Chiang Ch'ing intended to succeed Mao. Scholars were therefore ordered to unearth historical evidence to prove that certain empresses such as Empress Lü or Wu Tse-t'ien were magnificent. Cautiously and painstakingly the scholars collected all evidence in favor of such a claim. These empresses were, in the end, glorified so that the way was paved for another female ruler to reign in China.

In short, along with the nationalization of private property came the nationalization of individual minds. Individuals could not use their own minds independently but had to conform to collective thinking under governmental direction and control. This could not help but have a chilling effect on genuine intellectual development and a stifling effect on social development and progress. In retrospect, this has been the most significant disappointment of the hopes of all Chinese intellectuals, and it has been paralleled in the political sphere by a lack of political democracy. Of course, freedom of thought is one of the important aspects of democracy. However, because this aspect is so basic to a discussion of ideology it is treated here in a separate section.

Lack of Democracy

Along with the lack of freedom of thought, the lack of political democracy has been the most signal disappointment of the hopes of Chinese intellectuals in the modern era. Among the democratic rights, freedom of speech (a goal basic to the struggle of Chinese intellectuals through the present century) has been notably and conspicuously absent. All forms of the media are controlled by the Party. Newspapers, magazines, academic journals, books, pamphlets, radio and TV programs, etc. are all operated by the government and subject to prior censorship, and thus only approved opinions can be disseminated. Freedom of assembly does not exist at all; meetings must have prior governmental approval. Change of living quarters is virtually impossible due to rationing of housing. Intercity or interprovincial travel is tightly regulated by food rationing cards and hotel room accommodations. Consequently, only those who have governmental approval or are on official duty can travel. International travel is virtually unheard of except by government sponsorship and even then one's spouse is not allowed along. There is no protection of civil liberties. Anyone may be arrested at the whim of the authorities. Once arrested, an individual is not supposed to defend himself. It is a practice in communist China to show "leniency towards those who acknowledge their crimes, and severe punishment to those who stubbornly refuse to confess guilt." In the United States, one is innocent until proven guilty. In China at present, one is guilty as soon as an accusation is made by the authorities. If the accused tries to defend himself, the attempt at defense is immediately seen as guilt and is a basis for severe punishment. People, in reality and in the large proportion, do not have the right to vote or to be elected for office, nor to they have the right to exercise referendum or initiative.

The lack of freedom of speech can have disastrous effects. Two striking cases are cited as examples. The first one is the extermination of sparrows as grain-destroying pests. According to official records, this movement was first discussed before the Supreme State Conference on 13 October 1957. Mao insisted that they had to be destroyed and he brushed aside any suggestion that the value of the sparrows as the destroyers of other pests harmful to crops outweighed their own destructiveness. Included in the Revised Agricultural Program, this plan was sent to the Standing Committee of the National Congress and of the Political Consultative Conference and finally to the whole people for discussion and implementation. Not a single word of dissent was heard in the entire country. With the whole country mobilized to kill sparrows, the job was done with appalling thoroughness. Millions of sparrows were killed. With their natural predators destroyed, other harmful insects multiplied and did far more harm to the crops than the sparrows ever had. Eventually the whole program was quietly dropped. Had there been some semblance of freedom of speech the folly of sparrow killing could have been avoided.

The second example is the problem of population explosion. In 1957, Ma Yin-ch'u made public his fear that China's rate of population growth was too high; he speculated that from 1953 to 1957 it was probably over 20 percent per thousand. At a meeting of the National Congress, of which he was a member, he raised the issue and strongly recommended birth control. Unfortunately, Ma's warning was refuted as supporting a Malthusian bourgeois, imperialist and anti-socialist theory of population. The most important objection to Ma lay in his contradiction of Mao's important dictum that "more people can do things easily." Mao's idea was true for primitive societies in which more hands means more productive power. In a modern industrial society it means disaster. Because of his insistence on the dangers of an uncontrolled population explosion, Ma was fired from his post as president of Peking University. And until quite recently, China's population was permitted to grow without any effective control. In 1982, it was 1.08 billion, as compared with Mao's figure of 600 million in 1957, an increase of 80 percent. Had there been free speech and free discussion, the effects of this staggering population explosion might have been averted.

Some apologists have argued that bourgeois democratic rights are not necessary and are even detrimental to the vast majority of the Chinese people. What China really needed was to work together as a unit to defeat external enemies and to develop a more stable and better livelihood for her people. In such circumstances, they argue, political democracy is a luxury and a divisive force that China could ill afford.

This argument has certain merits. China's problems have been and are still monumental. Faced with economic and political chaos, it was necessary to make a disciplined, cooperative, and concerted effort. By its nature, that effort would have had to involve a considerable, but temporary, sacrifice of personal liberties. But under the people's democratic dictatorship this temporary retreat from democratic principles in the face of overwhelming necessity was taken to mean a perpetual total acquiescence to a disregard of human dignity and basic human rights. As has been seen, even in the short run, this massive centralization had significant drawbacks. If it had been capable of spectacular breakthroughs, it was also capable of spectacular errors, as demonstrated by the failure of the Great Leap Forward movement.

The Communist Party is the only ruling party on mainland China that is supposed to rule indefinitely. It is considered a constitutional duty of the people to support the party. The Constitution of 1978 stipulates that "citizens must support the leadership of the Communist Party of China." Though the Constitution of 1982 has deleted this article, it actually maintains the same principle. Since the Communist Party considers that it represents the true interests of all the Chinese people, it refuses to allow any effective political opposition party to develop. While it is true that parties other than the Communist Party exist in China today, their role is strictly limited and they would be accused of usurpation of leadership should they attempt to function as a political party in the Western sense of the term. So there is no opposition party in China at present. When there is no competition in politics, degeneration and corruption usually follow.

Related to the problem of one party dictatorship is the problem of peaceful transition of power. This problem has never been solved in China. In traditional China the transition from one emperor to another was frequently accompanied by plotting for power and murder. Dynastic succession was even bloodier, frequently accompanied by long devastating wars. The impact of these struggles for power on the people is staggering. Although no one would contend that the power struggles in communist China compare with some of those in imperial days, there is still no generally recognized, institutionalized method for the peaceful transfer of power. Long before Mao's death, Liu Shao-ch'i was generally recognized to be a prime candidate to succeed Mao, but he was liquidated and died in prison during the turmoil of the Cultural Revolution. Lin Piao, even cited in the Constitution as Mao's successor, died in a mysterious plane crash after he allegedly plotted a coup. Chou En-lai, the only qualified successor to Mao in later years, was attacked and, according to rumor, all but hounded to death by the Gang of Four (the Maoist press said that he died of cancer in January 1976). The Gang of Four, supposed successors to Mao, were in turn arrested by their close comrade Hua Kuo-feng and charged with usurpation of power after Mao's death.

It is not only the contenders of power who are harmed in these struggles for supreme power. Communist critics have themselves complained that had not the Gang of Four been arrested there would have been great bloodshed and millions of heads would have fallen. Allowing for a natural tendency to dramatize, it is still clear that a great many innocent people are caught up and suffer in these struggles. Were the subordinates and associates of Liu Shao-ch'i, Teng Hsiao-p'ing, Lin Piao, etc., all counterrevolutionary reactionary capitalist roaders? Was it not possible that the majority of them worked honestly and obediently under their bosses and strove to serve the country and the party? Did they not suddenly become heinous criminals to be struggled against just because their bosses lost in a power struggle? Official reports have admitted that the wrong verdicts (of being counterrevolutionary) against those implicated by the downfall of Liu, which have been reversed and corrected, amounted to over 26,000 cases.[60] Usually figures from official reports of this kind are con-servative; it is not known how many wronged cases remained uncorrected. When Liu Shao-ch'i was rehabilitated, some of those who had been labeled as his clique were also rehabilitated. In a sense, these fortunate people were vindicated but their sacrifices and sufferings were irreparable. Those who have not been vindicated yet must continue to suffer. In the latest power struggle it has become the turn of the victims of the Gang of Four to victimize the gang and those who might have associated with them by chance or necessity.

The turmoil that political struggle brings to the disruption of production and consequently on the daily lives and livelihood of the people is bound to be great. Under dictatorial power it is impossible to solve the problem of who shall wield power short of bloodshed, coups, plots, and other methods that entail suffering for the participants, their families, and millions of ordinary people. Only in a democracy can the transition of power be handled peacefully—the sort of transfer that Chinese have yearned for for a very long time. Until this problem is solved, one of the basic dreams of all our thinkers will remain disappointed.

Recapitulation

Two main goals permeate the thoughts of all these thinkers—to maintain China's national existence and to retain her cultural identity. The first goal has been completely achieved, because China is no longer apprehensive of extinc-tion or of being cut up like a watermelon by foreign powers. As Mao put it, China now stands on her own feet.

With regard to culture, the liberal thinkers advocated a kind of liberal culture which mainly consisted of political democracy, a free economy with certain governmental interventions, but with socialism as the final goal, and freedom in thought and academic work. These liberal goals are completely denied by the communist ideologues. On Taiwan the defeated Nationalists have tried to adhere to this liberal line in practice and in principle. All these goals fall within the scope of Sun Yat-sen's Three Principles of the People. Although Taiwan has not fully exercised all these principles, it has made certain noteworthy achievements. Compared to the mainland Chinese, the Chinese on Taiwan enjoy many more democratic rights and have achieved a far higher standard of living. There is also a greater degree of academic freedom and freedom of thought and much less regimentation on Taiwan. On the whole, Taiwan aims at achieving, and indeed is on the way to building, an open society.

After more than thirty years of Communist control of China, what form of society has been reconstructed? To a great extent, China evidently imitated the Soviet Union. The Soviet form of society is described by an Italian professor, Umberto Melotti, as bureaucratic collectivism. According to Melotti, the term *bureaucratic collectivism* comes from Bruno Rizzi, who gave a precise answer to Trotsky's question: What kind of society is the USSR? "Rizzi says it is the most complete manifestation so far seen of a new type of antagonistic society, where social power belongs to a 'new class' of exploiters which, through the existence of collective property, has 'securely entrenched itself within the state,' taking control of the means of production and appropriating the surplus value. . . . Rizzi called it a 'bureaucratic collectivism'." [61] With regard to its significance for the Asian mode of production, Melotti argues that "We could assert that bureaucratic collectivism is the typical form of development of countries based on the Asiatic or semi-Asiatic mode of production that have not long been subjected to the capitalist mode of production as a prolonged and penetrating external influence. . . . This was particularly the case in Russia and China." [62]

Michael Harrington makes the same observation: Joseph Stalin was the architect of a new form of class society which I shall call "bureaucratic collectivism." Under it, the state owns the means of production, and the elite Party bureaucracy owns the state. By totalitarian means it is able to extract a surplus from the direct producers and to invest it in industrial modernization and its own class privileges. It does these things in the name of "socialism," and yet it is based on the continuing expropriation of the political power of the workers and the peasants. Such a society, it must be emphasized, does not require Russian sponsorship. It can be run by Maoists. [63] Both Melotti and Harrington include China in this category. Bureaucratic collectivism is an apt description of China's new society, for China is not a socialist country in the proper sense of the word.

The Chinese government under Mao's stewardship achieved unprecedented unity in Chinese history; in carrying out its policies, the government proved to be the most efficient but also the most tyrannical. All economic policies and activities came under government central planning and control. The people

320

became more egalitarian in material things, but their political power, which was severely limited before, has now dropped to a new nadir. At the present, the Communist government has absolute power over the people while the people have absolutely no power over the government. Academic freedom and freedom of thought have been completely obliterated. In short, all political, economic, and cultural power has been concentrated in the hands of a few Communist leaders. The Communist cadres share this mammoth and monolithic power at various administrative levels. It created a new but more stringent class society—between the ruling Communist class and the ruled masses of the people. The cadres have been described by tourists, journalists, and native citizens as markedly lawless, incompetent, and corrupt. This phenomenon is not surprising in light of the fact that a government can be inefficient and corrupt if it has monopolized all power for a long period without the people's supervision. A socialist state, such as the Soviet Union, which has vested absolute power in a dictator, can produce an engine of tyranny more dreadful, vast, and minute than any feudal or capitalist society that ever existed before.

However, the current Chinese government under Teng Hsiao-p'ing is retreating, in many respects, from Mao's original ambition and is steering a somewhat different course, which reflects a kind of ideological shift closer to the noncommunist thinkers. This change will be dealt with in the subsequent section.

Communist Ideas Modified

As we have analyzed, noncommunist thinkers, labeled "reformists" by the Communists, frown on revolution, holding that revolution entails heavy human sacrifice, and creates great social disruption; real social progress is not born of revolution, but comes from peaceful construction. If revolution is unavoidable, the shorter the revolution is, the better. The Communists on the other hand see revolution as a positive good and favor continual revolution. However, one can see significant change in communist ideology as revealed in the "Resolution on Certain Questions in the History of Our Party since the Founding of the People's Republic of China," adopted by the Sixth Plenary Session of the Eleventh Central Committee in 1981.

First, the Cultural Revolution was condemned by the Central Committee as the severest setback and the heaviest loss suffered by the party, the state and the people since the founding of the People's Republic.[64] Second, the basic principle underlining the Cultural Revolution—the general theory of "continued revolution under the dictatorship of the proletariat"—was denounced as an erroneous Left theory by the Central Committee.[65] Third, the Central Committee also denounced the use of cruel class-struggle methods, which had been used habitually but should not have been followed mechanically in the new situations of the Cultural Revolution.[66]

The Central Committee completely denounced the Cultural Revolution—its initiation, principles, content, methods, and results. It resolved that the chaotic conditions of the Cultural Revolution must never be allowed to happen again in any sphere.[67] The task henceforth of resolving or removing the "dark sides" extant in the Party and state organisms should be tackled by measures in conformity with the Constitution, the laws, and the Party Constitution, but under no circumstances should the theories and methods of the Cultural Revolution be applied.[68]

The new outlook of the Central Committee signifies a significant turning point with regards to certain basic communist ideas. The Third Session of the Eleventh Central Committee in 1979 already firmly discarded the slogan of "take class struggle as the key link" as being unsuitable in a socialist society and made the strategic decision to shift the focus of work to socialist modernization.[69] In other words, the emphasis on class struggle has given way to the emphasis on peaceful economic construction.

To use Marxist terms, the Party has shifted the focus of government endeavor from the change of production relations to an immense expansion of production forces.[70] Class struggle mainly involves the change of production relations, i.e., which class owns the means of production. The expansion of production forces means simply economic construction. During the Cultural Revolution emphasis was laid on the change of production relations, and it was assumed that the change of production relations would automatically result in the enhancement of production forces. The task of the government at the present stage is seen no longer to be carried out through fierce class confrontation and conflict, which characterized the revolution before the overthrow of the exploitative systems, but through the great expansion of production forces under the socialist system, for the present stage has entered into the period of peaceful development.[71]

In national economic affairs, with the introduction of the new production responsibility system (sheng-ch'an tse-jen chih) in 1979, the Communist Central Committee has retreated from its previous policy of nationalization and central control. This policy allows industrial enterprises and peasant households to take more responsibility for production and to have more power in the running of their businesses and farms. Enterprises are given more autonomous power with respect to their direction and management, but they are also responsible for their own profit or loss. Also, small retail shops have mushroomed since permission for small business was given by the government. As a result of this change, it is reported by Jen-min jih-pao that three advantages have been produced from a sample survey of more than three thousand enterprises—more revenue to the state, more proceeds to the enterprises, and more income to the workers.[72]

In the agricultural sector, a production responsibility system beyond the allocation of more private plots was introduced in 1979. It takes various forms, one of them being called household production responsibility system (pao-kan tao-hu). Under this form the ownership of the means of production still belongs to the collectives but the right of actual use of the land is transferred to the peasants. As a unit, the household, by entering into a contract with the collective, can have virtually independent control of production without government interference. This practice frees the peasants from the so-called blind guidance of the powerful but technically ignorant cadres. Again, as stipulated in the contract, the peasant household can pocket whatever is left over from the harvest after fulfilling the state quota and the shares retained by the collective.

As the result of the implementation of the production responsibility system, production has gone up and peasant income has increased tremendously. The income of the peasants during the last few years has surpassed that of the two previous decades. As of 1982, some 70 percent of rural China had adopted this system.[73] In Yunnan, for instance, 98.8 percent of all production teams had adopted this system by 1982.[74]

The peasants, although pleased with the new system, are skeptical of its lasting long. They fear the government will soon change its policy, as it has so often in the past. When Premier Chao Tzu-yang visited a county in Honan province in 1981, the peasants surrounded him and asked, "How many years can contracting production to the household be allowed? Is it all right to do it for a few more years?" The premier promised that "You may contract to the household for as long as you want. You may contract to the collective when you want." The peasants' distrust and worries are understandable. In the beginning of land reform, peasants were given land; they thought they would own the land indefinitely. But shortly, when the advanced type of the agricultural-producers' cooperative was implemented, all peasants lost their lands. The current production responsibility system is reminiscent of the New Economic Policy of the Soviet Union between 1921 and 1928, whereby concessions were made to capitalism in small industry, retail trades, and agriculture.

Apparently all these new measures, industrial as well as agricultural, deviate from the earlier central control policy and practices of the government, signifying a shift from rigorous government control to a certain amount of individual initiative, or a shift from centralization to decentralization. To a certain degree they move closer to what the noncommunist thinkers have advocated.

One more important change in economic affairs is the policy on economic cooperation with foreign countries, including imperialist countries. Fighting imperialism is a cornerstone of the ideology of the Communist Party, since it sees imperialism as a major cause of China's poverty. In the thirty years since 1949 China had a kind of self-imposed isolation from non-communist countries in economic affairs. In that period we can say categorically that there was not a single imperialist country imposing exploitation on China, for there was practically no trade between the two sides. Yet, despite the absence of imperialist exploitation for thirty years, the Chinese economy has not appreciably improved as would have been predicted according to the theory of imperialist exploitation. Consequently, in recent years the Communist Party has been engaging in economic cooperation with the capitalist countries, notably the United States, which at one time was considered as the imperialist enemy par excellence. The economic stagnation may have led the Communist leaders to realize that imperialism was not entirely the cause of China's poverty and to seek international economic cooperation. The noncommunist thinkers examined in this book are all for international economic exchange and cooperation, and are less intense in censuring imperialism. Hu Shih even went so far as not to include imperialism as one of the five archenemies, or devils, harming China. In recent years the Communist Party has decided to change the course of economic isolation to the promotion of economic and technical exchange with foreign countries.[75] So, to a certain degree, the idea of economic isolation from imperialist and capitalist countries has given way to the idea of international economic and technical cooperation, irrespective of countries being imperialist and capitalist.

In 1981, *Jen-min jih-pao* published an important article signed by a "special reviewer," refuting and correcting the erroneous Left guiding thought in economic construction.[76] Though the writer remains anonymous, it clearly reflects the official line of the new economic thought held by the top leaders. This article first quotes a statement made by Ch'en Yun at a work conference called by the Central Committee in 1980, pointing out that the erroneous thinking in the economic realm, and also in socialist construction in general, is what is called the "theory of quick results" *(su-ch'eng lun)*. The fallacies of this theory, according to Ch'en Yun, are: it disregards objective conditions, it violates objective laws, it substitutes wishful thinking for the truth, it does things based on subjective considerations, and it addresses in a forced-draft manner work that can only be realized in the future.

This erroneous Left guiding thought, the article points out, has become increasingly serious since 1958. The mistakes it has generated consist of the attempt to change China in a very short time from the conditions of being both poor and blank, and the attempt to catch up and surpass economically the highly developed industrial countries. The Great Leap Forward was the most disastrous such attempt, causing serious economic dislocations and heavy human and material losses. Most significantly, the article warns that *real* economic development requires travelling a long and arduous road and can by no means be accomplished quickly. No one should expect miracles. The central theme of the new official line is to expose the mistakes of the theory of quick results, and to warn people to be candid and realistic.

One of the ideological conflicts between the Communist and noncommunist thinkers that we analyzed lies in the notion of revolution versus gradualism. Gradualists advocate social reforms to be carried out gradually; Hu Shih's theory of achieving social progress by drop-by-drop evolutionary method is representative of this view. The revolutionaries believe, among other things, that a leap to a better society can be achieved through revolution. The theory of quick results, a term recently coined, furnishes, in a simplistic way, a new antithesis to gradualism. The Communists' turning away from this idea actually narrows, to a certain degree, the gap between communist and noncommunist ideology.

324

Where Does China Go From Here?

A Struggle between Two Lines

Based on an objective and careful analysis of the ideological conflicts in modern China I can find no real conflicts between what the Communists call the two roads of capitalism and communism. First, capitalism never developed to a high degree in China. If we were to call the Chinese economy capitalistic, it would only be capitalism in the rudimentary stage, or, as Mao put it, the budding of capitalism. Thus the economic evils that have plagued Western nations have never been conspicuous in China. For instance, the occurrence of boom and bust in business due to overproduction has not appeared in Chinese economic history. Granted, the Chinese economy has had its good and bad years, but the causes lay in reasons other than what Marx described as the typical internal law of contradiction in Western economy. China's marked difference between rich and poor did not, as a rule, stem from capitalistic exploitation as was the case in the industrialized West. Except in a few large cities, China was in a precapitalist state prior to the industrial revolution. Even if China pursued the capitalist road to develop her economy, she probably would not repeat the economic miseries, crimes, or evils of the West because the many bitter experiences of the West can serve as a warning. There are also the positive examples of antitrust and antidepression legislative measures that have been taken in the West to mitigate the intensity of economic depressions and to eliminate many of the serious evils of capitalism. At present there is no pure capitalist society of the eighteenth century sort existing in the West, and many societies have developed economic systems of a more or less socialist nature. The Chinese social thinkers discussed in this book all favored some kind of socialism. Their differences lay in the means used to achieve socialism, whether by violence or by peaceful ways. Thus, I believe that ideological conflicts between capitalism and socialism in the strict sense did not exist in China at all.

Democratic Tradition in China

What was the real conflict then? The real conflict, either ideologically or pragmatically, was the conflict between democracy and despotism. In historical terms it would be the conflict between the ruling and the ruled, between the government and the people. This has been true in the past, and continues to be true in communist China. Under the Communist regime, the people have suffered severely from the atrocities of lawlessness, the complete lack of legal protection of individual rights, and draconian, mental regimentation. Consequently, they value human rights much more than ever before and aspire to democratic practices more eagerly.

The Chinese translation of the term *democracy* is *min-chu*, meaning that it is the people who command, or put another way, the people are the masters. Actually, the concept of democracy is an ancient ideal in Chinese political philosophy. The famous quotation of Mencius that the people are the most important element in a nation and the sovereign is the least important illustrates the ideal of the supremacy of the people. This ideal can be seen in the often repeated aphorism, also quoted in *Mencius,* from the *Book of History* in the chapter of *T'ai-shih* that "Heaven sees with the eyes of its people; Heaven hears with the ears of its people." Heaven is supposed to have the supreme power, but Heaven's will is seen by the will of the people. Thus, what the people see or hear is reflected in what Heaven does. So the people are identified with Heaven and have the supreme power. Again, *Li Chi,* in the chapter of "Li Yun," says that "When the great course is pursued, the world will be for all." This illustrates the principle that the country belongs to the people, not a particular person, or a family or a party.

True, the Confucianists elevated the position of the sovereign to a supreme degree, but the prerequisite was that he be wise, able, and virtuous. Confucius and Mencius sang high praises of Emperors Yao and Shun simply because their moral grandeur was impeccable and the works they accomplished for the people were great. Unable to work out a system to eliminate mediocre or tyrannical rulers, and with an eye toward the peaceful transition of political power, Confucius and Mencius merely eulogized the two sage emperors Yao and Shun for their voluntary abdication of their thrones to other popular and virtuous men. Some historians consider this story as too perfect and good to be true. The moral of the story, though probably exaggerated or even fabricated, was to teach and to warn emperors to do a good job while in power and to abdicate after one's term. The underlying principle is that the kingdom is not to be privately monopolized. In actual practice, no ruler in Chinese history since the time of Confucius ever obeyed this edifying advice, and every dynasty tried to monopolize its ruling power for its own family and was in the end overthrown by violence. There were no exceptions.

In the Ch'ing dynasty, a great scholar, Huang Li-chou (1610–1695), made a very bold and devastating attack on the hereditary monarchy. He asserted that monarchs were the greatest evil in a country, because they considered the kingdom as private property, to be fought for by ruthless and violent means, and to be kept for personal comforts and family privileges at the expense and misfortunes of the people. The root of this evil was the so-called family kingdom where the rule of a country had degenerated into a monopoly of private families instead of being a public service.

In recent times, the essence of this form of government has appeared under new names—one party dictatorship or people's democratic dictatorship. Actually, as Ch'u An-p'ing put it in 1953 during the Hundred Flowers Movement, this is a party kingdom. Having made this comment, this gentleman disappeared and was never heard of again. Basically, all of China's troubles result from the lack of a workable system to put the democratic principle into operation. While it has never been institutionalized, the concept of democracy germinated 2,000 years ago.

The Attraction of Democracy to the Chinese

After the introduction of Western ideas into China, the idea that was widely accepted and acclaimed was democracy, not communism. Communism was accepted by a number of left-oriented people, while democracy was accepted by the overwhelming majority—albeit a silent majority. Western democracy had a systematic and profound theoretical foundation, and provided a set of specific measures to embody the Chinese ideal. In theory and in practice democracy thus captivated the Chinese mind for many years. The attraction of democracy was that it solved the centuries-old problem of the peaceful transition of political power through the practice of universal election. The election of the highest executive chief coincided with and fulfilled the Chinese traditional ideal that the country is open to all, not just to an individual or family, and that office holders are to be chosen for their wisdom and worthiness. Moreover, democracy professed the protection of independent free thinking and human rights. In imperial times, the standards of "right and wrong," that is, values, emananted from the emperor or the court; they were to be obediently followed by the people, who were not supposed to think beyond those limits. Only in democratic countries could people think freely.

Freedom of thought is especially cherished by Chinese intellectuals. Recent disasters in China, especially during the Cultural Revolution, have made the intellectuals, nearly all of them, victims in the so-called fascist cultural-tyranny. Their experience has made democratic rights even more precious. The peasants, often considered apolitical, also aspire to democratic rights; they demonstrated this by traveling from distant villages to Peking to redress their grievances with an equally strong demand for a democratic government. Thus, I believe that the democratic movement, which has been the mainstream in the past and remains viable at the present, is irresistible.

Democratic Voices in the National Silence

Despite the harsh suppression of any free thinking, which resulted in an awesome deathly silence throughout the country, a few loud and clear voices have broken out, indicating that the democratic spirit is still alive. The first one, chronologically, was the appearance in 1974 of a large-character poster (running to over twenty thousand characters) in Canton. The poster was signed by Li I-che and entitled, "Socialist Democracy and Legal System." On the surface, the copies of this poster (which were widely circulated and attracted the attention of both the populace and the government) assailed Lin Piao. However, it was obvious that it actually alluded to Chairman Mao and his government. Basically the main points of the poster

1. called for democracy, freedom, and rule by law;
2. showed disrespect for Ch'in Shih Huang-ti (who at that time was acclaimed by the Party as a unifier and innovator);
3. denounced the Cultural Revolution;

4. opposed the "new class" and its privileges;
5. demanded a guarantee of the people's power to supervise the activities of the Party and government at all levels;
6. charged that the absolute worship of "genius" (I read that to mean "personality cult") resulted in forbidding the people to think, study, explore and question, and that this amounted to the liquidation of 800,000,000 brains.[77]

The poster then concluded that the antidemocratic force of the reactionaries was only a reverse current in the modern world stream. Under the existing conditions of strict thought control, this was a truly daring and dangerous poster. And, as such, it demonstrated that a desire for democracy existed even under the prevailing antidemocratic conditions.

The second, and most impressive and bloody one, was the T'ien-an Men Square demonstration of 5 April 1976, which resulted in the killing of many participants. A famous poem was displayed consisting of these lines: "People are no longer extremely ignorant; The time of Ch'in Shih Huang-ti has gone for good." The Ch'in emperor was clearly an allusion to Mao.

The third and most recent courageous protest was made in 1978 by Wei Ching-sheng, a young man of 29. A product of the Communist regime, raised under and influenced by Maoism, he was completely disillusioned with Chinese socialism. His first poster appeared on the Democratic Wall in Peking and was entitled "The Fifth Modernization—Democracy." He utilized the form of large-character posters and also published an underground magazine, *Explorer (T'an-so)*, to express his and his group's opinions.[78] He protested that the people had been deceived by all sorts of beautiful promises and political lies such as that Marxism-Leninism and the thought of Mao Tse-tung were the foundation of foundations; that Chairman Mao was the great savior of the people; that without the Communist Party or the chairman, there would have been no new China; that what China needed was dictatorship instead of democracy, except for democracy under collective leadership; and that if the people worked as hard as oxen for the revolution and followed the principles of stability and solidarity, they would find their way to paradise, which actually meant communist prosperity and the four modernizations. After detecting the deceptions, and being burned by the furnace of the Cultural Revolution, the Chinese people, Wei believed, were no longer ignorant and were capable of finding their own way out.

At present, Wei asserted, China had become more impoverished, more miserable and more backward. The reason for all this was due to the adoption of the road to socialism and the leadership of the great dictator. Wei refused to recognize the road as socialism, but called it different names, such as despotism under the great helmsman, despotic fascism, fascist authoritarianism, dictatorship of the proletariat, a variant of the Soviet despotism, Chinese socialist dictatorship, feudal socialism, feudal monarchy under the cloak of socialism, etc. His evaluation of Marxism also was extremely caustic and inflammatory. He said that Marxism was a kind of quack deception, built on an ideal that it could never reach. Marx was just like a quack drug dealer who boasted that his drug could cure any disease. The thought of Mao Tse-tung was also a quack deception like Marxism-Leninism and communism.

Wei concluded that democracy meant that the people should become the masters of their own destinies. They did not need a savior. The self-glorifying dictatorship had to go. The people wanted democracy and did not want to serve as modern pawns for a dictatorial ruler. Without being their own masters, the people's livelihood could not improve even if they did increase production by tightening their belts as they were forced to do in past years. They had produced a great deal of wealth, but where did the wealth go? It fattened small dictatorial regimes such as Vietnam and Albania, that had the same political lines, and the "new bourgeoisie class," including such as Chiang Ch'ing and Lin Piao, or it was wasted by all sorts of political swindlers, big and small. Hence, the four modernizations would be meaningless without a fifth modernization, the modernization of the people and the social system—democracy.

In 1979, one of the writers of the famous Li I-che large-character poster, Wang Hsi-che, published another article entitled "To Strive for the Class Dictatorship of the Proletariat." He indirectly charged that the present dictatorship in China had degenerated into the dictatorship of Communist bureaucrats under the cloak of communism. He further charged that as a result of Mao's theoretical fallacy, the present Communist Party's dictatorship had inevitably developed into the dictatorship of the leader, permitting the leader to be free from the control of the Party and the people. So he urged that the dictatorship of the proletariat should be built on the system in which the workers can exercise direct democratic control over the means of production.[79] Though his vision of democracy was still in the framework of Marxism, it was suppressed and Wang Hsi-che and other writers were arrested and put in prison, where some of them are still in custody.

The latest democratic movement of the Chinese is the China's Spring movement started in the United States in 1982 after the suppression of the short-lived "Peking's Spring." The leader is Wang Ping-chang, age 33, a Chinese physician who earned a Ph.D. in Canada on a Chinese government scholarship. He decided to abandon his medical career and to devote himself to China's democratic movement because he reasoned that medicine could only cure a few patients; it could not cure all the diseases of the nation. The aim of his movement is to promote a democratic system in China to replace the Communist dictatorship. (A journal is being published by the movement and is entitled *China's Spring*.) Since this is a new movement not much more can be said of it as yet, except that it shows the democratic movement extends beyond mainland China.

Democracy the Chinese Want

The Western democratic system is not perfect. People who know the system well have found many shortcomings and flaws in it, but the basic principles of democracy cannot be denied to China just because of its shortcomings. As a Chinese proverb puts it, "One should not stop eating just because he chokes sometimes." Furthermore, China does not need to copy Western democratic practices exactly in such matters as campaign fanfare and extravagance. What is important are the essential principles. Based on my observations and beliefs, what China should have and what the people aspire to are as follows:

1. The independence and dignity of man should be maintained so that people are not used as tools for a totalitarian form of government.
2. Individualism should be respected so that each person can freely and fully develop his or her talent without government control or regimentation.
3. Human rights (civil liberties) should be legally protected so that individuals cannot be arrested, tortured, persecuted, or killed at the whim of those in power. The atrocities of the Cultural Revolution should be prohibited forever.
4. People should have the right to elect their representative government. Transitions of political power should be carried out peacefully. No political party should seize or monopolize political power by violence or force.
5. People's opinions should be expressed, instead of being suppressed, through proper democratic means, including the organization of political parties, making bloody revolutions unnecessary and avoiding costly sacrifices to the people and the nation.
6. People should enjoy freedom of speech, of thinking, and of beliefs. The practice of maintaining the orthodoxy of Marxism-Leninism and the thought of Mao Tse-tung by force should be abandoned forever.

The above items, reduced to simple principles, would bring stability and progress. An armed revolution is destructive and signifies, in itself, the overthrow of stability. In summarizing Mao's ideas, the Central Committee in one of its important documents expounded that Mao held that "since there was no bourgeois democracy in China and the reactionary ruling classes enforced their terroristic dictatorship over the people by armed force, the revolution could not but essentially take the form of protracted armed struggle."[80] Thus armed struggle was necessary because there was no democracy to which the people could turn for peaceful and legal means of social reconstruction. Again, the Central Committee has pointed out that "inadequate attention was paid to this matter [a democratic socialist political system] after the founding of the People's Republic, and this was one of the major factors contributing to the initiation of the 'cultural revolution.'"[81] This shows that the lack of democracy can cause a cataclysm. These observations of the Central Committee reflect clearly that democracy can act as a deterrent against possible armed revolutions, and has the power to maintain political stability. With stability achieved, progress can be pursued. A highly cultured society can only be built step by step under the favorable conditions of peace and order.

Difficulties in Attaining Democracy

The problem of achieving democracy is that it is easier said than done. All the emperors of past dynasties invariably grasped absolute power. Common people had only to serve them but were never allowed to have their own independent political rights. In the Republican period, Yuan Shih-k'ai wanted absolute power; so did Chiang Kai-shek and Mao Tse-tung. Ironically, although Mao was supposed to be the people's humble servant, he ultimately attained the highest peak of personal power in history. Given such a tradition, it will be very difficult to change the course of politics from despotism to democracy. Teng Hsiao-p'ing, despite his democratic gestures, cannot give up the basic principle of dictatorship and sticks to the "four persistencies" (the socialist road, the people's democratic dictatorship, i.e., the dictatorship of the proletariat, and Marxism-Leninism and Mao Tse-tung-thought), which, in a nutshell, mean the concentration of power. Although he tolerated freedom of speech for a short while after returning to power, once his position was stronger he practiced stern suppression whenever people began to talk freely. Wei Ching-sheng was sentenced to fifteen years in prison just because he demanded democracy. With Teng Hsiao-p'ing's approval, the "four greats," i.e., the four great democratic freedoms (great contending, blooming, big-character posters, and debate), were removed from the Constitution in 1980. It is difficult for people to give up political power once they have grasped and tasted its sweetness. Thus, it will take a long struggle for the Chinese people to procure democratic political rights from existing or would-be rulers.

The Chinese Communist government reiterated in 1978 the goals of the four modernizations—industry, agriculture, national defense, and science-technology. Certainly this was a commendable move, but modernization itself cannot guarantee a good life for the people. Wei Ching-sheng proposed a fifth modernization—democracy. History reveals that Hitler's Germany achieved modernization, but it was accompanied by a life of misery for a majority of the people. The Soviets also have achieved modernization, but as Nobel prize-winner Solzhenitsyn and the top physicist Sakharov have shown, it did not give a happy life to the Russian people. The aim of the modernization program in China, as far as the ruling minority is concerned, is to strengthen the position of the government by creating better agriculture, industry, and national defense. These three areas are to be supported by science, primarily technology. As a rule, in China the stronger the government the fewer freedoms the people enjoy. When the government finds itself in trouble or in a crisis it concedes a little by giving people a little more freedom in order to win their support, and to motivate their enthusiasm and initiative. When the country is in a better condition, and the government becomes stronger again, controls and regimentation are reimposed. So the four modernizations, even if successful, cannot guarantee a democratic life to the people.

Democracy is merely the prerequisite for solving China's problems; it is only a political system that prevents the government from becoming totalitarian, permits opposition parties to exist, and allows people to hold and to express openly different political views and thus influence the government through the vehicle of public opinion. Democracy cannot by itself bring about high culture, but it guarantees the free and natural growth of a culture without the danger of suffocation. Thus, the value of democracy lies in its basic but negative nature. In and of itself, democracy cannot guarantee the development of a high culture; without it, however, especially under a totalitarian regime, no culture can develop freely.

After China attains democracy, she would have a stable political situation which would permit the people to develop their talents and initiatives to the fullest extent. At that time it is hoped a new independent and splendid culture would emerge. As mentioned in the Introduction, cultural identity was one of the two aims of the thinkers. Culture cannot be built while the country is in chaos, with the minds of the people severely regimented. The Chinese thinkers did not want to establish capitalism but a higher type of society, namely, socialism. Unfortunately, a workable system containing both democracy and socialism has not yet been invented. The Chinese suffered immensely for democracy and also in their experiment with socialism. As Toynbee has indicated, man creates a new civilization as a response to the challenge of a situation of special difficulty that rouses him to make a hitherto unprecedented effort. The Chinese people have surmounted many difficulties in history and will also respond to this new challenge successfully. It is my firm hope that their wisdom will lead them to create a society that combines both political democracy and social justice. Since this ideal system has never been in existence, it may take several decades yet for the Chinese to fulfill their dreams by inventing a specific system to fit their needs. For the time being, let hope sustain us.

Notes

[1] *Mencius,* bk. 2, pt. 2, ch. 2, secs. 1–10.

[2] Mao Tse-tung, "Lun jen-min min-chu chuan-cheng," *Mao Tse-tung hsuan-chi,* 4:1369.

[3] Mao Tse-tung, "Tu Cheng-chih ching-chi hsueh," *Mao Tse-tung szu-hsiang wan-sui,* 1:171.

[4] Chang Tung-sun, *Li-hsing yü min-chu* (Chungking, 1946), p. 5.

[5] See note no. 32, ch. 4.

[6] The original quotation, romanized below, is somewhat in rhyme and almost translatable: "Tz'u-ch'u pu yang yeh/Tzu yu yang-yeh ch'u;/Ch'u-ch'u pu yang yeh/Chih-yu t'o Pao-lu."

[7] The original in romanized Chinese is: "Tz'u-lu pu-t'ung, ch'ü-chao Mao Tse-tung." "Tz'u-lu pu-t'ung" is a Chinese phrase meaning not a through street. It is generally used to refer to a situation in which one is at the dead end.

[8] *Confucian Analects,* bk. 4, ch. 16.

[9] *Mencius,* bk. 1, pt. 1, ch. 1, sec. 3.

[10] Mao, "Lun jen-min min-chu chuan-cheng," *MTTHC,* 4:1358–60.

[11] Hu Hua *Chung-kuo hsin min-chu chu-i ko-ming shih* (Peking: Jen-min ch'u-pan she, 1950), pp. 156, 174–5.

[12] Mao, "Chieh-chien Jih-pen she-hui tang jen-shih Tso-tso-mu-keng-san, Hei-t'ien-shou-nan, Hsi-p'o-chien-kuang teng te t'an hua," *Wan-sui,* 2:540.

[13] Chalmers Johnson, *Peasant Nationalism and Communist Power* (Stanford: Stanford University Press, 1962), p. 49.

[14] Tetsuya Kataoka, *Resistance and Revolution in China* (Berkeley: University of California Press, 1974), p. 311.

[15] Chang Tung-sun, *Li-hsing,* p. 2.

[16] Mao, "Tsai pa-ta erh-tz'u hui-i shang te chiang-hua," *Wan-sui,* 2:187.

[17] Stalin, *Program of the Communist International,* 1928.

[18] Sun Yat-sen, *Ch'üan-chi,* vol. 1, pt. 1, pp. 139–40.

[19] Bertrand Russell, *Unpopular Essays,* (New York, 1962), p. 14.

[20] David Spitz, ed., *John Stuart Mill on Liberty* (New York: Norton, 1975), p. 238.

[21] "Quarterly Chronicle and Documentation (January–March 1979)," *China Quarterly* (London), no. 78 (June 1979):410.

[22] *Yomiuri Shimbun* (Tokyo), 16 October 1981. The paper claims that the news is based on the official statistics of twenty-nine provinces and cities compiled by the Central Committee. But we cannot find this information in the *Jen-min jih-pao.*

[23] Richard L. Walker, *The Human Cost of Communism in China* (Washington D. C.: U.S. Government Printing Office, 1971), estimated table on p. 16.

[24] Sun Yat-sen, "Min-pao fa-k'an tz'u," *Ch'üan-chi,* bk. 1, pt. 1, p. 173.

[25] Mao, "Hu-nan nung-min yun-tung k'ao-ch'a pao-kao," *MTTHC,* 1:21.

[26] Mao, "Tu Cheng-chih ching-chi hsueh," *Wan-sui,* 1:182.

[27] Mao, "Chung-yang kung-tso tso-t'an hui chi-yao," *Wan-sui,* 2:591.

[28] Mao, "Hu-nan nung-min yun-tung k'ao-ch'a pao-kao," *MTTHC,* 1:20–1.

[29] Szu-ma Lu, *Chung-kung tang-shih chi wen-hsien hsuan-ts'ui* (Hong Kong: Tzu Lien Press, 1977), 5:110.

[30] Mao, "Tsai tsui-kao kuo-wu hui-i shang te chiang-hua," *Wan-sui,* 2:157.

[31] A remark made by Ts'ao Yü at a meeting in honor of him on the University of California, Berkeley campus on 21 April 1980.

[32] Chiang Kai-shek, *Chung-kuo chih ming-yun,* in *Chiang tsung-t'ung szu-hsiang yen-lun chi,* vol. 4 (Taipei: Chiang tsung-t'ung szu-hsiang yen-lun chi pien-chi wei-yuan hui, 1966), p. 72.

[33] The personal income per capita is computed from national income figures provided by

the State Statistical Bureau. The figure for 1979 is obtained by interpolation. See Table 1, *Beijing Review,* no. 48, 1982.

34 Sun Yeh-fang, "Chia-ch'iang t'ung-chi kung-tso, kai-ko t'ung-chi t'i-chih," *Ching-chi kuan-li* (Peking) (15 February 1981).

35 Stephens Broening, "The Death of 30 Million Chinese," Opinion-Commentary, *The (Baltimore) Sun,* 24 April 1984, p. A19.

36 *Jen-min jih-pao,* editorial, 1 January 1979.

37 "Tuan-cheng ching-chi kung-tso te chih-tao szu-hsiang," *Jen-min jih-pao,* 9 April 1981, p. 5.

38 Cheng Chu-yuan, "Ta-lu p'in-k'un lo-hou te ken-yuan," *Lien-ho pao* (Taipei), 10 July 1981.

39 Seymour Topping, "China's Long March into the Future," *New York Times Magazine,* 3 February 1980, p. 14.

40 For economic conditions see: U.S., Congress, Joint Economic Committee, *Economic Developments in Modern China,* 1972; *China: a Reassessment of the Economy,* 1975; *Chinese Economy Post-Mao,* 1978; *China Under the Four Modernizations,* 1982 (Washington, D.C.: Government Printing Office); World Bank, *China: Socialist Economic Development* (Washington, D.C.: World Bank, 1981); Chung-kuo ching-chi nien-chien pien-chi wei-yuan hui, *Chung-kuo ching-chi nien-chien* (1981) (Peking: Ching-chi kuan-li tsa-chih she, 1982) (translated: *Annual Economic Report of China* [Hong Kong: Hsien-tai wen-hua ch'i-yeh kung-szu, 1982]); Chung-kuo ching-chi nien-chien pien-chi wei-yuan hui, *Chung-kuo ching-chi nien-chien* (1982) (Peking: Ching-chi kuan-li tsa-chih she, 1983) (translated: *Almanac of China's Economy* [Hong Kong: Chung-kuo ching-chi nien-chien yu-hsien kung-szu, 1983].). For a concise eye-witness report of the economic conditions of Mainland China made in 1973, readers may wish to refer to: Wen-shun Chi, "Highlights of Economic Conditions in China," *Chinese Economic Studies* 8:3 (Spring 1975), pp. 65, 74.

41 Linda Mathews, "The Persistent Chinese 'Siesta,'" *San Francisco Chronicle,* Sunday Punch, 3 August 1980, p. 7.

42 The romanized Chinese is I-ch'ieh hsiang ch'ien-k'an.

43 *New York Times,* 26 December 1979, p. A12.

44 Ibid., 29 August 1979, p. A12.

45 D. W. Y. Kwok, *Scientism in Chinese Thought 1900–1950* (New Haven: Yale University Press, 1965), p. 3.

46 Jan S. Prybyla, "Man and Society in China," *Vital Speeches of the Day* 41, no. 18 (1 July 1975): 551–2.

47 Bertrand Russell, *Authority and the Individual* (Boston: Beacon, 1960), p. 73.

48 David Reisman, *Individualism Reconsidered and Other Essays* (Glencoe, IL: Free Press, 1954), p. 38.

49 Mao, "Tsai tsui-kao kuo-wu hui-i shang te chiang-hua," *Wan-sui,* 2:158.

50 Mao, "Tsai tsui-kao kuo-wu hui-i shang te chiang-hua," *Wan-sui,* 2:132.

51 Mao, "Tsai pa-ta erh-tz'u hui-i shang te chiang-hua," *Wan-sui,* 2:210.

52 Edgar Snow, *Red Star Over China* (New York: Random House, 1938), pp. 134–5. See also Li Jui, "Wu-szu yun-tung chung te ch'ing-nien Mao Tse-tung," *Li-shih yen-chiu* Peking), no. 5 (1979):19.

53 This quotation was related to me by a visitor from mainland China. The primary source cannot be located in the publications on Mao in this country. However, I was told that sources of many remarks credited to Mao cannot be located on the mainland, either, because many of his articles and speeches have not been published.

54 Ch'en Jo-hsi, *Kuei* (Hong Kong: Min-pao ch'u-pan she, 1979), pp. 172–3. This book is a novel. I checked with the author and she told me that this episode was factual.

55 *Kuang-ming jih-pao,* 8 September 1982.

56 *Kuan-yü chien-kuo i-lai tang te jo-kan li-shih wen-t'i te chueh-i* (Hong Kong: San-lien

shu-tien, 1981), p. 54. Hereafter referred to as *Chueh-i*. "Resolution on Certain Questions in the History of Our Party Since the Founding of the People's Republic of China," *Resolution on CPC History (1949–1981)* (Peking: Foreign Languages, 1981).

[57] *Jen-min jih-pao,* editorial, 21 October 1982.

[58] Mao, "Tsai pa-chieh ch'i-chung ch'üan-hui shang te chiang-hua," *Wan-sui,* 1:52.

[59] Mao, "Tsai i-tz'u hui-pao shih te ch'a-hua," *Wan-sui,* 2:472.

[60] Chung-kuo hsin-wen she dispatch, 2 September 1980.

[61] Umberto Melotti, *Marx and the Third World,* trans. Pat Ransford (London: Macmillan Press 1977), pp. 146–7.

[62] Ibid., pp. 149–50.

[63] Michael Harrington, *Socialism* (New York: Saturday Review Press, 1972), p. 169.

[64] *Chueh-i,* p. 21.

[65] Ibid., pp. 21–3.

[66] Ibid., p. 30.

[67] Ibid., p. 54.

[68] Ibid., p. 24.

[69] Ibid., p. 33.

[70] Ibid., p. 51.

[71] Ibid., pp. 56–7.

[72] *Jen-min jih-pao,* 11 April 1980.

[73] Chao Pao-hsu, "China's Agricultural Policies, Past and Present," statement based on lecture at the Center for Chinese Studies, University of California, Berkeley, 16 November 1982. Chao Pao-hsu is the chairman of the Department of International Relations, and also director of the Institute of Asian and African Studies of Peking University.

[74] Long Chun, "Kuan-yü nung-yeh sheng-ch'an tse-jen chih te chi-ko wen-t'i" (Kunming, Yunnan), *Ching-chi wen-t'i t'an-so,* no. 1 (1982):1.

[75] *Chueh-i,* p. 35.

[76] *Jen-min jih-pao,* editorial, 1 January 1979.

[77] Li I-che, "Kuan-yü she-hui chu-i te min-chu yü fa-chih," poster, reprinted in *Chanwang* (Hong Kong), no. 332 (1 December 1975): 11–20. This poster was written jointly by three people, Li Cheng-t'ien, Ch'en I-yang, and Wang Hsi-che. Li I-che was formed by taking one character from each one of the three names.

[78] Wei Ching-sheng, "Ti-wu ko hsien-tai-hua," *T'an-so* (Peking), no. 1, 1979.

[79] Wang Hsi-che, "Wei wu-ch'an chieh-chi te chuan-cheng erh nu-li" (Canton), *Jen-min chih-sheng,* no. 8, July 1979. Reprinted in *Ch'i-shih nien-tai* (Hong Kong), no. 116 (September 1979):25–30.

[80] *Chueh-i,* p. 39.

[81] Ibid., p. 53.

List of Characters

an-fen shou-chi 安分守己
Anhwei 安徽
Canton 廣東
Chang, Carsun (see Chang Chün-mai) 張嘉森
Chang Chih-tung 張之洞
Chang chuň-mai (see Carsun Chang) 張君勱
Chang Erh-t'ien 張爾田
Chang Fa-k'uei 張發奎
Chang Hsi-jo 張奚若
Chang Hsueh-liang 張學良
Chang Hsun 張勳
Chang Kuo-t'ao 張國燾
Chang Ping-lin 章炳麟
Chang san-shih 張三世
Chang Shih-chao 章士釗
Chang T'ieh-sheng 張鐵生
Chang Tsung-sui 張宗遂
Chang Tung-sun 張東蓀
Ch'ang-sha 長沙
Chao K'uang-yin 趙匡胤
Chao Tzu-yang 趙紫陽
Chekiang 浙江
Chen Cheng (Ch'en Ch'eng) 陳誠
Chen-tan 震旦
Ch'en Chi-t'ang 陳濟棠
Ch'en Fa-chih 陳發之
Ch'en Hou-chu 陳後主
Ch'en Ming-shu 陳銘樞
Ch'en Tu-hsiu 陳獨秀
Ch'en Yun 陳雲
cheng-chih 政治
Cheng-chih ta-hsueh 政治大學
cheng-ch'üan 政權
Cheng Hsuan 鄭玄
Cheng-i 正義

Cheng Kuan-ying 鄭觀應
cheng-li kuo-ku 整理國故
Cheng-lun 政論
cheng-t'i 政體
Cheng-wen she 政聞社
Ch'eng-tu 成都
chi-ch'üan chu-i 集權主義
Chi Hsi 績溪
chi-t'i so-yu chih 集體所有制
Ch'i 齊
Chia-ching 嘉靖
Chia-ting 嘉定
Chia-yin tsa-chih 甲寅雜誌
Chiang Chin 江津
Chiang Chi'ing 江青
Chiang Hsueh-she 講學社
Chiang Kai-shek 蔣介石
Chiang-nan chih-tsao chü 江南織造局
Chiang Tung-hsiu 江冬秀
Ch'iang-hsueh hui 強學會
Ch'iang-kuo hui 強國會
Chiao-chou 膠州
chiao-yü tzu-chih 教育自治
chien-hsiung 奸雄
Chien-kuo fang-lueh 建國方署
Chien-kuo ta-kang 建國大綱
ch'ien-jang 謙讓
Ch'ien-t'ang 錢塘
Ch'ien Tuan-sheng 錢端升
chih 智
chih-ch'üan 治權
chih-nan hsing-i 知難行易
ch'ih-t'ung 赤統
Chin 晉
Chin-pu tang 進步黨
chin-shih 進士
Chin-wen 今文
Ch'in 秦
Ch'in Shih Huang-ti 秦始皇帝
Ching-kang (mountain) 井崗山
Ch'ing 清
ch'ing-chih 情志
Ch'ing-i pao 清議報
Chiu-wang lun 救亡論
Ch'iu-shih 求實
Chou 周
Chou 紂
Chou En-lai 周恩來

338

Chou Yang 周揚
Chu Hsi 朱熹
Chu Te 朱德
chu-t'i 主體
Ch'u An-p'ing 儲安平
Chuang-tzu 莊子
chuang-yuan 狀元
Ch'un-ch'iu 春秋
ch'un-hou 淳厚
chung-hsiao 忠孝
Chungking 重慶
Chung-kuo kung-hsueh 中國公學
Chung-kuo pen-wei wen-hua 中國本位文化
Chung-wai chi-wen 中外紀聞
Chung-wai kung-pao 中外公報
Chung-yang hsing-cheng yuan 中央行政院
ch'ung-fen hsien-tai-hua 充分現代化
ch'ung-fen shih-chieh-hua 充分世界化
chü-jen 舉人
chü-luan-shih 據亂世
Ch'ü Ch'iu-pai 瞿秋白
Ch'ü-fu 曲阜
ch'üan 權
ch'üan-min so-yu chih 全民所有制
ch'üan-p'an hsi-hua 全盤西化
chün 軍
chün-chu li-hsien 君主立憲
chün-hsien chih 郡縣制
fa-chia chih-fu 發家致富
fa-ts'ai 發財
Fan Chung-yen 范仲淹
Fukien 福建
Fu Tso-i 傅作義
Genghis Khan 成吉思汗
Han 漢
Han Fu-chü 韓復榘
Hankow 漢口
Han-lin 翰林
Han-shu 漢書
Han Yü 韓愈
Hangchow 杭州
hao-jan chih-ch'i 浩然之氣
hei-t'ung 黑統
ho-ch'ün 合群
Ho Hsiu 何休
Honan 河南
Ho Ping-sung 何炳松
ho-p'ing 和平

339

Ho-tse 荷澤

Hou-Han shu 後漢書

Hsi-an 西安

Hsi-ch'iao (mountain) 西樵山

Hsi-k'ang 西康

Hsi Shih 西施

Hsia 夏

Hsiang-chiang p'ing-lun 湘江評論

Hsiang-hsiang 湘鄉

Hsiang-shan 香山

Hsiang-t'an 湘潭

Hsiang-tao chou-pao 嚮導週報

Hsiang-ts'un chien-she p'ai 鄉村建設派

hsiang-yueh 鄉約

hsiao-k'ang 小康

hsien 縣

hsien i-hui 縣議會

Hsien-ts'ao hsiao-tsu hui-i 憲草小組會議

Hsin che-hsueh lun-ts'ung 新哲學論叢

Hsin hsiao-shuo 新小說

Hsin-hua 新華

Hsin-hui 新會

hsin-i 信義

hsin-li 心力

Hsin-lu 新路

hsin-min 新民

Hsin-min hsueh-hui 新民學會

Hsin-min ts'ung-pao 新民叢報

Hsing-Chung hui 興中會

hsiu-ts'ai 秀才

hsu-chün kung-ho 虛君共和

Hsu Hsing 許行

Hsu Kuang-ch'i 徐光啟

Hsu Shao 許劭

Hsu Ti-hsin 許滌新

Hsueh-hai shu-yuan 學海書院

Hsueh-hai t'ang 學海堂

Hsueh-heng 學衡

hsun-ku tz'u-chang 訓古詞章

Hsun-tzu 荀子

Hu Feng 胡風

Hunan 湖南

Hu Shih 胡適

Hu Szu-tu 胡思杜

Hu Yao-pang 胡燿邦

Hua Kuo-feng 華國鋒

Huai-ning 懷寧

Huang Li-chou (see Huang Tsung-hsi) 黃梨州

340

Huang Tsung-hsi (see Huang Li-chou) 黃宗羲
Hui (king) 惠
Huo Kuang 霍光
i-chang 議長
i-hui mi 議會迷
I Yin 伊尹
jen 仁
jen-ai 仁愛
Jen-kung 任公
jen-min 人民
jen-pen yuan 人本院
jen-sheng kuan 人生觀
jen-t'ung 人統
Jui-chin 瑞金
Kai-tsao 改造
Kai-tsao yü chieh-fang 改造與解放
K'ai fang cheng-ch'üan 開放政權
Kang-chien i-chih lu 綱鑑易知錄
K'ang T'ung-pi 康同璧
K'ang Yu-wei 康有為
Kao Chün-man 高君曼
Kiangsi 江西
Kiangsu 江蘇
ko-ming 革命
Ku Meng-yü 顧孟餘
Ku T'ing-lin (see Ku Yen-wu) 顧亭林
Ku-wen 古文
Ku Yen-wu (see Ku T'ing-lin) 顧炎武
Kuan Han-ch'ing 關漢卿
Kuan Yin 關尹
Kuang-hsu 光緒
Kuang-hua (university) 光華大學
Kuang-ming jih-pao 光明日報
Kuang-tung 廣東
Kuang-wu 光武
Kunming 昆明
kuo-chia 國家
kuo-chia she-hui chu-i 國家社會主義
Kuo-chia she-hui tang 國家社會黨
Kuo-feng pao 國風報
Kuo-li tzu-chih hsueh-yuan 國立自治學院
kuo-min 國民
Kuomintang 國民黨
Kuo-min ts'an-cheng hui 國民參政會
Kuo Mo-jo 郭沫若
kuo-t'i 國體
kuo-tsu chu-i 國族主義
kung 工

kung 公
kung-ch'an 共產
kung-ch'e shang-shu 公車上書
kung cheng-fu 公政府
kung-ch'i 公醫
kung-ho li-hsien 共和立憲
Kung-ho tang 共和黨
Kung-hsueh she 共學社
kung-i cheng-fu 公議政府
Kung-yang 公羊
Kung-yang chuan 公羊傳
K'ung-tzu 孔子
Kwangsi 廣西
Kweilin 桂林
Lan Chih-hsien 藍志先
lao-ts'u 老粗
Lao-tzu 老子
Lei Chen 雷震
li 禮
li 里
Li Chi 禮記
li-chih 理智
Li Hou-chu 李後主
li-hsing 理性
Li Hung-chang 李鴻章
Li I-che 李一哲
Li Li-san 李立三
Li Po 李白
Li Shih-min 李世民
Li Szu 李斯
Li Ta-chao 李大釗
Li Yun 禮運
li-yung hou-sheng 利用厚生
Liang 梁
Liang Ch'i-ch'ao 梁啟超
Liang Shu-ming 梁漱溟
Liang Wu-ti 梁武帝
Liao P'ing 廖平
Liaotung peninsula 遼東半島
Lin Piao 林彪
Liu Hsin 劉歆
liu-mang 流氓
Liu Pang 劉邦
Liu Shao-ch'i 劉少奇
Liu Tsung-yuan 柳宗元
Lo Kuan-chung 羅貫中
Lo Lung-chi 羅隆基
Lu Chiu-yuan 陸九淵

342

Lu Hsun 魯迅
lun-li pen-wei 倫理本位
Lü 呂
Lü Ta-fang 呂大防
Ma Yin-ch'u 馬寅初
Mao-erh-kai 毛兒蓋
Mao Tse-tung 毛澤東
mei 美
Mei-chou p'ing-lun 每周評論
min 民
min-chu 民主
Min-chu cheng-t'uan t'ung-meng 民主政團同盟
min-chu chi-ch'üan 民主集權
Min-chu Chung-kuo yun-tung 民主中國運動
Min-chu hsien-cheng tang 民主憲政黨
Min-chu she-hui tang 民主社會黨
Min-chu tang 民主黨
Min-chu t'ung-meng 民主同盟
min-chung 民眾
min-ch'üan 民權
Min-ch'üan ch'u-pu 民權初步
min-ch'üan lun 民權論
min-kuo 民國
Min-pao 民報
min-sheng shih-kuan 民生史觀
min-tsu ching-shen 民族精神
Min-tsu wen-hua hsueh-yuan 民族文化學院
Ming Ch'eng-tsu 明成祖
Ming T'ai-tsu 明太祖
Mo-tzu 墨子
Nan-ching kao-teng hsueh-hsiao 南京高等學校
Nan-hai 南海
Nanking 南京
Nanning 南寧
nei-hang 內行
neng 能
pa-tao 霸道
Pai-hsing 百姓
pai-hua 白話
pai-t'ung 白桃
P'an Kuang-tan 潘光旦
Pao-huang hui 保皇會
pao-kan tao-hu 包干到戶
Pao-kuo hui 保國會
P'eng Te-huai 彭德懷
Pieh T'ing-fang 別庭芳
Pien-fa t'ung-i 變法通議
p'ing-min 平民

pu-jen 不忍
Pu-jen tsa-chih 不忍雜志
pu-min 部民
pu-tsu 不足
P'u Sung-ling 蒲松齡
P'u Te-chih 濮德志
Sa Meng-wu 薩孟武
San-min chu-i 三民主義
shang 商
Shang-hai chiang-nan chih-tsao chü kuang-fang yen-kuan 上海江南織造局廣方言館
shang-t'ung 尚同
Shao-shan 韶山
shen 紳
Shen-nung 神農
Shensi 陝西
sheng-ch'an tse-jen chih 生產責任制
Sheng Liang-jui 盛良瑞
sheng i-hui 省議會
sheng-p'ing shih 升平世
Sheng-shih wei-yen 盛世危言
sheng-yuan 生員
shih-che sheng-ts'un 適者生存
Shih-chi 史記
shih-chia chuang 石家莊
shih chieh-chi 士階級
shih-chieh chu-i 世界主義
shih i-hui 市議會
shih-shih hsin-pao 時事新報
shih ta-fu 士大夫
Shih-wu hsueh-t'ang 時務學堂
Shih-wu pao 時務報
Shih-yeh chi-hua 實業計劃
shu 術
shu-yuan 書院
Shui-hu chuan 水滸傳
Shun 舜
Soochow 蘇州
su-ch'eng lun 速成論
sui 歲
Sui Yang-ti 隋煬帝
Sun Wen hsueh-shuo 孫文學說
Sun Yat-sen (Sun Chung-shan) 孫中山
Sun Yeh-fang 孫冶方
Sung 宋
Sung Hui-tsung 宋徽宗
Szechwan 四川
szu 私
Tai-chai 大寨

344

Ta Chung-hua tsa-chih 大中華雜誌
ta-chung min-chu 大眾民主
Ta-hsueh 大學
Ta-kung-ho jih-pao 大共和日報
Ta-kung pao 大公報
Ta-li 大理
ta-t'ung 大同
Taipei 台北
Taiwan 台灣
T'ai-p'ing 太平
T'ai-p'ing shih 太平世
T'ai-shih 泰誓
T'an-so 探索
T'an Szu-t'ung 譚嗣同
tang-kuo 黨國
T'ang 湯，唐
Tao-t'ung 道統
T'ao Meng-ho 陶孟和
Teng Hsiao-p'ing 鄧小平
ti-t'ung 地統
T'ien-an Men 天安門
t'ien-hsia 天下
T'ien-hsia wei-kung 天下為公
t'ien-tao 天道
t'ien-t'ung 天統
t'ien-yu 天遊
Ting, V.K. (Ting Wen-chiang) 丁文江
Ting Wen-chiang (V.K. Ting) 丁文江
t'o-ku kai-chih 託古改制
Tsai-sheng 再生
Ts'ai Yuan-p'ei 蔡元培
Ts'ao-chou 曹州
Ts'ao Hsueh-ch'in 曹雪芹
Ts'ao Ts'ao 曹操
Ts'ao Yü 曹禺
ts'e-lun 策論
Tseng Kuo-fan 曾國藩
Tseng-tzu 曾子
Tsiang, T.F. (Chiang T'ing-fu) 蔣廷黻
Tsing Hua 清華
Tsou-p'ing 鄒平
Ts'ui-heng 翠亨
Tsun-i 遵義
Ts'un-chih yueh-k'an 村治月刊
Tu Fu 杜甫
tu-shu-jen 讀書人
Tu Yü 杜預
t'u-ti ko-ming 土地革命

Tung Chung-shu 董仲舒
t'ung 統
T'ung-ch'eng 桐城
T'ung-meng hui 同盟會
t'ung san-t'ung 通三統
tzu-li keng-sheng 自力更生
Tzu Lu 子路
tzu-te 自得
tzu-yu 自由
Tzu-yu chung 自由鐘
wai-hang 外行
Wang An-shih 王安石
wang-che shih 王者師
Wang-chih 王制
Wang Ching-wei 汪精衛
Wang Ch'uan-shan 王船山
Wang Hsi-che 王希哲
Wang Jo-shui 王若水
Wang Mang 王莽
Wang Ming 王明
Wang Ping-chang 王炳章
Wang Shih-fu 王實甫
Wang Su 王肅
wang-tao 王道
Wang Yang-ming 王陽明
Wei 魏
Wei Ching-sheng 魏京生
wen 文
Wen (king) 文王
Wen-hui pao 文滙報
Wu 武
wu-ch'an che 無產者
wu-chih chien-she 物質建設
Wu Ching-ch'ao 吳景超
Wu Han 吳晗
Wuhan 武漢
Wuhsien 吳縣
Wu Hsun 武訓
Wu Tse-t'ien 武則天
wu-wei 無為
Yang Ch'ang-chi 楊昌濟
Yang Kuei-fei 楊貴妃
yang-mou 陽謀
Yao 堯
Yeh Chien-ying 葉劍英
Yenan 延安
Yenching (university) 燕京大學
Yen-chiu hsi 研究系

346

Yen Fu 嚴復
Yen Hsi-chai 顏習齊
Yen Jo-chü 閻若璩
yin-mou 陰謀
yu-min 遊民
Yuan 元
Yuan-ming yuan 圓明園
Yuan Shih-k'ai 袁世凱
Yunnan 雲南
Yung-yen 庸言
Yü 禹
Yü-chou 宇宙
Yü-yen mei 語言美
Xinjiang 新疆

Bibliography

The materials included here are based largely on the materials cited in this book, supplemented by other items the author believes essential to the study of these areas. No attempt has been made to be comprehensive. The reader may wish to consult the bibliographies of the books cited for a more comprehensive survey of the material available.

Ai Szu-ch'i [艾思奇]. *Hu Shih Liang Shu-ming che-hsueh szu-hsiang p'i-p'an* [胡適梁漱溟哲學思想批判]. Peking, 1977.

Alitto, Guy S. *The Last Confucian: Liang Shu-ming and the Chinese Dilemma of Modernity*. Berkeley, 1979.

Beard, Charles A., ed. *Whither Mankind*. New York, 1928.

Benton, Gregor. *Chinese Revolutionary Memoirs 1919–1949*. London, 1980.

Boorman, Howard, ed. *Biographical Dictionary of Republican China*. New York, 1967.

Broening, Stephens. "The Death of 30 Million Chinese." Opinion-Commentary, *The (Baltimore) Sun*, 24 April 1984, p. A19.

Chang, Carsun. *Development of Neo-Confucian Thought*. New York, 1962. (see also Chang, Chün-mai.)

———. *The Third Force in China*. New York, 1952.

Chang Chen-chih et al. [張振之等]. *P'ing Hu Shih fan tung-i chin-chu* [評胡適反党義近著]. Shanghai, 1929.

Chang Chün-mai [張君勱]. "Chung-hua min-tsu chih li-kuo neng-li" [中華民族之立國能力]. *Tsai-sheng* [再生], 20 August 1932. (See also Chang, Carsun.)

———. "Fa k'an-tz'u" [發刊詞]. *Hsin-lu* [新路], 1 February 1928.

———. "I-tang chuan-cheng yü wu-kuo" [一党專政與吾國]. *Hsin-lu*, 15 February 1928.

———. "Jen-sheng-kuan lun-chan chih hui-ku" [人生觀論戰之回顧]. *Tung-fang tsa-chih* [東方雜誌], July 1934.

———. "Jen-sheng-kuan lun-chan chi hui-ku—Szu-shih nien lai hsi-fang che-hsueh chieh chih szu-hsiang-chia" [人生觀論戰之回顧　四十年來西方哲學界之思想家]. *Jen-sheng* [人生] (Hong Kong), no. 313 (November 1963); no. 314 (December 1963).

———. "Kuo-chia min-chu cheng-chih yü kuo-chia she-hui chu-i" [國家民主政治與國家社會主義]. *Tsai-sheng*, 20 June 1932.

———. "Kuo-min-tang tang-cheng chih hsin ch'i-lu" [國民黨黨政之新歧路].
Tsai-sheng, 20 June 1932.

———. *Li-kuo chih tao* [立國之道] or *Kuo-chia she-hui chu-i* [國家社會主義].
Kweilin, 1938.

———. *Ming-jih chih Chung-kuo wen-hua* [明日之中國文化]. Shanghai, 1934.

———. "P'i hsun-cheng shuo" [關訓政說]. *Hsin-lu,* 1 May 1982.

———. *Pien-cheng wei-wu chu-i po-lun* [辯證唯物主義駁論]. Hong Kong,
1958.

———, and Chang Tung-sun [張東蓀]. "Wo-men so yao shuote hua"
[我們所要說的話]. *Tsai-sheng,* 20 May 1932.

———, Tang Chun-i [唐君毅], Mou Chun-san [牟宗三], and Hsu Fu-kwan
[徐復觀]. *Chung-kuo wen-hua yü shih-chieh* [中國文化與世界]. Hong Kong,
1958.

Chang Hao. *Liang Ch'i-ch'ao and Intellectual Transition in China 1890–1907.*
Cambridge, Mass., 1971.

Chang Lei [張磊]. *Sun Chung-shan szu-hsiang yen-chiu* [孫中山思想研究].
Peking, 1981.

Chang P'eng-yuan [張朋園]. *Li-hsien pai yü hsin-hai ko-ming*
[立憲派與辛亥革命]. Taipei, 1969.

———. *Liang Ch'i-ch'ao yü Ch'ing-chi ko-ming* [梁啟超與清季革命]. Taipei,
1964.

———. *Liang Ch'i-ch'ao yü min-kuo cheng-chih* [梁啟超與民國政治]. Taipei,
1978.

Chang Tung-sun [張東蓀]. *Chih-shih yü wen-hua* [知識與文化]. Shanghai, 1947.

———. *Li-hsing yü min-chu* [理性與民主]. Chungking, 1946.

———. *Min-chu chu-i yü she-hui chu-i* [民主主義與社會主義]. Shanghai, 1948.

———. *Szu-hsiang yü she-hui* [思想與社會]. Shanghai, 1947.

———. *Tao-te che-hsueh* [道德哲學]. Shanghai, 1931.

———. *Wei-wu pien-cheng fa lun-chan* [唯物辯證法論戰]. Peking, 1934.

Chao Feng-nien [趙豐年]. "K'ang Ch'ang-su hsien-sheng nien-p'u"
[康長素先生年譜]. *Shih-hsueh nien-pao* [史學年報] 2, no. 1 (1934).

Chen Cheng. *Land Reform in Taiwan.* Taipei, 1961.

Ch'en Jo-hsi [陳若曦]. *Kuei* [歸]. Hong Kong, 1979.

Ch'en Po-ta [陳伯達]. "Kuan-yü chih-hsing wen-t'i te yen-chiu"
[關於知行問題的研究]. In *Tsai wen-hua chen-hsien shang* [在文化陣線上].
Chunking, 1939.

———. "Lun kung-ch'an chu-i-che tui-yü San-min chu-i kuan-hsi te chi-ko wen-
t'i" [論共產主義者對於三民主義關係的幾個問題]. In Mao Tse-tung
[毛澤東], Ch'en Po-ta et al, *Lun San-min chu-i* [論三民主義]. N.p., n.d.

———. *Lun Sun Chung-shan chu-i* [論孫中山主義]. (N.p.) 1946.

Ch'en Tu-hsiu [陳獨秀]. *Ch'en Tu-hsiu hsien-sheng pien-su chuang*
[陳獨秀先生辯訴狀]. Pamphlet N.p. 1933.

———. *Ch'en Tu-hsiu tsui-hou tui-yü min-chu cheng-chih te chien-chieh*
[陳獨秀最後對於民主政治的見解]. Hong Kong, 1950. (Henceforth *Tsui-hou chien-
chieh.*)

———. "Chin-jih chih chiao-yü fang-chen" [今日之教育方針]. *Hsin ch'ing-nien*
[新青年], October 1915.

———. "Ching-kao ch'ing-nien" [敬告青年]. *Hsin ch'ing-nien,* September 1915.

————. "Hsien-fa yü K'ung-chiao" [憲法與孔教]. *Hsin ch'ing-nien*, November 1916.

———— et al. *Kao ch'üan-tang t'ung-chih shu* [告全黨同志書]. Pamphlet. N.p. 10 December 1929.

————. "Kei Hsi-liu teng te hsin" [給西流等的信]. In *Tsui-hou chien-chieh*.

————. "Kei Hsi-liu te hsin" [給西流的信]. In *Tsui-hou chien-chieh*.

————. "Kei Lien-ken te hsin" [給連根的信]. In *Tsui-hou chien-chieh*.

————. "Kei S ho H te hsin" [給 S 和 H 的信]. In *Tsui-hou chien-chieh*.

————. "K'ung-tzu chih-tao yü hsien-tai sheng-huo" [孔子之道與現代生活]. *Hsin ch'ing-nien*, December 1919.

————. "Lao-tung-che te chueh-wu" [勞動者的覺悟]. *Hsin ch'ing-nien*, September 1920.

————. "Pen-chih tsui-an chih ta-pien shu" [本誌罪案之答辯書]. *Hsin ch'ing-nien*, January 1919.

————. *Shih-an tzu-chuan* [實庵自傳]. Taipei, 1967.

————. "Shih-hsing min-chih te chi-ch'u" [實行民治的基礎]. *Hsin ch'ing-nien*, December 1919.

————. "T'an cheng-chih" [談政治]. *Hsin ch'ing-nien*, September 1920.

————. *Tu-hsiu wen-ts'un* [最後見解]. Shanghai, 1922.

————. "Tung-hsi min-tsu ken-pen szu-hsiang chih ch'a-i" [東西民族根本思想之差異]. *Hsin ch'ing-nien*, December 1915.

————. "Wu-jen tsui-hou chih chueh-wu" [吾人最後之覺悟]. *Hsin ch'ing nien*, February 1916.

————. "Wo-te ken-pen i-chien" [我的根本意見]. In *Tsui-hou chien-chieh*.

———— et al. *Wo-men te cheng-chih i-chien shu* [我們的政治意見書]. Pamphlet. N.p. 15 December 1929.

————. "Wu-jen tsui-hou chih chueh-wu" [吾人最後之覺悟]. *Hsin ch'ing-nien*, February 1916.

Ch'en Wan-hsiung [陳萬雄]. *Hsin wen-hua yun-tung ch'ien te Ch'en Tu-hsiu (1879–1915)* [新文化運動前的陳獨秀]. Hong Kong 1979.

Cheng Chu-yuan. *China's Economic Development: Growth and Structural Change*. Boulder, 1982.

Cheng Chu-yuan [鄭竹園]. "Ta-lu p'in-k'un lo-hou te ken-yuan" [大陸貧困落後的根源]. *Lien-ho pao* (Taipei), 10 July 1981.

Cheng-feng wen hsien [整風文獻]. Hong Kong, 1949.

Ch'eng Wen-hsi [程文熙]. "Chang Chün-mai hsien-sheng chih yen-hsing" [張君勱先生之言行]. In *Chang Chün-mai hsien-sheng ch'i-shih shou-ch'ing chi-nien lun-wen chi* [張君勱先生七十壽慶紀念論文集], Wang Yun-wu et al. [王雲五等]. Taipei, 1956.

————. "Chang Chün-mai hsien-sheng chu: 'Min-chu li-kuo wen-chi' mu-lu ch'u-kao" [張君勱先生著：「民主立國文集」目錄初稿]. *Tsai-sheng* (Taipei), no. 125 (20 February 1982): 5–8, 14.

Chi, Wen-shun. "The Great Proletarian Cultural Revolution in Ideological Perspective." *Asian Survey*, August 1969.

————. "Highlights of Economic Conditions in China." *Chinese Economic Studies*. Spring, 1975.

————. "The Ideological Source of the People's Communes in Communist China." *Pacific Coast Philology*, April 1967.

———. "Liang Shu-ming and Chinese Communism." *The China Quarterly,* January-March, 1970.

———. "New Economic Ideas and Their Traditional Sources in China." *Current Scene,* May-June, 1975.

———. "Sun Yeh-fang and his Revisionist Economics." *Asian Survey,* October 1972.

Chiang Kai-shek [蔣介石]. *Chung-kuo chih ming-yün* [中國之命運]. In *Chiang tsung-t'ung szu-hsiang yen lun chi* [蔣總統思想言論集]. Reprint. Taipei, 1966. Translated by Philip Jaffe, under the title *China's Destiny and Chinese Economic Theory.* New York, 1947.

Ch'iang Chung-hua et al. [强重華等]. *Ch'en Tu-hsiu pei-pu tzu-lien hui-pien* [陳獨秀被捕資料滙編]. Ho-nan, 1982.

Chien Po-tsan [翦伯贊]. *Wu-hsu pien-fa* [戊戌變法]. Shanghai, 1953.

Ch'ien Mu [錢穆]. *Chung-kuo chin san-pai nien hsueh-shu shih* [中國近三百年學術史]. Chungking, 1945.

———. *Chung-kuo szu-hsiang shih* [中國思想史]. Taipei, 1957.

Ch'ien Tuan-sheng [錢端升]. "Min-chu cheng-chih hu, chi-ch'üan kuo-chia hu?" [民主政治乎 集權國家乎?]. *Tung-fang tsa-chih,* 1 January 1934.

Chi-lin sheng ko-ming wei-yuan hui hsieh-tso hsiao-tsu [吉林省革命委員會寫作小組]. "She-hui chu-i chien-she yü ching-chi hsueh liang-yü chung te chieh-chi tou-cheng" [社會主義建設與經濟學領域中的階級鬥爭]. *Hung-ch'i* [紅旗], no. 2 (1970).

Chi Yü-ju [邱玉汝]. *Ch'en Tu-hsiu nien-p'u* [陳獨秀年譜]. Hong Kong, 1974.

Ch'in Shih-huang tsai li-shih shang te chin-pu tso-yung [秦始皇在歷史上的進步作用]. Hu-nan, 1973.

Chou Ch'ing-wen [周鯨文]. *Feng-po shih nien* [風暴十年]. Hong Kong, 1959. Translated by Lai Ming, under the title *Ten Years of Storm.* New York, 1960.

Chou Yang [周揚]. "Niu-kuei she-shen tsai K'ung-tzu t'ao-lun hui shang fang-le hsieh shen-ma tu?" [牛鬼蛇神在孔子討論會上放了些甚麼毒?]. *Jen-min jih-pao* [人民日報], 10 January 1967.

Chou Yü-jui [周楡瑞]. *Hung-ch'ao jen-wu chih* [紅朝人物誌]. New York, 1976.

Chow, Tse-tsung. *The May Fourth Movement: Intellectual Revolution in Modern China.* Cambridge, Mass., 1960.

Chung-kuo ching-chi nien-chien pien-chi wei-yuan hui [中國經濟年鑑編輯委員會]. *Chung-kuo ching-chi nien-chien* (1981) [中國經濟年鑑]. Peking, 1982. Translated under the title *Annual Economic Report of China.* Hong Kong, 1982.

———. *Chung-kuo ching-chi nien-chien* (1982). Peking, 1983. Translated under the title *Almanac of China's Economy.* Hong Kong, 1983.

"Chung-kuo i-hui-mi te p'o-ch'an" [中國議會迷的破產]. *Jen-min jih-pao,* 12 August 1967.

Chung-kuo jen-min cheng-chih hsieh-shang hui-i Kuang-tung sheng wei-yuan hui wen-shih tzu-liao yen-chiu wei-yuan hui et al. [中國人民政治協商會議廣東省委員會文史資料研究委員會等]. *Sun Chung-shan yü Hsin-hai ko-ming shih-liao chuan-chi* [孫中山與辛亥革命史料專輯]. Canton, 1981.

Chung-kuo k'o-hsueh yuan che-hsueh yen-chiu so Chung-kuo che-hsueh shih tsu, and Pei-ching ta-hsueh che-hsueh hsi Chung-kuo che-hsueh shih chiao-yen shih [中國科學院哲學研究所中國哲學史組北京大學哲學系中國哲學史教研室].

Chung-kuo che-hsueh shih tzu-liao chien-pien [中國哲學史資料簡編]. Peking, 1972.

"Chung-kuo kung-ch'an tang chang-ch'eng" [中國共產黨章程]. In *Chung-kuo kung-ch'an tang ti-pa chieh ch'üan-kuo tai-piao ta-hui wen-hsien* [中國共產黨第八屆全國代表大會文献]. Peking, 1956.

Chung-kuo kung-ch'an tang chung-yang wei-yuan hui, "Kuan-yü wu-ch'an chieh-chi wen-hua ta ko-ming te chueh-ting" [中國共產黨中央委員會關於無產階級文化大革命的決定]. *Jen-min jih-pao,* 11 August 1966.

Chung-kuo kung-ch'an tang ti pa-chieh ch'üan-kuo tai-piao ta-hui wen-hsien. Peking, 1956.

Ch'ü Hao-jan [曲浩然]. "Hui-ku 'Wu-szu' yü chan-wang pao-wei Tiao-yü t'ai yun-tung" [回顧五四與展望保衛釣魚台運動]. *Ming-pao yueh-k'an* [明報月刊] (Hong Kong), May 1971.

Directorate General of Budget, Accounting & Statistics, Executive Yuan of the Republic of China. *Statistical Yearbook of the Republic of China, 1982.* Taipei, 1983.

Dittmer, Lowell. *Liu Shao-ch'i and the Chinese Cultural Revolution—the Politics of Mass Criticism.* Berkeley, 1974.

Fairbank, John King. *The United States and China.* 4th ed. Cambridge, Mass., 1979.

Fu Ch'i-hsueh [傅啟學]. *Kuo-fu Sun Chung-shan hsien-sheng chuan* [國父孫中山先生傳]. Taipei, 1965.

Fung Yu-lan [馮友蘭]. "P'i-p'an Liang Shu-ming hsien-sheng te wen-hua kuan ho 'ts'un-chih' li-lun" [批判梁漱溟先生的文化觀和"村治"理論]. In *Liang Shu-ming szu-hsiang p'i p'an* [梁漱溟思想批判]. Peking, 1955.

Gelbras, V. *Mao's Pseudo-Socialism.* Moscow, n.d.

Gregor, A. James, et al. *Ideology and Development, Sun Yat-sen and the Economic History of Taiwan.* Berkeley, 1981.

Grieder, Jerome B. *Hu Shih and the Chinese Renaissance.* Cambridge, Mass., 1970.

————. *Intellectuals and the State in Modern China.* London, 1981.

Harrington, Michael. *Socialism.* New York, 1970, 1972.

Ho Lin [賀麟]. *Tang-tai Chung-kuo che-hsueh* [當代中國哲學]. Nanking, 1947.

Ho-nan sheng nung-yeh wei-yuan hui [河南省農業委員會]. *Nung-yeh sheng-ch'an tse-jen chih shih-hsing pan-fa* [農業生產責任制實行辦法]. Peking, 1981.

Hou Wai-lu [侯外廬], ed. *Chung-kuo chin-tai che-hsueh shih* [中國近代哲學史]. Peking, 1978.

Howard, Richard C. "K'ang Yu-wei (1858–1927): His Intellectual Background and Early Thought." In *Confucian Personalities.* Edited by Arthur F. Wright and Denis Twitchett. Stanford, 1962.

Hsiang-kang Chung-wen ta-hsueh hsueh-sheng hui [香港中文大學學生會]. *Min-chu Chung-hua* [民主中華]. Hong Kong, 1982.

Hsiao, Kung-chuan. *A Modern China and a New World.* Seattle, 1957. (See also Hsiao Kung-ch'üan.)

Hsiao Kung-ch'üan [蕭公權]. *Chung-kuo cheng-chih szu-hsiang shih* [中國政治思想史]. Shanghai, 1946. (See also Kung-chuan Hsiao.)

Hsiao San [蕭三]. *Mao Tse-tung t'ung-chih te ch'ing shao-nien shih-tai* [毛澤東同志的青少年時代]. Peking, 1950.

Hsin-hua yueh-pao [新華月報], 15 January 1950, p. 819.

Hsu Kao-juan [徐高阮]. "Hu Shih-chih yü ch'üan-p'an hsi-hua" [胡適之與全盤 西化]. In *Hu Shih yü Chung-hsi wen-hua* [胡適與中西文化]. Taipei, 1967.

Hsu Kwan-san [許冠三]. "K'ang Nan-hai te san-shih chin-hua kuan" [康南海的三世進化觀]. *Chung-wen ta-hsueh hsueh-pao* [中文大學學報] 4, no. 1 (1977).

———. *Liu Shao-ch'i yü Liu Shao-ch'i lu-hsien* [劉少奇與劉少奇路線]. Hong Kong, 1980.

"Hsu Ti-hsin lun li-jun wen-t'i" [許滌新論利潤問題]. *Ta Kung Pao* [大公報], 24 November 1977.

Hsü, Immanuel C.Y. *Intellectual Trends in the Ch'ing Period.* Cambridge, Mass., 1959.

———. *The Rise of Modern China.* 3d ed. London, 1983.

Hu Ch'iao-mu [胡喬木]. *Chung-kuo kung-ch'an tang te san-shih nien* [中國共産黨的三十年]. Peking, 1951.

Hu Hua [胡華]. *Chung-kuo hsin min-chu chu-i ko-ming shih* [中國新民主義革命史]. Peking, 1951.

Hu Pin [胡濱]. *Chung-kuo chin-tai kai-liang chu-i szu -hsiang* [中國近代改良主義思想]. Peking. 1964.

———. *Wu-hsu pien-fa* [戊戌變法]. Shanghai, 1956.

Hu Shih [胡適]. "Chieh-shao wo tzu-chi szu-hsiang" [介紹我自己的思想]. In *Hu Shih wen-ts'un* [胡適文存]. Taipei, 1953. (Henceforth *Wen-ts'un.)*

———. "Chien-kuo yü chuan-chih" [建國與專制]. *Tu-li p'ing-lun* [獨立評論], 27 December 1933.

———. *The Chinese Renaissance.* New York, 1934.

———. "Ch'ing-tai hsueh-che te chih-hsueh fang-fa" [清代學者的治學方法]. In *Wen-ts'un.*

———. "Chung-kuo ku-tai cheng-chih szu-hsiang shih te i-ko k'an-fa" [中國古代政治思想史的一個看法]. In *Hu Shih yü Chung-hsi wen-hua.* Taipei, 1967.

———. "Chih-nan hsing i pu-i" [知難行亦不易]. *Hsin-yueh yueh k'an* [新月] (Shanghai) 2, no. 4 (1929).

———. "Ch'ung-fen shih-chieh-hua yü ch'üan-p'an hsi-hua" [充分世界化與全盤西化]. In *Hu Shih yü Chung-hsi wen-hua.* Taipei, 1967.

———. "The Civilization of the East and the West." In *Whither Mankind.* Edited by Charles A. Beard. New York, 1928.

———. "Hsin szu-ch'ao te i-i" [新思潮的意義]. In *Wen-ts'un.*

———. "Hsin wen-hua yun-tung yü Kuo-min-tang" [新文化運動與國民黨]. In *Jen-ch'üan lun-chi* [人權論集]. Shanghai, 1930.

———. *Hu Shih hsuan-chi* [胡適選集]. Taipei, 1966.

———. *Hu Shih lun-hsueh chin-chu* [胡適論學近著]. Shanghai, 1935.

———. *Hu Shih wen-ts'un* [胡適文存]. Taipei, 1953.

———. "I-nien lai kuan-yü min-chu yü tu-ts'ai te t'ao-lun" [一年來關於民主與獨裁的討論]. *Tung-fang tsa-chih,* 1 January 1935.

———. "I-pu-sheng chi-i" [易卜生主義]. In *Wen-ts'un.*

———. "Jen-ch'üan yü yueh-fa" [人權與約法]. *Hsin-yueh* 2, no. 2. Reprinted in *Jen-ch'üan lun-chi.* Shanghai, 1930.

———. "Kung-ch'an tang chih-hsia chueh mei-yu tzu-yu" [共產黨治下決沒有自由]. In *Wo-men pi-hsu hsuan-tse wo-men te fang-hsiang*

[我們必須選擇我們的方向]. Hong Kong, 1950.

————. "Our Attitude Towards Modern Western Civilization." In *Whither Mankind*. Edited by Charles A. Beard. New York, 1928.

————. "Pu-hsiu—Wo-te tsung-chiao" [不朽 — 我的宗教]. In *Wen-ts'un*.

————. "San-lun wen-t'i yü chu-i" [三論問題與主義]. In *Wen-ts'un*.

————. "San-pai nien-lai shih-chieh te ch'ü-shih yü Chung-kuo ying ts'ai te fang-hsiang" [三百年來世界的趨勢與中國應採的方向]. In *Hu Shih yü Chung-hsi wen-hua*. Taipei, 1967.

————. "The Scientific Spirit and Method in Chinese Philosophy." In *The Chinese Mind: Essentials of Chinese Philosophy and Culture*. Edited by Charles A. Moore. Honolulu, 1967.

————. "Shih-p'ing so-wei Chung-kuo pen-wei te wen-hua chien-she" [試評所謂中國本位的文化建設]. In *Hu Shih yü Chung-hsi wen-hua*. Taipei, 1967.

————. "Shih-yen chu-i" [實驗主義]. In *Wen-ts'un*.

————. "The Social Changes and Science." *The China News* (Taipei), March 1962.

Hu Shih szu-hsiang p'i-p'an [胡適思想批判]. Peking, 1955–56.

Hu Shih. *Szu-shih tzu-shu* [四十自述]. Shanghai, 1933.

————. "Ta Liang Shu-ming hsien-sheng" [答梁漱溟先生]. In *Hu Shih lun-hsueh chin-chu*. Shanghai, 1935.

————. "To-yen-chiu hsieh wen-t'i, shao t'an hsieh chu-i" [多研究些問題，少談些主義]. In *Wen-ts'un*.

————. "Tsai-lun chien-kuo yü chuan-chih" [再論建國與專制]. *Tu-li p'ing-lun*, 24 December 1933.

————. "Tsai-t'an hsien-cheng" [再談憲政]. *Tu-li p'ing-lun*, 30 May 1937.

————. "Ts'ung i-tang tao wu-tang cheng-chih" [從一黨到無黨政治]. *Tu-li p'ing-lun*, 6 October 1935.

————. "Ts'ung min-chu tu-ts'ai te t'ao-lun li ch'iu-te i-ko kung-t'ung te cheng-chih hsin-yang" [從民主獨裁的討論裡求得一個共同的政治信仰]. *Tu-li p'ing-lun*, 17 February 1935.

————. "Tzu-yu chu-i shih shen-mo?" [自由主義是甚麼]. In *Wo-men pi-hsu hsuan-tse wo-men te fang-hsiang* [我們必須選擇我們的方向]. Hong Kong, 1950.

————. *Wo-men pi-hsu hsuan-tse wo-men ti fang-hsiang*. Hong Kong, 1950.

————. "Wo-men shen-ma shih-hou ts'ai-k'o yu hsien-fa?" [我們甚麼時候才可有憲法]. *Hsin-yueh*, 1928. Reprinted in *Jen-ch'üan lun-chi*. Shanghai, 1930.

————. "Wo-men tsou nei-t'iao-lu?" [我們走那條路]. In *Hu Shih yü Chung-hsi wen-hua*. Taipei, 1967.

————. "Wo-men tui-yü hsi-yang chin-tai wen-ming te t'ai-tu" [我們對於西洋近代文明的態度]. In *Hu Shih yü Chung-hsi wen-hua*. Taipei, 1967.

————. "Yen-ch'ien shih-chieh wen-hua te ch'ü-hsiang" [眼前世界文化的趨向]. In *Wo-men pi-hsu hsuan-tse wo-men te fang-hsiang*. Hong Kong, 1950.

Hu Shih yü Chung-hsi wen-hua. Taipei, 1967.

Hu Sung-p'ing [胡頌平]. *Hu Shih hsien-sheng nien-p'u chien-pien* [胡適先生年譜簡編]. Taipei, 1971.

Hu Szu-tu [胡思杜]. "Tui wo-te fu-ch'in Hu Shih te p'i-p'ing" [對我的父親胡適的批評]. *Jen-min jih-pao*, 22 September 1950.

Hu Ying-han [胡應漢]. "Liang Shu-ming hsien-sheng nien-p'u ch'u-kao"

[梁漱溟先生年譜初稿]. *Jen-sheng* [人生] (Hong Kong), nos. 295–301 (10 February 1963–16 March 1963).

Hua Kuo-feng [華國鋒]. "Pa wu-ch'an chieh-chi chuan-cheng hsia te chi-hsu ko-ming chin-hsing tao-ti" [把無產階級專政下的繼續革命進行到底]. *Jen-min jih-pao,* 4 May 1977.

Huang, Philip. *Liang Ch'i-ch'ao and Modern Chinese Liberalism.* Seattle, 1972.

Hunt, R.N. Carew. *The Theory and Practice of Communism.* Baltimore, 1963.

Jen Chi-yü [任繼愈], ed. *Chung-kuo che-hsueh shih chien-pien*
[中國哲學史簡編]. Peking, 1973.

Jen Cho-hsuan [任卓宣]. *Chung-kuo wen-hua ti chu-liu* [中國文化底主流].
Taipei, 1968.

———. *Kuo-fu te ta-t'ung szu-hsiang* [國父的大同思想]. Taipei, 1969.

Johnson, Chalmers. *Peasant Nationalism and Communist Power.* Stanford, 1962.

K'ang T'ung-chia [康同家]. *K'ang Yu-wei yü wu-hsu pien-fa* [康有為與戊戌變法].
Hong Kong, 1959.

K'ang T'ung-pi [康同璧], comp. *Nan-hai K'ang hsien-sheng tzu-pien nien-pu pu-i*
[南海康先生自編年譜補遺]. Peking, 1958.

K'ang Yu-wei [康有為]. "Chin-ch'eng O-lo-szu Ta-pi-te pien-fa-chi hsu"
[進呈俄羅斯大彼德變法記序]. In *Wu-hsu pien-cheng.* Compiled by Chien Po-tsan et al. Shanghai, 1953.

———. *Chung-yung chu* [中庸注]. Shanghai, ca. 1901.

———. *Hsin-hsueh wei-ching k'ao* [新學偽经考]. Peking, 1967.

———. *K'ang Nan-hai tzu-pien nien-p'u* [康南海自編年譜]. In *Wu-hsu pien-fa*
[戊戌變法]. Compiled by Chien Po-tsan et al. Shanghai, 1953. His autobiography is translated into English and enlarged as *K'ang Yu-wei: A Biography and a Symposium* by Jung-pang Lo. Tucson, 1967.

———. *K'ung-tzu kai-chih k'ao* [孔子改制考]. Peking, 1969.

———. *Li-ts'ai chiu-kuo lun* [理財救國論]. Shanghai, ca. 1914.

———. *Li-yun chu* [禮運注]. Shanghai, 1912.

———. *Lun-yü chu* [論語注]. In *Wan-mu ts'ao-t'ang ts'ung-shu* [萬木草堂叢書].
Peking, 1917.

———. *Meng-tzu wei* [孟子微]. Shanghai, 1916.

———. *Ni Chung-hua Min-kuo hsien-fa ts'ao-an* [擬中華民國憲法草案].
Shanghai, 1916.

———. "Shang Ch'ing-ti ti-liu shu" [上清帝第六書]. In *Wu-hsu pien-fa.* Compiled by Chien Po-tsan et al. Shanghai, 1953.

———. *Ta-hsueh chu* [大學注]. Shanghai (?), 1913.

———. *Ta-t'ung shu* [大同書]. Shanghai, 1935. Translated by Laurence G. Thompson under the title *Ta T'ung Shu: The One World Philosophy of K'ang Yu-wei.* London, 1958.

———. *Wan-mu ts'ao-t'ang ts'ung-shu* [萬木草堂叢書]. Peking, 1917.

———. *Wei-ching k'ao* [偽经考]. Shanghai, 1936.

———. *Wu-chih chiu-kuo lun* [物質救國論]. Shanghai, 1919.

Kataoka, Tetsuya. *Resistance and Revolution in China.* Berkeley, 1974.

K'o-hsueh yü jen-sheng-kuan [科学與人生觀]. Shanghai, 1923.

Kuan-yü chien-kuo i-lai tang te jo-kan li-shih wen-t'i te chueh-i
[關於建國以來党的若干歷史問題的決議]. Hong Kong, 1981. Translated under the title "Resolutions on Certain Questions in the History of Our Party Since the

356

Founding of the People's Republic of China." In *Resolution on CPC History (1949–1981)*. Peking, 1981.

Kuang-tung sheng che-hsueh she-hui k'o-hsueh yen-chiu so li-shih yen-chiu shih et al. [廣東省哲学社會科学研究所歷史研究室等]. *Sun Chung-shan nien-p'u* [孫中山年譜]. Peking, 1980.

Kung Wen-sheng [龔文聲]. "Po Sun Yeh-fang te hsiu-cheng chu-i 'ching-chi kang-ling'" [駁孫冶方的修正主義經濟綱領]. *Jen-min jih-pao,* 10 August 1966.

Kuo Chan-po [郭湛波]. *Chin wu-shih nien Chung-kuo szu-hsiang shih* [近五十年中國思想史]. Hong Kong, 1965.

Kuo Mo-jo [郭沫若]. "Chung-kuo ku-tai shih te fen-ch'i wen-t'i" [中國古代史的分期問題]. *Hung-ch'i*, no. 7 (1972).

———. "San-tien chien-i" [三点建議]. In *Hu Shih szu-hsiang p'i-p'an* Peking, 1955–56.

———. *Shih p'i-p'an shu* [十批判書]. Shanghai, 1950.

Kuo, Thomas C. *Ch'en Tu-hsiu and the Chinese Communist Movement*. South Orange, New Jersey, 1975.

Kwok, D. W. Y. *Scientism in Chinese Thought 1900–1950*. New Haven, 1965.

Lai Ming. *Ten Years of Storm*. New York, 1960.

Lau, D. C. Introduction to *Mencius*, D. C. Lau, trans. Harmondworth, England, 1970.

Lee Feigon. *Chen Duxiu, the Founder of the Chinese Communist Party*. Princeton University Press, 1983.

Legge, James, trans. *The Chinese Classics*. Oxford, 1892. Reprint. Taipei, 1970.

Lei Yü-tung [雷宇同], comp. *Chung-kuo kung-ch'an tang kung-chi Ch'en Tu-hsiu te fan-hsiang* [中國共產党攻擊陳獨秀的反響]. Canton, 1938.

Lenin. V. I. "Democracy and Narodism in China." In *Collected Works*. Moscow, 1963.

Levenson, Joseph R. *Liang Ch'i-ch'ao and the Mind of Modern China*. Berkeley, 1953.

———, and Schurmann, Franz, eds. *China: An Interpretive History*. Berkeley, 1969.

Leys, Simon. *Chinese Shadows*. New York, 1977.

Li, Chien-nung [李劍農]. *Chung-kuo chin-pai nien cheng-chih shih* [中國近百年政治史]. Shanghai, 1948; Taipei, 1957. Translated by Ssu-yü Teng and Jeremy Ingalls under the title *The Political Thought of China 1840–1920*. Princeton, 1956.

Li I-che [李一哲]. "Kuan-yü she-hui chu-i te min-chu yü fa'chih" [関于社会主義的民主與法制]. *Chan-wang* [展望] (Hong Kong), no. 332 (1 December 1975).

Li Jui [李銳]. *Mao Tse-tung t'ung-chih te ch'u-ch'i ko-ming huo-tung* [毛澤東同志的初期革命活動]. Peking, 1957.

———. "Wu-szu yun-tung chung te ch'ing-nien Mao Tse-tung" [五四運動中的青年毛澤東]. *Li-shih yen-chiu* [歷史研究] (Peking), no. 5 (May 1979).

Li Tse-hou [李澤厚]. *Chung-kuo chin-tai szu-hsiang shih-lun* [中國近代思想史論]. Peking, 1979.

———. *K'ang Yu-wei, T'an Szu-t'ung szu-hsiang yen-chiu* [康有為 譚嗣同思想研究]. Shanghai, 1958.

Liang Ch'i-ch'ao [梁啟超]. "Cheng-chih hsueh ta-chia Po-lun-chi-li chih hsueh-shuo" [政治學大家伯倫知理之學說]. In *Yin-ping shih ho-chi* [飲冰室合集]. Compiled by Lin Chih-chün [林志鈞]. Shanghai, 1936. (Henceforth *YPSHC*).

———. *Ch'ing-tai hsueh-shu kai-lun* [清代學術概論]. Shanghai, 1921. Translated by Immanuel C. Y. Hsü under the title *Intellectual Trends in the Ch'ing Period*. Cambridge, 1959.

———. "Chung-kuo li-shih shang ko-ming chih yen-chiu" [中國歷史上革命之研究]. In *YPSHC*.

———. "Fu Chang Tung-sun shu lun she-hui chu-i yün-tung" [復張東蓀書論社會主義運動]. In *YPSHC*.

———. "Hsin-min shuo" [新民說]. In *YPSHC*.

———. "K'ai-ming chuan-chi lun" [開明專制論]. In *YPSHC*.

———. "Lun cheng-chih neng-li" [論政治能力]. In *YPSHC*.

———. "Lun chin-ch'ü mao-hsien" [論進取冒險]. In *YPSHC*.

———. "Lun chin-pu" [論進步]. In *YPSHC*.

———. "Lun ch'üan-li szu-hsiang" [論權力思想]. In *YPSHC*.

———. "Lun ho-ch'ün" [論合群]. In *YPSHC*.

———. "Lun i-li" [論毅力]. In *YPSHC*.

———. "Lun i-wu szu-hsiang" [論義務思想]. In *YPSHC*.

———. "Lun kung-te" [論公德]. In *YPSHC*.

———. "Lun kuo-chia szu-hsiang" [論國家思想]. In *YPSHC*.

———. "Lun shang-wu" [論尚武]. In *YPSHC*.

———. "Lun sheng-li fen-li" [論生利分利]. In *YPSHC*.

———. "Lun szu-te" [論私德]. In *YPSHC*.

———. "Lun tzu-chih" [論自治]. In *YPSHC*.

———. "Lun tzu-tsun" [論自尊]. In *YPSHC*.

———. "Lun tzu-yu" [論自由]. In *YPSHC*.

———. "*Nan-hai K'ang hsien-sheng chuan*" [南海康先生傳]. In *YPSHC*.

———. "Ou-yu hsin-ying lu" [歐遊心影錄]. In *YPSHC*.

———. "Po mou-pao chih t'u-ti kuo-yu lun" [駁某報之土地國有論]. In *YPSHC*.

———. "Shen-lun chung-tsu ko-ming yü cheng-chi ko-ming chih te-shih" [申論種族革命與政治革命之得失]. In *YPSHC*.

———. "Shih hsin-min chih-i" [釋新民之義]. In *YPSHC*.

———. "*Wu-hsu cheng-pien chi*" [戊戌政變記]. In *YPSHC*.

Liang Shih-ch'iu et al. [梁實秋等]. *Jen ch'üan lun-chi* [人權論集]. Shanghai, 1941.

Liang Shu-ming [梁漱溟]. "Ching i ch'ing-chiao Hu Shih-chih hsien sheng" [敬以請教胡適之先生]. In *Ts'un-chih yueh-k'an* [村治月刊], no. 2 (1930). Reprinted in *Hu Shih lun-hsueh chin-chu* [胡適論學近著]. Shanghai, 1935.

———. "Chiu-yuan chueh-i lun" [究元決疑論]. *Tung-fang tsa-chih* (May 1916), (June 1916), (July 1916).

———. *Chung-kuo min-tsu tzu-chiu yun-tung chih tsui-hou chueh-wu* [中國民族自救運動之最後覺悟]. Shanghai, 1936.

———. *Chung-kuo wen-hua yao-i* [中國文化要義]. Hong Kong, 1963.

———. *Hsiang ts'un chien-she li-lun* [鄉村建設理論]. Ts'ou-p'ing, 1937.

———. *Hsiang-ts'un chien-she ta-i* [鄉村建設大意]. Ts'ou-p'ing, 1936.

———. *Jen-hsin yü jen-sheng* [人心與人生], unpublished manuscript written between 1955 and 1957.

———. *Kung-hsueh i-chih* [孔學繹旨], unpublished manuscript of lecture notes for Peking University, 1923–24.

———. "Liang-nien lai wo-te szu-hsiang yu shen-ma chuan-pien?"
[兩年來我的思想有甚麼轉變?. *Kuang-ming Jih-pao* [光明日報], 5 October 1951.

Liang Shu-ming szu-hsiang p'i-p'an [梁漱溟 思想批判]. Peking, 1955.

"Liang Shu-ming te fa-yen" [梁漱溟的發言]. *Kuang-ming jih-pao*, 7 February 1956.

Liang Shu-ming. *Tung-hsi wen-hua chi-ch'i che-hsueh* [東西文化及其哲學]. Shanghai, 1923.

———. "Wo-men liang ta k'ung-nan" [我們兩大困難]. In Liang Shu-ming, *Hsiang-ts'un chien-she li-lun* [鄉村建設理論]. Ts'ou-p'ing, 1937.

Lin Tzu-hsun [林子勛]. *Kuo-fu hsueh-shou yü hsi-fang wen-hua*
[國父學說與西方文化]. Taipei, 1953.

Liu Shao-ch'i [劉少奇]. "Lun tang" [論黨]. In *She-hui chu-i chiao-yü k'o-ch'eng te yueh-tu wen-chien hui-pien* [社會主義教育課程的閱讀文件匯編]. Peking, 1958.

Lo, Jung-pang. *K'ang Yu-wei: A Biography and a Symposium*. Tucscon, 1967.

Long Chun [龍春]. "Kuan-yü nung-yeh sheng-ch'an tse-jen chih te chi-ko wen-t'i"
[閱於農業生產責任制的經濟問題探索]. *Ching-chi wen-t'i t'an-so*
[經濟問題探索], January 1982.

Mao Tse-tung [毛澤東]. "Chan-cheng ho chan-lueh wen-t'i" [戰爭和戰略問題]. In *Mao Tse-tung hsuan-chi* [毛澤東選集]. 1969. (Henceforth *MTTHC*.)

———. "Chao-chien shou-tu hung tai-hui fu-tse jen te chiang-hua"
[召見首都紅代會負責人的講話]. In *Mao Tse-tung szu-hsiang wan-sui*
[毛澤東思想萬歲]. N.p. 1967 and 1969. (Henceforth *Wan-sui*.)

———. "Cheng-tun hsueh-feng, tang-feng, wen-feng" [整頓學風、党風、文風].
Cheng-feng wen-hsien [整風文獻]. Hong Kong, 1949.

———. "Cheng-tun tang te tso-feng" [整頓党的作風]. In *MTTHC*.

———. "Chi-nien Sun Chung-san hsien-sheng" [紀念孫中山 先生]. In *MTTHC*.

———. "Chieh-chien Jih-pen she-hui tang jen-shih Tso-tso-mu-keng-san, Hei-t'ien-shou-nan, Hsi-p'o-chien-kuang teng te t'an hua"
[接見日本社會党人士佐佐木更三、黑田壽男、細迫萌光等的談話]. In *Wan-sui*.

———. "Ch'un-chieh t'an-hua chi-yao" [春節談話紀要]. In *Wan-sui*.

———. "Chung-kuo ko-ming ho Chung-kuo kung-ch'an tang"
[中國革命和中國共產党]. In *MTTHC*.

———. "Chung-yang kung-tso tso-t'an hui chi-yao" [中央工作座談會紀要]. In *Wan-sui*.

———. *A Critique of Soviet Economics*. Translated by Moss Roberts. New York, 1977.

———. "Fan-tui tzu-yu chu-i" [反對自由主義]. In *MTTHC*.

———. "Hsin min-chu chu-i lun" [新民主主義論]. In *MTTHC*.

———. "Hu-nan nung-min yun-tung k'ao-ch'a pao-kao" [湖南農民運動考察報告].
In *MTTHC*.

———. "I-chiu-wu-ch'i nien hsia-chi te hsing-shih" [一九五七年夏季的形勢]. In *MTTHC*.

———. "Kai-tsao wo-men te hsueh-hsi" [改造我們的學習]. In *MTTHC*.

———. "Kuan-yü cheng-ch'ueh ch'u-li jen-min nei-pu mao-tun te wen-t'i"
[閱於正確處理人民內部矛盾的問題]. In *MTTHC*.

———. "Kuan-yü chiu-cheng tang-nei te ts'o-wu szu-hsiang"

[關於糾正黨內的錯誤思想]. In *MTTHC*.

———. "Kuan-yü ling-tao fang-fa te jo-kan wen-t'i" [關於領導方法的若干問題]. In *MTTHC*.

———. "Lun jen-min min-chu chuan-cheng" [論人民民主專政]. In *MTTHC*.

———. "Lun lien-ho cheng-fu" [論聯合政府]. In *MTTHC*.

———. "Lun shih ta kuan-hsi" [論十大關係]. In *MTTHC*.

———. *Mao Tse-tung hsuan-chi* [毛澤東選集]. Peking, 1969, 1977. Translated by Foreign Languages Press under the title *Selected Works of Mao Tse-tung*. Peking, 1967.

———. *Mao Tse-tung szu-hsiang wan-sui* [毛澤東思想萬歲]. N.p. 1967 and 1969.

———. "Mao-tun lun" [矛盾論]. In *MTTHC*.

———. "Ni ta ni-te, wo ta wo-te" [你打你的，我打我的]. In *Wan-sui*.

———. "P'i-p'an Liang Shu-ming te fan-tung szu-hsiang"
[批判梁漱溟的反動思想]. In *MTTHC*.

———. "Pien-cheng fa chü-li" [辯證法舉例]. In *Wan-sui*.

———. *Selected Works of Mao Tse-tung*. Peking, 1967.

———. "Shih-chien lun" [實踐論]. In *MTTHC*.

———. "Su-lien Cheng-chih ching-chi hsueh tu-shu pi-chi"
[蘇聯政治經濟學讀書筆記]. In *Wan-sui*. Translated by Moss Roberts under the title *A Critique of Soviet Economics*. New York, 1977.

———. "Ta-liang hsi-shou chih-shih fen-tzu" [大量吸收知識分子]. In *MTTHC*.

———. "Tsai Ch'eng-tu hui-i shang te chiang-hua" [在成都會議上的講話]. In *Wan-sui*.

———. "Tsai Chung-kuo kung-ch'an tang ti-pa-chieh chung-yang wei-yuan hui ti-erh tz'u ch'üan-t'i hui-i shang te chiang-hua"
[在中國共產黨第八屆中央委員會第二次全體會議上的講話]. In *MTTHC*.

———. "Tsai Hang-chou hui-i shang te chiang-hua" [在杭州會議上的講話]. In *Wan-sui*.

———. "Tsai i-tz'u hui-pao shih te ch'a-hua" [在一次會報時的插話]. In *Wan-sui*.

———. "Tsai Lu-shan hui-i shang te chiang-hua" [在廬山會議上的講話]. In *Wan-sui*.

———. "Tsai Nan-ning hui-i shang te chiang-hua" [在南寧會議上的講話]. In *Wan-sui*.

———. "Tsai pa-chieh ch'i-chung ch'üan-hui shang te chiang-hua"
[在八屆七中全會上的講話]. In *Wan-sui*.

———. "Tsai pa-ta erh-tz'u hui-i shang te chiang-hua" [在八屆二次會議上的講話]. In *Wan-sui*.

———. "Tsai tsui-kao kuo-wu hui-i shang te chiang-hua"
[在最高國務會議上的講話]. In *Wan-sui*.

———. "Tsai Yenan wen-i tso-t'an hui shang te chiang-hua"
[在延安文藝座談會上的講話]. In *MTTHC*.

———. "Tseng-ch'iang tang te t'uan-chieh, chi-ch'eng tang te ch'uan-t'ung"
[增強黨的團結繼承黨的傳統]. In *MTTHC*.

———. "Tu Cheng-chih ching-chi hsueh chiao-k'o-shu (she-hui chu-i pu-fen) te pi-chi" [讀政治經濟學教科書（社會主義部分）的筆記]. In *Wan-sui*. (Same as "Su-lien Cheng-chih ching-chi hsueh tu-shu pi-chi.")

———. "Tui A-erh-pa-ni-ya chün-shih tai-piao t'uan te chiang-hua"
[對阿爾巴尼亞軍事代表團的講話]. In *Wan-sui*.

———. "Tui wei-sheng kung-tso te chih-shih" [對衛生工作的指示]. In *Wan-sui*.

————. "Wei cheng-ch'ü ch'ien-pai-wan ch'ün-chang chin-ju k'ang-Jih min-tsu t'ung-i chan-hsien erh tou-cheng"
[為爭取千百萬群眾進入抗日民族統一戰線而斗爭]. In *MTTHC*.

————. "Wu-ch'i chih-shih" [五七指示]. In *Wan-sui*.

————. "Yen-chung te chiao-hsun" [嚴重的教训]. In *Chung-kuo nung-ts'un te she-hui chu-i kao-ch'ao*. Peking, 1956.

————. "Yü Ch'en Po-ta, Ai Szu-ch'i t'ung-chih te t'an-hua"
[與陳伯達艾思奇同志的談話]. In *Wan-sui*.

————, Ch'en Po-ta, et al. [陳伯達等]. *Lun San-min chu-i*. N.p., n.d.

"Mao Tse-tung yü P'eng-pi-tu te hui-t'an" [毛澤東與彭比度的會談]. *Ming-pao yueh-k'an* (Hong Kong), 131 (1976).

Marx, Karl. "Introduction to 'Critique of Political Economy.'" In *Capital and Other Writings of Karl Marx*. New York, 1932.

Mathews, Linda. "The Persistent Chinese 'Siesta.'" *San Francisco Chronicle*, 3 August 1980.

McDougall, William. *Introduction to Social Psychology*. Boston, 1918.

Melotti, Umberto. *Marx and the Third World*. Translated by Pat Ransford. London, 1977.

Michael, Franz. *Mao and the Perpetual Revolution*. New York, 1977.

Moore, Charles A., ed. *The Chinese Mind: Essentials of Chinese Philosophy and Culture*. Honolulu, 1967.

MTTHC. See Mao Tse-tung. *Mao Tse-tung hsuan-chi*.

Mu, Fu-sheng. *The Wilting of the Hundred Flowers*. New York, 1962.

Needham, Joseph. *Within the Four Seas*. London, 1969.

Ni Szu [尼司]. *Ch'en Tu-hsiu yü so-wei T'o-pai wen-t'i*
[陳獨秀與所謂托派問題]. Canton, 1937.

Palmer, R. R. *A History of the Modern World*. New York, 1978.

Pei Wen-chung [裴文中], et al. *Wo-te szu-hsiang tsen-mo chuan-pien kuo-lai te?*
[我的思想是怎麼轉变过來的？]. Peking, 1952.

People's Communes in China. Peking, 1958.

Price, Frank W. *San-min chu-i*. Taipei, n.d.

Prybyla, Jan S. *The Chinese Economy: Problems and Politics*. Los Angeles, 1981.

————. "Man and Society in China." *Vital Speeches of the Day*, 1 July 1975.

Rice, Edward E. *Mao's Way*. Berkeley, 1972.

Riesman, David. *Individualism Reconsidered and Other Essays*. Glencoe, Ill., 1954.

Russell, Bertrand. *Authority and the Individual*. Boston, 1960.

————. *New Hopes for a Changing World*. New York, 1951.

————. *Unpopular Essays*. New York, 1962.

Schiffrin, Harold Z. *Sun Yat-sen and the Origins of the Chinese Revolution*. Berkeley and Los Angeles, 1968.

Schram, Stuart R. *The Political Thought of Mao Tse-tung*. New York, 1963.

Schumpeter, Joseph A. *Capitalism, Socialism, and Democracy*. New York, 1950.

Schwartz, Benjamin I. *Chinese Communism and the Rise of Mao*. Cambridge, Mass., 1958.

Shang Ming-hsuan [尚明軒]. *Sun Chung-shan chuan* [孫中山傳]. Peking, 1979.

Sharmon, Lyon. *Sun Yat-sen: His Life and its Meaning. A Critical Biography*. New York, 1934. Reprint. Stanford, 1968.

She-hui chu-i chiao-yü k'o-ch'eng te yueh-tu wen-chien hui-pien

[社會主義教育課程的閱讀文件匯編]. Peking, 1958.

Shen, T. H. *The Sino-American Joint Commission on Rural Reconstruction, Twenty Years of Cooperation for Agricultural Development*. Ithaca, N.Y., 1970.

Shen-hsi shih-fan ta-hsueh hsieh-tso tsu [陝西師範大學寫作組]. "Ch'in Shih-huang shih chien-chueh ta-chi nu-li chu fu-p'i te cheng-chih-chia" [秦始皇是堅決打擊奴隸主義復辟的政治家]. *Jen-min jih-pao,* 31 October 1973.

Sheng Liang-jui [盛良瑞]. "Wan-hsi kuai-chieh Pieh T'ing-fang (shang)" [宛西怪傑別庭芳（上）]. *Chung-wai tsa-chih* [中外雜誌]. (Taipei) 84 (February 1974):37–41.

Shih Chün, Jen Chi-yu, and Chu Po-k'un [石峻、任繼愈、朱伯崑]. *Chung-kuo chin-tai szu-hsiang shih chiang-shou t'i-kang* [中國近代思想史講授提綱]. Peking, 1957.

Shih Ting [施丁]. "Fen-shu k'eng-ju pien" [焚書坑儒辯]. In *Ch'in Shih-huang tsai li-shih shang te chin-pu tso-yung* [秦始皇在歷史上的進步作用]. Hu-nan, 1973.

Shih Ts'ang [石倉]. "Lun tsun-ju fan-fa" [論尊儒反法]. *Hung-ch'i,* no. 10 (1973).

Shih, Vincent. "A Talk with Hu Shih." *The China Quarterly,* no. 10 (1962).

Shu, Austin C. W. *On Mao Tse-tung: A Bibliography Guide*. Lansing, 1972.

Snow, Edgar. "China's Communes, Success or Failure?" *The New Republic,* 26 June 1971.

———. *Red Star Over China*. New York, 1938.

Some Basic Facts about China. China Reconstructs (Supplement). Peking, January 1974.

Spitz, David, ed. *John Stuart Mill on Liberty*. New York, 1975.

Stalin, Joseph. *Program of the Communist International*. 1928.

Starr, John Bryan. *Continuing the Revolution, the Political Thought of Mao*. Princeton, 1979.

Sun Yat-sen [孫中山]. "Chien-kuo ta-kang". [建國大綱]. In *Kuo-fu ch'üan-chi* [國父全集]. Taipei, 1965.

———. "Chu-i sheng-kuo wu-li" [主義勝過武力]. In *Kuo-fu ch'üan-chi*. Taipei, 1965.

———. "Chung-kuo ko-ming shih" [中國革命史]. In *Kuo-fu ch'üan-chi*. Taipei, 1965.

———. "Keng-che yu ch'i-t'ien" [耕者有其田]. In *Kuo-fu ch'üan-chi*. Taipei, 1965.

———. *Kuo-fu ch'üan-chi*. Edited by Chung-yang wen-wu kung-ying she [中央文物供應社]. Taipei, 1957.

———. *Kuo-fu ch'üan-chi*. Edited by Chung-kuo kuo-min tang chung-yang tang-shih shih-liao pien-tsuan wei-yuan hui [中國國民黨中央黨史史料編纂委員會]. Taipei, 1965.

———. "Min-pao fa-k'an tz'u" [民報發刊詞]. In *Kuo-fu ch'üan-chi*. Taipei, 1965.

———. *San-min chu-i* [三民主義]. In *Kuo-fu ch'üan-chi*. Taipei, 1965. Translated by Frank W. Price under the title *San Min Chu I*. Taipei, n.d.

———. "Sun Wen hsueh-shuo" [孫文學說]. In *Kuo-fu ch'üan-chi*. Taipei, 1965.

———. "Ta-p'o chiu szu-hsiang yao-yung San-min chu-i" [打破舊思想要用三民主義]. In *Kuo-fu ch'üan-chi*. Taipei, 1965.

———. "Tzu-chuan" [自傳]. In *Kuo-fu ch'üan-chi*. Taipei, 1957.

Sun Yeh-fang [孫冶方]. "Chia-ch'iang t'ung-chi kung-tso, kai-ko t'ung-chi t'i-chih" [加強統計工作，改造 統計體制制]. *Chiang-chi kuan-li* [経済管理], 15 February 1981.

Sung Yun-pin [宋雲彬]. *K'ang Yu-wei* [康有為]. Shanghai, 1951.

"Szu-jen pang tsun-fa ch'ou-chü te mu'ch'ien mu-hou" [四人邦尊法醜劇的幕前幕后]. *Li-shih yen-chiu*, no. 5 (May 1978).

Szu-ma Lu [司馬璐]. *Chung-kung tang-shih chi wen-hsien hsuan-ts'ui* [中共党史暨文獻選粹]. Hong Kong, 1982.

T'ang Chih-chün [湯志鈞]. *Wu-hsu pien-fa chien-shih* [戊戌变法簡史]. Peking, 1960.

———. *Wu-hsu pien-fa jen-wu chuan-kao* [戊戌变法人物傳稿]. Peking, 1961.

———. *Wu-hsu pien-fa shih lun-ts'ung* [戊戌变法史論叢]. Hong Kong, 1973.

T'ang Te-kang [唐德剛]. *Hu Shih k'ou-shu tzu-chuan* [胡適口述自傳]. Taipei, 1981.

———. *Hu Shih tsa-i* [胡適雜憶]. Taipei, 1979.

Teng Kuang-ming [鄧廣銘]. *Wang An-shih* [王安石]. Peking: Jen-min ch'u-pan she, 1975.

Teng, Ssu-yu and Jeremy Ingalls. *The Political History of China 1840–1928*. Princeton, 1956.

Thompson, Laurence G. *Ta T'ung Shu: The One World Philosophy of K'ang Yu-wei*. London, 1958.

Ting Shou-ho [丁守和] and Yin Hsu-i [殷叙彝]. *Ts'ung Wu-szu ch'i-meng yun-tung tao Ma-k'o-szu chu-i te ch'uan-po* [從五四啟蒙運動到馬克思主義的傳播]. Peking, 1979.

Ting, V. K. See Ting Wen-chiang.

Ting Wen-chiang (V. K. Ting) [丁文江]. *Liang Jen-king hsien-sheng nien-p'u ch'ang-pien ch'u-kao* [梁任公先生年譜長編初稿]. Taipei, 1958.

———. "Min-chu cheng-chih yü tu-ts'ai cheng-chih" [民主政治與獨裁政治]. *Tu-li p'ing-lun*, 30 December 1934.

Topping, Seymour. "China's Long March into the Future." *New York Times Magazine*, 3 February 1980.

Toynbee, Arnold J. *A Study of History*. New York, 1957.

Tsiang, T. F. (Chiang T'ing-fu) [蒋廷黻]. "Ko-ming yü chuan-chih" [革命與專制]. *Tu-li p'ing-lun*, 20 December 1933.

———. "Lun chuan-chih ping ta Hu Shih-chih hsien-sheng" [論專制並答胡適之先生]. *Tu-li p'ing-lun*, 31 December 1933.

Tsui-hou chien-chieh. See Ch'en Tu-hsiu, *Ch'en Tu-hsiu tsui-hou tui-yü min-chu cheng-chih te chien-chieh*.

Ts'ui Shu-ch'in [崔書琴]. *San-min chu-i hsin-lun* [三民主義新論]. Taipei, 1960.

———. *Sun Chung-shan yü kung-ch'an chu-i* [孫中山與共產主義]. 3d ed. Hong Kong, 1956.

"Tsung Shang-hai chi-ch'uang ch'ang k'an pei-yang kung-ch'eng chi-shu jen-yuan te tao-lu" [從上海機床廠看培養工程技術人民的道路]. *Jen-min jih-pao*, 22 July 1968.

Tuan Ch'ang-t'ung [段昌同]. "Wu-hsu pai-jih wei-hsin ta-shih piao" [戊戌百日維新大事表]. In Chien Po-tsan, *Wu-hsu pien-fa*. Shanghai, 1953.

"Tuan-cheng ching-chi kung-tso te chih-tao szu-hsiang" [端正經濟工作的指導思想]. *Jen-min jih-pao*, 9 April 1981.

"Tui Sun Yeh-fang te p'i-p'an ho ching-chi chan-hsien te tou-p'i-kai"

[對孫治方的批判和經濟戰線上的鬥批改]. *Jen-min jih-pao*, 24 February 1970.

"T'ung-chih" [通知]. *Jen-min jih-pao*, 17 May 1967.

U.S. Congress, Joint Economic Committee, *China: A Reassessment of the Economy*, Washington, D.C., 1978.

———. *China Under the Four Modernizations*, Washington, D.C., 1982.

———. *Chinese Economy Post-Mao*, Washington, D.C., 1978.

———. *Economic Developments in Modern China*, Washington, D.C., 1972.

Wakeman, Frederic, Jr. *History and Will: Philosophical Perspectives of Mao Tsetung Thought*. Berkeley, 1973.

Waley, Arthur, trans. *The Confucian Analects*. New York, 1938.

Walker, Richard L. *The Human Cost of Communism in China*. Washington, D.C., 1971.

Wang, Fan-hsi [王凡西]. *Shuang-shan hui-i lu* [雙山回憶錄]. Hong Kong, 1977. Translated by Gregor Benton under the title *Chinese Revolutionary Memoirs 1919–1949*. London, 1980.

Wang Hsi-che [王希哲]. "Wei wu-ch'an chieh-chi te chuan-cheng erh nu-li" [為無產階級的專政而努力]. *Jen-min chih-sheng* [人民之聲] (Canton), no. 8 (July 1979). Reprinted in *Ch'i-shih nien-tai* [七十年代] (Hong Kong), no. 116 (September 1979).

Wang Hsin-ming et al. [王新命等]. "Chung-kuo pen-wei te wen-hua chien-she hsuan-yen" [中國本位的文化建設宣言]. In *Hu Shih yü Chung-hsi wen-hua*. Taipei, 1967.

Wang Hsueh-hua [王學華]. *Sun Chung-shan te che-hsueh szu-hsiang* [孫中山的哲學思想]. Shanghai, 1960.

Wang Jo-shui [王若水]. "Ch'ing-ch'u Hu Shih che-hsueh te fan-tung i-tu" [清除胡適哲學的反動遺毒]. *Jen-min jih-pao*, 5 November 1954.

Wang Shu-huai [王樹槐]. *Wai-jen yü wu-hsu pien-fa* [外人與戊戌變法]. Taipei, 1965.

Wan-sui. See Mao Tse-tung. *Mao Tse-tung szu-hsiang wan-sui*.

Wei Chieh-t'ing [韋杰廷]. *Sun Chung-san che-hsueh szu-hsiang yen-chiu* [孫中山哲學思想研究]. Ch'ang-sha, 1981.

Wei Ching-sheng [魏京生]. "Ti-wu ko hsien-tai-hua" [第五個現代化]. *T'an-so* [探索] (Peking), no. 1 (1979).

Wen-ts'un. See *Hu Shih wen-ts'un*.

Wilbur, Martin. *Sun Yat-sen: Frustrated Patriot*. New York, 1976.

William, Maurice. *The Social Interpretation of History: A Refutation of the Marxian Economic Interpretation of History*. New York, 1921.

———. *Sun Yat-sen Versus Communism*. Baltimore, 1932.

Wilson, Dick. *Mao, The People's Emperor*. London, 1979.

Wilson, Edmund. *To the Finland Station*. New York, 1953.

World Bank. *China: Socialist Economic Development*. Washington, 1981.

Wu Ching-ch'ao [吳景超]. "Ko-ming yü chien-kuo" [革命與建國]. *Tu-li p'ing-lun*, 7 January 1934.

———. "P'i-p'an Liang Shu-ming te Chung-kuo wen-hua lun" [批判梁漱溟的中國文化論]. In *Liang Shu-ming szu-hsiang p'i-p'an*. Peking, 1955.

———. "Wo yü Hu Shih—ts'ung p'eng-yu tao ti-jen" [我與胡適—從朋友到敵人].

In *Hu Shih Szu-hsiang p'i-p'an*. Peking, 1955–56.

Wu, John C. H. *Sun Yat-sen: The Man and his Ideas*. Taipei, 1971.

Wu T'ing-ch'iu [吳廷璆]. "P'i-p'an Liang Shu-ming fan-tung li-shih kuan-tien"
[批判梁漱溟反動歷史觀点]. In *Liang Shu-ming szu-hsiang p'i-p'an*. Peking,
1955.

Yang Jung-kuo [楊榮國]. "Ch'un-ch'iu chan-kuo shih-ch'i szu-hsiang ling-yü nei
liang-t'iao lu-hsien te tou-cheng" [春秋戰國時期思想領域內兩條路綫的斗爭].
Hung-ch'i, no. 12 (1972).

———. "K'ung-tzu—wan-ku te wei-hu nu-li chih-tu te szu-hsiang-chia"
[孔子—頑固的維護奴隸制度的思想家]. *Jen-min jih-pao*, 7 August 1973. Translated under the title "Confucius—A Thinker Who Stubbornly Upheld the Slave
System." *Peking Review*, 12 October 1973.

Yao P'eng-tzu [姚蓬子]. *P'i-p'an Hu Shih shih-yung chu-i te fan-tung hsing ho
fan k'o-hsueh hsing* [批判胡適實用主義的反動性和反科學性]. Shanghai, 1955.

Yao Wen-yuan [姚文元]. "Lun Lin Piao fan-tang chi-t'uan te she-hui chi-ch'u"
[論林彪反党集團的社會基礎]. *Hung-ch'i*, no. 3 (March 1975).

Yen Fu [嚴復]. *Ch'ün-chi ch'üan-chieh lun* [群己權界論]. Shanghai, 1931.

YPSHC. See Liang Ch'i-chao. *Yin-ping shih ho-chi*.

Index

Mao Tse-tung, 70; on liberty and freedom, 60; on material civilization, 68; on
moral revolution, 56–66; on political
ability, 63–64; political activities, 49–
51; on production, 62–63; on progress
and conservatism, 61–62; publications,
49–51, 57; on renovation of the people,
54–56; on revolution, 52–53, 70; on socialism, 66–67; on Western spirit, 58
Liang Shu-ming, 107–8, 121, 175, 205,
289, 292, 297, 301; biography, 179–82;
on Chinese culture, 185–87; on Communism, 188; Communist criticism of, 182f,
192; criticism of Mao Tse-tung, 193–94;
on culture, 182–85; on democracy, 188–
90; political activities, 181–82; publica-
tions, 180–82, 185, 188, 191, 193; on
rural reconstruction, 190–92
Liang Wu-ti, 268, 276
Liao P'ing, 18
Lin Piao, 231, 251, 264, 273, 278f, 310,
318f, 327, 329
Lincoln, Abraham, 58, 84
Literary Revolution, 100f, 126, 200
Liu Hsin, 16f
Liu Pang, 268
Liu Shao-ch'i, 82, 153, 231, 246–48, 254,
264, 273, 278, 298–99, 310, 318f
Liu Tsung-yuan, 268
Livingstone, David, 58
Lo Kuan-chung, 268
Lo Lung-chi, 313
Lord Shang, 116f
Lu Chiu-yuan, 48
Lu Hsun, 252
Lu Ta-fang, 175
Luther, Martin, 58, 61, 267

Ma Yin-ch'u, 317
Magellan, Ferdinand, 58
Mao Tse-tung, 42f, 70, 102, 137, 160, 182,
192; analysis of Chinese history, 239; on
art and literature, 263–64; biography,
225–31; on burning of books, 251–53;
on change, 237; Chinese influence, 269–
71; on Chinese revolution, 240–41; on
culture, 263–68; on democratic centralism, 245–49; economic policies of,
254–63; on economic reconstruction,
258–60; on education, 264–65; on elections, 253–54; on industry and agriculture, 259–62; on intellectuals, 266–69;

on liberalism, 249–50; Marxian influence, 271–73; on mass line, 245–46; on
materialist dialectics, 236; on New Democracy, 240–45, 249; on New Democratic Culture, 243–44; personality,
273–76; political activities, 226–31;
position in history, 276–83; on production, 256–58; publications, 227–30,
246, 249, 302; theory of contradictions,
235–38; theory of evolution, 236–37;
theory of knowledge, 232–35; theory of
practice, 232–35; on Three Principles of
the People, 90, 245. *See also* individual
works by Mao
Maring, H., 85, 201
Marshall, George C., 138, 182
Marx, Karl. *See* Marxism
Marxism, 19, 42, 66, 170, 183, 201. *See
also* individual thinkers' views on
Marxism-Leninism. *See* Marxism
May Fourth Movement, 85, 101, 180, 243,
270, 303, 315
McDougall, William, 185
Melotti, Umberto, 320
Mencius, 35, 40, 58, 82, 85f, 89, 116, 123,
161, 216, 273, 289–90, 294, 326. *See
also* Confucius
Mill, J. S., 226, 270, 300, 308
Miller, James C., 226
Ming Ch'eng-tsu, 268
Ming T'ai-tsu, 268
Mo-tzu, 19, 58, 68, 116, 276
Montesquieu, Charles-Louis, 69, 226, 270
Mussolini, Benito, 109, 142

Napoleon, Bonaparte, 142, 253, 274
Nationalist government. *See* Kuomintang
Neo-confucianism, 123–24
New Culture Movement, 108, 122, 200f,
207, 212
New Democracy, 258, 295
Newton, Isaac, 119, 124
Nixon, Richard, 254

October Revolution, 227, 230, 241, 294,
303
On Coalition Government, 230, 266
On Contradiction, 229, 235ff
On New Democracy, 229, 240ff
On Practice, 232, 229, 232ff
On the People's Democratic Dictatorship,
103, 188, 230, 242

Pai-hua Movement. *See* Literary Revolution
P'an Kuang-tan, 121
Pasteur, Louis, 119
P'eng Te-huai, 278
People's Republic of China: founding of, 230
People's communes, 30–31, 231, 261, 273, 281
Peter the Great, 13, 38
Plato, 165, 173, 277
Political parties, 50, 137f, 158f, 291–92, 318
Pompidou, Georges, 253
Population problem, 306, 317–18
Prybyla, Jan S., 312
P'u Sung-ling, 268
Pu Yi, 14, 42

Red Army, 228f
Revolution of 1911, 93, 175, 240–41
Revolution, Chinese, 301–3
Riesman, David, 313
Rizzi, Bruno, 320
Rousseau, Jean Jacques, 69, 160, 226
Russell, Bertrand, 32, 51, 70, 148, 185, 253, 300, 312

Sa Meng-wu, 121
Sakharov, Andrei, 331
Schurmann, Franz, 252
Seekt, Hans von, 229
Shakyamuni, 267
Schram, Stuart, 281
Smith, Adam, 63, 69, 207, 226
Snow, Edgar, 194, 262, 278
Socialism. *See* Marxism
Socrates, 122f, 184
Solzhenitsyn, Alexander, 331
Spencer, Herbert, 226
Spitz, David, 300
Stalin, Joseph, 142, 202, 217, 267, 277, 320
Sui Yang-ti, 153, 268
Sun Yat-sen, 14, 17, 42, 49, 63, 108–9, 153, 175, 214, 226, 234, 242, 244, 289, 292, 297, 301, 303, 305; biography, 75; Communist criticism of, 88–90, 93; on Confucianism, 85–86; on democracy, 78–82, 92; on equality, 79; on liberty, 79; on nationalism, 76–78, 91; on peo-ple's livelihood, 82–84; political ac-tivities, 75; publications, 75f, 84, 88; on socialism, 82; theory of knowledge, 87–

88; theory of revolution, 87–88; on three principles of the people, 75, 76–84, 90, 92; Western influence on, 87
Sun Yeh-fang, 254–56, 306
Sung Hui-tsung, 268

Ta-hsueh. See *The Great Learning*
Ta-t'ung shu, 14, 19–31, 37f, 40, 43, 270
Ta-t'ung, 17, 19, 34–37 *passim*, 40ff, 48, 78, 84, 86, 294
Tagore, Rabindranath, 51, 185
Taiwan, 92–93, 153, 320
Talks on Art and Literature at the Yenan Forum, 230, 263
T'an Szu-t'ung, 227
T'ang Ts'ai-ch'ang, 50
Taoism, 145
Teng Hsiao-p'ing, 231, 273, 281, 319, 321, 331
The Great Learning, 50, 55, 78, 86
Three Principles of the People, 42, 215, 242, 244, 320
T'ien-an Men, 231, 328
Ting Wen-chiang. *See* Ting, V. K.
Ting, V. K., 111f, 136, 291
Topping, Seymour, 307
Toynbee, Arnold, 332
Trotsky, Leon, 110, 202, 218, 220, 277
Ts'ai Yuan-p'ei, 179, 200
Ts'ao Hsueh-ch'in, 268
Ts'ao Yu, 303
Tseng Kuo-fan, 203
Tseng Tzu, 116
Tsiang, T. F., 112, 278; on absolutism, 109–11
Tu Fu, 268
Tu Yu, 17
Tung Chung-shu, 18, 236

Unequal treaties, 1–2, 305

Voitinksy, George, 66, 158, 201

Walker, Richard, 301
Wang An-shih, 15, 39
Wang Ch'uan-shan, 226f
Wang Ching-wei, 112, 137, 232
Wang Hsi-che, 329
Wang Jo-shui, 125
Wang Mang, 15, 17, 39
Wang Ming, 230
Wang Ping-chang, 329

371